# Math 76

## An Incremental Development

*Third Edition*

# Math 76

## An Incremental Development

*Third Edition*

**Stephen Hake**

**John Saxon**

Saxon Publishers, Inc.

*Math 76: An Incremental Development*

*Third Edition*

Teacher's Edition

Copyright © 1997 by Saxon Publishers, Inc. and Stephen Hake

Printed in the United States of America.

ISBN: 1-56577-154-0

Pre-Press Manager: J. Travis Rose

Production Coordinator: Joan Coleman

Second printing: June 1998

Printed on recycled paper.

┌─ *Reaching us via the Internet* ─┐

**WWW:** http://www.saxonpub.com

**E-mail:** info@saxonpub.com

Saxon Publishers, Inc.
2450 John Saxon Blvd.
Norman, OK 73071

# Contents

# Preface

## To The Teacher

This book grew out of a decade of intense classroom interaction with students in which the goal was for students to learn and **remember** the foundational skills of mathematics. The term "foundational" is appropriate because mathematics, perhaps more than any other subject, is a cognitive structure that builds upon prior learning. The ultimate height and stability of the mathematical structure within each individual are determined by the strength of the foundation. This book, as well as each book that precedes or follows it, provides the student with the time and opportunities necessary to build a rock-solid foundation in beginning mathematics. **For this to occur it is essential that all practice problems and all problem sets be completed by the student.**

## How To Use This Book

This book consists of a series of daily lessons and investigations that are carefully sequenced to incrementally develop a spectrum of skills and concepts. Each daily lesson has four components as described below.

First is a collection of warm-up activities that includes facts practice, mental math practice, and a problem-solving opportunity. The masters for the suggested facts practice speed tests are presented in the *Math 76 Test Masters* and need to be reproduced for students. We suggest beginning class with this activity as students race to improve their personal performance on each facts practice sheet. Emphasizing speed helps to automate the recall of basic facts. Confine this activity to five minutes or less. The back of the facts practice paper may be used to record mental math answers and problem solving work. The suggested mental math questions may be orally posed by the teacher or read by the students. The students record their answers on paper while performing the calculations "in their heads." Class discussion of various mental calculation strategies is helpful. The problem-solving activity is intended to be a whole-group effort. Eager students often work ahead on these problems. However, the goal is to provide a problem-solving experience for all students without intimidating those who are more hesitant. The three warm-up activities should be completed in 10 to 12 minutes.

The second component of the daily lesson is an explanation of the new increment. Example problems are included to illustrate the day's topic. The presentation of the new increment should be brief and lead promptly to the practice problems.

The practice problems, the third component of the daily lesson, are designed to provide massed, guided practice on the new skill or concept. Closely monitor student work on the practice questions to provide immediate feedback. An asterisk after the word "practice" in a lesson indicates that additional massed practice for that lesson can be found in the appendix. This additional practice is intended for remedial use only. Most students do not require the additional practice to acquire the skills and concepts presented.

The fourth and most important component of the daily lesson is the problem set. The problem set provides distributed practice on previously presented skills and concepts. The conscientious completion of the daily problem set is essential for student success in this program. The majority of class time should be devoted to student work on the problem set. To focus students on the problem set, some teachers choose to begin class each day with five selected problems from the new problem set. This is an acceptable variation from beginning class with facts practice, which then moves to a later portion of the class period. Students should deliberately work on the more difficult problems in the set while they are in class and save the easier problems for homework. Designating student tutors and cooperative groups to assist students who are having difficulty can help all students be successful.

Investigations are variations of the daily lesson. The investigations included in *Math 76* are activities that may fill an entire class period and contain their own set of questions rather than an integrated problem set. Note that investigations often require materials that need to be assembled prior to class time. The prescribed pacing is to complete a lesson, an investigation, or a test each day.

## Assessment

An available test booklet contains two forms of tests for every five lessons. The second test form may be used for make-up testing. Tests should be given about five lessons after the last concept has been taught. Thus Test 1, which covers topics from Lesson 1 through Lesson 5, should be given after Lesson 10. Test 2 should be given after Lesson 15, Test 3 after Lesson 20, and so on. This allows the students time to learn the new topic before being tested on it. Students will make excellent progress if they are able to score 80% or better on the tests. Students who fall below the 80% level should be given remedial attention immediately. Some teachers choose to test every ten lessons using only the even-numbered or odd-numbered tests. This is an acceptable alternative to testing every five lessons.

*Stephen Hake*                                                    *John Saxon*
*Temple City, California*                          *Norman, Oklahoma*

# Acknowledgments

We thank Shirley McQuade Davis for her ideas on teaching word problem thinking patterns and Dan Gallup for his content editing. We would also like to thank the following people for their contributions in the production of this revision: Edward Burr, Adriana Castaneda, John Chitwood, Chris Cope, Serena Freeberg, Mike Lott, Erin McCain, Emerson Mounger, Tara Nance, Anna Maria Rodriguez, Heather Shaver, Ryan Solomon, Travis Southern, Letha Steinbron, and Julie Webster.

# Adding Whole Numbers and Money • Subtracting Whole Numbers and Money • Fact Families

Mental Math:
a. 60
b. 600
c. 120
d. 1200
e. 90
f. 900
Problem Solving:
18

**Facts Practice:** 64 Addition Facts (Test A in Test Masters)[†]

**Mental Math:** Count by 10's from 10 to 100 and from 100 to 0. Count by 100's from 100 to 1000 and from 1000 to 0.

    **a.** 30 + 30      **b.** 300 + 300      **c.** 80 + 40
    **d.** 800 + 400     **e.** 20 + 30 + 40     **f.** 200 + 300 + 400

**Problem Solving:** Sam thought of a number between ten and twenty. Then he gave a clue: You say the number when you count by twos and when you count by threes, but not when you count by fours. Of what number was Sam thinking?

**Adding whole numbers and money**

To combine two or more numbers we **add.** The numbers added together are called **addends.** The answer is called the **sum.**

When adding numbers, we add digits that have the same place value.

**Example 1**    345 + 67

*Solution*    When we add whole numbers on paper, we write the numbers so that the last digits are aligned one above the other. Then we add the digits in each column.

$$\begin{array}{r} \overset{1\,1}{345} \\ +\phantom{0}67 \\ \hline 412 \end{array}$$   addend
  addend
  sum

Changing the order of the addends does not change the sum. One way to check an addition answer is to change the order of the addends, and add again.

$$\begin{array}{r} \overset{1\,1}{67} \\ +\,345 \\ \hline 412 \end{array}$$   check

---

[†]For instructions on how to use the boxed activities, please consult the preface.

1

Example 2   $1.25 + $12.50 + $5

*Solution*   When we add money we write the numbers so that the decimal points are aligned. We write $5 as $5.00 and add the digits in each column.

$$\begin{array}{r} \$1.25 \\ \$12.50 \\ + \ \$5.00 \\ \hline \mathbf{\$18.75} \end{array}$$

**Subtracting whole numbers and money**   We find the **difference** between two numbers when we subtract.

$$5 - 3 = 2$$

The difference between 5 and 3 is 2.

When subtracting on paper, we align digits with the same place value. Order matters in subtraction: $2 - 4$ is not the same as $4 - 2$. Here are two forms we use to show we are subtracting 3 from 5.

$$5 - 3 \qquad \begin{array}{r} 5 \\ - \ 3 \\ \hline \end{array}$$

Example 3   $345 - 67$

*Solution*   When we subtract whole numbers, we align the last digits. We subtract the bottom number from the top number. We regroup when it is necessary.

$$\begin{array}{r} {}^{2}\cancel{3}\ {}^{13}\cancel{4}\ {}^{1}5 \\ - \quad 6\ 7 \\ \hline \mathbf{2\ 7\ 8} \leftarrow \text{difference} \end{array}$$

Example 4   Jim spent $1.25 for a hamburger. He paid for it with a five-dollar bill. Find how much change he should get back by subtracting $1.25 from $5.

*Solution*   Order matters when we subtract. The starting amount is put on top. We write $5 as $5.00. We line up the decimal points to line up place values. Then we subtract. Jim should get back $3.75.

$$\begin{array}{r} {}^{4}\cancel{\$5}.{}^{9}\cancel{0}\ {}^{1}0 \\ - \ \$1.2\ 5 \\ \hline \mathbf{\$3.7\ 5} \end{array}$$

We may check the answer to a subtraction problem by adding. If we add the answer (difference) to the amount subtracted, the total should equal the starting amount. We do not need to rewrite the problem. We just add the two bottom numbers to see if their sum equals the top number.

| SUBTRACT DOWN:<br>To find the<br>difference | $5.00<br>$- $1.25$<br>$3.75 | ADD UP:<br>To check<br>the answer |
|---|---|---|

**Fact families**   The numbers 4, 5, and 9 are a fact family. They can be arranged to form two addition facts and two subtraction facts.

$$
\begin{array}{cccc}
4 & 5 & 9 & 9 \\
+\,5 & +\,4 & -\,5 & -\,4 \\
\hline
9 & 9 & 4 & 5
\end{array}
$$

**Example 5**   Rearrange the numbers in this addition fact to form another addition fact and two subtraction facts.

$$11 + 14 = 25$$

*Solution*   We form another addition fact by reversing the addends.

**14 + 11 = 25**

We form two subtraction facts by making the sum, 25, the first number of the two subtraction facts. Each of the other numbers may be subtracted from 25.

**25 − 11 = 14**

**25 − 14 = 11**

**Example 6**   Rearrange the numbers in this subtraction fact to make another subtraction fact and two addition facts.

$$
\begin{array}{r}
11 \\
-\ 6 \\
\hline
5
\end{array}
$$

*Solution*  We may not reverse the first two numbers of a subtraction problem, but we may reverse the last two numbers.

$$
\begin{array}{r} 11 \\ -\ 6 \\ \hline 5 \end{array}
\qquad\qquad
\begin{array}{r} 11 \\ -\ 5 \\ \hline 6 \end{array}
$$

We make 11 the sum of the two addition facts.

$$
\begin{array}{r} 5 \\ +\ 6 \\ \hline 11 \end{array}
\qquad\qquad
\begin{array}{r} 6 \\ +\ 5 \\ \hline 11 \end{array}
$$

**Practice**

a. 3675 + 426 + 1357
5458

b. $6.25 + $8.23 + $12
$26.48

c. 5374 − 168    5206

d. $6 − $1.35    $4.65

e. Arrange the numbers 6, 8, and 14 to make two addition facts and two subtraction facts.
6 + 8 = 14, 8 + 6 = 14, 14 − 6 = 8, 14 − 8 = 6

f. Rearrange the numbers in this subtraction fact to make another subtraction fact and two addition facts.
25 − 15 = 10,
10 + 15 = 25,     25 − 10 = 15
15 + 10 = 25

**Problem set 1**

1. What is the sum of 25 and 40?    65

2. Johnny had 137 apple seeds in one pocket and 89 in another. He found 9 more seeds in his cuff. Find how many seeds he had in all by adding 137, 89, and 9.    235 seeds

3. What is the difference when 93 is subtracted from 387?
294

4. John paid $5 for a movie ticket that cost $3.75. To find out how much money John should get back, subtract $3.75 from $5.    $1.25

$6.37  5. Monica had $5.22 and earned $1.15 more. To find how much money Monica had in all, add $1.15 to $5.22.

**6.** The hamburger cost $1.25, the fries cost $0.70, and the drink cost $0.60. To find the total price of the lunch, add $1.25, $0.70, and $0.60.   $2.55

**7.**
```
   63
   47
 + 50
 ────
  160
```

**8.**
```
  632
   57
 + 198
 ─────
  887
```

**9.**
```
   78
    9
 + 967
 ─────
 1054
```

**10.**
```
  432
  579
 + 3604
 ──────
 4615
```

**11.** 345 − 67   278

**12.** 678 − 416   262

**13.** 3764 − 96   3668

**14.** 875 + 1086 + 980
  2941

**15.** 10 + 156 + 8 + 27   201

**16.**
```
  $3.47
 − $0.92
 ──────
  $2.55
```

**17.**
```
  $24.15
 −  $1.45
 ───────
  $22.70
```

**18.**
```
  $0.75
 + $0.75
 ──────
  $1.50
```

**19.**
```
  $0.12
  $0.46
 + $0.50
 ──────
  $1.08
```

**20.** What is the name for the answer when we add?   sum

**21.** What is the name for the answer when we subtract?
  difference

**22.** The numbers 5, 6, and 11 are a fact family. Make two addition facts and two subtraction facts with these three numbers.
  5 + 6 = 11, 6 + 5 = 11, 11 − 6 = 5, 11 − 5 = 6

**23.** Rearrange the numbers in this addition fact to make another addition fact and two subtraction facts.
  16 + 27 = 43,
  43 − 16 = 27,       27 + 16 = 43
  43 − 27 = 16

**24.** Rearrange the numbers in this subtraction fact to make another subtraction fact and two addition facts.
  50 − 29 = 21,
  29 + 21 = 50,       50 − 21 = 29
  21 + 29 = 50

25. Add the answer (difference) to the amount subtracted. The total should equal the starting amount.

**25.** Describe a way to check the correctness of a subtraction answer.

# Multiplying Whole Numbers and Money • Dividing Whole Numbers and Money • Fact Families

**Mental Math:**
**a.** 540
**b.** 260
**c.** 270
**d.** 770
**e.** 480
**f.** 480
**Problem Solving:**
15; 21

---

**Facts Practice:** 64 Addition Facts (Test A in Test Masters)

**Mental Math:** Count by 5's from 5 to 100 and from 100 to 0. Count by 2's from 2 to 20 and from 20 to 2.

   **a.** 500 + 40     **b.** 60 + 200     **c.** 30 + 200 + 40
   **d.** 70 + 300 + 400   **e.** 400 + 50 + 30   **f.** 60 + 20 + 400

**Problem Solving:** Robert made three triangle patterns using 3 coins, 6 coins, and 10 coins. If he continues the patterns, how many coins will he need to make each of the next two triangle patterns?

---

**Multiplying whole numbers and money**

When we add the same number several times, we get the sum. We can get the same answer by multiplying.

$$\underbrace{67 + 67 + 67 + 67 + 67}_{\text{Five 67's equal 335.}} = 335$$

$$5 \times 67 = 335$$

Numbers that are multiplied together are called **factors.** The answer is called the **product.**

When we multiply by a two-digit number on paper we multiply twice. To multiply 28 by 14, we first multiply 28 by 4. Then we multiply 28 by 10. For each multiplication, we write a partial product. We add the partial products to find the final product.

$$
\begin{array}{r}
28 \\
\times\ 14 \\
\hline
112 \\
280 \\
\hline
392
\end{array}
\quad
\begin{array}{l}
\text{factor} \\
\text{factor} \\
\text{partial product } (4 \times 28) \\
\text{partial product } (10 \times 28) \\
\text{product } (14 \times 28)
\end{array}
$$

When multiplying dollars and cents by a whole number the answer will have cents' places, that is, two places after the decimal point.

$$\begin{array}{r} \$1.35 \\ \times \quad 6 \\ \hline \$8.10 \end{array}$$

**Example 1**    Find the cost of two dozen pencils at 35¢ each.

*Solution*    Two dozen is two 12's, which is 24. To find the cost of 24 pencils we multiply 35¢ by 24.

$$\begin{array}{r} 35¢ \\ \times \quad 24 \\ \hline 140 \\ 700 \\ \hline 840¢ \end{array}$$

The cost of two dozen pencils is 840¢, which is **$8.40.**

Reversing the order of the factors does not change the product.

$$4 \times 2 = 2 \times 4$$

One way to check multiplication is to reverse the order of factors and multiply again.

$$\begin{array}{r} 23 \\ \times \quad 14 \\ \hline 92 \\ 230 \\ \hline 322 \end{array} \qquad \begin{array}{r} 14 \\ \times \quad 23 \\ \hline 42 \\ 280 \\ \hline 322 \end{array} \quad \begin{array}{l} \text{factors reversed} \\ \\ \\ \\ \text{check} \end{array}$$

When one of the two factors of a multiplication is one, the product equals the other factor. When one of the two factors is zero, the product is zero.

$$\text{Any number} \times 0 = 0$$

**Example 2**   Multiply:   $\begin{array}{r} 400 \\ \times\ 874 \\ \hline \end{array}$

*Solution*   Reversing the order of the factors may make a multiplication problem easier. Writing trailing zeros so that they "hang out" to the right simplifies the multiplication.

$$\begin{array}{r} {\scriptstyle 2\ 1} \\ 874 \\ \times\quad 400 \\ \hline \textbf{349,600} \end{array}$$

**Dividing whole numbers and money**   When a number is to be separated into a certain number of equal parts, we divide. We can indicate division in several ways. Here are three ways to show that 24 is to be divided by 2.

$$24 \div 2 \qquad 2\overline{)24} \qquad \frac{24}{2}$$

The answer to a division problem is the **quotient.** The number that is divided is the **dividend.** The number by which the dividend is divided is the **divisor.** We show these terms in the three division forms in this table.

| dividend ÷ divisor = quotient |
| --- |
| $\text{divisor}\overline{)\text{dividend}}^{\,\text{quotient}}$ |
| $\dfrac{\text{dividend}}{\text{divisor}} = \text{quotient}$ |

When the dividend is zero, the quotient is zero. The divisor may not be zero. When the dividend and divisor are equal (and not zero), the quotient is one.

**Example 3**    $3456 \div 7$

*Solution*    We show both the long division and short division methods.

LONG DIVISION:              SHORT DIVISION:

$$
\begin{array}{r}
493 \text{ r } 5 \\
7\overline{)3456} \\
\underline{28} \\
65 \\
\underline{63} \\
26 \\
\underline{21} \\
5
\end{array}
\qquad
\begin{array}{r}
4 \ 9 \ 3 \text{ r } 5 \\
7\overline{)3 \ 4^6 5^2 6}
\end{array}
$$

Using the short division method we perform the multiplication and subtraction steps mentally, recording only the result of each subtraction.

To check our work we multiply the quotient by the divisor, then add the remainder to this answer. The result should be the dividend. For this example we multiply 493 by 7. Then we add 5.

$$
\begin{array}{r}
{}^{6\,2}\phantom{00} \\
493 \\
\times \quad 7 \\
\hline
3451 \\
+ \quad \ 5 \\
\hline
3456
\end{array}
$$

When dividing dollars and cents, there will be cents in the answer. Notice that the decimal point is directly up from the decimal point in the division box, separating the dollars from the cents.

$$
\begin{array}{r}
\$1.60 \\
3\overline{)\$4.80} \\
\underline{3}\phantom{.00} \\
1\ 8 \\
\underline{1\ 8} \\
00 \\
\underline{0} \\
0
\end{array}
$$

**Fact families**   There are multiplication and division fact families just as there are addition and subtraction fact families. The numbers 5, 6, and 30 are a fact family. We can form two multiplication facts and two division facts with these numbers.

$$5 \times 6 = 30 \qquad 30 \div 5 = 6$$
$$6 \times 5 = 30 \qquad 30 \div 6 = 5$$

**Example 4**   Rearrange the numbers in this multiplication fact to make another multiplication fact and two division facts.

$$5 \times 12 = 60$$

*Solution*   By reversing the factors we make another multiplication fact.

$$\mathbf{12 \times 5 = 60}$$

By making 60 the dividend we can form two division facts.

$$\mathbf{60 \div 5 = 12}$$
$$\mathbf{60 \div 12 = 5}$$

**Practice**\*†   **a.** $20 \times 37¢$
$7.40

**b.** $37 \times 0$   0

**c.** $407 \times 37$
15,059

**d.** $\dfrac{\$1.68}{5)\$8.40}$

**e.** $200 \div 12$
16 r 8

**f.** $\dfrac{234}{3}$   78

**g.** Which numbers are the divisors in problems (d), (e), and (f)?   5; 12; 3

**h.** Use the numbers 8, 9, and 72 to make two multiplication facts and two division facts.   $8 \times 9 = 72$,   $72 \div 9 = 8$,
$9 \times 8 = 72$,   $72 \div 8 = 9$

---

†All lessons with practice sets starred with an asterisk (\*) have supplemental practice sets in the appendix. These sets may be used as needed for additional practice.

**Problem set 2**

†**1.** If the factors are 7 and 11, what is the product?    77
*(2)*

**2.** What is the difference between 97 and 79?    18
*(1)*

**3.** If the addends are 170 and 130, then what is the sum?
*(1)*   300

**4.** If 36 is the dividend and 4 is the divisor, what is the
*(2)*   quotient?    9

**5.** Find the sum of 386, 98, and 1734.    2218
*(1)*

**6.** Jim spent $2.25 for a hamburger. He paid for it with a
*(1)*   five-dollar bill. Find how much change he should get
back by subtracting $2.25 from $5.    $2.75

**7.** Luke wants to buy a $70.00 radio for his car. He has
*(1)*   $47.50. Find how much more money he needs by
subtracting $47.50 from $70.00.    $22.50

**8.** Each energy bar costs 75¢. Find the cost of one dozen
*(2)*   energy bars by multiplying 75¢ by 12.    $9.00

**9.**  $\begin{array}{r} 312 \\ -\ 86 \\ \hline 226 \end{array}$
*(1)*

**10.**  $\begin{array}{r} 4106 \\ +\ 1398 \\ \hline 5504 \end{array}$
*(1)*

**11.**  $\begin{array}{r} 4000 \\ -\ 1357 \\ \hline 2643 \end{array}$
*(1)*

**12.**  $\begin{array}{r} \$10.00 \\ -\ \$2.83 \\ \hline \$7.17 \end{array}$
*(1)*

**13.**  $\begin{array}{r} 405 \\ \times\ \ \ 8 \\ \hline 3240 \end{array}$
*(2)*

**14.**  $\begin{array}{r} 25 \\ \times\ 25 \\ \hline 625 \end{array}$
*(2)*

**15.**  $\dfrac{288}{6}$    48
*(2)*

**16.**  $\dfrac{225}{15}$    15
*(2)*

**17.** $1.25 × 8    $10.00
*(2)*

**18.** 400 × 50    20,000
*(2)*

**19.** 1000 ÷ 8    125
*(2)*

**20.** $45.00 ÷ 20    $2.25
*(2)*

---

†The italicized numbers within parentheses underneath each problem number are called *lesson reference numbers*. These numbers refer to the lesson(s) in which the major concept of that particular problem is introduced. A lesson reference number of *N.R.* means "no reference." If additional assistance is needed, reference should be made to the discussion, examples, practice, or problem set of that lesson.

**21.** Use the numbers 6, 8, and 48 to make two
<sup>(2)</sup> multiplication facts and two division facts.
$6 \times 8 = 48$, $8 \times 6 = 48$, $48 \div 6 = 8$, $48 \div 8 = 6$

**22.** Rearrange the numbers in this division fact to make
<sup>(2)</sup> another division fact and two multiplication facts.
$36 \div 9 = 4$,
$4 \times 9 = 36$,
$9 \times 4 = 36$
$$4\overline{)36}^{\,9}$$

$24 + 12 = 36$,
$36 - 24 = 12$,
$36 - 12 = 24$

**23.** Rearrange the numbers in this addition fact to make
<sup>(1)</sup> another addition fact and two subtraction facts.
$$12 + 24 = 36$$

**24.** Find the sum of 9 and 6 and the difference between 9
<sup>(1)</sup> and 6.    15; 3

**25.** The divisor, dividend, and quotient are in these
<sup>(2)</sup> positions when we use a division sign.

Dividend ÷ divisor = quotient   $\text{divisor}\overline{)\text{dividend}}^{\,\text{quotient}}$

On your paper, draw a division box and show the
position of the divisor, dividend, and quotient.

**26.** Multiply to find the answer to this addition problem:
<sup>(2)</sup>
$$39¢ + 39¢ + 39¢ + 39¢ + 39¢ + 39¢$$
$39¢ \times 6 = \$2.34$

**27.** $365 \times 0$   0     **28.** $0 \div 50$   0     **29.** $365 \div 365$   1
<sup>(2)</sup>            <sup>(2)</sup>           <sup>(2)</sup>

**30.** Describe a way to check the correctness of a division
<sup>(2)</sup> answer that has no remainder.   Multiply the divisor and
the quotient. The answer should equal the dividend.

LESSON
3

# Missing Numbers in Addition •
# Missing Numbers in Subtraction

Mental Math:
a. 7000
b. 2600
c. 3020
d. 920
e. 4500
f. 4370
Problem Solving:
6

**Facts Practice:** 100 Addition Facts (Test B in Test Masters)

**Mental Math:** Count by 5's from 5 to 100 and from 100 to 0.
　　　　　　　Count by 50's from 50 to 1000 and from 1000 to 0.
　**a.** 3000 + 4000　　**b.** 600 + 2000　　　**c.** 20 + 3000
　**d.** 600 + 300 + 20　**e.** 4000 + 300 + 200　**f.** 70 + 300 + 4000

**Problem Solving:** Shoes in a typical shoe box cannot "get out"
　　　　　　　because they are closed in by a number of flat
　　　　　　　surfaces. How many surfaces enclose a pair of
　　　　　　　shoes in a closed shoe box?

**Missing numbers in addition**

Below is an addition fact with three numbers. If one of the addends is missing we can use the other addend and the sum to figure out the missing number.

$$\begin{array}{r} 4 \\ + \ 3 \\ \hline 7 \end{array}$$

Cover the 4 with your finger. How can you use the 7 and the 3 to figure out that the number under your finger is 4?

Now cover the 3 instead of the 4. How can you use the other two numbers to figure out that the number under your finger is 3?

Notice that we can find a missing addend by subtracting the known addend from the sum. We will use a letter to stand for a missing number. The letter may be lowercase or uppercase.

**Example 1**　Find the number for $m$:
$$\begin{array}{r} 12 \\ + \ m \\ \hline 31 \end{array}$$

*Solution*　One of the addends is missing. The known addend is 12. The sum is 31. If we subtract 12 from 31 we find that the missing addend is **19.** We check our answer by using 19 in place of $m$ in the original problem.

$$\begin{array}{r} \overset{2}{\cancel{3}}\,\overset{1}{1} \\ -\ 1\,2 \\ \hline 1\,9 \end{array} \quad \begin{array}{c} \text{Use 19 in} \\ \text{place of } m. \end{array} \quad \begin{array}{r} \overset{1}{1}2 \\ +\ 19 \\ \hline 31 \end{array} \quad \text{check}$$

**Example 2**    Find the number for $n$:

$$36 + 17 + 5 + n = 64$$

*Solution*    First we add all the known addends.

$$\underbrace{36\ +\ 17\ +\ 5}_{58}\ +\ n = 64$$
$$58 \qquad +\ n = 64$$

Then we find $n$ by subtracting 58 from 64.

$$64 - 58 = 6 \quad \text{So } n \text{ is } \mathbf{6.}$$

We check our work by using 6 in place of $n$ in the original problem to be sure the sum is 64.

$$36 + 17 + 5 + 6 = 64 \quad \text{The answer checks.}$$

**Missing numbers in subtraction**    Below is a subtraction fact. Cover the 8 with your finger and describe how to use the other two numbers to figure out that the number under your finger is 8.

$$\begin{array}{r} 8 \\ -\ 3 \\ \hline 5 \end{array}$$

Now cover the 3 instead of the 8. Describe how to use the other two numbers to figure out that the covered number is 3.

**Example 3**    Find the number for $W$:

$$\begin{array}{r} W \\ -\ 16 \\ \hline 24 \end{array}$$

*Solution*  We can find the first number of a subtraction problem by adding the other two numbers. We add 16 and 24 and get **40.** We check our answer by using 40 in place of *W*.

$$
\begin{array}{r}
{}^{1}\\
16\\
+\ 24\\
\hline
40
\end{array}
\qquad
\begin{array}{c}
\text{Use 40 in}\\
\text{place of } W.
\end{array}
\qquad
\begin{array}{r}
{}^{3}\,{}^{1}\\
\cancel{4}\,0\\
-\ 1\ 6\\
\hline
2\ 4 \quad \text{check}
\end{array}
$$

**Example 4**  Find the number for *y*:

$$236 - y = 152$$

*Solution*  One way to figure out how to find a missing number is to think of a simpler problem that is similar. Here is a simpler subtraction fact.

$$5 - 3 = 2$$

In the problem, *y* is in the same position as the 3 in the simpler subtraction fact. Just as we can find 3 by subtracting 2 from 5, so we can find *y* by subtracting 152 from 236.

$$
\begin{array}{r}
{}^{1}\,{}^{1}\\
\cancel{2}\,3\ 6\\
-\ 1\ 5\ 2\\
\hline
8\ 4
\end{array}
$$

We find that *y* is **84.** Now we check our answer by using 84 in place of *y* in the original problem.

$$
\begin{array}{r}
{}^{1}\,{}^{1}\\
\cancel{2}\,3\ 6\\
-\ \ \ \ 8\ 4\\
\hline
1\ 5\ 2
\end{array}
$$

← Use 84 in place of *y*.

← The answer checks.

To summarize, we find the first number of a subtraction problem by adding the other two numbers. We find the second number by subtracting the difference from the first number.

**Practice*** Find the missing number in each problem:

a.
$$\begin{array}{r} A \\ +\ 12 \\ \hline 45 \end{array}$$  33

b.
$$\begin{array}{r} 32 \\ +\ B \\ \hline 60 \end{array}$$  28

c.
$$\begin{array}{r} C \\ -\ 15 \\ \hline 24 \end{array}$$  39

d.
$$\begin{array}{r} 38 \\ -\ D \\ \hline 29 \end{array}$$  9

e. $e + 24 = 52$    28

f. $29 + f = 70$    41

g. $g - 67 = 43$    110

h. $80 - h = 36$    44

i. $36 + 14 + n + 8 = 75$    17

**Problem set 3**

1. If the two factors are 25 and 12, then what is the product?
(2)    300

2. If the addends are 25 and 12, then what is the sum?
(1)    37

3. What is the difference of 25 and 12?    13
(1)

4. Each of the 31 students brought 75 aluminum cans to class. Find how many cans the class collected by multiplying 31 and 75.    2325 cans
(2)

5. Find the total price of one dozen pepperoni pizzas at $7.85 each by multiplying $7.85 by 12.    $94.20
(2)

6. The basketball team scored 63 of its 102 points in the first half of the game. Find how many points the team scored in the second half by subtracting 63 points from 102 points.    39 points
(1)

7.
$$\begin{array}{r} \$3.68 \\ \times\ \ \ \ \ 9 \\ \hline \$33.12 \end{array}$$
(2)

8.
$$\begin{array}{r} 407 \\ \times\ \ 80 \\ \hline 32{,}560 \end{array}$$
(2)

9.
$$\begin{array}{r} 28¢ \\ \times\ 14 \\ \hline \$3.92 \end{array}$$
(2)

10.
$$\begin{array}{r} 370 \\ \times\ 140 \\ \hline 51{,}800 \end{array}$$
(2)

11. $100 \times 100$    10,000
(2)

12. $144 \div 12$    12
(2)

13. $12 \times 5$    60
(2)

14.
$$\begin{array}{r} 3627 \\ 598 \\ +\ 4881 \\ \hline 9106 \end{array}$$
(1)

15.
$$\begin{array}{r} 5010 \\ -\ 1376 \\ \hline 3634 \end{array}$$
(1)

16.
$$\begin{array}{r} \$10.00 \\ -\ \ \$0.26 \\ \hline \$9.74 \end{array}$$
(1)

Find the missing number in each problem:

**17.**  $\quad A$  32  **18.**  $\quad$ 23  **19.**  $\quad C$  48  **20.**  $\quad$ 42
*(3)*  $\underline{+\ 16}$  *(3)*  $\underline{+\ B}$  29  *(3)*  $\underline{-\ 17}$  *(3)*  $\underline{-\ D}$  17
$\quad\quad$ 48  $\quad\quad$ 52  $\quad\quad$ 31  $\quad\quad$ 25

**21.** $x + 38 = 75$   37
*(3)*

**22.** $x - 38 = 75$   113
*(3)*

**23.** $75 - y = 38$   37
*(3)*

**24.** $6 + 8 + w + 5 = 32$
*(3)*   13

**25.** Rearrange the numbers in this addition fact to make
*(1)*  another addition fact and two subtraction facts.
$\quad$ 48 + 24 = 72,
$\quad$ 72 − 24 = 48,   $\quad$ 24 + 48 = 72
$\quad$ 72 − 48 = 24

**26.** Rearrange the numbers in this multiplication fact to
*(2)*  make another multiplication fact and two division facts.
$\quad$ 15 × 6 = 90,
$\quad$ 90 ÷ 6 = 15,   $\quad$ 6 × 15 = 90
$\quad$ 90 ÷ 15 = 6

**27.** Find the quotient when the divisor is 20 and the
*(2)*  dividend is 200.   10

**28.** Multiply to find the answer to this addition problem:
*(2)*
$\quad\quad$ 15 + 15 + 15 + 15 + 15 + 15 + 15 + 15
$\quad$ 15 × 8 = 120

**29.** 144 ÷ 144   1
*(2)*

**30.** Describe how to find a missing addend in an addition
*(3)*  problem.   To find a missing addend, subtract the known
addend(s) from the sum.

# LESSON 4

# Missing Numbers in Multiplication • Missing Numbers in Division

Mental Math:
a. 2920
b. 8420
c. 7740
d. 2850
e. 1490
f. 9050
Problem Solving:
  315, 351, 513, 531

---

**Facts Practice:** 64 Addition Facts (Test A in Test Masters)

**Mental Math:** Count up and down by 5's between 5 and 100.
         Count up and down by 50's between 50 and 1000.

  **a.** 600 + 2000 + 300 + 20      **b.** 3000 + 20 + 400 + 5000
  **c.** 7000 + 200 + 40 + 500      **d.** 700 + 2000 + 50 + 100
  **e.** 60 + 400 + 30 + 1000      **f.** 900 + 8000 + 100 + 50

**Problem Solving:** The digits 1, 3, and 5 can be arranged to make six different three-digit numbers. Two of the six numbers are 135 and 153. What are the other four numbers?

---

**Missing numbers in multiplication**

This multiplication fact has three numbers. If one of the factors is missing, we can use the other factor and the product to figure out the missing factor.

$$
\begin{array}{r}
4 \\
\times\ 3 \\
\hline
12
\end{array}
$$

Cover up the factors in this multiplication fact one at a time. Describe how you can use the two numbers to find the number that is covered. Notice that we can find a missing factor by dividing the product by the known factor.

**Example 1**  Find the missing number:

$$
\begin{array}{r}
A \\
\times\ 6 \\
\hline
72
\end{array}
$$

**Solution**  The missing number is a factor. The product is 72. The factor that we know is 6. Dividing 72 by 6 we find that the missing factor is **12.** We check our work by using 12 in the original problem.

$$
6\overline{)72} \quad \longrightarrow \quad \begin{array}{r} 12 \\ \times\ 6 \\ \hline 72 \end{array} \ \text{check}
$$

Example 2   Find the missing number: $6w = 84$

Solution   When a number and a letter are written side by side it means that they are to be multiplied. In this problem, $6w$ means 6 times $w$. We divide 84 by 6 and find that the missing factor is **14.** We check the answer by multiplying.

$$
\begin{array}{c}
1\,4 \\
6\,\overline{)8^24}
\end{array}
\longrightarrow
\begin{array}{r}
\overset{2}{1}4 \\
\times\ 6 \\
\hline
84
\end{array}
\quad \text{check}
$$

**Missing numbers in division**   This division fact has three numbers. If we know two of the numbers we can figure out the third number. Cover each of the numbers with your finger and describe how to use the other two numbers to find the covered number.

$$
\begin{array}{c}
4 \\
6\,\overline{)24}
\end{array}
$$

Notice that we can find the dividend, the number inside the division box, by multiplying the other two numbers. We can find either the divisor or quotient, the numbers outside of the box, by dividing.

Example 3   Find the missing number:

$$\frac{k}{6} = 15$$

Solution   The letter $k$ is in the position of the dividend. If we rewrite this problem with a division box it looks like this.

$$
\begin{array}{c}
15 \\
6\,\overline{)k}
\end{array}
$$

We find a missing dividend by multiplying the divisor and quotient. We multiply 15 by 6 and find that the missing number is **90.** Then we check our work.

$$
\begin{array}{r}
\overset{3}{1}5 \\
\times\ 6 \\
\hline
90
\end{array}
\qquad
\begin{array}{c}
1\,5 \\
6\,\overline{)9^30}
\end{array}
\quad \text{check}
$$

**Example 4**   Find the missing number: $126 \div m = 7$

**Solution**   The letter $m$ is in the position of the divisor. If we rewrite the problem with a division box it looks like this.

$$m\overline{)126}^{\,7}$$

We can find $m$ by dividing 126 by 7.

$$7\overline{)1\,2^5 6}^{\,1\,8}$$

We find that $m$ is **18**. We will check our answer by multiplying.

$$\begin{array}{r} {}^{5}\;\; \\ 18 \\ \times\ 7 \\ \hline 126 \end{array}$$

**Practice\***   Find each missing number:

**a.**  $\begin{array}{r} A\ \ 13 \\ \times\ 7 \\ \hline 91 \end{array}$   **b.**  $\begin{array}{r} 20 \\ \times\ \ B\ \ 22 \\ \hline 440 \end{array}$   **c.**  $7\overline{)C}^{\,15}$  105   **d.**  $D\overline{)144}^{\,8}$  18

**e.** $7w = 84$   12   **f.** $112 = 8m$   14

**g.** $\dfrac{360}{x} = 30$   12   **h.** $\dfrac{n}{5} = 60$   300

**Problem set 4**

**1.** Five dozen carrot sticks are to be divided evenly
$^{(2)}$ among 15 children. Find how many carrot sticks each child should receive by dividing 60 by 15.
4 carrot sticks

**2.** Matt separated 100 pennies into 4 equal piles. Find how
$^{(2)}$ many pennies are in each pile by dividing 100 by 4.
25 pennies

20 stacks   **3.** Sandra put 100 pennies into stacks of 5 pennies each.
$^{(2)}$ Find how many stacks are formed by dividing 100 by 5.

**4.** Find the number of 14-player soccer teams that can be
(2) formed if 294 players sign up for soccer by dividing 294 by 14.   21 teams

**5.** Tom is reading a 280-page book. He has just finished
(1) page 156. Find how many pages he still has to read by subtracting 156 from 280.   124 pages

**6.** Each month Bill earns $0.75 per customer for
(2) delivering newspapers. Find how much money he would earn in a month in which he had 42 customers by multiplying $0.75 by 42.   $31.50

Find the missing number:

**7.**   $J$ 12         **8.**      27         **9.**   $L$ 1     **10.**      64
(4)   × 5         (3)   + $K$ 45     (3)   + 36     (3)   − $M$ 18
   ————         ————         ————         ————
     60             72             37             46

**11.** $n - 48 = 84$   132         **12.** $7p = 91$   13
(3)                                 (4)

**13.** $q \div 7 = 0$   0         **14.** $144 \div r = 6$   24
(4)                                 (4)

**15.** $\overset{\$2.06}{6)\overline{\$12.36}}$         **16.** $\dfrac{5760}{8}$   720         **17.** $526 \div 18$
(2)                     (2)                     (2)   29 r 4

**18.** $563 + 563 + 563 + 563$   2252         **19.** $\$3.75 \times 16$
(1)                                             (2)   $60.00

**20.** $3 + \$2.86 + \$0.98$   $6.84         **21.** $10 − \$6.43
(1)                                             (1)   $3.57

**22.** If the divisor is 3 and the quotient is 12, then what is
(4) the dividend?   36

**23.** If the product is 100 and one factor is 5, then what is
(4) the other factor?   20

17 − 8 = 9,   **24.** Rearrange the numbers in this subtraction fact to make
8 + 9 = 17,   (1) another subtraction fact and two addition facts.
9 + 8 = 17

$$17 - 9 = 8$$

**25.** Rearrange the numbers in this division fact to make
(2) another division fact and two multiplication facts.

$72 \div 9 = 8,$
$8 \times 9 = 72,$                    $72 \div 8 = 9$
$9 \times 8 = 72$

**26.** $w + 6 + 8 + 10 = 40$    16
(3)

**27.** Find the answer to this addition problem by multiplying:
(2)

23¢ + 23¢ + 23¢ + 23¢ + 23¢ + 23¢ + 23¢

23¢ × 7 = \$1.61

**28.** $25m = 25$    1          **29.** $15n = 0$    0
(4)                                      (4)

**30.** Describe how to find a missing factor in a multiplication
(4) problem.    To find a missing factor, divide the product by the
known factor.

---

## LESSON
## 5

**Mental Math:**
**a.** 760
**b.** 870
**c.** 7200
**d.** 790
**e.** 5800
**f.** 640
**Problem Solving:**

155
+ 938
1093

# Order of Operations, Part 1

---

**Facts Practice:** 100 Addition Facts (Test B in Test Masters)

**Mental Math:** Count by 25's from 25 to 1000.

| | | |
|---|---|---|
| **a.** 560 + 200 | **b.** 840 + 30 | **c.** 5200 + 2000 |
| **d.** 650 + 140 | **e.** 3800 + 2000 | **f.** 440 + 200 |

**Problem Solving:** Copy this addition problem and fill        1_5
in the five missing digits.              + _3_
_ _93

---

When there is more than one addition or subtraction step
within a problem, we take the steps in order from left to
right. In this problem we first subtract 4 from 9. Then we
add 3.

$$9 - 4 + 3 = 8$$

If a different order of steps is desired, parentheses are used to show which step should be taken first. In the problem below we first add 4 and 3, which equals 7. Then we subtract 7 from 9.

$$9 - (4 + 3) = 2$$

**Example 1** (a) $18 - 6 - 3$ (b) $18 - (6 - 3)$

*Solution* (a) We subtract in order from left to right.

$\underline{18 - 6} - 3$ First subtract 6 from 18.

$\phantom{18 -} 12 \phantom{-} - 3$ Then subtract 3 from 12.

$\phantom{18 - 12 - }$ **9** The answer is 9.

(b) We subtract within the parentheses first.

$18 - \underline{(6 - 3)}$ First subtract 3 from 6.

$18 - \phantom{(} 3 \phantom{)}$ Then subtract 3 from 18.

$\phantom{18 - 3 }$ **15** The answer is 15.

When there is more than one multiplication or division step within a problem, we take the steps in order from left to right.

$$24 \div 6 \times 2 = 8$$

If there are parentheses we first do the work within the parentheses. In this problem we first multiply 6 by 2 and get 12. Then we divide 24 by 12.

$$24 \div (6 \times 2) = 2$$

**Example 2** (a) $18 \div 6 \div 3$ (b) $18 \div (6 \div 3)$

*Solution* (a) We take the steps in order from left to right.

$\underline{18 \div 6} \div 3$ First divide 18 by 6.

$\phantom{18 \div} 3 \phantom{\div} \div 3$ Then divide 3 by 3.

$\phantom{18 \div 3 \div}$ **1** The answer is 1.

(b) We divide within the parentheses first.

$$18 \div (6 \div 3) \quad \text{First divide 6 by 3.}$$

$$18 \div \quad 2 \quad \text{Then divide 18 by 2.}$$

$$\mathbf{9} \quad \text{The answer is 9.}$$

**Example 3**   $\dfrac{5 + 7}{1 + 2}$

*Solution*   Before dividing we add above the bar and below the bar. Then we divide 12 by 3. The quotient is 4.

$$\frac{5 + 7}{1 + 2} = \frac{12}{3} = \mathbf{4}$$

**Practice**   **a.** $16 - 3 + 4$   17   **b.** $16 - (3 + 4)$   9

**c.** $24 \div (4 \times 3)$   2   **d.** $24 \div 4 \times 3$   18

**e.** $24 \div 6 \div 2$   2   **f.** $24 \div (6 \div 2)$   8

**g.** $\dfrac{6 + 9}{3}$   5   **h.** $\dfrac{12 + 8}{12 - 8}$   5

**Problem set 5**

1. Jack paid $5 for a hamburger that cost $1.25 and a
   (1) drink that cost $0.60. How much change should he get
   back?   $3.15

2. In one day the elephant ate 82 pounds of straw, 8
   (1) pounds of apples, and 12 pounds of peanuts. How
   many pounds of food did it eat in all?   102 pounds

3. What is the difference of 110 and 25?   85
   (1)

4. What is the total price of one dozen apples that cost
   (2) 25¢ each?   $3.00

5. What number must be added to 149 to total 516?   367
   (3)

**6.** Judy plans to read a 235-page book in 5 days. Describe
(2) how to find the average number of pages she needs to
read each day.   To find the average number of pages to read
each day, divide 235 pages by 5.

**7.** 5 + (3 × 4)   17
(5)

**8.** (5 + 3) × 4   32
(5)

**9.** 800 − (450 − 125)
(5)   475

**10.** 600 ÷ (20 ÷ 5)   150
(5)

**11.** 800 − 450 − 125
(5)   225

**12.** 600 ÷ 20 ÷ 5   6
(5)

**13.** 144 ÷ (8 × 6)   3
(5)

**14.** 144 ÷ 8 × 6   108
(5)

**15.** $5 − ($1.25 + $0.60)   $3.15
(5)

**16.** Use the numbers 63, 7, and 9 to make two multiplication
(2)   facts and two division facts.
7 × 9 = 63, 9 × 7 = 63, 63 ÷ 7 = 9, 63 ÷ 9 = 7

**17.** If the quotient is 12 and the dividend is 288, then
(4)   what number is the divisor?   24

**18.** $\begin{array}{r} \$0.40 \\ 25\overline{)\$10.00} \end{array}$
(2)

**19.** $\begin{array}{r} 378 \\ \times\ 64 \\ \hline 24{,}192 \end{array}$
(2)

**20.** $\begin{array}{r} 506 \\ \times\ 370 \\ \hline 187{,}220 \end{array}$
(2)

**21.** $\begin{array}{r} \$10.10 \\ -\ \$9.89 \\ \hline \$0.21 \end{array}$
(1)

**22.** $n − 63 = 36$   99
(3)

**23.** $63 − p = 36$   27
(3)

**24.** $56 + m = 432$   376
(3)

**25.** $8w = 480$   60
(4)

**26.** $5 + 12 + 27 + y = 50$   6
(3)

**27.** $36 ÷ a = 4$   9
(4)

**28.** $x ÷ 4 = 8$   32
(4)

**29.** Use the numbers 7, 11, and 18 to make two addition
(1)   facts and two subtraction facts.
7 + 11 = 18, 11 + 7 = 18, 18 − 11 = 7, 18 − 7 = 11

**30.** 3 × 4 × 5   60
(5)

# LESSON
# 6

# Fractional Parts

**Facts Practice:** 100 Subtraction Facts (Test C in Test Masters)

**Mental Math:** Count up and down by 25's between 25 and 1000.

   **a.** 2500 + 400    **b.** 6000 + 2400    **c.** 370 + 400

   **d.** 9500 + 240    **e.** 360 + 1200    **f.** 480 + 2500

**Problem Solving:** Alex had seven coins in his pocket totaling exactly one dollar. Name a possible collection of coins in his pocket. How many different collections of coins are possible?

When we first began to learn about numbers as young children we counted objects. When we count we are using whole numbers. As we grew older we discovered that there are parts of wholes—like parts of a candy bar—which cannot be named with whole numbers. We can name these parts with **fractions.** A common fraction is written with two numbers and a fraction bar. The "bottom" number is the **denominator.** The denominator shows the number of equal parts in the whole. The "top" number, the **numerator,** shows the number of the parts being described.

We see that this whole circle has been divided into **4** equal parts; **1** part is shaded. The fraction of the circle which is shaded is 1 out of 4 parts. We call this part one fourth and write it as $\frac{1}{4}$.

Example 1   What fraction of the circle is shaded?

*Solution*   The circle has been divided into 6 equal parts. We use 6 for the bottom of the fraction. One of the parts is shaded, so we use 1 for the top of the fraction. The fraction of the circle which is shaded is one sixth, which we write as $\frac{1}{6}$.

We can also use a fraction to name a part of a group. There are 6 members in this group. We can divide this group in half by dividing it into two equal groups with 3 in each half. We write that $\frac{1}{2}$ of 6 is 3.

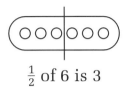

$\frac{1}{2}$ of 6 is 3

We can divide this group into thirds by dividing the 6 members into three equal groups. We write that $\frac{1}{3}$ of 6 is 2.

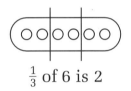

$\frac{1}{3}$ of 6 is 2

**Example 2**   (a)  What number is $\frac{1}{2}$ of 450?

(b)  What number is $\frac{1}{3}$ of 450?

(c)  How much money is $\frac{1}{5}$ of $4.50?

*Solution*   (a)  To find $\frac{1}{2}$ of 450 we divide 450 into two equal parts and find the amount in one of the parts. We find that $\frac{1}{2}$ of 450 is **225.**

$$\frac{225}{2\overline{)450}}$$

$\frac{1}{2}$ of 450 is 225

(b)  To find $\frac{1}{3}$ of 450 we divide 450 into three equal parts. Since each part is 150, we find that $\frac{1}{3}$ of 450 is **150.**

$$\frac{150}{3\overline{)450}}$$

$\frac{1}{3}$ of 450 is 150

(c) To find $\frac{1}{5}$ of \$4.50 we divide \$4.50 by 5. We find that $\frac{1}{5}$ of \$4.50 is **\$0.90.**

$$\begin{array}{r} \$0.90 \\ 5\overline{)\$4.50} \end{array}$$

$\frac{1}{5}$ of \$4.50 is \$0.90

**Practice**   Use both words and digits to write the fraction that is shaded:

**a.**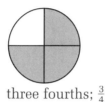

three fourths; $\frac{3}{4}$

**b.**

two fifths; $\frac{2}{5}$

**c.**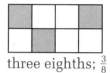

three eighths; $\frac{3}{8}$

**d.** What number is $\frac{1}{2}$ of 72?   36

**e.** What number is $\frac{1}{2}$ of 1000?   500

**f.** What number is $\frac{1}{3}$ of 180?   60

**g.** How much money is $\frac{1}{3}$ of \$3.60?   \$1.20

**Problem set 6**

**1.** What number is $\frac{1}{2}$ of 540?   270
*(6)*

**2.** What number is $\frac{1}{3}$ of 540?   180
*(6)*

**3.** In four days of sight-seeing the Richmonds drove 346
*(1)* miles, 417 miles, 289 miles, and 360 miles, respectively. How many miles did they drive in all?
1412 miles

**4.** Brad paid \$20 for a book that cost \$12.08. How much
*(1)* money should he get back?   \$7.92

**5.** How many days are in 52 weeks?   364 days
*(2)*

**6.** How many \$20 bills would it take to make \$1000?   50
*(2)*

**7.** Use words and digits to write the
*(6)* fraction that is shaded.
five sixths; $\frac{5}{6}$

**8.**  3604
*(1)*  5186
 + 7145
 —————
 15,935

**9.**   $30.01
*(1)*  − $15.76
 —————
  $14.25

**10.**  376
*(2)*  × 87
 ——————
 32,712

**11.**  470
*(2)*  × 203
 ——————
 95,410

**12.** $20 − $11.98  $8.02
*(1)*

**13.** 596 − (400 − 129)  325
*(5)*

**14.** 32 ÷ (8 × 4)  1
*(5)*

**15.** 8)4016  502
*(2)*

**16.** 15)6009  400 r 9
*(2)*

**17.** 36)9000  250
*(2)*

**18.**  *W*  60
*(4)*  × 8
 ————
 480

**19.**  *X*  110
*(3)*  − 64
 ————
 46

**20.** $\frac{49}{N}$ = 7  7
*(4)*

**21.** $\frac{M}{7}$ = 15  105
*(4)*

**22.** $6.35 × 12  $76.20
*(2)*

**23.** 365 + *P* = 653  288
*(3)*

**24.** 9 × ☐ = 720  80
*(4)*

**25.** This square was divided in half.
*(6)* Then each half was divided in
 half. What fraction of the square is
 shaded?  $\frac{1}{4}$

**26.** 36¢ + 25¢ + *m* = 99¢  38¢
*(3)*

**27.** Use the numbers 2, 4, and 6 to make two addition facts
(1)  and two subtraction facts.    2 + 4 = 6, 4 + 2 = 6,
6 − 4 = 2, 6 − 2 = 4

**28.** Write two multiplication facts and two division facts
(2)  using the numbers 2, 4, and 8.    2 × 4 = 8, 4 × 2 = 8
8 ÷ 2 = 4, 8 ÷ 4 = 2

**29.** Multiply to find the answer to this addition problem.
(2)
38 + 38 + 38 + 38 + 38 + 38 + 38 + 38 + 38 + 38
38 × 10 = 380

**30.** Make up a fractional part question about money like
(6)  Example 2 (c). Then find the answer.    See student work.

## LESSON 7

# Linear Measure

**Facts Practice:** 100 Subtraction Facts (Test C in Test Masters)

**Mental Math:** Count up and down by $\frac{1}{2}$'s between $\frac{1}{2}$ and 10.
Count up and down by 2's between 2 and 40.

**a.** 800 − 300      **b.** 3000 − 2000      **c.** 450 − 100
**d.** 2500 − 300     **e.** 480 − 80         **f.** 750 − 250

**Problem Solving:** Sharon made three square patterns using 4 coins, 9 coins, and 16 coins. If she continues the patterns, how many coins will she need for each of the next two square patterns?

As civilized people we have agreed upon certain units of measure. In the United States we have two systems of units that we use to measure length. One system is the **U.S. Customary System.** Some of the units in this system are inches (in.), feet (ft), yards (yd), and miles (mi). The other system is the **metric system.** Some of the units in the metric system are millimeters (mm), centimeters (cm), meters (m), and kilometers (km).

## Activity: Inch Ruler

Materials needed by each student:

- Inch ruler
- Narrow strip of tagboard about 6 in. long by 1 in. wide
- Pencil

We will use estimation to make an inch ruler out of tagboard marked to fourths of an inch. Use your pencil and ruler to draw inch marks on the strip of tagboard. Number the inch marks. When you are done, the tagboard strip should look like this.

Now set your ruler aside. We will use estimation to make the rest of the marks on the tagboard strip. Estimate the halfway point between inch marks and make the half inch marks a little bit shorter than the inch marks. Write "$\frac{1}{2}$" below each of these marks.

Every half inch is marked on your ruler. Now we will show every quarter inch by making a shorter mark halfway between each mark on the tagboard ruler. Label the marks as we show here.

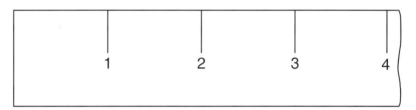

You may use this ruler to help you with the measurements in the problem sets. Save this tagboard ruler. We will be making more marks on it in a few days.

A metric ruler is divided into centimeters. Each centimeter is divided into ten millimeters. So one centimeter equals 10 millimeters, and two centimeters equals 20 millimeters.

*Example 1*  How long is the line segment?

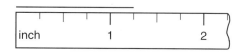

*Solution*  The line is one whole inch plus a fraction. The fraction is one fourth. The length of the line is **$1\frac{1}{4}$ in.**

**Note:** In this book, the abbreviation for "inches" ends with a period. The abbreviations for other units do not end with periods.

*Example 2*  How long is the line segment?

*Solution*  We simply read the scale to see that the line is **2 cm** long. The segment is also **20 mm** long.

**Practice**  How long is each line segment?

**a.** 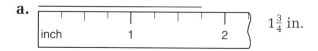  $1\frac{3}{4}$ in.

**b.**   25 mm

**Problem set 7**

1. To earn money for gifts, Debbie sold decorated pine cones. If she sold 100 cones at $0.25 each, how much money did she earn?  $25.00
   (2)

**2.** There are 365 days in a normal year. April 1 is the 91st
*(1)* day. How many days are left in the year after April 1?
274

**3.** The Smiths are planning to complete a 1890-mile trip
*(5)* in 3 days. If they drive 596 miles the first day and 612
miles the second day, how far must they travel the
third day? (*Hint*: This is a two-step problem. First find
how far the Smiths traveled the first two days.)   682 mi

**4.** What number is $\frac{1}{2}$ of 234?   117
*(6)*

**5.** How much money is $\frac{1}{3}$ of $2.34?   $0.78
*(6)*

**6.** Use words and digits to write the
*(6)* fraction of the circle that is shaded.
three eighths; $\frac{3}{8}$

**7.**  3654     **8.**  $41.01    **9.**   28¢     **10.**   906
*(1)*  2893    *(1)* − $15.76    *(2)*  × 74     *(2)*   × 47
   + 5614         ────────        ────────       ────────
   ────────        $25.25         $20.72          42,582
    12,161

         833 r 2
**11.** 6$\overline{)5000}$                      **12.** 800 ÷ 16   50
*(2)*                                  *(2)*

          52 r 54
**13.** 60$\overline{)3174}$                     **14.** 3 + 6 + 5 + w + 4 = 30
*(2)*                                  *(3)*  12

**15.** 300 − 30 + 3   273            **16.** 300 − (30 + 3)   267
*(5)*                                  *(5)*

**17.**   $4.32     **18.**    48¢        **19.** $8.75 ÷ 25
*(2)*  ×    20     *(2)*   × 24        *(2)*  $0.35
   ────────         ────────
    $86.40           $11.52

Find the missing numbers:

**20.** $W \div 6 = 7$     **21.** $6n = 96$     **22.** $58 + r = 213$
*(4)*  42            *(4)*  16          *(3)*  155

60 − 36 = 24,   **23.** Rearrange the numbers in this subtraction fact to make
36 + 24 = 60,   *(1)* another subtraction fact and two addition facts.
24 + 36 = 60

$$60 - 24 = 36$$

**24.** How long is the line segment?    $1\frac{1}{2}$ in.
*(7)*

**25.** Find the length, in centimeters and in millimeters, of
*(7)* the line segment.    3 cm; 30 mm

**26.** Use the numbers 9, 10, and 90 to make two
*(2)* multiplication facts and two division facts.
9 × 10 = 90, 10 × 9 = 90, 90 ÷ 9 = 10, 90 ÷ 10 = 9

**27.** Describe how to find a missing dividend in a division
*(3)* problem.    To find a missing dividend, multiply the quotient
and the divisor.

**28.** $w - 12 = 8$    20          **29.** $12 - x = 8$    4
*(3)*                                *(3)*

**30.** A meter stick is 100 centimeters long. One hundred
*(7)* centimeters is how many millimeters?    1000 mm

# LESSON
# 8

# Perimeter

Mental Math:
a. 2800
b. 786
c. 8920
d. 920
e. 2400
f. 360
Problem Solving:
Answers will vary.

**Facts Practice:** 64 Addition Facts (Test A in Test Masters)

**Mental Math:** Count up by $\frac{1}{4}$'s from $\frac{1}{4}$ to 10.

**a.** 400 + 2400    **b.** 750 + 36    **c.** 8400 + 520

**d.** 980 − 60    **e.** 4400 − 2000    **f.** 480 − 120

**Problem Solving:** As you sit straight in your desk, you can describe the locations of people and objects in your classroom compared to your position. Perhaps a friend is in front and to the left. Perhaps a door is directly to your right. Describe the location of your teacher's desk, the pencil sharpener, and a person or object of your choice.

The distance around a shape is its **perimeter.** The perimeter of a square is the distance around it. The perimeter of a room is the distance around the room.

## Activity: Perimeter

Walk the perimeter of the classroom. Start at a point along a wall of the classroom. Staying close to the walls, walk around the room until you return to your starting point. Count your steps as you travel around the room. How many of your steps is the perimeter of the room? When you are finished, discuss these questions:

b. The perimeter does not change. An agreed upon unit of measure is needed for consistent measurements.

c. 2. Although molding does not cross doorways, it is a good physical model for the perimeter of the room.

**a.** Did everyone count the same number of steps?

Different-sized steps will result in different counts.

**b.** Does the perimeter depend upon who is measuring it?

**c.** Which of these is the best physical example of perimeter?

1. The tile or carpet that covers the floor.

2. The molding along the base of the wall.

Here we have a rectangle that is 3 cm long and 2 cm wide.

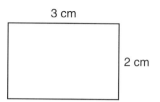

3 cm

2 cm

If we were to trace the perimeter of the rectangle, our pencil would travel 3 cm, then 2 cm, then 3 cm, then 2 cm to get all the way around the rectangle. We add these lengths to find the perimeter of the rectangle.

$$3 \text{ cm} + 2 \text{ cm} + 3 \text{ cm} + 2 \text{ cm} = \textbf{10 cm}$$

**Example**   What is the perimeter of the triangle?

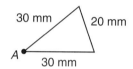

30 mm   20 mm

$A$   30 mm

**Solution**   The perimeter of a shape is the distance around it. If we use a pencil to trace a triangle of the given dimensions from point $A$, the point of the pencil would travel 30 mm, then 20 mm, then 30 mm. Adding these distances, we find that the perimeter is **80 mm.**

**Practice**   What is the perimeter of each shape?

   **a.** Square   48 mm    **b.** Rectangle 70 mm   **c.** Pentagon 5 cm

12 mm

15 mm

20 mm

1 cm   1 cm

1 cm   1 cm

1 cm

   **d.** Equilateral triangle 6 cm     **e.** Trapezoid   55 mm

2 cm

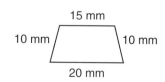

15 mm

10 mm   10 mm

20 mm

**Problem set 8**

**1.** In an auditorium there are 25 rows of chairs with 18
*(2)* chairs in each row. How many chairs are in the
auditorium?  450 chairs

**2.** All the king's horses numbered 765. All the king's
*(1)* men numbered 1750. Find how many fewer horses
than men the king had by subtracting 765 from 1750.
985 fewer horses than men

**3.** Robin Hood divided 140 of his merry men into 5 equal
*(2)* groups. How many were in each group?  28 men

**4.** What is the perimeter of the
*(8)* triangle?  80 mm

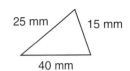

25 mm  15 mm
40 mm

**5.** How much money is $\frac{1}{2}$ of $6.54?  $3.27
*(6)*

**6.** What number is $\frac{1}{3}$ of 654?  218
*(6)*

**7.** What fraction of the rectangle is
*(6)* shaded?  $\frac{3}{10}$

$2.25                   37 r 3                    125                    20 r 20
**8.** 4$\overline{)\$9.00}$  **9.** 10$\overline{)373}$  **10.** 12$\overline{)1500}$  **11.** 39$\overline{)800}$
*(2)*           *(2)*            *(2)*             *(2)*

**12.** 400 ÷ 20 ÷ 4  5       **13.** 400 ÷ (20 ÷ 4)  80
*(5)*                         *(5)*

20 × 12 = 240,     **14.** Use the numbers 240, 20, and 12 to make two
12 × 20 = 240,     *(2)* multiplication facts and two division facts.
240 ÷ 20 = 12,
240 ÷ 12 = 20

**15.** Rearrange the numbers in this addition fact to make
*(1)* another addition fact and two subtraction facts.
80 + 60 = 140,
140 − 80 = 60,          60 + 80 = 140
140 − 60 = 80

**16.** What is the perimeter of a square tile with sides 12
*(8)* inches long?  48 in.

10; 24  **17.** Find the sum of 6 and 4 and find the product of 6 and 4.
*(1,2)*

**18.** $5 − M = $1.48
(3)   $3.52

**19.** 10 × 20 × 30   6000
(5)

**20.** 825 ÷ 8   103 r 1
(2)

Find the missing numbers:

**21.** $w − 63 = 36$   99
(3)

**22.** 150 + 165 + $a$ = 397
(3)   82

**23.** $12w = 120$
(4)   10

**24.** If the divisor is 8 and the quotient is 24, then what is
(4)   the dividend?   192

**25.** How many millimeters long is the line segment?
(7)   27 mm

```
mm   10     20     30     40
|..il..|..il..|..il..|..il..|..il.|)
```

**26.** Use your ruler to help you draw a line segment that is
(7)   $2\frac{3}{4}$ in. long. ——————————————

**27.** $w − 27 = 18$   45
(3)

**28.** $27 − x = 18$   9
(3)

**29.** Multiply to find the answer to this addition problem:
(2)   35 × 4 = 140
35 + 35 + 35 + 35

**30.** Describe how to find the perimeter of a rectangle.
(8)   To find the perimeter of a rectangle, add the lengths of the four
sides.

# LESSON
# 9

# The Number Line: Ordering and Comparing

**Facts Practice:** 100 Subtraction Facts (Test C in Test Masters)

**Mental Math:** Count up and down by 25's between 25 and 1000.

    **a.** 48 + 120      **b.** 76 + 10 + 3      **c.** 7400 + 320

    **d.** 860 − 50      **e.** 960 − 600      **f.** 365 − 200

**Problem Solving:** The digits 2, 4, and 6 can be arranged to form six different three-digit numbers. List the six numbers in order from least to greatest.

A **number line** is a way to show numbers in order.

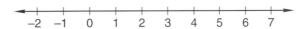

The arrowheads show that the line continues without end and that the numbers continue without end. The small marks crossing the horizontal line are called **tick marks.** Number lines may be labeled with various types of numbers. The numbers we say when we count (1, 2, 3, 4, and so on) are called **counting numbers. Whole numbers** are all of the counting numbers plus the number zero. To the left of zero on this number line are **negative numbers,** which will be described in later lessons. As we move to the right on this number line, the numbers are greater and greater in value. As we move to the left, the numbers are less and less in value.

**Example 1** Arrange the numbers in order from least to greatest:

        121         112         211

*Solution* On a number line these three numbers appear in order from least (on the left) to greatest (on the right).

For our answer we write

        **112**         **121**         **211**

When we **compare** two numbers we decide whether the numbers are equal or if one number is greater and the other is less. We may show a comparison with symbols. If the numbers are equal, the comparison sign we use is the **equals sign** (=).

$$1 + 1 = 2$$

If the numbers are not equal, we use the **greater than/ less than sign** (>). The greater than/less than sign may point to the right or to the left (> or <). When the symbol is properly placed between two numbers, the small point of the symbol points to the smaller number.

**Example 2**    Compare: 5012 ◯ 5102

*Solution*    In place of the circle we should write =, >, or < to make the statement true. Since 5012 is less than 5102, we point the small end to the 5012.

**5012 < 5102**

**Example 3**    Compare: 16 ÷ 8 ÷ 2 ◯ 16 ÷ (8 ÷ 2)

*Solution*    Before we compare the two expressions, we find the number each expression equals.

$$\underbrace{16 \div 8 \div 2}_{1} \bigcirc \underbrace{16 \div (8 \div 2)}_{4}$$

Since 1 is less than 4, the point of the comparison symbol points to the left.

**16 ÷ 8 ÷ 2 < 16 ÷ (8 ÷ 2)**

**Example 4**    Use digits and other symbols to write this comparison:

One fourth is less than one half.

*Solution*    We write the numbers in the order stated.

$$\frac{1}{4} < \frac{1}{2}$$

**Practice**    **a.** Arrange these amounts of money in order from least to greatest:    12¢, $1.20, $12

12¢        $12        $1.20

**b.** Compare:  16 − 8 − 2 ⓒ 16 − (8 − 2)

**c.** Compare:  8 ÷ 4 × 2 ⓢ 8 ÷ (4 × 2)

**d.** 2 × 3 ⓢ 2 + 3          **e.** 1 × 1 × 1 ⓒ 1 + 1 + 1

**f.** Use digits and other symbols to write this comparison:
$\frac{1}{2} > \frac{1}{4}$      One half is greater than one fourth.

**Problem set 9**

**1.** Tamara arranged 144 books into 8 equal stacks. How many books were in each stack?    18 books per stack
*(2)*

**2.** Find how many years there were from 1492 to 1603 by subtracting 1492 from 1603.    111 years
*(1)*

**3.** Martin is carrying groceries in from the car. If he can carry 2 bags at a time, how many trips will it take him to carry in 9 bags?    5 trips
*(2)*

**4.** What is the perimeter of the rectangle?    60 mm
*(8)*

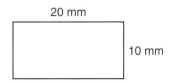

20 mm
10 mm

**5.** How much money is $\frac{1}{2}$ of $5.80?    $2.90
*(6)*

**6.** How many cents is $\frac{1}{4}$ of a dollar?    25¢
*(6)*

**7.** Use words and digits to name the fraction of the triangle that is shaded.    one fourth; $\frac{1}{4}$
*(6)*

**8.** Compare: 5012 ⓒ 5120
*(9)*

**9.** Arrange these numbers in order from least to greatest:
*(9)*    0, $\frac{1}{2}$, 1                1, 0, $\frac{1}{2}$

**10.** Compare: $100 - 50 - 25$ (<) $100 - (50 - 25)$
*(9)*

**11.** $478$  **12.** $\$50.00$  **13.** $\$4.20$  **14.** $78$
*(1)* $3692$  *(1)* $- \$31.76$  *(2)* $\times\ \ \ 60$  *(2)* $\times\ 36$
$+\ \ 45$  $\overline{\ \ \$18.24}$  $\overline{\$252.00}$  $\overline{2808}$
$\overline{4215}$

**15.** $9\overline{)7227}$  (803)  **16.** $25\overline{)7600}$  (304)  **17.** $20\overline{)8014}$  (400 r 14)
*(2)*  *(2)*  *(2)*

**18.** $7136 \div 100$   71 r 36   **19.** $736 \div 736$   1
*(2)*  *(2)*

Find the missing numbers:

**20.** $165 + a = 300$   135   **21.** $b - 68 = 86$   154
*(3)*  *(3)*

**22.** $9c = 144$   16   **23.** $d \div 15 = 7$   105
*(4)*  *(4)*

**24.** How long is the line segment?   $\frac{3}{4}$ in.
*(7)*

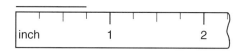

**25.** How many millimeters long is the line segment?   40 mm
*(7)*

**26.** Use digits and symbols to write this comparison:   $\frac{1}{2} > \frac{1}{3}$
*(9)*  One half is greater than one third.

**27.** Arrange the numbers 9, 11, and 99 to form two
*(2)* multiplication facts and two division facts.
$9 \times 11 = 99$, $11 \times 9 = 99$, $99 \div 11 = 9$, $99 \div 9 = 11$

**28.** Compare: $25 + 0$ (>) $25 \times 0$
*(9)*

**29.** $100 = 20 + 30 + 40 + x$   10
*(3)*

30. Since 5012
is less than 5120,
we point the
small end of the
sign to the
smaller number,
5012.

**30.** Describe how to properly position a greater than/less
*(9)* than sign (>) to correctly show the comparison in
problem 8.

# LESSON
# 10

**Sequences • Scales**

Mental Math:
a. 68
b. 870
c. 279
d. 50
e. 250
f. 3200
Problem Solving:

$$\begin{array}{r} 58 \\ +\ 9 \\ \hline 67 \end{array} \qquad \begin{array}{r} 76 \\ +\ 9 \\ \hline 85 \end{array}$$

**Facts Practice:** 100 Subtraction Facts (Test C in Test Masters)

**Mental Math:** Count by $\frac{1}{4}$'s from $\frac{1}{4}$ to 10.

   **a.** 43 + 20 + 5     **b.** 670 + 200     **c.** 254 + 20 + 5
   **d.** 100 − 50     **e.** 300 − 50     **f.** 3600 − 400

**Problem Solving:** Use the digits 5, 6, 7, and 8 to complete this addition problem. There are two possible arrangements.

$$\begin{array}{r} \_\ \_ \\ +\ \ 9 \\ \hline \_\ \_ \end{array}$$

**Sequences**

A **sequence** is an ordered list of numbers that follows a certain rule. Here are two different sequences.

(a) 5, 10, 15, 20, 25, …

(b) 5, 10, 20, 40, 80, …

Sequence (a) is an **addition sequence** because the same number is added to each term of the sequence to get the next term. In this case, 5 is added to each term. Sequence (b) is a **multiplication sequence** because each term of the sequence is multiplied by the same number to get the next term. In (b) each term is multiplied by 2. When we are asked to find missing numbers in a sequence, we inspect the numbers to discover the rule for the sequence. Then we use the rule to find other numbers in the sequence.

**Example 1** What is the next number in this sequence?

1, 3, 9, 27, _____, …

*Solution* Inspecting the numbers, we find that each term in the sequence can be found by multiplying the term before it by 3. Multiplying 27 by 3, we find that the next term in the sequence is **81.**

    The numbers …, 0, 2, 4, 6, 8, … form a special sequence called **even numbers.** We say the even numbers when we "count by twos." Notice that zero is an even number. A whole number with a last digit of 0, 2, 4, 6, or 8 is an even number. The whole numbers which are not even numbers are **odd numbers.** The odd numbers are ... 1, 3, 5, 7, 9, .... An even number of objects can be divided into two equal groups. An odd number of objects cannot be divided into two equal groups.

**Example 2**     Think of a whole number. Double that number. Is the answer even or odd?

*Solution*     The answer is **even.** Doubling any whole number—odd or even—results in an even number.

**Scales**     Numerical information is often presented to us in the form of a **scale** or **graph.** A scale is a display of numbers with an indicator to show where a certain measure falls on the scale. **The trick to reading a scale is to discover the value of the marks on the scale.** Marks on a scale may show every unit or only every two, five, ten, or another number of units. We study the scale to find the value of the units before we try to read the indicated number.

Two commonly used scales on thermometers are the Fahrenheit scale and the Celsius scale. The temperature at which water freezes under standard conditions is 32 degrees Fahrenheit (abbreviated 32°F) and zero degrees Celsius (0°C). The boiling temperature of water is 212°F and 100°C. Normal body temperature is 98.6°F and 37°C. A cool room may be 68°F and 20°C.

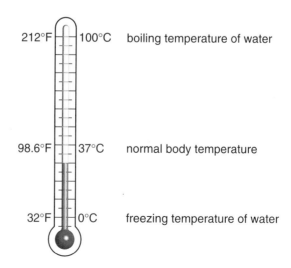

**Example 3** What temperature is shown on the thermometer?

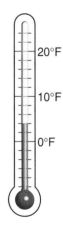

*Solution* As we look at the scale on this Fahrenheit thermometer, we see that the tick marks on the scale divide the distance from 0°F to 10°F into five equal sections. So the number of degrees from one tick mark to the next tick mark must be 2°F. Since the fluid in the thermometer is two marks above the zero mark, the temperature shown is **4°F.**

**Practice** Find the next three numbers in each sequence:

**a.** 18, 27, 36, 45, __54__, __63__, __72__, ...

**b.** 1, 2, 4, 8, __16__, __32__, __64__, ...

**c.** Think of a whole number. Double that number. Then add 1 to the answer. Is the final number even or odd? odd

**d.** Find the temperature indicated on this thermometer to the nearest degree Fahrenheit and to the nearest degree Celsius.   72°F; 22°C

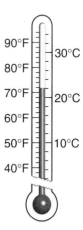

**Problem set 10** **1.** Find the next three numbers in this sequence:
*(10)*
　　　16, 24, 32, __40__, __48__, __56__, ...

**2.** Find how many years there were from 1620 to 1776 by
*(1)* subtracting 1620 from 1776.   156 years

**3.** Is the number 1492 even or odd? How can you tell?
(10)    1492 is even because the last digit, 2, is even. If the last digit of a whole number is even, then the number is even.

**4.** What weight is indicated on this scale?    154 pounds
(10)

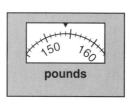

**5.** What is the perimeter of the square?    10 mm
(8)    40 mm

**6.** How much money is $\frac{1}{2}$ of $6.50?
(6)    $3.25

**7.** Compare: 4 × 3 + 2 ⓒ 4 × (3 + 2)
(9)

**8.** Use words and digits to write the fraction of the circle that is **not** shaded.    three fourths; $\frac{3}{4}$
(6)

**9.** What is the product of 100 and 100 and the sum of 100 and 100?    10,000; 200
(1,2)

**10.**    365
(2)    × 100
    ‾‾‾‾‾
    36,500

**11.**    146
(2)    × 240
    ‾‾‾‾‾
    35,040

**12.**    78¢
(2)    × 48
    ‾‾‾‾‾
    $37.44

**13.**    907
(2)    × 36
    ‾‾‾‾‾
    32,652

**14.** $\frac{4260}{10}$    426
(2)

**15.** $\frac{4260}{20}$    213
(2)

**16.** $\frac{4260}{15}$    284
(2)

**17.** 56 + 28 + 37 + $n$ = 200    79
(3)

**18.** 28,347 − 9,637    18,710
(1)

**19.** $8 + $w$ = $11.49    $3.49
(3)

**20.** $10 − $0.75    $9.25
(1)

**21.** $0.56 × 60    $33.60
(2)

**22.** $6.20 ÷ 4    $1.55
(2)

**23.** $a$ − 67 = 49    116
(3)

**24.** 67 − $b$ = 49    18
(3)

**25.** 8$c$ = 120    15
(4)

**26.** $\frac{d}{8}$ = 24    192
(4)

**27.** Here are three ways to write "12 divided by 4."
(2)

$$4\overline{)12} \qquad 12 \div 4 \qquad \frac{12}{4}$$

Show three ways to write "20 divided by 5."
$5\overline{)20};\ 20 \div 5;\ \frac{20}{5}$

**28.** What number is one third of 36?   12
(6)

$346 + 463 = 809,$
$463 + 346 = 809,$
$809 - 463 = 346,$
$809 - 346 = 463$

**29.** Arrange the numbers 346, 463, and 809 to form two
(1)   addition equations and two subtraction equations.

**30.** At what temperature on the Fahrenheit scale does
(10)   water freeze?   32°F

## LESSON 11

# "Some and Some More" and "Some Went Away" Stories

Mental Math:
· **a.** 120
**b.** 1200
**c.** $5.75
**d.** 691
**e.** 4100
**f.** $3.50
g. 2

Problem Solving:
3: 29¢
2: 10¢
2: 3¢
1: 2¢
8 stamps total

---

**Facts Practice:** 64 Multiplication Facts (Test D in Test Masters)

**Mental Math:** Count up and down by $\frac{1}{2}$'s between $\frac{1}{2}$ and 12.

**a.** 3 × 40   **b.** 3 × 400   **c.** $4.50 + $1.25
**d.** 451 + 240   **e.** 4500 − 400   **f.** $5.00 − $1.50
**g.** Start with 10; add 2; divide by 2; add 2; divide by 2; subtract 2.

**Problem Solving:** Sandra has 2¢ stamps, 3¢ stamps, 10¢ stamps, and 29¢ stamps. What is the fewest number of stamps she can use to mail a package that requires $1.15 postage?

---

Millions of people go to the theaters to watch stories. Millions buy books to read stories. Stories can entertain us, inspire us, and instruct us. When we analyze stories we talk about the characters, the settings, and the plots. The plot is often about a problem that develops for the main characters and how that problem is resolved.

Many of the stories we analyze in mathematics also have plots. Two common mathematical stories are stories with "some and some more" plots and stories with "some went away" plots. Here are some examples.

A "some and some more" story:

*Before he went to work, Tom had $24.50. He earned $12.50 more putting up a fence. Then Tom had $37.00. (Plot: Tom had some money and then he earned some more money.)*

A "some went away" story:

*Tom took $37.00 to the music store. He bought a pair of headphones for $26.17. Then Tom had $10.83. (Plot: Tom had some money, but some went away when he spent it.)*

A "some and some more" story has an addition thought pattern. We fit the numbers from the story into the pattern.

| PATTERN | PROBLEM |
|---|---|
| Some | $24.50 |
| + Some More | + $12.50 |
| Total | $37.00 |

A "some went away" story has a subtraction thought pattern. We fit the numbers from the story into the pattern.

| PATTERN | PROBLEM |
|---|---|
| Some | $37.00 |
| − Some Went Away | − $26.17 |
| What is left | $10.83 |

Questions arise when one of the numbers in the story is missing. Since each of these stories has three numbers, three different questions could be asked for each story.

To answer a question about a "some and some more" story or about a "some went away" story we follow these four steps.

**Step 1.** Read the story and recognize the pattern.

**Step 2.** Sketch the pattern and record the given information.

**Step 3.** Find the missing number to complete the pattern.

**Step 4.** Answer the question.

**Note:** When referring to "some and some more" stories and to "some went away" stories, we will sometimes use the abbreviations SSM and SWA, respectively.

Example 1    Jenny rode her bike on a trip with her bicycling club. After the first day her trip odometer showed that she had traveled 86 miles. After the second day the trip odometer showed that she had traveled a total of 163 miles. How far did Jenny ride the second day?

*Solution*    **Step 1.** Jenny rode some miles and then rode some more miles. We **recognize** that this is a "some and some more" story.

**Step 2.** The trip odometer showed how far she traveled the first day and the total of the first two days. We **record** the information in the pattern. We'll use a letter in place of the missing number.

$$
\begin{array}{rr}
\text{Some} & 86 \text{ miles} \\
+ \text{ Some More} & + m \text{ miles} \\
\hline
\text{Total} & 163 \text{ miles}
\end{array}
$$

**Step 3.** We **find the missing number** that completes the pattern. From Lesson 3 we know that we can find the missing addend by subtracting 86 miles from 163 miles. We check the answer.

$$
\begin{array}{rr}
163 \text{ miles} & 86 \text{ miles} \\
- \phantom{0}86 \text{ miles} & + 77 \text{ miles} \\
\hline
77 \text{ miles} & 163 \text{ miles}
\end{array}
$$

**Step 4.** We answer the question. On the second day of the trip Jenny rode **77 miles.**

Example 2  Nancy counted 47 prairie dogs standing in the field. When a hawk flew over the field some of the prairie dogs ducked into their burrows. Then Nancy counted 29 prairie dogs. How many prairie dogs ducked into their burrows when the hawk flew over the field?

*Solution*  **Step 1.** We recognize this as a "some went away" story.

**Step 2.** We sketch the pattern and record the information.

$$\begin{array}{r} \text{Some} \\ - \text{ Some Went Away} \\ \hline \text{What is left} \end{array} \qquad \begin{array}{r} 47 \text{ prairie dogs} \\ - \quad d \text{ prairie dogs} \\ \hline 29 \text{ prairie dogs} \end{array}$$

**Step 3.** We find the missing number by subtracting 29 from 47. We check the answer.

$$\begin{array}{r} 47 \text{ prairie dogs} \\ - 29 \text{ prairie dogs} \\ \hline 18 \text{ prairie dogs} \end{array} \qquad \begin{array}{r} 47 \text{ prairie dogs} \\ - 18 \text{ prairie dogs} \\ \hline 29 \text{ prairie dogs} \end{array}$$

**Step 4.** We answer the question. When the hawk flew over the field **18 prairie dogs** ducked into their burrows.

**Practice**  Identify each story below as a SSM or a SWA story, and answer the question.

**a.** When Tim finished page 129 of a 314-page book, how many pages did he still have to read?  SWA; 185 pages

**b.** The football team scored 19 points in the first half of the game and 42 points by the end of the game. How many points did the team score in the second half of the game?  SSM; 23 points

**Problem set 11**

**1.** John ran 8 laps and rested. Then he ran some more
$^{(11)}$ laps. If John ran 21 laps in all, how many laps did he run after he rested? (Use the SSM pattern.)  13 laps

**2.** What is the product of 8 and 4? What is the sum of 8
$^{(1,2)}$ and 4?  32; 12

**3.** Here we show the product of 6 and 4 divided by the
$^{(5)}$ difference of 8 and 5. What is the quotient?  8

$$(6 \times 4) \div (8 - 5)$$

**4.** Marcia went to the store with $20.00 and returned
$^{(11)}$ home with $7.75. How much money did Marcia spend
at the store? (Use a SWA pattern.)  $12.25

**5.** When Jack went to bed at night, the beanstalk was one
$^{(11)}$ meter tall. When he woke up in the morning, the
beanstalk was one thousand meters tall. How many
meters had the beanstalk grown during the night? (Use
a SSM pattern.)  999 m

**6.** $0.65 + $0.40  $1.05
$^{(1)}$

**7.** 87 + $w$ = 155  68
$^{(3)}$

**8.** 1000 − $x$ = 386  614
$^{(3)}$

**9.** $y$ − 1000 = 386
$^{(3)}$  1386

**10.** 42 + 596 + $m$ = 700  62
$^{(3)}$

**11.** Compare: 1000 − (100 − 10) $\,\textgreater\,$ 1000 − 100 − 10
$^{(9)}$

**12.** $8\overline{)1000}$  125
$^{(2)}$

**13.** $10\overline{)987}$  98 r 7
$^{(2)}$

**14.** $12\overline{)w}$  35  420
$^{(4)}$

**15.** 600 × 300  180,000
$^{(2)}$

**16.** 365$w$ = 365  1
$^{(4)}$

**17.** What are the next three numbers in the sequence?
$^{(10)}$

$$2, 6, 10, \underline{\;\;14\;\;}, \underline{\;\;18\;\;}, \underline{\;\;22\;\;}, \ldots$$

**18.** 2 × 3 × 4 × 5  120
$^{(5)}$

**19.** What number is $\frac{1}{2}$ of 360?  180
$^{(6)}$

**20.** What number is $\frac{1}{4}$ of 360?  90
$^{(6)}$

**21.** What is the product of eight and one hundred twenty-
$^{(2)}$ five? 1000

**22.** How long is the line segment?    $2\frac{1}{4}$ in.
*(7)*

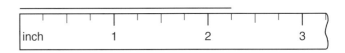

**23.** What fraction of the circle is not
*(6)* shaded?    $\frac{5}{8}$

**24.** What is the perimeter of the square?
*(8)*    36 mm

9 mm

**25.** What is the sum of the first five odd numbers greater
*(10)* than zero?    $1 + 3 + 5 + 7 + 9 = 25$

**26.** Here are three ways to write "24 divided by 4."
*(2)*

$$4\overline{)24}    \qquad 24 \div 4 \qquad \frac{24}{4}$$

Show three ways to write "30 divided by 6."

$6\overline{)30}$;    $30 \div 6$;    $\frac{30}{6}$

**27.** Seventeen of the 30 students in a class are girls. So the
*(6)* girls are $\frac{17}{30}$ of the students in the class. The boys are
what fraction of the students in the class?    $\frac{13}{30}$

**28.** At what temperature on the Celsius scale does water
*(10)* freeze?    0°C

**29.** Use the numbers 24, 6, and 4 to write two
*(2)* multiplication facts and two division facts.
$6 \times 4 = 24$, $4 \times 6 = 24$, $24 \div 4 = 6$, $24 \div 6 = 4$

**30.** In the third paragraph of this lesson there is a "some and
*(11)* some more" story. Rewrite the story as a problem by
removing one of the numbers from the story and asking
a question instead.    Answers will vary. See student work.

# LESSON 12

# Place Value Through Trillions' • Multiple-Step Problems

**Mental Math:**
**a.** 240
**b.** 2400
**c.** $17.50
**d.** 475
**e.** 2500
**f.** $7.50
**g.** 0
**Problem Solving:**
  21

---

**Facts Practice:** 64 Multiplication Facts (Test D in Test Masters)

**Mental Math:** Count by $\frac{1}{4}$'s from $\frac{1}{4}$ to 12.

  **a.** 6 × 40      **b.** 6 × 400      **c.** $12.50 + $5.00
  **d.** 451 + 24      **e.** 7500 − 5000      **f.** $10.00 − $2.50
  **g.** Start with 12; divide by 2; subtract 2; divide by 2; subtract 2.

**Problem Solving:** A number cube (a die) has six surfaces (faces) marked with one through six dots. Altogether, how many dots are on a number cube?

---

**Place value through trillions'**

In our number system the value of a digit depends upon its position. The value of each position is called its **place value.**

**Example 1** In the number 123,456,789,000 which digit is in the ten-millions' place?

**Solution** Either by counting places or looking at the chart we find that the digit in the ten-millions' place is **5.**

**Example 2** In the number 5,764,283 what is the place value of the digit 4?

**Solution** By counting places or looking at the chart we can see that the place value of 4 is **thousands'.**

Large numbers are easy to read and write if we use commas to group the digits. To place commas, we begin at the right and move to the left, writing a comma after each three digits.

Putting commas in 1234567890 we get 1,234,567,890.

Commas help us read large numbers by marking the end of the trillions, billions, millions, and thousands. We need only to read the three-digit number in front of each comma, then say "trillion," "billion," "million," or "thousand" when we reach the comma.

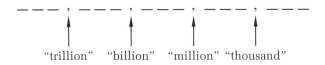

Example 3    Use words to write the number 1024305.

Solution    First we insert commas.

1,024,305

We write **one million, twenty-four thousand, three hundred five.**

**Note:** We write commas after the words "trillion," "billion," "million," and "thousand." We hyphenate compound numbers from 21 through 99. We do not say or write "and" when naming whole numbers.

Example 4    Use digits to write the number one trillion, two hundred fifty billion.

Solution    When writing large numbers it may help to sketch the pattern before writing the digits.

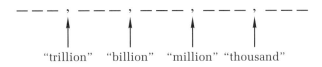

We write a 1 to the left of the trillions' comma and 250 in the three places to the left of the billions' comma. The remaining places are filled with zeros.

**1,250,000,000,000**

**Multiple-step problems**    The **operations of arithmetic** are addition, subtraction, multiplication, and division. In this table we list the terms for the answers we get when we perform these operations.

| | |
|---|---|
| **Sum** | The answer when we add |
| **Difference** | The answer when we subtract |
| **Product** | The answer when we multiply |
| **Quotient** | The answer when we divide |

We will use these terms in problems that have several steps.

**Example 5**    What is the difference between the product of 6 and 4 and the sum of 6 and 4?

*Solution*    We see the words "difference," "product," and "sum" in this question. We first look for phrases like "the product of 6 and 4." We will rewrite the question, emphasizing these phrases.

What is the difference between the **product of 6 and 4** and the **sum of 6 and 4?**

For each phrase we find one number. "The product of 6 and 4" is 24, and "the sum of 6 and 4" is 10. So we can replace the two phrases with the numbers 24 and 10.

What is the difference between 24 and 10?

We find this answer by subtracting 10 from 24. The difference between 24 and 10 is **14**.

**Practice***

a. Which digit is in the millions' place in 123,456,789?
  3

b. What is the place value of the 1 in 12,453,000,000?
  ten billions'

c. Use words to write 21,350,608.
  twenty-one million, three hundred fifty thousand, six hundred eight

d. Use digits to write four billion, five hundred twenty million.   4,520,000,000

e. When the product of 6 and 4 is divided by the difference of 6 and 4, what is the quotient?   12

**Problem set 12**

1. What is the difference between the product of 1, 2, and 3 and the sum of 1, 2, and 3?   0
   *(12)*

2. The earth is about ninety-three million miles from the sun. Use digits to write that number.   93,000,000
   *(12)*

3. Gilbert and Sharon cooked 342 pancakes for the pancake breakfast. If Gilbert cooked 167 pancakes, how many pancakes did Sharon cook? (Use a SSM pattern.)   175 pancakes
   *(11)*

4. Robin bought two arrows for $1.75 each. If he paid the good merchant with a five-dollar bill, how much did he receive in change?   $1.50
   *(5)*

5. What is the perimeter of the rectangle?   56 mm
   *(8)*

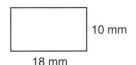
10 mm

18 mm

6. $6m = 60$   10
   *(4)*

7. (a) What number is $\frac{1}{2}$ of 100?   50
   *(6)*

   (b) What number is $\frac{1}{4}$ of 100?   25

8. Compare: $300 \times 1 \;\text{(=)}\; 300 \div 1$
   *(9)*

9. $(3 \times 3) - (3 + 3)$   3
   *(5)*

**10.** What are the next three numbers in this sequence?
(10)

$$1, 2, 4, 8, \underline{\hphantom{0}16\hphantom{0}}, \underline{\hphantom{0}32\hphantom{0}}, \underline{\hphantom{0}64\hphantom{0}}, \dots$$

**11.** $1 + m + 456 = 480$      **12.** $1010 - n = 101$
(3)   23                 (3)    909

**13.** $1234 \div 10$   123 r 4      **14.** $1234 \div 12$   102 r 10
(2)                           (2)

**15.** What is the sum of the first five even numbers greater
(10) than zero?    $2 + 4 + 6 + 8 + 10 = 30$

**16.** How many millimeters long is the line segment?    32 mm
(7)

**17.** In the number 123,456,789,000 which digit is in the
(12) ten-billions' place?    2

**18.** In the number 5,764,283,000 what is the place value of
(12) the digit 4?    millions'

**19.** Which digit is in the hundred-thousands' place in
(12) 987,654,321?    6

**20.** $1 \times 10 \times 100 \times 1000$    1,000,000
(5)

**21.** $\$3.75 \times 3$   $\$11.25$      **22.** $22y = 0$   0
(2)                          (4)

**23.** $100 + 200 + 300 + 400 + w = 2000$    1000
(3)

**24.** $24 \times 26$    624
(2)

**25.** $m\overline{)625}$    25
(4)
$$\overset{25}{m\overline{)625}}$$

**26.** If the divisor is 4 and the quotient is 8, then what is
(4) the dividend?    32

**27.** Show three ways to write "27 divided by 3."
(2)   $3\overline{)27}$;  $27 \div 3$;  $\frac{27}{3}$

**28.** Seven of the ten marbles in a bag are red. So $\frac{7}{10}$ of the
(6)   marbles are red. What fraction of the marbles are not
red?   $\frac{3}{10}$

**29.** Use digits to write four trillion.   4,000,000,000,000
(12)

**30.** Make up a question similar to Example 5 in this lesson
(12)   using different numbers. Then find the answer.
Answers will vary. See student work.

---

LESSON
**13**

# "Larger-Smaller-Difference" Stories • "Later-Earlier-Difference" Stories

**Mental Math:**
a. 1500
b. 15,000
c. $9.25
d. 3830
e. 4000
f. $15.00

**Problem Solving:**
Facing north; 10
steps away from
the tree

**Facts Practice:** 64 Addition Facts (Test A in Test Masters)

**Mental Math:** Count up and down by 25's between 25 and 1000.
Count up and down by 2's between 2 and 40.

| | | |
|---|---|---|
| **a.** 5 × 300 | **b.** 5 × 3000 | **c.** $7.50 + $1.75 |
| **d.** 3600 + 230 | **e.** 4500 − 500 | **f.** $20.00 − $5.00 |

**Problem Solving:** Tom studied the treasure map. He started at
the tree and walked north 5 steps. He turned
right and walked 7 steps. He turned right
again and walked 9 steps. Then he turned left
and walked 3 steps. Finally, he turned left
and walked 4 steps and stopped. In what
direction was he facing? How many steps
away was the tree?

**"Larger-smaller-difference" stories**

"Larger-smaller-difference" stories compare two numbers.
We can find how much greater or how much less one
number is than another number by subtracting. "Larger-
smaller-difference" stories have a subtraction pattern.

Larger
− Smaller
Difference

We will sometimes use the abbreviation L-S-D to refer to "larger-smaller-difference" stories.

**Example 1**  There were 324 girls and 289 boys in the school. How many fewer boys than girls were there in the school?

*Solution*  **Step 1.**  We are asked to compare the number of boys to the number of girls. We recognize this as a "larger-smaller-difference" story.

**Step 2.**  We draw the L-S-D pattern and record the numbers.

| PATTERN | PROBLEM |
|---|---|
| Larger | 324 girls |
| − Smaller | − 289 boys |
| Difference | $d$ fewer boys |

**Step 3.**  We find the missing number by subtracting.

$$\begin{array}{r} 324 \text{ girls} \\ - \ 289 \text{ boys} \\ \hline 35 \text{ fewer boys} \end{array}$$

**Step 4.**  We answer the question. There were **35 fewer boys** than girls in the school. We can also state that there were 35 more girls than boys in the school.

**"Later-earlier-difference" stories**  We use a "larger-smaller-difference" pattern to compare sizes. We use a "later-earlier-difference" pattern to compare times.

$$\begin{array}{r} \text{Later} \\ - \ \text{Earlier} \\ \hline \text{Difference} \end{array}$$

We will sometimes abbreviate this pattern as L-E-D.

**Example 2**  How many years were there from 1492 to 1620?

*Solution*  **Step 1.**  We recognize the question has a "later-earlier-difference" pattern.

**Step 2.** We sketch the pattern and record the years. The year 1620 is later than the year 1492.

|  PATTERN |  PROBLEM |
|---|---|
| Later | 1620 |
| − Earlier | − 1492 |
| Difference | $d$ |

**Step 3.** We find the missing number by subtracting.

$$\begin{array}{r} 1620 \\ - 1492 \\ \hline 128 \end{array}$$

**Step 4.** We answer the question. There were **128 years** from 1492 to 1620.

**Example 3**  Abraham Lincoln was born in 1809 and died in 1865. How many years did he live?

*Solution*  **Step 1.** We recognize that this is a "later-earlier-difference" story.

**Step 2.** We sketch the pattern and record the numbers.

|  PATTERN |  PROBLEM |
|---|---|
| Later | 1865 (death) |
| − Earlier | − 1809 (birth) |
| Difference | $L$ (years lived) |

**Step 3.** We find the missing number by subtracting.

$$\begin{array}{r} 1865 \\ - 1809 \\ \hline 56 \end{array}$$

**Step 4.** We answer the question. Abraham Lincoln lived **56 years.**

**Practice**  **a.** The population of Castor is 26,290. The population of Weston is 18,962. How many more people live in Castor than live in Weston?   7328

**b.** How many years were there from 1066 to 1215?   149

**Problem set
13**

**1.** When the sum of 8 and 5 is subtracted from the
(12)  product of 8 and 5, what is the difference?    27

**2.** The moon is about two hundred fifty thousand miles
(12)  from the earth. Use digits to write that number.
250,000

**3.** Use words to write 521,000,000,000.
(12)    five hundred twenty-one billion

**4.** Use digits to write five million, two hundred thousand.
(12)    5,200,000

**5.** Robin Hood roamed Sherwood Forest with sevenscore
(2)  merry men. A score is twenty. So sevenscore is seven
twenties. Find how many merry men roamed with Robin.
140

**6.** The beanstalk was 1000 meters tall. The giant had
(11)  climbed down 487 meters before Jack could chop
down the beanstalk. How far did the giant fall? (Use a
SWA pattern.)    513 m

**7.** At Big River Middle School there are 503 girls and 478
(13)  boys. How many more girls than boys attend Big River
Middle School? (Use a L-S-D pattern.)    25 more girls
than boys

**8.** 99 + 100 + 101    300        **9.** 9 × 10 × 11    990
(5)                                (5)

**10.** Which digit is in the thousands' place in 54,321?    4
(12)

**11.** What is the place value of the 1 in 1,234,567,890?
(12)    billions'

**12.** The three sides of an equilateral
(8)  triangle are equal in length. What is
the perimeter of this equilateral
triangle?    54 mm

18 mm

**13.** 5432 ÷ 100    54 r 32      **14.** $\dfrac{60,000}{30}$    2000
(2)                               (2)

**15.** 1000 ÷ 7    142 r 6       **16.** $4.56 ÷ 3    $1.52
(2)                               (2)

**17.** Compare: 3 + 2 + 1 + 0 $\bigcirc{>}$ 3 × 2 × 1 × 0
(9)

**18.** The sequence in this problem has a rule that is
(10) different from the rules for an addition sequence or a multiplication sequence. What is the next number in the sequence?

$$1, 4, 3, 6, 5, 8, \underline{\quad 7 \quad}, \ldots$$

**19.** What is $\frac{1}{2}$ of 5280?    2640
(6)

**20.** 365 ÷ $w$ = 365    1
(4)

**21.** (5 + 6 + 7) ÷ 3    6
(5)

**22.** Use your ruler to find the length of this rectangle in
(7) inches.    $1\frac{3}{4}$ in.

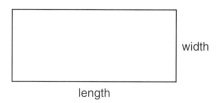

length

**23.** Describe two ways to find the perimeter of a square,
(8) one way by adding and the other way by multiplying.

23. To find the perimeter of a square, either add the lengths of the four sides or multiply the length of one side by four.

**24.** Multiply to find the answer to this addition problem:
(2)
$$125 + 125 + 125 + 125 + 125 + 125$$
125 × 6 = 750

**25.** At what temperature on the Fahrenheit scale does
(10) water boil?    212°F

**26.** Show three ways to write "21 divided by 7."
(2)    $\frac{21}{7}$; 21 ÷ 7; $7\overline{)21}$

Find each missing number:

**27.** 8$a$ = 816    102
(4)

**28.** $\frac{b}{4}$ = 12    48
(4)

**29.** $\frac{12}{c}$ = 4    3
(4)

**30.** $d$ − 16 = 61    77
(3)

**LESSON
14**

# The Number Line: Negative Numbers

**Mental Math:**
**a.** 3200
**b.** 18,000
**c.** $15.00
**d.** 590
**e.** 250
**f.** $2.50
**g.** 11
**Problem Solving:**
   Andy, Bob, Carol;
   Andy, Carol, Bob;
   Bob, Andy, Carol;
   Bob, Carol, Andy;
   Carol, Andy, Bob;
   Carol, Bob, Andy

**Facts Practice:** 64 Multiplication Facts (Test D in Test Masters)

**Mental Math:** Count up and down by $\frac{1}{4}$'s between $\frac{1}{4}$ and 6.

   **a.** 8 × 400      **b.** 6 × 3000      **c.** $7.50 + $7.50
   **d.** 360 + 230      **e.** 1250 − 1000      **f.** $10.00 − $7.50
   **g.** Start with 10; add 2; divide by 3; multiply by 4; subtract 5.

**Problem Solving:** Andy, Bob, and Carol stood side by side for a picture. Then they changed their order for another picture. Then they changed their order again. List all the possible side-by-side arrangements. Three students may demonstrate the arrangements.

We have seen that a number line can be used to arrange numbers in order.

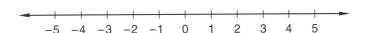

On the number line above, the points to the right of zero represent **positive** numbers. The points to the left of zero represent **negative** numbers. Zero is neither positive nor negative.

The number −5 is read "negative five." Notice that the points marked 5 and −5 are the same distance from zero but are on opposite sides of zero. We say that 5 and −5 are **opposites.** The numbers −2 and 2 are opposites. The tick marks on this number line show the location of **integers.** Integers include all of the counting numbers and their opposites and zero.

If you subtract a larger number from a smaller number (like 2 − 3), the answer will be a negative number. One way to find the answer to such questions is to use the number line. We start at 2 and count back (left) three integers. Maybe you can figure out a faster way to find the answer.

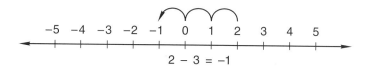

$$2 - 3 = -1$$

**Example 1**   Subtract 5 from 2.

*Solution*   **Order matters in subtraction.** Start at 2 and count to the left 5 integers. You should end up at **−3.** Try this problem with a calculator. Enter [ 2 ] [ − ] [ 5 ] [ = ]. What number is displayed after the [ = ] is pressed?

**Example 2**   Arrange these four numbers in order from least to greatest:

$$1, -2, 0, -1$$

*Solution*   A number line shows numbers in order. By arranging these numbers in the order they appear on a number line, we arrange them in order from least to greatest.

$$-2, -1, 0, 1$$

**Example 3**   What number is 7 less than 3?

*Solution*   The phrase "7 less than 3" means to start with 3 and subtract 7.

$$3 - 7$$

We count to the left 7 integers from 3. The answer is **−4.**

**Practice**   **a.** Use words to write this number: −8.   negative eight

**b.** What number is the opposite of 3?   −3

**c.** Arrange these numbers in order from least to greatest:
$$-3, -1, 0, 2$$
$$0, -1, 2, -3$$

**d.** What number is 5 less than 0?   −5

**e.** What number is 10 less than 5?   –5

**f.** 5 – 8   –3                              **g.** 1 – 5   –4

**h.** All five of these numbers are integers: true or false?
true
$$-3, 0, 2, -10, 50$$

**Problem set**    **1.** What is the quotient when the sum of 15 and 12 is
**14**    (12)   divided by the difference of 15 and 12?   9

**2.** What is the place value of the 7 in 987,654,321,000?
(12)   billions'

**3.** Light travels at a speed of about one hundred eighty-
(12)   six thousand miles per second. Use digits to write that
number.   186,000

**4.** What number is three integers to the left of 2 on the
(14)   number line?   –1

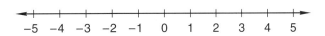

**5.** What number is halfway between 1 and 5 on the
(9)    number line?   3

**6.** What number is halfway between –4 and 0 on the
(14)   number line?   –2

**7.** Seventy-two of the 140 Merry Men remained in
(11)   Sherwood Forest while the rest rode out with Robin.
How many of the Merry Men rode out of the forest
with Robin? (Use a SWA pattern.)   68

**8.** Compare: 1 + 2 + 3 + 4 ⟨<⟩ 1 × 2 × 3 × 4
(9)

**9.** What is the perimeter of the right
(8)    triangle?   60 mm

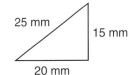

**10.** What are the next two numbers in this sequence?
(10)

$$16, 8, 4, \underline{\quad 2 \quad}, \underline{\quad 1 \quad}, ...$$

**11.** There are 365 days in a common year. How much less
(13) than 500 is 365? (Use a L-S-D pattern.)   135

**12.** What number is 8 less than 6?   −2
(14)

**13.** 1020 ÷ 100     **14.** $\dfrac{36{,}180}{12}$   3015   **15.** $18\overline{)564}$ $\overset{31\text{ r }6}{\phantom{)}}$
(2)    10 r 20        (2)                                (2)

**16.** 1234 + 567 + 89        **17.** $n - 310 = 186$   496
(5)   1890                   (3)

**18.** 10 × 11 × 12   1320      **19.** $\$3.05 - m = \$2.98$
(5)                           (3)   $0.07

**20.** (a) How many centimeters long is the nail?   4 cm
(7)
    (b) How many millimeters long is the nail?   40 mm

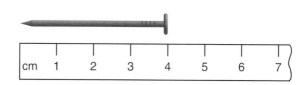

**21.** 100 × 100 × 100   1,000,000
(5)

**22.** What digit is in the ten-thousands' place in
(12) 123,456,789?   5

**23.** If you know the length of an object in centimeters,
(7) how can you figure out the length of the object in
millimeters without remeasuring?   To find the length of
an object in millimeters, multiply the number of centimeters by 10.

**24.** Use the numbers 19, 21, and 399 to write two
(2) multiplication facts and two division facts.
19 × 21 = 399, 21 × 19 = 399, 399 ÷ 19 = 21, 399 ÷ 21 = 19

**25.** Compare: 12 ÷ 6 × 2 $\overset{>}{\bigcirc}$ 12 ÷ (6 × 2)
(9)

**26.** Show three ways to write "60 divided by 6."
(2)  $6\overline{)60}$;  $60 \div 6$;  $\frac{60}{6}$

**27.** The human brain has about nine trillion nerve cells.
(12) Use digits to write that number.  9,000,000,000,000

**28.** One third of the 12 eggs in the carton were cracked.
(6) How many eggs were cracked?  4 eggs

**29.** What number is the opposite of 10?  −10
(14)

**30.** Arrange these numbers in order from least to greatest.
(14)  $-1, 0, \frac{1}{2}, 1$                    $1, 0, -1, \frac{1}{2}$

---

# LESSON 15

# "Equal Groups" Stories

Mental Math:
a. 28,000
b. 2400
c. $25.00
d. 92
e. 6100
f. $17.50
g. 0
Problem Solving:

$$
\begin{array}{r}
417 \\
-\ 396 \\
\hline
21
\end{array}
$$

**Facts Practice:** 100 Subtraction Facts (Test C in Test Masters)

**Mental Math:** Count up and down by $\frac{1}{4}$'s between $\frac{1}{4}$ and 10.

   **a.** 7 × 4000     **b.** 8 × 300     **c.** $12.50 + $12.50
   **d.** 80 + 12      **e.** 6250 − 150   **f.** $20.00 − $2.50
   **g.** Start with a dozen; subtract 3; divide by 3; subtract 3; multiply by 3.

**Problem Solving:** Copy this subtraction problem and fill in the missing digits.

$$
\begin{array}{r}
4\_7 \\
-\ \_9\_ \\
\hline
21
\end{array}
$$

We have studied some mathematical story problems. "Some and some more" stories have an addition pattern. "Some went away" stories and "larger-smaller-difference" stories have subtraction patterns. Another type of mathematical story is the "equal groups" story.

*In the auditorium there were 15 rows of chairs with 20 chairs in each row. Altogether, there were 300 chairs in the auditorium.*

The chairs were arranged in groups (rows) of 20 chairs in each group. There were 15 groups. Here is how we draw the pattern.

| PATTERN | PROBLEM |
|---|---|
| Number in each group | 20 chairs in each row |
| × Number of groups | × 15 rows |
| Number in all groups | 300 chairs in all rows |

Any one of the numbers may be missing in an "equal groups" problem. Since an "equal groups" story has a multiplication pattern, we multiply to find the total, and we divide to find either the number of groups or the number in each group. We will sometimes use the abbreviation EG to stand for "equal groups."

**Example**   At Russell Middle School there were 232 seventh-grade students in 8 classrooms. If there were the same number of students in each classroom, how many students would be in each seventh-grade classroom at Russell Middle School?

*Solution*   **Step 1.**   A number of students is divided into equal groups (classrooms). We recognize this as an "equal groups" story. The words "in each" often appear in "equal groups" stories, signifying the top number of the pattern.

**Step 2.**   We draw the pattern and record the numbers, writing a letter in place of the missing number.

| PATTERN | PROBLEM |
|---|---|
| Number in each group | $n$ in each classroom |
| × Number of groups | × 8 classrooms |
| Number in all groups | 232 in all classrooms |

**Step 3.**   We find the missing number. We find the missing factor by dividing. We check our work.

$$
\begin{array}{r} 29 \\ 8\overline{)232} \end{array}
\qquad
\begin{array}{r} 29 \\ \times\ \ 8 \\ \hline 232 \end{array}
$$

**Step 4.** We answer the question. If there were the same number of students in each classroom, there would be **29 students** in each seventh-grade classroom.

**Practice**   **a.** Marcie collected $4.50 selling lemonade at 25¢ for each cup. How many cups of lemonade did Marcie sell? (*Hint*: Record $4.50 as 450¢.)   18 cups

**b.** In the store parking lot there were 18 parking spaces in each row and there were 12 rows of parking spaces. Altogether, how many parking spaces were in the parking lot?   216 parking spaces

**Problem set 15**   **1.** The second paragraph of this lesson contains an *(15)* "equal groups" story. Rewrite the story as a problem by removing one of the numbers and writing a question.   Answers will vary. See student work.

**2.** On the Fahrenheit scale of temperature, water freezes *(13)* at 32°F and boils at 212°F. How many degrees difference is there between the freezing and boiling points? (Use a L-S-D pattern.)   180°F

**3.** There are about three hundred twenty little O's of *(15)* cereal in an ounce. About how many O's are there in a one-pound box? (1 pound = 16 ounces) (Use an EG pattern.)   5120

**4.** There are 31 days in August. How many days are left *(11)* in August after August 3? (Use a SSM pattern.)
28

**5.** Compare: $3 - 1 \ \textgreater \ 1 - 3$
*(9,14)*

**6.** Subtract 5 from 2. Use words to write the answer.
*(14)*   negative three

**7.** What number is 8 less than 5?   –3
*(14)*

**8.** What are the next three numbers in this sequence?
*(10)*
6, 4, 2, 0, __–2__, __–4__, __–6__, ...

**9.** What is the temperature reading on this thermometer? Write your answer twice, once with digits and an abbreviation and once with words. –6°F; negative six degrees Fahrenheit or six degrees below zero Fahrenheit
(10)

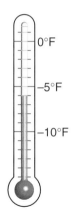

**10.** $10 − 10¢   $9.90
(1)

**11.** How much money is $\frac{1}{2}$ of $3.50?   $1.75
(6)

**12.** To which hundred is 587 closest?   600
(9)

**13.** 9 + 87 + 654 + 3210   3960
(5)

**14.** $w$ + $65 = $1000   $935
(3)

**15.** $\dfrac{4320}{9}$   480
(2)

**16.** $36\overline{)493}$   13 r 25
(2)

**17.** (8 + 9 + 16) ÷ 3   11
(5)

**18.** 63$w$ = 63   1
(4)

**19.** $\dfrac{76}{m}$ = 1   76
(4)

**20.** 574 × 76   43,624
(2)

**21.** 3 + $n$ + 12 + 27 = 50   8
(3)

**22.** There are 10 millimeters in 1 centimeter. How many millimeters long is the paper clip?   30 mm
(7)

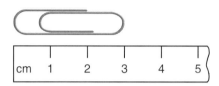

**23.** 1200 ÷ $w$ = 300   4
(4)

**24.** What is the place value of 5 in 12,345,678?   thousands'
(12)

**25.** Which digit occupies the ten-billions' place in 123,456,789,000?   2
(12)

**26.** Use the numbers 19, 21, and 40 to write two addition
(1)   facts and two subtraction facts.
19 + 21 = 40, 21 + 19 = 40, 40 − 19 = 21, 40 − 21 = 19

**27.** Arrange these numbers in order from least to greatest:
(14)   −3, −1, 0, 2                    0, −1, 2, −3

**28.** Susan sold seven of her seventeen seashells down by
(6)   the seashore. What fraction of her seashells did she
sell?   $\frac{7}{17}$

**29.** Susan sold seashells for 75¢ each. How much money
(15)   did Susan receive selling seven seashells?   $5.25

**30.** Which number is neither positive nor negative?   0
(14)

# LESSON 16

# Rounding Whole Numbers • Estimating • Bar Graphs

Mental Math:
a. 96
b. 92
c. 170
d. 84
e. 750
f. 7500
g. 1
Problem Solving:
2Q, 4D, 2N

**Facts Practice:** 64 Multiplication Facts (Test D in Test Masters)

**Mental Math:** Count by 3's from 3 to 60.

   **a.** $3 \times 30$ plus $3 \times 2$      **b.** $4 \times 20$ plus $4 \times 3$
   **c.** $150 + 20$                **d.** $75 + 9$
   **e.** $800 - 50$             **f.** $8000 - 500$
   **g.** Start with 1; add 2; multiply by 3; subtract 4; divide by 5.

**Problem Solving:** Fran has 8 coins that total exactly $1.00. If at least one of the coins is a dime, what are Fran's 8 coins?

**Rounding whole numbers**

When we **round** a number, we are finding another number, usually ending in zero, that is close to the number we are rounding. The number line can help us visualize rounding.

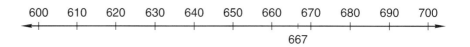

If we are to round 667 to the nearest ten, we can see that 667 is closer to 670 than it is to 660. If we are to round 667 to the nearest hundred, we can see that 667 is closer to 700 than 600.

**Example 1**    Round 6789 to the nearest thousand.

**Solution**    The number we are rounding is between 6000 and 7000. It is closer to **7000.**

**Example 2**    Round 550 to the nearest hundred.

**Solution**    The number we are to round is halfway between 500 and 600. When the number we are rounding is halfway between two round numbers, we round **up.** So 550 rounds to **600.**

**Estimating** Rounding can help us estimate the answer to a problem. Estimating is a quick, easy way to get "close" to the answer. Estimating can help us decide if an answer is reasonable. To estimate, we round the numbers before we add, subtract, multiply, or divide.

**Example 3** Estimate the sum of 467 and 312.

*Solution* Estimating is a skill we can learn to do "in our head." First we round each number. Since both numbers are in the hundreds we will round each number to the nearest hundred.

467 rounds to 500

312 rounds to 300

To estimate the sum we add the rounded numbers.

$$\begin{array}{r} 500 \\ + \ 300 \\ \hline 800 \end{array}$$

The estimated sum of 467 and 312 is **800.**

**Bar graphs** Bar graphs display numerical information with shaded rectangles (bars) of various lengths. Bar graphs are often used to show comparisons.

**Example 4** According to this graph, about how many more people lived in Ashton in 1990 than in 1970?

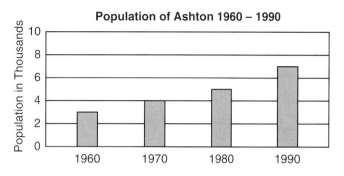

*Solution* In 1990 the population was about 7000. In 1970 the population was about 4000. The question is a "larger-smaller-difference" question. We subtract and find that about **3000** more people lived in Ashton in 1990 than in 1970.

**Practice\***   Round each of these numbers to the nearest ten:

    **a.** 57   60            **b.** 63   60            **c.** 45   50

Round each of these numbers to the nearest hundred:

    **d.** 282   300         **e.** 350   400         **f.** 426   400

Round each of these numbers to the nearest thousand:

    **g.** 4387   4000      **h.** 7500   8000      **i.** 6750   7000

Use rounded numbers to estimate each answer:

    **j.** 397 + 206   600            **k.** 703 − 598   100

    **l.** 29 × 31   900            **m.** $29\overline{)591}$   20

Use the information in the graph in Example 4 to answer these questions:

    **n.** About how many fewer people lived in Ashton in 1980 than in 1990?   2000

    **o.** The graph shows an upward trend in the population of Ashton. Based upon the trend, what would be a reasonable projection for the population of Ashton in the year 2000?   9000

**Problem set 16**

    **1.** What is the difference between the product of 20 and 5 $^{(12)}$ and the sum of 20 and 5?   75

    **2.** Columbus landed in the Americas in 1492. The $^{(13)}$ Pilgrims landed in 1620. How many years after Columbus did the Pilgrims land in America? (Use a L-E-D pattern.)   128 years

    **3.** Robin Hood separated his 140 merry men into 5 equal $^{(15)}$ groups. One group he sent north, one south, one east, and one west. The remaining group stayed in camp. How many merry men stayed in camp? (Use an EG pattern.)   28 merry men

**4.** Which digit is in the hundred-thousands' place in
*(12)* 159,342,876?  3

**5.** Use words to write the number 5,010,000,000.
*(12)* five billion, ten million

**6.** What number is halfway between 5 and 11 on the
*(9)* number line?  8

**7.** Round 56,789 to the nearest thousand.  57,000
*(16)*

**8.** Round 550 to the nearest hundred.  600
*(16)*

**9.** Estimate the product of 295 and 406 by rounding each
*(16)* number to the nearest hundred before multiplying.
120,000

**10.** 45 + 5643 + 287        **11.** 40,312 − 14,908   25,404
*(5)*  5975                *(1)*

**12.** $\dfrac{7308}{12}$  609        **13.** $100\overline{)5367}$  53 r 67
*(2)*                 *(2)*

**14.** (5 + 11) ÷ 2  8
*(5)*

**15.** How much money is $\frac{1}{2}$ of \$5?  \$2.50
*(6)*

**16.** How much money is $\frac{1}{4}$ of \$5?  \$1.25
*(6)*

**17.** \$0.25 × 10  \$2.50        **18.** 325 × (324 − 323)   325
*(2)*                  *(5)*

**19.** Compare: 1 + (2 + 3) $\boxed{=}$ (1 + 2) + 3
*(9)*

**20.** What number is five less than 1?  −4
*(14)*

**21.** Your heart beats about 72 times per minute. At that
*(15)* rate, how many times will it beat in one hour? (Use an
EG pattern.)  4320 beats per hour

**22.** What number comes next in this sequence?
*(10)*
100, 80, 60, 40, __20__ , ...

Use the graph to answer questions 23, 24, 25, and 26.

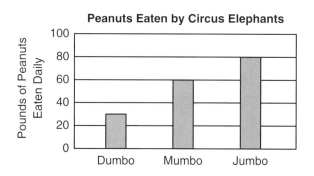

**23.** How many more pounds of peanuts does Jumbo eat all
(16) day than Dumbo?    50 pounds

**24.** Altogether, how many pounds do the three elephants
(16) eat each day?    170 pounds

**25.** How many pounds would Mumbo eat in one week?
(16)    420 pounds

**26.** Write a "larger-smaller-difference" problem using the
(16) information in this graph.    Answers will vary. See student work.

Find the missing number:

**27.** $6w = 66$        **28.** $m - 60 = 37$        **29.** $60 - n = 37$
(4)    11                (3)    97                (3)    23

**30.** Chico, Fuji, and Rolo each day eat 6, 8, and 9 bananas,
(16) respectively. Sketch a bar graph to illustrate this
information.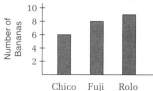

# LESSON 17

# Number Line: Fractions and Mixed Numbers

**Facts Practice:** 100 Multiplication Facts (Test E in Test Masters)

**Mental Math:** Count up and down by $\frac{1}{4}$'s between $\frac{1}{4}$ and 12.

   **a.** $5 \times 30$ plus $5 \times 4$        **b.** $4 \times 60$ plus $4 \times 4$
   **c.** $180 + 12$               **d.** $64 + 9$
   **e.** $3000 - 1000 - 100$    **f.** $\$10.00 - \$7.50$
   **g.** Start with 5; multiply by 4; add 1; divide by 3; subtract 2.

**Problem Solving:** If you pick up a number cube with two fingers by holding your fingers against opposite faces, your fingers will cover a total of how many dots? (Use a number cube to find out.)

On this number line the tick marks show the location of the integers.

There are points on the number line between the integers that can be named with fractions or mixed numbers. Halfway between 0 and 1 is $\frac{1}{2}$. Halfway between 1 and 2 is $1\frac{1}{2}$. Halfway between $-1$ and $-2$ is $-1\frac{1}{2}$.

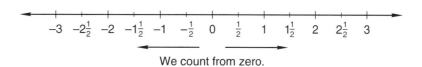

We count from zero.

The distance between consecutive integers on a number line may be divided into halves, thirds, fourths, fifths, or any other number of equal divisions. To determine which fraction or mixed number is represented by a point on the number line, we follow the steps described in the next example.

**Example 1**    What mixed number is marked as point *A* on this number line?

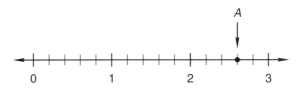

*Solution*    Point *A* represents a mixed number. A mixed number is a whole number plus a fraction.

**Step 1.**  As we move from zero to point *A*, we pass points for the whole numbers 1 and 2. We do not pass 3. So the whole number part of the answer is 2.

**Step 2.**  From the tick mark for 2 we count three small segments to point *A*. So 3 is the numerator of the fraction.

**Step 3.**  From the tick mark for 2 to the tick mark for 3 are five small segments. So 5 is the denominator of the fraction.

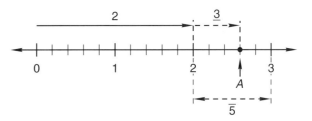

Point *A* represents the mixed number $2\frac{3}{5}$.

## Activity: Inch Ruler to Sixteenths

Materials needed:

- Inch ruler made in Lesson 7

In Lesson 7 we made an inch ruler divided into fourths. In this activity we will divide the ruler into eighths and sixteenths. First we will review what we did in Lesson 7.

We used a ruler to make one-inch divisions on a strip of tag board.

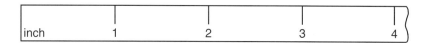

Then we estimated the halfway point between inch marks and drew new marks. The new marks were half-inch divisions. Then we estimated the halfway point between the half-inch marks and made quarter-inch divisions.

We made the half-inch marks a little shorter than the inch marks and the quarter-inch marks a little shorter than the half-inch marks.

Now divide your ruler into eighths of an inch by estimating the halfway point between the quarter-inch marks. Make these eighth-inch marks a little shorter than the quarter-inch marks.

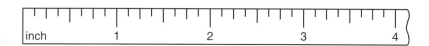

Finally, divide your ruler into sixteenths by estimating the halfway point between the eighth-inch marks. Make these marks the shortest marks on the ruler.

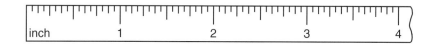

**Example 2**    Use your ruler to find the length of this line segment to the nearest sixteenth of an inch.

_____

*Solution*  The ruler has been divided into sixteenths. We align the zero mark (or end of the ruler) with one end of the line segment. Then we find the mark on the ruler closest to the other end of the line segment and read this mark. We will enlarge a portion of a ruler to show how each mark is read.

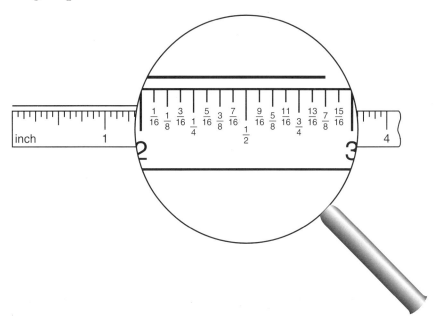

We find that the line segment is about $2\frac{7}{8}$ **inches long.** This is the nearest sixteenth because the end of the segment aligns more closely to the $\frac{7}{8}$ mark $\left(\text{which equals } \frac{14}{16}\right)$ than it does to the $\frac{13}{16}$ mark or to the $\frac{15}{16}$ mark.

**Practice**  **a.** Continue this sequence to $1\frac{1}{2}$:

$$\frac{1}{16}, \frac{1}{8}, \frac{3}{16}, \frac{1}{4}, \frac{5}{16}, \frac{3}{8}, \frac{7}{16}, \frac{1}{2}, \dots$$

$\frac{9}{16}, \frac{5}{8}, \frac{11}{16}, \frac{3}{4}, \frac{13}{16}, \frac{7}{8},$
$\frac{15}{16}, 1, 1\frac{1}{16}, 1\frac{1}{8}, 1\frac{3}{16},$
$1\frac{1}{4}, 1\frac{5}{16}, 1\frac{3}{8}, 1\frac{7}{16}, 1\frac{1}{2}$

**b.** What number is halfway between $-2$ and $-3$?   $-2\frac{1}{2}$

**c.** What number is halfway between 2 and 5?   $3\frac{1}{2}$

Use your ruler to find the length of each of these line segments to the nearest sixteenth of an inch.

**d.** ———————   $\frac{13}{16}$ in.

**e.** ————————————————   $2\frac{1}{4}$ in.

**f.** ————————————————————   $3\frac{3}{16}$ in.

**Problem set 17**

1. What is the sum of twelve thousand, five hundred and
(12) ten thousand, six hundred ten?   23,110

2. In 1903 the Wright brothers made the first powered
(13) airplane flight. In 1969 Americans first landed on the
moon. How many years was it from the first powered
airplane flight to the first moon landing? (Use the L-E-D
pattern.)   66 years

3. Captain Hook often ran from the sound of ticking
(15) clocks. If he could run 6 yards in one second, how far
could he run in 12 seconds? (Use an "equal groups"
pattern.)   72 yards

4. Jack found two dozen golden eggs. If the value of each
(15) egg was $1000, what was the value of all the eggs Jack
found? (Use an "equal groups" pattern.)   $24,000

5. Estimate the sum of 5280 and 1760 by rounding each
(16) number to the nearest thousand before adding.
7000

6. $\dfrac{480}{3}$   160
(2)

7. $\dfrac{6 - 6}{3}$   0
(5)

8. The letters $a$, $b$, and $c$ represent three different
(1) numbers. The sum of $a$ and $b$ is $c$.   $b + a = c$,
$$a + b = c \qquad \begin{array}{l} c - a = b, \\ c - b = a \end{array}$$

Rearrange the letters to make another addition fact and
two subtraction facts.

9. Rewrite $2 \div 3$ with a division bar but do not divide.
(2) $\frac{2}{3}$

10. A square has sides 10 cm long. What is its perimeter?
(8) 40 cm

11. Use your ruler to find the length of this line segment
(17) to the nearest sixteenth of an inch.   $2\frac{5}{8}$ in.

_____

12. $3 - y = 1.75$   $1.25
(3)

13. $365 + 4576 + 50,287$
(5)   55,228

**14.** $12n = 0$   0
(4)

**15.** Compare: $19 \times 21$ $\textcircled{<}$ $20 \times 20$
(9)

**16.** $\dfrac{5280}{44}$   120
(2)

**17.** What number is missing in this sequence?
(10)

$$5, 10, \underline{\ 15\ }, 20, 25, \ldots$$

**18.** Which digit is in the hundred-millions' place in
(12)  987,654,321?   9

**19.** $250{,}000 \div 100$   2500     **20.** $\$3.75 \times 10$   $\$37.50$
(2)                                    (2)

**21.** $16 + 14 = 14 + w$   16
(3)

**22.** The magician pulled 38 rabbits out of a hat. Half of the
(15)  rabbits were white. How many were not white? (Use
an EG pattern.)   19

**23.** $100 - (50 - 25)$   75     **24.** $m - 20 = 30$   50
(5)                              (3)

**25.** What is the sum of the first six positive odd numbers?
(10)   36

**26.** Describe how to find $\frac{1}{4}$ of 52.
(6)   One way to find $\frac{1}{4}$ of 52 is to divide 52 by 4.

**27.** A quarter is $\frac{1}{4}$ of a dollar.
(6)

(a) How many quarters are in one dollar?   4

(b) How many quarters are in three dollars?   12

**28.** On an inch ruler, which mark is halfway between the
(17)  $\frac{1}{4}$-inch mark and the $\frac{1}{2}$-inch mark?   $\frac{3}{8}$-inch mark

**29.** Point $A$ represents what mixed number on this line?
(17)   $4\frac{1}{6}$

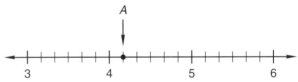

**30.** A segment that is $\frac{1}{2}$ of an inch long is how many
(17)  sixteenths of an inch long?   8

LESSON
**18**

# Average • Line Graphs

**Mental Math:** Count by 3's from 3 to 60.

 **a.** 4 × 23 equals 4 × 20 plus 4 × 3. Find 4 × 23.
 **b.** 4 × 32     **c.** 3 × 42     **d.** 3 × 24
 **e.** Start with half a dozen; add 2; multiply by 3; divide by 4; subtract 5.

**Problem Solving:** Jeana folded a square paper in half so that the left edge aligned with the right edge. Then she folded the paper again so that the top edge aligned with the bottom edge. (The four corners of the paper aligned at the lower right.) Then she used scissors and cut off the upper left corners. What will the paper look like when it is unfolded?

cut

4 corners

Mental Math:
a. 92
b. 128
c. 126
d. 72
e. 1
Problem Solving:

**Average**
Here we show three stacks of books. In the three stacks there are 8 books, 7 books, and 3 books, respectively. Altogether, there are 18 books, but the number of books in each stack is not equal.

  If we move some of the books from the taller stacks to the shortest stack we can make the three stacks the same height. Then there will be 6 books in each stack.

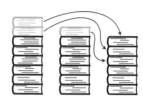

By making the stacks equal we have found the **average** number of books in the three stacks. One way to find an average is to make equal groups.

**Example 1**   In four classrooms there were 28 students, 27 students, 26 students, and 31 students, respectively. What was the average number of students in each classroom?

**Solution**   The average number of students in each classroom is how many students there would be in each room if we made the numbers equal. So we will take all of the students and make four equal groups. To find all of the students, we add the numbers in each classroom.

$$\begin{array}{r} 28 \text{ students} \\ 27 \text{ students} \\ 26 \text{ students} \\ + \ 31 \text{ students} \\ \hline 112 \text{ students in all} \end{array}$$

We make four equal groups by dividing the total number of students by four.

$$\overset{\textstyle 2\ 8 \text{ students}}{4\overline{)11^32 \text{ students}}}$$

If the groups were equal there would be 28 students in each classroom. The average number of students in each classroom was **28.**

Notice that this average problem is an "equal groups" problem. First we found the number of students in all the groups (classrooms). Then we found the number of students that would be in each group if the groups were equal.

**Example 2**   What is the average of 3, 7, and 8?

**Solution**   The question does not tell us if the numbers 3, 7, and 8 refer to books or students or coins or quiz scores. We can still find the average by making equal groups. Since there are three numbers, there will be three groups. First we find the total. Then we divide the total by three.

$$3 + 7 + 8 = 18 \text{ (Find the total.)}$$

Then we divide the total into three equal groups.

$$18 \div 3 = 6$$

The average of 3, 7, and 8 is **6.**

Example 3   What number is halfway between 27 and 81?

*Solution*   The number halfway between two numbers is also the average of the two numbers. For example, the average of 7 and 9 is 8, and 8 is halfway between 7 and 9. So the average of 27 and 81 will be the number halfway between 27 and 81. We add 27 and 81 and divide by 2.

$$\text{Average of 27 and 81} = \frac{27 + 81}{2}$$

$$= \frac{108}{2}$$

$$= 54$$

The number halfway between 27 and 81 is **54.**

**Line graphs**   **Line graphs** display numerical information as points on a line. Line graphs are often used to show how a measurement is changing.

Example 4   This line graph shows Margie's height in inches from her 8th birthday to her 14th birthday. During which year did Margie grow the most?

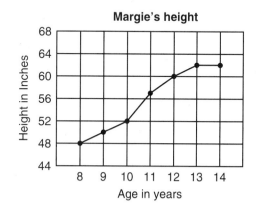

*Solution*   From Margie's 8th birthday to her 9th birthday she grew about two inches. She also grew about two inches from her 9th to her 10th birthday. From her 10th to her 11th birthday Margie grew about five inches. Notice that this is the steepest part of the growth line. So the year Margie grew the most was **the year she was ten.**

Your teacher may like for you to keep a line graph of your math test scores from week to week. "Activity Master 1" in the *Math 76 Test Masters* may be used for this purpose.

**Practice\***  **a.** There were 26 books on the first shelf, 36 books on the second shelf, and 43 books on the third shelf. Martin rearranged the books so that there were the same number of books on each shelf. After Martin rearranged the books, how many were on the first shelf?   35

**b.** What is the average of 96, 44, 68, and 100?   77

**c.** What number is halfway between 28 and 82?   55

**d.** What number is halfway between 86 and 102?   94

**e.** Find the average of 3, 6, 9, 12, and 15.   9

Use the information in the graph in Example 4 to answer these questions:

**f.** How many inches did Margie grow from her 8th to her 12th birthday?   12 in.

**g.** During which year did Margie grow the least?
between her 13th and her 14th birthday

**h.** Predicting from the information in the graph, does it seem likely that Margie will grow to be 68 inches tall?
no

**Problem set**  **1.** Jumbo ate two thousand, sixty-eight peanuts in the
**18**  (11)  morning and three thousand, nine hundred forty in the afternoon. How many peanuts did Jumbo eat in all? What kind of a pattern did you use?   6008; SSM

**2.** Jimmy counted his permanent teeth. He had eleven on
(11)  top and twelve on the bottom. An adult has 32 permanent teeth. How many more of Jimmy's teeth need to grow in? What kind of pattern did you use?
9; SSM

**3.** Olive bought one dozen cans of spinach as a birthday
(15) present for her boyfriend. The spinach cost 53¢ per
can. How much did Olive spend on spinach? What
kind of pattern did you use?   $6.36; EG

**4.** Estimate the difference of 5035 and 1987 by rounding to
(16) the nearest thousand before subtracting.   3000

**5.** Find the average of 9, 7, and 8.   8
(18)

**6.** What number is halfway between 59 and 81?   70
(18)

**7.** What number is 6 less than 2?   −4
(14)

**8.** $\dfrac{234}{n} = 6$   39    **9.** 10,010 ÷ 10    **10.** 34,180 ÷ 17
(4)              (2)   1001           (2)   2010 r 10

**11.** $3.64 + $94.28 + 87¢   **12.** 41,375 − 13,576
(5)   $98.79                   (1)   27,799

**13.** $w - 84 = 48$   132    **14.** 4 × 3 × 2 × 1 × 0   0
(3)                           (5)

**15.** 125 × 16   2000    **16.** $0.35 × 100   $35
(2)                       (2)

**17.** Draw a rectangle 5 cm long and 3 cm wide. What is its
(8)   perimeter?   16 cm

**18.** What is the sum of the first six positive even
(10)  numbers?   42

**19.** What number is missing in this sequence?
(10)
                1, 2, 4, __8__, 16, 32, 64, ...

**20.** Compare: 500 × 1 ⊜ 500 ÷ 1
(9)

**21.** (1 + 2) × 3 = (1 × 2) + $m$   7
(3)

**22.** What number is $\frac{1}{2}$ of 1110?   555
(6)

millions' **23.** What is the place value of the 7 in 987,654,321?
(12)

Use the graph to answer questions 24, 25, and 26.

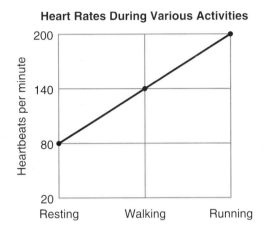

**Heart Rates During Various Activities**

24. Running increases a resting person's heartbeat by
(18) about how many beats per minute?    120

25. About how many times would a person's heart beat
(18) during a 10-minute run?    2000

26. Write a larger-smaller-difference problem using the
(18) information in the line graph and answer the problem.
Answers will vary. See student work.

27. In three classrooms there are 24, 27, and 33 students,
(18) respectively. How many students would be in each
classroom if some students were moved from one
classroom to the other classrooms so that the number
of students in the three classrooms were equal?    28

28. A dime is $\frac{1}{10}$ of a dollar.
(6)
   (a) How many dimes are in a dollar?    10

   (b) How many dimes are in three dollars?    30

29. Use your ruler to draw a rectangle that is $2\frac{1}{4}$ inches
(17) long and $1\frac{3}{4}$ inches wide.

$2\frac{1}{4}$ in.

$1\frac{3}{4}$ in.

30. What number is the opposite of 12?    −12
(14)

# LESSON
# 19

# Factors • Divisibility

**Mental Math:**
a. 192
b. 138
c. 138
d. 83
e. 83
f. $7.50
g. 10
**Problem Solving:**
 DNQ; NQD; DQN;
 QND

**Facts Practice:** 64 Multiplication Facts (Test C in Test Masters)

**Mental Math:** Count up and down by $\frac{1}{4}$'s between $\frac{1}{4}$ and 12.

a. $3 \times 64$       b. $3 \times 46$       c. $120 + 18$
d. $34 + 40 + 9$     e. $34 + 50 - 1$     f. $20.00 - $12.50
g. Start with 100; divide by 2; subtract 1; divide by 7; add 3.

**Problem Solving:** Alex wanted to make a 40¢ phone call at a pay phone. He had a nickel, a dime, and a quarter. He could put in the nickel, then the dime, then the quarter. Or he could put in the quarter, then the dime, then the nickel. What are the other possible orders of coin drops for his phone call?

**Factors**   A whole number **factor** is a whole number that divides another whole number. For example, there are four whole numbers that divide 6. These four numbers are 1, 2, 3, and 6. All these numbers are factors of 6.

$$1\overline{)6} \quad \overset{3}{2\overline{)6}} \quad \overset{2}{3\overline{)6}} \quad \overset{1}{6\overline{)6}}$$

We can illustrate the factors of 6 by arranging 6 tiles to form rectangles. With 6 tiles we can make a 1-by-6 rectangle. With 6 tiles we can also make a 2-by-3 rectangle.

The number of tiles along the sides of these two rectangles (1, 6, 2, 3) are the four factors of 6.

**Example 1**  What are the factors of 10?

**Solution**  The factors of 10 are all the numbers that divide 10 with no remainder. They are **1, 2, 5,** and **10.**

$$\underset{\mathbf{1})\overline{10}}{10} \qquad \underset{\mathbf{2})\overline{10}}{5} \qquad \underset{\mathbf{5})\overline{10}}{2} \qquad \underset{\mathbf{10})\overline{10}}{1}$$

We can illustrate the factors of 10 with two rectangular arrays of tiles.

The number of tiles along the sides of the two rectangles (1, 10, 2, 5) are the factors of 10.

**Example 2**  How many different whole numbers are factors of 12?

**Solution**  Twelve can be divided by 1, 2, 3, 4, 6, and 12. The question asked "How many?" Counting, we find that 12 has **6** different factors.

Twelve tiles can be arranged in three rectangular arrays demonstrating that the six factors of 12 are 1, 12, 2, 6, 3, and 4.

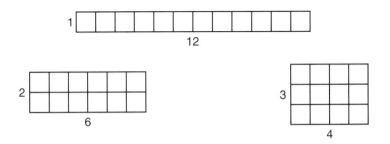

**Divisibility**  There are ways of discovering whether some numbers are factors of other numbers without actually dividing. For instance, even numbers can be divided by 2. Therefore, 2 is a factor of every even counting number. Since even numbers are "able" to be divided by 2, we say that even numbers are "divisible" by 2. The tests for **divisibility** can help us find the factors of a number. Here we list the tests for divisibility of 2, 3, 5, 9, and 10.

**Last-Digit Tests**

Inspect the last digit of the number. A number is able to be divided by …

2 if the last digit is even

5 if the last digit is 0 or 5

10 if the last digit is 0

**Sum-of-Digits Tests**

Add the digits of the number and inspect the total. A number is able to be divided by…

3 if the sum of the digits can be divided by 3

9 if the sum of the digits can be divided by 9

**Example 3** Which of these numbers is divisible by 2?

365          1179          1556

*Solution* To decide if a number can be divided by 2, we inspect the last digit of the number. If the last digit is an even number, then the number can be divided by 2. The last digit of these three numbers are 5, 9, and 6. Since 5 and 9 are not even numbers, 365 and 1179 are not divisible by 2. Since 6 is an even number, 1556 is divisible by 2. It is not necessary to perform the division to answer the question. By inspecting the last digits we see that the number that is divisible by 2 is **1556.**

**Example 4** Which of these numbers is divisible by 3?

365          1179          1556

*Solution* To decide if a number can be divided by 3, we add the digits of the number and inspect the sum. If the sum of the digits is divisible by 3, then the number is also divisible by 3.

The digits of 365 are 3, 6, and 5. We add these digits and get 14.

$$3 + 6 + 5 = 14$$

We try to divide 14 by 3 and find that there is a remainder of 2. Since 14 is not divisible by 3, we know that 365 is not divisible by 3 either.

The digits of 1179 are 1, 1, 7, and 9. The sum of these digits is 18.

$$1 + 1 + 7 + 9 = 18$$

We divide 18 by 3 and there is no remainder. We see that 18 is divisible by 3, so 1179 is also divisible by 3.

The sum of the digits of 1556 is 17.

$$1 + 5 + 5 + 6 = 17$$

Since 17 is not divisible by 3, the number 1556 is not divisible by 3.

By using the divisibility test for 3, we find that the number that is divisible by 3 is **1179.**

**Example 5**   Which of the numbers 2, 3, 5, 9, and 10 are factors of 135?

*Solution*   First we will use the last-digit tests. The last digit of 135 is 5, so 135 is divisible by 5 but not by 2 or by 10. Next we use the sum-of-digit tests. The sum of the digits in 135 is 9 $(1 + 3 + 5 = 9)$. Since 9 can be divided by both 3 and 9, we know that 135 can also be divided by 3 and 9. So **3, 5,** and **9** are factors of 135.

**Practice**   Most of the time we just say **factors** instead of saying **whole number factors.** List the factors of the following numbers:

**a.** 14   1, 2, 7, 14          **b.** 15   1, 3, 5, 15

**c.** 16   1, 2, 4, 8, 16          **d.** 17   1, 17

How many different factors do each of these numbers have?

e. 18  6

f. 19  2

g. 20  6

h. 21  4

Use the tests for divisibility to decide which of the numbers 2, 3, 5, 9, and 10 are factors of the following numbers:

i. 120  2, 3, 5, 10

j. 102  2, 3

**Problem set 19**

1. If two hundred fifty-two is the dividend and six is the quotient, then what is the divisor?  42
   (4)

2. Lincoln began his speech, "Fourscore and seven years ago ...." A score is twenty. How many years is fourscore and seven?  87
   (15)

3. Overnight the temperature dropped from 4°C to −3°C. This was a drop of how many degrees?  7°C
   (14)

4. If 203 turnips are to be shared equally among seven dwarfs, how many should each receive? What kind of pattern did you use?  29; EG
   (15)

5. What is the average of 1, 2, 4, and 9?  4
   (18)

6. What is the next number in the sequence?
   (10)

   $$1, 4, 9, 16, 25, \underline{\phantom{0}36\phantom{0}}, ...$$

7. A regular hexagon has six sides of equal length. If each side of a hexagon is 25 mm, what is the perimeter?
   (8)
   150 mm

8. One centimeter equals ten millimeters. How many millimeters long is the line segment?  30 mm
   (7)

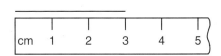

**9.** What are the whole number factors of 20?
(19)  1, 2, 4, 5, 10, 20

**10.** How many different whole numbers are factors of 15?
(19)  4

**11.** Which of these numbers is divisible by 9?   B. 1179
(19)

  A. 365            B. 1179            C. 1556

**12.** 250,000 ÷ 100   2500      **13.** 1234 ÷ 60   20 r 34
(2)                              (2)

**14.** $\dfrac{6 + 18 + 9}{3}$   11
(5)

**15.** $42 + $375   $417      **16.** $3.45 × 10   $34.50
(1)                          (2)

**17.** $10.00 − $w$ = $1.93   $8.07
(3)

**18.** The letters $a$, $b$, and $c$ represent three different
(2)  numbers. The product of $a$ and $b$ is $c$.

$$ab = c$$

Rearrange the letters to make another multiplication fact
and two division facts.   $ba = c$, $c ÷ a = b$, $c ÷ b = a$

**19.** $\dfrac{w}{3}$ = 4   12
(4)

**20.** Compare: 123 ÷ 1 $\gt$ 123 − 1
(9)

**21.** Which digit is in the ten-millions' place in
(12)  135,792,468,000?   9

**22.** Round 123,456,789 to the nearest million.
(16)  123,000,000

**23.** How much money is $\frac{1}{2}$ of $11.00?   $5.50
(6)

**24.** If a square has a perimeter of 40 inches, how long is
(8)  each side of the square?   10 in.

**25.** (51 + 49) × (51 − 49)   200
(5)

**26.** Which of these numbers is divisible by both 2 and 3?
(19)
   A. 4671        B. 3858        C. 6494
   B. 3858

**27.** By which whole numbers is 24 divisible?
(19)   1, 2, 3, 4, 6, 8, 12, 24

**28.** The dictionaries were piled in three stacks. There
(18)   were 6 dictionaries in one stack and 12 dictionaries in
each of the other two stacks. How many dictionaries
would be in each stack if some dictionaries were
moved from the taller stacks to the shortest stack so
that there were the same number of dictionaries in
each stack?   10

$1\frac{3}{8}$ in.  **29.** Draw a square with sides that are $1\frac{3}{8}$ inches long.
(17)

**30.** Describe a method for deciding if a number is
(19)   divisible by 3.   Add the digits of the number. If the sum of
the digits can be divided by 3, then the original number is
divisible by 3.

# LESSON 20

# Greatest Common Factor (GCF)

**Mental Math:**
a. 138
b. 192
c. 1840
d. 92
e. 92
f. $25.00
g. 12
**Problem Solving:**

$$\begin{array}{r} 67 \\ -\ 9 \\ \hline 58 \end{array} \qquad \begin{array}{r} 85 \\ -\ 9 \\ \hline 76 \end{array}$$

**Facts Practice:**  100 Subtraction Facts (Test C in Test Masters)

**Mental Math:**  Count up and down by 3's between 3 and 60.
    **a.** 6 × 23        **b.** 6 × 32        **c.** 640 + 1200
    **d.** 63 + 20 + 9    **e.** 63 + 30 − 1    **f.** $100.00 − $75.00
    **g.** Start with 10; multiply by 10; subtract 1; divide by 9; add 1.

**Problem Solving:**  Use the digits 5, 6, 7, and 8 to complete this subtraction problem. There are two possible arrangements.

$$\begin{array}{r} \_\_ \\ -\ 9 \\ \hline \_\_ \end{array}$$

The factors of 8 are

1, 2, 4, and 8

The factors of 12 are

1, 2, 3, 4, 6, and 12

We see that 8 and 12 have some of the same factors. They have three factors in common. Their three common factors are 1, 2, and 4. Their **greatest common factor**—the largest factor which they both have—is 4. Greatest common factor is often abbreviated **GCF.** The letters GCF stand for **G**reatest **C**ommon **F**actor.

**Example 1**    Find the greatest common factor of 12 and 18.

*Solution*    The factors of 12 are

1, 2, 3, 4, 6, and 12

The factors of 18 are

1, 2, 3, 6, 9, and 18

We see that 12 and 18 share four common factors. The greatest of these is **6.**

**Example 2**    Find the GCF of 6, 9, and 15.

*Solution*   The factors of 6 are

1, 2, 3, and 6.

The factors of 9 are

1, 3, and 9.

The factors of 15 are

1, 3, 5, and 15.

The GCF of 6, 9, and 15 is **3**.

**Note:** The search for the greatest common factor of two or more numbers is a search for the **largest** number which divides them. In this problem we can quickly determine by inspecting the numbers that 3 is the largest number that divides 6, 9, and 15. A complete listing of the factors may be helpful but is not required.

**Practice\***   Find the greatest common factor (GCF) of the following:

**a.** 10 and 15   5                    **b.** 18 and 27   9

**c.** 18 and 24   6                    **d.** 12, 18, and 24   6

**e.** 15 and 25   5                    **f.** 20, 30, and 40   10

**g.** 12 and 15   3                    **h.** 20, 40, and 60   20

**Problem set 20**   **1.** What is the difference between the product of 12 and 8 $^{(12)}$ and the sum of 12 and 8?   76

**2.** Saturn's average distance from the sun is one billion, $^{(12)}$ four hundred twenty-seven million kilometers. Write that number.   1,427,000,000 km

**3.** Which digit in 497,325,186 is in the ten-millions' $^{(12)}$ place?   9

**4.** Ernie actually had $427,872, but when Bert asked him
(16) how much money he had, Ernie rounded the amount
to the nearest thousand dollars. How much did he say
he had?   $428,000

**5.** The morning temperature was −3°C. By afternoon it
(14) had warmed to 8°C. How many degrees had the
temperature risen?   11°C

**6.** What is the average of 31, 52, and 40?   41
(18)

**7.** Find the greatest common factor of 12 and 20.   4
(20)

**8.** Find the GCF of 9, 15, and 21.   3
(20)

**9.** How much money is $\frac{1}{4}$ of $3.24?   $0.81
(6)

**10.** 5432 ÷ 10          **11.** $\dfrac{28 + 42}{14}$   5
(2)  543 r 2            (5)

**12.** 56,042 + 49,985    **13.** 14,009 − w = 9670
(1)  106,027            (3)  4339

**14.** w − 76 = 528   604   **15.** 5 × 4 × 3 × 2 × 1  120
(3)                        (5)

**16.** $6.47 × 10   $64.70   **17.** 37,080 ÷ 12
(2)                          (2)  3090

**18.** Which number is missing in this sequence?
(10)
____4____ , 10, 16, 22, 28, ...

**19.** 6w = 90   15
(4)

**20.** Compare: 50 − 1 $\underset{<}{}$ 49 + 1
(9)

**21.** q − 365 = 365   730   **22.** 365 − p = 365   0
(3)                          (3)

**23.** The first positive odd number is 1. What is the tenth
(10) positive odd number?   19

**24.** The perimeter of a square is 100 cm. What is the
(8) length of each side?   25 cm

**25.** Use your ruler to find the length of the key to the nearest sixteenth of an inch.   $2\frac{1}{4}$ in.
(17)

**26.** A "bit" is $\frac{1}{8}$ of a dollar.
(6)
(a) How many bits are in a dollar?   8

(b) How many bits are in three dollars?   24

**27.** In four boxes there are 12, 24, 36, and 48 ping pong
(18) balls, respectively. If the ping pong balls are rearranged so that there are the same number of ping pong balls in each of the four boxes, then how many ping pong balls would be in each box?   30

**28.** Which of these numbers is divisible by both 9 and 5?
(19)
A. 567          B. 875          C. 675   C. 675

**29.** List the whole number factors of 24.   1, 2, 3, 4, 6, 8, 12, 24
(19)

**30.** Ten billion is how much less than one trillion?
(12)   990,000,000,000

# LESSON
# 21

# Comparing Fractions with Pictures

**Facts Practice:** 64 Multiplication Facts (Test D in Test Masters)

**Mental Math:** Count up and down by $\frac{1}{4}$'s between $\frac{1}{4}$ and 12.
**a.** 4 × 42        **b.** 3 × 76            **c.** 64 + 19 *(19 is 20 – 1)*
**d.** 450 + 37    **e.** $10.00 − $6.50      **f.** $\frac{1}{2}$ of 24
**g.** Start with 25, × 2, − 1, ÷ 7, + 1, ÷ 2*

**Problem Solving:** Alexis has 6 coins that total exactly one dollar. Name three sets of coins that she **could** have.

*As a shorthand, we will use commas to separate operations to be performed sequentially from left to right. In this case, 25 × 2 = 50, then 50 − 1 = 49, then 49 ÷ 7 = 7, then 7 + 1 = 8, then 8 ÷ 2 = 4. The answer is 4.

Sketching pictures that represent fractions can help us compare fractions. Recall that common fractions are written with two numbers. The denominator (the bottom number) tells the number of equal parts in the whole. The numerator (the top number) tells how many of the equal parts we are counting. We will usually sketch and shade circles or rectangles to represent fractions. Discussing sketching strategies can help us improve our sketches. Here are sample illustrations for six fractions. Notice that the segments we draw to divide a circle pass through the center of the circle or meet (intersect) at the center of the circle.

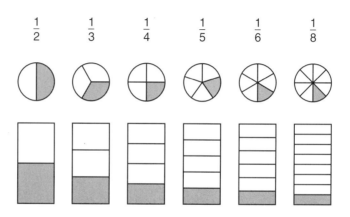

**Example 1** Draw and shade circles to illustrate this comparison:

$$\frac{1}{4} < \frac{1}{3}$$

*Solution* We begin by drawing two circles the same size. We will divide one circle into four equal parts and the other circle into three equal parts. To divide a circle into four equal parts, we may draw a "**+**" in the circle. The segments intersect at the center of the circle. To divide a circle into three equal parts, we may draw an open "**Y**" in the circle with the three segments intersecting at the center of the circle. Then we shade one part of each circle.

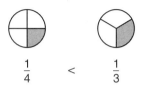

$$\frac{1}{4} \quad < \quad \frac{1}{3}$$

We see that less of the circle is shaded when $\frac{1}{4}$ is shaded than when $\frac{1}{3}$ is shaded. This illustrates that $\frac{1}{4}$ is less than $\frac{1}{3}$.

**Example 2** Draw and shade rectangles to illustrate this comparison:

Compare: $\frac{3}{4} \bigcirc \frac{3}{5}$

*Solution* We begin by drawing two congruent rectangles (two rectangles that are the same size and shape). We will divide one rectangle into four equal sections and the other rectangle into five equal sections. We describe a possible strategy for each sketch.

To divide the rectangle into fourths, we may first divide the rectangle in half. (To sketch fractions with denominators that are even numbers, we may begin by drawing a segment that divides the figure in half.)

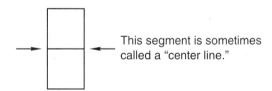

This segment is sometimes called a "center line."

Then we divide each half in half to make four equal sections.

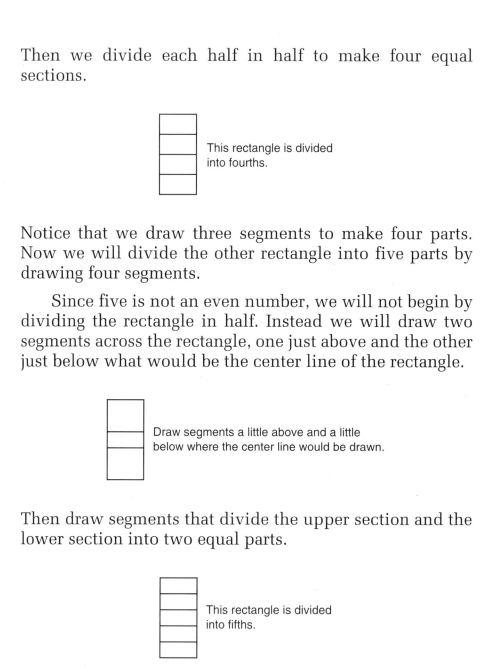

This rectangle is divided into fourths.

Notice that we draw three segments to make four parts. Now we will divide the other rectangle into five parts by drawing four segments.

Since five is not an even number, we will not begin by dividing the rectangle in half. Instead we will draw two segments across the rectangle, one just above and the other just below what would be the center line of the rectangle.

Draw segments a little above and a little below where the center line would be drawn.

Then draw segments that divide the upper section and the lower section into two equal parts.

This rectangle is divided into fifths.

Once the rectangles are divided, we shade them and compare the fractions by comparing the shaded sketches.

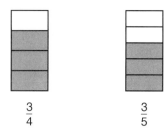

$$\frac{3}{4} \qquad \frac{3}{5}$$

We see that the $\frac{3}{4}$-shaded rectangle is slightly more shaded than the $\frac{3}{5}$-shaded rectangle. This illustrates that $\frac{3}{4}$ is greater than $\frac{3}{5}$.

$$\frac{3}{4} > \frac{3}{5}$$

**Practice**  Draw and shade circles to illustrate these comparisons:

   **a.** Compare: $\frac{1}{2}$ ⊜ $\frac{2}{4}$       **b.** Compare: $\frac{2}{3}$ ⊙ $\frac{3}{5}$

Draw and shade rectangles to illustrate these comparisons:

   **c.** Compare: $\frac{1}{2}$ ⊜ $\frac{3}{6}$       **d.** Compare: $\frac{2}{5}$ ⊙ $\frac{1}{4}$

> **Teacher Note:** Fraction manipulatives will be used by students beginning in Lesson 23. Masters to produce these manipulatives are included in the *Math 76 Test Masters.* Please refer to Lessons 23, 25, and 28 for a list of materials that will be required.

**Problem set 21**

**1.** What is the product of the sum of 8 and 5 and the difference of 8 and 5?    39
*(12)*

**2.** Delaware became the first state in 1787. Hawaii became the fiftieth state admitted to the Union in 1959. How many years were there between these two events? 172 years
*(11)*

**3.** Tom figured that the bowling balls on the rack weighed a total of 240 pounds. How many 16-pound bowling balls weigh a total of 240 pounds?    15
*(15)*

**4.** An apple pie was cut into four equal slices. One slice was quickly eaten. What fraction of the pie was left?    $\frac{3}{4}$
*(6)*

**5.** There are 17 girls in a class of 30 students. What fraction of the class is made up of girls?    $\frac{17}{30}$
*(6)*

**6.** Use digits to write the fraction three hundredths.   $\frac{3}{100}$
(6)

**7.** How much money is $\frac{1}{2}$ of $2.34?   $1.17
(6)

**8.** What is the place value of the 7 in 987,654,321?   millions'
(12)

**9.** What number comes next in this multiplication
(10) sequence?

$$1, 4, 16, 64, \underline{\ \ 256\ \ }, \dots$$

**10.** Compare: 64 × 1 $\textcircled{<}$ 64 + 1
(9)

**11.** 50 − 1 = 49 + $n$   0
(3)

**12.** Estimate the sum of 396, 197, and 203 by rounding to
(16) the nearest hundred before adding.   800

**13.** What is the greatest common factor (GCF) of 12 and 16?
(20)   4

**14.** $100\overline{)4030}$   $\overset{40\ r\ 30}{}$
(2)

**15.** 48,840 ÷ 24   2035
(2)

**16.** $\dfrac{678}{6}$   113
(2)

**17.** $4.75 × 10   $47.50
(2)

**18.** $10 − $w$ = 87¢
(3)   $9.13

**19.** 463 + 27 + $m$ = 500
(3)   10

**20.** What number is 10 less than 3?   −7
(14)

**21.** What is the average of 12, 16, and 23?   17
(18)

**22.** List the whole numbers that are factors of 28.
(19)   1, 2, 4, 7, 14, 28

**23.** A regular octagon has eight equal-length sides. What is
(8)   the perimeter of a regular octagon with sides 18 cm long?
144 cm

**24.** How long is the arrow?   $2\frac{1}{2}$ in.
(7)

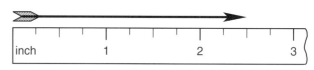

**25.** $(12 \times 12) - (11 \times 13)$   1
(5)

**26.** To divide a circle into thirds, John
(21) first imagined the face of a clock.
From the center of the "clock" he
drew one segment down to the
six. Then starting from the center
John drew two other segments. To
which two numbers on the
"clock" did John draw the two
segments when he divided the
circle into thirds?
10 and 2

**27.** Draw and shade rectangles to illustrate this comparison:
(21)   ▯▯ < ▯▯▯
$$\frac{2}{3} < \frac{3}{4}$$

**28.** A "bit" is $\frac{1}{8}$ of a dollar.
(6)
(a) How many bits are in a dollar?   8

(b) How many bits are in a half dollar?   4

**29.** What numbers are factors of both 20 and 30?   1, 2, 5, 10
(19)

**30.** Describe a method for dividing a circle into eight
(21) equal parts that involves drawing a plus sign and a
times sign. Illustrate the explanation.   Draw a circle. In
the circle draw a plus sign ⊕. Then draw a times sign in the
circle ⊛.

# LESSON 22

# "Equal Groups" Stories with Fractions

**Mental Math:**
**a.** 216
**b.** 168
**c.** 65
**d.** 317
**e.** $6.50
**f.** 24
**g.** 25
**Problem Solving:**
   8

---

**Facts Practice:** 100 Subtraction Facts (Test C in Test Masters)

**Mental Math:** Count by 2's from 2 to 40. Count by 4's from 4 to 40. Count up and down by $\frac{1}{4}$'s between $\frac{1}{4}$ and 12.

**a.** $4 \times 54$    **b.** $3 \times 56$         **c.** $36 + 29$ (*29 is 30 − 1*)
**d.** $359 - 42$    **e.** $10.00 - 3.50$    **f.** $\frac{1}{2}$ of 48
**g.** Start with 100, − 1, ÷ 9, + 1, ÷ 2, − 1, × 5

**Problem Solving:** Two number cubes are rolled. The total number of dots on the two top faces is 6. What is the total of the dots on the bottom faces of the two number cubes?

---

Here we show a collection of six objects. The collection is divided into three equal groups. We see that there are two objects in $\frac{1}{3}$ of the collection. We also see that there are four objects in $\frac{2}{3}$ of the collection.

This collection of 12 objects has been divided into four equal groups. There are three objects in $\frac{1}{4}$ of the collection. There are nine objects in $\frac{3}{4}$ of the collection.

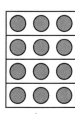

**Example 1**  Two thirds of the 12 musicians played guitars. How many of the musicians played guitars?

**Solution**  This is a two-step problem. First we divide the 12 musicians into three equal groups (thirds). There are four musicians in each group. Then we count the number of musicians in two of the three groups.

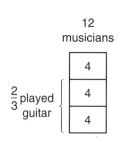

Since there are four musicians in each third, the number of musicians in two thirds is eight. We find that **eight** of the 12 musicians played guitars.

**Example 2**  Cory has finished $\frac{3}{4}$ of the 28 problems on the assignment. How many problems has Cory finished?

*Solution*  First we will divide the 28 problems into four equal groups (fourths). Then we will find the number of problems in three of the four groups. Since 28 ÷ 4 is 7, there are 7 problems in each group (in each fourth).

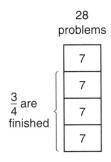

In one group there are 7 problems; in two groups there are 14 problems; and in three groups there are 21 problems. We see that Cory has finished **21 problems.**

**Example 3**  How much money is $\frac{3}{5}$ of $3.00?

*Solution*  First we will divide $3.00 into 5 equal groups. Then we will find the amount of money in 3 of the 5 groups. We will divide $3.00 by 5 to find the amount of money in each group.

$$5\overline{)\$3.00}\qquad \$0.60 \text{ in each group.}$$

Now we multiply $0.60 by 3 to find the amount of money in 3 groups.

$$\begin{array}{r} \$0.60 \\ \times \quad 3 \\ \hline \$1.80 \end{array}$$

We find that $\frac{3}{5}$ of $3.00 is **$1.80.**

**Practice*** Answer the following questions. Draw a diagram to illustrate each problem.

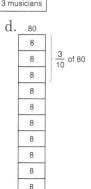

a. 12 musicians

**a.** Three fourths of the 12 musicians could play the piano. How many of the musicians could play the piano? 9

b. $4.50

**b.** How much money is $\frac{2}{3}$ of $4.50? $3.00

**c.** What number is $\frac{4}{5}$ of 60? 48

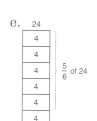

**d.** What number is $\frac{3}{10}$ of 80? 24

**e.** Five sixths of 24 is what number? 20

**Problem set 22**

**1.** When the sum of 15 and 12 is subtracted from the
(12) product of 15 and 12, what is the difference? 153

**2.** There were 13 original states. There are now 50 states.
(6) What fraction of the states are the original states? $\frac{13}{50}$

4. 12 jelly beans

**3.** A marathon race is 26 miles plus 385 yards. A mile is
(11,15) 1760 yards. Altogether, how many yards long is a marathon? (First use an EG pattern to find the number of yards in 26 miles. Then use a SSM pattern to include the 385 yards.) 46,145 yd

**4.** If $\frac{2}{3}$ of the 12 jelly beans are eaten, how many are
(22) eaten? Draw a diagram to illustrate the problem. 8

**5.** What number is $\frac{3}{4}$ of 16? Draw a diagram to illustrate
(22) the problem. 12

**6.** How much money is $\frac{3}{10}$ of $3.50? Draw a diagram to
(22) illustrate the problem. $1.05

**7.** The temperature rose from −3°F to 4°F. How many
(14) degrees did the temperature rise? 7°F

**8.** $w - 15 = 8$   23          **9.** 36¢ + $4.78 + $34.09
(3)                              (5)   $39.23

**10.** $w \div 67 = 345$
(4)   23,115

**11.** $\$12.45 \div 3$   $4.15
(2)

**12.** $35\overline{)1000}$   $\dfrac{28 \text{ r } 20}{}$
(2)

**13.** $\dfrac{7 + 9 + 14}{3}$   10
(5)

**14.** Find the product of 36 and 124, and then round the
(16)   answer to the nearest hundred.   4500

**15.** Which digit is in the ten-millions' place in
(12)   375,426,198,000?   2

**16.** Find the greatest common factor of 12 and 15.   3
(20)

**17.** List the factors of 30.   1, 2, 3, 5, 6, 10, 15, 30
(19)

**18.** The number 100 is divisible by which of these
(19)   numbers: 2, 3, 5, 9, 10?   2, 5, 10

**19.** Compare: $\dfrac{1}{3}$ $\overset{<}{\bigcirc}$ $\dfrac{1}{2}$
(21)

**20.** $\dfrac{64}{m} = 64$   1
(4)

**21.** Here are the first five numbers of a sequence. What
(10)   would be the **seventh** number in the sequence?

1, 4, 7, 10, 13, ..., __19__, ...

**22.** $(3 + 3) - (3 \times 3)$   –3
(5)

**23.** Find the number halfway between 27 and 43.   35
(18)

**24.** What is the perimeter of the rectangle?   50 cm
(8)

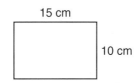

15 cm

10 cm

**25.** Use your ruler to find the length of this line
(7)   segment.   $2\frac{1}{4}$ in.

**26.** An apple pie was cut into six equal slices. A cherry
(21) pie, baked in the same size pie pan, was cut into five
equal slices. Which was larger, a slice of apple pie or a
slice of cherry pie?    a slice of cherry pie

**27.** Compare these fractions. Draw and shade rectangles to
(21) illustrate the comparison.    ▮▯▯ < ▮▮▯▯

$$\frac{2}{4} \; \textcircled{<} \; \frac{3}{5}$$

**28.** A quarter of a year is $\frac{1}{4}$ of a year. There are 12 months
(22) in a year. How many months are in a quarter of a year?
3

**29.** A "bit" is one eighth of a dollar.
(6)
(a) How many bits are in a dollar?    8

(b) How many bits are in a quarter of a dollar?    2

**30.** The letters $c$, $p$, and $t$ represent three different
(1) numbers. When $p$ is subtracted from $c$, the answer is $t$.

$$c - p = t$$

Use these letters to write another subtraction fact and
two addition facts.    $c - t = p$, $p + t = c$, $t + p = c$

LESSON
**23**

# Fraction Manipulatives, Part 1

**Mental Math:**
a. 310
b. 180
c. 96
d. 1550
e. $4.50
f. 42
g. 2
**Problem Solving:**
  27

**Facts Practice:** 64 Multiplication Facts (Test D in Test Masters)

**Mental Math:** Count up and down by 3's between 3 and 60.
Count up and down by $\frac{1}{4}$'s between $\frac{1}{4}$ and 12.

**a.** 5 × 62          **b.** 5 × 36          **c.** 87 + 9 (*9 is 10 − 1*)
**d.** 1200 + 350    **e.** $20.00 − $15.50    **f.** $\frac{1}{2}$ of 84
**g.** 10 × 3, + 2, ÷ 4, + 1, ÷ 3, × 4, ÷ 6

**Problem Solving:** Sarah used 8 sugar cubes to make a larger cube as shown. The cube she made was two cubes high, two cubes wide, and two cubes deep. How many cubes will she need to make a cube that has three cubes along each edge?

In this lesson you will make your own set of fraction manipulatives to use as you answer the questions in this lesson and in future problem sets.

## Activity:  Fraction Manipulatives $\left(\frac{1}{2}, \frac{1}{4}, \frac{1}{8}\right)$

Materials needed:

- Each student needs a copy of "Activity Master 2," which includes patterns for halves, fourths, and eighths (available in the *Math 76 Test Masters*).
- Scissors
- Envelopes or locking plastic bags in which to store fraction pieces
- Colored pencils or markers if the fraction manipulatives are to be color-coded

**Note:** Color-coding the fraction manipulatives makes sorting easier. If you wish to color-code the manipulatives, agree upon a different color for each fraction circle. Students may lightly color the front and back of each circle before cutting. Following the activity, each student should store the fraction manipulatives in an envelope or plastic bag for use in later lessons.

Preparation for activities:

- Distribute materials. Have students color-code the manipulatives if desired. Then have students separate the fraction manipulatives by cutting out the fraction circles and cutting apart the fraction slices along the lines. After the activities, store the manipulatives for later use.

Use your fraction manipulatives to help you with these activities and questions.

**a.** What percent of a circle is $\frac{1}{2}$ of a circle?   50%

**b.** What fraction is half of $\frac{1}{2}$?   $\frac{1}{4}$

**c.** What fraction is half of $\frac{1}{4}$?   $\frac{1}{8}$

**d.** Fit three $\frac{1}{4}$ pieces together to form $\frac{3}{4}$ of a circle. Three fourths of a circle is what percent of a circle?   75%

**e.** Fit four $\frac{1}{8}$ pieces together to form $\frac{4}{8}$ of a circle. Four eighths of a circle is what percent of a circle?   50%

**f.** If you add $\frac{1}{8} + \frac{1}{8} + \frac{1}{8}$, the sum is $\frac{3}{8}$. If you add $\frac{3}{8} + \frac{2}{8}$, what is the sum?   $\frac{5}{8}$

Using your halves, fourths, and eighths manipulatives, a whole circle can be formed using two through eight pieces. Write a number sentence for each blank in the chart.

g. $\frac{1}{2} + \frac{1}{4} + \frac{1}{8} + \frac{1}{8} = 1$

h. $\frac{1}{2} + \frac{1}{8} + \frac{1}{8} + \frac{1}{8} + \frac{1}{8} = 1$

i. $\frac{1}{4} + \frac{1}{4} + \frac{1}{8} + \frac{1}{8} + \frac{1}{8} + \frac{1}{8} = 1$

j. $\frac{1}{4} + \frac{1}{8} + \frac{1}{8} + \frac{1}{8} + \frac{1}{8} + \frac{1}{8} + \frac{1}{8} = 1$

k. $\frac{1}{8} + \frac{1}{8} + \frac{1}{8} + \frac{1}{8} + \frac{1}{8} + \frac{1}{8} + \frac{1}{8} + \frac{1}{8} = 1$

| NUMBER OF PIECES USED | NUMBER SENTENCE WITH A SUM OF 1 |
|---|---|
| 2 | $\frac{1}{2} + \frac{1}{2} = 1$ |
| 3 | $\frac{1}{2} + \frac{1}{4} + \frac{1}{4} = 1$ |
| 4 | $\frac{1}{4} + \frac{1}{4} + \frac{1}{4} + \frac{1}{4} = 1$ or **g.** |
| 5 | $\frac{1}{4} + \frac{1}{4} + \frac{1}{4} + \frac{1}{8} + \frac{1}{8} = 1$ or **h.** |
| 6 | **i.** |
| 7 | **j.** |
| 8 | **k.** |

**l.** Show that both $\frac{4}{8}$ and $\frac{2}{4}$ make $\frac{1}{2}$ of a circle. (We say that $\frac{4}{8}$ and $\frac{2}{4}$ both "reduce" to $\frac{1}{2}$.)  ⊛ = ⬯ and ⊕ = ⬯

**m.** The fraction $\frac{2}{8}$ is equivalent to which single fraction piece?  $\frac{1}{4}$

**n.** The fraction $\frac{6}{8}$ is equivalent to how many $\frac{1}{4}$'s?  3

Work in groups of two or three students for the remaining exercises.

**o.** Show that the improper fraction $\frac{5}{4}$ is equal to the mixed number $1\frac{1}{4}$ by combining four of the $\frac{1}{4}$ pieces to make a whole circle.  ⊕◗ = ◯◗

**p.** To what mixed number is the improper fraction $\frac{7}{4}$ equal?  $1\frac{3}{4}$

After the activities have been completed, each student should gather and store his or her own fraction manipulatives in a bag for later use.

**Problem set 23**

**1.** How many millimeters long is a ruler that is 30 cm long?
(7)    300 mm

**2.** Dan has finished $\frac{2}{3}$ of the 27 problems on an
(22)    assignment. How many problems has Dan finished?
18 problems

**3.** William Tell shot at the apple from 100 paces. If each pace
(15)    was 36 inches, how many inches away was the apple?
3600 in.

**4.** There are 31 days in December. After December 25,
(6)    what fraction of the month remains?  $\frac{6}{31}$

**5.** What number is $\frac{3}{5}$ of 25?  15
(22)

**6.** How much money is $\frac{7}{10}$ of $36.00?  $25.20
(22)

You may use your fraction manipulatives to help you answer questions 7 through 9.

**7.** What is the sum of $\frac{3}{8}$ and $\frac{4}{8}$?  $\frac{7}{8}$
(23)

**8.** The improper fraction $\frac{9}{8}$ equals what mixed number?
(23)    $1\frac{1}{8}$

**9.** Two eighths of a circle is what percent of a circle?  25%
(23)

**10.** $10.20      **11.**   $3.75      **12.** $\frac{$3.75}{25}$  $0.15
(3)   − _____ m    (2)   × _____ 16    (2)
    $3.46          $60.00
$6.74

**13.** What is the place value of the 6 in 36,174,591?
(12)   millions'

14. One way to find **14.** Describe a way to find $\frac{2}{3}$ of a number.
$\frac{2}{3}$ of a number is to    (22)
first divide the
number by 3; then   **15.** $0.35n = $35.00   100
multiply that    (4)
answer by 2.

**16.** Compare: $\frac{3}{4}$ $\;\textcircled{<}\;$ 1
(21)

**17.** The length of a rectangle is 20 inches. The width is
(8)   half the length. What is the perimeter of the rectangle?
    60 in.

**18.** What is the sixth number in this sequence?   64
(10)

    2, 4, 8, 16, ...

**19.** Estimate the sum of 3174 and 4790 to the nearest
(16)   thousand.   8000

**20.** Compare: 12 ÷ 6 − 2 $\;\textcircled{<}\;$ 12 ÷ (6 − 2)
(9)

**21.** What is the greatest common factor (GCF) of 24 and 32?
(20)   8

**22.** What is the sum of the first seven positive odd
(10)   numbers?   49

You may use your fraction manipulatives to help you
answer questions 23, 24, and 25.

**23.** (a) How many $\frac{1}{4}$'s are in 1?   4
(23)   (b) How many $\frac{1}{4}$'s are in $\frac{1}{2}$?   2

**24.** One eighth of a circle is what percent of a circle?   $12\frac{1}{2}$%
(23)

**25.** Write a fraction with a denominator of 8 that is equal
(23)   to $\frac{1}{2}$.   $\frac{4}{8}$

# LESSON
# 24

# Adding and Subtracting Fractions That Have Common Denominators

**Mental Math:**

**a.** 144

**b.** 300

**c.** 86

**d.** 1250

**e.** $5.50

**f.** 34

**g.** 5

**Problem Solving:**

(a) XYZ, XZY
    YXZ, YZX
    ZXY, ZYX

(b) 4

**Facts Practice:** 100 Subtraction Facts (Test C in Test Masters)

**Mental Math:** Count by 4's from 4 to 80.

Count up and down by $\frac{1}{4}$'s between $\frac{1}{4}$ and 12.

**a.** $6 \times 24$       **b.** $4 \times 75$       **c.** $47 + 39$

**d.** $1500 - 250$       **e.** $20.00 - $14.50       **f.** $\frac{1}{2}$ of 68

**g.** $6 \times 7, - 2, \div 5, \times 2, - 1, \div 3$

**Problem Solving:** Xavier, Yolanda, and Zollie finished first, second, and third in the race, though not necessarily in that order. (a) List all the possible orders of finish. (b) If Xavier was not first, how many possible orders of finish were there?

Using our fraction manipulatives, we see that when we add $\frac{2}{8}$ to $\frac{3}{8}$ the sum is $\frac{5}{8}$.

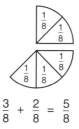

$$\frac{3}{8} + \frac{2}{8} = \frac{5}{8}$$

Three eighths plus two eighths equals five eighths.

Likewise, if we subtract $\frac{2}{8}$ from $\frac{5}{8}$, then $\frac{3}{8}$ are left.

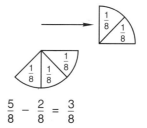

$$\frac{5}{8} - \frac{2}{8} = \frac{3}{8}$$

Five eighths minus two eighths equals three eighths.

Notice that we add the numerators when we add fractions and we subtract the numerators when we subtract fractions. The denominator of the fraction is not changed by adding or subtracting.

**Example 1**    $\frac{1}{4} + \frac{1}{4} + \frac{1}{4}$

*Solution*    The denominators are the same. We add the numerators.

$$\frac{1}{4} + \frac{1}{4} + \frac{1}{4} = \frac{3}{4}$$

**Example 2**    $\frac{1}{2} + \frac{1}{2}$

*Solution*    One half and one half is two halves, which is one whole.

$$\frac{1}{2} + \frac{1}{2} = \frac{2}{2}$$

$$\frac{2}{2} = 1$$

**Example 3**    $\frac{7}{8} - \frac{2}{8}$

*Solution*    The denominators are the same. We subtract two eighths from seven eighths.

$$\frac{7}{8} - \frac{2}{8} = \frac{5}{8}$$

**Example 4**    $\frac{2}{4} - \frac{1}{4}$

*Solution*    The denominators are the same. We subtract $\frac{1}{4}$ from $\frac{2}{4}$ and get $\frac{1}{4}$.

$$\frac{2}{4} - \frac{1}{4} = \frac{1}{4}$$

**Example 5**    $\frac{1}{2} - \frac{1}{2}$

*Solution*  If we start with $\frac{1}{2}$ and subtract $\frac{1}{2}$, then what is left is zero.

$$\frac{1}{2} - \frac{1}{2} = \frac{0}{2}$$

$$\frac{0}{2} = \mathbf{0}$$

**Practice**  Add or subtract as shown:

**a.** $\frac{3}{8} + \frac{4}{8}$  $\frac{7}{8}$

**b.** $\frac{3}{4} + \frac{1}{4}$  1

**c.** $\frac{1}{8} + \frac{1}{8} + \frac{1}{8}$  $\frac{3}{8}$

**d.** $\frac{4}{8} - \frac{1}{8}$  $\frac{3}{8}$

**e.** $\frac{3}{4} - \frac{2}{4}$  $\frac{1}{4}$

**f.** $\frac{1}{4} - \frac{1}{4}$  0

**Problem set 24**

**1.** Martin worked in the yard for five hours and was paid
$(11,15)$ $6.00 per hour. Then he washed the car for $5.
Altogether, how much money did Martin earn? What
pattern did you use to find Martin's yard-work
earnings? Then what pattern did you use to find his
total earnings?  $35.00; EG; SSM

2.
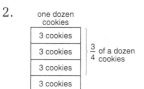

**2.** In one bite, Cookie ate $\frac{3}{4}$ of a dozen chocolate chip
$(22)$ cookies. How many cookies did Cookie eat in that
bite? Draw a diagram that illustrates the problem.  9

**3.** One mile is one thousand, seven hundred sixty yards.
$(22)$ How many yards is $\frac{1}{8}$ of a mile?  220 yards

You may use your fraction manipulatives to help answer
problems 4 through 8.

**4.** $\frac{1}{4} + \frac{2}{4}$  $\frac{3}{4}$
$(24)$

**5.** $\frac{7}{8} - \frac{4}{8}$  $\frac{3}{8}$
$(24)$

**6.** $\frac{1}{2} + \frac{1}{2}$  1
$(24)$

**7.** $\frac{1}{2} - \frac{1}{2}$  0
$(24)$

**8.** What percent of a circle is $\frac{1}{2}$ of a circle plus $\frac{1}{4}$ of a
(23)　circle?　75%

**9.** Which of these numbers is divisible by both 2 and 5?
(19)
　　A. 1760　　　　　B. 365　　　　　C. 1492
　　A. 1760

**10.** What number is halfway between 123 and 321?　222
(18)

**11.** Paul wanted to fence in a square pasture for Babe, his
(8)　blue ox. Each side was to be 25 miles long. How many
　　miles of fence did Paul need?　100 miles

**12.** Round 32,987,145 to the nearest million.　33,000,000
(16)

**13.** What number is missing in this sequence?
(10)
　　　　　　1, 7, __13__, 19, 25, ...

**14.** $9\overline{)1000}$　111 r 1
(2)

**15.** 22,422 ÷ 32　700 r 22
(2)

**16.** $w \div 8 = 20$　160
(4)

**17.** $350.00 ÷ 100　$3.50
(2)

**18.** $7x = 84$　12
(4)

**19.** Compare: $\frac{1}{2}$ ⊙ $\frac{1}{4}$
(21)

**20.** What temperature is shown on the
(10)　thermometer?　44°F

**21.** $(35 \times 35) - (5 \times 5)$　1200
(5)

**22.** Estimate the product of 385 and
(16)　214.　80,000

**23.** What is the GCF of 21 and 28?　7
(20)

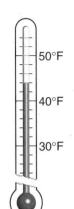

**24.** Which of these numbers is divisible by 9?　B. 234
(19)
　　A. 123　　　　　B. 234　　　　　C. 345

**25.** Write a fraction equal to 1 that has 4 as the
(23)　denominator.　$\frac{4}{4}$

Find the missing numbers:

**26.** 376 + _w_ = 481    105       **27.** _m_ − 286 = 592    878
(3)                                                          (3)

Use the information in this graph to help answer questions 28 through 30.

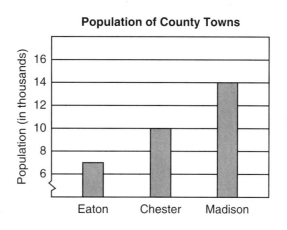

**28.** Which town has about twice the population of Eaton?
(16)    Madison

**29.** About how many more people live in Madison than in
(16)    Chester?    4000

**30.** Sketch this graph on your paper and add a fourth town
(16)    to your graph: Wilson, population 11,000.

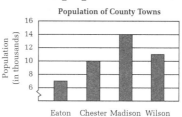

# LESSON 25

# Fraction Manipulatives, Part 2

**Mental Math:**
a. 364
b. 198
c. 82
d. 306
e. $2.75
f. 43
g. 10

**Problem Solving:**

$$\begin{array}{r} 819 \\ -\ 452 \\ \hline 367 \end{array}$$

---

**Facts Practice:** 100 Multiplication Facts (Test E in Test Masters)

**Mental Math:** Count up and down by 3's between 3 and 60. Count up and down by 6's between 6 and 60.

| | | |
|---|---|---|
| **a.** $7 \times 52$ | **b.** $6 \times 33$ | **c.** $63 + 19$ |
| **d.** $256 + 50$ | **e.** $\$10.00 - \$7.25$ | **f.** $\frac{1}{2}$ of 86 |
| **g.** $8 \times 8, -1, \div 7, \times 2, +2, \div 2$ | | |

**Problem Solving:** The digits 1 through 9 are used in this subtraction problem. Copy the problem and fill in the missing digits.

$$\begin{array}{r} \_\,\_\,\_ \\ -\ 452 \\ \hline 3\_\,\_ \end{array}$$

---

In this lesson you will make fraction manipulatives for thirds, sixths, and twelfths.

## Activity: Fraction Manipulatives $\left(\frac{1}{3}, \frac{1}{6}, \frac{1}{12}\right)$

Materials needed:

- Each student needs a copy of "Activity Master 3" (available in the *Math 76 Test Masters*).
- Scissors
- Envelopes or locking plastic bags in which to store fraction pieces (re-use bag from Lesson 23)
- Colored pencils or markers
- Fraction manipulatives made in Lesson 23

Preparation for activities:

- Distribute materials. If fraction manipulatives will be color-coded, we suggest agreeing upon colors and lightly coloring the front and back of each circle before cutting. After the activities, store the manipulatives for later use.

Use all the fraction manipulatives you have made to help you with these activities and questions.

**a.** What fraction is half of $\frac{1}{3}$?   $\frac{1}{6}$

**b.** What fraction is half of $\frac{1}{6}$?   $\frac{1}{12}$

**c.** How many sixths equal $\frac{1}{2}$?   3

**d.** How many twelfths equal $\frac{1}{2}$?    6

$\frac{5}{6}$   **e.** Form a whole circle using six of the $\frac{1}{6}$ pieces. Then remove (subtract) $\frac{1}{6}$. What fraction of the circle is left?

**f.** Demonstrate subtracting $\frac{1}{3}$ from 1 by forming a circle of $\frac{3}{3}$ and then removing $\frac{1}{3}$. What fraction is left?    $\frac{2}{3}$

**g.** Use four fourths to demonstrate the subtraction $1 - \frac{1}{4}$ and write the answer.    $\frac{3}{4}$

**h.** Use eight eighths to demonstrate the subtraction $1 - \frac{3}{8}$ and write the answer.    $\frac{5}{8}$

**i.** What percent of a circle is $\frac{1}{3}$ of a circle?    $33\frac{1}{3}\%$

**j.** What percent of a circle is $\frac{3}{6}$ of a circle?    50%

**k.** Make a fraction equivalent to $\frac{4}{6}$ using thirds.    $\frac{2}{3}$

**l.** Find a single fraction piece that matches $\frac{3}{12}$.    $\frac{1}{4}$

**m.** What percent of a circle is $\frac{3}{12}$ of a circle?    25%

**n.** Find a single fraction piece that matches $\frac{4}{12}$.    $\frac{1}{3}$

**o.** How many twelfths equal $\frac{2}{3}$?    8

**p.** How many twelfths equal $\frac{3}{4}$?    9

$1\frac{1}{3}$   **q.** The improper fraction $\frac{4}{3}$ equals what mixed number?

**r.** Convert $\frac{11}{6}$ to a mixed number.    $1\frac{5}{6}$

Store your manipulatives for later use.

**Problem set 25**

**1.** What is the product of the sum of 55 and 45 and the
(12) difference of 55 and 45?    1000

**2.** Potatoes are three fourths water. If a sack of potatoes
(22) weighs 20 pounds, how many pounds of water are in the potatoes?    15 lb

**3.** Frankie found three hundred six fleas on his dog. He
(11) caught two hundred forty-nine of them. How many fleas got away?    57

**4.** What number is halfway between 8 and 9?    $8\frac{1}{2}$
(17)

**5.** Which of these numbers is divisible by both 2 and 3?
(19)
   A.  122              B.  123              C.  132
   C. 132

**6.** Round 1,234,567 to the nearest ten thousand.    1,230,000
(16)

**7.** If ten pounds of apples cost $4.90, then what is the
(15)   price per pound?    49¢

**8.** What is the denominator of $\frac{23}{24}$?    24
(6)

**9.** What number is $\frac{3}{5}$ of 65?    39
(22)

**10.** How much money is $\frac{2}{3}$ of $15?    $10
(22)

You may use your fraction manipulatives to help answer problems 11 through 18.

**11.** $\frac{1}{6} + \frac{2}{6} + \frac{3}{6}$    1          **12.** $\frac{11}{12} - \frac{5}{12}$    $\frac{1}{2}$
(24)                                        (24)

**13.** $\frac{6}{6} - \frac{5}{6}$    $\frac{1}{6}$          **14.** $\frac{2}{8} + \frac{5}{8}$    $\frac{7}{8}$
(25)                                        (24)

**15.** (a)  What percent of a circle is $\frac{1}{12}$ of a circle?    $8\frac{1}{3}$%
(25)   (b)  What percent of a circle is $\frac{2}{12}$ of a circle?    $16\frac{2}{3}$%

**16.** (a)  How many $\frac{1}{12}$'s are in 1?    12
(25)   (b)  How many $\frac{1}{12}$'s are in $\frac{1}{2}$?    6

**17.** What fraction is half of $\frac{1}{4}$?    $\frac{1}{8}$
(23)

**18.** What fraction of a circle is 50% of a circle?    $\frac{1}{2}$
(23)

**19.** $52\overline{)2100}$  $\quad$ 40 r 20          **20.** $\frac{432}{18}$    24
(2)                                        (2)

**21.** If a 36-inch-long string is made into the shape of a
(8)    square, how long will each side be?    9 in.

**22.** Convert $\frac{7}{6}$ to a mixed number.    $1\frac{1}{6}$
(25)

**23.** $(55 + 45) \div (55 - 45)$    10
(5)

**24.** Which of these numbers is divisible by both 2 and 5?
(19)
   A. 502            B. 205            C. 250
   C. 250

**25.** Describe a method for deciding if a number is
(19)   divisible by 9.    Add the digits of the number. If the sum of
       the digits can be divided by 9, the number can be divided by 9.

---

**LESSON
26**

# Writing Division Answers as Mixed Numbers • Multiples

**Mental Math:**
**a.** 258
**b.** 225
**c.** 86
**d.** 2500
**e.** $3.75
**f.** 15
**g.** 4
**Problem Solving:**
   dime

> **Facts Practice:** 90 Division Facts (Test F in Test Masters)
>
> **Mental Math:** Count by $\frac{1}{8}$'s from $\frac{1}{8}$ to 2.
>
>   **a.** $6 \times 43$      **b.** $3 \times 75$      **c.** $57 + 29$ (*29 is 30 − 1*)
>   **d.** $2650 - 150$   **e.** $10.00 - \$6.25$   **f.** $\frac{1}{2}$ of 30
>   **g.** $10 \times 2, + 1, \div 3, + 2, \div 3, \times 4, \div 3$
>
> **Problem Solving:** Alexis has 6 coins that total exactly $1.00.
>                    Name the one coin she **must** have.

**Writing division answers as mixed numbers**

We have been writing division answers with remainders. However, not all questions involving division can be appropriately answered using remainders. Some story problems have answers that are mixed numbers, as we see in the following example:

**Example 1** A 15-inch length of ribbon was cut into four equal lengths. How long was each piece of ribbon?

**Solution** We divide 15 by 4 and write the answer as a mixed number.

$$
\begin{array}{r}
3\frac{3}{4} \\
4\overline{)15} \\
\underline{12} \\
3
\end{array}
$$

Notice that the remainder is the numerator of the fraction and the divisor is the denominator of the fraction. We find that the length of each piece of ribbon is $3\frac{3}{4}$ **inches.**

**Example 2**   A whole circle is 100% of a circle. One third of a circle is what percent of a circle?

**Solution**   If we divide 100% by 3, we will find the percent equivalent of $\frac{1}{3}$.

$$
\begin{array}{r}
33\frac{1}{3}\% \\
3\overline{)100\%} \\
\underline{9}\phantom{00\%} \\
10\phantom{\%} \\
\underline{9}\phantom{\%} \\
1\phantom{\%}
\end{array}
$$

We write the answer **$33\frac{1}{3}\%$**. Notice that our answer matches our fraction manipulative piece for $\frac{1}{3}$.

**Example 3**   Write $\frac{25}{6}$ as a mixed number.

**Solution**   The fraction line in $\frac{25}{6}$ is also a division sign. We divide 25 by 6 and write the remainder as the numerator of the fraction.

$$
\begin{array}{r}
4\frac{1}{6} \\
6\overline{)25} \\
\underline{24} \\
1
\end{array}
$$

We find that the improper fraction $\frac{25}{6}$ equals the mixed number **$4\frac{1}{6}$**.

**Multiples**   We find **multiples** of a number by multiplying the number by 1, 2, 3, 4, 5, 6, and so on.

The first six multiples of 2 are 2, 4, 6, 8, 10, and 12.
The first six multiples of 3 are 3, 6, 9, 12, 15, and 18.
The first six multiples of 4 are 4, 8, 12, 16, 20, and 24.
The first six multiples of 5 are 5, 10, 15, 20, 25, and 30.

**Example 4**   What are the first four multiples of 8?

**Solution**   Multiplying 8 by 1, 2, 3, and 4 gives the first four multiples: **8, 16, 24,** and **32.**

**Example 5** What number is the eighth multiple of 7?

*Solution* The eighth multiple of 7 is 8 times 7, which is **56.**

**Practice*** **a.** A 28-inch long ribbon was cut into eight equal lengths. How long was each piece of ribbon? $3\frac{1}{2}$ in.

**b.** A whole circle is 100% of a circle. What percent of a circle is $\frac{1}{7}$ of a circle? $14\frac{2}{7}\%$

**c.** Divide 467 by 10 and write the quotient as a mixed number. $46\frac{7}{10}$

**d.** What are the first four multiples of 12? $12, 24, 36, 48$

**e.** What are the first six multiples of 8? $8, 16, 24, 32, 40, 48$

**f.** What number is both the third multiple of 8 and the second multiple of 12? $24$

Write each of these improper fractions as a mixed number:

**g.** $\dfrac{35}{6}$ $5\frac{5}{6}$  **h.** $\dfrac{49}{10}$ $4\frac{9}{10}$  **i.** $\dfrac{65}{12}$ $5\frac{5}{12}$

**Problem set 26**

**1.** $(25)$ What is the difference between the sum of $\frac{1}{2}$ and $\frac{1}{2}$ and the sum of $\frac{1}{3}$ and $\frac{1}{3}$? $\frac{1}{3}$

2. Carlos can find the average distance of the three punts by adding 35 yd, 30 yd, and 37 yd, and then dividing the sum by 3.

**2.** $(18)$ In three tries Carlos punted the football 35 yards, 30 yards, and 37 yards, respectively. How can Carlos find the average distance of his punts?

**3.** $(12)$ The earth's average distance from the sun is one hundred forty-nine million, six hundred thousand kilometers. Use digits to write that number. $149,600,000$

**4.** $(8)$ What is the perimeter of the rectangle? $1$ in.

$\frac{3}{8}$ in.

$\boxed{\phantom{xxxx}}$ $\frac{1}{8}$ in.

**5.** A 30-inch length of ribbon was cut into 4 equal
(26) lengths. How long was each piece of ribbon?   $7\frac{1}{2}$ in.

**6.** Two thirds of the class finished the test on time. What
(25) fraction of the class did not finish the test on time?   $\frac{1}{3}$

**7.** Compare: $\frac{1}{2}$ of 12 $\bigcirc\!\!>$ $\frac{1}{3}$ of 12
(22)

**8.** What fraction is half of the fraction that is half of $\frac{1}{2}$?   $\frac{1}{8}$
(23)

**9.** A whole circle is 100% of a circle. What percent of a
(26) circle is $\frac{1}{9}$ of a circle?   $11\frac{1}{9}\%$

**10.** (a) How many $\frac{1}{6}$'s are in 1?   6
(25)
    (b) How many $\frac{1}{6}$'s are in $\frac{1}{2}$?   3

**11.** What fraction of a circle is $33\frac{1}{3}\%$ of a circle?   $\frac{1}{3}$
(26)

**12.** Divide 365 by 7 and write the answer as a mixed
(26) number.   $52\frac{1}{7}$

**13.** $\frac{2}{3} + \frac{2}{3} + \frac{2}{3}$   2        **14.** $\frac{6}{6} - \frac{5}{6}$   $\frac{1}{6}$
(24)                                (24)

**15.** $\frac{5}{8} + m = 1$   $\frac{3}{8}$        **16.** $\frac{5}{12} - \frac{5}{12}$   0
(25)                                (24)

**17.** What number comes next in this sequence?
(10)
                81, 64, 49, 36, __25__ , ...

**18.** Cheryl bought 10 pens for 25¢ each. How much did
(15) she pay for all ten pens?   $2.50

**19.** What is the greatest common factor (GCF) of 24 and 30?
(20)   6

**20.** 30 × 40 ÷ 60   20
(5)

**21.** What number is $\frac{1}{100}$ of 100?   1
(22)

**22.** Estimate the sum of 3142, 6328, and 4743 to the
(16) nearest thousand.   14,000

23.

60 students

20 students
20 students      } $\frac{2}{3}$ liked hamburgers
20 students

**23.** Two thirds of the students liked hamburgers. If 60
(22) students were asked, how many liked hamburgers?
Draw a diagram that illustrates the problem.   40

**24.** $\dfrac{144}{n} = 12$   12
(4)

**25.** Use your ruler to find the length of this line segment.
(17) $1\frac{7}{8}$ in.

_____

**26.** To divide a circle into thirds, Jan imagined the circle
(21) was the face of a clock. She drew one segment from
the center of the "clock" up to where the "12" would
be on a clock. Then she drew two more segments from
the center of the circle. To which two numbers on the
face of a clock did Jan draw the segments to divide the
circle into thirds?   4 and 8

**27.** Write $\frac{15}{4}$ as a mixed number.   $3\frac{3}{4}$
(26)

**28.** Draw and shade rectangles to illustrate and complete
(21) this comparison:

▓▓▢ < ▓▢▢▢        $\dfrac{3}{4}$ ⓧ $\dfrac{4}{5}$

**29.** What are the first four multiples of 25?   25, 50, 75, 100
(26)

**30.** Which of these numbers is divisible by both 9 and 10?
(19)  A. 910          B. 8910          C. 78,910
B. 8910

# LESSON 27

# Using Manipulatives to Reduce Fractions • Adding and Subtracting Mixed Numbers

**Mental Math:**
**a.** 238
**b.** 224
**c.** 93
**d.** 600
**e.** $3.25
**f.** 16
**g.** 2
**Problem Solving:**
    14

---

**Facts Practice:**  100 Subtraction Facts (Test C in Test Masters)

**Mental Math:**   Count up and down by $\frac{1}{8}$'s between $\frac{1}{8}$ and 2.

| | | |
|---|---|---|
| **a.** 7 × 34 | **b.** 4 × 56 | **c.** 74 + 19 |
| **d.** 475 + 125 | **e.** $5.00 − $1.75 | **f.** $\frac{1}{2}$ of 32 |
| **g.** 7 × 5, + 1, ÷ 6, × 3, ÷ 2, + 1, ÷ 5 | | |

**Problem Solving:**   Tad picked up a number cube. His thumb and forefinger covered opposite faces. He counted the dots on the other four faces. How many dots did he count?

---

**Using manipulatives to reduce fractions**

Use your fraction manipulatives to form these fraction models.

$$\frac{6}{12} \qquad \frac{4}{8} \qquad \frac{3}{6} \qquad \frac{2}{4} \qquad \frac{1}{2}$$

We see that each of these models illustrates half of a circle. The model that uses the fewest number of pieces is $\frac{1}{2}$. We say that each of the other fractions **reduces** to $\frac{1}{2}$.

We can use our fraction manipulatives to reduce a given fraction by making an equivalent model that uses fewer pieces.

**Example 1**   Use your fraction manipulatives to reduce $\frac{2}{6}$.

**Solution**   First we use our manipulatives to form $\frac{2}{6}$.

Then we search for a fraction piece that is equivalent to the $\frac{2}{6}$ model. We find $\frac{1}{3}$.

The models illustrate that $\frac{2}{6}$ reduces to $\frac{1}{3}$.

**Adding and subtracting mixed numbers**   When adding mixed numbers, we add the whole number parts together and the fractions parts together. When subtracting mixed numbers, we subtract fraction parts from fractions and whole number parts from whole numbers.

**Example 2**   Two thirds of a circle is what percent of a circle?

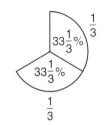

**Solution**   One third is equivalent to $33\frac{1}{3}\%$. So two thirds is equivalent to $33\frac{1}{3}\%$ + $33\frac{1}{3}\%$. We add.

$$
\begin{array}{r}
33\frac{1}{3}\% \\
+\ 33\frac{1}{3}\% \\
\hline
\mathbf{66\frac{2}{3}\%}
\end{array}
$$

**Example 3**   Two sixths of a circle is what percent of a circle?

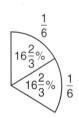

*Solution*   We add $16\frac{2}{3}\%$ and $16\frac{2}{3}\%$.

$$
\begin{array}{r}
16\dfrac{2}{3}\% \\[2mm]
+\ 16\dfrac{2}{3}\% \\[1mm]
\hline
32\dfrac{4}{3}\%
\end{array}
$$

We notice that the fraction part of the answer, $\frac{4}{3}$, is an improper fraction that equals $1\frac{1}{3}$.

So $32\frac{4}{3}\%$ equals $32 + 1\frac{1}{3}\%$, which is **$33\frac{1}{3}\%$**. This makes sense because $\frac{2}{6}$ of a circle equals $\frac{1}{3}$, which is equivalent to $33\frac{1}{3}\%$.

**Example 4**   Tom lives $2\frac{3}{4}$ miles from school. Tom rode his bike from home to school and back to home. How far did he ride?

*Solution*   This is a "some and some more" story.

$$
\begin{array}{r}
2\dfrac{3}{4}\ \text{mi} \\[2mm]
+\ 2\dfrac{3}{4}\ \text{mi} \\[1mm]
\hline
4\dfrac{6}{4}\ \text{mi}
\end{array}
$$

We notice that the fraction part of the answer, $\frac{6}{4}$, reduces to $1\frac{1}{2}$. We find that Tom rode his bike **$5\frac{1}{2}$ miles.**

**Example 5**   $5\frac{3}{8} - 1\frac{1}{8}$

*Solution*   We subtract $\frac{1}{8}$ from $\frac{3}{8}$, and we subtract 1 from 5. The difference is $4\frac{2}{8}$.

$$
5\frac{3}{8} - 1\frac{1}{8} = 4\frac{2}{8}
$$

We reduce the fraction $\frac{2}{8}$ to $\frac{1}{4}$. We write the answer **$4\frac{1}{4}$.**

**Practice** Use your fraction manipulatives to reduce these fractions:

**a.** $\dfrac{2}{8}$  $\frac{1}{4}$

**b.** $\dfrac{6}{8}$  $\frac{3}{4}$

Add. Reduce the answer when possible.

**c.** $12\dfrac{1}{2}\% + 12\dfrac{1}{2}\%$  25%

**d.** $16\dfrac{2}{3}\% + 66\dfrac{2}{3}\%$  $83\frac{1}{3}\%$

**e.** $3\dfrac{3}{4} + 2\dfrac{3}{4}$  $6\frac{1}{2}$

**f.** $1\dfrac{1}{8} + 2\dfrac{7}{8}$  4

**g.** $3 + 2\dfrac{2}{3}$  $5\frac{2}{3}$

**h.** $\dfrac{3}{4} + 4$  $4\frac{3}{4}$

**Problem set 27**

**1.** Jan rode her bike to the park and back. If the trip was $3\frac{3}{4}$ miles each way, how far did she ride in all?  $7\frac{1}{2}$ mi
(27)

**2.** The young elephant was 36 months old. How many years old was the elephant?  3 years
(15)

**3.** Gwen bought $2\frac{1}{2}$ dozen cupcakes for the party. That was enough for how many children to have one cupcake each?  30 children
(6)

**4.** There are 100 centimeters in a meter. There are 1000 meters in a kilometer. How many centimeters are in a kilometer?  100,000 cm
(15)

**5.** What is the perimeter of the equilateral triangle?  2 in.
(8)

$\frac{2}{3}$ in.

**6.** Compare: $\dfrac{1}{2}$ plus $\dfrac{1}{2}$ $\bigcirc{>}$ $\dfrac{1}{2}$ of $\dfrac{1}{2}$
(23)

**7.** $5\dfrac{7}{8} + 7\dfrac{5}{8}$  $13\frac{1}{2}$
(27)

**8.** One eighth of a circle is $12\frac{1}{2}\%$ of a circle. What percent of a circle is $\frac{3}{8}$ of a circle?  $37\frac{1}{2}\%$
(27)

**9.** Write a fraction equal to 1 that has a denominator of 12.   $\frac{12}{12}$
*(25)*

**10.** What is the greatest common factor of 15 and 25?   5
*(20)*

**11.** What is the **seventh** number in this sequence?   56
*(10)*
$$8, 16, 24, 32, 40, \ldots$$

**12.** Write $\frac{14}{5}$ as a mixed number.   $2\frac{4}{5}$
*(26)*

**13.** Add and simplify: $\frac{2}{5} + \frac{4}{5}$   $1\frac{1}{5}$
*(27)*

**14.** $\frac{2}{3} + n = 1$   $\frac{1}{3}$
*(25)*

**15.** What is the largest factor of both 12 and 18?   6
*(19)*

**16.** $1 - \frac{3}{4}$   $\frac{1}{4}$        **17.** $3\frac{3}{4} + 3$   $6\frac{3}{4}$        **18.** $2\frac{1}{2} - 2\frac{1}{2}$   0
*(25)*                                *(27)*                                  *(24)*

**19.** What number is 25 less than 100?   75
*(14)*

**20.** $(123 + 123 + 123) - (123 + 123)$   123
*(5)*

**21.** Estimate the difference of 5063 and 3987 to the nearest
*(16)*   thousand.   1000

**22.** Use your fraction manipulatives to reduce $\frac{3}{12}$.   $\frac{1}{4}$
*(27)*

**23.** Find the average of 85, 85, 90, and 100.   90
*(18)*

**24.** How much money is $\frac{3}{5}$ of $30?   $18
*(22)*

**25.** How many millimeters long is the line segment?   26 mm
*(7)*

**26.** Arrange these numbers in order from least to greatest:
*(17)*   $-1, 0, \frac{1}{2}, 1$
$$\frac{1}{2}, 0, -1, 1$$

Sandra began measuring the rainfall when she moved to her new home. The graph below shows the annual rainfall during her first three years in her home. Use the information in this graph to answer questions 27 through 30.

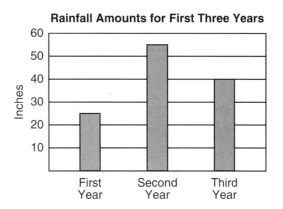

**Rainfall Amounts for First Three Years**

**27.** About how many more inches of rain fell during the
(18) second year than during the first year?    30 in.

**28.** What was the approximate average annual rainfall
(18) during the first three years?    40 in.

**29.** The first year's rainfall was about how many inches
(18) below the average annual rainfall of the first three years?
15 in.

**30.** Write a "some and some more" problem that refers to
(11) this graph and then answer the problem.    Answers may
vary. See student work.

# LESSON 28

# Fraction Manipulatives, Part 3

**Mental Math:**

**a.** 336

**b.** 255

**c.** 85

**d.** 1250

**e.** $1.75

**f.** 18

**g.** 5

**Problem Solving:**

Three of the six faces of each block were painted.

**Facts Practice:** 90 Division Facts (Test F in Test Masters)

**Mental Math:** Count up and down by 3's between 3 and 60.
Count up and down by 6's between 6 and 60.

| | | |
|---|---|---|
| **a.** $8 \times 42$ | **b.** $3 \times 85$ | **c.** $36 + 49$ |
| **d.** $1750 - 500$ | **e.** $\$10.00 - \$8.25$ | **f.** $\frac{1}{2}$ of 36 |
| **g.** $8 \times 4, + 1, \div 3, + 1, \times 2, + 1, \div 5$ | | |

**Problem Solving:** Grant glued eight wooden blocks together to make a cube. Then he painted all six faces of the cube. Later the cube broke apart into eight blocks. Describe which sides of the small blocks had been painted.

In this lesson you will make fraction manipulatives for fifths and tenths.

### Activity:  Fraction Manipulatives $\left(\frac{1}{5}, \frac{1}{10}\right)$

Materials needed:

- Each student needs a copy of "Activity Master 4" (available in the *Math 76 Test Masters*).

- Scissors

- Envelopes or locking plastic bags in which to store fraction pieces (re-use bag from Lesson 23)

- Colored pencils or markers

- Fraction manipulatives made in Lessons 23 and 25

Preparation for activities:

- Distribute materials. Color-code circles, if desired, before cutting. Save fraction manipulatives for later use.

Use all the fraction manipulatives you have made to help you with these activities and questions.

**a.** What fraction is half of $\frac{1}{5}$?    $\frac{1}{10}$

**b.** How many tenths equal $\frac{1}{2}$?    5

**c.** Two fifths of a circle is what percent of a circle?    40%

**d.** What percent of a circle is $\frac{7}{10}$ of a circle?    70%

$\frac{3}{5}$  **e.** Demonstrate the subtraction $1 - \frac{2}{5}$ and write the answer.

$\frac{7}{10}$  **f.** Demonstrate the subtraction $1 - \frac{3}{10}$ and write the answer.

Use all of your fraction manipulatives to find the fractional answer.

$\frac{1}{6}$  **g.** $\frac{1}{3}$ of $\frac{1}{2}$ (Start with $\frac{1}{2}$. Which fraction piece covers $\frac{1}{3}$ of it?)

$\frac{1}{8}$  **h.** $\frac{1}{2}$ of $\frac{1}{4}$ (Start with $\frac{1}{4}$. Which fraction piece covers $\frac{1}{2}$ of it?)

**i.** $\frac{1}{3}$ of $\frac{1}{4}$    $\frac{1}{12}$

**j.** $\frac{1}{2}$ of $\frac{1}{3}$    $\frac{1}{6}$

**k.** $\frac{1}{2}$ of $\frac{2}{3}$ (Start with $\frac{2}{3}$. Then find $\frac{1}{2}$ of it.)    $\frac{1}{3}$

**l.** $\frac{1}{2}$ of $\frac{4}{5}$    $\frac{2}{5}$

**m.** $\frac{1}{3}$ of $\frac{3}{4}$    $\frac{1}{4}$

**n.** $\frac{2}{3}$ of $\frac{3}{4}$    $\frac{1}{2}$

**o.** $\frac{1}{3}$ of $\frac{9}{10}$    $\frac{3}{10}$

Write each improper fraction as a mixed number:

**p.** $\frac{17}{10}$    $1\frac{7}{10}$          **q.** $\frac{17}{5}$    $3\frac{2}{5}$          **r.** $\frac{17}{12}$    $1\frac{5}{12}$

Use your manipulatives to reduce each fraction:

**s.** $\frac{5}{10}$    $\frac{1}{2}$          **t.** $\frac{2}{10}$    $\frac{1}{5}$          **u.** $\frac{4}{6}$    $\frac{2}{3}$

Write each improper fraction as a mixed number with the fraction part of the mixed number reduced:

**v.** $\frac{12}{10}$    $1\frac{1}{5}$          **w.** $\frac{15}{10}$    $1\frac{1}{2}$          **x.** $\frac{14}{10}$    $1\frac{2}{5}$

**Problem set
28**

2.

```
            140 men
       ┌──────────┐
       │  28 men  │ ┐
       ├──────────┤ │ 2
       │  28 men  │ ├ ─ rode with
       ├──────────┤ │ 5 Little John
       │  28 men  │ │
       ├──────────┤ ┘
       │  28 men  │
       ├──────────┤
       │  28 men  │
       └──────────┘
```

**1.** What is the sum of $\frac{1}{3}$ and $\frac{2}{3}$ and $\frac{3}{3}$?   2
(24)

**2.** Two fifths of Robin Hood's one hundred forty men
(22) rode with Little John to the castle. How many men
went with Little John? Draw a diagram to illustrate the
problem.   56

**3.** Seven hundred sixty-eight peanuts are to be shared
(15) equally by the thirty-two children at the party. How
many should each child receive? What type of pattern
do we use?   24; EG

**4.** Columbus discovered the Americas in 1492. The
(13) Declaration of Independence was signed in 1776. How
many years were there from Columbus's discovery of
the Americas to the signing of the Declaration of
Independence? What type of pattern do we use?
284 years;  L-E-D

**5.** Convert $\frac{23}{3}$ to a mixed number.   $7\frac{2}{3}$
(26)

**6.** $1\frac{2}{3} + 1\frac{2}{3}$   $3\frac{1}{3}$   **7.** $3 + 4\frac{2}{3}$   $7\frac{2}{3}$   **8.** $3\frac{5}{6} - 1\frac{4}{6}$   $2\frac{1}{6}$
(27)                      (27)                   (27)

**9.** Use your fraction manipulatives to reduce $\frac{4}{8}$.   $\frac{1}{2}$
(27)

**10.** How much money is $\frac{2}{3}$ of $24.00?   $16.00
(22)

**11.** What percent of a circle is $\frac{3}{10}$ of a circle?   30%
(28)

**12.** Twenty-five percent of a circle is what fraction of a
(23) circle?   $\frac{1}{4}$

**13.** What number is 240 less than 250?   10
(14)

**14.** $\frac{1}{4} + m = 1$   $\frac{3}{4}$         **15.** $423 - w = 297$   126
(25)                              (3)

**16.** Compare: $20 \times 20$ $\bigcirc\!\!>$ $21 \times 19$
(9)

**17.** On the last four papers Christie had 22 right, 20 right,
*(18)* 23 right, and 23 right, respectively. She averaged how
many right on each paper?　22

**18.** A 36-inch-long string is formed into the shape of an
*(8)* equilateral triangle. How long is each side of the
triangle?　12 in.

**19.** What is the greatest common factor (GCF) of 24, 36,
*(20)* and 60?　12

**20.** 10,010 − 9909　101　　　**21.** (100 × 100) − (100 × 99)
*(1)* 　　　　　　　　　　　　　　　*(5)* 　100

**22.** If $\frac{1}{10}$ of the class was absent, what percent of the class
*(26)* was absent?　10%

**23.** Divide 5097 by 10 and write the answer as a mixed
*(26)* number.　$509\frac{7}{10}$

24. 2 dozen eggs

**24.** Three fourths of two dozen eggs is how many eggs?
*(22)* Draw a diagram to illustrate the problem.　18

**25.** Use your ruler to find the length of this line segment
*(17)* to the nearest sixteenth of an inch.　$3\frac{3}{16}$ in.

**26.** List the first five multiples of 6 and the first five
*(26)* multiples of 8. Circle any numbers that are multiples
of both 6 and 8.　6, 12, 18, **24**, 30
　　　　　　　　　　　　8, 16, **24**, 32, 40

**27.** Which fraction manipulative covers $\frac{1}{2}$ of $\frac{1}{5}$?　$\frac{1}{10}$
*(28)*

# INVESTIGATION
# 1

# Frequency Tables •
# Histograms • Surveys

**Frequency**
**tables**

Mr. Lawson made a frequency table to record student scores on a math test. As he graded tests he made a tally mark in the row that shows the number of correct answers on the test.

**Frequency Table**

| Number Correct | Tally | Frequency |
|:---:|:---:|:---:|
| 19–20 | ~~JHT~~ IIII | 9 |
| 17–18 | ~~JHT~~ II | 7 |
| 15–16 | IIII | 4 |
| 13–14 | II | 2 |

When Mr. Lawson finished grading the tests, he counted the number of tally marks in each row, and he recorded the count in the frequency column. For example, the table shows that nine students had either 19 or 20 correct answers on the test. A **frequency table** is a way of pairing selected data, in this case specified test scores, with the number of times the selected data occurred.

**Histograms**

Using the information in the frequency table, Mr. Lawson created a histogram to display the results of the test.

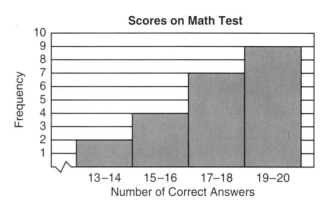

A **histogram** is a special type of bar graph. This histogram displays the data (test scores) in equal sized intervals (range of scores). There are no spaces between the bars. The break in the horizontal scale ($\sim$) shows that the scale on the graph is broken between 0 and 13. The height of the bar indicates the number of test scores in each interval.

Refer to the histogram to answer questions 1, 2, and 3.

1. Which interval had the lowest frequency of scores?
   13–14

2. Which interval had the highest frequency of scores?
   19–20

3. Which interval had twice as many scores as the 13–14 interval?   15–16

4. Make a frequency table and histogram for the following set of scores. Use 50–59, 60–69, 70–79, 80–89, and 90–99 for the intervals.   See student work.

   Test scores:  63, 75, 58, 89, 92, 84, 95, 63, 78, 88, 96, 67, 59, 70, 83, 89, 76, 85, 94, 80

**Surveys** A **survey** is a way of collecting data about a population. Rather than study every member of a population, a survey studies a small part of the population, called a **sample.** From the sample, conclusions are formed about the entire population.

Mrs. Patterson's class conducted a survey of 100 male and female students to determine the favorite participant sport of middle school students. Survey participants were given a choice of six different sports and were asked to select the sport they enjoyed participating in the most. The surveyors made a frequency table for the responses.

| Sport | Tally | Frequency |
|---|---|---|
| Basketball | JHT JHT JHT I | 16 |
| Bowling | JHT JHT II | 12 |
| Football | JHT JHT JHT | 15 |
| Softball | JHT JHT JHT JHT JHT I | 26 |
| Table Tennis | JHT JHT II | 12 |
| Volleyball | JHT JHT JHT IIII | 19 |

From the frequency table Mrs. Patterson's students constructed a bar graph to display the results.

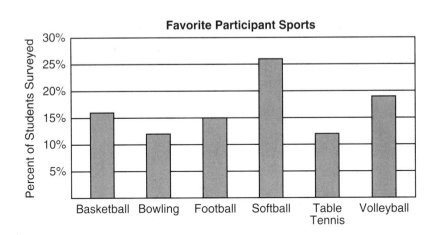

Since 16 out of 100 students selected basketball as their favorite participant sport, basketball was the choice of 16% (which means 16 out of 100) of the students surveyed. Refer to the frequency table and bar graph for this survey to answer questions 5 through 8.

5. Which sport was the favorite sport of about $\frac{1}{4}$ of the students surveyed (1 in 4 students)?   softball

6. Which sport was the favorite sport of the girls who were surveyed?   D.

   A. Softball
   B. Volleyball
   C. Basketball
   D. Cannot be determined from information provided.

7. How might changing the sample group change the results of the survey?   Consider all boys, all girls. Discuss.

8. How might changing the question—the choice of sports—change the results of the survey?   Consider eliminating some sports and adding some sports. Discuss.

This survey was **closed-option** because survey responses were limited to the six choices offered. An **open-option** survey does not limit the choices. An example of an open-option survey question is, "What is your favorite sport?"

**Extensions**

a. Consider making a frequency table and histogram based on results from a recent class test. Would raw scores or percentage scores be used? What intervals would be used? What questions can be answered by referring to the histogram?

b. Conduct a class survey of favorite foods. Determine which foods will be included in the survey if the survey question is closed-option. What will be the size of the sample? How will the data gathered by the survey be displayed?

c. Plan a series of surveys that can be conducted throughout the year. Surveys could ask individuals about favorite television shows or books. Opinion surveys could be conducted about current issues. Brainstorm a list of possible topics and design questions to be asked about each topic.

d. Look for surveys in the newspaper or in magazines and bring the publication to class to discuss these questions. What was the population that was surveyed? Did those doing the survey ask open or closed questions? How were the results of the survey displayed? What was the purpose of the survey?

# LESSON 29

# Multiplying Fractions • Reducing Fractions by Dividing by Common Factors

**Mental Math:**
a. 301
b. 256
c. 92
d. 375
e. $2.75
f. 35
g. 50
**Problem Solving:**
HHH, TTT, HTT,
THH, HHT, TTH,
HTH, THT

**Facts Practice:** 100 Addition Facts (Test B in Test Masters)

**Mental Math:** Count up and down by $\frac{1}{8}$'s between $\frac{1}{8}$ and 3.

a. $7 \times 43$        b. $4 \times 64$        c. $53 + 39$
d. $325 + 50$        e. $\$20.00 - \$17.25$        f. $\frac{1}{2}$ of 70
g. $4 \times 5, - 6, \div 7, \times 8, + 9, \times 2$

**Problem Solving:** Todd flipped a coin three times. It landed up heads, heads, then tails. If he flips the coin three more times, what are the possible outcomes?

**Multiplying fractions**

We have shaded $\frac{1}{2}$ of $\frac{1}{2}$ of a circle.

We see that $\frac{1}{2}$ of $\frac{1}{2}$ is $\frac{1}{4}$.

When we find $\frac{1}{2}$ of $\frac{1}{2}$ we are actually multiplying. The "of" in $\frac{1}{2}$ of $\frac{1}{2}$ means to multiply. The problem becomes

$$\frac{1}{2} \times \frac{1}{2} = \frac{1}{4}$$

When we multiply fractions, we multiply the numerators to find the numerator of the product, and we multiply the denominators to find the denominator of the product.

**Example 1** What fraction is $\frac{1}{2}$ of $\frac{3}{5}$?

*Solution* The word "of" means to multiply. By multiplying $\frac{1}{2}$ and $\frac{3}{5}$ we find $\frac{1}{2}$ of $\frac{3}{5}$.

$$\frac{1}{2} \times \frac{3}{5} = \frac{3}{10} \quad \begin{matrix} \leftarrow (1 \times 3 = 3) \\ \leftarrow (2 \times 5 = 10) \end{matrix}$$

We find that $\frac{1}{2}$ of $\frac{3}{5}$ is $\frac{3}{10}$. You can illustrate this with your fraction manipulatives.

**Example 2**  Multiply: $\dfrac{3}{4} \times \dfrac{2}{3}$

*Solution*  By performing this multiplication we will find $\frac{3}{4}$ of $\frac{2}{3}$. We multiply the numerators to find the numerator of the product, and we multiply the denominators to find the denominator of the product.

$$\frac{3}{4} \times \frac{2}{3} = \frac{6}{12}$$

The fraction $\frac{6}{12}$ can be reduced to $\frac{1}{2}$, as you can see with your fraction manipulatives.

A whole number may be written as a fraction by writing the whole number as the numerator of the fraction and 1 as the denominator of the fraction. Thus, the whole number 2 may be written as the fraction $\frac{2}{1}$. Writing whole numbers as fractions is helpful when multiplying whole numbers and fractions.

**Example 3**  Multiply: $4 \times \dfrac{2}{3}$

*Solution*  We write 4 as $\frac{4}{1}$ and multiply.

$$\frac{4}{1} \times \frac{2}{3} = \frac{8}{3}$$

Then we convert the improper fraction $\frac{8}{3}$ to a mixed number.

$$\frac{8}{3} = 2\frac{2}{3}$$

**Example 4**  Three pennies are laid in a row. The diameter of one penny is $\frac{3}{4}$ inch. How long is the row of pennies?

*Solution*  We may find the answer by adding or by multiplying. We will show both ways.

$$\text{Adding: } \frac{3}{4} \text{ in.} + \frac{3}{4} \text{ in.} + \frac{3}{4} \text{ in.} = \frac{9}{4} \text{ in.}$$

Then we convert $\frac{9}{4}$ inches to $2\frac{1}{4}$ inches.

$$\text{Multiplying: } \frac{3}{1} \times \frac{3}{4} \text{ in.} = \frac{9}{4} \text{ in.}$$

$$\frac{9}{4} \text{ in.} = 2\frac{1}{4} \text{ in.}$$

We find that the row of pennies is **$2\frac{1}{4}$ inches** long.

**Reducing fractions by dividing by common factors**  We can reduce fractions by dividing the numerator and the denominator by a factor of both numbers. To reduce $\frac{6}{12}$, we will divide both the numerator and denominator by 6.

$$\frac{6}{12} \div \frac{6}{6} = \frac{1}{2} \quad \begin{matrix} \leftarrow (6 \div 6 = 1) \\ \leftarrow (12 \div 6 = 2) \end{matrix}$$

We divide the numerator and the denominator by 6 because 6 is the largest factor (the GCF) of both 6 and 12.

If we had divided by 2 instead of by 6 we would not have completely reduced the fraction.

$$\frac{6}{12} \div \frac{2}{2} = \frac{3}{6}$$

The fraction $\frac{3}{6}$ can be reduced by dividing the numerator and the denominator by 3.

$$\frac{3}{6} \div \frac{3}{3} = \frac{1}{2}$$

It took two steps to reduce $\frac{6}{12}$ to $\frac{1}{2}$. It takes two or more steps to reduce some fractions if we do not divide by the greatest common factor.

**Example 5**  Reduce: $\frac{8}{12}$

*Solution*   We will show two ways.

<table>
<tr><td>Divide numerator<br>and denominator by 2.</td><td>Divide numerator<br>and denominator by 4.</td></tr>
<tr><td>$$\frac{8}{12} \div \frac{2}{2} = \frac{4}{6}$$</td><td>$$\frac{8}{12} \div \frac{4}{4} = \frac{2}{3}$$</td></tr>
</table>

Continue reducing $\frac{4}{6}$ by dividing 4 and 6 by 2.

$$\frac{4}{6} \div \frac{2}{2} = \frac{2}{3}$$

Either way we find that $\frac{8}{12}$ reduces to $\frac{2}{3}$. Since the greatest common factor of 8 and 12 is 4, we reduce $\frac{8}{12}$ in one step by dividing the numerator and denominator by 4.

**Example 6**   Multiply:  $2 \times \dfrac{5}{12}$

*Solution*   We write 2 as $\frac{2}{1}$ and multiply.

$$\frac{2}{1} \times \frac{5}{12} = \frac{10}{12}$$

We can reduce $\frac{10}{12}$ because both 10 and 12 are divisible by 2.

$$\frac{10}{12} \div \frac{2}{2} = \frac{5}{6}$$

**Practice\***   Multiply; then reduce if possible.

**a.** $\dfrac{1}{2}$ of $\dfrac{4}{5}$  $\frac{2}{5}$     **b.** $\dfrac{1}{4}$ of $\dfrac{2}{3}$  $\frac{1}{6}$     **c.** $\dfrac{2}{3} \times \dfrac{3}{4}$  $\frac{1}{2}$

Multiply; then convert each answer from an improper fraction to a whole number or to a mixed number.

**d.** $\dfrac{5}{6} \times \dfrac{6}{5}$  $1$     **e.** $5 \times \dfrac{2}{3}$  $3\frac{1}{3}$     **f.** $2 \times \dfrac{4}{3}$  $2\frac{2}{3}$

Reduce each fraction:

**g.** $\dfrac{9}{12}$  $\frac{3}{4}$     **h.** $\dfrac{6}{10}$  $\frac{3}{5}$     **i.** $\dfrac{18}{24}$  $\frac{3}{4}$

**Problem set**
**29**

1. _(25)_ If the product of $\frac{1}{2}$ and $\frac{1}{2}$ is subtracted from the sum of $\frac{1}{2}$ and $\frac{1}{2}$, what is the difference?    $\frac{3}{4}$

2. _(15)_ The African elephant can weigh eight tons. A ton is two thousand pounds. How many pounds can an African elephant weigh?    16,000 lb

3. _(15)_ Sixteen jelly beans weigh one ounce. How many jelly beans weigh one pound? (1 pound = 16 ounces)    256

4. _(29)_ Reduce: $\frac{6}{8}$    $\frac{3}{4}$          5. _(29)_ Reduce: $\frac{16}{24}$    $\frac{2}{3}$

6. _(24)_ $\frac{1}{8} + \frac{3}{8}$    $\frac{1}{2}$       7. _(29)_ $\frac{1}{2} \times \frac{2}{3}$    $\frac{1}{3}$       8. _(24)_ $\frac{7}{12} - \frac{3}{12}$    $\frac{1}{3}$

9. _(22)_ How much money is $\frac{1}{10}$ of $40.00?    $4.00

10. _(10)_ Write the next three numbers in the sequence:

$$1, 4, 7, 10, \underline{\ 13\ }, \underline{\ 16\ }, \underline{\ 19\ }, \ldots$$

11. _(25)_ When five months have passed, what fraction of the year remains?    $\frac{7}{12}$

12. _(2)_ $3.60 × 100    $360          13. _(2)_ 50,000 ÷ 100    500

14. _(26)_ Convert $\frac{18}{4}$ to a mixed number. Remember to reduce the fraction part of the mixed number.    $4\frac{1}{2}$

15. _(14)_ The temperature rose from −8°F to 15°F. This was a rise of how many degrees?    23°F

16. _(3)_ $m + 496 + 2684 = 3217$    37

17. _(3)_ $1000 − n = 857$    143

18. _(5)_ $7 × 11 × 13$    1001          19. _(4)_ $24x = 480$    20

20. To estimate 4963 ÷ 39, first round 4963 to 5000 and round 39 to 40. Then divide 5000 by 40.

**20.** Describe how to estimate the quotient of 4963 ÷ 39.
(16)

**21.** Compare: $\dfrac{2}{3} \times \dfrac{3}{2}$ ⊜ 1
(29)

**22.** The perimeter of the rectangle is 60 mm. Its width is 10 mm. What is the length?   20 mm
(8)

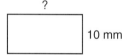

**23.** 12 − 40   −28
(14)

**24.** $\left( \dfrac{1}{2} \times \dfrac{1}{2} \right) - \dfrac{1}{4}$   0
(29)

**25.** How long is the line segment?   46 mm
(7)

**26.** What fraction is $\frac{2}{3}$ of $\frac{3}{5}$?   $\frac{2}{5}$
(29)

**27.** What is the product of $\frac{3}{4}$ and $\frac{4}{3}$?   1
(29)

**28.** What fraction is $\frac{1}{2}$ of $\frac{5}{6}$?   $\frac{5}{12}$
(29)

**29.** Convert $\frac{30}{8}$ to a mixed number. Reduce the fraction part of the mixed number.   $3\frac{3}{4}$
(26)

**30.** What percent of a circle is $\frac{2}{5}$ of a circle?   40%
(26)

# LESSON 30

# Least Common Multiples • Reciprocals

**Mental Math:**
a. 288
b. 210
c. 94
d. 535
e. $7.25
f. 36
g. 49
**Problem Solving:**

$$\begin{array}{r} 238 \\ \times\ \ \ 7 \\ \hline 1666 \end{array}$$

**Facts Practice:** 100 Multiplication Facts (Test E in Test Masters)

**Mental Math:** Count up and down by 3's between 3 and 30. Count up and down by 4's between 4 and 40.

a. $9 \times 32$      b. $5 \times 42$      c. $45 + 49$
d. $436 + 99$      e. $20.00 - $12.75$      f. $\frac{1}{2}$ of 72
g. $7 \times 7, - 1, \div 6, \times 3, + 1, \times 2, - 1$

**Problem Solving:** Use the digits 6, 7, and 8 to complete this multiplication problem.

$$\begin{array}{r} 23\_ \\ \times\ \ \ \_ \\ \hline 166\_ \end{array}$$

**Least common multiples**

Common multiples are numbers that are multiples of more than one number. Here we show some multiples of 2 and 3. We have emphasized the common multiples.

Multiples of 2:  2, 4, **6,** 8, 10, **12,** 14, 16, **18,** 20, …

Multiples of 3:  3, **6,** 9, **12,** 15, **18,** 21, …

We see that 6, 12, and 18 are common multiples of 2 and 3. Since the number 6 is the least of these common multiples, it is called the **least common multiple.** The term "least common multiple" is abbreviated LCM.

**Example 1** What is the least common multiple of 3 and 4?

*Solution* We will list some multiples of each number and emphasize the common multiples.

Multiples of 3:  3, 6, 9, **12,** 15, 18, 21, **24,** …

Multiples of 4:  4, 8, **12,** 16, 20, **24,** 28, …

We see that the numbers 12 and 24 are in both lists. Both 12 and 24 are common multiples of 3 and 4. The least of the common multiples, which is the first common multiple, is **12.**

Example 2    What is the LCM of 2 and 4?

*Solution*    We will list some multiples of 2 and 4.

Multiples of 2: 2, **4**, 6, **8**, 10, **12**, …

Multiples of 4: **4**, **8**, **12**, 16, 20, …

The first number that is a common multiple of both 2 and 4 is **4.**

**Reciprocals**    Reciprocals are two numbers whose product is 1. For example, 2 and $\frac{1}{2}$ are reciprocals because $2 \times \frac{1}{2}$ equals 1.

$$2 \times \frac{1}{2} = 1$$

reciprocals

We say that 2 is the reciprocal of $\frac{1}{2}$, and $\frac{1}{2}$ is the reciprocal of 2. Sometimes we want to find the reciprocal of a certain number. One way we will practice finding the reciprocal of a number is by solving equations like this.

$$3 \times \boxed{\phantom{x}} = 1$$

The number that goes in the box is $\frac{1}{3}$ because 3 times $\frac{1}{3}$ is 1. One third is the reciprocal of three.

Reciprocals also answer questions like this one.

How many $\frac{1}{4}$'s are in 1?

The answer 4 is the reciprocal of $\frac{1}{4}$.

Fractions have two terms, the numerator and the denominator. To form the reciprocal of a fraction, we make a new fraction with the terms of the fraction reversed.

$$\frac{3}{4} \quad\diagup\!\!\!\!\diagdown\quad \frac{4}{3}$$

The new fraction, $\frac{4}{3}$, is the reciprocal of $\frac{3}{4}$.

If we multiply $\frac{3}{4}$ and $\frac{4}{3}$, we see that the product, $\frac{12}{12}$, equals 1.

$$\frac{3}{4} \times \frac{4}{3} = 1$$

**Example 3**    How many $\frac{2}{3}$'s are in 1?

*Solution*    To find the number of $\frac{2}{3}$'s in 1, we need to find the reciprocal of $\frac{2}{3}$. The easiest way to find the reciprocal of $\frac{2}{3}$ is to reverse the positions of the 2 and the 3. The reciprocal of $\frac{2}{3}$ is $\frac{3}{2}$. (We may convert $\frac{3}{2}$ to $1\frac{1}{2}$, but we usually write reciprocals as fractions rather than as mixed numbers.)

**Example 4**    What number goes into the box to make the equation true?

$$\frac{5}{6} \times \boxed{\phantom{x}} = 1$$

*Solution*    When $\frac{5}{6}$ is multiplied by its reciprocal, the product is 1. So the answer is the reciprocal of $\frac{5}{6}$, which is $\frac{6}{5}$. When we multiply $\frac{5}{6}$ and $\frac{6}{5}$ we get $\frac{30}{30}$.

$$\frac{5}{6} \times \frac{6}{5} = \frac{30}{30}$$

The fraction $\frac{30}{30}$ equals 1.

**Example 5**    What is the reciprocal of 5?

*Solution*    Recall that a whole number may be written as a fraction that has a denominator of 1. So 5 can be written $\frac{5}{1}$. (This means five wholes.) Reversing the positions of the 5 and the 1 gives us the reciprocal of 5, which is $\frac{1}{5}$. This makes sense because five $\frac{1}{5}$'s make 1, and $\frac{1}{5}$ of 5 is 1.

**Practice\***    Find the least common multiple of each pair of numbers:

   **a.** 6 and 8    24        **b.** 3 and 5    15        **c.** 5 and 10    10

Write the reciprocal of each number:

   **d.** 6    $\frac{1}{6}$        **e.** $\frac{2}{3}$    $\frac{3}{2}$        **f.** $\frac{8}{5}$    $\frac{5}{8}$        **g.** $\frac{1}{3}$    $\frac{3}{1}$

Find the number that goes into the box that makes each equation true.

   **h.** $\frac{3}{8} \times \boxed{\phantom{x}} = 1$    $\frac{8}{3}$            **i.** $4 \times \boxed{\phantom{x}} = 1$    $\frac{1}{4}$

**j.** $\square \times \dfrac{1}{6} = 1$   $\frac{6}{1}$

**k.** $\square \times \dfrac{7}{8} = 1$   $\frac{8}{7}$

**l.** How many $\frac{2}{5}$'s are in 1?   $\frac{5}{2}$

**m.** How many $\frac{5}{12}$'s are in 1?   $\frac{12}{5}$

**Problem set 30**

**1.** *(26)* If the fourth multiple of 3 is subtracted from the third multiple of 4, what is the difference?   0

**2.** *(22)* About $\frac{2}{3}$ of a person's body weight is water. Albert weighs 117 pounds. About how many pounds of Albert's weight is the weight of the water?   78 lb

**3.** *(15)* Cynthia ate 42 pieces of popcorn in the first 15 minutes of a movie. If she kept eating at the same rate, how many pieces of popcorn did she eat in the 2-hour movie?   336

**4.** *(26)* What are the first four multiples of 8?   8, 16, 24, 32

**5.** *(30)* What is the least common multiple of 4 and 6?   12

**6.** *(30)* What is the LCM of 6 and 10?   30

**7.** *(24)* $\dfrac{2}{5} + \dfrac{2}{5} + \dfrac{2}{5}$   $1\frac{1}{5}$   **8.** *(28)* $1 - \dfrac{1}{10}$   $\frac{9}{10}$   **9.** *(24)* $\dfrac{11}{12} - \dfrac{1}{12}$   $\frac{5}{6}$

**10.** *(29)* $\dfrac{3}{4} \times \dfrac{4}{3}$   1   **11.** *(29)* $5 \times \dfrac{3}{4}$   $3\frac{3}{4}$   **12.** *(29)* $\dfrac{5}{2} \times \dfrac{5}{3}$   $4\frac{1}{6}$

**13.** *(19)* The number 24 has how many different whole number factors?   8

**14.** *(5)* \$3 + \$24 + \$6.50   \$33.50

**15.** *(1)* \$5 − \$1.50   \$3.50

**16.** *(16)* Estimate the product: 596 × 405.   240,000

**17.** *(12)* Find the difference of one billion and nine hundred eight million, fifty-three thousand.   91,947,000

**18.** Compare: $\dfrac{2}{3} \times \dfrac{2}{3}$ $\bigcirc\!\!<$ $\dfrac{2}{3} \times 1$
(29)

**19.** 500,000 ÷ 100    5000    **20.** $35\overline{)8540}$  (244)
(2)                                (2)

**21.** $\dfrac{100\%}{7}$    $14\frac{2}{7}\%$
(26)

**22.** Reduce: $\dfrac{4}{12}$    $\frac{1}{3}$
(29)

**23.** What is the average of 375, 632, and 571?    526
(18)

**24.** A regular hexagon has six sides of equal length. If a
(8)  regular hexagon is made from a 36-inch-long string, what will be the length of each side?    6 in.

**25.** What is the product of a number and its reciprocal?    1
(30)

**26.** How many $\frac{2}{5}$'s are in 1?    $\frac{5}{2}$
(30)

**27.** What number goes in the box to make the equation true?
(30)  $\frac{8}{3}$

$$\frac{3}{8} \times \boxed{\phantom{x}} = 1$$

**28.** What is the reciprocal of 6?    $\frac{1}{6}$
(30)

**29.** Convert the improper fraction $\frac{45}{10}$ to a mixed number
(26)  with the fraction part of the mixed number reduced.    $4\frac{1}{2}$

**30.** Four pennies are placed in a row. The diameter of one
(29)  penny is $\frac{3}{4}$ inch. What is the length of the row of pennies?    3 in.

$\longmapsto \frac{3}{4}$ in. $\longmapsto$

# LESSON 31

# Areas of Rectangles • Comparing Differences

**Mental Math:**
a. 100
b. 222
c. 57
d. $8.75
e. 21
f. 60
g. 8
**Problem Solving:**
   10; 20

**Facts Practice:**  90 Division Facts (Test F in Test Masters)

**Mental Math:**   Count up and down by $\frac{1}{8}$'s between $\frac{1}{8}$ and 2.

   **a.** 4 × 25        **b.** 6 × 37     **c.** 28 + 29 *(29 is 30 – 1)*
   **d.** $6.25 + $2.50    **e.** $\frac{1}{3}$ of 63    **f.** $\frac{600}{10}$
   **g.** 10 × 10, − 20, + 1, ÷ 9, × 2, ÷ 3, × 5, + 2, ÷ 4

**Problem Solving:**  The bus has 40 seats for passengers. Two passengers can sit in each seat. Sixty passengers got on the bus. What is the largest number of seats that could be empty? What is the largest number of seats that could have just one passenger?

**Areas of rectangles**   We have measured the distance around a shape. The distance around a shape is called its perimeter.

The perimeter of a shape is the distance around it.

We can also measure how much surface is enclosed by the sides of a shape. When we measure the "inside" of a flat shape we are measuring its **area.**

The area of a shape is the amount of surface enclosed by its sides.

We use different kinds of units to measure perimeter and area. To measure perimeter we use units of length like centimeters. To measure area we use units that have area, like square centimeters.

—————

This is one centimeter.

This is one square centimeter.

Units of area such as square centimeters, square feet, and square yards are like floor tiles. The area of a shape is the number of "floor tiles" of a certain size that completely cover the shape. Note that we can use "sq." to abbreviate the word "square."

**Example 1**    How many floor tiles, one foot on a side, are needed to cover the floor of a room that is 8 feet wide and 12 feet long?

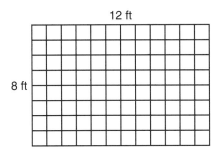

**Solution**    The surface of the floor is covered with tiles. By answering this question we are finding the area of the room in square feet. We could count the tiles, but a faster way to find the number of tiles is to multiply. There are 8 rows of tiles with 12 tiles in each row.

$$
\begin{array}{r}
12 \quad \text{tiles in each row} \\
\times \quad 8 \quad \text{rows} \\
\hline
96 \quad \text{tiles}
\end{array}
$$

The number of tiles needed to cover the floor is **96**. This means that the area of the room is 96 sq. ft.

**Example 2**    What is the area of this rectangle?

8 cm

4 cm

*Solution*  The diagram shows the length and width of the rectangle in centimeters. So the unit of area we will use is square centimeters. To calculate the number of square-centimeter tiles needed to cover the rectangle, we multiply the length and width of the rectangle.

Length × width = area

8 cm × 4 cm = **32 sq. cm**

**Comparing differences**  Recall that when we subtract two numbers the answer is the difference. The difference of 100 and 85 is 15. The difference of 114 and 100 is 14. By comparing the differences, 15 and 14, we can determine that 114 is closer to 100 than 85 is.

*Example 3*  Which of these numbers is closest to 64?

A. 56 B. 71 C. 58

*Solution*  We can see that 58 is closer than 56 to 64. So we can eliminate 56 from consideration. To determine whether 58 or 71 is closer to 64 we subtract.

$$
\begin{array}{r} 64 \\ -\ 58 \\ \hline 6 \end{array}
\qquad
\begin{array}{r} 71 \\ -\ 64 \\ \hline 7 \end{array}
$$

We subtract in the order that results in a positive difference. The smaller the difference the closer the number is to 64. Since the difference 6 is less than 7, we find that 58 is closer to 64 than 71 is. So given our three choices the answer is **C. 58.**

**Practice**  Find the number of square units needed to cover the area of these shapes.

**a.**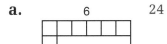

**b.**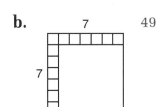

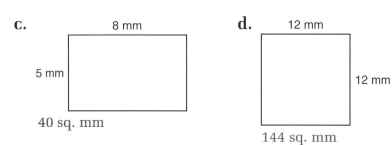

**c.**  8 mm  5 mm  40 sq. mm

**d.**  12 mm  12 mm  144 sq. mm

**e.** Which of these numbers is closest to 500?    C. 459

A. 449        B. 559        C. 459        D. 549

**Problem set 31**

**1.** When the third multiple of 4 is divided by the fourth multiple of 3, what is the quotient?    1
*(26)*

**2.** How many $\frac{3}{4}$'s are in 1?    $\frac{4}{3}$
*(30)*

**3.** The distance the earth travels around the sun each year is about five hundred eighty million miles. Use digits to write that number.    580,000,000
*(12)*

**4.** Convert $\frac{10}{3}$ to a mixed number.    $3\frac{1}{3}$
*(26)*

**5.** How many square stickers 1 centimeter on a side would be needed to cover this rectangle?    8 square stickers
*(31)*

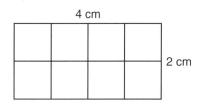

4 cm

2 cm

**6.** How many square floor tiles 1 foot on a side would be needed to cover this square?    100 square floor tiles
*(31)*

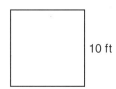

10 ft

**7.** What is the area of a rectangle 12 inches long and 8 inches wide?    96 sq. in.
*(31)*

**8.** What is the next number in the sequence?
(10)
$$1, 4, 9, 16, 25, 36, \underline{\phantom{xx}49\phantom{xx}}, \ldots$$

**9.** What number is $\frac{2}{3}$ of 24?     **10.** $24 + f = 42$    18
(22)  16                                      (3)

Write each answer in simplest form:

**11.** $\frac{1}{8} + \frac{1}{8}$     **12.** $\frac{5}{6} - \frac{1}{6}$     **13.** $\frac{2}{3} \times \frac{1}{2}$     **14.** $\frac{2}{3} \times 5$
(24)  $\frac{1}{4}$            (24)  $\frac{2}{3}$            (29)  $\frac{1}{3}$            (29)  $3\frac{1}{3}$

**15.** Estimate the product of 387 and 514.    200,000
(16)

**16.** $20.00 ÷ 10     **17.** 47¢ × 63     **18.** 4623 ÷ 22
(2)   $2.00            (2)   $29.61        (2)   210 r 3

**19.** What is the reciprocal of 2?    $\frac{1}{2}$
(30)

**20.** Two thirds of a circle is what percent of a circle?
(27)  $66\frac{2}{3}\%$

**21.** Which of these numbers is closest to 100?    D. 109
(31)
　　A. 90          B. 89          C. 111          D. 109

**22.** Which digit is in the ten-millions' place in 987,654,321?
(12)  8

**23.** The first three positive odd numbers are 1, 3, and 5.
(10)  What is the sum of the first five positive odd numbers?
　　25

**24.** Three of the nine players play outfield. What fraction
(29)  of the players play outfield? (Reduce.)    $\frac{1}{3}$

**25.** Use your ruler to find the length of this line segment.
(17)  $2\frac{5}{8}$ in.

**26.** $\frac{3}{10} \times \frac{3}{10}$    $\frac{9}{100}$
(29)

**27.** Write a fraction equal to 1 with a denominator of 8.
(29)  $\frac{8}{8}$

**28.** Five sixths of the 24 students in the class scored 80% or
(22)  higher on the test. How many students scored 80% or
　　higher? Draw a diagram to illustrate the problem.    20

28.    24 students

| 4 students |
| 4 students |
| 4 students |
| 4 students |
| 4 students |
| 4 students |

$\frac{5}{6}$ of 24

**29.** Reduce $\frac{30}{100}$.  $\frac{3}{10}$
(29)

**30.** Using a ruler, how could you calculate the floor area
(31) of your classroom?  If the room is rectangular, first measure
the length of the room and the width of the room. Then multiply
the two measurements to find the area of the room.

# LESSON
# 32

# Expanded Notation • Elapsed Time

**Mental Math:**
**a.** 300
**b.** 1580
**c.** 73
**d.** $6.50
**e.** 120
**f.** 6
**g.** 10
**Problem Solving:**
  1, 2, 3;
  15

**Facts Practice:** 30 Fractions to Reduce (Test G in Test Masters)

**Mental Math:** Count up and down by 25's between 25 and 400.

  **a.** 4 × 75        **b.** 380 + 1200        **c.** 54 + 19
  **d.** $8.00 − $1.50    **e.** $\frac{1}{2}$ of 240        **f.** $\frac{600}{100}$
  **g.** 12 × 3, − 1, ÷ 5, × 2, + 1, ÷ 3, × 2

**Problem Solving:** Cheryl picked up a number cube and held it
                so that she could see the dots on three faces.
                The total number of dots on the three faces
                was 6. What was the number of dots on each
                of the three faces? What was the total number
                of dots on the other three faces?

**Expanded notation**   Recall that in our number system the location of a digit in
a number has a value called its place value. Consider the
value of the 5 in these two numbers.

250        520

In 250 the value of the 5 is 5 × 10. In 520 the value of the
5 is 5 × 100.

The value of a digit in a number is the value of the
digit times the value of the place the digit occupies. When

we write a number in **expanded notation,** we write each non-zero digit times its place value.

**Example 1**     Write 250 in expanded notation.

*Solution*     The 2 is in the hundreds' place, and the 5 is in the tens' place. In expanded notation we write

$$(2 \times 100) + (5 \times 10)$$

Since there is a zero in the ones' place we could add a third set of parentheses $(0 \times 1)$. However, since zero times any number equals zero, it is not necessary to include zeros when writing numbers in expanded notation.

**Example 2**     Write $(5 \times 1000) + (2 \times 100) + (8 \times 10)$ in standard notation.

*Solution*     Standard notation is our usual way of writing numbers. One way to think about this number is $5000 + 200 + 80$. Another way to think about this number is 5 in the thousands' place, 2 in the hundreds' place, and 8 in the tens' place. We may assume a 0 in the ones' place. Either way we think about the number, the standard form is **5280.**

**Elapsed time**     The 24 hours of the day are divided into two parts: the hours from midnight to noon (a.m.) and the hours from noon to midnight (p.m.). When we calculate the amount of time between two events we are calculating elapsed time—the amount of time that has passed. Elapsed time problems are "later-earlier-difference" problems that we have practiced since Lesson 13. The time elapsed is the difference.

**Example 3**     The marathon started at 7:15 a.m. Jason finished the race at 10:10 a.m. How long did it take Jason to run the marathon?

*Solution*   This is a "later-earlier-difference" problem. We find Jason's race time (elapsed time) by subtracting the earlier time from the later time.

$$
\begin{array}{ll}
\text{Later} & \text{10:10 a.m.} \\
\underline{-\ \text{Earlier}} & \underline{-\ \ \text{7:15 a.m.}} \\
\text{Difference} &
\end{array}
$$

Since we cannot subtract 15 minutes from 10 minutes, we rename one hour as 60 minutes. The 60 minutes and 10 minutes equals 70 minutes. (This means 70 minutes after 9, which is the same as 10:10.)

$$
\begin{array}{r}
\overset{9\ :70}{\cancel{10{:}10}} \\
-\ \ \ 7{:}15 \\
\hline
2{:}55
\end{array}
$$

We find that it took Jason **2 hours and 55 minutes** to run the marathon.

**Example 4**   What time is two and a half hours after 10:43 a.m.?

*Solution*   This is a "later-earlier-difference" problem. The elapsed time, $2\frac{1}{2}$ hours, is the difference. We write $2\frac{1}{2}$ hours as 2:30. The earlier time is 10:43 a.m.

$$
\begin{array}{ll}
\text{Later} & \text{Later} \\
\underline{-\ \text{Earlier}} & \underline{-\ \text{10:43 a.m.}} \\
\text{Difference} & \qquad 2{:}30
\end{array}
$$

We need to find the later time, so we add $2\frac{1}{2}$ hours to 10:43 a.m. We will describe two methods to do this addition: a mental calculation and a pencil-and-paper calculation. As a mental calculation we could first count two hours after 10:43 a.m. One hour later is 11:43 a.m. Another hour later is 12:43 **p.m.** From 12:43 p.m. we now count 30 minutes (one half hour). We will count 10 minutes at a time, from 12:43 p.m. to 12:53 p.m. to 1:03 p.m. to 1:13 p.m. We find that $2\frac{1}{2}$ hours after 10:43 a.m. is **1:13 p.m.** (Another mental calculation is to add 3 hours, then subtract 30 minutes.)

To perform a pencil-and-paper calculation, we add two hours and 30 minutes to 10:43 a.m.

$$
\begin{array}{r}
10\!:\!43 \text{ a.m.} \\
+\quad 2\!:\!30 \\
\hline
12\!:\!73 \text{ p.m.}
\end{array}
$$

The time of day turns to p.m., but the sum 12:73 p.m. is improper. Seventy-three minutes is more than an hour. We think of 73 minutes as one hour plus 13 minutes. We add one to the number of hours and write 13 as the number of minutes. So $2\frac{1}{2}$ hours after 10:43 a.m. is **1:13 p.m.**

**Practice\***   Write each of these numbers in expanded notation:

**a.** 205   $(2 \times 100) + (5 \times 1)$

**b.** 1760   $(1 \times 1000) + (7 \times 100) + (6 \times 10)$

**c.** 8050   $(8 \times 1000) + (5 \times 10)$

Write each of these numbers in standard form:

**d.** $(6 \times 1000) + (4 \times 100)$   **e.** $(7 \times 100) + (5 \times 1)$
   6400                                      705

**f.** The marathon started at 7:15 a.m. George finished the race at 11:05 a.m. How long did it take George to run the marathon?   3 hr 50 min, or 3:50

**g.** What time is $3\frac{1}{2}$ hours after 11:50 p.m.?   3:20 a.m.

**Problem set 32**

**1.** When the sum of 24 and 7 is multiplied by the
$^{(12)}$ difference of 18 and 6, what is the product?   372

**2.** Davy Crockett was born in Tennessee in 1786 and died
$^{(13)}$ at the Alamo in 1836. How many years did he live?
   50 years

**3.** A 16-ounce box of a certain cereal costs $2.24. What is
$^{(15)}$ the cost per ounce of this cereal?   $0.14

10:20 a.m.   **4.** What time is three hours and 30 minutes after 6:50 a.m.?
$^{(32)}$

**5.** How many $\frac{2}{5}$'s are in 1?   $\frac{5}{2}$
(30)

**6.** Reduce $\dfrac{40}{100}$.   $\frac{2}{5}$
(29)

**7.** How many square centimeters would be needed to
(31) cover the area of the rectangle?   40 sq. cm

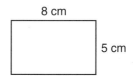

8 cm

5 cm

**8.** How many centimeters is the distance around the
(8) same rectangle?   26 cm

**9.** What is the eighth number in this sequence?   15
(10)

1, 3, 5, 7, ...

**10.** Write 7500 in expanded notation.  (7 × 1000) + (5 × 100)
(32)

**11.** Which of these numbers is closest to 1000?   C. 1009
(31)   A. 990        B. 909        C. 1009        D. 1090

**12.** In three separate bank accounts Robin has $623, $494,
(18) and $380. What is the average amount of money Robin
has in each account?   $499

**13.** $0.05 × 100   $5          **14.** $8q = 240$   30
(2)                              (4)

**15.** How much money is $\frac{3}{4}$ of $24?   $18
(22)

Write each answer in simplest form:

**16.** $\dfrac{3}{5} + \dfrac{3}{5}$    **17.** $\dfrac{3}{4} - \dfrac{1}{4}$    **18.** $\dfrac{3}{4} \times \dfrac{1}{3}$    **19.** $\dfrac{3}{10} \times \dfrac{7}{10}$
(24)                (24)                (29)                (29)
$1\frac{1}{5}$            $\frac{1}{2}$            $\frac{1}{4}$            $\frac{21}{100}$

**20.** Three fourths of a circle is what percent of a circle?  75%
(23)

**21.** $w - 53 = 12$   65          **22.** $1\frac{2}{3} - 1\frac{1}{3}$   $\frac{1}{3}$
(3)                                (27)

**23.** Reduce $\dfrac{15}{21}$.   $\frac{5}{7}$
(29)

**24.** What is the least common multiple of 4 and 6?   12
(30)

**25.** Use your ruler to find the length of this line segment:
(17)   $3\frac{3}{8}$ in.

_____

**26.** If 24 of the 30 students finished the assignment in class,
(29) then what fraction of the students finished in class?
$\frac{4}{5}$

**27.** Brad and Sharon began the hike at 6:45 a.m. and
(32) finished at 11:15 a.m. For how long did they hike?
4 hr, 30 min

**28.** Compare: $(3 \times 100) + (5 \times 1)$ $\lessdot$ 350
(32)

**29.** What fraction is represented by Point $A$ on this
(17) number line?   $\frac{3}{10}$

**30.** Some grocery stores post the price per ounce of
(15) different kinds of cereal to help customers compare
costs. How can we calculate the cost per ounce of a
box of cereal?   To find the cost per ounce, divide the price of
the box of cereal by the weight of the cereal in ounces.

# LESSON 33

# Writing Percents as Fractions, Part 1

Mental Math:
a. 500
b. 203
c. 84
d. $7.25
e. 240
f. 12
g. 7
Problem Solving:
8; 12; 6

**Facts Practice:** 30 Fractions to Reduce (Test G in Test Masters)

**Mental Math:** Count by 7's from 7 to 84.

**a.** $(4 \times 100) + (4 \times 25)$    **b.** $7 \times 29$    **c.** $56 + 28$
**d.** $5.50 + $1.75    **e.** Double 120    **f.** $\frac{120}{10}$
**g.** $2 \times 3, + 1, \times 8, + 4, \div 6, \times 2, + 1, \div 3$

**Problem Solving:** Grant glued 27 small blocks together to make a cube. Then he painted the six faces of the cube. Later the cube broke apart into 27 blocks. How many of the blocks had paint on three faces? on two faces? on one face?

Our fraction manipulatives describe parts of circles as fractions and as percents. The manipulatives show that 50% is equivalent to $\frac{1}{2}$ and that 25% is equivalent to $\frac{1}{4}$. We can find fraction equivalents of other percents by writing a percent as a fraction and then reducing the fraction.

A **percent** actually is a fraction with a denominator of 100. The word "percent" and its abbreviation, %, mean *per hundred*. To write a percent as a fraction, we remove the percent sign and write the number as the numerator and 100 as the denominator.

**Example 1** Write 60% as a fraction.

**Solution** We remove the percent sign and write 60 over 100.

$$60\% = \frac{60}{100}$$

We can reduce $\frac{60}{100}$ in one step by dividing 60 and 100 by 20. If we begin by dividing by a number smaller than 20, it will take more than one step to reduce the fraction.

$$\frac{60}{100} \div \frac{20}{20} = \frac{3}{5}$$

We find that 60% is equivalent to $\frac{3}{5}$.

**Example 2**  Find the fraction equivalent to 4%.

*Solution*  We remove the percent sign and write 4 over 100.

$$4\% = \frac{4}{100}$$

We reduce the fraction by dividing 4 by 4 and 100 by 4, which is the GCF of 4 and 100.

$$\frac{4}{100} \div \frac{4}{4} = \frac{1}{25}$$

We find that 4% is equivalent to $\frac{1}{25}$.

**Practice***  Write each percent as a fraction. Reduce when possible.

**a.** 80%  $\frac{4}{5}$    **b.** 5%  $\frac{1}{20}$    **c.** 25%  $\frac{1}{4}$

**d.** 24%  $\frac{6}{25}$    **e.** 23%  $\frac{23}{100}$    **f.** 10%  $\frac{1}{10}$

---

**Teacher Note:**  As a class activity, conduct a survey of class members to find out what pets are in their homes. Prepare a frequency table to tally the number of each type of pet. Then create a bar graph to display the results. (Settle questions that arise along the way by consensus.)

---

**Problem set 33**

**1.** When the product of 10 and 15 is divided by the sum
  (12)  of 10 and 15, what is the quotient?   6

**2.** The Nile River is 6651 kilometers long. The
  (13)  Mississippi River is 5986 kilometers long. How much longer is the Nile? What type of pattern do we use?
  665 km; L-S-D

**3.** Some astronomers think the universe may be fifteen
  (12)  billion years old. Use digits to write that number.
  15,000,000,000

**4.** Write 3040 in expanded notation.   $(3 \times 1000) + (4 \times 10)$
  (32)

602   **5.** Write $(6 \times 100) + (2 \times 1)$ in standard notation.
  (32)

**6.** Write two fractions equal to 1, one with a denominator
(29) of 10 and the other with a denominator of 100.     $\frac{10}{10}$ ; $\frac{100}{100}$

**7.** By what number should $\frac{5}{3}$ be multiplied for the product
(30) to be 1?     $\frac{3}{5}$

**8.** What is the perimeter of the
(8) rectangle?     40 in.

**9.** How many square tiles 1 inch on a
(31) side would be needed to cover the
rectangle?     96 tiles

12 in.

8 in.

**10.** Which of these numbers is divisible by both 2 and 3?
(19)
A. 56          B. 75          C. 83          D. 48
D. 48

**11.** Estimate the difference of 4968 and 2099.     3000
(16)

**12.** $4.30 × 100     **13.** $Q - 24 = 23$     **14.** $\frac{3}{5}$ of 20     12
(2)  $430.00        (3)    47               (22)

Write each answer in simplest form:

**15.** $\frac{4}{5} + \frac{4}{5}$     $1\frac{3}{5}$          **16.** $\frac{5}{8} - \frac{1}{8}$     $\frac{1}{2}$
(24)                                    (24)

**17.** $\frac{5}{2} \times \frac{3}{2}$     $3\frac{3}{4}$          **18.** $\frac{3}{10} \times \frac{3}{100}$     $\frac{9}{1000}$
(29)                                    (29)

**19.** What is the tenth number of this sequence?     20
(10)
2, 4, 6, 8, ...

**20.** $402.00 ÷ 25     **21.** 348 × 67     **22.** $\frac{1}{2}w = 1$     2
(2)  $16.08           (2)    23,316       (30)

**23.** A meter is about one big step. About how many meters
(7) high is a door?     2 m

**24.** Five of the 30 students in the class were absent. What
(29) fraction of the class was absent? (Reduce.)     $\frac{1}{6}$

**25.** To what mixed number on the line is the arrow pointing?
(17)   $1\frac{7}{10}$

**26.** Write 70% as a reduced fraction.    $\frac{7}{10}$
(33)

27.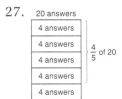

**27.** Four fifths of Gina's 20 answers were correct. How
(22)   many of Gina's answers were correct? Draw a diagram
that illustrates the problem.    16

28. If the
numerator is more
than half of the
denominator, the
fraction is greater
than $\frac{1}{2}$. If the
numerator is less
than half of the
denominator, the
fraction is less
than $\frac{1}{2}$.

**28.** By looking at the numerator and denominator of a
(28)   fraction, how can you tell if the fraction is greater than
or less than $\frac{1}{2}$?

**29.** What time is $6\frac{1}{2}$ hours after 8:45 p.m.?    3:15 a.m.
(32)

**30.** Arrange these fractions in order from least to greatest:
(17)   $\frac{1}{16}, \frac{1}{8}, \frac{1}{4}, \frac{1}{2}$         $\dfrac{1}{8}, \dfrac{1}{4}, \dfrac{1}{16}, \dfrac{1}{2}$

# LESSON 34

# Decimal Place Value

**Facts Practice:** 64 Multiplication Facts (Test D in Test Masters)

**Mental Math:** Count up and down by $\frac{1}{8}$'s between $\frac{1}{8}$ and 2.

**a.** $(4 \times 200) + (4 \times 25)$      **b.** $1480 - 350$
**c.** $45 + 18$ (*18 is 20 − 2*)      **d.** $12.00 − $2.50$
**e.** Double 250      **f.** $\frac{1500}{100}$
**g.** $3 \times 3, \times 9, - 1, \div 2, + 2, \div 7, \times 2$

**Problem Solving:** In the deck there were red cards and black cards. Kathy selected three cards. Two were red and one was black. If she selects three more cards, what possible combinations of three cards could she select?

Since Lesson 12 we have studied place value from the ones' place leftward to the hundred trillions' place, noting as we move to the left that each place is ten times as large as the preceding place. If we move to the right instead of to the left, each place is one tenth of the preceding place.

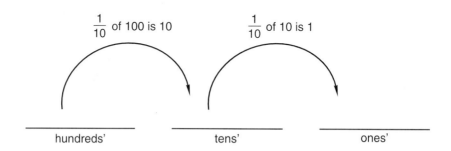

Places to the right of the ones' place also have a value one tenth of the value of the place to their left. These places have a value less than one (but not less than zero). We use a decimal point to mark the separation between the ones' place and places with a value less than one.

Places to the right of a decimal point are often called **decimal places.** Here we show three decimal places.

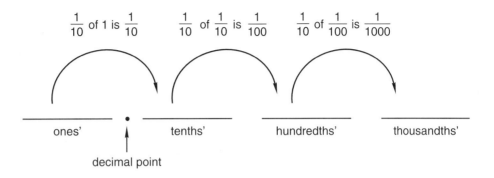

Thinking about money is a helpful way to remember decimal place values.

A mill is $\frac{1}{1000}$ of a dollar and $\frac{1}{10}$ of a cent. We do not have a coin for a mill. However, purchasers of gasoline are charged mills at the gas pump. A price of $1.49$\frac{9}{10}$ per gallon is one mill less than $1.50 and nine mills more than $1.49.

**Example 1**    Which digit in 123.45 is in the hundredths' place?

*Solution*    The *-ths* ending of "hundredths" indicates that the hundredths' place is to the right of the decimal point. The first place to the right of the decimal point is the tenths' place. The second place is the hundredths' place. The digit in the hundredths' place is **5.**

**Example 2**    What is the place value of the 8 in 67.89?

*Solution*    The 8 is in the first place to the right of the decimal point, which is the **tenths' place.**

**Practice**  **a.** What is the place value of the 5 in 12.345?   thousandths'

**b.** Which digit in 5.4321 is in the tenths' place?   4

**c.** In 0.0123, what is the digit in the thousandths' place?   2

**d.** What is the value of the place held by zero in 50.375?
ones'

**Problem set 34**

**1.** Three eighths of the 24 choir members were tenors.
*(22)* How many tenors were in the choir? Draw a diagram
to illustrate the problem.   9

1.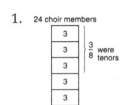

**2.** Mom wants to triple a recipe for cheesecake. If the
*(15)* recipe calls for 8 ounces of cream cheese, how many
ounces of cream cheese should she put in the mix?
24 oz

**3.** What time is two and one half hours after 10:40 a.m.?
*(32)*   1:10 p.m.

**4.** Write 80% as a reduced fraction.   $\frac{4}{5}$
*(33)*

**5.** Compare: $\frac{100}{100}$ ⊜ $\frac{10}{10}$
*(24)*

**6.** Write $(6 \times 100) + (5 \times 1)$ in standard notation.   605
*(32)*

**7.** Which digit is in the ones' place in $42,876.39?   6
*(12)*

**8.** How many square millimeters is
*(31)* the area of the square?   144 sq. mm

**9.** How many millimeters is the
*(8)* perimeter of the square?   48 mm

12 mm

**10.** What is the least common multiple of 6 and 8?   24
*(30)*

**11.** $5.60 ÷ 10   $0.56          **12.** $\frac{9}{10} \times \frac{9}{10}$   $\frac{81}{100}$
*(2)*                          *(29)*

**13.** Estimate the quotient when 898 is divided by 29.   30
*(16)*

**14.** Round 36,847 to the nearest hundred.   36,800
(16)

**15.** $6d = 144$   24         **16.** $\dfrac{d}{6} = 144$   864
(4)                            (4)

**17.** Compare: $\dfrac{5}{2} + \dfrac{5}{2}$ $\;\boxed{=}\;$ $2 \times \dfrac{5}{2}$
(29)

**18.** $\dfrac{3}{8} + \dfrac{3}{8}$  $\frac{3}{4}$     **19.** $\dfrac{11}{12} - \dfrac{1}{12}$  $\frac{5}{6}$     **20.** $\dfrac{5}{4} \times \dfrac{3}{2}$  $1\frac{7}{8}$
(24)                        (24)                          (29)

**21.** What number is missing in this sequence?
(10)

$$6, 12, \underline{\;\;18\;\;}, 24, 30, \ldots$$

**22.** $\$4.37 \times 86$   $\$375.82$
(2)

**23.** To what number on the number line is the arrow
(14) pointing?   −6

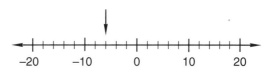

**24.** $(80 \div 40) - (8 \div 4)$   0
(5)

**25.** Which digit is in the thousandths' place in 2,345.678?
(34)   8

**26.** Draw a circle and shade $\frac{2}{3}$ of it.
(21)

**27.** Divide 5225 by 12 and write the quotient as a mixed
(26) number.   $435\frac{5}{12}$

**28.** The first glass contained 12 ounces of water. The
(18) second glass contained 11 ounces of water. The third
glass contained 7 ounces of water. If some water was
poured from the first and second glasses into the third
glass until all three glasses contained the same amount
of water, then how many ounces of water would be in
each glass?   10 oz

**29.** The letters *r*, *t*, and *d* represent three different
(2) numbers. The product of *r* and *t* is *d*.   *tr = d, d ÷ t = r,*
*d ÷ r = t*

$$rt = d$$

Arrange the letters to form another multiplication fact
and two division facts.

15; 15   **30.** Instead of dividing 75 by 5, Sandy mentally doubled
(2) both numbers and divided 150 by 10. Find the
quotient of 75 ÷ 5 and the quotient of 150 ÷ 10.

## LESSON 35

# Writing Decimal Numbers as Fractions, Part 1 • Reading and Writing Decimal Numbers

**Mental Math:**
**a.** 1300
**b.** 344
**c.** 76
**d.** $15.00
**e.** 120
**f.** 360
**g.** 4
**Problem Solving:**

$$\begin{array}{r} 999 \\ +\quad 1 \\ \hline 1000 \end{array}$$

---

**Facts Practice:**  30 Fractions to Reduce (Test G in Test Masters)

**Mental Math:**  Count by 3's from 3 to 60. Count by 7's from 7 to 84.

   **a.** (4 × 300) + (4 × 25)      **b.** 8 × 43      **c.** 37 + 39

   **d.** $7.50 + $7.50      **e.** $\frac{1}{3}$ of 360      **f.** $\frac{3600}{10}$

   **g.** 5 × 5, − 1, ÷ 3, × 4, + 1, ÷ 3, + 1, ÷ 3

**Problem Solving:**  Copy this problem and fill in the
missing digits.

$$\begin{array}{r} \_\_\_ \\ +\quad 1 \\ \hline \_\_\_\_ \end{array}$$

---

**Writing decimal numbers as fractions, part 1**

Decimal numbers are actually fractions with denominators
of 10, 100, 1000, or other numbers in this sequence. The
denominator of a decimal fraction is not written. Instead,
the denominator is indicated by the number of decimal
places.

One decimal place indicates that the denominator is 10.

$$0.\underline{3} = \frac{3}{10}$$

Two decimal places indicates that the denominator is 100.

$$0.0\underline{3} = \frac{3}{100}$$

Three decimal places indicates that the denominator is 1000.

$$0.0\underline{03} = \frac{3}{1000}$$

Notice that the number of zeros in the denominator equals the number of decimal places in the decimal number.

**Example 1**  Write 0.23 as a fraction.

*Solution*  The decimal number 0.23 has two decimal places, so the denominator is 100. The numerator is 23.

$$0.23 = \frac{\textbf{23}}{\textbf{100}}$$

**Example 2**  Write $\frac{9}{10}$ as a decimal number.

*Solution*  The denominator is 10, so the decimal number has one decimal place.

$$0.\underline{\phantom{0}}$$

We write the digit 9 in this place.

$$\frac{9}{10} = \textbf{0.9}$$

**Reading and writing decimal numbers**  We read numbers to the right of a decimal point the same way we read whole numbers, and then we say the place value of the last digit. We read 0.23 as "twenty-three hundredths" because the last digit is in the hundredths' place. To read a mixed decimal number like 20.04, we read the whole number part, say "and," and then read the decimal part.

**Example 3**    Write 0.023 with words.

**Solution**    We see 23 and three decimal places. We write **twenty-three thousandths.**

**Example 4**    Use words to write 20.04.

**Solution**    The decimal point separates the whole number part of the number from the decimal part of the number. We name the whole number part, write "and," and then name the decimal part.

**Twenty and four hundredths**

**Example 5**    Write twenty-one hundredths
(a)  as a fraction, and
(b)  as a decimal number.

**Solution**    The same words name both a fraction form and a decimal form of the number.

(a)  The word "hundredths" indicates that the denominator is 100.

$$\frac{21}{100}$$

(b)  The word "hundredths" indicates that the decimal number has two decimal places.

**0.21**

**Example 6**    Write fifteen and two tenths as a decimal number.

**Solution**    The whole number part is fifteen. The fractional part is two tenths, which we write in decimal form.

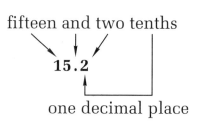

**Practice\*** Write each decimal number as a fraction:

    **a.** 0.1   $\frac{1}{10}$        **b.** 0.21   $\frac{21}{100}$        **c.** 0.321   $\frac{321}{1000}$

Write each fraction as a decimal number:

    **d.** $\frac{3}{10}$   0.3        **e.** $\frac{17}{100}$   0.17        **f.** $\frac{123}{1000}$   0.123

Use words to write these numbers:

    **g.** 0.05    five hundredths

    **h.** 0.015    fifteen thousandths

    **i.** 1.2    one and two tenths

Write these numbers first as fractions, then as decimal numbers:

    **j.** Seven tenths    $\frac{7}{10}$; 0.7

    **k.** Thirty-one hundredths    $\frac{31}{100}$; 0.31

    **l.** Seven hundred thirty-one thousandths    $\frac{731}{1000}$; 0.731

Write each of these numbers as a decimal number:

    **m.** Five and six tenths    5.6

    **n.** Eleven and twelve hundredths    11.12

    **o.** One hundred twenty-five thousandths    0.125

**Problem set 35**

**1.** What is the product of three fourths and three fifths?
(29)   $\frac{9}{20}$

**2.** Bugs planted 360 carrot seeds in his garden. Three
(22) fourths of them grew. How many carrots grew? Draw a diagram to illustrate the problem.   270

2.
| 360 carrot seeds | |
| --- | --- |
| 90 seeds | |
| 90 seeds | $\frac{3}{4}$ of 360 |
| 90 seeds | |
| 90 seeds | |

**3.** Jan's birthday cake must bake for 2 hours and 15
(32) minutes. If it is put into the oven at 11:45 a.m., at what time will it be done?   2:00 p.m.

**4.** Write twenty-three hundredths
(35)
    (a) as a fraction.   $\frac{23}{100}$

    (b) as a decimal number.   0.23

**5.** Write 20.04 with words.   twenty and four hundredths
(35)

**6.** Write ten and five tenths as a decimal number.   10.5
(35)

**7.** Write 75% as a reduced fraction.   $\frac{3}{4}$
(33)

**8.** Write the following in standard notation:   5640
(32)
$$(5 \times 1000) + (6 \times 100) + (4 \times 10)$$

**9.** Which digit in 1.23 is in the same place as the 5 in 0.456?
(34)   3

**10.** What is the area of the rectangle?   200 sq. mm
(31)

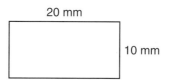

20 mm

10 mm

**11.** What is the perimeter of the rectangle?   60 mm
(8)

**12.** There are 100 centimeters in a meter. How many
(7)   centimeters are in 10 meters?   1000 cm

**13.** Arrange these numbers in order from least to greatest:
(34)
$$0.001, \, 0.1, \, 1.0, \, 0.01$$
0.001, 0.01, 0.1, 1.0

**14.** A meter is about one **big** step. About how many meters
(7)   wide is a door?   1 m

**15.** $\frac{3}{5} + \frac{2}{5}$   1     **16.** $\frac{5}{8} - \frac{5}{8}$   0     **17.** $\frac{2}{3} \times \frac{3}{4}$   $\frac{1}{2}$
(24)               (24)              (29)

**18.** (a) How many $\frac{2}{5}$'s are in 1?   $\frac{5}{2}$
(30)
    (b) Use the answer from part (a) to find the number of
       $\frac{2}{5}$'s in 2.   $\frac{10}{2}$, which is 5

**19.** Convert $\frac{20}{6}$ to a mixed number; then reduce the fraction.
(29)   $3\frac{1}{3}$

**20.** $\dfrac{100\%}{6}$   $16\frac{2}{3}\%$
(29)

**21.** $3\frac{4}{4} - 1\frac{1}{4}$   $2\frac{3}{4}$
(27)

**22.** Compare: $5 \;\textcircled{=}\; 4\dfrac{4}{4}$
(29)

**23.** One sixth of a circle is what percent of a circle?   $16\frac{2}{3}\%$
(25)

**24.** Compare: $3 \times 18 \div 6 \;\textcircled{=}\; 3 \times (18 \div 6)$
(9)

**25.** To what number on the line is the arrow pointing?
(14)   $-14$

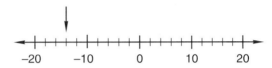

**26.** Which of these division problems has the greatest
(2)   quotient?

   A. $\dfrac{6}{2}$      B. $\dfrac{60}{20}$      C. $\dfrac{12}{4}$      D. $\dfrac{25}{8}$   D. $\frac{25}{8}$

**27.** Write 0.3 and 0.7 as fractions. Then multiply the
(35)   fractions. What is the product?   $\frac{21}{100}$

**28.** Write 21% as a fraction. Then write the fraction as a
(33)   decimal number.   $\frac{21}{100}$; 0.21

**29.** Instead of dividing 400 by 50, Sandy doubled each
(2)   number and divided 800 by 100. Find both quotients.
   8; 8

**30.** A 30-inch-long ribbon was cut into four smaller
(26)   ribbons of equal length. How long was each of the
   smaller ribbons?   $7\frac{1}{2}$ in.

# LESSON 36

# Subtracting Fractions and Mixed Numbers from Whole Numbers

**Facts Practice:** 90 Division Facts (Test F in Test Masters)

**Mental Math:** Count up and down by $\frac{1}{8}$'s between $\frac{1}{8}$ and 3.

  **a.** $(4 \times 400) + (4 \times 25)$    **b.** $2500 + 375$    **c.** $86 - 39$
  **d.** $15.00 - $2.50$    **e.** $\frac{1}{2}$ of 320    **f.** $\frac{4800}{100}$
  **g.** $2 \times 4, \times 5, + 10, \times 2, - 1, \div 9, \times 3, - 1, \div 4$

**Problem Solving:** Nathan has seven coins that total exactly one dollar. Name three sets of coins that he **could** have.

Read this "some went away" story about pies.

*There were four pies on the shelf. The server sliced one of the pies into sixths and took $2\frac{1}{6}$ pies from the shelf. Then how many pies were on the shelf?*

We will illustrate this story with circles. There were four pies on the shelf.

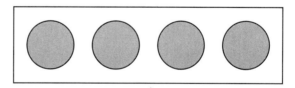

The server sliced one of the pies into sixths. (Then there were $3\frac{6}{6}$ pies, which is another name for 4 pies.)

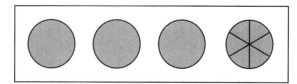

The server took $2\frac{1}{6}$ pies from the shelf.

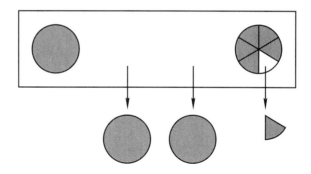

We see $1\frac{5}{6}$ pies left on the shelf.

Now we will show the arithmetic for subtracting $2\frac{1}{6}$ from 4.

$$\begin{array}{r} 4 \ \ \text{pies} \\ -\ 2\frac{1}{6}\ \text{pies} \\ \hline \end{array}$$

Just as the server sliced one of the pies into sixths, so we change four wholes into three wholes plus six sixths. Then we subtract.

$$\begin{array}{r} \overset{\overset{3}{}}{\cancel{4}}\tfrac{6}{6} \quad \text{Change 4 to } 3\tfrac{6}{6}. \\ -\ 2\tfrac{1}{6} \\ \hline 1\tfrac{5}{6} \end{array}$$

**Example**   $5 - 1\dfrac{2}{3}$

*Solution*   To subtract $1\frac{2}{3}$ from 5, we first change 5 to 4 plus $\frac{3}{3}$. Then we subtract.

$$\begin{array}{r} \overset{\overset{4}{}}{\cancel{5}}\tfrac{3}{3} \quad \text{Change 5 to } 4\tfrac{3}{3}. \\ -\ 1\tfrac{2}{3} \\ \hline \mathbf{3\tfrac{1}{3}} \end{array}$$

**Practice*** Show the arithmetic of each subtraction:

**a.** $4 - 2\frac{1}{4}$    $1\frac{3}{4}$

**b.** $3 - \frac{5}{12}$    $2\frac{7}{12}$

**c.** $10 - 2\frac{1}{2}$    $7\frac{1}{2}$

**d.** $6 - 1\frac{3}{10}$    $4\frac{7}{10}$

**e.** There were four whole pies on the shelf. The server took $1\frac{5}{6}$ pies. Then how many pies were on the shelf? $2\frac{1}{6}$

**f.** Write a problem similar to problem (e) and find the answer.    See student work.

**Problem set 36**

**1.** Twenty-five percent of the students played musical instruments. What fraction of the students played musical instruments?   $\frac{1}{4}$
(33)

**2.** Jack accidentally sat on his lunch and smashed $\frac{3}{4}$ of his sandwich. What fraction of his sandwich was not smashed?   $\frac{1}{4}$
(36)

**3.** A mile is 5280 feet. There are 3 feet in a yard. How many yards are in a mile?   1760 yd
(15)

**4.** Which digit in 23.47 has the same place value as the 6 in 516.9?   3
(34)

**5.** Write 1.3 with words.   one and three tenths
(35)

**6.** Write the decimal number five hundredths.   0.05
(35)

**7.** Write thirty-one hundredths
(35)

   (a) as a fraction.   $\frac{31}{100}$

   (b) as a decimal number.   0.31

**8.** Write $(4 \times 100) + (3 \times 1)$ in standard notation.   403
(32)

**9.** Which digit in 4.375 is in the tenths' place?   3
*(34)*

**10.** How many 1-inch square tiles are needed to cover this square?
*(31)* 1296 sq. tiles

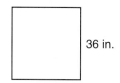

36 in.

**11.** What is the perimeter of the square?   144 in.
*(8)*

**12.** $3\frac{1}{4} + 2\frac{1}{4}$   $5\frac{1}{2}$    **13.** $3 - 1\frac{1}{4}$   $1\frac{3}{4}$    **14.** $3\frac{1}{3} + 2\frac{2}{3}$   6
*(27)*                     *(36)*                  *(27)*

**15.** $\frac{3}{4}$ of 28   21         **16.** $\frac{3}{4} \times \frac{4}{6}$   $\frac{1}{2}$
*(22)*                        *(29)*

17.

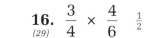

**17.** Monte went to the mall with $24.00. He spent $\frac{5}{6}$ of his money in the music store. How much money did he spend in the music store? Draw a diagram to illustrate the problem.   $20
*(22)*

**18.** What is the average of 42, 57, and 63?   54
*(18)*

**19.** The factors of 6 are 1, 2, 3, and 6. List the factors of 20.
*(19)*   1, 2, 4, 5, 10, 20

**20.** (a) What is the least common multiple of 9 and 6?   18
*(30,20)*
     (b) What is the greatest common factor of 9 and 6?   3

**21.** $\frac{m}{12} = 6$   72           **22.** $\frac{12}{n} = 6$   2
*(4)*                            *(4)*

**23.** Round 58,742,177 to the nearest million.   59,000,000
*(16)*

**24.** Estimate the product of 823 and 680.   560,000
*(16)*

**25.** How many millimeters long is the line segment?
*(7)* (1 cm = 10 mm)   50 mm

| cm | 1 | 2 | 3 | 4 | 5 | 6 | 7 | 8 |
|----|---|---|---|---|---|---|---|---|

**26.** Using your fraction manipulatives you will find that
(25) the sum of $\frac{1}{3}$ and $\frac{1}{6}$ is $\frac{1}{2}$.

$$\frac{1}{3} + \frac{1}{6} = \frac{1}{2}$$

$\frac{1}{6} + \frac{1}{3} = \frac{1}{2},$
$\frac{1}{2} - \frac{1}{3} = \frac{1}{6},$
$\frac{1}{2} - \frac{1}{6} = \frac{1}{3}$

Arrange these numbers to form another addition fact and two subtraction facts.

**27.** Write 0.9 and 0.09 as fractions. Then multiply the
(35) fractions. What is the product? $\frac{81}{1000}$

**28.** Write $\frac{81}{1000}$ as a decimal number. (*Hint*: Write a zero in
(35) the tenths' place.) 0.081

**29.** (a) How many $\frac{3}{4}$'s are in 1? $\frac{4}{3}$
(30)
  (b) Use the answer to part (a) to help you find the number of $\frac{3}{4}$'s in 3. $\frac{12}{3}$, which equals 4

**30.** Instead of dividing 350 by 25, Sandy multiplied both
(2) numbers by 4 and divided 1400 by 100. Find both products. 14; 14

# LESSON
# 37

# Adding and Subtracting Decimal Numbers

Mental Math:
a. 2100
b. 387
c. 47
d. $20.00
e. 260
f. 250
g. 1
Problem Solving:
   1, 4, 5

**Facts Practice:** 30 Fractions to Reduce (Test G in Test Masters)

**Mental Math:** Count up and down by 25's between 25 and 400.
   **a.** (4 × 500) + (4 × 25)    **b.** 9 × 43    **c.** 76 − 29
   **d.** $17.50 + $2.50        **e.** $\frac{1}{2}$ of 520    **f.** $\frac{2500}{10}$
   **g.** 6 × 8, + 1, ÷ 7, × 3, − 1, ÷ 5, + 1, ÷ 5

**Problem Solving:** Cheryl turned a number cube so that she could see the dots on three faces. The total number of dots she could see was 10. What was the total number of dots on each of the three faces?

When we add or subtract numbers using pencil and paper, it is important to align digits that have the same place value. When we add or subtract whole numbers with pencil and paper we line up the ending digits. When we line up the ending digits, which are in the ones' place, we automatically line up other digits that have the same place value.

$$
\begin{array}{r}
2\!\!\overset{\displaystyle\downarrow}{3} \\
241 \\
+\ 317 \\
\hline
\end{array}
$$

When we line up the ones' place we also align other digits with the same place values.

However, lining up the ending digits of decimal numbers may not properly line up all the digits. We use another method for decimal numbers. **We line up decimal numbers for addition or subtraction by lining up the decimal points.** The decimal point in the answer is in line with the other decimal points. Empty places are treated as zeros.

$$
\begin{array}{r}
2.\!\!\overset{\displaystyle\downarrow}{3} \\
2.41 \\
+\ 31.7 \\
\hline
\end{array}
$$

When we line up the decimal points, we also align digits that have the same place values.

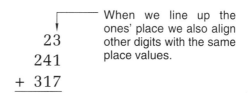

**Example 1** Add: 3.4 + 0.26 + 0.3

*Solution* Line up the decimal points in the problem and add. The decimal point in the answer is placed in line with the other decimal points.

$$\begin{array}{r} 3.4 \\ 0.26 \\ + \ 0.3 \\ \hline \mathbf{3.96} \end{array}$$

**Example 2** Subtract: 4.56 − 2.3

*Solution* Line up the decimal points in the problem and subtract.

$$\begin{array}{r} 4.56 \\ - \ 2.3 \\ \hline \mathbf{2.26} \end{array}$$

**Practice** Add or subtract. Remember to line up the decimal points.

**a.** 3.46 + 0.2   3.66

**b.** 8.28 − 6.1   2.18

**c.** 0.735 + 0.21   0.945

**d.** 0.543 − 0.21   0.333

**e.** 0.43 + 0.1 + 0.413   0.943

**f.** 0.30 − 0.27   0.03

**g.** 0.6 + 0.7   1.3

**h.** 1.00 − 0.24   0.76

**i.** 0.9 + 0.12   1.02

**j.** 1.23 − 0.4   0.83

**Problem set 37**

**1.** Sixty percent of the students in the class were girls. What fraction of the students in the class were girls?
$\frac{3}{5}$
(33)

**2.** Penny broke 8 pencils on her math test. She broke half that many on her spelling test. How many did she break in all?   12
(27)

**3.** What number must be added to three hundred seventy-five to total one thousand?   625
(3)

**4.** 3.4 + 0.62 + 0.3   4.32
(37)

**5.** 4.56 − 3.2   1.36
(37)

$1.08   **6.** $0.37 + $0.23 + $0.48
(5)

**7.** $5 − m = 5¢   $4.95
(3)

**8.** What is the next number in this sequence?
(10)
$$1, 10, 100, 1000, \underline{10,000}, \ldots$$

**9.** Each side of a square is 100 cm long. How many tiles
(31) 1 cm on each edge are needed to cover the area?
10,000 tiles

**10.** Which digit is in the ten-millions' place in 1,234,567,890?
(12) 3

**11.** Three of these numbers are equal. Which number is
(35) different? D. 0.01

A. $\dfrac{1}{10}$     B. 0.1     C. $\dfrac{10}{100}$     D. 0.01

**12.** Estimate the product of 29, 42, and 39. 48,000
(16)

**13.** $3210 \div 3$     **14.** $32,100 \div 30$     **15.** $\$10,000 - \$345$
(2) 1070     (2) 1070     (1) $9655

**16.** $\dfrac{3}{4} + \dfrac{3}{4}$ $1\frac{1}{2}$     **17.** $3 - 1\dfrac{3}{5}$ $1\frac{2}{5}$     **18.** $\dfrac{3}{3} - \dfrac{2}{2}$ 0
(24)          (36)          (29)

**19.** $1\dfrac{1}{3} + 2\dfrac{1}{3} + 3\dfrac{1}{3}$ 7
(27)

**20.** Compare: $\dfrac{1}{4} + \dfrac{3}{4}$ ⊙> $\dfrac{1}{4} \times \dfrac{3}{4}$
(29)

**21.** Convert the improper fraction $\frac{100}{7}$ to a mixed number.
(26) $14\frac{2}{7}$

**22.** What is the average of 90 lb, 84 lb, and 102 lb? 92 lb
(18)

**23.** What is the least common multiple of 4 and 5? 20
(30)

**24.** The temperature changed from 11°C at noon to −4°C at
(14) 8:00 p.m. How many degrees did the temperature drop?
15°C

**25.** The arrow points to what mixed number on this
(17) number line? $10\frac{1}{10}$

**26.** Write 0.3 and 0.9 as fractions. Then multiply the
(35)   fractions. Change the product to a decimal number.
0.27

27. Fraction
answers will vary.
Examples are $\frac{2}{2}$, $\frac{3}{3}$,
$\frac{4}{4}$. When the
numerator and
denominator of a
fraction are equal
(but not zero) the
fraction equals 1.

**27.** Write three different fractions equal to 1. How can you
(23)   tell if a fraction is equal to 1?

**28.** Instead of dividing 6 by $\frac{1}{2}$, Sandy doubled both
(2)    numbers and divided 12 by 1. Do you think both
quotients are the same? Write a one or two sentence
reason for your answer.   See student work.

**29.** The movie started at 2:50 p.m. and ended at 4:23 p.m.
(32)   How long was the movie?   1 hr, 33 min

30.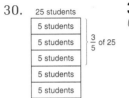

**30.** Three fifths of the 25 students in the class were girls.
(22)   How many girls were in the class? Draw a diagram to
illustrate the problem.   15 girls

# Adding and Subtracting Decimal Numbers and Whole Numbers • Squares

**Facts Practice:** 64 Addition Facts (Test A in Test Masters)

**Mental Math:** Count by 6's from 6 to 72. Count by 7's from 7 to 84.

**a.** $(4 \times 600) + (4 \times 25)$     **b.** $875 - 125$     **c.** $56 - 19$
**d.** $10.00 - 6.25$     **e.** $\frac{1}{2}$ of 150     **f.** $\frac{$40.00}{10}$
**g.** $10 + 10, - 2, \div 3, \times 4, + 1, \times 4, \div 2, + 6, \div 7$

**Problem Solving:** Teresa wanted to paint each face of a cube so that the faces that were next to each other were different colors. She wanted to use less than six different colors. What is the fewest number of different colors she could use? Describe how the cube could be painted.

**Adding and subtracting decimal numbers and whole numbers**

Here we show two ways to write three dollars.

$$\$3 \qquad \$3.00$$

We see that we may write three dollars with or without a decimal point. We may also write whole numbers with or without a decimal point. Here are several ways we may write the whole number three.

$$3 \qquad 3. \qquad 3.0 \qquad 3.00$$

A decimal point follows the ones' place. A whole number may be written with a decimal point after the ones' place. With a calculator, when we enter a whole number a decimal point is displayed. It may be helpful to write a whole number with a decimal point when adding and subtracting decimal numbers with pencil and paper.

**Example 1**   $12 + 7.5$

*Solution*   We line up decimal points when adding decimal numbers so that we add digits with the same place values. The whole number 12 may be written with a decimal point to the right of the digit 2. We line up the decimal points and add.

$$\begin{array}{r} 12. \\ + \phantom{0}7.5 \\ \hline \mathbf{19.5} \end{array}$$

**Example 2**  12.75 − 5

*Solution*  We write the whole number 5 with a decimal point to its right. Then we line up the decimal points and subtract.

$$\begin{array}{r} 12.75 \\ - \phantom{0}5. \\ \hline \mathbf{7.75} \end{array}$$

**Squares**  We know that the four sides of a square are equal in length. Therefore we can find the perimeter and area of a square if we know the length of one side. Likewise, if we know the perimeter of a square we can find the length of each side and then the area of the square. We divide the perimeter of a square by four to find the length of one side.

**Example 3**  The perimeter of a square is 20 cm. What is the length of each side?

*Solution*  Each side of a square is $\frac{1}{4}$ of the perimeter. By dividing the perimeter 20 cm by 4, we find the length of each side of the square is **5 cm,** as we show below.

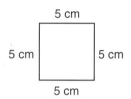

**Example 4**  The perimeter of a square is 12 inches. What is the area of the square?

*Solution* This is a two-step problem. First we find the length of each side. Then we can find the area. We divide the perimeter 12 inches by 4 and find that the length of each side is 3 inches.

3 in.

3 in.

Now we multiply 3 inches by 3 inches and find that the area of the square is **9 square inches.**

**Practice**

**a.** 4 + 2.1   6.1

**b.** 4.3 − 2   2.3

**c.** 3 + 0.4   3.4

**d.** 43.2 − 5   38.2

**e.** 0.23 + 4 + 3.7   7.93

**f.** 6.3 − 6   0.3

**g.** 12.5 + 10   22.5

**h.** 75.25 − 25   50.25

**i.** The perimeter of a square is 40 inches. How long is each side?   10 in.

**j.** The perimeter of a square is 24 inches. What is the area of the square?   36 in.²

**Problem set 38**

**1.** What is the largest factor of both 54 and 45?   9
(20)

**2.** Roberto began saving $3 each week for summer camp, which costs $126. How many weeks will it take to save that amount of money?   42 weeks
(15)

**3.** Ghandi was born in 1869. How old was he when he was assassinated in 1948?   79 years
(13)

**4.** 3 + 1.2   4.2
(38)

**5.** 3.6 + 4   7.6
(38)

**6.** 5.63 − 1.2   4.43
(37)

**7.** 5.376 + 0.24
(37)   5.616

**8.** 4.75 − 0.6
(37)   4.15

**9.** $4 − w = 4¢
(3)   $3.96

**10.** Write forty-seven hundredths
(35)

    (a) as a fraction.   $\frac{47}{100}$

    (b) as a decimal number.   0.47

**11.** Write $(9 \times 1000) + (4 \times 10) + (3 \times 1)$ in standard
(32)  notation.   9043

**12.** Which digit is in the hundredths' place in $123.45?   5
(34)

**13.** The perimeter of a square is 100 inches. How long is
(38)  each side?   25 in.

**14.** What is the least common multiple of 2, 3, and 4?   12
(30)

**15.** $1\frac{2}{3} + 2\frac{2}{3}$   $4\frac{1}{3}$          **16.** $5 - 1\frac{1}{4}$   $3\frac{3}{4}$
(27)                              (36)

**17.** $\frac{3}{4}$ of $\frac{4}{5}$   $\frac{3}{5}$           **18.** $\frac{7}{10} \times \frac{11}{10}$   $\frac{77}{100}$
(29)                              (29)

**19.** (a) How many $\frac{2}{3}$'s are in 1?   $\frac{3}{2}$
(30)

    (b) Use the answer to part (a) to help you find the
        number of $\frac{2}{3}$'s in 2.   3

**20.** Six of the nine players got on base. What fraction of
(29)  the players got on base?   $\frac{2}{3}$

**21.** List the factors of 30.   1, 2, 3, 5, 6, 10, 15, 30
(19)

**22.** Write 35% as a reduced fraction.   $\frac{7}{20}$
(33)

**23.** Round 186,497 to the nearest thousand.   186,000
(16)

**24.** $\frac{1}{3}m = 1$   3           **25.** $\frac{22 + 23 + 24}{3}$   23
(30)                              (5)

**26.** Compare: $24 \div 8 \,\, \boxed{=} \,\, 240 \div 80$
(9)

**27.** Write 0.7 and 0.21 as fractions. Then multiply the
(35) fractions. Change the product to a decimal number.
0.147

**28.** Peter bought ten carrots for $0.80. What was the cost
(15) for each carrot?   $0.08

**29.** Which of these fractions is closest to 1?   D. $\frac{4}{5}$
(31)  A. $\frac{1}{5}$       B. $\frac{2}{5}$       C. $\frac{3}{5}$       D. $\frac{4}{5}$

**30.** If you know the perimeter of a square, you can find the
(38) area of the square in two steps. Describe the two steps.
First divide the perimeter by four to find the length of each side.
Then multiply the length of a side times the length of a side to
find the area.

---

# LESSON
# 39

# Multiplying Decimal Numbers

---

> **Facts Practice:** 30 Fractions to Reduce (Test G in Test Masters)
>
> **Mental Math:** Count up and down by $\frac{1}{8}$'s between $\frac{1}{8}$ and 3.
> **a.** $(4 \times 700) + (4 \times 25)$       **b.** $6 \times 45$       **c.** $67 - 29$
> **d.** $\$8.75 + \$0.75$       **e.** $\frac{1}{2}$ of 350       **f.** $\frac{2500}{100}$
> **g.** $8 \times 5, \div 2, + 1, \div 7, \times 3, + 1, \div 10, \div 2$
>
> **Problem Solving:** Sam has many red socks, white socks, and
> blue socks in a drawer. In the dark, Sam
> pulled out two socks that did not match. How
> many more socks does Sam need to pull
> from the drawer to be certain to have a
> matching pair?

**Mental Math:**
a. 2900
b. 270
c. 38
d. $9.50
e. 175
f. 25
g. $\frac{1}{2}$
**Problem Solving:**
  2

To find the area of a rectangle that is 0.75 meter long and
0.5 meter wide, we multiply 0.75 m and 0.5 m.

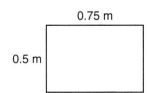

0.75 m

0.5 m

One way to multiply these numbers would be to write each decimal number as a fraction and multiply the fractions.

$$0.75 \times 0.5$$

$$\frac{75}{100} \times \frac{5}{10} = \frac{375}{1000}$$

The product $\frac{375}{1000}$ can be written as the decimal number 0.375. We find the area of the rectangle is 0.375 square meter.

Notice that the product 0.375 has three decimal places and that the factors 0.75 and 0.5 have a **total** of three decimal places. Whenever we multiply decimal numbers, the product has the same number of decimal places as there are in all of the factors. This fact allows us to multiply decimal numbers the same way we multiply whole numbers. After multiplying, we count the total number of decimal places in the factors and place the decimal point in the answer so that the product has the same number of decimal places.

Three decimal places in the factors
$$\begin{array}{r} 0.75 \\ \times\ 0.5 \\ \hline 0.375 \end{array}$$
We do not align decimal points. We just multiply, then count decimal places.

Three decimal places in the product

**Example 1**  Multiply: $0.25 \times 0.7$

*Solution*  We set up the arithmetic as though we were multiplying whole numbers, ignoring the decimal points until after we multiply. Next, we count the number of digits to the right of the decimal point in the two factors. There are three. Then we put a decimal point in the product three places from the right-hand end. We write .175 as **0.175.**

$$\begin{array}{r} 0.25 \\ \times\ 0.7 \\ \hline 0.175 \end{array} \Big\} \text{3 places}$$

**Example 2**  Multiply: 1.6 × 3

*Solution*  We multiply as though we were multiplying whole numbers. Then we count decimal places in the factors. There is only one. We count one place in the product and place a decimal point. The answer is **4.8.**

$$\begin{array}{r} 1.6 \\ \times\ \ 3 \\ \hline 4.8 \end{array} \Big\} \text{ 1 place}$$

**Practice**   **a.** 15 × 0.3   4.5

**b.** 1.5 × 3   4.5

**c.** 1.5 × 0.3   0.45

**d.** 0.15 × 3   0.45

**e.** 1.5 × 1.5   2.25

**f.** 0.15 × 10   1.50 or 1.5

**g.** 0.25 × 0.5   0.125

**h.** 0.025 × 100   2.500 or 2.5

**Problem set 39**

**1.** Mount Everest, the world's tallest mountain, is
(12) twenty-nine thousand, twenty-eight feet high. Use digits to write that number.   29,028

**2.** There are three feet in a yard. How many yards high is
(7) Mt. Everest?   9676 yd

**3.** Bam Bam says his pet dinosaur weighs $\frac{3}{4}$ as much as a
(22) garbage truck. If the truck weighs 12 tons, how much does his dinosaur weigh?   9 tons

**4.** 0.25 × 0.5
(39) 0.125

**5.** $1.80 × 10
(2) $18.00

**6.** 63 × 0.7
(39) 44.1

**7.** 1.23 + 4 + 0.5
(38) 5.73

**8.** 12.34 − 5.6
(37) 6.74

**9.** $3.00 − $3   0
(38)

**10.** Write ten and three tenths
(35)
(a) as a decimal number.   10.3
(b) as a mixed number.   $10\frac{3}{10}$

11. Answers will vary, but the product will be the least.

**11.** Think of two different fractions that are greater than
(17) zero but less than one. Multiply the two fractions to form a third fraction. For your answer to this problem, write the three fractions in order from least to greatest.

**12.** Write the decimal number one hundred twenty-three
(35) thousandths.   0.123

**13.** Write $(6 \times 100) + (4 \times 10)$ in standard form.   640
(32)

**14.** The perimeter of a square is 40 inches. How many square
(38) tiles 1 inch on each edge are needed to cover its area?
100 tiles

**15.** What is the least common multiple (LCM) of 2, 3, and 6?
(30)   6

**16.** Convert $\frac{20}{8}$ to a mixed number and reduce the fraction.
(26)   $2\frac{1}{2}$

**17.** $\left( \dfrac{1}{3} + \dfrac{2}{3} \right) - 1$     **18.** $\dfrac{3}{5} \times \dfrac{2}{3}$   $\frac{2}{5}$     **19.** $\dfrac{8}{9} \times \dfrac{9}{8}$   1
(24)                          (29)                      (29)

0

**20.** A pie was cut into six equal slices. Two slices were
(36) eaten. Then what fraction of the pie was left? (Reduce
answers when possible.)   $\frac{2}{3}$

**21.** What time is $2\frac{1}{2}$ hours before 1 a.m.?   10:30 p.m.
(32)

**22.** On Tim's last four assignments he had 26, 29, 28, and
(18) 25 correct answers, respectively. He averaged how
many correct answers on these papers?   27

**23.** Estimate the quotient when 7987 is divided by 39.
(16)   200

**24.** Compare: $365 - 364 \;\bigcirc\!\!>\; 364 - 365$
(14)

**25.** Which digit in 3.675 has the same place value as the 4
(34) in 14.28?   3

**26.** Use your ruler to find the length of the segment to the
(17) nearest sixteenth of an inch.   $2\frac{3}{16}$ in.

_____

**27.** Morton bought 12 pencils for $0.96. What was the cost
(15) for each pencil?   $0.08

**28.** (a) How many $\frac{3}{5}$'s are in 1?    $\frac{5}{3}$
(30)
   (b) Use the answer to part (a) to help you find the number of $\frac{3}{5}$'s in 2.    $3\frac{1}{3}$

**29.** Instead of dividing 390 by 15, Sandy divided both
(2) numbers by 3 to make the problem $130 \div 5$. Then she multiplied both of those numbers by two to make $260 \div 10$. Find all three quotients.    26; 26; 26

**30.** Find the area of this rectangle.    0.15 sq. m
(39)

0.5 m

0.3 m

# LESSON 40

# Using Zero as a Place Holder • Circle Graphs

**Facts Practice:** 64 Multiplication Facts (Test D in Test Masters)

**Mental Math:** Count by 8's from 8 to 96.

    **a.** $(4 \times 800) + (4 \times 25)$     **b.** $1500 + 750$     **c.** $74 - 39$
    **d.** $8.25 - $1.50               **e.** Double 240      **f.** $\frac{480}{10}$
    **g.** $4 \times 4, - 1, \div 5, \times 6, + 2, \times 2, + 2, \div 6$

**Problem Solving:** Copy this problem and fill in the missing digits.

$$\begin{array}{r} \_\_\_ \\ \times \quad 9 \\ \hline \_\_2 \end{array}$$

**Using zero as a place holder**

When subtracting, multiplying, and dividing decimal numbers, we often find a decimal place with no digit in it, like these.

$$\begin{array}{r} 0.5\_ \\ -\ 0.32 \\ \hline \end{array} \qquad \begin{array}{r} \overset{.}{0}.2 \\ \times\ 0.3 \\ \hline 0.\_6 \end{array} \qquad \begin{array}{r} \$0.\_4 \\ 3)\overline{\$0.12} \end{array}$$

We may fill an empty decimal place with zero.

### In Subtraction

In order to subtract it is sometimes necessary to attach zeros to the top number.

$$\begin{array}{r} 0.5\textcolor{gray}{0} \\ -\ 0.32 \\ \hline \end{array}$$

**Example 1** $3 - 0.4$

*Solution* We place the decimal on the back of the whole number and line up the decimal points. We fill the empty place with zero and subtract.

$$\begin{array}{r} 3.0 \\ -\ 0.4 \\ \hline \mathbf{2.6} \end{array}$$

### In Multiplication

When multiplying, we may need to insert one or more zeros between the multiplication answer and the decimal point to hold the other digits in their proper places.

$$\begin{array}{r} 0.2 \\ \times\ 0.3 \\ \hline 0.06 \end{array}$$

**Example 2**   $0.12 \times 0.3$

*Solution*   We multiply and count three places. We fill the empty place with zero.

$$\begin{array}{r} 0.12 \\ \times\ 0.3 \\ \hline \mathbf{0.036} \end{array}$$

**Example 3**   Use digits to write the decimal number twelve thousandths.

*Solution*   The word "thousandths" tells us that there are three places to the right of the decimal point.

$$\cdot\_\ \_\ \_$$

We fit the two digits of twelve in the last two places.

$$\cdot\_\ \mathbf{1}\ \mathbf{2}$$

Then we fill the empty place with zero.

**0.012**

**Circle graphs**   **Circle graphs,** which are sometimes called **pie graphs** or **pie charts,** display quantitative information in fractions of a circle. In the chart in Example 4, we see that dogs represent half of the pets belonging to the students in Brett's classroom. Circle graphs often express the portions of a graph in percent form. Instead of stating the number of dogs as 16, the graph might have stated the portion of pets that are dogs as 50%.

**Example 4**   Brett collected information from his classmates about their pets. He displayed the information about the number of pets in a circle graph. Use the information in this graph to answer the following questions:

(a) How many pets are represented in the graph?

(b) What fraction of the pets are birds?

(c) What percent of the pets are dogs?

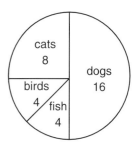

*Solution*  (a) We add the number of dogs, cats, birds, and fish. The total is **32.**

(b) Birds are 4 of the 32 pets. The fraction $\frac{4}{32}$ reduces to $\frac{1}{8}$. So the circle graph was divided in a way to make the bird portion of the circle $\frac{1}{8}$ of the circle.

(c) Dogs are 16 of the 32 pets, which means that $\frac{1}{2}$ of the pets are dogs. From our fraction manipulatives we know that $\frac{1}{2}$ is equivalent to **50%.**

**Practice\***   **a.** $0.2 \times 0.3$   0.06          **b.** $4.6 - 0.46$   4.14

**c.** $0.1 \times 0.01$   0.001          **d.** $0.4 - 0.32$   0.08

**e.** $0.12 \times 0.4$   0.048          **f.** $1 - 0.98$   0.02

**g.** Write the decimal number ten and eleven thousandths.
10.011

**h.** Refer to the circle graph in this lesson. What percent of the pets are cats?   25%

**Problem set 40**   **1.** Refer to the circle graph in this lesson and to your fraction manipulatives. What percent of the pets are birds?   $12\frac{1}{2}\%$
*(40)*

**2.** The first slaves were taken to the colony of Virginia in 1619. African slave trade ended in 1871. How many years did the slave trade last?   252 years
*(13)*

**3.** White Rabbit is three and a half hours late for a very important date. If the time is 2:00 p.m., what was the time of his date?   10:30 a.m.
*(32)*

**4.** $3 - 0.3$   2.7      **5.** $1.2 - 0.12$   1.08 **6.** $1 - 0.1$   0.9
*(40)*                     *(40)*                      *(40)*

**7.** $0.12 \times 0.2$      **8.** $0.01 \times 0.1$      **9.** $4.8 \times 0.23$
*(40)*   0.024              *(40)*   0.001              *(39)*   1.104

**10.** Write one and two hundredths as a decimal number.
*(40)*   1.02

60,800  **11.** Write $(6 \times 10,000) + (8 \times 100)$ in standard form.
*(32)*

**12.** A square room has a perimeter of 32 feet. How many
(38) floor tiles 1 foot on a side are needed to cover the floor
of the room?    64 tiles

**13.** What is the least common multiple (LCM) of 2, 4, and 8?
(30)    8

**14.** $6\frac{2}{3} + 4\frac{2}{3}$    $11\frac{1}{3}$         **15.** $5 - 3\frac{3}{8}$    $1\frac{5}{8}$
(27)                          (36)

**16.** $\frac{5}{8} \times \frac{2}{3}$    $\frac{5}{12}$         **17.** $2\frac{5}{6} + 5\frac{2}{6}$    $8\frac{1}{6}$
(29)                          (27)

**18.** Compare: $\frac{1}{2} \times \frac{2}{2}$ $\;\boxed{=}\;$ $\frac{1}{2} \times \frac{3}{3}$
(29)

**19.** $1000 - w = 567$    433
(3)

**20.** Eighteen of the thirty students in the class received
(29) A's. What fraction of the class received A's?    $\frac{3}{5}$

**21.** How many whole numbers are factors of 100?    9
(19)

**22.** Round $4167 to the nearest hundred dollars.    $4200
(16)

The circle graph below gives us some information about
the test scores of some students who took a test. Use the
information in this graph to answer questions 23–26.

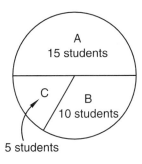

**23.** How many students took the test?    30
(40)

**24.** What fraction of the students received a grade of C on
(40) the test?    $\frac{1}{6}$

**25.** What percent of the students received an A on the test?
(40)     50%

**26.** Write a "larger-smaller-difference" question that refers
(40)     to this graph. Then answer the question.   Answers will
vary.

0.3 × 0.12 = 0.036,  **27.** In Example 2 of this lesson is the following multi-
0.036 ÷ 0.3 = 0.12,  (40)     plication fact:
0.036 ÷ 0.12 = 0.3

$$0.12 \times 0.3 = 0.036$$

Arrange these numbers to form another multiplication
fact and two division facts.

**28.** Instead of dividing 240 by 15, Sandy divided both
(2)     numbers by 3 to make 80 ÷ 5. Then she doubled both
numbers to make 160 ÷ 10. Find all three quotients.
16; 16; 16

**29.** Forty percent of the 25 students in the class are boys.
(33)     Write 40% as a reduced fraction. Then find the
numbers of boys in the class.   $\frac{2}{5}$; 10 boys

**30.** What mixed number is represented by point $A$ on this
(17)     number line?   $5\frac{9}{10}$

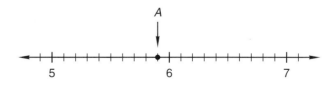

# LESSON
# 41

# Renaming Fractions by Multiplying by 1

**Mental Math:**
a. 500
b. 875
c. 75
d. $9.25
e. 500
f. 58
g. 3
Problem Solving:
  31

**Facts Practice:** 30 Fractions to Reduce (Test G in Test Masters)

**Mental Math:** Count by 12's from 12 to 96.

a. $4 \times 125$
b. $825 + 50$
c. $67 + 8$
d. $\$6.75 + \$2.50$
e. $\frac{1}{2}$ of 1000
f. $\frac{580}{10}$
g. $3 \times 4, - 2, \times 5, - 2, \div 6, + 1, \div 3$

**Problem Solving:** The average of two numbers is 25. If one of the numbers is 19, what is the other number?

With our fraction manipulatives we have seen that the same fraction may be named many different ways. Here we show six ways to name the fraction $\frac{1}{2}$.

$$\frac{1}{2} \qquad \frac{2}{4} \qquad \frac{3}{6} \qquad \frac{4}{8} \qquad \frac{5}{10} \qquad \frac{6}{12}$$

In this lesson we will practice renaming a fraction by multiplying the fraction by a fraction equal to 1. Here we show six ways to name 1 as a fraction.

$$\frac{1}{1} \qquad \frac{2}{2} \qquad \frac{3}{3} \qquad \frac{4}{4} \qquad \frac{5}{5} \qquad \frac{6}{6}$$

We know that when we multiply a number by 1, the product equals the number multiplied. So if we multiply $\frac{1}{2}$ by 1, the answer is $\frac{1}{2}$.

$$\frac{1}{2} \times 1 = \frac{1}{2}$$

However, if we multiply $\frac{1}{2}$ by a fraction equal to 1, the answer will be a different name for $\frac{1}{2}$. We multiply $\frac{1}{2}$ by $\frac{2}{2}$, $\frac{3}{3}$, and $\frac{4}{4}$ to make three different fractions equal to $\frac{1}{2}$.

$$\frac{1}{2} \times \frac{2}{2} = \frac{2}{4} \qquad \frac{1}{2} \times \frac{3}{3} = \frac{3}{6} \qquad \frac{1}{2} \times \frac{4}{4} = \frac{4}{8}$$

The fractions $\frac{2}{4}$, $\frac{3}{6}$, and $\frac{4}{8}$ are all equivalent to $\frac{1}{2}$.

**Example 1**   Write a fraction equal to $\frac{1}{2}$ that has a denominator of 20.

$$\frac{1}{2} = \frac{?}{20}$$

**Solution**   To rename a fraction, we multiply the fraction by a fraction equal to 1. The denominator of $\frac{1}{2}$ is 2. We want to make an equivalent fraction with a denominator of 20.

$$\frac{1}{2} = \frac{?}{20}$$

Since we need to multiply the denominator by 10, we multiply $\frac{1}{2}$ by $\frac{10}{10}$.

$$\frac{1}{2} \times \frac{10}{10} = \frac{\mathbf{10}}{\mathbf{20}}$$

**Example 2**   Write $\frac{1}{2}$ and $\frac{1}{3}$ as fractions with denominators of 6. Then add the renamed fractions.

**Solution**   We multiply each fraction by a fraction equal to one to form fractions that have a denominator of 6.

$$\frac{1}{2} = \frac{?}{6} \qquad \frac{1}{3} = \frac{?}{6}$$

We multiply $\frac{1}{2}$ by $\frac{3}{3}$. We multiply $\frac{1}{3}$ by $\frac{2}{2}$.

$$\frac{1}{2} \times \frac{3}{3} = \frac{3}{6} \qquad \frac{1}{3} \times \frac{2}{2} = \frac{2}{6}$$

The renamed fractions are $\frac{3}{6}$ and $\frac{2}{6}$. We are told to add these fractions.

$$\frac{3}{6} + \frac{2}{6} = \frac{5}{6}$$

**Practice**   Complete each equivalent fraction by multiplying each fraction by a fraction equal to 1.

**a.** $\frac{1}{3} = \frac{?}{12}$   4

**b.** $\frac{2}{3} = \frac{?}{6}$   4

**c.** $\frac{3}{4} = \frac{?}{8}$   6

**d.** $\frac{3}{4} = \frac{?}{12}$   9

**e.** Write $\frac{2}{3}$ and $\frac{1}{4}$ as fractions with denominators of 12. Then add the renamed fractions.   $\frac{8}{12} + \frac{3}{12} = \frac{11}{12}$

**f.** Write $\frac{1}{6}$ as a fraction with 12 as the denominator. Subtract the renamed fraction from $\frac{5}{12}$. Reduce the subtraction answer.   $\frac{2}{12}; \frac{5}{12} - \frac{2}{12} = \frac{3}{12} = \frac{1}{4}$

**Problem set 41**   **1.** Write $\frac{1}{2}$ and $\frac{2}{3}$ as fractions with denominators of 6. Then add the renamed fractions. Write the answer as a mixed number.   $\frac{3}{6}, \frac{4}{6}; 1\frac{1}{6}$
(41)

**2.** Our own galaxy, the Milky Way, may contain two hundred billion stars. Write that number.   200,000,000,000
(12)

**3.** The rectangular school yard is 120 yards long and 40 yards wide. How many square yards is its area?   4800 sq. yd
(31)

**4.** Write 40% as a reduced fraction.   $\frac{2}{5}$
(33)

In problems 5 and 6, multiply $\frac{1}{2}$ by a fraction equal to 1 to complete each equivalent fraction.

**5.** $\frac{1}{2} = \frac{?}{8}$   4
(41)

**6.** $\frac{1}{2} = \frac{?}{10}$   5
(41)

**7.** 4.32 + 0.6 + 11   15.92
(36)

**8.** 6.3 − 0.54   5.76
(37)

**9.** $0.15 \times 0.15$    0.0225
(40)

**10.** What is the reciprocal of $\frac{6}{7}$?    $\frac{7}{6}$
(30)

**11.** Which digit in 12,345 has the same place value as the
(34)    6 in 67.89?    4

**12.** What is the least common multiple of 3, 4, and 6?    12
(30)

**13.** $5\frac{3}{5} + 4\frac{4}{5}$    $10\frac{2}{5}$    **14.** $6 - 4\frac{2}{3}$    $1\frac{1}{3}$    **15.** $\frac{8}{3} \times \frac{1}{2}$    $1\frac{1}{3}$
(27)                        (27)                    (29)

**16.** $\frac{6}{5} \times 3$    $3\frac{3}{5}$    **17.** $1 - \frac{1}{4}$    $\frac{3}{4}$    **18.** $\frac{10}{10} - \frac{5}{5}$    0
(29)                    (27)                (28)

**19.** Make three different fractions that are equal to $\frac{1}{3}$ by
(41)    multiplying $\frac{1}{3}$ by three different fraction names for 1.
Answers vary. See student work.

**20.** List the factors of 35.    1, 5, 7, 35
(19)

**21.** In three games Alma's scores were 12,643, 9870, and
(18)    14,261. What was her average score per game?    12,258

**22.** Estimate the quotient of $\frac{8176}{41}$.    200
(16)

**23.** How many doughnuts are in $\frac{2}{3}$ of a dozen? Draw a
(22)    diagram to illustrate the problem.    8

23.
12 doughnuts
4 doughnuts
4 doughnuts    $\frac{2}{3}$ of a dozen
4 doughnuts

**24.** Write $\frac{3}{4}$ with a denominator of 8. Subtract the renamed
(41)    fraction from $\frac{7}{8}$.    $\frac{6}{8}$; $\frac{1}{8}$

**25.** What is the perimeter of this
(8)    rectangle?    1.2 m

0.4 m

0.2 m

0.08 sq. m    **26.** What is the area of this rectangle?
(31)

**27.** The regular price ($r$) minus the discount ($d$) equals the
(1)    sale price (s).   $r - s = d,\ s + d = r,\ d + s = r$

$$r - d = s$$

Arrange these letters to form another subtraction fact and two addition facts.

**28.** Here we show the same division problem written three
(2)    different ways. Identify which number is the divisor, which is the dividend, and which is the quotient.

divisor, 4;
dividend, 20;      $\dfrac{20}{4} = 5$     $4\overline{)20}^{\,5}$     $20 \div 4 = 5$
quotient, 5

**29.** What time is $2\frac{1}{2}$ hours after 11:45 a.m.?   2:15 p.m.
(32)

**30.** (a) How many $\frac{5}{6}$'s are in 1?   $\frac{6}{5}$
(30)
   (b) Use your answer to part (a) to help you find the number of $\frac{5}{6}$'s in 3.   $3\frac{3}{5}$

# LESSON 42

# Equivalent Division Problems • Missing Number Problems with Fractions and Decimals

Mental Math:
a. 900
b. 520
c. 65
d. $25
e. 600
f. $7.00
g. 6
Problem Solving:
  Sixteen, (3–18)

---

**Facts Practice:** 100 Subtraction Facts (Test C in Test Masters)

**Mental Math:** Count by 6's to 72. Count by 8's to 96.

  **a.** $4 \times 225$      **b.** $720 - 200$      **c.** $37 + 28$

  **d.** $\$200 - \$175$    **e.** $\frac{1}{2}$ of 1200      **f.** $\frac{\$70.00}{10}$

  **g.** $8 \times 4, - 2, \times 2, + 3, \div 7, \times 2, \div 3$

**Problem Solving:** You can "roll" six different numbers with one number cube (1–6). You can roll eleven different numbers with two number cubes (2–12). How many different numbers can you roll with three number cubes?

---

**Equivalent division problems**

The following two division problems have the same quotient. We call them **equivalent division problems.** Which problem seems easier to perform mentally?

$$\text{(a)} \ \ 700 \div 14$$

$$\text{(b)} \ \ 350 \div 7$$

We can change problem (a) to problem (b) by dividing both 700 and 14 by 2.

$$700 \div 14$$

$$\downarrow$$

Divide both 700 and 14 by 2.

$$\downarrow$$

$$350 \div 7$$

By dividing both the dividend and divisor by the same number, in this case 2, we formed an equivalent division problem that was easier to divide mentally.

We may also form equivalent division problems by multiplying the dividend and divisor by the same number. Consider the following equivalent problems:

$$\text{(c)} \quad 7\frac{1}{2} \div \frac{1}{2}$$

$$\text{(d)} \quad 15 \div 1$$

We changed problem (c) to problem (d) by doubling both $7\frac{1}{2}$ and $\frac{1}{2}$, that is, by multiplying both numbers by 2.

$$7\frac{1}{2} \div \frac{1}{2}$$

$$\downarrow$$

Multiply both $7\frac{1}{2}$ and $\frac{1}{2}$ by 2.

$$\downarrow$$

$$15 \div 1$$

**Example 1**  Make an equivalent division problem; then calculate the quotient.

$$1200 \div 16$$

*Solution*  Instead of dividing 1200 by the two-digit number 16, we can divide both the dividend and the divisor by 2 to form the equivalent division of 600 divided by 8.

$$16\overline{)1200} \quad \xrightarrow{\substack{\text{Divide both} \\ \text{numbers by 2.}}} \quad 8\overline{)600}$$

$$\begin{array}{r} 75 \\ 8\overline{)600} \\ \underline{56} \\ 40 \\ \underline{40} \\ 0 \end{array}$$

Both quotients are 75, but dividing by 8 is easier than dividing by 16.

Notice that there are often equivalent problems that can be made.

$$1200 \div 16 \longrightarrow 600 \div 8 \longrightarrow 300 \div 4 \longrightarrow 150 \div 2$$

All of these problems have the same quotient.

Example 2   Find an equivalent problem for this division problem and calculate the quotient.

$$7\frac{1}{2} \div 2\frac{1}{2}$$

Solution   Instead of performing the division with these mixed numbers, we will double both numbers to make a whole number division problem.

$$7\frac{1}{2} \div 2\frac{1}{2}$$

Multiply both $7\frac{1}{2}$ and $2\frac{1}{2}$ by 2.

$$15 \div 5 = 3$$

**Missing number problems with fractions and decimals**   Since Lessons 3 and 4 we have practiced finding missing numbers in whole number arithmetic problems. Beginning in this lesson we will find missing numbers in fraction and decimal problems. If you encounter a problem and you feel unsure how to find the solution, try making up a similar, easier problem to help you think of how to find the answer.

Example 3   $d - 5 = 3.2$

Solution   This problem is similar to $d - 5 = 3$. We remember that we find the first number of a subtraction problem by adding the other two numbers.

$$\begin{array}{r} 5 \\ + \ 3.2 \\ \hline 8.2 \end{array}$$

We find that $d$ equals **8.2.**

Example 4   $f + \dfrac{1}{5} = \dfrac{4}{5}$

*Solution*  This problem is like $f + 1 = 4$. We can find a missing addend by subtracting the known addend from the sum.

$$\frac{4}{5} - \frac{1}{5} = \frac{3}{5}$$

We find that $f$ equals $\frac{3}{5}$.

**Example 5**  $\frac{3}{5}n = 1$

*Solution*  Two numbers are multiplied and the product is 1. This is only true when the two factors are reciprocals. So the problem is to find the reciprocal of the known factor, $\frac{3}{5}$. Reversing the terms of $\frac{3}{5}$ makes the fraction $\frac{5}{3}$.

$$\frac{3}{5} \cdot \frac{5}{3} = \frac{15}{15}, \text{ which equals 1}$$

We find that $n$ equals $\frac{5}{3}$.

**Practice**  **a.** Make an equivalent division problem for $5 \div \frac{1}{3}$ by multiplying both the dividend and divisor by 3. Then find the quotient.  $15 \div 1 = 15$

**b.** Make an equivalent division problem for $266 \div 14$ that has a one-digit divisor. Then find the quotient.  $133 \div 7 = 19$

**c.** $5 - d = 3.2$  1.8  **d.** $f - \frac{1}{5} = \frac{4}{5}$  1

**e.** $m + 1\frac{1}{5} = 4$  $2\frac{4}{5}$  **f.** $\frac{3}{8}w = 1$  $\frac{8}{3}$

**Problem set 42**  **1.** What number must be added to six thousand, eighty-four to get a sum of ten thousand?  3916
(3)

22  **2.** If one hundred fifty knights could sit at the Round Table and only one hundred twenty-eight knights were seated, then how many empty places were at the table?
(11)

**3.** Frank started running the marathon at 11:50 a.m. and
(32) finished 2 hours and 11 minutes later. At what time did he finish?  2:01 p.m.

**4.** $3\frac{7}{8} - 1\frac{3}{8}$  $2\frac{1}{2}$
(42)

**5.** $6 - w = 1\frac{4}{5}$
(42)
$4\frac{1}{5}$

**6.** $m - 4\frac{1}{4} = 6\frac{3}{4}$
(42)
11

**7.** $\frac{5}{8} \times \frac{1}{5}$  $\frac{1}{8}$
(29)

**8.** $\frac{3}{4} \times 5$  $3\frac{3}{4}$
(29)

**9.** $\frac{2}{3}n = 1$  $\frac{3}{2}$
(42)

**10.** $\frac{2}{3} = \frac{?}{6}$  4
(41)

**11.** $\frac{1}{2} = \frac{?}{6}$  3
(41)

**12.** Compare: $\frac{2}{2}$ Ⓞ$=$ $\frac{2}{2} \times \frac{2}{2}$
(29)

**13.** The temperature was 8°F at midnight but dropped 15°F
(14) by morning. What was the morning temperature?  −7°F

**14.** Write the decimal number for nine and twelve
(35) hundredths.  9.12

**15.** Round 67,492,384 to the nearest million.  67,000,000
(16)

**16.** $46.37 + 5.93 + 14$
(38)  66.3

**17.** $12 - d = 1.43$  10.57
(42)

**18.** $0.37 \times 100$  37
(39)

**19.** $0.6 \times 0.4 \times 0.2$  0.048
(40)

**20.** The perimeter of a square room is 80 feet. The area of
(38) the room is how many square feet?  400 sq. ft

**21.** Divide 100 by 16 and write the answer as a mixed
(26) number. Reduce the fraction part of the mixed number.
$6\frac{1}{4}$

$25 \div 4 = 6\frac{1}{4}$ **22.** Instead of dividing 100 by 16, Sandy divided the
(42) dividend and divisor by 4. What new division problem did Sandy make? What is the quotient?

**23.** Make an equivalent division problem for $4\frac{1}{2} \div \frac{1}{2}$ by
$^{(42)}$ doubling both the dividend and divisor and then find
the quotient.   $9 \div 1 = 9$

**24.** What is the least common multiple (LCM) of 4, 6, and 8?
$^{(30)}$   24

**25.** What are the next three numbers in this sequence?
$^{(17)}$

$$\frac{1}{16}, \frac{1}{8}, \frac{3}{16}, \frac{1}{4}, \frac{5}{16}, \frac{3}{8}, \frac{7}{16}, \underline{\quad\frac{1}{2}\quad}, \underline{\quad\frac{9}{16}\quad}, \underline{\quad\frac{5}{8}\quad}, \ldots$$

**26.** Find the length of this segment to the nearest eighth of
$^{(17)}$ an inch.   $1\frac{5}{8}$ in.

_____

**27.** To what mixed number on this number line is the
$^{(17)}$ arrow pointing?   $4\frac{7}{10}$

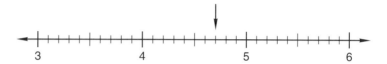

**28.** Write $\frac{1}{2}$ and $\frac{1}{5}$ as fractions with denominators of 10.
$^{(41)}$ Then add the renamed fractions.   $\frac{5}{10}, \frac{2}{10}; \frac{7}{10}$

29. 20 seats

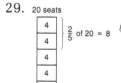

**29.** Forty percent of the 20 seats on the bus were
$^{(22,33)}$ occupied. Write 40% as a reduced fraction. Then find
the number of seats that were occupied. Draw a
diagram to illustrate the problem.   $\frac{2}{5}$; 8 seats

**30.** Describe how to form the reciprocal of a fraction.
$^{(30)}$ To form the reciprocal of a fraction, write a new fraction using
the same number as the original fraction but with the numerator
and denominator reversed.

# LESSON 43

# Simplifying Decimal Numbers • Comparing Decimal Numbers

**Mental Math:**
**a.** 1300
**b.** 461
**c.** 85
**d.** $11.25
**e.** 700
**f.** $0.15
**g.** 7
**Problem Solving:**

---

**Facts Practice:** 30 Fractions to Reduce (Test G in Test Masters)

**Mental Math:** Count up and down by $\frac{1}{8}$'s between $\frac{1}{8}$ and 3.

**a.** $4 \times 325$
**b.** $426 + 35$
**c.** $28 + 57$
**d.** $8.50 + 2.75$
**e.** $\frac{1}{2}$ of 1400
**f.** $\frac{\$15.00}{100}$
**g.** $6 \times 8, - 3, \div 5, + 1, \times 6, + 3, \div 9$

**Problem Solving:** Jeana folded a square paper in half from top to bottom. Then she folded the folded paper in half from left to right so that the four corners were together at the lower right. Then she cut off the lower right corners as shown. What will the paper look like when it is unfolded?

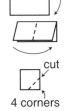
cut
4 corners

---

**Simplifying decimal numbers**

Perform these two subtractions with a calculator. Which calculator answer differs from the printed answer?

$$
\begin{array}{r}
425 \\
- 125 \\
\hline
300
\end{array}
\qquad
\begin{array}{r}
4.25 \\
- 1.25 \\
\hline
3.00
\end{array}
$$

A calculator automatically simplifies decimal numbers. Zeros at the end of a decimal number are removed. A decimal point at the end of a whole number is shown on a calculator although we usually remove the decimal point if no digits follow it. So 3.00 simplifies to 3. on a calculator. We remove the decimal point and write 3 only.

**Example 1** Multiply 0.25 and 0.04 and simplify the product.

*Solution* We multiply.

$$
\begin{array}{r}
0.25 \\
\times \quad 0.04 \\
\hline
0.0100
\end{array}
$$

If we perform this multiplication on a calculator the answer 0.01 is displayed. The calculator simplifies the answer by removing zeros at the end of a decimal number.

0.0100 simplifies to **0.01**

Decimal answers in this book are printed in simplified form unless otherwise stated.

**Comparing decimal numbers** Zeros at the end of a decimal number do not affect the value of the decimal number. Each of these decimal numbers has the same value because the 3 is in the tenths' place.

0.3     0.30     0.300

Although 0.3 is the simplified form, sometimes it is useful to attach extra zeros to a decimal number. For instance, comparing decimal numbers can be easier if the numbers being compared have the same number of decimal places.

Example 2    Compare:  0.3 ◯ 0.303

Solution    When comparing decimal numbers it is important to pay close attention to place values. Writing both numbers with the same number of decimal places can make the job of comparing easier. We will attach two zeros to 0.3 so that it has three decimal places like 0.303.

0.3     ◯ 0.303

0.300 ◯ 0.303

We see that 300 thousandths is less than 303 thousandths. We write our answer this way.

**0.3  <  0.303**

Example 3    Arrange these numbers in order from least to greatest:

0.3     0.042     0.24     0.235

*Solution*  We will write each number with three decimal places.

0.300     0.042     0.240     0.235

Then we arrange the numbers in order, omitting ending zeros.

**0.042     0.235     0.24     0.3**

**Practice**  Write these numbers in simplified form:

**a.** 0.0500   0.05                    **b.** 50.00   50

**c.** 1.250   1.25                     **d.** 4.000   4

Compare these decimal numbers:

**e.** 0.2 $\gtrless$ 0.15

**f.** 12.5 $\gtrless$ 1.25

**g.** 0.012 $\lessgtr$ 0.12

**h.** 0.31 $\gtrless$ 0.039

**i.** 0.4 $\doteq$ 0.40

**j.** Write these numbers in order from least to greatest.
0.12, 0.125, 0.015, 0.2   0.015, 0.12, 0.125, 0.2

**Problem set 43**

1. What is the sum of the third multiple of four and the third multiple of five?   27
   *(26)*

2. One mile is 5280 feet. How many feet is five miles?
   *(15)*   26,400 ft

Mt. Everest is 29,028 feet high. Mt. Whitney is 14,495 feet high. Use this information to answer questions 3 and 4.

3. Mt. Everest is how many feet higher than Mt. Whitney?
   *(13)*   14,533 ft

4. How many feet more than 5 miles high is Mt. Everest?
   *(13)*   (Refer to question 2.)   2628 ft

**5.** $5\dfrac{1}{3} - w = 4$   $1\frac{1}{3}$
(42)

**6.** $m - 6\dfrac{4}{5} = 1\dfrac{3}{5}$   $8\frac{2}{5}$
(42)

**7.** $7\dfrac{3}{4} - 1\dfrac{1}{4}$   $6\frac{1}{2}$
(27)

**8.** What is the reciprocal of $\frac{5}{16}$?   $\frac{16}{5}$
(30)

**9.** Write thirty-two thousandths as a decimal number.
(35)   0.032

**10.** $6\overline{)24{,}042}$   $\overset{4007}{}$
(2)

**11.** $10\overline{)\$36.00}$   $\overset{\$3.60}{}$
(2)

**12.** Compare: $0.25 \,\textcircled{>}\, 0.125$
(43)

**13.** Write the standard numeral for $(6 \times 100) + (4 \times 1)$.
(32)   604

**14.** Write a division problem that is equivalent to $8\frac{1}{2} \div \frac{1}{2}$
(42)   by doubling the dividend and divisor. Then find the quotient.   $17 \div 1 = 17$

**15.** (a) How many $\frac{5}{8}$'s are in 1?   $\frac{8}{5}$
(30)

    (b) Use your answer to part (a) to help you find the number of $\frac{5}{8}$'s in 3.   $4\frac{4}{5}$

**16.** What is the least common multiple of 2, 3, 4, and 6?
(30)   12

**17.** $6.74 + 0.285 + f = 11.025$   4
(42)

**18.** $0.4 - d = 0.33$   0.07
(42)

**19.** $1.6 \times 4.2$
(39)   6.72

**20.** $\dfrac{3}{4} = \dfrac{?}{12}$   9
(41)

**21.** $\dfrac{2}{3} = \dfrac{?}{12}$   8
(41)

**22.** Find the average of 26, 37, 42, and 43.   37
(18)

**23.** Round 364,857 to the nearest thousand.   365,000
(16)

**24.** Write the next two numbers in this sequence.
(10)

$$1, 6, 4, 9, 7, 12, \underline{\;\;10\;\;}, \underline{\;\;15\;\;}, \dots$$

**25.** List the factors of 100.    1, 2, 4, 5, 10, 20, 25, 50, 100
*(19)*

**26.** Write 9% as a fraction. Then write the fraction as a
*(33)* decimal number.    $\frac{9}{100}$; 0.09

**27.** Write $\frac{3}{4}$ and $\frac{2}{3}$ as fractions with denominators of 12.
*(41)* Then add the renamed fractions.    $\frac{9}{12}$, $\frac{8}{12}$; $1\frac{5}{12}$

28. B. 40%. Nearly **28.** Which percent best describes the
half of the rectangle *(28)* shaded portion of this rectangle and
is shaded. Since $\frac{1}{2}$     why?
is equivalent to          A. 80%                    B. 40%
50%, the shaded
part of the rectangle      C. 60%                    D. 20%
is close to but less
than 50%.

**29.** Walt started working at 10:30 a.m. and finished
*(32)* working at 2:15 p.m. How many hours and minutes
did Walt work?    3 hours and 45 minutes

**30.** Which of these numbers is closest to 1?    C. 1.1
*(43)* A. 0.1          B. 0.8          C. 1.1          D. 1.2

**31.** What mixed number corresponds to point $x$ on this
*(17)* number line?    $10\frac{1}{10}$

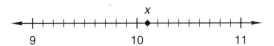

LESSON
**44**

# Dividing a Decimal Number by a Whole Number

Mental Math:
a. 1700
b. 875
c. 95
d. $10.75
e. 750
f. $4.00
g. 7
Problem Solving:
21

**Facts Practice:** 90 Division Facts (Test F in Test Masters)

**Mental Math:** Count up and down by 25's between 25 and 300.

**a.** 4 × 425      **b.** 375 + 500      **c.** 77 + 18

**d.** $12.00 − $1.25      **e.** $\frac{1}{2}$ of 1500      **f.** $\frac{\$40.00}{10}$

**g.** 4 × 8, − 2, ÷ 3, + 2, ÷ 3, × 5, + 1, ÷ 3

**Problem Solving:** Sheldon used six blocks to build this three-step shape. How many blocks would be in a six-step shape?

Dividing a decimal number by a whole number is like dividing dollars and cents by a whole number.

$$\begin{array}{r} \$0.45 \\ 5\overline{)\$2.25} \end{array} \qquad \begin{array}{r} 0.45 \\ 5\overline{)2.25} \end{array}$$

Notice that the decimal point in the quotient is directly above the decimal point in the dividend. Decimal division answers are not written with remainders. Instead, we attach zeros to the end of the number we are dividing and continue dividing.

**Example 1**    $3\overline{)4.2}$

**Solution**    The decimal point in the quotient is straight up from the decimal point in the dividend.

$$\begin{array}{r} 1.4 \\ 3\overline{)4.2} \\ \underline{3\phantom{.0}} \\ 1\,2 \\ \underline{1\,2} \\ 0 \end{array}$$

**Example 2**    $3\overline{)0.24}$

**Solution**    The decimal point in the quotient is straight up. We fill the empty place with zero.

$$\begin{array}{r} 0.08 \\ 3\overline{)0.24} \\ \underline{24} \\ 0 \end{array}$$

**Example 3**  5$\overline{)0.6}$

*Solution*  The decimal point in the quotient is straight up. To complete the division, we attach a zero to 0.6 making the equivalent decimal number 0.60. Then we continue dividing.

$$\begin{array}{r} 0.12 \\ 5\overline{)0.60} \\ \underline{5\phantom{.00}} \\ 10 \\ \underline{10} \\ 0 \end{array}$$

**Practice\***  **a.** The distance from Margaret's house to school and back is 3.6 miles. How far does Margaret live from school?
1.8 miles

**b.** The perimeter of a square is 6.4 meters. How long is each side of the square?  1.6 meters

Find each quotient:

**c.** $\dfrac{4.5}{3}$  1.5    **d.** $0.6 \div 4$  0.15   **e.** 2$\overline{)0.14}$  0.07

**f.** $0.4 \div 5$  0.08   **g.** 4$\overline{)0.3}$  0.075    **h.** $\dfrac{0.012}{6}$  0.002

**i.** 10$\overline{)1.4}$  0.14    **j.** $\dfrac{0.7}{5}$  0.14    **k.** $0.1 \div 4$  0.025

---

**Teacher Note:** As a class activity, conduct a survey of class members and members of their families to find the favorite movies of the population. Set the rules for the survey in class. Students should collect responses at home. Assemble and display the data collected at a later class meeting.

---

**Problem set 44**

**1.** By what fraction must $\frac{5}{3}$ be multiplied to have a product equal to 1?  $\frac{3}{5}$
(30)

**2.** How many twenty-dollar bills equal one thousand dollars?  50
(15)

32 pt

**3.** Cindy made $\frac{2}{3}$ of her 24 shots at the basket. Each basket was worth 2 points. How many points did she make?
(29)

**4.** $3\overline{)4.5}$  $\overset{1.5}{}$
(44)

**5.** $8\overline{)0.24}$  $\overset{0.03}{}$
(44)

**6.** $5\overline{)0.8}$  $\overset{0.16}{}$
(44)

**7.** What is the least common multiple (LCM) of 2, 4, 6,
(30)  and 8?   24

**8.** $6 - m = 2\dfrac{3}{10}$   $3\frac{7}{10}$
(42)

**9.** $g - 2\dfrac{2}{5} = 5\dfrac{4}{5}$   $8\frac{1}{5}$
(42)

**10.** $4\dfrac{3}{8} - 2\dfrac{1}{8}$   $2\frac{1}{4}$
(27)

**11.** Estimate the product of 694 and 412.   280,000
(16)

**12.** 5.36 + 9 + 0.742
(38)  15.102

**13.** $m - 1.56 = 1.44$   3
(42)

**14.** 0.7 × 0.6 × 0.5   0.21
(39)

**15.** 0.46 × 0.17   0.0782
(40)

**16.** Convert the improper fraction $\dfrac{40}{6}$ to a mixed number
(26)  with the fraction reduced.   $6\frac{2}{3}$

**17.** Brenda's car traveled 177.6 miles on 8 gallons of gas.
(15)  Her car traveled an average of how many miles per
gallon? Use an "equal groups" pattern.   22.2 miles per
gallon

**18.** $\dfrac{3}{8}$ of 6   $2\frac{1}{4}$
(29)

**19.** $\dfrac{9}{4} \times \dfrac{2}{3}$   $1\frac{1}{2}$
(29)

**20.** Write a fraction equal to $\frac{5}{6}$ that has 12 as the
(41)  denominator. Then subtract $\frac{7}{12}$ from the fraction.
Reduce the answer.   $\frac{10}{12} - \frac{7}{12} = \frac{3}{12}; \frac{1}{4}$

**21.** The perimeter of a square is 24 feet. The area of the
(38)  square is how many square feet?   36 sq. ft

**22.** Write 27% as a fraction. Then write the fraction as a
(33)  decimal number.   $\frac{27}{100}$; 0.27

**23.** Use your ruler to find the length
(17)  of this rectangle to the nearest
eighth of an inch.   $1\frac{1}{8}$ in.

**24.** 20 answers

$\frac{3}{4}$ of 20

**24.** Seventy-five percent of the 20 answers were correct.
*(22,23)* Write 75% as a reduced fraction. Then find the number of answers that were correct. Illustrate the fractional part problem.   $\frac{3}{4}$; 15

**25.** $\frac{2}{3} \times \frac{1}{2} = \frac{1}{3}$,
$\frac{1}{3} \div \frac{1}{2} = \frac{2}{3}$,
$\frac{1}{3} \div \frac{2}{3} = \frac{1}{2}$

**25.** The product of $\frac{1}{2}$ and $\frac{2}{3}$ is $\frac{1}{3}$.
*(29)*

$$\frac{1}{2} \times \frac{2}{3} = \frac{1}{3}$$

Arrange these numbers to form another multiplication fact and two division facts.

**26.** B. 60%.
Since a little more than half the circle is shaded, a little more than 50% is shaded.

**26.** Which percent best describes the
*(23)* shaded portion of this circle? Why?

A. 80%                    B. 60%
C. 40%                    D. 20%

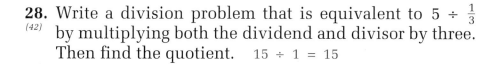

**27.** Write nine hundredths
*(35)*
(a) as a fraction.   $\frac{9}{100}$

(b) as a decimal number.   0.09

**28.** Write a division problem that is equivalent to $5 \div \frac{1}{3}$
*(42)* by multiplying both the dividend and divisor by three.
Then find the quotient.   $15 \div 1 = 15$

**29.** The average number of students in three classrooms
*(18)* was 24. Altogether, how many students were in the three classrooms?   72

**30.** Ask your family members about their favorite movies.
*(44)* Record the information to add to the class survey.
See student work.

LESSON
**45**

# Writing Decimal Numbers in Expanded Notation • Other Multiplication Forms

**Facts Practice:** 30 Fractions to Reduce (Test G in Test Masters)

**Mental Math:** Count by 12's from 12 to 108.

   **a.** 4 × 525        **b.** 567 − 120        **c.** 38 + 17
   **d.** $5.75 + $2.50     **e.** $\frac{1}{2}$ of 950        **f.** $\frac{2000}{100}$
   **g.** 9 × 7, + 1, ÷ 8, × 3, + 1, × 2, − 1, ÷ 7

**Problem Solving:** Copy this problem and fill in the missing digits.

$$\begin{array}{r} \_\,\_\,\_ \\ +\;\;\_ \\ \hline \_\,\_\,\_\,8 \end{array}$$

**Writing decimal numbers in expanded notation**

We may use expanded notation to write decimal numbers just as we use expanded notation to write whole numbers. The values of some decimal places are shown in this table.

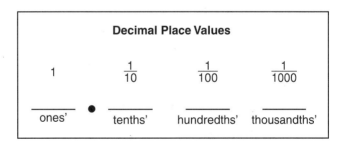

|  | Decimal Place Values | | |
|:---:|:---:|:---:|:---:|
| 1 | $\frac{1}{10}$ | $\frac{1}{100}$ | $\frac{1}{1000}$ |
| ones' | tenths' | hundredths' | thousandths' |

We write 4.025 in expanded notation this way:

$$(4 \times 1) + \left(2 \times \frac{1}{100}\right) + \left(5 \times \frac{1}{1000}\right)$$

The zero that serves as a place holder is usually not included in expanded notation.

**Example 1**    Write 5.06 in expanded notation.

*Solution*    The 5 is in the ones' place and the 6 is in the hundredths' place.

$$(5 \times 1) + \left(6 \times \frac{1}{100}\right)$$

**Example 2**    Write $\left(4 \times \frac{1}{10}\right) + \left(5 \times \frac{1}{1000}\right)$ as a decimal number.

*Solution*    We write a decimal number with a 4 in the tenths' place and a 5 in the thousandths' place. No digits in the ones' place or hundredths' place are indicated, so we write zeros in those places.

**0.405**

**Other multiplication forms**    To indicate multiplication we may use a times sign, a dot, or write the numbers side by side without a sign. Each of these expressions means that *l* and *w* are multiplied.

$$(1) \; l \times w \qquad (2) \; l \cdot w \qquad (3) \; lw$$

Notice that the multiplication dot in form (2) is elevated and is not in the position of a decimal point. Form (3) may be used to show the multiplication of two or more letters, of a number and a letter, or of two numbers.

$$lwh \qquad 4s \qquad 3(5)$$

When two numbers like 3 and 5 are multiplied, one or more sets of parentheses may be used so that 3 times 5 is not confused with 35. Each of these ways is a proper use of parentheses to indicate the multiplication of 3 and 5, although the first form is most commonly used.

$$3(5) \qquad (3)(5) \qquad (3)5$$

Recall that the order of two factors may be reversed without changing the product.

$$3 \cdot 5 = 5 \cdot 3$$

This property of multiplication is known as the **commutative property of multiplication.** We may use this property to rearrange factors in an expression.

$$2 \cdot 3 \cdot 2 \cdot 5 \cdot 3 \cdot 5 = 2 \cdot 2 \cdot 3 \cdot 3 \cdot 5 \cdot 5$$

**Example 3**   If $l$ equals 8 and $w$ equals 5, than what number does $lw$ equal?

*Solution*   The expression $lw$ means $l$ times $w$. We are given that $l = 8$ and $w = 5$. So $lw$ equals 8 times 5, which is **40.**

**Example 4**   Use the commutative property of multiplication to arrange these factors in order from least to greatest.

$$2 \cdot 5 \cdot 2 \cdot 7 \cdot 2 \cdot 3 \cdot 2 \cdot 3$$

*Solution*   We are not told to multiply the factors, just to rearrange the factors.

$$\mathbf{2 \cdot 2 \cdot 2 \cdot 2 \cdot 3 \cdot 3 \cdot 5 \cdot 7}$$

**Practice\***   Write these numbers in expanded notation:

**a.** 2.05   $(2 \times 1) + \left(5 \times \frac{1}{100}\right)$

**b.** 20.5   $(2 \times 10) + \left(5 \times \frac{1}{10}\right)$

**c.** 0.205   $\left(2 \times \frac{1}{10}\right) + \left(5 \times \frac{1}{1000}\right)$

Write these numbers in decimal form:

**d.** $(7 \times 10) + \left(8 \times \dfrac{1}{10}\right)$   70.8

**e.** $\left(6 \times \dfrac{1}{10}\right) + \left(4 \times \dfrac{1}{100}\right)$   0.64

Multiply as indicated:

**f.** 4(2.5)   10        **g.** 7 · 5   35        **h.** $\left(\dfrac{1}{3}\right)\left(\dfrac{1}{2}\right)$   $\frac{1}{6}$

**i.** If $l = 6$, $w = 5$, and $h = 4$, then what number does *lwh* equal?   120

**j.** Use the commutative property to arrange the factors in the numerator and the denominator in order from least to greatest. (Do not move factors between the numerator and denominator.)   $\frac{2 \cdot 2 \cdot 3 \cdot 3 \cdot 5 \cdot 5}{2 \cdot 2 \cdot 2 \cdot 3 \cdot 7}$

$$\frac{3 \cdot 5 \cdot 2 \cdot 5 \cdot 2 \cdot 3}{2 \cdot 2 \cdot 3 \cdot 2 \cdot 7}$$

---

**Teacher Note:** Conclude the Favorite Movie Survey by tallying the responses in a frequency table and by displaying the results in a graph.

---

**Problem set 45**

**1.** *(26)* When a fraction with a numerator of 30 and a denominator of 8 is converted to a mixed number and reduced, what is the result?   $3\frac{3}{4}$

**2.** *(13)* Normal body temperature is 98.6° on the Fahrenheit scale. A person with a temperature of 100.2°F would have a temperature how many degrees above normal? Use a "larger-smaller-difference" pattern.   1.6°F

**3.** *(15)* Four and twenty blackbirds is how many dozen?   2 dozen

**4.** *(45)* Write $(5 \times 10) + \left(6 \times \frac{1}{10}\right) + \left(7 \times \frac{1}{1000}\right)$ in decimal form.   50.607

**5.** *(33)* Twenty-one percent of the earth's atmosphere is oxygen. Write 21% as a fraction. Then write the fraction as a decimal number.   $\frac{21}{100}$; 0.21

**6.** *(33)* Twenty-one percent is slightly more than 20%. Twenty percent is equivalent to what reduced fraction?   $\frac{1}{5}$

**7.** *(44)* $5)\overline{6.35}$   1.27

**8.** *(44)* $4)\overline{0.5}$   0.125

**9.** *(44)* $8)\overline{1.0}$   0.125

**10.** *(42)* $x + 3\frac{5}{8} = 9$   $5\frac{3}{8}$

**11.** *(27)* $16\frac{1}{4} + 4\frac{3}{4}$   21

**12.** $y - 1\frac{7}{8} = 2\frac{3}{8}$   $4\frac{1}{4}$
(42)

**13.** $5.63 + 26.9 + 12 + w = 44.53$   0
(42)

**14.** $1 - q = 0.235$   0.765
(42)

**15.** $3.7 \times 0.25$   **16.** $\frac{3}{4} = \frac{?}{8}$   6   **17.** $\frac{3}{4} = \frac{?}{12}$   9
(39)   0.925   (41)   (41)

**18.** What is the least common multiple of 3, 4, and 8?   24
(30)

**19.** Compare: $\frac{1}{10}$ ⊜ 0.1
(43)

**20.** Which digit is in the thousandths' place in 1,234.5678?
(34)   7

**21.** Estimate the quotient when 3967 is divided by 48.
(16)   80

**22.** The area of a square is 100 square centimeters. How
(38)   long is each side?   10 cm

**23.** There are 100 centimeters in 1 meter and 1000 meters in
(7)   1 kilometer. How many centimeters are in 2 kilometers?
   200,000 cm

**24.** $\frac{1}{2} \cdot \frac{4}{5}$   $\frac{2}{5}$   **25.** $\left(\frac{3}{4}\right)\left(\frac{5}{3}\right)$   $1\frac{1}{4}$
(29)   (45)

**26.** If $b = 8$ and $h = 4$, then what number does $bh$ equal?
(45)   32

**27.** Use the commutative property of multiplication to
(45)   rearrange these factors in order from least to greatest.

$$3 \cdot 7 \cdot 2 \cdot 5 \cdot 2 \cdot 3 \cdot 3 \cdot 5$$
$2 \cdot 2 \cdot 3 \cdot 3 \cdot 3 \cdot 5 \cdot 5 \cdot 7$

**28.** Use your ruler to find the width of
(17)   this rectangle to the nearest eighth
   of an inch.   $\frac{3}{4}$ in.

**29.** (a) How many $\frac{3}{8}$'s are in 1?    $\frac{8}{3}$
(30)
    (b) Use your answer to part (a) to find the number of $\frac{3}{8}$'s in 3.    8

**30.** Rename $\frac{1}{2}$ and $\frac{1}{3}$ so that the denominators of the
(41)    renamed fractions are 6. Then add the renamed fractions.    $\frac{3}{6}, \frac{2}{6}; \frac{5}{6}$

## LESSON 46

# Mentally Multiplying Decimal Numbers by 10 and by 100

**Mental Math:**
**a.** 3700
**b.** 261
**c.** 37
**d.** $7.75
**e.** $6.25
**f.** $2.50
**g.** 1
**Problem Solving:**
    54

**Facts Practice:** 100 Multiplication Facts (Test E in Test Masters)

**Mental Math:** Count by 9's from 9 to 108.
    **a.** 4 × 925            **b.** 3 × 87            **c.** 56 − 19
    **d.** $9.00 − $1.25      **e.** $\frac{1}{2}$ of $12.50      **f.** $\frac{\$25.00}{10}$
    **g.** 6 × 8, + 2, × 2, −10, ÷ 9, + 5, ÷ 3, + 1, ÷ 6

**Problem Solving:** The average of two numbers is 44. If one of the numbers is 34, what is the other number?

When we multiply whole numbers by 10 or by 100 we may mentally attach zeros to the number we are multiplying to find the product.

$$24 \times 10 = 240$$

$$24 \times 100 = 2400$$

It may seem that we are just attaching zeros, but we are actually shifting the digits to the left. When we multiply 24 by 10, the digits shift one place to the left. When we multiply 24 by 100, the digits shift two places to the left. The zeros hold the 2 and the 4 in their proper places.

|                 | 1000s | 100s | 10s | 1s |          |
|-----------------|-------|------|-----|----|----------|
|                 |       |      | 2   | 4  | 24       |
| one-place shift |       | 2    | 4   | 0  | 24 × 10  |
| two-place shift | 2     | 4    | 0   | 0  | 24 × 100 |

When we multiply a decimal number by 10, the digits shift one place to the left. When we multiply by 100, the digits shift two places to the left. Here we show the products when 0.24 is multiplied by 10 and by 100.

| 10s | 1s | . | $\frac{1}{10}$s | $\frac{1}{100}$s | |
|---|---|---|---|---|---|
| | 0 | . | 2 | 4 | 0.24 |
| | 2 | . | 4 | | 0.24 × 10 |
| 2 | 4 | . | | | 0.24 × 100 |

Although it is the digits that are shifting one or two places to the left, we get the same effect by shifting the decimal point one or two places to the right.

$$0.24 \times 10 = 2.4 \qquad 0.24 \times 100 = 24$$
$$\text{one-place shift} \qquad \text{two-place shift}$$

**Example 1**   3.75 × 10

*Solution*   Since we are multiplying by 10, the product will have the same digits as 3.75, but the digits will be shifted one place. The product will be 10 times as large, so we mentally shift the decimal point one place to the right.

$$3.75 \times 10 = \textbf{37.5 } \text{(one-place shift)}$$

We do not need to attach any zeros because the decimal point serves to hold the digits in their proper places.

**Example 2**   3.75 × 100

*Solution*   Multiplying by 100, we mentally shift the decimal point two places to the right.

$$3.75 \times 100 = 375. \text{ (two-place shift)}$$

We do not need to attach zeros. Since there are no decimal places we may remove·the decimal point to simplify the answer.

Example 3   $\dfrac{1.2}{0.4} \times \dfrac{10}{10}$

*Solution*   Multiplying 1.2 and 0.4 by 10 shifts both decimal points one place.

$$\dfrac{1.2}{0.4} \times \dfrac{10}{10} = \dfrac{12}{4}$$

The expression $\frac{12}{4}$ means to divide 12 by 4.

$$\dfrac{12}{4} = \mathbf{3}$$

**Practice**   Mentally calculate the product of each multiplication:

**a.** $0.35 \times 10$   3.5

**b.** $0.35 \times 100$   35

**c.** $2.5 \times 10$   25

**d.** $2.5 \times 100$   250

**e.** $0.125 \times 10$   1.25

**f.** $0.125 \times 100$   12.5

Answer "true" or "false" to the following statements:

**g.** If 0.04 is multiplied by 10, the product is a whole number. false

**h.** If 0.04 is multiplied by 100, the product is a whole number. true

Multiply as shown. Then complete the division.

**i.** $\dfrac{1.5}{0.5} \times \dfrac{10}{10}$   3

**j.** $\dfrac{2.5}{0.05} \times \dfrac{100}{100}$   50

**Problem set 46**

**1.** *(10)* The first positive odd number is 1. The second is 3. What is the tenth positive odd number?   19

**2.** *(15)* Giant tidal waves can travel 500 miles per hour. How long would it take a tidal wave traveling at that speed to cross 3000 miles of ocean?   6 hr

**3.** *(15)* José bought Carmen one dozen red roses, two for each month he had known her. How long had he known her?   6 months

**4.** *(42)* $m - 1.25 = 3.75$   5

**5.** *(39)* $(0.5)(0.12)$   0.06

**6.** If $s = \frac{1}{2}$, then what number does $4s$ equal?  2
(45)

7. $(6 \times 1)$
  $+ \left(2 \times \frac{1}{10}\right)$
  $+ \left(5 \times \frac{1}{100}\right)$

**7.** Write 6.25 in expanded notation.
(45)

**8.** Write 99% as a fraction. Then write the fraction as a
(33)  decimal number.   $\frac{99}{100}$; 0.99

**9.** $12\overline{)0.18}$  0.015
(44)

**10.** $10\overline{)12.30}$  1.23
(44)

**11.** $w \div 12 = 36$
(4)   432

**12.** $5y = 1.25$   0.25
(42)

**13.** Three of the twelve months begin with the letter $J$.
(29)  What fraction of the months begin with $J$?   $\frac{1}{4}$

**14.** $n + 5\frac{11}{12} = 10$   $4\frac{1}{12}$
(42)

**15.** $m - 6\frac{2}{5} = 3\frac{3}{5}$   10
(42)

**16.** $8\frac{3}{4} + 5\frac{3}{4}$   $14\frac{1}{2}$
(27)

**17.** $\frac{5}{3} \times \frac{5}{4}$   $2\frac{1}{12}$
(29)

**18.** $\frac{3}{4} = \frac{?}{20}$   15
(41)

**19.** $\frac{3}{5} = \frac{?}{20}$   12
(41)

**20.** Bob's scores on his first five tests were 18, 20, 18, 20,
(18)  and 20. His average score is closest to which of these
  numbers?   C. 19

  A. 17        B. 18        C. 19        D. 20

**21.** Which factors of 20 are also factors of 30?   1, 2, 5, 10
(19)

**22.** Mentally calculate the product of 6.25 and 10.   62.5
(46)

**23.** Multiply as shown. Then complete the division.   2.5
(46)

$$\frac{1.25}{0.5} \cdot \frac{10}{10}$$

**24.** What number is equal to "threescore and ten"?
(5)  (Remember, a score is 20.)   70

**25.** Use the chart to find out how many more days it takes
(13) Mars to go around the sun than it takes the earth to go
around the sun.   322 days

| Planet | Earth days to orbit the sun |
|--------|-----------------------------|
| Mercury | 88 |
| Venus | 225 |
| Earth | 365 |
| Mars | 687 |

**26.** In the time it takes Mars to travel around the sun once,
(15) Venus travels around the sun about how many times?
3

**27.** Use your ruler to find the length
(17) and width of this rectangle.
length, 1 in.; width, $\frac{3}{4}$ in.

**28.** Calculate the perimeter of the rectangle in problem 27.
(8)   $3\frac{1}{2}$ in.

**29.** Rename $\frac{2}{5}$ so the denominator of the renamed fraction
(41) is 10. Then subtract the renamed fraction from $\frac{9}{10}$.
Remember to reduce the answer.   $\frac{4}{10}$; $\frac{1}{2}$

**30.** When we mentally multiply 15 by 10, we may think of
(46) attaching a zero to 15 to make the product 150. When we
multiply 1.5 by 10, why can't we attach a zero to make the
product 1.50?   The numbers 1.5 and 1.50 are equivalent.
Attaching a zero to a decimal number does not shift place values. To
multiply 1.5 by 10, we may move the decimal point one place to the
right, which shifts the place values and makes the product 15.

## LESSON 47

# Subtracting Mixed Numbers with Regrouping, Part 1

**Facts Practice:** 30 Fractions to Reduce (Test G in Test Masters)

**Mental Math:** Count up and down by $\frac{1}{8}$'s between $\frac{1}{8}$ and 3.

**a.** $8 \times 25$  **b.** $630 - 50$  **c.** $62 + 19$
**d.** $\$4.50 + 75¢$  **e.** $\frac{1}{2}$ of $15.00  **f.** $\frac{\$25.00}{100}$
**g.** $4 \times 7, -1, \div 3, \times 4, \div 6, \times 3, \div 2$

**Problem Solving:** Brad's first two test scores were 85 and 85. What score does he need on his third test to have an average score of 90 on his first three tests?

Here is another "some went away" story about pies.

*There were $4\frac{1}{6}$ pies on the restaurant shelf. The server sliced one of the whole pies into sixths. Then the server removed $1\frac{2}{6}$ pies. How many pies were left on the shelf?*

We will illustrate this story with circles. There were $4\frac{1}{6}$ pies on the shelf.

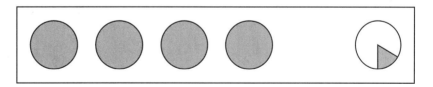

The server sliced one of the pies into sixths. This makes $3\frac{7}{6}$ pies, which equals $4\frac{1}{6}$ pies.

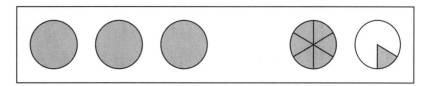

The server removed $1\frac{2}{6}$ pies. So $2\frac{5}{6}$ pies were left on the shelf.

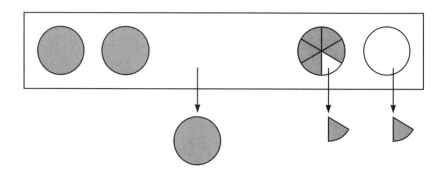

Now we will show the arithmetic for subtracting $1\frac{2}{6}$ from $4\frac{1}{6}$.

$$4\frac{1}{6} \text{ pies}$$
$$-1\frac{2}{6} \text{ pies}$$

We cannot subtract $\frac{2}{6}$ from $\frac{1}{6}$, so we will rename $4\frac{1}{6}$. Just as the server sliced one of the pies into sixths, so we will take one of the four wholes and change it to $\frac{6}{6}$. This makes three wholes plus $\frac{6}{6}$ plus $\frac{1}{6}$. We combine the $\frac{6}{6}$ and $\frac{1}{6}$, which makes $3\frac{7}{6}$.

$$
\begin{array}{c}
4\frac{1}{6} \\
-\,1\frac{2}{6}
\end{array}
\xrightarrow{\;3 + \frac{6}{6} + \frac{1}{6}\;}
\begin{array}{c}
3\frac{7}{6} \text{ pies} \\
-\,1\frac{2}{6} \text{ pies} \\
\hline
2\frac{5}{6} \text{ pies}
\end{array}
$$

**Example**     $5\frac{1}{3} - 2\frac{2}{3}$

*Solution*  We cannot subtract $\frac{2}{3}$ from $\frac{1}{3}$, so we will rename $5\frac{1}{3}$. We take one of the five wholes and make $\frac{3}{3}$. Then we combine $\frac{3}{3}$ and $\frac{1}{3}$ to make $4\frac{4}{3}$. Now we subtract.

$$
\begin{array}{c}
5\frac{1}{3} \\
-\,2\frac{2}{3}
\end{array}
\xrightarrow{\;4 + \frac{3}{3} + \frac{1}{3}\;}
\begin{array}{c}
4\frac{4}{3} \\
-\,2\frac{2}{3} \\
\hline
2\frac{2}{3}
\end{array}
$$

**Practice\*** **a.** $4\frac{1}{3}$  $2\frac{2}{3}$     **b.** $3\frac{2}{5}$  $\frac{4}{5}$     **c.** $5\frac{2}{4}$  $3\frac{3}{4}$

$\qquad\qquad -1\frac{2}{3} \qquad\qquad\qquad -2\frac{3}{5} \qquad\qquad\qquad -1\frac{3}{4}$

**d.** $5\frac{1}{8}$  $2\frac{5}{8}$     **e.** $7\frac{3}{12}$  $2\frac{5}{12}$     **f.** $6\frac{1}{4}$  $3\frac{1}{2}$

$\qquad\qquad -2\frac{4}{8} \qquad\qquad\qquad -4\frac{10}{12} \qquad\qquad\qquad -2\frac{3}{4}$

**Problem set 47**

**1.** The average of two numbers is ten. What is the sum of
(18) the two numbers?    20

**2.** What would be the cost of 10.0 gallons of gasoline
(46) priced at $1.449 per gallon?    $14.49

**3.** The movie started at 11:45 a.m. and ended at 1:20 p.m.
(32) The movie was how many hours and minutes long?
1 hr, 35 min

**4.** Three of these numbers are equal to each other. Which
(43) number is different?    B. 0.2

A. $\frac{1}{2}$     B. 0.2     C. 0.5     D. $\frac{10}{20}$

**5.** Arrange these numbers in order from least to greatest:
(43)
1.02   0.102   0.12   1.20
0.102, 0.12, 1.02, 1.20

**6.** 0.1 + 0.2 + 0.3 + 0.4     **7.** (8)(0.125)   1
(37) 1               (39)

**8.** The hike to the waterfall was 3 miles. After hiking 2.1
(11) miles, how many more miles was it to the waterfall?
0.9 mi

**9.** Estimate the sum of 4967, 8142, and 6890.    20,000
(16)

**10.** $8\overline{)0.144}$  0.018     **11.** $6\overline{)0.9}$  0.15     **12.** $4\overline{)0.9}$  0.225
(44)             (44)            (44)

**13.** What is the price of 100 pens at 39¢ each?    $39.00
(46)

**14.** Write $(5 \times 10) + (6 \times \frac{1}{10}) + (4 \times \frac{1}{100})$ as a standard
(45) number.    50.64

**15.** What is the least common multiple of 6 and 8?    24
(30)

**16.**
(42)
$w - 7\dfrac{7}{12} = 5\dfrac{5}{12}$   13

**17.**
(42)
$12 - m = 5\dfrac{2}{3}$   $6\dfrac{1}{3}$

**18.**
(42)
$n + 2\dfrac{3}{4} = 5\dfrac{1}{4}$   $2\dfrac{1}{2}$

**19.**
(45)
$\left(\dfrac{9}{10}\right)\left(\dfrac{3}{2}\right)$   $1\dfrac{7}{20}$

**20.** What number is $\frac{5}{6}$ of 60?   50
(22)

**21.** The temperature rose from −12°F to 5°F. How many
(14) degrees did the temperature rise?   17°F

**22.** What number is halfway between 440 and 660?   550
(18)

**23.**
(41)
$\dfrac{3}{8} = \dfrac{?}{24}$   9

**24.** The perimeter of this square is
(8) four feet. What is the perimeter in
inches?   48 in.

**25.** The area of this square is one
(31) square foot. What is the area in
square inches?   144 sq. in.

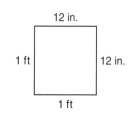

**26.** If $r = 60$ and $t = 4$, then what does $rt$ equal?   240
(45)

**27.** Seventy-five percent of the 32 chairs in the room were
(33) occupied. Write 75% as a reduced fraction. Then find
the number of chairs that were occupied.   $\frac{3}{4}$; 24

**28.** Rename $\frac{1}{3}$ and $\frac{1}{4}$ as fractions with denominators of 12.
(41) Then add the renamed fractions.   $\frac{4}{12}, \frac{3}{12}; \frac{7}{12}$

**29.** Multiply as shown. Then simplify the answer.   5
(46)

$$\dfrac{3.5}{0.7} \cdot \dfrac{10}{10}$$

**30.** There were $3\frac{1}{6}$ pies on the shelf. Explain how the server
(47) can take $1\frac{5}{6}$ pies from the shelf.   The server can cut one of
the whole pies into $\frac{6}{6}$. Then there will be $2\frac{7}{6}$ pies on the shelf.
The server can remove $1\frac{5}{6}$ pies, and there will be $1\frac{2}{6}$ pies left on
the shelf.

LESSON
**48**

# Dividing by a Decimal Number

**Mental Math:**
**a.** 1000
**b.** 340
**c.** 39
**d.** $1.75
**e.** $15.00
**f.** 40
**g.** 5
**Problem Solving:**
    0

**Facts Practice:** 72 Mixed Multiplication and Division (Test H in Test Masters)

**Mental Math:** Count by 12's from 12 to 120.
  **a.** $(8 \times 100) + (8 \times 25)$     **b.** $290 + 50$     **c.** $58 - 19$
  **d.** $5.00 - $3.25         **e.** $\frac{1}{2}$ of $30.00     **f.** $\frac{4000}{100}$
  **g.** $5 \times 10, \div 2, + 5, \div 2, + 5, \div 2, \div 2$

**Problem Solving:** The P.E. class ran around the school block, starting and finishing at point *A*. Instead of running all the way around the block, Brad took what he called his "shortcut," shown by the dotted line in the diagram. How many meters of running did Brad save by taking his "shortcut"?

When the **divisor** of a division problem is a decimal number, we change the problem so that the divisor is a whole number.

$$0.4\overline{)1.24}$$

$$\frac{1.24}{0.4}$$

The divisor is a decimal number. We will change the problem before we divide.

One way to change the problem is to multiply the divisor and the dividend by 10. Notice that multiplying both numbers by 10 does not change the division answer.

$$4\overline{)8}^{\,2} \quad \longrightarrow \quad 40\overline{)80}^{\,2}$$

Multiplying 4 and 8 by 10 does not change the answer.

If we multiply the divisor and dividend by 10 in $\frac{1.24}{0.4}$, the new problem has a whole number divisor.

$$\text{decimal} \rightarrow \frac{1.24}{0.4} \times \frac{10}{10} = \frac{12.4}{4} \leftarrow \text{whole number divisor}$$

We divide 12.4 by 4 to find the quotient.

$$\begin{array}{r} 3.1 \\ 4\overline{)12.4} \end{array}$$

**Example 1** $\dfrac{1.24}{0.04}$

*Solution* The divisor, 0.04, is a decimal number with two decimal places. To make the divisor a whole number, we will multiply $\frac{1.24}{0.04}$ by $\frac{100}{100}$ to shift the decimal point two places.

$$\frac{1.24}{0.04} \times \frac{100}{100} = \frac{124}{4}$$

We divide and find the quotient is **31**.

$$\begin{array}{r} 31 \\ 4\overline{)124} \\ \underline{12\phantom{4}} \\ 04 \\ \underline{4} \\ 0 \end{array}$$

**Example 2** $0.6\overline{)1.44}$

*Solution* The divisor, 0.6, has one decimal place. If we multiply the divisor and dividend by 10, we will shift the decimal point one place in both numbers.

$$0.6\overline{)1.44}$$

This makes a new problem with a whole number divisor.

$$\begin{array}{r} 2.4 \\ 6{\overline{\smash{\big)}\,14.4}} \\ \underline{12\phantom{.4}} \\ 2\,4 \\ \underline{2\,4} \\ 0 \end{array}$$

Some people think of the phrase "over, over, and up" to remind themselves of how to keep track of the decimal points when dividing by decimal numbers.

$$\overset{\text{up}}{0{,}6{\overline{\smash{\big)}\,1{,}44}}}$$
over  over

**Practice\***   **a.** We would multiply the divisor and dividend of $\frac{1.44}{1.2}$ by what number to make the divisor a whole number?   10

**b.** We would multiply the divisor and dividend of $0.12{\overline{\smash{\big)}\,0.144}}$ by what number to make the divisor a whole number?   100

Change each problem so that the divisor is a whole number. Then divide.

**c.** $\dfrac{0.24}{0.4}$   $\frac{2.4}{4} = 0.6$       **d.** $\dfrac{9}{0.3}$   $\frac{90}{3} = 30$

**e.** $0.05{\overline{\smash{\big)}\,2.5}}$   $5{\overline{\smash{\big)}\,250}} = 50$     **f.** $0.3{\overline{\smash{\big)}\,12}}$   $3{\overline{\smash{\big)}\,120}} = 40$

**g.** $0.24 \div 0.8$   $2.4 \div 8 = 0.3$    **h.** $0.3 \div 0.03$   $30 \div 3 = 10$

**i.** $0.05{\overline{\smash{\big)}\,0.4}}$   $5{\overline{\smash{\big)}\,40}} = 8$       **j.** $0.2 \div 0.4$   $2 \div 4 = 0.5$

**Problem set**   **1.** When the product of 0.2 and 0.3 is subtracted from the
**48**   $^{(39)}$   sum of 0.2 and 0.3, what is the difference?   0.44

**2.**
$1.00

| 20¢ |
| 20¢ |
| 20¢ |
| 20¢ |
| 20¢ |

$\frac{4}{5}$ of $1.00 = 80¢

**2.** Four fifths of a dollar is how many cents? Draw a
(22) diagram to illustrate the problem.   80¢

**3.** Dolores went to sleep at 9:15 p.m. and woke up at
(32) 7:15 a.m. How many hours did she sleep?   10 hr

**4.** If each side of a square is 2.4 cm, then what is the
(38) perimeter of the square?   9.6 cm

**5.** Compare: 0.31 $\bigcirc >$ 0.301
(43)

**6.** 0.67 + 2 + 1.33   4         **7.** 12(0.25)   3
(38)                               (39)

**8.** 0.07$\overline{)3.5}$  $\overset{50}{}$        **9.** 0.5$\overline{)12}$  $\overset{24}{}$
(48)                               (48)

**10.** 8$\overline{)0.14}$  $\overset{0.0175}{}$      **11.** $m + 7\frac{1}{4} = 15$   $7\frac{3}{4}$
(44)                               (42)

**12.** $n - 6\frac{1}{8} = 4\frac{3}{8}$   $10\frac{1}{2}$    **13.** $\frac{5}{6} = \frac{?}{24}$   20
(42)                               (41)

**14.** $5 - m = 1.37$   3.63      **15.** $(0.012)(1.5)$   0.018
(42)                               (39)

**16.** Write the decimal number one and twelve thousandths.
(35)   1.012

**17.** $5\frac{7}{10} + 4\frac{9}{10}$   $10\frac{3}{5}$     **18.** $\frac{5}{2} \cdot \frac{5}{3}$   $4\frac{1}{6}$
(27)                               (29)

**19.** $\frac{0.125}{0.05}$   2.5
(48)

**20.** There are 24 hours in a day. Jim sleeps 8 hours each
(29) night. Eight hours is what fraction of a day?   $\frac{1}{3}$

1, 2, 3, 6   **21.** List the factors that 12 and 18 have **in common.** (That
(19) is, list the numbers that are factors of **both** 12 and 18.)

**22.** What is the average of 1.2, 1.3, and 1.7?     1.4
(18)

**23.** Estimate the difference of 5670 and 3940 to the nearest
(16)     thousand.     2000

**24.** (a) How many $\frac{3}{4}$'s are in 1?     $\frac{4}{3}$
(30)

    (b) Use your answer to part (a) to find the number of
      $\frac{3}{4}$'s in 4.     $5\frac{1}{3}$

**25.** Refer to this number line to answer the following
(17)     questions about points $x$, $y$, and $z$.

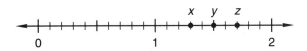

    (a) Which point is halfway between 1 and 2?     $y$

    (b) Which point is closer to 1 than 2?     $x$

    (c) Which point is closer to 2 than 1?     $z$

**26.** Multiply and divide as indicated: $\dfrac{2 \cdot 3 \cdot 2 \cdot 5 \cdot 7}{2 \cdot 5 \cdot 7}$     6
(45)

**27.** We can find the number of quarters in three dollars by
(48)     dividing $3.00 by $0.25. Show this division using the
    pencil-and-paper method taught in this lesson.     12

**28.** Use your ruler to find the length
(8)     of each side of this square to the
    nearest eighth of an inch. Then
    calculate the perimeter of the
    square.     side, $\frac{3}{4}$ in.; perimeter, 3 in.

**29.** Ninety percent of the 20 answers on the test were
(33)     correct. Write 90% as a reduced fraction. Then find
    the number of correct answers on the test.     $\frac{9}{10}$; 18

**30.** Sam was given the following division problem:
(48)

$$\frac{2.5}{0.5}$$

Instead of multiplying the numerator and denominator by 10, he accidentally multiplied by 100.

$$\frac{2.5}{0.5} \times \frac{100}{100} = \frac{250}{50}$$

Then he divided 250 by 50 and found that the quotient was 5. Did Sam find the correct answer to 2.5 ÷ 0.5? Why or why not?    Yes, Sam found the correct answer. Both $\frac{10}{10}$ and $\frac{100}{100}$ are equal to 1. When we multiply a number by different fraction names for one, the numbers may look different, but they are equal. So $\frac{2.5}{0.5}$, $\frac{25}{5}$, and $\frac{250}{50}$ are three equivalent problems with the same quotient.

## LESSON
## 49

# Decimal Number Line (Tenths) •
# Dividing by a Fraction

**Mental Math:**
a. 1800
b. 315
c. 85
d. $2.44
e. $12.50
f. 500
g. 1

**Problem Solving:**

| Steps | Blocks |
|-------|--------|
| 1 | 1 |
| 2 | 3 |
| 3 | 6 |
| 4 | 10 |
| 5 | 15 |
| 6 | 21 |
| 7 | 28 |
| 8 | 36 |
| 9 | 45 |
| 10 | 55 |

---

**Facts Practice:** 30 Fractions to Reduce (Test G in Test Masters)

**Mental Math:** Count by 7's from 7 to 84.

a. $(8 \times 200) + (8 \times 25)$     b. $565 - 250$     c. $58 + 27$
d. $1.45 + 99¢                          e. $\frac{1}{2}$ of $25.00     f. $\frac{5000}{10}$
g. $8 \times 9, + 3, \div 3, - 1, \div 3, + 1, \div 3, \div 3$

**Problem Solving:** Sheldon began building stair-step patterns with blocks. He used one block for a one-step pattern, three blocks for a two-step pattern, and six blocks for a three-step pattern. He wrote the information in a table. Copy the table and complete it through a ten-step pattern.

**Blocks needed to make pattern**

| Steps | Blocks |
|-------|--------|
| 1 | 1 |
| 2 | 3 |
| 3 | 6 |
| 4 | |
| 5 | |
| 6 | |
| 7 | |
| 8 | |
| 9 | |
| 10 | |

---

**Decimal number line (tenths)**

We can locate different kinds of numbers on the number line. We have learned to locate whole numbers, negative numbers, and fractions on the number line. We can also locate decimal numbers on the number line.

The distance between the whole numbers has been divided into 10 equal lengths. Each length is $\frac{1}{10}$ of the distance between the whole numbers. The arrow is pointing to a mark three spaces beyond the 1. The mark it is pointing to is $1\frac{3}{10}$. We can rename $\frac{3}{10}$ as the decimal 0.3, so we can say that the arrow is pointing to the mark 1.3. When a unit has been divided into 10 spaces, we normally use the decimal form instead of the fractional form to name the mark.

**Example 1**    What decimal number is represented by point $y$ on this number line?

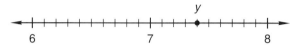

**Solution**    The distance from 7 to 8 has been divided into ten smaller segments. Point $y$ is four segments to the right of the whole number 7. So point $y$ represents $7\frac{4}{10}$. We write $7\frac{4}{10}$ as the decimal number **7.4.**

**Dividing by a fraction**    The following question can be answered by dividing by a decimal number or by dividing by a fraction.

How many quarters are in three dollars?

If we think of a quarter as $\frac{1}{4}$ of a dollar, we have this division problem.

$$3 \div \frac{1}{4} \quad \text{"How many quarters are in three?"}$$

We take two steps to solve this type of problem. First we answer this question, "How many quarters are in one dollar?" The answer to this question is the reciprocal of $\frac{1}{4}$, which is $\frac{4}{1}$ or just 4.

$$1 \div \frac{1}{4} = \frac{4}{1}, \text{ which is 4}$$

Then we use the answer to this question to find the number of quarters in three dollars. There are four quarters in one dollar, so there are three times as many quarters in three dollars. For the second step, we multiply 3 times 4 and find there are 12 quarters in three dollars.

number of quarters in one dollar

$$3 \times 4 = 12$$

number of quarters in three dollars

We will review the steps we took to solve the problem.

Original problem: How many quarters are in $3? $3 \div \dfrac{1}{4}$

Step 1: Find the number of quarters in $1. $1 \div \dfrac{1}{4} = 4$

Step 2: Use the number of quarters in 1$ to find the number in $3.

$3 \times 4 = 12$

**Example 2** The diameter of a penny is $\frac{3}{4}$ of an inch. How many pennies are needed to make a row of pennies 6 inches long?

*Solution* In effect, this problem asks, "How many $\frac{3}{4}$-inch segments are in 6 inches?" We can write the question this way.

$$6 \div \dfrac{3}{4}$$

We will take two steps. First we will find the number of pennies—the number of $\frac{3}{4}$-inch segments—in one inch. The number of $\frac{3}{4}$'s in 1 is the reciprocal of $\frac{3}{4}$, which is $\frac{4}{3}$.

$$1 \div \dfrac{3}{4} = \dfrac{4}{3}$$

Four thirds of a penny is $1\frac{1}{3}$ pennies. There are $1\frac{1}{3}$ pennies in an inch. However, we will not convert $\frac{4}{3}$ to the mixed number $1\frac{1}{3}$. Instead, we will use $\frac{4}{3}$ in the second step of the solution. Since there are $\frac{4}{3}$ pennies in 1 inch, there are six times as many in 6 inches. So we multiply 6 times $\frac{4}{3}$. We find the number of pennies in a 6-inch row is **8.**

$$6 \times \dfrac{4}{3} = \dfrac{24}{3}, \text{ which is } 8$$

We will review the steps of the solution.

Original problem: How many $\frac{3}{4}$'s are in 6?    $6 \div \dfrac{3}{4}$

   Step 1:  Find the number of $\frac{3}{4}$'s in 1.    $1 \div \dfrac{3}{4} = \dfrac{4}{3}$

   Step 2:  Use the number of $\frac{3}{4}$'s in 1 to find the number in 6. Then simplify the answer.

$$6 \times \dfrac{4}{3} = \dfrac{24}{3}$$
$$\dfrac{24}{3} = 8$$

**Practice**  To which decimal number is each arrow pointing?

a. 0.1
b. 0.5
c. 0.9
d. 1.2
e. 1.6
f. 1.8

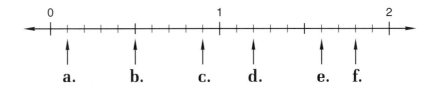

   **g.** Write and solve a fraction division problem to find the number of quarters in four dollars. Follow this pattern.

      Original problem    $4 \div \frac{1}{4}$
      Step 1    $1 \div \frac{1}{4} = 4$
      Step 2    $4 \times 4 = 16$

h.   Original problem:

$$12 \div \dfrac{3}{8}$$

Step 1: $1 \div \dfrac{3}{8} = \dfrac{8}{3}$

Step 2: $12 \times \dfrac{8}{3} = 32$

   **h.** Write and solve a fraction division problem for this question:

     *Pads of writing paper were stacked 12 inches high on a shelf. The thickness of each pad was $\frac{3}{8}$ of an inch. How many pads were in a 12-inch stack?*    32 pads

**Problem set 49**

   **1.** The first three positive odd numbers are 1, 3, and 5.
   *(10)* Their sum is 9. The first five positive odd numbers are 1, 3, 5, 7, and 9. Their sum is 25. What is the sum of the first ten positive odd numbers?    100

**2.** Jack keeps each of his cassette
(49) tapes in a plastic box that is $\frac{5}{8}$ of
an inch high. How many boxes
are in a stack 10 inches high?   16

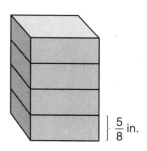

$\frac{5}{8}$ in.

**3.** The boxing match ended after two minutes of the 12th
(15) round. Each of the first eleven rounds lasted three
minutes. For how many minutes did the contenders box?
35 minutes

**4.** Compare: 3.4 $\left(>\right)$ 3.389   **5.** Compare: 0.60 $\left(=\right)$ 0.600
(43)                                    (43)

**6.** 7.25 + 2 + $w$ = 10       **7.** (3.75)(2.4)   9
(42) 0.75                    (39)

**8.** 1 − 0.97   0.03        **9.** $0.12\overline{)7.2}$   60
(38)                          (48)

**10.** $0.4\overline{)7}$   17.5            **11.** $6\overline{)0.138}$   0.023
(48)                          (44)

**12.** $w + \dfrac{5}{12} = 1$   **13.** $6\dfrac{1}{8} - x = 1\dfrac{7}{8}$   **14.** $\dfrac{3}{4} = \dfrac{?}{24}$   18
(42)   $\frac{7}{12}$        (42)   $4\frac{1}{4}$      (41)

**15.** Write 7% as a fraction. Then change the fraction to a
(33) decimal number.   $\frac{7}{100}$; 0.07

**16.** Which digit in 4.637 is in the same place as the 2 in 85.21?
(34)   6

**17.** One hundred centimeters equal
(31) one meter. How many square
centimeters equal one square
meter?   10,000 sq. cm

100 cm

1 m   100 cm

1 m

**18.** What is the least common multiple of 6 and 9?   18
(30)

**19.** $6\dfrac{5}{8} + 4\dfrac{5}{8}$   $11\frac{1}{4}$   **20.** $\dfrac{8}{3} \cdot \dfrac{3}{1}$   8   **21.** $\dfrac{2}{3} \cdot \dfrac{3}{4}$   $\frac{1}{2}$
(27)                      (29)              (29)

**22.** If you sleep 8 hours each day, what fraction of the day
(29) do you **not** sleep?   $\frac{2}{3}$

**23.** Find the average of 2.4, 6.3, and 5.7.   4.8
(18)

**24.** What factors do 18 and 24 have in common?   1, 2, 3, 6
(19)

**25.** What decimal number corresponds to point $A$ on this
(49) number line?   5.3

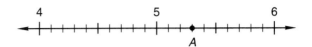

**26.** $\dfrac{2 \cdot 3 \cdot 5 \cdot 7}{2 \cdot 5}$   21
(45)

**27.** 0.375 × 100   37.5
(46)

**28.** Rename $\frac{1}{3}$ as a fraction with 6 as the denominator.
(41) Then subtract the renamed fraction from $\frac{5}{6}$. Remember
to reduce your answer.   $\frac{2}{6}$; $\frac{1}{2}$

**29.** Points $x$, $y$, and $z$ are three points on this number line.
(49) Refer to the number line to answer the following
questions.

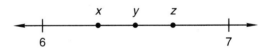

(a) Which point is halfway between 6 and 7?   $y$

(b) Which point corresponds to $6\frac{7}{10}$?   $z$

(c) Which point corresponds to a number that would
be closest to 6?   $x$

**30.** Which of these numbers is divisible by both 2 and 5?
(19)      A. 552        B. 255        C. 250        D. 525
C. 250

LESSON
**50**

# Rounding Decimal Numbers

**Mental Math:**
**a.** 1000
**b.** 272
**c.** 35
**d.** $5.63
**e.** $75.00
**f.** $1.00
**g.** 20
**Problem Solving:**

$$\begin{array}{r} 99 \\ 9\overline{)891} \\ \underline{81} \\ 81 \\ \underline{81} \\ 0 \end{array}$$

**Facts Practice:** 72 Mixed Multiplication and Division (Test H in Test Masters)

**Mental Math:** Count up and down by $\frac{1}{8}$'s between $\frac{1}{8}$ and 3.

**a.** $8 \times 125$      **b.** $4 \times 68$      **c.** $64 - 29$
**d.** $4.64 + 99¢      **e.** $\frac{1}{2}$ of $150.00      **f.** $\frac{\$100.00}{100}$
**g.** $8 \times 8, - 4, \div 2, + 2, \div 4, + 2, \div 5, \times 10$

**Problem Solving:** Copy this problem and fill in the missing digits.

$$\begin{array}{r} 9\,\_ \\ 9\overline{)\_9\_} \\ \underline{==} \\ --\\ \underline{==} \\ 0 \end{array}$$

It is often necessary to round decimal numbers. For instance, money is usually rounded to two places after the decimal point because we do not have a coin smaller than one hundredth of a dollar.

**Example 1** Dan wanted to buy a tape for $6.89. The sales tax rate was 8%. Dan calculated the sales tax. He knew that 8% equaled the fraction $\frac{8}{100}$ and the decimal 0.08. To figure the amount of tax, he multiplied the price $6.89 by the sales tax rate 0.08.

$$\begin{array}{r} \$6.89 \\ \times\ 0.08 \\ \hline \$0.5512 \end{array}$$

How much tax would Dan need to pay?

**Solution** Sales tax is rounded to the nearest cent, which is two places to the right of the decimal point. We will mark the places that will be included in the answer.

$$\underline{\$0.55}\,|\,12$$

Next we decide the possible answers. We see that $0.5512 is a little more than $0.55 but less than $0.56. We will decide whether $0.5512 is closer to $0.55 or $0.56 by looking at the next digit. If the next digit is 5 or more, we round up to $0.56. If the next digit is less than 5, we round down to $0.55. Since the next digit is 1, we round $0.5512 down. If Dan buys the tape he will need to pay **$0.55** sales tax.

**Example 2**    Sheila pulled into the gas station and filled the car's tank with 10.381 gallons of gasoline. Round the amount of gasoline she purchased to the nearest tenth of a gallon.

*Solution*    Tenths is one place to the right of the decimal point. We will mark the places that will be included in the answer.

$$\underline{10.3} \mid 81$$

Next we determine what our possible answers may be. The number we are rounding is more than 10.3 but less than 10.4. Our answer will be one of these two numbers. We decide that 10.381 is closer to 10.4 because the digit in the next place is 8, and we round up when the next digit is 5 or more. Sheila bought about **10.4** gallons of gasoline.

**Example 3**    Estimate the product of 6.85 and 4.2 by rounding the numbers to the nearest whole number before multiplying.

*Solution*    We mark the whole-number places.

$$\underline{6} \mid 85 \qquad \underline{4} \mid 2$$

We see that 6.85 is more than 6 but less than 7. The next digit, 8, shows that 6.85 is closer to 7. The number 4.2 is more than 4 but less than 5. The next digit, 2, shows that 4.2 is closer to 4. So 6.85 rounds to 7, and 4.2 rounds to 4.

We multiply the rounded numbers.

$$7 \cdot 4 = 28$$

We estimate that the product of 6.85 and 4.2 is about **28.**

**Practice***    Round to the nearest cent:

   **a.** $6.6666   $6.67   **b.** $0.4625   $0.46   **c.** $0.08333 $0.08

Round to the nearest tenth:

   **d.** 0.12    0.1       **e.** 12.345    12.3     **f.** 2.375    2.4

Round to the nearest whole number:

   **g.** 16.75    17       **h.** 4.875    5       **i.** 73.29    73

**Problem set 50**

**1.** $^{(26)}$ When the third multiple of 8 is subtracted from the fourth multiple of 6, what is the difference?   0

**2.** $^{(37)}$ From Brad's home to school is 3.5 miles. How far does Brad travel riding from home to school and back home?
7 mi

**3.** $^{(13)}$ Napoleon I was born in 1769. How old was he when he was crowned emperor of France in 1804?   35 years

**4.** $^{(50)}$ Round $0.1625 to the nearest cent.   $0.16

**5.** $^{(50)}$ Round 2.375 to the nearest tenth.   2.4

6. The whole number part of 12.75 is 12. The next digit, 7, is 5 or more, so we round up to the next whole number, 13.

**6.** $^{(50)}$ Explain how to round 12.75 to the nearest whole number.

**7.** $^{(37)}$ 0.125 + 0.25 + 0.375     **8.** $^{(42)}$ 0.399 + $w$ = 0.4   0.001
0.75

**9.** $^{(48)}$ $\dfrac{4}{0.25}$   16     **10.** $^{(44)}$ $4\overline{)0.5}$  $\overset{0.125}{}$     **11.** $^{(44)}$ 3.25 ÷ 10   0.325

**12.** $^{(47)}$ $3\dfrac{5}{12} - 1\dfrac{7}{12}$    **13.** $^{(41)}$ $\dfrac{5}{8} = \dfrac{?}{24}$   15    **14.** $^{(47)}$ $20 - 17\dfrac{3}{4}$   $2\dfrac{1}{4}$
$1\dfrac{5}{6}$

**15.** $^{(39)}$ (0.19)(0.21)   0.0399     **16.** $^{(35)}$ Write 0.01 as a fraction.   $\dfrac{1}{100}$

**17.** $^{(45)}$ Write $(6 \times 10) + \left(7 \times \dfrac{1}{100}\right)$ as a decimal number.
60.07

**18.** $^{(31)}$ How many square inches are needed to cover the area of the rectangle?   288 sq. in.

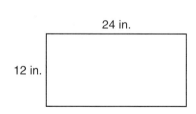

24 in.

12 in.

**19.** What is the least common multiple of 2, 3, and 4?
*(30)*  12

**20.** $5\dfrac{3}{10} + 6\dfrac{9}{10}$   $12\frac{1}{5}$
*(27)*

**21.** $\dfrac{10}{3} \times \dfrac{1}{2}$   $1\frac{2}{3}$
*(29)*

**22.** A collection of paperback books was stacked 12 inches
*(49)*  high. Each book in the stack was $\frac{3}{4}$ inch thick. Use the method described in Lesson 49 to find the number of books in the stack.   16

**23.** Estimate the quotient when 4876 is divided by 98.
*(16)*  50

**24.** What factors do 16 and 24 have in common?
*(19)*  1, 2, 4, 8

**25.** Estimate the product of 11.8 and 3.89 by rounding the
*(50)*  factors to the nearest whole number before multiplying.
48

**26.** Find the average of the decimal numbers that
*(49)*  correspond to points $x$ and $y$ on this number line.   1

**27.** $\dfrac{2 \cdot 2 \cdot 3 \cdot 3 \cdot 5}{2 \cdot 2 \cdot 3 \cdot 5}$   3
*(45)*

**28.** Mentally calculate the total price of ten pounds of
*(46)*  bananas at $0.79 per pound.   $7.90

**29.** Rename $\frac{2}{3}$ and $\frac{3}{4}$ as fractions with 12 as the
*(41)*  denominator. Then add the renamed fractions. Write the sum as a mixed number.   $\frac{8}{12}, \frac{9}{12}$; $1\frac{5}{12}$

**30.** How many $0.40 pens can Sam buy for $10.00? Show
*(48)*  the division using the method taught in Lesson 48.

$\dfrac{\$10.00}{\$0.40} \times \dfrac{100}{100} = \dfrac{\$1000}{\$40} = 25$ pens

# Mentally Dividing Decimal Numbers by 10 and by 100

**Mental Math:**
a. 1000
b. 218
c. 349
d. $22.50
e. $2\frac{1}{2}$
f. 800
g. 25
**Problem Solving:**
96%

**Facts Practice:** 30 Fractions to Reduce (Test G in Test Masters)

**Mental Math:** Count by 12's from 12 to 132.

| | | |
|---|---|---|
| **a.** 4 × 250 | **b.** 368 − 150 | **c.** 250 + 99 |
| **d.** $15.00 + $7.50 | **e.** $\frac{1}{2}$ of 5 | **f.** 20 × 40 |
| **g.** 5 × 10, + 4, ÷ 6, × 8, + 3, ÷ 3 | | |

**Problem Solving:** Debbie averaged 88% on her first three tests. What score does she need on her fourth test to have a four-test average of 90%?

When we divide a decimal number by 10 or by 100, the answer (quotient) has the same digits as the number that is divided (dividend). However, the position of the digits is shifted. Here we show 12.5 divided by 10 and by 100.

$$10\overline{)12.50} = 1.25 \qquad 100\overline{)12.500} = .125$$

When we divide by 10, the digits shift one place to the right. When we divide by 100, the digits shift two places to the right. Although it is the digits that are shifting places, we produce the shift by moving the decimal point. When we divide by 10, the decimal point moves one place to the left. When we divide by 100, the decimal point moves two places to the left.

**Example 1**  37.5 ÷ 10

*Solution*  Dividing by 10, the answer will be less than 37.5, so we mentally shift the decimal point one place to the left.

$$37.5 ÷ 10 = \mathbf{3.75}$$

**Example 2**  3.75 ÷ 100

*Solution*  We mentally shift the decimal point two places to the left. This creates an empty place between the decimal point and the 3, which we fill with a zero. We also write a zero in the ones' place.

$$\mathbf{0.0375}$$

**Practice\***  Mentally calculate each quotient. Write each answer as a decimal number.

**a.** $2.5 \div 10$   0.25              **b.** $2.5 \div 100$   0.025

**c.** $87.5 \div 10$   8.75            **d.** $87.5 \div 100$   0.875

**e.** $0.5 \div 10$   0.05             **f.** $0.5 \div 100$   0.005

**g.** $25 \div 10$   2.5               **h.** $25 \div 100$   0.25

**Problem set 51**

**1.** What is the product of one half and two thirds?  $\frac{1}{3}$
(29)

**2.** A piano has 88 keys. Fifty-two of the keys are white. How many more white keys are there than black keys?  16
(13)

**3.** The deepest part of the Atlantic Ocean is thirty thousand, two hundred forty-six feet. Write that number.   30,246
(12)

**4.** $3.75 \times 10$   37.5            **5.** $3.75 \div 10$   0.375
(46)                                (51)

**6.** $2 \cdot 2 \cdot 2 \cdot 2 \cdot 2$   32      **7.** Convert and reduce: $\dfrac{150}{12}$
(45)                                (26)   $12\frac{1}{2}$

**8.** Multiply and simplify: $(0.125)(4)$   0.5
(39)

**9.** $\dfrac{(1 + 0.2)}{(1 - 0.2)}$   1.5        **10.** $5\dfrac{1}{3} - m = 1\dfrac{2}{3}$   $3\frac{2}{3}$
(48)                                (42)

**11.** $\dfrac{5}{2} \times \dfrac{4}{1}$   10      **12.** $m - 5\dfrac{1}{3} = 1\dfrac{2}{3}$   7
(29)                                (42)

**13.** $\$10 - \$0.10$   $9.90
(1)

**14.** Round $6.789 to the nearest cent.   $6.79
(50)

**15.** Round 12.475 to the nearest tenth.   12.5
(50)

16. 0.201,
0.21,
1.02,
1.2

**16.** Arrange these numbers in order from least to greatest:
(43)
$$1.02, \ 1.2, \ 0.21, \ 0.201$$

**17.** What is the missing number in this sequence?
(10)

$$1, 2, 4, 7, 11, \underline{\phantom{0}16\phantom{0}}, 22, ...$$

**18.** The perimeter of a square room is 80 feet. How many
(38) floor tiles 1 foot square would be needed to cover the area of the room?   400 floor tiles

**19.** One foot is 12 inches. What fraction of a foot is 3
(22) inches?   $\frac{1}{4}$

**20.** How many cents is $\frac{2}{5}$ of a dollar?   40¢
(22)

**21.** The diameter of a penny is $\frac{3}{4}$ of an inch. How many
(49) pennies are needed to make a row of pennies 12 inches long? (Write and solve a fraction division problem to answer this question.)   16 pennies

**22.** What is the least common multiple of 2, 4, and 6?   12
(30)

**23.** $\dfrac{4}{4} - \dfrac{2}{2}$   0
(29)

**24.** A meter is about one **big** step. About how many meters
(7) above the floor is the top of the chalkboard?   probably 2

**25.** To what decimal number is the arrow pointing?   1.8
(49)

**26.** $\dfrac{2 \cdot 2 \cdot 2 \cdot 3 \cdot 3}{2 \cdot 3 \cdot 2}$   6
(45)

**27.** Rename $\frac{1}{2}$ and $\frac{2}{3}$ as fractions with denominators of 6.
(41) Then add the renamed fractions. Write the sum as a mixed number.   $\frac{3}{6}, \frac{4}{6}; 1\frac{1}{6}$

**28.** Seventy-eight percent of the earth's atmosphere is
*(33)* nitrogen. Write 78% as an unreduced fraction. Then
write the fraction as a decimal number.  $\frac{78}{100}$; 0.78

**29.** What time was $12\frac{1}{2}$ hours before 7 a.m.?  6:30 p.m.
*(32)*

**30.** Draw a square with a perimeter of 4 inches. Then
*(38)* shade 50% of the square.  One of many shading
possiblities.

1 in.
1 in.

# LESSON 52

# Decimals Chart • Simplifying Fractions

**Mental Math:**
**a.** 1800
**b.** 290
**c.** 151
**d.** $12.50
**e.** 5
**f.** 40
**g.** 11
**Problem Solving:**
   49

**Facts Practice:** 64 Multiplication Facts (Test D in Test Masters)

**Mental Math:** Count by 9's from 9 to 108.

   **a.** $8 \times 225$            **b.** $256 + 34$          **c.** $250 - 99$
   **d.** $25.00 - $12.50        **e.** Double $2\frac{1}{2}$          **f.** $\frac{800}{20}$
   **g.** $10 \times 10, - 20, + 1, \div 9, \times 5, - 1, \div 4$

**Problem Solving:** Here is part of the multiplication table. What number is
missing?

| 36 | 42 | 48 |
|----|----|----|
| 42 | ?  | 56 |
| 48 | 56 | 64 |

**Decimals chart**   For many lessons we have been developing our decimal
arithmetic skills. We find that arithmetic with decimal
numbers is similar to arithmetic with whole numbers.
However, in decimal number arithmetic, we need to keep
track of the decimal point. The chart on the next page
summarizes the rules for arithmetic with decimal numbers
by providing keywords to help you keep track of the
decimal point.

Across the top of the chart are the four operation signs (+, −, ×, ÷). Below each sign is the rule or memory cue to follow when performing that operation. (There are two kinds of division problems, so there are two different cues.)

**Decimals Chart**

| + − | × | ÷ by whole | ÷ by decimal |
|---|---|---|---|
| Line up the decimal points. | Multiply. Then count decimal places. | Decimal point is up. | over, over, up |
| 1. Place a decimal point to the right of a whole number. 2. Fill empty places with zeros. | | | |

The bottom of the chart contains two rules that apply to more than one operation.

**Simplifying fractions**  We simplify fractions in two ways. We reduce fractions to lowest terms and we convert improper fractions to mixed numbers. Sometimes a fraction can be reduced and converted to a mixed number.

**Example**  $\dfrac{2}{3} + \dfrac{5}{6}$

**Solution**  We rename $\frac{2}{3}$ to $\frac{4}{6}$. We add $\frac{4}{6}$ and $\frac{5}{6}$. The sum $\frac{9}{6}$ can be simplified.

We may reduce first and then convert the fraction to a mixed number, or we may convert first and then reduce.

$$\begin{array}{r} \dfrac{2}{3} \times \dfrac{2}{2} = \dfrac{4}{6} \\[2mm] + \dfrac{5}{6} \qquad = \dfrac{5}{6} \\[1mm] \hline \dfrac{9}{6} \end{array}$$

**REDUCE FIRST:**

1. Reduce $\dfrac{9}{6} = \dfrac{3}{2}$

2. Convert $\dfrac{3}{2} = 1\dfrac{1}{2}$

**CONVERT FIRST:**

1. Convert $\dfrac{9}{6} = 1\dfrac{3}{6}$

2. Reduce $1\dfrac{3}{6} = 1\dfrac{1}{2}$

**Practice**    **a.** Discuss how the rules in the decimals chart apply to each of these problems.    See student work.

$$5 - 4.2 \qquad 0.4 \times 0.2 \qquad 0.12 \div 3 \qquad 5 \div 0.4$$

**b.** Draw the decimals chart on your paper.    See decimals chart.

Add and simplify:

**c.** $\dfrac{5}{6} + \dfrac{5}{12}$    $1\frac{1}{4}$    **d.** $\dfrac{9}{10} + \dfrac{3}{5}$    $1\frac{1}{2}$    **e.** $\dfrac{2}{3} + \dfrac{7}{12}$    $1\frac{1}{4}$

> **Teacher Note:**  Plan a survey about a subject the class selects. Students should collect information about the subject from other students in the school.

**Problem set 52**

1. We only add or subtract digits that have the same place value. If we line up the decimal points, we also line up the digits with the same place value.

**1.** The decimals chart in this lesson shows that we line
$^{(52)}$ up the decimal points when we add or subtract decimal numbers. Why do we do that?

**2.** The turkey must cook for 4 hours and 45 minutes.
$^{(32)}$ What time must it be put in the oven in order to be done by 3:00 p.m.?    10:15 a.m.

**3.** Billy won the contest by eating $\frac{1}{4}$ of a berry pie in 7
$^{(49)}$ seconds. At this rate, how long would it take Billy to eat a whole berry pie?    28 s

**4.** In four games the basketball team scored 47, 52, 63,
$^{(18)}$ and 66 points. What was the average number of points scored per game?    57 points

**5.** $0.375x = 37.5$    100          **6.** $0.375 \div 10$    0.0375
$^{(42)}$                                   $^{(51)}$

**7.** Write 1% as a fraction. Then write the fraction as a
$^{(33)}$ decimal number.    $\frac{1}{100}$; 0.01

**8.** $3.6 + 4 + 0.39$    7.99
$^{(38)}$

**9.** $\dfrac{36}{0.12}$    300          **10.** $\dfrac{0.15}{4}$    0.0375
$^{(48)}$                            $^{(44)}$

**11.** $6\frac{1}{4} - 3\frac{3}{4}$   $2\frac{1}{2}$   **12.** $\frac{2}{3} \times \frac{3}{5}$   $\frac{2}{5}$   **13.** $5\frac{5}{8} + 7\frac{7}{8}$   $13\frac{1}{2}$
(47)              (29)            (27)

**14.** Which digit in 3456 has the same place value as the 2
(34)   in 28.7?   5

**15.** Round 0.416 to the nearest hundredth.   0.42
(50)

**16.** Which number is closest to 1?   B. 0.9
(49)

    A.  1.2         B.  0.9         C.  0.1         D. $\frac{1}{2}$

**17.** What is the sum of the first eight positive odd numbers?
(10)   64

**18.** What is the perimeter of the square?
(38)   $1\frac{1}{2}$ in.

                                  $\square$   $\frac{3}{8}$ in.

**19.** A yard is 36 inches. What fraction of a yard is 3 inches?
(29)   $\frac{1}{12}$

**20.** $8m = 1000$   125         **21.** List the factors of 11.
(4)                             (19)   1, 11

**22.** What is the smallest number that is a multiple of both
(30)   6 and 9?   18

$\frac{3}{2} \cdot \frac{2}{3} = 1,$   **23.** The product of $\frac{2}{3}$ and $\frac{3}{2}$ is 1.
(30)

$1 \div \frac{2}{3} = \frac{3}{2},$

$1 \div \frac{3}{2} = \frac{2}{3}$                     $\frac{2}{3} \cdot \frac{3}{2} = 1$

        Use these numbers to form another multiplication fact
        and two division facts.

**24.** $\dfrac{2 \cdot 3 \cdot 2 \cdot 5 \cdot 2 \cdot 5}{2 \cdot 5 \cdot 2 \cdot 5}$   6   **25.** $\dfrac{5}{6} = \dfrac{?}{24}$   20
(45)                                 (41)

**26.** What fraction of the circles are
(29)   shaded?   $\frac{1}{3}$

$\frac{3}{10}$; 105   **27.** Thirty percent of the 350 students ride the bus to
(22,33)   Thompson School. Write 30% as a reduced fraction.
        Then find the number of students who ride the bus.

**28.** Rename $\frac{1}{4}$ and $\frac{1}{6}$ as fractions with denominators of 12.
(41) Then add the renamed fractions.    $\frac{3}{12}, \frac{2}{12}; \frac{5}{12}$

**29.** The number that corresponds to point $A$ is how much
(49) less than the number that corresponds to point $B$?
1.3

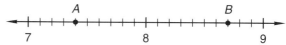

**30.** The classroom set of Huckleberry Finn books fills a
(49) shelf that is 24 inches long. Each book is $\frac{3}{4}$ of an inch
thick. How many books are in the classroom set?
(Write and solve a fraction division problem to answer
the question.)    32 books

# LESSON 53

# More on Reducing • Dividing Fractions

**Mental Math:**
**a.** 1500
**b.** 336
**c.** 474
**d.** $13.75
**e.** $4\frac{1}{2}$
**f.** 900
**g.** 100
**Problem Solving:**
Walk to school =
walk home

---

**Facts Practice:**  30 Fractions to Reduce (Test G in Test Masters)

**Mental Math:**  Count up and down by $\frac{1}{8}$'s between $\frac{1}{8}$ and 3.
  **a.** $6 \times 250$         **b.** $736 - 400$       **c.** $375 + 99$
  **d.** $8.75 + $5.00       **e.** $\frac{1}{2}$ of 9       **f.** $30 \times 30$
  **g.** $8 \times 8, - 1, \div 9, \times 7, + 1, \div 5, \times 10$

**Problem Solving:**  Ned walked from his home
(H) to school (S) following
the path from H to I to J to K
to L to M to S. After school
he walked home from S to C
to H. Compare the distance
of his walk to school and the
distance of his walk home.

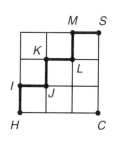

---

**More on reducing**  The factors in the problem below are arranged in order
from least to greatest. Notice that some factors appear in
both the dividend and the divisor.

$$\frac{2 \cdot 2 \cdot 3 \cdot 5}{2 \cdot 2 \cdot 3}$$

Since $2 \div 2$ is 1 and $3 \div 3$ is 1, we will mark the combinations of factors equal to 1 in this problem.

$$\frac{2 \cdot 2 \cdot 3 \cdot 5}{2 \cdot 2 \cdot 3}$$

Looking at the factors this way, the problem becomes $1 \cdot 1 \cdot 1 \cdot 5$, which is 5.

**Example 1** Reduce this fraction: $\dfrac{2 \cdot 2 \cdot 2 \cdot 5}{2 \cdot 2 \cdot 3 \cdot 5}$

*Solution* We will mark combinations of factors equal to 1.

$$\frac{2 \cdot 2 \cdot 2 \cdot 5}{2 \cdot 2 \cdot 3 \cdot 5}$$

Grouping factors equal to 1, the problem becomes $1 \cdot 1 \cdot 1 \cdot \frac{2}{3}$, which is $\mathbf{\frac{2}{3}}$.

**Dividing fractions** When we divide 10 by 5, we are answering the question "How many 5's are in 10?" When we divide $\frac{3}{4}$ by $\frac{1}{2}$, we are answering the same type of question, "How many $\frac{1}{2}$'s are in $\frac{3}{4}$?" While it is easy to see how many 5's are in 10, it is not as easy to see how many $\frac{1}{2}$'s are in $\frac{3}{4}$. When the divisor is a fraction, we take two steps to find the answer. First we find how many of the divisors are in 1. This is the reciprocal of the divisor. Then we use the reciprocal to find the answer to the original division problem by multiplying, as we show in these examples.

**Example 2** How many $\dfrac{1}{2}$'s are in $\dfrac{3}{4}$? $\left( \dfrac{3}{4} \div \dfrac{1}{2} \right)$

*Solution* Before we show the two-step process we will solve the problem with our fraction manipulatives. The question in the example can be stated this way:

How many of these ⊟ are needed to make this ⊕?

We see that the answer is more than one but less than two. If we take one ⊟ and cut another one into two parts ⊟, then we can fit the ⊟ and one of the parts ▽ together to make three fourths.

We see that we need $1\frac{1}{2}$ of these ⊟ to make this ⊕.

Now we will show $\frac{3}{4} \div \frac{1}{2} = 1\frac{1}{2}$ by arithmetic. The original problem asks, "How many $\frac{1}{2}$'s are in $\frac{3}{4}$?"

$$\frac{3}{4} \div \frac{1}{2}$$

The first step is to find the number of $\frac{1}{2}$'s in 1.

$$1 \div \frac{1}{2} = 2$$

The number of $\frac{1}{2}$'s in 1 is 2, which is the reciprocal of $\frac{1}{2}$. So the number of $\frac{1}{2}$'s in $\frac{3}{4}$ should be $\frac{3}{4}$ of 2. We find $\frac{3}{4}$ of 2 by multiplying.

$$\frac{3}{4} \text{ of } 2 = \frac{6}{4}, \text{ which equals } 1\frac{1}{2}$$

We simplified $\frac{6}{4}$ by reducing $\frac{6}{4}$ to $\frac{3}{2}$ and by converting $\frac{3}{2}$ to **$1\frac{1}{2}$**. We will review the steps we took to solve the problem.

Original problem: How many $\frac{1}{2}$'s are in $\frac{3}{4}$? $\qquad \frac{3}{4} \div \frac{1}{2}$

Step 1: Find the number of $\frac{1}{2}$'s in 1. $\qquad 1 \div \frac{1}{2} = 2$

Step 2: Use the number of $\frac{1}{2}$'s in 1 to find the number of $\frac{1}{2}$'s in $\frac{3}{4}$. $\qquad \frac{3}{4} \times 2 = \frac{6}{4}$

Then simplify the answer. $\qquad = 1\frac{1}{2}$

**Example 3** How many $\frac{3}{4}$'s are in $\frac{1}{2}$? $\left( \frac{1}{2} \div \frac{3}{4} \right)$

**Solution** Using our fraction manipulatives, the question can be stated this way:

How much of ⬤ is needed to make ⬤?

The answer is less than 1. We need to cut off part of ⬤ to make ⬤. If we cut off one of the three parts of three fourths, ⬤, then two of the three parts equal ⬤. So $\frac{2}{3}$ of $\frac{3}{4}$ is needed to make $\frac{1}{2}$.

Now we will show the arithmetic. The original problem asks, "How many $\frac{3}{4}$'s are in $\frac{1}{2}$?"

$$\frac{1}{2} \div \frac{3}{4}$$

First we find the number of $\frac{3}{4}$'s in 1. The number is the reciprocal of $\frac{3}{4}$.

$$1 \div \frac{3}{4} = \frac{4}{3}$$

The number of $\frac{3}{4}$'s in 1 is $\frac{4}{3}$. So the number of $\frac{3}{4}$'s in $\frac{1}{2}$ should be $\frac{1}{2}$ of $\frac{4}{3}$. We find $\frac{1}{2}$ of $\frac{4}{3}$ by multiplying.

$$\frac{1}{2} \times \frac{4}{3} = \frac{4}{6}, \text{ which equals } \frac{2}{3}$$

The product, $\frac{4}{6}$, reduces to $\frac{2}{3}$. Again we will review the steps we took to solve the problem.

Original problem: How many $\frac{3}{4}$'s are in $\frac{1}{2}$?     $\frac{1}{2} \div \frac{3}{4}$

   Step 1: Find the number of $\frac{3}{4}$'s in 1.     $1 \div \frac{3}{4} = \frac{4}{3}$

   Step 2: Use the number of $\frac{3}{4}$'s in 1 to find the number of $\frac{3}{4}$'s in $\frac{1}{2}$.     $\frac{1}{2} \times \frac{4}{3} = \frac{4}{6}$

   Then simplify the answer.     $= \frac{2}{3}$

**Practice**   **a.** $\dfrac{2 \cdot 2 \cdot 3 \cdot 5}{2 \cdot 2 \cdot 5}$   3   **b.** $\dfrac{2 \cdot 2 \cdot 3 \cdot 3 \cdot 5}{2 \cdot 2 \cdot 3 \cdot 5 \cdot 5}$   $\frac{3}{5}$

**c.** How many $\dfrac{3}{8}$'s are in $\dfrac{1}{2}$?  $\left(\dfrac{1}{2} \div \dfrac{3}{8}\right)$   $1\frac{1}{3}$

**d.** How many $\dfrac{1}{2}$'s are in $\dfrac{3}{8}$?  $\left(\dfrac{3}{8} \div \dfrac{1}{2}\right)$   $\frac{3}{4}$

**Problem set 53**

**1.** Draw the decimals chart from Lesson 52.   See Lesson 52.
(52)

**2.** If 0.4 is the dividend and 4 is the divisor, what is the quotient?   0.1
(44)

**3.** In 1900 the U.S. population was 76,212,168. In 1950 the population was 151,325,798. **Estimate** the increase in population between 1900 and 1950 to the nearest million.   75,000,000
(16)

**4.** Mark was $59\frac{3}{4}$ inches tall when he turned 11 and $61\frac{1}{4}$ inches tall when he turned 12. How many inches did he grow during the year?   $1\frac{1}{2}$ in.
(47)

**5.** $1000 - (100 - 1)$   901
(5)

**6.** $\dfrac{1000}{24}$   $41\frac{2}{3}$
(26)

**7.** What number is halfway between 37 and 143?   90
(18)

**8.** $\$3 - n = 24\cyrchar¢$   $2.76
(3)

**9.** $(1.2 \div 0.12)(1.2)$   12
(52)

**10.** $4.2 \div 100$   0.042
(44)

**11.** $m + 3\dfrac{4}{5} = 6\dfrac{2}{5}$   $2\frac{3}{5}$
(42)

**12.** $\dfrac{4}{3} \cdot \dfrac{4}{3}$   $1\frac{7}{9}$
(29)

**13.** $\dfrac{4}{3} = \dfrac{?}{18}$   24
(41)

**14.** Which digit is in the hundred-thousands' place in 123,456,789?   4
(12)

**15.** Round $26.777 to the nearest cent.  $26.78
(50)

**16.** Use your rulers to compare:
(9)

One centimeter $<$ one inch

**17.** What is the twelfth number in this sequence?  23
(10)

1, 3, 5, 7, 9, ...

**18.** How many square feet of tile would be needed to
(31) cover the area of a room 14 feet long and 12 feet wide?
168 sq. ft

**19.** Nine of the 30 students received A's on the test. What
(29) fraction of the students received A's?  $\frac{3}{10}$

**20.** $\dfrac{5}{6} = \dfrac{?}{24}$  20
(41)

**21.** What is the least common multiple of 3, 4, and 6?  12
(30)

**22.** How many $\dfrac{1}{2}$'s are in $\dfrac{2}{3}$?  $\left( \dfrac{2}{3} \div \dfrac{1}{2} \right)$  $1\frac{1}{3}$
(53)

**23.** Eighty percent of the 30 questions were correct. Write
(22,33) 80% as a reduced fraction; then find the number of
questions that were correct.  $\frac{4}{5}$; 24

**24.** One inch equals 2.54 centimeters. A line 100 inches
(46) long would be how many centimeters long?  254 cm

**25.** $\dfrac{2 \cdot 3 \cdot 5 \cdot 3 \cdot 2}{2 \cdot 3 \cdot 2 \cdot 5}$  3      **26.** $\dfrac{2 \cdot 3 \cdot 3 \cdot 5}{2 \cdot 2 \cdot 2 \cdot 3 \cdot 5}$  $\frac{3}{4}$
(53)                                      (53)

**27.** Rename $\frac{2}{3}$ and $\frac{1}{2}$ as fractions with denominators of 6.
(41) Then add the renamed fractions and convert the
answer to a mixed number.  $\frac{4}{6}$, $\frac{3}{6}$; $1\frac{1}{6}$

**28.** A music store sells cassette tapes in clear plastic boxes
(49) that are $4\frac{1}{2}$ inches long, $2\frac{3}{4}$ inches wide, and $\frac{5}{8}$ inch deep.
The store also sells a carrying case for cassettes that has
an inside length of 15 inches. How many cassettes in
boxes can the carrying case hold?     24 cassettes

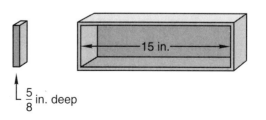

$\frac{5}{8}$ in. deep

**29.** Draw a rectangle that is $1\frac{1}{2}$ inches long and 1 inch
(27) wide. What is the perimeter of the rectangle?     5 in.

**30.** Instead of dividing $2\frac{1}{2}$ by $\frac{1}{4}$, Sandra made an equivalent
(42) division problem with whole numbers by multiplying the
dividend and the divisor by 4. What equivalent problem
did she make, and what is the quotient?     $10 \div 1$; 10

# LESSON 54

# Common Denominators, Part 1

**Mental Math:**
a. 2600
b. 379
c. 276
d. $7.50
e. 7
f. 30
g. 4
**Problem Solving:**
16 cups

**Facts Practice:** 28 Fractions to Simplify (Test I in Test Masters)

**Mental Math:** Count by 7's from 7 to 84.

a. $8 \times 325$
b. $329 + 50$
c. $375 - 99$
d. $12.50 - $5.00
e. Double $3\frac{1}{2}$
f. $\frac{600}{20}$
g. $8 \times 5, + 2, \div 6, \times 7, + 7, \div 8, \times 4, \div 7$

**Problem Solving:** Half of a gallon is a half gallon. Half of a half gallon is a quart. Half of a quart is a pint. Half of a pint is a cup. How many cups of water equal a gallon of water?

1 gallon    $\frac{1}{2}$ gallon    1 quart    1 pint    1 cup

When the denominators of two or more fractions are equal, we say that the fractions have **common denominators.** The fractions $\frac{3}{5}$ and $\frac{2}{5}$ have common denominators.

$\frac{3}{5}$          $\frac{2}{5}$

The common denominator is 5.

The fractions $\frac{3}{4}$ and $\frac{1}{2}$ do not have common denominators because the denominators 4 and 2 are not equal.

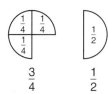

$\frac{3}{4}$          $\frac{1}{2}$

These fractions do not have common denominators.

Fractions that do not have common denominators can be renamed to make fractions that do have common denominators. Since $\frac{2}{4}$ equals $\frac{1}{2}$, we may rename $\frac{1}{2}$ as $\frac{2}{4}$. The fractions $\frac{3}{4}$ and $\frac{2}{4}$ have common denominators.

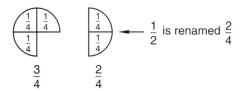

The common denominator is 4.

Fractions that have common denominators can be added by counting the number of parts, that is, by adding the numerators.

$$\frac{3}{4} + \frac{2}{4} = \frac{5}{4}$$

To add or subtract fractions that do not have common denominators, we rename one or more fractions to make fractions that do have common denominators. Then we add or subtract. Recall that we rename fractions by multiplying the fractions to be renamed by a fraction equal to 1. Here we rename $\frac{1}{2}$ by multiplying $\frac{1}{2}$ by $\frac{2}{2}$. This forms the equivalent fraction $\frac{2}{4}$, which can be added to $\frac{3}{4}$.

Rename $\frac{1}{2}$.

$$\frac{1}{2} \times \frac{2}{2} = \frac{2}{4}$$
$$+ \frac{3}{4} \phantom{\times \frac{2}{2}} = \frac{3}{4}$$

Then add.

$$\frac{5}{4} = 1\frac{1}{4}$$

Simplify your answer, if possible.

To find the common denominator of two fractions, we find a common multiple of the denominators. The least common multiple of denominators is the lowest common denominator of the fractions.

**Example** $\frac{1}{2} - \frac{1}{6}$

*Solution* The denominators are 2 and 6. The least common multiple of 2 and 6 is 6. So 6 is a common denominator of the two fractions. We change halves to sixths by multiplying by $\frac{3}{3}$. We do not need to rename $\frac{1}{6}$.

$$\xrightarrow{\text{Rename } \frac{1}{2}.}$$

$$\begin{array}{r} \frac{1}{2} \times \frac{3}{3} = \frac{3}{6} \\ - \frac{1}{6} \qquad = \frac{1}{6} \\ \hline \frac{2}{6} = \frac{1}{3} \end{array}$$

Subtract $\frac{1}{6}$ from $\frac{3}{6}$.

$$\xrightarrow{\text{Reduce.}}$$

**Practice**

**a.** $\begin{array}{r} \frac{1}{2} \\ + \frac{3}{8} \\ \hline \frac{7}{8} \end{array}$
  **b.** $\begin{array}{r} \frac{3}{8} \\ + \frac{1}{4} \\ \hline \frac{5}{8} \end{array}$
  **c.** $\begin{array}{r} \frac{3}{4} \\ + \frac{1}{8} \\ \hline \frac{7}{8} \end{array}$

**d.** $\begin{array}{r} \frac{1}{2} \\ - \frac{1}{4} \\ \hline \frac{1}{4} \end{array}$
  **e.** $\begin{array}{r} \frac{5}{8} \\ - \frac{1}{4} \\ \hline \frac{3}{8} \end{array}$
  **f.** $\begin{array}{r} \frac{3}{4} \\ - \frac{3}{8} \\ \hline \frac{3}{8} \end{array}$

**Problem set 54**

1. When we divide a decimal number by a whole number using a division box, we place a decimal point in the quotient directly "up" from the decimal point in the dividend.

**1.** In the decimals chart, the memory cue for dividing by a whole number is "up." What does that mean?
(52)

**2.** How many $\frac{3}{8}$-inch-thick CD holders will fit on a 12-inch-long shelf? (Write and solve a fraction division problem to answer the question.)   32 CD holders
(49)

**3.** The average pumpkin weighs 6 pounds. The Great Pumpkin weighs 324 pounds. The Great Pumpkin weighs as much as how many average pumpkins?   54
(15)

**4.** $\frac{1}{8} + \frac{1}{2}$   $\frac{5}{8}$
(54)

**5.** $\begin{array}{r} \frac{1}{2} \\ - \frac{1}{8} \end{array}$   $\frac{3}{8}$
(54)

**6.** $\begin{array}{r} \frac{2}{3} \\ - \frac{1}{6} \end{array}$   $\frac{1}{2}$
(54)

**7.** 6.28 + 4 + 0.13    10.41
(38)

**8.** 81 ÷ 0.9    90
(48)

**9.** 0.2 ÷ 10    0.02
(51)

**10.** (0.17)(100)    17
(46)

**11.** $x + \dfrac{3}{4} = 3\dfrac{1}{4}$    $2\dfrac{1}{2}$
(42)

**12.** $\dfrac{5}{6} \cdot \dfrac{2}{3}$    $\frac{5}{9}$
(29)

**13.** $\dfrac{5}{8} = \dfrac{?}{24}$    15
(41)

**14.** Write the following in standard notation:    60,420
(32)
$$(6 \times 10{,}000) + (4 \times 100) + (2 \times 10)$$

**15.** Multiply 0.14 and 0.8 and round the product to the nearest hundredth.    0.11
(50)

**16.** Compare: $\dfrac{2}{3} \,\textcircled{=}\, \dfrac{2}{3} \times \dfrac{2}{2}$
(29)

**17.** Which of these fractions is closest to 1?    C. $\frac{3}{4}$
(17)

A. $\dfrac{1}{4}$        B. $\dfrac{1}{2}$        C. $\dfrac{3}{4}$

**18.** A 20-foot rope was used to make a square. How many square feet of area are enclosed by the rope?    25 sq. ft
(38)

**19.** What fraction of a dollar is six dimes?    $\frac{3}{5}$
(29)

**20.** What is the least common multiple (LCM) of 3 and 4?    12
(30)

**21.** List the factors of 23.    1, 23
(19)

**22.** How many 12's are in 1212?    101
(15)

**23.** By what fraction should $\frac{2}{5}$ be multiplied to make the product 1?    $\frac{5}{2}$
(30)

**24.** Compare: 2 cm $\,\textcircled{<}\,$ 1 in.
(7)

**25.** How many $\dfrac{2}{5}$'s are in $\dfrac{1}{2}$? $\left( \dfrac{1}{2} \div \dfrac{2}{5} \right)$    $1\frac{1}{4}$
(53)

**26.** Draw a rectangle that is $1\frac{1}{2}$ inches long and 1 inch
$(31)$ wide. What is the area of the rectangle? $1\frac{1}{2}$ sq. in.

**27.** What fraction of this group of
$(29)$ circles is shaded? $\frac{1}{3}$

**28.** Reduce: $\dfrac{2 \cdot 3 \cdot 2 \cdot 5 \cdot 3 \cdot 7}{2 \cdot 2 \cdot 3 \cdot 5 \cdot 5 \cdot 5}$ $\frac{21}{25}$
$(53)$

**29.** The performance began at 7:45 p.m. and concluded at
$(32)$ 10:25 p.m. How many hours and minutes long was the
performance? 2 hr, 40 min

**30.** Draw the decimals chart from Lesson 52. See Lesson 52.
$(52)$

# LESSON 55

# Common Denominators, Part 2

**Mental Math:**
a. 2000
b. 112
c. 199
d. $8.25
e. 7½
f. 1200
g. 8
**Problem Solving:**

  956
+  44
─────
 1000

---

**Facts Practice:**  30 Fractions to Reduce (Test G in Test Masters)

**Mental Math:**  Count up and down by 25's between 25 and 300.

  **a.** 8 × 250          **b.** 462 − 350          **c.** 150 + 49
  **d.** $3.75 + $4.50          **e.** ½ of 15          **f.** 30 × 40
  **g.** 10 × 8, + 1, ÷ 9, × 3, + 1, ÷ 4, × 6, − 2, ÷ 5

**Problem Solving:**  Copy this problem and fill in the missing digits.

```
   _56
+  __
──────
 _000
```

---

In Lesson 54 we added and subtracted fractions which required us to rename one of the fractions so that the fractions would have common denominators. In this lesson we will rename both fractions before we add or subtract. To add ½ and ⅓ we cannot simply count the number of parts because the parts are not the same size—the denominators are different.

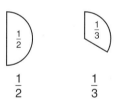

These fractions do not have common denominators.

Renaming ½ as ²⁄₄ does not help us to add because the parts still are a different size.

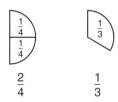

These fractions do not have common denominators.

We need to rename both fractions in order to have two fractions whose parts are the same size.

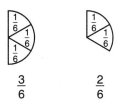

$$\frac{3}{6} \qquad \frac{2}{6}$$

The common denominator is 6.

Often both fractions of an addition or subtraction problem need to be renamed. The least common multiple of the denominators may be used as the common denominator of the renamed fractions.

**Example 1** $\quad \dfrac{1}{2} + \dfrac{1}{3}$

*Solution* The denominators are 2 and 3. The least common multiple of 2 and 3 is 6. We rename each fraction so that 6 is the common denominator. Then we add. The sum is $\frac{5}{6}$.

Rename $\dfrac{1}{2}$ and $\dfrac{1}{3}$.

$$\dfrac{1}{2} \times \dfrac{3}{3} = \dfrac{3}{6}$$
$$\dfrac{1}{3} \times \dfrac{2}{2} = \dfrac{2}{6}$$
$$\overline{\phantom{xxxxx}} \dfrac{5}{6}$$
Add.

**Example 2** $\quad \begin{array}{r} \frac{3}{4} \\ -\frac{2}{3} \\ \hline \end{array}$

*Solution* The least common multiple of 4 and 3 is 12. We rename both fractions so that their denominators are 12. Then we subtract. The difference is $\frac{1}{12}$.

Rename $\dfrac{3}{4}$ and $\dfrac{2}{3}$.

$$\dfrac{3}{4} \times \dfrac{3}{3} = \dfrac{9}{12}$$
$$\dfrac{2}{3} \times \dfrac{4}{4} = \dfrac{8}{12}$$
$$\overline{\phantom{xxxxx}} \dfrac{1}{12}$$
Subtract.

**Practice**   **a.** $\dfrac{2}{3}$ $\dfrac{1}{6}$   **b.** $\dfrac{1}{4}$ $\dfrac{13}{20}$   **c.** $\dfrac{3}{4}$ $\dfrac{5}{12}$   **d.** $\dfrac{2}{3}$ $\dfrac{11}{12}$   **e.** $\dfrac{1}{3}$ $\dfrac{1}{12}$

$-\dfrac{1}{2}$   $+\dfrac{2}{5}$   $-\dfrac{1}{3}$   $+\dfrac{1}{4}$   $-\dfrac{1}{4}$

**Problem set 55**

**1.** Add $\frac{1}{4}$ and $\frac{1}{3}$. Make the common denominator 12.
(55)   $\frac{7}{12}$

**2.** Subtract $\frac{1}{3}$ from $\frac{1}{2}$. Make the common denominator 6.
(55)   $\frac{1}{6}$

**3.** Of the 88 keys on a piano, 52 are white. What fraction of a piano's keys are white?   $\frac{13}{22}$
(29)

**4.** If $4\frac{1}{2}$ apples are needed to make an apple pie, how many apples would be needed to make two apple pies?   9
(29)

**5.** Subtract $\frac{1}{4}$ from $\frac{2}{3}$. Make the common denominator 12.
(55)   $\frac{5}{12}$

**6.** Add $\frac{1}{3}$ and $\frac{1}{6}$. Reduce your answer.
(54)   $\frac{1}{2}$

**7.** Subtract $\frac{1}{2}$ from $\frac{5}{6}$. Reduce your answer.
(54)   $\frac{1}{3}$

**8.** $3 + $1.75 + 65¢   $5.40
(5)

**9.** $(0.625)(0.4)$   0.25
(39)

**10.** $24 \div 0.08$   300
(48)

**11.** $3\frac{1}{8} - 1\frac{7}{8}$   $1\frac{1}{4}$
(47)

**12.** $\frac{5}{8} \cdot \frac{2}{3}$   $\frac{5}{12}$
(29)

**13.** Moe answered 40% of the 100 questions correctly. Write 40% as a reduced fraction. How many questions did Moe answer correctly?   $\frac{2}{5}$; 40
(22,33)

**14.** Write the following as a decimal number:   80.65
(45)

$$(8 \times 10) + \left(6 \times \tfrac{1}{10}\right) + \left(5 \times \tfrac{1}{100}\right)$$

**15.** Estimate the sum of 3627 and 4187 to the nearest hundred.   7800
(16)

**16.** Which of these numbers is between 1 and 2?   A. 1.875
(49)

A. 1.875          B. 2.01          C. 0.15

**17.** What is the average of 1.2, 1.3, 1.4, and 1.5?   1.35
(18)

**18.** The perimeter of a square is 36 inches. What is its area?
(38)  81 sq. in.

**19.** Returning from the store, Dad found that four of the
(29)  dozen eggs were cracked. What fraction of the eggs
were cracked?  $\frac{1}{3}$

Find a number for each letter to make each equation true:

**20.** $\frac{2}{3}w = 0$  0    **21.** $\frac{2}{3}m = 1$  $\frac{3}{2}$    **22.** $\frac{2}{3} - n = 0$  $\frac{2}{3}$
(42)                        (30)                          (42)

Use this graph of test results to answer questions 23, 24, 25, and 26.

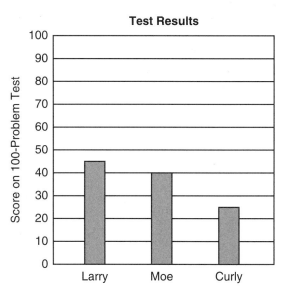

**23.** How many problems did Moe miss on the test?  60
(16)

**24.** How many more problems did Larry have right on the
(16)  test than Curly?  20

**25.** What fraction of the questions on the test did Curly
(29)  answer correctly?  $\frac{1}{4}$

**26.** Write a percent question that refers to the bar graph
(29)  and answer the question. Answers vary. See student work.

**27.** $\dfrac{2 \cdot 3 \cdot 5}{2 \cdot 3 \cdot 5 \cdot 7}$  $\frac{1}{7}$
(53)

**28.** How many $\frac{2}{3}$'s are in $\frac{1}{2}$? $\left(\frac{1}{2} \div \frac{2}{3}\right)$    $\frac{3}{4}$
(53)

**29.** Draw three rectangles that are two centimeters long
(7) and one centimeter wide. Show three different ways to divide the rectangle in half. Then shade half of each rectangle.

**30.** What is the area of the shaded part of one of the
(31) rectangles you drew in problem 29?    1 sq. cm

---

## LESSON 56

# Adding and Subtracting Fractions: Three Steps

**Facts Practice:** 72 Mixed Multiplication and Division (Test H in Test Masters)

**Mental Math:** Count by 12's from 12 to 144.

**a.** $8 \times 425$     **b.** $465 + 250$     **c.** $150 - 49$
**d.** $9.75 - $3.50     **e.** Double $4\frac{1}{2}$     **f.** $\frac{600}{30}$
**g.** $2 \times 2, \times 2, \times 2, \times 2, \times 2, \div 8, \div 8$

**Problem Solving:** Brad was thinking of two different two-digit odd numbers whose average was 15. Find two pairs of numbers of which Brad could have been thinking.

To solve a fraction problem there are three steps to consider:

**Step 1.** We need to be sure that the problem is in the right **shape** or form. When adding or subtracting fractions, the correct form is with common denominators.

**Step 2.** We perform the **operation** indicated—we add, subtract, multiply, or divide.

**Step 3.** We **simplify** the answer, if necessary, by reducing the fraction or by writing an improper fraction as a mixed number.

**Example 1**    $\dfrac{1}{2} + \dfrac{2}{3}$

*Solution*    We will identify the shape, operate, and simplify steps:

> **Step 1.** Shape—Write the fractions with common denominators.
>
> **Step 2.** Operate—Add the renamed fractions.
>
> **Step 3.** Simplify—Convert the improper fraction to a mixed number.

$$
\begin{array}{l}
\phantom{+}\dfrac{1}{2} \times \dfrac{3}{3} = \dfrac{3}{6} \\[2mm]
+\dfrac{2}{3} \times \dfrac{2}{2} = \dfrac{4}{6} \\[1mm]
\hline
\phantom{+\dfrac{2}{3} \times \dfrac{2}{2} = }\dfrac{7}{6} = 1\dfrac{1}{6}
\end{array}
$$

**Example 2**    $\dfrac{1}{2} - \dfrac{1}{6}$

*Solution*

> **Step 1.** Shape—Write fractions with common denominators.
>
> **Step 2.** Operate—Subtract the renamed fractions.
>
> **Step 3.** Simplify—Reduce the fraction.

$$
\begin{array}{l}
\phantom{-}\dfrac{1}{2} \times \dfrac{3}{3} = \dfrac{3}{6} \\[2mm]
-\dfrac{1}{6} \phantom{\times \dfrac{3}{3}} = \dfrac{1}{6} \\[1mm]
\hline
\phantom{-\dfrac{1}{6} = }\dfrac{2}{6} = \dfrac{1}{3}
\end{array}
$$

**Practice***    **a.** $\dfrac{1}{2} + \dfrac{1}{6}$    $\frac{2}{3}$    **b.** $\dfrac{2}{3} + \dfrac{3}{4}$    $1\frac{5}{12}$    **c.** $\dfrac{1}{5} + \dfrac{3}{10}$    $\frac{1}{2}$

**d.** $\dfrac{5}{6} - \dfrac{1}{2}$    $\frac{1}{3}$    **e.** $\dfrac{7}{10} - \dfrac{1}{2}$    $\frac{1}{5}$    **f.** $\dfrac{5}{12} - \dfrac{1}{6}$    $\frac{1}{4}$

**Problem set 56**

**1.** What is the difference between the sum of $\frac{1}{2}$ and $\frac{1}{2}$ and
(29) the product of $\frac{1}{2}$ and $\frac{1}{2}$?    $\frac{3}{4}$

**2.** Thomas Jefferson was born in 1743. How old was he
(13) when he was elected president of the United States in
1800?    57 years

**3.** Subtract $\frac{3}{4}$ from $\frac{5}{6}$. Make the common denominator 12.
(55)    $\frac{1}{12}$

**4.** $\frac{1}{2} + \frac{2}{3}$    $1\frac{1}{6}$        **5.** $\frac{1}{2} + \frac{1}{6}$    $\frac{2}{3}$        **6.** $\frac{5}{6} + \frac{2}{3}$    $1\frac{1}{2}$
(56)                    (56)                    (56)

**7.** How many $\frac{3}{5}$'s are in $\frac{3}{4}$?    $\left( \frac{3}{4} \div \frac{3}{5} \right)$    $1\frac{1}{4}$
(53)

**8.** $32.50 \div 10$    \$3.25        **9.** $2 - (1 - 0.2)$    1.2
(51)                        (5)

**10.** $6 \div 0.12$    50    **11.** $5\frac{3}{8} - 2\frac{5}{8}$    $2\frac{3}{4}$    **12.** $\frac{3}{4} \cdot \frac{5}{3}$    $1\frac{1}{4}$
(48)                (47)                    (29)

**13.** Fifty percent of this rectangle is
(31,33) shaded. Write 50% as a reduced
fraction. What is the area of the
shaded part of the rectangle?    $\frac{1}{2}$;
100 sq. mm

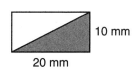
10 mm
20 mm

**14.** Name the place value of the 7 in 3.567.    thousandths'
(34)

**15.** Divide 0.5 by 4 and round the quotient to the nearest
(50) tenth.    0.1

**16.** Rearrange these numbers in order from least to
(43) greatest:    0.03, 0.3, 3.0

0.3, 3.0, 0.03

**17.** What is the twentieth number in this sequence?    40
(10)

2, 4, 6, 8, ...

**18.** What is the perimeter of the
(56) rectangle? $1\frac{1}{2}$ in.

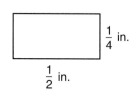

$\frac{1}{4}$ in.

$\frac{1}{2}$ in.

**19.** Multiply the length and width of
(31) the rectangle to find the area of
the rectangle in square inches.
$\frac{1}{8}$ in.²

**20.** What number is $\frac{5}{8}$ of 80?   50
(22)

**21.** List the factors of 29.   1, 29
(19)

**22.** What is the least common multiple of 12 and 18?   36
(30)

**23.** Compare: $\dfrac{5}{8}$ ⊘ $\dfrac{7}{8}$   <
(21)

**24.** What temperature is shown on the
(10) thermometer?   −4°F

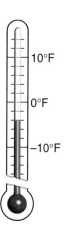

10°F

0°F

−10°F

**25.** If the temperature rose from the
(14) temperature shown on the thermometer to 12°F, then how many
degrees did the temperature rise?
16°F

**26.** Reduce: $\dfrac{2 \cdot 2 \cdot 3 \cdot 3 \cdot 5 \cdot 7}{2 \cdot 2 \cdot 5 \cdot 5 \cdot 7 \cdot 7}$   $\frac{9}{35}$
(53)

**27.** What fraction of the group of
(29) circles is shaded?   $\frac{1}{3}$

**28.** Cheryl has a 6-inch stack of CD's on the shelf. Each CD
(49) is in a $\frac{3}{8}$-inch-thick plastic holder. How many CD's are
in the 6-inch stack? (Write and solve a fraction
division problem to answer the question.)   16 CD's

**29.** Subtract $\frac{1}{2}$ from $\frac{4}{5}$. Make the common denominator 10.
(55) $\frac{3}{10}$

**30.** Three of these numbers are equivalent. Which one is
(33,35) different? A. $\frac{1}{5}$

A. $\frac{1}{5}$ B. $\frac{1}{2}$ C. 0.5 D. 50%

# LESSON 57

# Comparing Fractions by Renaming with Common Denominators

**Mental Math:**
a. 150
b. 165
c. 449
d. $20.00
e. $12\frac{1}{2}$
f. 1000
g. 5

**Problem Solving:**
$\frac{2}{3}, \frac{5}{6}, 1$

**Facts Practice:** 28 Fractions to Simplify (Test I in Test Masters)

**Mental Math:** Count up and down by $\frac{1}{8}$'s between $\frac{1}{8}$ and 2.

   **a.** 2 × 75        **b.** 315 − 150       **c.** 250 + 199
   **d.** $7.50 + $12.50    **e.** $\frac{1}{2}$ of 25       **f.** 20 × 50
   **g.** 10 × 10, − 1, ÷ 11, × 8, + 3, ÷ 3, ÷ 5

**Problem Solving:** What are the next three numbers in this sequence?

$$\frac{1}{6}, \frac{1}{3}, \frac{1}{2}, \underline{\quad}, \underline{\quad}, \underline{\quad}, \cdots$$

To compare fractions that have common denominators, we simply compare the numerators.

$$\frac{4}{6} < \frac{5}{6}$$

One way to compare fractions that do not have common denominators is to rename one or both fractions so that they do have common denominators.

**Example 1** Compare: $\frac{3}{8} \bigcirc \frac{1}{2}$

*Solution* We rename $\frac{1}{2}$ so that the denominator is 8.

$$\frac{1}{2} \cdot \frac{4}{4} = \frac{4}{8}$$

We see that $\frac{3}{8}$ is less than $\frac{4}{8}$.

$$\frac{3}{8} < \frac{4}{8}$$

Therefore, $\frac{3}{8}$ is less than $\frac{1}{2}$.

$$\frac{\mathbf{3}}{\mathbf{8}} < \frac{\mathbf{1}}{\mathbf{2}}$$

**Example 2**  Compare: $\frac{2}{3} \bigcirc \frac{3}{4}$

*Solution*  The denominators are 3 and 4. We rename both fractions with a common denominator of 12.

$$\frac{2}{3} \cdot \frac{4}{4} = \frac{8}{12} \qquad \frac{3}{4} \cdot \frac{3}{3} = \frac{9}{12}$$

We see that $\frac{8}{12}$ is less than $\frac{9}{12}$.

$$\frac{8}{12} < \frac{9}{12}$$

Therefore, $\frac{2}{3}$ is less than $\frac{3}{4}$.

$$\frac{\mathbf{2}}{\mathbf{3}} < \frac{\mathbf{3}}{\mathbf{4}}$$

**Practice**  Before comparing the fractions, write each pair of fractions with common denominators.

**a.** $\frac{2}{3} \bigcirc\!> \frac{1}{2}$    **b.** $\frac{4}{6} \bigcirc\!< \frac{3}{4}$    **c.** $\frac{2}{3} \bigcirc\!> \frac{3}{5}$

**Problem set 57**

**1.** What is the difference between the sum and product of $\frac{1}{2}$ and $\frac{1}{3}$?  $\frac{2}{3}$
*(55)*

**2.** The flat of eggs held $2\frac{1}{2}$ dozen eggs. How many eggs are in $2\frac{1}{2}$ dozen?  30
*(22)*

**3.** In three nights Rumpelstiltskin spun $44,400 worth of
(18) gold thread. What was the average value of thread he
spun each night?   $14,800

**4.** Compare: $\dfrac{5}{8}$ ⊙ $\dfrac{1}{2}$
(57)

**5.** Compare: $\dfrac{4}{3}$ ⊙ $\dfrac{5}{4}$
(57)

**6.** $m + \dfrac{3}{8} = \dfrac{1}{2}$
(42)
$\dfrac{1}{8}$

**7.** $\dfrac{2}{3} + \dfrac{3}{4}$   $1\frac{5}{12}$
(56)

**8.** $3 - f = \dfrac{5}{6}$
(42)
$2\frac{1}{6}$

**9.** $32.50 × 10
(46)   $325.00

**10.** $(6.2)(0.48)$
(39)   2.976

**11.** $1.0 ÷ 0.8$   1.25
(48)

**12.** $120 ÷ 0.5$
(48)   240

**13.** $\dfrac{7}{8} \cdot \dfrac{8}{7}$   1
(30)

**14.** $\dfrac{5}{6} \cdot \dfrac{3}{4}$   $\frac{5}{8}$
(29)

**15.** Instead of dividing $7\frac{1}{2}$ by $1\frac{1}{2}$, Julie doubled both
(42) numbers, then divided mentally. What was the division
problem Julie did mentally, and what was the quotient?
15 ÷ 3; 5

**16.** Round 36.486 to the nearest hundredth.   36.49
(50)

**17.** What number is next in this sequence?   1 (or 1.0)
(10)
$$0.6, \ 0.7, \ 0.8, \ 0.9, \ \underline{\quad}, \ \ldots$$

**18.** The perimeter of this square is
(38) 4 cm. What is the area of this
square?   1 sq. cm

**19.** How many $\dfrac{3}{5}$'s are in $\dfrac{3}{4}$? $\left(\dfrac{3}{4} \div \dfrac{3}{5}\right)$   $1\frac{1}{4}$
(53)

**20.** $0.32w = 32$   100
(42)

**21.** $x + 3.4 = 5$   1.6
(42)

**22.** List the factors of 27.   1, 3, 9, 27
(19)

**23.** Arrange in order from shortest to longest:
(7)
$$1 \text{ in., } 3 \text{ cm, } 20 \text{ mm}$$
20 mm, 1 in., 3 cm

**24.** Larry correctly answered 45% of the 100 questions.
(29,33) Write 45% as a reduced fraction. How many questions
did Larry answer correctly?   $\frac{9}{20}$; 45

**25.** Finding $\frac{1}{10}$ of $12.50 is like dividing $12.50 by 10. We shift the decimal point in $12.50 one place to the left, which makes $1.250. Then we remove the trailing zero. The answer is $1.25.

**25.** Describe how to mentally calculate $\frac{1}{10}$ of $12.50.
(51)

**26.** Reduce: $\dfrac{2 \cdot 5 \cdot 2 \cdot 3 \cdot 3 \cdot 7}{2 \cdot 2 \cdot 2 \cdot 5 \cdot 5 \cdot 7}$  $\frac{9}{10}$
(53)

**27.** What is the sum of the decimal numbers represented by points $x$ and $y$ on this number line?  4
(49)

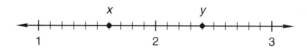

**28.** Draw a rectangle that is $1\frac{1}{2}$ inches long and $\frac{3}{4}$ inch wide. Then draw a segment that divides the rectangle into two triangles.  See student answer.
(7)

**29.** What is the perimeter of the rectangle drawn in problem 28?  $4\frac{1}{2}$ in.
(8)

**30.** If $l = 1.5$ and $w = 0.75$, then what does $lw$ equal?  1.125
(45)

# LESSON
# 58

Mental Math:
a. 300
b. 629
c. 51
d. $7.25
e. $3.00
f. 20
g. 15
Problem Solving:
  12

# Adding Mixed Numbers

**Facts Practice:** 30 Fractions to Reduce (Test G in Test Masters)

**Mental Math:** Count up and down by 3's between 3 and 36.

  **a.** 4 × 75         **b.** 279 + 350       **c.** 250 − 199
  **d.** $15.00 − $7.75     **e.** Double $1.50    **f.** $\frac{800}{40}$
  **g.** 4 × 12, ÷ 6, × 8, − 4, ÷ 6, × 3, ÷ 2

**Problem Solving:** A number cube has six faces. Where two faces meet there is an edge. How many edges does a number cube have?

We have been practicing adding mixed numbers since Lesson 27. In this lesson we will rename the fraction parts of the mixed numbers so that the fractions have common denominators. Then we will add.

**Example 1**    $2\frac{1}{2} + 1\frac{1}{6}$

*Solution*    **Step 1.** Shape—Write the fractions with common denominators.

**Step 2.** Operate—Add the fractions and add the whole numbers.

**Step 3.** Simplify—Reduce the fraction.

$$
\begin{array}{rcl}
2\frac{1}{2} \times \frac{3}{3} &=& 2\frac{3}{6} \\[2mm]
+\ 1\frac{1}{6} &=& 1\frac{1}{6} \\[1mm]
\hline
3\frac{4}{6} &=& \mathbf{3\frac{2}{3}}
\end{array}
$$

**Example 2**    $1\frac{1}{2} + 2\frac{2}{3}$

*Solution*    **Step 1.** Shape—Write the fractions with common denominators.

**Step 2.** Operate—Add the fractions and add the whole numbers.

**Step 3.** Simplify—Convert the improper fraction to a mixed number and combine the mixed number with the whole number.

$$
\begin{array}{rcl}
1\frac{1}{2} \times \frac{3}{3} &=& 1\frac{3}{6} \\[2mm]
+\ 2\frac{2}{3} \times \frac{2}{2} &=& 2\frac{4}{6} \\[1mm]
\hline
3\frac{7}{6} &=& 3 + 1\frac{1}{6} \\[2mm]
&=& \mathbf{4\frac{1}{6}}
\end{array}
$$

**Practice**    **a.** $1\frac{1}{2} + 1\frac{1}{3}$   $2\frac{5}{6}$    **b.** $1\frac{1}{2} + 1\frac{2}{3}$   $3\frac{1}{6}$    **c.** $5\frac{1}{3} + 2\frac{1}{6}$   $7\frac{1}{2}$

**d.** $3\frac{3}{4} + 1\frac{1}{3}$  $5\frac{1}{12}$    **e.** $5\frac{1}{2} + 3\frac{1}{6}$  $8\frac{2}{3}$    **f.** $7\frac{1}{2} + 4\frac{5}{8}$  $12\frac{1}{8}$

---

**Teacher Note:** "Activity Master 5" may be helpful to students in Lesson 61. Refer to the activity in that lesson to determine if copies need to be prepared.

---

**Problem set 58**

**1.** What is the product of the decimal numbers four
(40) tenths and four hundredths?   0.016

**2.** Larry looked at the clock. It was 9:45 p.m. His book
(32) report was due the next morning at 8:30. How many hours and minutes were there until Larry's book report was due?   10 hr, 45 min

**3.** Pluto's greatest distance from the sun is seven billion,
(12) four hundred million kilometers. Write that number.
7,400,000,000

**4.** $2\frac{1}{2} + 1\frac{1}{6}$  $3\frac{2}{3}$ 　　　　　**5.** $1\frac{1}{2} + 2\frac{2}{3}$  $4\frac{1}{6}$
(58)　　　　　　　　　　　　　　(58)

**6.** Compare: $\frac{1}{2}$ $<$ $\frac{3}{5}$ 　　　　**7.** Compare: $\frac{2}{3}$ $=$ $\frac{6}{9}$
(57)　　　　　　　　　　　　　(57)

**8.** $8\frac{1}{5} - 3\frac{4}{5}$  $4\frac{2}{5}$ 　　　　　**9.** $\frac{3}{4} \cdot \frac{5}{2}$  $1\frac{7}{8}$
(47)　　　　　　　　　　　　　(29)

**10.** How many $\frac{1}{2}$'s are in $\frac{2}{5}$?  $\left(\frac{2}{5} \div \frac{1}{2}\right)$  $\frac{4}{5}$
(53)

**11.** $(0.875)(40)$ 　　**12.** $0.07 \div 4$ 　　**13.** $30 \div d = 0.6$
(39)  35 　　　　　　(44)  0.0175 　　　(42)  50

**14.** What number is halfway between 0.1 and 0.24?   0.17
(49)

**15.** Round 36,428,591 to the nearest million.   36,000,000
(16)

**16.** What temperature is 23°F less than 8°F?   −15°F
(14)

**17.** What number is missing in this sequence?
(10)
　　　　　320, 160, 80, __40__, 20, 10, 5, …

**18.** How many square inches are needed to cover a square
(38) foot?   144 sq. in.

**19.** One centimeter is what fraction of one meter?   $\frac{1}{100}$
(51)

Mentally calculate the answers to problems 20 and 21:

**20.** 6.25 × 10   62.5          **21.** 6.25 ÷ 10   0.625
(46)                             (51)

**22.** Compare: 32 ÷ 10 ÷ 10 $\textcircled{<}$ 32 ÷ (10 ÷ 10)
(9)

Use the chart below to answer questions 23, 24 and 25.

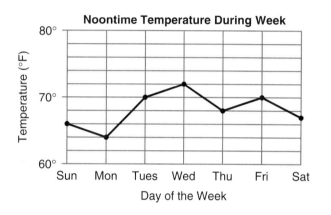

**23.** What was the difference in degrees between the
(18) highest and lowest noontime temperatures during
the week?   8°F

**24.** What was the Saturday noontime temperature?   67°F
(18)

**25.** Write a question that refers to this line graph and
(18) answer the question.   See student work.

**26.** Rumpelstiltskin could pronounce his name in six
(49) tenths of a second. At that rate, how many times could
he pronounce his name in 15 seconds? (Write and
solve a fraction division problem to answer
the question.)   25 times

**27.** One eighth is equivalent to $12\frac{1}{2}$%. To what percent is
(27) three eighths equivalent?   $37\frac{1}{2}$%

**28.** Mentally calculate the total cost of exactly 10 gallons
$^{(46)}$ of gas priced at $1.599 per gallon.   $15.99

**29.** Arrange these three numbers in order from least
$^{(57)}$ to greatest:   $\frac{3}{4}$, 1, the reciprocal of $\frac{3}{4}$

$$\frac{3}{4}, \text{ the reciprocal of } \frac{3}{4}, 1$$

**30.** If $l$ = 4 and $w$ = 3, then what does $2l + 2w$ equal?
$^{(45)}$   14

---

**LESSON
59**

**Mental Math:**
**a.** 1500
**b.** 179
**c.** 949
**d.** $11.25
**e.** $2.50
**f.** 2000
**g.** 25
**Problem Solving:**
   One cup of water

# Adding Three or More Fractions

---

**Facts Practice:**  28 Fractions to Simplify (Test I in Test Masters)

**Mental Math:**  Count by 7's from 7 to 84.

   **a.** 2 × 750         **b.** 429 − 250      **c.** 750 + 199
   **d.** $9.50 + $1.75    **e.** $\frac{1}{2}$ of $5       **f.** 40 × 50
   **g.** 12 × 3, + 4, × 2, + 20, ÷ 10, × 5, ÷ 2

**Problem Solving:**  Half of a gallon is a half gallon. Half of a half
gallon is a quart. Half of a quart is a pint. Half
of a pint is a cup. Into an empty gallon
container is poured a half gallon of water, plus
a quart of water, plus a pint of water, plus a
cup of water. How much more water is
needed to fill the gallon container?

   1 gallon    $\frac{1}{2}$ gallon  1 quart  1 pint  1 cup

---

To add three or more fractions we find a common
denominator for all the fractions being added. The lowest
common denominator is the least common multiple of all
of the denominators. When we know what the common
denominator is we can rename the fractions and add.

**Example 1**    $\frac{1}{2} + \frac{1}{4} + \frac{1}{8}$

*Solution*    First we find a common denominator. The LCM of 2, 4, and 8 is 8. We rename all fractions as eighths. Then we add and simplify if possible.

$$\frac{1}{2} \times \frac{4}{4} = \frac{4}{8}$$
$$\frac{1}{4} \times \frac{2}{2} = \frac{2}{8}$$
$$+ \frac{1}{8} \times \frac{1}{1} = \frac{1}{8}$$
$$\frac{7}{8}$$

**Example 2**    $1\frac{1}{2} + 2\frac{1}{3} + 3\frac{1}{6}$

*Solution*    A common denominator is 6. We rename all fractions. We add whole numbers and fractions. We simplify when possible.

$$1\frac{1}{2} \times \frac{3}{3} = 1\frac{3}{6}$$
$$2\frac{1}{3} \times \frac{2}{2} = 2\frac{2}{6}$$
$$+ 3\frac{1}{6} \times \frac{1}{1} = 3\frac{1}{6}$$
$$6\frac{6}{6} = 7$$

**Practice**    **a.** $\frac{1}{2} + \frac{3}{4} + \frac{1}{8}$    **b.** $\frac{1}{2} + \frac{1}{3} + \frac{1}{6}$    **c.** $1\frac{1}{2} + 1\frac{1}{3} + 1\frac{1}{4}$
$1\frac{3}{8}$    $1$    $4\frac{1}{12}$

**d.** $\frac{1}{2} + \frac{2}{3} + \frac{5}{6}$  2    **e.** $\frac{1}{2} + \frac{3}{4} + \frac{7}{8}$  $2\frac{1}{8}$    **f.** $1\frac{1}{4} + 1\frac{1}{8} + 1\frac{1}{2}$
$3\frac{7}{8}$

**Problem set**    **1.** What is the cost per ounce for a 42-ounce box of
**59**    *(15)* oatmeal priced at $1.26?    $0.03

**2.** There are 30 days in November. How many days are
(13) there from November 19 to December 25?　36

**3.** The smallest three-digit number is 100. What is the
(12) largest three-digit number?　999

**4.** $\dfrac{1}{2} + \dfrac{3}{4} + \dfrac{5}{8}$　$1\frac{7}{8}$　　　　**5.** $1\dfrac{1}{2} + 2\dfrac{2}{3} + 3\dfrac{1}{6}$　$7\frac{1}{3}$
(59)　　　　　　　　　　　　　　　(59)

**6.** $m + 1\dfrac{3}{5} = 5$　$3\frac{2}{5}$　　　**7.** $6\dfrac{1}{8} - w = 3\dfrac{5}{8}$　$2\frac{1}{2}$
(42)　　　　　　　　　　　　　(42)

**8.** Compare: $\dfrac{5}{8}$ ⓛ $\dfrac{3}{4}$　　　**9.** $\dfrac{3}{5} \cdot \dfrac{1}{3}$　$\frac{1}{5}$
(57)　　　　　　　　　　　　(29)

**10.** How many $\dfrac{1}{3}$'s are in $\dfrac{3}{5}$?　$\left(\dfrac{3}{5} \div \dfrac{1}{3}\right)$　$1\frac{4}{5}$
(53)

**11.** How much money is $\frac{5}{8}$ of $24.00?　$15.00
(22)

**12.** $(0.65)(0.14)$　0.091　　　**13.** $65 \div 0.05$　1300
(40)　　　　　　　　　　　　(48)

**14.** What is the place value of the 9 in 46.934?　tenths'
(34)

**15.** Round the product of 0.24 and 0.26 to the nearest
(50) hundredth.　0.06

**16.** What is the average of 1.3, 2, and 0.81?　1.37
(18)

**17.** What is the sum of the first seven numbers of this
(10) sequence?　49

$$1, 3, 5, 7, \dots$$

**18.** How many square feet are needed to cover a square yard?
(38)　9 sq. ft

**19.** Ten centimeters is what fraction of one meter?　$\frac{1}{10}$
(51)

**20.** $3x = 1.2 + 1.2 + 1.2$　1.2
(42)

**21.**
(30) $\frac{4}{3}y = 1$    $\frac{3}{4}$

**22.** The number 37 has how many different factors?    2
(19)

**23.** $\frac{5}{5} \times \left( \frac{4}{4} - \frac{3}{3} \right)$    0
(29)

**24.** To what decimal number is the arrow pointing?    5.4
(49)

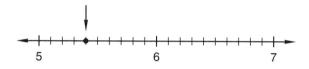

**25.** The decimal number answer to problem 24 rounds to
(50) what whole number?    5

**26.** Mary found that the elm tree in her yard added about $\frac{3}{8}$
(49) of an inch to the diameter of its trunk every year. If the diameter of the tree is about 12 inches, then the tree is about how many years old? (Write and solve a fraction division problem to answer the question.)    32 years

**27.** Duncan's favorite T.V. show starts at 8 p.m. and ends
(29) at 9 p.m. Duncan timed the commercials and found that there were 12 minutes of commercials between 8 p.m. and 9 p.m. What fraction of the hour was commercial time?    $\frac{1}{5}$

**28.** Instead of dividing 400 by 16, Chip thought of an
(42) equivalent division problem that was easier for him to divide. Write an equivalent division problem that has a one-digit divisor and find the quotient.    Possible answers 200 ÷ 8 or 100 ÷ 4; 25

**29.** Round $0.6666 to the nearest cent.    $0.67
(50)

**30.** Compare: $3\frac{1}{2}$ ⊜ $\frac{6}{2} + \frac{1}{2}$
(57)

**LESSON**

**60**

# Writing Mixed Numbers as Improper Fractions

**Mental Math:**
**a.** 3000
**b.** 533
**c.** 551
**d.** $5.75
**e.** 25
**f.** 30
**g.** 100
**Problem Solving:**

$$
\begin{array}{r}
93 \\
5\overline{)465} \\
\underline{45} \\
15 \\
\underline{15} \\
0
\end{array}
$$

**Facts Practice:** 72 Mixed Multiplication and Division (Test H in Test Masters)

**Mental Math:** Count up and down by $\frac{1}{4}$'s between $\frac{1}{4}$ and 4.

**a.** 4 × 750        **b.** 283 + 250        **c.** 750 − 199
**d.** $8.25 − $2.50        **e.** Double $12\frac{1}{2}$        **f.** $\frac{900}{30}$
**g.** 6 × 10, ÷ 3, × 2, ÷ 4, × 5, ÷ 2, × 4

**Problem Solving:** Copy this problem and fill in the missing digits.

$$
\begin{array}{r}
= = \\
5\overline{)\_\,\_\,\_} \\
4\,5 \\
1\,\_ \\
\underline{\_\,5} \\
0
\end{array}
$$

Here is another story about pies. In this story a mixed number is changed to an improper fraction.

*There were $3\frac{5}{6}$ pies on the shelf. The restaurant manager asked the server to cut the whole pies into serving slices—into sixths. Altogether, how many slices of pie will there be when the server cuts the pies?*

We will illustrate this story with circles. There were $3\frac{5}{6}$ pies on the shelf.

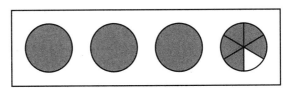

The server will cut the whole pies into sixths. Each whole pie will have six slices.

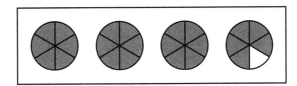

The three whole pies will make 18 slices (3 × 6 = 18). The five additional slices from the $\frac{5}{6}$ of a pie will make the total 23 slices—23 sixths. This story illustrates that $3\frac{5}{6}$ is equivalent to $\frac{23}{6}$.

Now we will describe the arithmetic for changing a mixed number like $3\frac{5}{6}$ to an improper fraction. Recall that a mixed number has a whole number part and a fraction part.

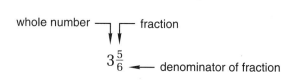

The denominator of the mixed number is also the denominator of the improper fraction.

$$3\frac{5}{6} = \frac{\phantom{0}}{6}$$

same denominator

The denominator indicates the size of the fraction "pieces." In this case the fraction pieces are sixths. We change the whole number 3 into sixths. We know that one whole is $\frac{6}{6}$, so three wholes is $3 \times \frac{6}{6}$, which is $\frac{18}{6}$. Now we add $\frac{18}{6}$ and $\frac{5}{6}$, which equals $\frac{23}{6}$.

$$\frac{18}{6} + \frac{5}{6} = \frac{23}{6}$$

**Example 1**  Write $2\frac{3}{4}$ as an improper fraction.

*Solution*  The denominator of the fraction part of the mixed number is fourths, so the denominator of the improper fraction will also be fourths.

$$2\frac{3}{4} = \frac{\phantom{0}}{4}$$

We change the whole number 2 into fourths. Since 1 equals $\frac{4}{4}$, the whole number 2 equals $2 \times \frac{4}{4}$, which is $\frac{8}{4}$. We add $\frac{8}{4}$ and $\frac{3}{4}$, which equals $\frac{11}{4}$.

$$2\frac{3}{4} = \frac{11}{4}$$

**Example 2**   Write $5\frac{2}{3}$ as an improper fraction.

*Solution*   We see that the denominator of the improper fraction will be thirds.

$$5\frac{2}{3} = \frac{\ }{3}$$

Some people use a quick, mechanical method to find the numerator of the improper fraction. Looking at the mixed number, they multiply the whole number by the denominator and then add the numerator. The result is the numerator of the improper fraction.

$$5\frac{+2}{\times 3} = \frac{17}{3}$$

**Practice**   Write each mixed number as an improper fraction.

**a.** $2\frac{4}{5}$   $\frac{14}{5}$     **b.** $3\frac{1}{2}$   $\frac{7}{2}$     **c.** $1\frac{3}{4}$   $\frac{7}{4}$

**d.** $6\frac{1}{4}$   $\frac{25}{4}$     **e.** $1\frac{5}{6}$   $\frac{11}{6}$     **f.** $3\frac{3}{10}$   $\frac{33}{10}$

**g.** $2\frac{1}{3}$   $\frac{7}{3}$     **h.** $12\frac{1}{2}$   $\frac{25}{2}$     **i.** $3\frac{1}{6}$   $\frac{19}{6}$

**Problem set 60**

1. Convert the improper fraction $\frac{20}{6}$ to a mixed number
(26) with the fraction reduced.   $3\frac{1}{3}$

2. A fathom is 6 feet. How many feet deep is water that is
(22) $2\frac{1}{2}$ fathoms?   15 ft

3. After 3 days and 7425 guesses, the queen guessed
(18) Rumpelstiltskin's name. What was the average number of names she guessed each day?   2475

4. $5\frac{1}{2} - 1\frac{2}{3}$   $3\frac{5}{6}$      5. $5\frac{1}{3} - 2\frac{1}{2}$   $2\frac{5}{6}$
(56)                                  (56)

**6.** $1\frac{1}{2} + 2\frac{1}{3} + 3\frac{1}{4}$   $7\frac{1}{12}$
(59)

**7.** $3\frac{3}{4} + 3\frac{1}{3}$   $7\frac{1}{12}$
(58)

**8.** Compare: $\frac{2}{3}$ ⊙ $\frac{3}{5}$
(57)

**9.** $\frac{5}{6} \times 42$   35
(29)

**10.** $\frac{3}{8} \cdot \frac{2}{3}$   $\frac{1}{4}$
(29)

**11.** How many $\frac{2}{3}$'s are in $\frac{3}{8}$? $\left( \frac{3}{8} \div \frac{2}{3} \right)$   $\frac{9}{16}$
(53)

**12.** $(4 - 0.4) \div 4$   0.9
(44)

**13.** $4 - (0.4 \div 4)$   3.9
(48)

**14.** Which digit in 49.63 has the same place value as the 7 in 8.7?   6
(34)

**15.** Estimate the sum of $642.23 and $861.17 to the nearest hundred dollars.   $1500
(16)

**16.** $\frac{1}{10} = \frac{?}{100}$   10
(41)

**17.** What is the next number in this sequence?   $0.1 \left( \text{or } \frac{1}{10} \right)$
(10)

$$100, 10, 1, \underline{\quad\quad}, \dots$$

**18.** The perimeter of a square is 1 foot. How many square inches cover its area?   9 sq. in.
(38)

**19.** Ten seconds is what fraction of one minute?   $\frac{1}{6}$
(29)

**20.** $15m = 300$   20
(4)

**21.** List the factors of 50.
(19)   1, 2, 5, 10, 25, 50

**22.** By what name for 1 must $\frac{2}{3}$ be multiplied to form a fraction with a 15 in the denominator?   $\frac{5}{5}$
(41)

**23.** What time is 5 hours and 15 minutes after 9:50 a.m.?
(32)   3:05 p.m.

**24.** Write $7\frac{1}{2}$ as an improper fraction.   $\frac{15}{2}$
(60)

**25.** Write $1\frac{1}{3}$ and $1\frac{1}{2}$ as improper fractions and multiply
(60) the improper fractions. What is the product? $\frac{4}{3}, \frac{3}{2}; 2$

**26.** The sales tax rate was 7%. Write 7% as a fraction.
(33) Then write the fraction as a decimal number. $\frac{7}{100}; 0.07$

Refer to the figure to answer problems 27 and 28:

**27.** The perimeter of this square is 8 cm.
(38) How long is each side? 2 cm

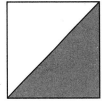

**28.** Half of the area of the square is
(38) shaded. What is the area of the
shaded part of the square? 2 sq. cm

**29.** Rawlings bought a sheet of 100 stamps from the post
(51) office for $35.00. What was the price for each stamp?
$0.35

**30.** Describe how to convert $2\frac{1}{3}$ to an improper fraction.
(60) The denominator of the improper fraction is 3. We change the
whole number 2 into thirds. Since 1 equals $\frac{3}{3}$, 2 equals $2 \times \frac{3}{3}$,
which is $\frac{6}{3}$. Then we add $\frac{6}{3}$ and $\frac{1}{3}$ and get the improper fraction $\frac{7}{3}$.

# LESSON
# 61

# Prime Numbers

**Facts Practice:**  30 Fractions to Reduce (Test G in Test Masters)

**Mental Math:**  Count by 12's from 12 to 144.

**a.** $5 \times 40$   *(10 × 40 ÷ 2)*    **b.** $475 + 1200$    **c.** $3 \times 84$
**d.** $8.50 + $2.50         **e.** $\frac{1}{3}$ of $36.00      **f.** $\frac{$25}{10}$
**g.** $6 \times 8, - 4, \div 4, \times 2, + 2, \div 6, \div 2$
**h.** Hold your hands one foot apart.

**Problem Solving:**  The average number of students in two classrooms was 27. If the students are separated into three classrooms instead of two classrooms, what will be the average number of students in each of the three classrooms?

Here we list the first ten counting numbers and their factors. Which of the numbers have exactly two factors?
2, 3, 5, 7

| NUMBER | FACTORS |
|--------|---------|
| 1 | 1 |
| 2 | 1, 2 |
| 3 | 1, 3 |
| 4 | 1, 2, 4 |
| 5 | 1, 5 |
| 6 | 1, 2, 3, 6 |
| 7 | 1, 7 |
| 8 | 1, 2, 4, 8 |
| 9 | 1, 3, 9 |
| 10 | 1, 2, 5, 10 |

Numbers that have exactly two factors are **prime numbers.** The first four prime numbers are 2, 3, 5, and 7. The number 1 is not a prime number because it has only one factor, itself. The only factors of a prime number are the number itself and 1. Therefore, to determine whether or not a number is prime, we may ask ourselves the question, "Is this number divisible by any number other than the number itself and 1?" If the number is divisible by any other number, the number is not prime.

**Example** The first four prime numbers are 2, 3, 5, and 7. What are the next four prime numbers?

**Solution** We will consider the next several numbers and eliminate those that are not prime.

$$8, 9, 10, 11, 12, 13, 14, 15, 16, 17, 18, 19, 20$$

All even numbers have 2 as a factor. So no even numbers greater than two are prime numbers. We can eliminate the even numbers from the list.

$$\cancel{8}, 9, \cancel{10}, 11, \cancel{12}, 13, \cancel{14}, 15, \cancel{16}, 17, \cancel{18}, 19, \cancel{20}$$

Since 9 is divisible by 3, and 15 is divisible by 3 and by 5, we can eliminate 9 and 15 from the list.

$$\cancel{8}, \cancel{9}, \cancel{10}, 11, \cancel{12}, 13, \cancel{14}, \cancel{15}, \cancel{16}, 17, \cancel{18}, 19, \cancel{20}$$

Each of the remaining four numbers on the list is divisible only by itself and by 1. Thus the next four prime numbers after 7 are **11, 13, 17,** and **19.**

## Activity: Prime Numbers

List the counting numbers from 1 to 50 (or use the Hundred Chart, "Activity Master 5," from the Test Masters). Then follow these directions:

**a.** Draw a line through the number 1. The number 1 is not a prime number.

**b.** Circle the prime number 2. Draw a line through all the other multiples of 2 (4, 6, 8, etc.).

**c.** Circle the prime number 3. Draw a line through all the other multiples of 3 ( 6, 9, 12, etc.).

**d.** Circle the prime number 5. Draw a line through all the other multiples of 5 (10, 15, 20, etc.).

**e.** Circle the prime number 7. Draw a line through all the other multiples of 7 (14, 21, 28, etc.).

**f.** All of the numbers on the list (or chart) from 1 through 50 (or 1 through 100) that do not have a line drawn through them are prime numbers. Circle the prime numbers.

**Practice**   Which number in each group is a prime number?

**a.** 21, 23, 25   23

**b.** 31, 32, 33   31

**c.** 43, 44, 45   43

Which number in each group is not a prime number?

**d.** 41, 42, 43   42

**e.** 31, 41, 51   51

**f.** 23, 33, 43   33

Prime numbers can be multiplied to equal whole numbers that are not prime. To make 12 we multiply 2 · 2 · 3. To make 15 we multiply 3 · 5. Show which prime numbers we multiply to make these products.

**g.** 16   2 · 2 · 2 · 2          **h.** 18   2 · 3 · 3

**Problem set 61**

**1.** In music there are whole notes, half notes, quarter
(53) notes, and eighth notes. How many quarter notes equal a whole note?   4

**2.** How many eighth notes equal a quarter note?   2
(53)

**3.** Don is 5 feet $2\frac{1}{2}$ inches tall. How many inches tall is that?
(60)   $62\frac{1}{2}$ in.

**4.** Which of these numbers is not a prime number?   B. 21
(61)
   A. 11          B. 21          C. 31          D. 41

**5.** Which of these numbers is a prime number? B. 41
(61)
A. 35 B. 41 C. 63 D. 72

**6.** The prices for three pairs of skates were $36.25,
(18) $41.50, and $43.75. What was the average price for a
pair of skates? $40.50

**7.** Instead of dividing 15 by $2\frac{1}{2}$, Solomon doubled both
(42) numbers, then divided mentally. What was Solomon's
mental division problem and its quotient? 30 ÷ 5 = 6

**8.** $m - 4\frac{3}{8} = 3\frac{1}{4}$  $7\frac{5}{8}$ **9.** $\frac{1}{2} + \frac{3}{4} + \frac{5}{8}$  $1\frac{7}{8}$
(42) (59)

**10.** $\frac{5}{6} - \frac{1}{2}$  $\frac{1}{3}$ **11.** $\frac{3}{5} - \frac{3}{10}$  $\frac{3}{10}$
(54) (54)

**12.** $\frac{1}{2} \cdot \frac{4}{5}$  $\frac{2}{5}$ **13.** $\frac{2}{3} \div \frac{1}{2}$  $1\frac{1}{3}$
(29) (53)

**14.** $1 - (0.2 - 0.03)$  0.83 **15.** $(0.14)(0.16)$  0.0224
(40) (38)

**16.** $\dfrac{0.456}{6}$  0.076 **17.** $\dfrac{1.5}{0.04}$  37.5
(44) (48)

**18.** One centimeter equals 10 millimeters. How many
(46) millimeters does 2.5 centimeters equal? 25 mm

**19.** List all of the common factors of 18 and 24 and circle
(19) the greatest. 1, 2, 3, ⑥

**20.** What fraction of the group is ◯●◯●◯
(21) shaded? $\frac{2}{5}$ ●●◯◯◯

**21.** If the perimeter of a square is 40 mm, what is the area
(38) of the square? 100 sq. mm

**22.** At 6 a.m. the temperature was −6°F. At noon the
(14) temperature was 14°F. From 6 a.m. to noon the
temperature rose how many degrees? 20°F

**23.** Compare: $\dfrac{3}{3} \times \dfrac{2}{2}$ ⊜ $\dfrac{3}{3} \div \dfrac{2}{2}$
*(49)*

Use this chart of favorite sports of 100 people to answer questions 24 through 28.

**24.** How many more people favored
*(40)* baseball than favored football?
18

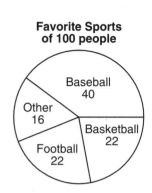

**Favorite Sports of 100 people**

**25.** What fraction of the people
*(40)* favored baseball?  $\frac{2}{5}$

**26.** Was any sport the favorite sport of
*(40)* the majority of the people surveyed? Write one or two sentences to explain your answer.  See student work.

**27.** Since baseball was the favorite sport of 40 **out of 100**
*(40)* people, it was the favorite sport of 40% of the people asked. What percent of the people answered that football was their favorite sport?  22%

**28.** Write a question that refers to this circle graph and
*(40)* answer the question.  See student work.

**29.** Tom thought of one number he could put in each of
*(38)* these boxes to make the equation true. Tom thought of what number?  10

$$\square \times \square = 100$$

**30.** If we multiply the prime numbers 2 · 3 · 3, the
*(61)* product is 18. Which prime numbers would we multiply to make a product of 20?  2 · 2 · 5

# Subtracting Mixed Numbers with Regrouping, Part 2

LESSON
62

Mental Math:
a. 700
b. 370
c. 252
d. $6.00
e. 15
f. $0.25
g. 0
Problem Solving:
$\frac{1}{3}, \frac{5}{12}, \frac{1}{2}$

**Facts Practice:** 64 Multiplication Facts (Test D in Test Masters)

**Mental Math:** Count up and down by $\frac{1}{8}$'s between $\frac{1}{8}$ and 2.

    **a.** 5 × 140 *(10 × 140 ÷ 2)*    **b.** 420 − 50    **c.** 4 × 63
    **d.** $8.50 − $2.50           **e.** Double $7\frac{1}{2}$    **f.** $\frac{\$25}{100}$
    **g.** 5 × 10, − 20, + 2, ÷ 4, + 1, ÷ 3, − 3
    **h.** Hold your hands one foot apart; then one inch apart.

**Problem Solving:** What are the next three numbers in this sequence?

$$\frac{1}{12}, \frac{1}{6}, \frac{1}{4}, \underline{\quad}, \underline{\quad}, \underline{\quad}, \cdots$$

Since Lesson 47 we have practiced subtracting mixed numbers with regrouping. In this lesson we will rename the fractions with common denominators before subtracting.

To subtract $1\frac{1}{2}$ from $3\frac{2}{3}$, we first write the fractions with common denominators. Then we subtract the whole numbers and fractions and simplify when possible.

$$
\begin{array}{r}
3\frac{2}{3} \times \frac{2}{2} = 3\frac{4}{6} \\
- 1\frac{1}{2} \times \frac{3}{3} = 1\frac{3}{6} \\
\hline
2\frac{1}{6}
\end{array}
$$

Sometimes when subtracting it is necessary to regroup. We write the fractions with common denominators before regrouping.

Example     $5\frac{1}{2} - 1\frac{2}{3}$

*Solution*    We write fractions with common denominators. We regroup if necessary. We simplify if possible.

$$
\begin{array}{r}
5\frac{1}{2} \times \frac{3}{3} = \overset{4}{\cancel{5}}\overset{9}{\cancel{\tfrac{3}{6}}} \\
- 1\frac{2}{3} \times \frac{2}{2} = 1\frac{4}{6} \\
\hline
3\frac{5}{6}
\end{array}
$$

**Practice\***    **a.** $5\frac{1}{2} - 3\frac{1}{3}$   $2\frac{1}{6}$    **b.** $4\frac{1}{4} - 2\frac{1}{3}$   $1\frac{11}{12}$    **c.** $6\frac{1}{2} - 1\frac{3}{4}$   $4\frac{3}{4}$

     **d.** $7\frac{2}{3} - 3\frac{5}{6}$   $3\frac{5}{6}$    **e.** $6\frac{1}{6} - 1\frac{1}{2}$   $4\frac{2}{3}$    **f.** $4\frac{1}{3} - 1\frac{1}{2}$   $2\frac{5}{6}$

     **g.** $4\frac{5}{6} - 1\frac{1}{3}$   $3\frac{1}{2}$    **h.** $6\frac{1}{2} - 3\frac{5}{6}$   $2\frac{2}{3}$    **i.** $8\frac{2}{3} - 5\frac{3}{4}$   $2\frac{11}{12}$

**Problem set 62**

**1.** What is the difference between the sum of 0.6 and 0.4
*(52)* and the product of 0.6 and 0.4?   0.76

**2.** Mt. Whitney, the highest point in California, has an
*(13)* elevation of 14,494 feet above sea level. From there one can see Death Valley, the lowest point, which has an elevation of 282 feet **below** sea level. The floor of Death Valley is how many feet below the peak of Mt. Whitney?   14,776 ft

**3.** The anaconda was 288 inches long. How many feet is
*(15)* 288 inches?   24 ft

**4.** Write the mixed number $4\frac{2}{3}$ as an improper fraction.   $\frac{14}{3}$
*(60)*

**5.** Write $2\frac{1}{2}$ and $1\frac{1}{5}$ as improper fractions. Then multiply
*(60)* the improper fractions and simplify the product.
   $\frac{5}{2}, \frac{6}{5}; 3$

**6.** What time is $2\frac{1}{2}$ hours after 10:15 a.m.?   12:45 p.m.
*(32)*

**7.** $(30 \times 15) \div (30 - 15)$     **8.** Compare: $\frac{5}{8}$ $\boxed{<}$ $\frac{2}{3}$
*(5)*   30           *(57)*

**9.** $w - 3\frac{2}{3} = 1\frac{1}{2}$   $5\frac{1}{6}$     **10.** $\frac{6}{8} - \frac{3}{4}$   0
*(42)*              *(54)*

**11.** $6\frac{1}{4} - 5\frac{5}{8}$   $\frac{5}{8}$     **12.** $\frac{3}{4} \times \frac{2}{5}$   $\frac{3}{10}$     **13.** $\frac{3}{4} \div \frac{2}{5}$   $1\frac{7}{8}$
*(62)*            *(29)*             *(53)*

**14.** $(1 - 0.4)(1 + 0.4)$     **15.** $\frac{3}{5}$ of \$45.00   \$27.00
*(39)*   0.84               *(22)*

**16.** $0.4 \div 8$   0.05
(44)

**17.** $8 \div 0.4$   20
(48)

**18.** What number is next in this sequence?
(10)   1 (or 1.0)

$$0.2, 0.4, 0.6, 0.8, \underline{\hspace{2em}}, \ldots$$

**19.** What is the tenth prime number?   29
(61)

**20.** What is the perimeter of the rectangle?   $3\frac{3}{4}$ in.
(8)

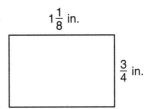

$1\frac{1}{8}$ in.

$\frac{3}{4}$ in.

**21.** This floor tile is one square foot.
(38)   The kitchen floor was covered
with 100 floor tiles. What was the
area of the kitchen floor in square
inches?   14,400 sq. in.

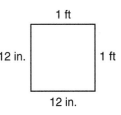

1 ft

12 in.

1 ft

12 in.

**22.** Round $678.25 to the nearest ten dollars.   $680.00
(16)

**23.** What is the area of the shaded
(31)   part of this rectangle?   150 sq. cm

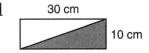

30 cm

10 cm

**24.** A ton is 2000 pounds. How many pounds is $2\frac{1}{2}$ tons?
(15)   5000 lb

**25.** Which arrow could be pointing to 0.2 on the number line?
(49)   C

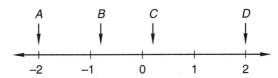

A   B   C   D

−2   −1   0   1   2

**26.** Think of a prime number for $n$ that makes this
(61)   equation true.   7

$$n \cdot n = 49$$

**27.** Jefferson got a hit 30% of the 240 times he came to bat
(29,33) during the season. Write 30% as a reduced fraction.
Then find the number of hits Jefferson got during the
season.   $\frac{3}{10}$; 72 hits

**28.** Dixon has run 11.5 miles of a 26.2-mile race. Find the
(42) remaining distance Dixon has to run to complete the
race by solving this equation.   14.7 mi

$$11.5 \text{ mi} + d = 26.2 \text{ mi}$$

**29.** Write 7% as a fraction. Then write the fraction as a
(33) decimal number.   $\frac{7}{100}$; 0.07

**30.** Arrange these numbers in order from least to greatest:
(57) $0, \frac{1}{2}, 1, 1\frac{1}{2}, 2$                   $1, \frac{1}{2}, 0, 1\frac{1}{2}, 2$

# Polygons

Mental Math:
a. 1200
b. 4950
c. 238
d. $15.00
e. $5.00
f. $7.50
g. 8
Problem Solving:
    8 vertices

**Facts Practice:** Write 24 Mixed Numbers as Improper Fractions
(Test J in Test Masters)

**Mental Math:** Count up and down by 25's between 25 and 300.

**a.** $5 \times 240$  **b.** $4500 + 450$  **c.** $7 \times 34$
**d.** $7.50 + $7.50  **e.** $\frac{1}{4}$ of $20.00  **f.** $\frac{\$75}{10}$
**g.** $6 \times 8, \div 2, + 1, \div 5, - 1, \times 4, \div 2$
**h.** Hold your hands one foot apart; then one yard apart.

**Problem Solving:** A number cube has six faces. Where two faces meet there is an edge. A "corner" where three edges meet is called a *vertex* (plural is *vertices*). A number cube has how many vertices?

**Polygons** are closed shapes with straight sides. Polygons are named by the number of sides they have. The chart below names some common polygons.

**Polygons**

| Shape | Number of Sides | Name of Polygon |
|-------|-----------------|-----------------|
|       | 3               | triangle        |
|       | 4               | quadrilateral   |
|       | 5               | pentagon        |
|       | 6               | hexagon         |
|       | 8               | octagon         |

Two sides of a polygon meet, or **intersect,** at a **vertex** (plural is **vertices**). A polygon has the same number of vertices as it has sides.

Example 1    What is the name of a polygon that has four sides?

Solution    The answer is not "square" or "rectangle." Squares and rectangles do have four sides, but not all four-sided polygons are squares or rectangles. The correct answer is **quadrilateral.** A rectangle is one kind of quadrilateral. A square is a rectangle with sides of equal length.

If all the sides of a polygon are the same length and if all the angles are the same measure, then the polygon is called a **regular polygon.** A square is a regular quadrilateral, but a rectangle that is longer than it is wide is not a regular quadrilateral.

Example 2    The area of a square is 25 square centimeters.

(a)  What is the length of each side of the square?

(b)  What is the perimeter of the square?

Solution    (a)  We find the area of a square, or of any rectangle, by multiplying the length by the width. With a square, the length and width are equal. Finding the length of a side is like finding the one number that goes into each of these boxes.

$$\square \times \square = 25$$

Since $5 \times 5 = 25$, the length of each side is **5 cm.**

(b)  The perimeter of the square is the sum of the lengths of the four sides. We may find the perimeter by adding the lengths of the four sides or by multiplying the length of one side by four.

$$5 \text{ cm} + 5 \text{ cm} + 5 \text{ cm} + 5 \text{ cm} = \textbf{20 cm}$$

$$4 \times 5 \text{ cm} = \textbf{20 cm}$$

Example 3    A **regular octagon** has a perimeter of 96 inches. How long is each side?

Solution    An octagon has eight sides. The sides of a regular octagon are the same length. Dividing the perimeter of 96 inches by 8, we find each side is **12 inches.** (Most of the red stop signs on our roads are regular octagons with sides 12 inches long.)

**Practice** **a.** What is the name of this six-sided shape? hexagon

**b.** How many sides does a pentagon have? 5

**c.** Can a polygon have 19 sides? yes

**d.** The area of a square is 16 square inches. What is its perimeter? 16 in.

**Problem set 63**

**1.** When the sum of 1.3 and 1.2 is divided by the difference of 1.3 and 1.2, what is the quotient? 25
(52)

**2.** William Shakespeare was born in 1564 and died in 1616. How many years did he live? 52 years
(13)

**3.** Robin Hood's arrow hit a target 45 yards away. How many feet did the arrow travel? 135 ft
(15)

4. A square is a four-sided polygon, so it is a quadrilateral. The four sides of a square are the same length, and the four angles are the same size, so a square is "regular."

**4.** Why is a square a regular quadrilateral?
(63)

**5.** A regular hexagon has a perimeter of 36 inches. How long is each side? 6 in.
(63)

**6.** $\frac{1}{4} = \frac{?}{100}$ 25
(41)

**7.** $\frac{8 \times 8}{8 + 8}$ 4
(5)

**8.** $5\frac{2}{3} + 3\frac{3}{4}$ $9\frac{5}{12}$
(58)

**9.** $\frac{1}{2} + \frac{2}{3} + \frac{1}{4}$ $1\frac{5}{12}$
(59)

**10.** $\frac{9}{10} - \frac{1}{2}$ $\frac{2}{5}$
(56)

**11.** $6\frac{1}{2} - 2\frac{7}{8}$ $3\frac{5}{8}$
(62)

**12.** Compare: $2 \times 0.4$ $\bigcirc<$ $2 + 0.4$
(43)

**13.** $4.8 \times 0.35$ 1.68
(39)

**14.** $1 \div 0.4$ 2.5
(48)

**15.** How many $0.12 pencils can Mr. Jones buy for $4.80? 40 pencils
(15)

**16.** Round the product of 0.33 and 0.38 to the nearest hundredth. 0.13
(50)

**17.** Multiply the length by the width to find the area of this rectangle. $\frac{3}{8}$ sq. in.
(31)

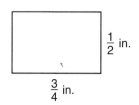

$\frac{1}{2}$ in.

$\frac{3}{4}$ in.

**18.** Which is the twelfth prime number?   37
(61)

**19.** Write $3\frac{4}{5}$ as an improper fraction.   $\frac{19}{5}$
(60)

**20.** The area of a square is 9 sq. cm.
(63)

    (a) How long is each side of the square?   3 cm

    (b) What is the perimeter of the square?   12 cm

**21.** Five minutes is what fraction of an hour?   $\frac{1}{12}$
(29)

**22.** The top, bottom, and sides of a box are also called the **faces** of the box. This box has how many faces?
(63)
6

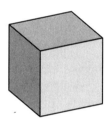

**23.** There are 100 centimeters to a meter. How many centimeters equal 2.5 meters?   250 cm
(15)

**24.** Write the mixed numbers $1\frac{1}{2}$ and $2\frac{1}{2}$ as improper fractions. Then multiply the improper fractions and simplify the product.   $\frac{3}{2}, \frac{5}{2}; 3\frac{3}{4}$
(60)

**25.** The numbers 2, 3, 5, 7, and 11 are prime numbers. The numbers 4, 6, 8, 9, 10, and 12 are not prime numbers, but they can be formed by multiplying prime numbers.
(61)

$$2 \cdot 2 = 4$$

$$2 \cdot 3 = 6$$

$$2 \cdot 2 \cdot 2 = 8$$

Show how to make 9, 10, and 12 by multiplying prime numbers.   $9 = 3 \times 3; 10 = 5 \times 2; 12 = 2 \times 2 \times 3$

**26.** Write 75% as an unreduced fraction. Then write the
(33)   fraction as a decimal number.   $\frac{75}{100}$ ; 0.75

**27.** Reduce: $\dfrac{2 \cdot 2 \cdot 2 \cdot 3 \cdot 3}{2 \cdot 2 \cdot 3 \cdot 5 \cdot 5}$   $\frac{6}{25}$
(53)

**28.** 16.6 mi + $l$ = 26.2 mi   9.6 mi
(42)

Refer to this double-line graph to find information for
problems 29 and 30.

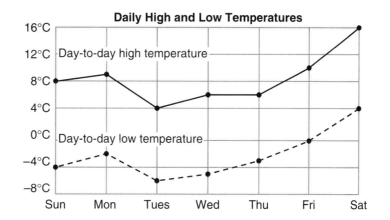

**29.** The difference between Tuesday's high and low
(18)   temperatures was how many degrees?   10°C

**30.** The difference between the lowest temperature of the
(18)   week and the highest temperature of the week was
   how many degrees?   22°C

# LESSON 64

# Prime Factorization • Division by Primes • Factor Tree

**Mental Math:**
a. 300
b. 536
c. 195
d. $17.50
e. $1.50
f. $0.75
g. 1
**Problem Solving:**
$\frac{1}{8}$;

Nelson

Sister

Little
Brother

---

**Facts Practice:** 72 Mixed Multiplication and Division (Test H in Test Masters)

**Mental Math:** Count by 9's from 9 to 108.

    **a.** $5 \times 60$           **b.** $586 - 50$        **c.** $3 \times 65$
    **d.** $20.00 - $2.50     **e.** Double 75¢     **f.** $\frac{75}{100}$
    **g.** $9 \times 9, - 1, \div 2, + 2, \div 6, + 3, \div 10$
    **h.** Hold your hands one yard apart; then one meter apart.

**Problem Solving:** Nelson bought a pizza and ate half of it. Then his sister ate half of what was left. Then his little brother ate half of what his sister had left. What fraction of the pizza did Nelson's little brother eat? Illustrate the portions of the pizza eaten by each family member.

---

**Prime factorization**

All whole numbers greater than 1 are either prime numbers or **composite numbers.** A composite number has **more than two** factors. As we studied in Lesson 61, the numbers 2, 3, 5, and 7 are prime numbers. The numbers 4, 6, 8, and 9 are composite numbers. All composite numbers can be made by multiplying prime numbers together.

$$4 = 2 \cdot 2$$

$$6 = 2 \cdot 3$$

$$8 = 2 \cdot 2 \cdot 2 \text{ (also } 2 \cdot 4, \text{ but 4 is not prime)}$$

$$9 = 3 \cdot 3$$

When we write a composite number as a product of its prime factors, we have written the **prime factorization** of the number. The prime factorizations of 4, 6, 8, and 9 are shown above.

In this lesson we will show two methods for factoring a composite number. One method is **division by primes,** and the other method is using a **factor tree.** We will illustrate both methods as we factor 60.

**Division by primes**

The smallest prime number is 2, then 3, then 5, and so on. Since 60 is divisible by 2, we begin by dividing 60 by 2. The quotient is 30.

$$\frac{30}{2\overline{)60}}$$

Since 30 is also divisible by 2, we divide 30 by 2. The quotient is 15. Notice how we "stack" the divisions.

$$\begin{array}{r} 15 \\ 2\overline{)30} \\ 2\overline{)60} \end{array}$$

Although 15 is not divisible by 2, it is divisible by the next prime number, which is 3. The quotient is 5.

$$\begin{array}{r} 5 \\ 3\overline{)15} \\ 2\overline{)30} \\ 2\overline{)60} \end{array}$$

Five is a prime number. The only prime number that divides 5 is 5.

$$\begin{array}{r} 1 \\ 5\overline{)5} \\ 3\overline{)15} \\ 2\overline{)30} \\ 2\overline{)60} \end{array}$$

By dividing by prime numbers we have found the prime factorization of 60.

$$60 = 2 \cdot 2 \cdot 3 \cdot 5$$

**Factor tree**  When using a factor tree, we simply think of any two numbers whose product is 60. Since 6 times 10 equals 60, we will use 6 and 10 as the first two "branches" of the factor tree.

The numbers 6 and 10 are not prime numbers, so we continue the process by factoring 6 into 2 · 3 and by factoring 10 into 2 · 5.

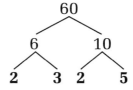

The numbers at the ends of the branches are all prime numbers. We have completed the factor tree. We will arrange the factors in order from least to greatest and write the prime factorization of 60.

$$60 = 2 \cdot 2 \cdot 3 \cdot 5$$

**Example 1**  Use a factor tree to find the prime factorization of 60. Use 4 and 15 as the first branches.

*Solution*  Some composite numbers can be divided into many different factor trees. However, when the factor tree is completed, the same prime numbers appear at the ends of the branches.

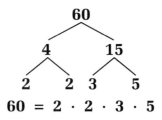

$$60 = 2 \cdot 2 \cdot 3 \cdot 5$$

**Example 2** Use division by primes to find the prime factorization of 36.

*Solution* We begin by dividing by the smallest prime number that is a factor of 36, which is 2. We will continue dividing by prime numbers until the quotient is 1.[†]

$$
\begin{array}{r}
1 \\
3\overline{)3} \\
3\overline{)9} \\
2\overline{)18} \\
2\overline{)36}
\end{array}
$$
$$36 = 2 \cdot 2 \cdot 3 \cdot 3$$

**Practice*** **a.** Which of these numbers are composite numbers?
20, 21, 22
19, 20, 21, 22, 23

**b.** Write the prime factorization of each composite number in problem (a). 20 = 2 · 2 · 5; 21 = 3 · 7; 22 = 2 · 11

**c.** Use a factor tree to find the prime factorization of 36.
36 = 2 · 2 · 3 · 3

**d.** Use division by primes to find the prime factorization of 48. 48 = 2 · 2 · 2 · 2 · 3

**e.** Write 125 as a product of prime factors. 125 = 5 · 5 · 5

**f.** Write the prime factorization of 10 and of 100. What similarities do you notice? Can you guess what the prime factorization of 1000 is? 10 = 2 · 5;
100 = 2 · 2 · 5 · 5;
1000 = 2 · 2 · 2 · 5 · 5 · 5

**Problem set 64** **1.** The total land area of the world is about fifty-seven
(12) million, two hundred eighty thousand square miles. Write that number. 57,280,000

78 in. **2.** Nelson photographed an African white rhinoceros
(15) that stood $6\frac{1}{2}$ feet high. How many inches is $6\frac{1}{2}$ feet?

[†]Some prefer to complete the division when the quotient is a prime number, in which case the final quotient, together with the divisors, is included in the prime factorization of the number.

**3.** Jenny shot 10 free throws and made 6. What fraction of her shots did she make? What percent of her shots did she make?   $\frac{3}{5}$; 60%
(29,41)

**4.** Draw a factor tree for 40. Then write the prime factorization of 40.   40 = 2 · 2 · 2 · 5
(64)

**5.** Which of these is a composite number?   21
(64)
$$21, 31, 41$$

**6.** Write $2\frac{2}{3}$ as an improper fraction and multiply the improper fraction by $\frac{3}{8}$. What is the product?   $\frac{8}{3}$, 1
(60)

**7.** 10,000 − (10,000 ÷ 10)   9000
(5)

**8.** $8\frac{1}{2} + 1\frac{1}{3} + 2\frac{1}{6}$   12          **9.** $\frac{1}{12} + \frac{1}{6} + \frac{1}{2}$   $\frac{3}{4}$
(59)                                              (59)

**10.** $15\frac{3}{4} - m = 2\frac{1}{8}$   $13\frac{5}{8}$
(42)

**11.** Compare: $\frac{1}{2} - \frac{1}{3}$ $\boxed{=}$ $\frac{2}{3} - \frac{1}{2}$
(57)

**12.** $\frac{3}{8} \times \frac{1}{3}$   $\frac{1}{8}$          **13.** $\frac{3}{8} \div \frac{1}{2}$   $\frac{3}{4}$
(29)                                  (53)

**14.** 1 − (0.2 + 0.48)   0.32
(38)

**15.** 0.0144 ÷ 12   0.0012
(44)

**16.** What is the total cost of two dozen erasers that are priced at 8¢ each?   $1.92
(15)

**17.** The store manager put $20.00 worth of $0.25 pieces in the change drawer. How many $0.25 pieces are in $20.00?   80
(15)

**18.** What time is $2\frac{1}{2}$ hours before 1:15 p.m.?   10:45 a.m.
(32)

**19.** Use division by primes to find the prime factorization
(64) of 50.   $50 = 2 \cdot 5 \cdot 5$

**20.** What is the name of a six-sided polygon? How many
(63) vertices does it have?   hexagon; 6

**21.** Write $3\frac{4}{7}$ as an improper fraction.   $\frac{25}{7}$
(60)

**22.** The area of a square is 36 square inches.
(63)
  (a) What is the length of each side?   6 in.

  (b) What is the perimeter of the square?   24 in.

**23.** Write 16% as a reduced fraction.   $\frac{4}{25}$
(33)

**24.** How many millimeters long is the line segment?   50 mm
(7)

**25.** A meter is about one **big** step. About how many meters
(7) long is an automobile?   about 4 m; Various answers.

**26.** Write the prime factorization of 375 and of 1000.
(64)   $375 = 3 \cdot 5 \cdot 5 \cdot 5$; $1000 = 2 \cdot 2 \cdot 2 \cdot 5 \cdot 5 \cdot 5$

**27.** Reduce: $\dfrac{3 \cdot 5 \cdot 5 \cdot 5}{2 \cdot 2 \cdot 2 \cdot 5 \cdot 5 \cdot 5}$   $\frac{3}{8}$
(53)

**28.** $\dfrac{4}{25} = \dfrac{?}{100}$   16
(41)

**29.** Eighty percent of the 20 answers were correct. Write
(29,33) 80% as a reduced fraction. Then find the number of
correct answers.   $\frac{4}{5}$; 16

**30.** The "rect-" part of *rectangle* means "right." A
(63) rectangle is a "right-angle" shape. Why is every square
also a rectangle?

30. A rectangle is a four-sided polygon with four right angles. Since every square is four-sided with four right angles, every square is a rectangle. (A rectangle need not be longer than it is wide.)

# LESSON 65

# Multiplying Mixed Numbers

Mental Math:
a. 800
b. 475
c. 184
d. $3.50
e. $20.00
f. $3.00
g. 1
Problem Solving:

$$\frac{146}{6\overline{)876}}$$
$$\frac{6}{27}$$
$$\frac{24}{36}$$
$$\frac{36}{0}$$

**Facts Practice:** Write 24 Mixed Numbers as Improper Fractions (Test J in Test Masters)

**Mental Math:** Count up and down by $\frac{1}{8}$'s between $\frac{1}{8}$ and 2.

   **a.** $5 \times 160$       **b.** $376 + 99$       **c.** $8 \times 23$
   **d.** $1.75 + $1.75    **e.** $\frac{1}{3}$ of $60.00    **f.** $\frac{\$30}{10}$
   **g.** $8 \times 8, -4, \div 2, + 3, \div 3, + 1, \div 6, \div 2$
   **h.** Hold your hands one meter apart; then one yard apart.

**Problem Solving:** Copy this problem and fill in the missing digits.

$$6\overline{)\_\_6}$$

Recall the three steps to solving an arithmetic problem with fractions.

   **Step 1.** Be sure the problem is in the correct shape.
   **Step 2.** Perform the operation indicated.
   **Step 3.** Simplify the answer if possible.

Remember that the correct shape for adding and subtracting fractions is to write the fraction with common denominators. To multiply or divide fractions we do not need to write the fractions with common denominators. The correct shape for multiplying and dividing fractions is to write the numbers in **fraction form.** This means we will write mixed numbers as improper fractions. We will also write whole numbers in fraction form by writing the whole number as the numerator of a fraction with the denominator 1.

**Example 1**   $2\frac{2}{3} \times 4$

*Solution*   First, we write $2\frac{2}{3}$ and 4 in fraction form.

$$\frac{8}{3} \times \frac{4}{1}$$

Second, we multiply the numerators to find the numerator of the product, and we multiply the denominators to find the denominator of the product.

$$\frac{8}{3} \times \frac{4}{1} = \frac{32}{3}$$

Third, we simplify the product by converting the improper fraction to a mixed number.

$$\frac{32}{3} = 10\frac{2}{3}$$

**Example 2**   $2\frac{1}{2} \times 1\frac{1}{3}$

*Solution*   First, write the numbers in fraction form.

$$\frac{5}{2} \times \frac{4}{3}$$

Second, multiply the terms of the fractions.

$$\frac{5}{2} \times \frac{4}{3} = \frac{20}{6}$$

Third, simplify the product.

$$\frac{20}{6} = 3\frac{2}{6}$$
$$3\frac{2}{6} = 3\frac{1}{3}$$

**Practice\***   **a.** $1\frac{1}{2} \times \frac{2}{3}$  1    **b.** $1\frac{2}{3} \times \frac{3}{4}$  $1\frac{1}{4}$    **c.** $1\frac{1}{2} \times 1\frac{2}{3}$  $2\frac{1}{2}$

**d.** $1\frac{2}{3} \times 3$  5    **e.** $2\frac{1}{2} \times 2\frac{2}{3}$  $6\frac{2}{3}$    **f.** $3 \times 1\frac{3}{4}$  $5\frac{1}{4}$

**g.** $3\frac{1}{3} \times 1\frac{2}{3}$  $5\frac{5}{9}$    **h.** $2\frac{3}{4} \times 2$  $5\frac{1}{2}$    **i.** $2 \times 3\frac{1}{2}$  7

**Problem set 65**

**1.** Fifty percent of the 60 questions on the test were
(29,33) multiple choice. Write 50% as a reduced fraction and
find the number of multiple choice questions.   $\frac{1}{2}$; 30

**2.** How many quarter notes equal a half note?   2
(53)

**3.** Some railroad rails weigh 155 pounds per yard and are
(15) 33 feet long. How much would a 33-foot-long rail weigh?
1705 lb

**4.** $1\frac{1}{2} \times 2\frac{2}{3}$   4
(65)

**5.** $2\frac{2}{3} \times 2$   $5\frac{1}{3}$
(65)

**6.** The sum of five numbers is 200. What is the average of
(18) the numbers?   40

**7.** $\dfrac{100 + 75}{100 - 75}$   7
(5)

**8.** $m - 1\frac{1}{5} = 3\frac{1}{2}$
(42)
$4\frac{7}{10}$

**9.** $\dfrac{1}{3} + \dfrac{1}{6} + \dfrac{1}{12}$
(59)
$\frac{7}{12}$

**10.** $35\frac{1}{4} - 12\frac{1}{2}$
(62)
$22\frac{3}{4}$

**11.** $\dfrac{4}{5} \times \dfrac{1}{2}$   $\frac{2}{5}$
(29)

**12.** $\dfrac{4}{5} \div \dfrac{1}{2}$   $1\frac{3}{5}$
(53)

**13.** $0.25 \div 5$   0.05
(44)

**14.** $5 \div 0.25$   20
(48)

**15.** What is the product of the answers to problems 13 and 14?
(39) 1

**16.** $\dfrac{1}{2} + \dfrac{1}{2}$ is equal to which of the following?   C. $\frac{1}{2} \div \frac{1}{2}$
(53)

A. $\dfrac{1}{2} - \dfrac{1}{2}$      B. $\dfrac{1}{2} \times \dfrac{1}{2}$      C. $\dfrac{1}{2} \div \dfrac{1}{2}$

**17.** Use a factor tree to find the prime factorization of 30.
(64) $30 = 2 \cdot 3 \cdot 5$

**18.** If three of the items cost a total of 75¢, how much
(15) would six of the items cost?   $1.50

**19.** Round $1.1675 to the nearest cent.   $1.17
(50)

**20.** One side of a regular pentagon is 0.8 meter. What is
(63) the perimeter?   4 m

**21.** Twenty minutes is what fraction of an hour? $\frac{1}{3}$
(29)

**22.** The temperature dropped from 12°C to −8°C. This was
(14) a drop of how many degrees? 20°C

Use the chart below to answer questions 23, 24, and 25.

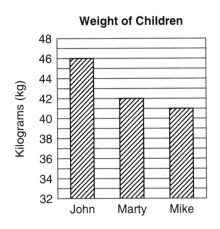

**Weight of Children**

**23.** John weighs how much more than Mike? 5 kg
(16)

**24.** What is the average weight of the three boys? 43 kg
(16)

**25.** Write a "larger-smaller-difference" problem that refers
(16) to the graph and answer the question. See student work.

**26.** Use division by primes to find the prime factorization
(64) of 400. 400 = 2 · 2 · 2 · 2 · 5 · 5

**27.** Simon covered the floor of a square room with 144
(38) floor tiles. How many floor tiles were along each wall
of the room? 12 tiles

**28.** The weight of a one-kilogram object on earth is about
(46) 2.2 pounds. A large man may be 100 kilograms. About
how many pounds is that? 220 pounds

**29.** Reduce: $\dfrac{5 \cdot 5 \cdot 5 \cdot 7}{2 \cdot 2 \cdot 2 \cdot 5 \cdot 5 \cdot 5}$  $\frac{7}{8}$
(53)

**30.** Which of these polygons is not a regular polygon?    B.
(63)

   A. △      B. ▭      C. ⬠      D. ⬡

## LESSON 66

# Using Prime Factorization to Reduce Fractions • Naming Solids

Mental Math:
a. 1300
b. 291
c. 144
d. $8.50
e. $2.50
f. $0.30
g. $2\frac{1}{2}$
Problem Solving:
   390 ft

---

**Facts Practice:** Write 24 Mixed Numbers as Improper Fractions (Test J in Test Masters)

**Mental Math:** Count down by 2's from 10 to negative 10.

   **a.** 5 × 260        **b.** 341 − 50        **c.** 3 × 48
   **d.** $9.25 − 75¢      **e.** Double $1.25     **f.** $\frac{\$30}{100}$
   **g.** 6 × 6, − 1, ÷ 5, × 2, + 1, ÷ 3, ÷ 2
   **h.** Hold your hands one foot apart; then nine inches apart.

**Problem Solving:** There are about 520 nine-inch-long noodles in a 1-pound package of spaghetti. Laid end to end, how many **feet** would the noodles in a package of spaghetti reach?

---

**Using prime factorization to reduce fractions**

One way to reduce fractions with large terms is to factor the terms and then reduce the common factors. To reduce $\frac{125}{1000}$, we could begin by writing the prime factorization of 125 and of 1000.

$$\frac{125}{1000} = \frac{5 \cdot 5 \cdot 5}{2 \cdot 2 \cdot 2 \cdot 5 \cdot 5 \cdot 5}$$

We see three pairs of 5's that can be reduced. Each $\frac{5}{5}$ reduces to $\frac{1}{1}$.

$$\frac{\overset{1}{\cancel{5}} \cdot \overset{1}{\cancel{5}} \cdot \overset{1}{\cancel{5}}}{2 \cdot 2 \cdot 2 \cdot \underset{1}{\cancel{5}} \cdot \underset{1}{\cancel{5}} \cdot \underset{1}{\cancel{5}}} = \frac{1}{8}$$

We multiply the remaining factors and find that $\frac{125}{1000}$ reduces to $\frac{1}{8}$.

**Example 1** Reduce: $\dfrac{375}{1000}$

*Solution* We write the prime factorization of the numerator and of the denominator.

$$\frac{375}{1000} = \frac{3 \cdot 5 \cdot 5 \cdot 5}{2 \cdot 2 \cdot 2 \cdot 5 \cdot 5 \cdot 5}$$

Then we reduce the common factors and multiply the remaining factors.

$$\frac{3 \cdot \overset{1}{\cancel{5}} \cdot \overset{1}{\cancel{5}} \cdot \overset{1}{\cancel{5}}}{2 \cdot 2 \cdot 2 \cdot \underset{1}{\cancel{5}} \cdot \underset{1}{\cancel{5}} \cdot \underset{1}{\cancel{5}}} = \frac{3}{8}$$

We find that $\dfrac{375}{1000}$ reduces to $\dfrac{3}{8}$.

**Naming solids**
Polygons are two-dimensional shapes. Polygons have length and width. However, polygons do not have height (or depth). The objects that we encounter in the world around us are three-dimensional. These objects have length, width, and height. This table illustrates some three dimensional shapes—shapes that take up space. Three-dimensional shapes are often called **solids.**

**Solids**

| Shape | Name | |
|-------|------|---|
| | Triangular Prism | |
| | Rectangular Prism | } Prisms |
| | Cube | |
| | Pyramid | |
| | Cylinder | |
| | Cone | |
| | Sphere | |

You should be able to recognize, name, and draw each of these shapes. Notice that when these shapes are drawn, the edges which are hidden from the viewer can be indicated by using dashed lines.

**Example 2** Name this shape.

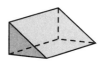

**Solution** This shape is a **triangular prism.**

**Example 3** Draw a cube.

**Solution** To draw a cube, we first sketch two squares like this. Then we draw lines to connect the vertices using dashed lines to draw the edges that are hidden from view.

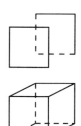

**Practice** Write the prime factorization of the numerator and denominator of each fraction and reduce each fraction.

**a.** $\dfrac{875}{1000}$ $\quad \dfrac{5 \cdot 5 \cdot 5 \cdot 7}{2 \cdot 2 \cdot 2 \cdot 5 \cdot 5 \cdot 5} = \dfrac{7}{8}$ **b.** $\dfrac{48}{400}$ $\quad \dfrac{2 \cdot 2 \cdot 2 \cdot 2 \cdot 3}{2 \cdot 2 \cdot 2 \cdot 2 \cdot 5 \cdot 5} = \dfrac{3}{25}$

**c.** A can of soup is an example of which geometric solid?
cylinder

**d.** Sketch a triangular prism. Begin by drawing two triangles like these.

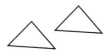

**Problem set 66**

**1.** What is the sum of the first nine positive odd numbers?
(10) 81

**2.** A fathom is about 6 feet. A nautical mile is 1000 fathoms. A nautical mile is about how many feet?
(46) 6000 ft

**3.** Instead of dividing $1.50 by $0.05, Marcus made an equivalent division problem by mentally multiplying the dividend and divisor by 100. Then he performed the equivalent division problem. What is the equivalent division problem Marcus made and what is the quotient? $150.00 ÷ $5 = 30
(42)

**4.** 6 cm + *l* = 11 cm   5 cm     **5.** 8*g* = 9.6   1.2
(3)                               (42)

**6.** The combined length of four sticks is 172 inches.
(18) What is the average length of each stick?   43 in.

**7.** 10,000 − (4675 + 968)   **8.** $3\frac{1}{3} + 2\frac{3}{4}$  $6\frac{1}{12}$
(5)  4357                        (58)

**9.** $\frac{7}{10} - w = \frac{1}{2}$  $\frac{1}{5}$     **10.** $4\frac{1}{4} - 2\frac{7}{8}$  $1\frac{3}{8}$
(42)                          (62)

**11.** $2\frac{2}{3} \times 3$  8     **12.** $1\frac{1}{3} \times 2\frac{1}{4}$  3
(65)                    (65)

**13.** $\frac{3}{5} = \frac{?}{100}$  60     **14.** (2 × 0.3) − (0.2 × 0.3)
(41)                        (39)  0.54

**15.** 1.44 ÷ 60   0.024     **16.** $6.00 ÷ $0.15
(44)                          (48)  40, not $40.00 or 40¢

**17.** Five dollars was divided evenly among four people.
(15) How much money did each receive?   $1.25

**18.** The area of a regular quadrilateral is 100 square
(63) inches. What is its perimeter?   40 in.

**19.** Write the prime factorization of 625 and of 1000.
(66) Then reduce $\frac{625}{1000}$.   $\frac{5 \cdot 5 \cdot 5 \cdot 5}{2 \cdot 2 \cdot 2 \cdot 5 \cdot 5 \cdot 5} = \frac{5}{8}$

**20.** What is the area of the rectangle shown below?
(31)  $1\frac{1}{8}$ sq. in.

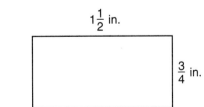

$1\frac{1}{2}$ in.

$\frac{3}{4}$ in.

**21.** Thirty-six of the eighty-eight piano keys are black.
(29) What fraction of the piano keys are black?   $\frac{9}{22}$

**22.** Sketch a rectangular prism. Begin by drawing two
(66) congruent rectangles.

**23.** $1\frac{1}{2} \times \boxed{\phantom{x}} = 1 \frac{2}{3}$
(30,60)

**24.** There are 1000 meters in a kilometer. How many
(15) meters are in 2.5 kilometers?   2500 m

**25.** Which arrow could be pointing to 0.1 on the number line?
(49)  *C*

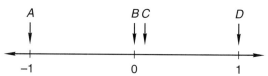

**26.** Which arrow in problem 25 is pointing to the number
(49) halfway between –1 and 1?   *B*

**27.** A basketball is an example of which geometric solid?
(66)  sphere

**28.** Write 51% as a fraction. Then write the fraction as a
(33) decimal number.   $\frac{51}{100}$ ; $0.51$

Refer to this map to answer questions 29 and 30.

**29.** Which building is on the corner of W. B St. and N. 2nd?
(N.R.)
A. 🏴    B. ✝    C. ☐    D. ⊠   A. 🏴

E. C St. and S. 1st   **30.** The building ◼ is on the corner of which two streets?
(N.R.)

# LESSON 67

# Dividing Mixed Numbers

**Facts Practice:**  28 Fractions to Simplify (Test I in Test Masters)

**Mental Math:**  Count down by 5's from 25 to negative 25.

 a.  5 × 80                   b.  275 + 1500            c.  7 × 42
 d.  $5.75 + 50¢             e.  $\frac{1}{4}$ of $48.00          f.  $\frac{\$120}{10}$
 g.  7 × 8, − 1, ÷ 5, × 2, − 1, ÷ 3, − 8
 h.  Hold your hands one meter apart; then 90 cm apart.

**Problem Solving:**  Which whole number greater than 90 but less
than 100 is a prime number?

Recall the three steps to solving an arithmetic problem with fractions.

> **Step 1.**  Be sure the problem is in the correct shape.
> **Step 2.**  Perform the operation indicated.
> **Step 3.**  Simplify the answer if possible.

In Lesson 65 we noted that the correct shape for multiplying and dividing fractions is fraction form. In this lesson we will practice dividing mixed numbers. We first write any mixed numbers or whole numbers as improper fractions. Then we divide.

**Example 1**   $2\frac{2}{3} \div 4$

*Solution*   We write the numbers in fraction form.

$$\frac{8}{3} \div \frac{4}{1}$$

We find the number of 4's in 1. Then we use the reciprocal of 4 to find the number of 4's in $\frac{8}{3}$.

$$1 \div \frac{4}{1} = \frac{1}{4}$$

$$\frac{8}{3} \times \frac{1}{4} = \frac{8}{12}$$

We simplify the answer.

$$\frac{8}{12} = \frac{2}{3}$$

Notice that dividing a number by 4 is equivalent to finding $\frac{1}{4}$ of the number. Instead of dividing $2\frac{2}{3}$ by 4, we find $\frac{1}{4}$ of $2\frac{2}{3}$.

**Example 2**     $2\frac{2}{3} \div 1\frac{1}{2}$

*Solution*  We write the mixed numbers as fractions.

$$\frac{8}{3} \div \frac{3}{2}$$

We find the number of $\frac{3}{2}$'s in 1. Then we use the reciprocal of $\frac{3}{2}$ to find the number of $\frac{3}{2}$'s in $\frac{8}{3}$.

$$1 \div \frac{3}{2} = \frac{2}{3}$$

$$\frac{8}{3} \times \frac{2}{3} = \frac{16}{9}$$

We simplify the answer.

$$\frac{16}{9} = 1\frac{7}{9}$$

**Practice\***   **a.** $\frac{1}{4}$ of $1\frac{3}{5}$   $\frac{2}{5}$   **b.** $1\frac{3}{5} \div 4$   $\frac{2}{5}$

**c.** $\frac{1}{3}$ of $2\frac{2}{5}$   $\frac{4}{5}$   **d.** $2\frac{2}{5} \div 3$   $\frac{4}{5}$

**e.** $1\frac{2}{3} \div 2\frac{1}{2}$   $\frac{2}{3}$   **f.** $2\frac{1}{2} \div 1\frac{2}{3}$   $1\frac{1}{2}$

**g.** $1\frac{1}{2} \div 1\frac{1}{2}$   $1$   **h.** $7 \div 1\frac{3}{4}$   $4$

**Problem set 67**

1. $^{(54)}$ What is the difference between the sum of $\frac{1}{2}$ and $\frac{1}{4}$ and the product of $\frac{1}{2}$ and $\frac{1}{4}$?   $\frac{5}{8}$

2. $^{(15)}$ Bill ran a half mile in two minutes and fifty-five seconds. How many seconds is that?   175 s

3. $^{(15)}$ The gauge of a railroad—the distance between the two tracks—is usually 4 feet $8\frac{1}{2}$ inches. How many inches is that?   $56\frac{1}{2}$ in.

4. $^{(67)}$ $1\frac{1}{2} \div 2\frac{2}{3}$   $\frac{9}{16}$

5. $^{(67)}$ $1\frac{1}{3} \div 4$   $\frac{1}{3}$

6. $^{(18)}$ In six games Yvonne scored a total of 108 points. How many points per game did she average?   18 points

7. $^{(66)}$ Write the prime factorization of 24 and 200. Then reduce $\frac{24}{200}$.   $\frac{2 \cdot 2 \cdot 2 \cdot 3}{2 \cdot 2 \cdot 2 \cdot 5 \cdot 5} = \frac{3}{25}$

8. $^{(42)}$ $m - 5\frac{3}{8} = 1\frac{3}{16}$   $6\frac{9}{16}$

9. $^{(42)}$ $3\frac{3}{5} + 2\frac{7}{10} = n$   $6\frac{3}{10}$

10. $^{(62)}$ $5\frac{1}{8} - 1\frac{1}{2}$   $3\frac{5}{8}$

11. $^{(65)}$ $3\frac{1}{3} \times 1\frac{1}{2}$   5

12. $^{(67)}$ $3\frac{1}{3} \div 1\frac{1}{2}$   $2\frac{2}{9}$

13. $^{(31)}$ What is the area of a rectangle that is 4 inches long and $1\frac{3}{4}$ inches wide?   7 sq. in.

14. $^{(52)}$ $(3.2 + 1) - (0.6 \times 7)$   0

15. $^{(48)}$ $12.5 \div 0.4$   31.25

16. $^{(44)}$ $0.375 \div 25$   0.015

17. $^{(51)}$ $3.2 \times 10$ equals which of the following?   B. $320 \div 10$

     A. $32 \div 10$      B. $320 \div 10$      C. $0.32 \div 10$

18. $^{(16)}$ Estimate the sum of 6416, 5734, and 4912 to the nearest thousand.   17,000

**19.** Instead of dividing 880 by 24, Sam made an
(42) equivalent division problem with smaller numbers by dividing the dividend and divisor by 8. Then he quickly found the quotient of the equivalent problem. What was the equivalent problem Sam made, and what was the quotient? Write the quotient as a mixed number.   $\frac{110}{3}$ ; $36\frac{2}{3}$

**20.** The perimeter of a square is 2.4 meters. How long is
(63) each side of the square?   0.6 m

**21.** What is the area of the square described in problem 20?
(63)   0.36 sq. m

**22.** What fraction of the months begin with the letter *M*?
(29)   $\frac{1}{6}$

**23.** $\dfrac{3}{4} = \dfrac{?}{100}$   75
(41)

**24.** Why is a circle not a polygon?   Polygons have straight sides.
(65)   Since a circle is curved, it is not a polygon.

**25.** Compare:   $\dfrac{1}{3} \times 4\dfrac{1}{2}$ $\bigcirc=$ $4\dfrac{1}{2} \div 3$
(67)

**26.** Use your ruler to find the length of this segment to the
(17) nearest eighth of an inch.   $1\frac{7}{8}$ in.

_____

**27.** 36 mm + *w* = 63 mm   27 mm
(3)

**28.** Write 3% as a fraction. Then write the fraction as a
(33) decimal number.   $\frac{3}{100}$ ; 0.03

**29.** A shoe box is an example of which geometric solid?
(66)   rectangular prism

**30.** Sunrise occurred at 6:20 a.m. and sunset occurred at
(32) 5:45 p.m. How many hours and minutes were there from sunrise to sunset?   11 hr, 25 min

# LESSON
# 68

# Lines

**Facts Practice:** Write 24 Mixed Numbers as Improper Fractions (Test J in Test Masters)

**Mental Math:** Count up and down by $\frac{1}{4}$'s between $\frac{1}{4}$ and 4.

  **a.** 5 × 180          **b.** 530 − 50          **c.** 6 × 44
  **d.** $6.00 − $1.75    **e.** Double $1.75      **f.** $\frac{\$120}{100}$
  **g.** 6 × 5, + 2, ÷ 4, × 3, ÷ 4, − 2, ÷ 2, ÷ 2
  **h.** Hold your hands one inch apart; then one cm apart.

**Problem Solving:** Nathan used a one-foot length of string to make a rectangle that was twice as long as it was wide. What was the area that was enclosed by the string?

Here we show ways to illustrate a **line,** a **ray,** and a **segment.**

A **line** continues in two directions without end. A **ray** begins at one point and continues without end. A **segment** is a part of a line and has two endpoints.

A **plane** in mathematics is a flat surface like a tabletop or a smooth sheet of paper. When two lines are drawn on the same plane, either they will cross at some point or they will not cross. When lines do not cross but stay the same distance apart, we say that the lines are **parallel.** When lines cross, we say they **intersect.** When they intersect and make square angles, we call the lines **perpendicular.** The square angles formed by perpendicular lines are called **right angles.** If lines intersect at a point but are not perpendicular, then the lines are **oblique.**

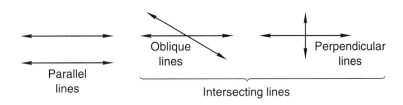

Letters are often used to designate points. We may use two points to identify a line, a ray, or a segment. Here we show a line that passes through points $A$ and $B$. This line may be referred to as line $AB$ or line $BA$. We may abbreviate line $AB$ as $\overleftrightarrow{AB}$.

The ray that begins at point $A$ and passes through point $B$ is ray $AB$, which may be abbreviated $\overrightarrow{AB}$. The portion of line $AB$ between and including points $A$ and $B$ is segment $AB$ (or segment $BA$), which can be abbreviated $\overline{AB}$ (or $\overline{BA}$).

**Example 1**  Which segment appears to be perpendicular to $\overline{PQ}$ in this figure?

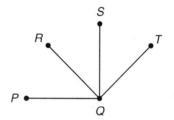

*Solution*  The segment that appears to be perpendicular to segment $PQ$ is **segment $SQ$** (or **segment $QS$**), which may be abbreviated $\overline{SQ}$ or $\overline{QS}$. Together, $\overline{PQ}$ and $\overline{QS}$ appear to form a right angle. (It may be necessary to "mentally erase" or ignore the other segments in the figure to see the relationship of the segments.)

**Example 2**  In rectangle $ABCD$, which side is parallel to $\overline{AB}$?

*Solution*  Points $A$, $B$, $C$, and $D$ are the vertices of the rectangle. In rectangle $ABCD$, $\overline{BC}$ and $\overline{AD}$ are perpendicular to $\overline{AB}$. The side that is parallel to $\overline{AB}$ is $\overline{DC}$, which may also be named $\overline{CD}$.

**Example 3**  In this figure, the length of $\overline{LM}$ is 4 cm, and the length of $\overline{LN}$ is 9 cm. What is the length of $\overline{MN}$?

*Solution*  The length of $\overline{LM}$ plus the length of $\overline{MN}$ equals the length of $\overline{LN}$. With the information in the problem we can make this equal. The letter *l* stands for the missing length.

$$4 \text{ cm} + l = 9 \text{ cm}$$

Since 4 cm plus 5 cm equals 9 cm, we find that the length of $\overline{MN}$ is **5 cm.**

**Practice**  **a.** What do we call a part of a line?  segment

**b.** Is a beam of sunlight like a segment, a line, or a ray?  ray

**c.** What do we call lines in the same plane that do not intersect?  parallel lines

Name the following:

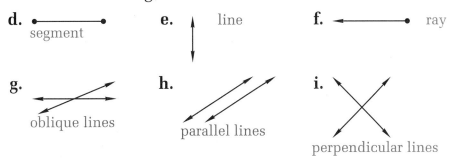

**d.** segment  **e.** line  **f.** ray

**g.** oblique lines  **h.** parallel lines  **i.** perpendicular lines

**j.** In this figure the length of $\overline{AC}$ is 60 mm, and the length of $\overline{BC}$ is 26 mm. Find the length of $\overline{AB}$.  34 mm

**k.** A **horizontal** line is parallel with the horizon. A **vertical** line is perpendicular to the horizon. If a horizontal line and a vertical line intersect, what kind of angles are formed by the lines?  right angles

1. Draw a pair of parallel lines. Then draw a second pair of parallel lines that are perpendicular to the first pair. Trace over the quadrilateral that is formed by the intersecting pairs of lines. What kind of quadrilateral did you trace?   rectangle

**Problem set 68**

1. (53) What is the quotient if the dividend is $\frac{1}{2}$ and the divisor is $\frac{1}{8}$?   4

2. (14) The highest weather temperature recorded was 136°F in Africa. The lowest was −127°F in Antarctica. How many degrees difference is there between these temperatures?   263°F

3. (15) A dollar bill is about 6 inches long. Laid end to end, about how many **feet** would 1000 dollar bills reach?   500 ft

4. (66) Write the prime factorization of the numerator and denominator of this fraction. Then reduce the fraction.
$$\frac{3 \cdot 3 \cdot 5}{2 \cdot 2 \cdot 2 \cdot 3 \cdot 3} = \frac{5}{8}$$
$$\frac{45}{72}$$

5. (68) In quadrilateral $QRST$, which segment appears to be parallel to $\overline{RS}$?   $\overline{QT}$ or $\overline{TQ}$

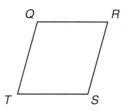

6. (18) In 10 days Carla saved $27.50. On the average, how much did she save each day?   $2.75

7. (5) $\dfrac{1 \times 2 \times 3 \times 4 \times 5}{1 + 2 + 3 + 4 + 5}$   8

8. (30) $\dfrac{2}{5}w = 1$   $\frac{5}{2}$

9. (59) $3\dfrac{1}{2} + 2\dfrac{3}{4} + 1\dfrac{5}{8}$   $7\frac{7}{8}$

10. (42) $\dfrac{3}{4} - f = \dfrac{1}{3}$   $\frac{5}{12}$

**11.** $m + 1\frac{3}{4} = 5\frac{3}{8}$  $3\frac{5}{8}$
(42)

**12.** $2\frac{2}{3} \times 1\frac{1}{5}$  $3\frac{1}{5}$
(65)

**13.** $1\frac{2}{3} \div 2$  $\frac{5}{6}$
(67)

**14.** $\dfrac{2.4}{0.08}$  30
(48)

**15.** What is the perimeter of this square?  10 m
(38)

**16.** What is the area of this square?  6.25 sq. m
(38)

2.5 m

**17.** How do you decide if a counting number is a composite
(64) number?   If a counting number is divisible by a counting number other than itself or 1, then the number is composite.

18. One possibility:

250
25  10
5  5 2  5

**18.** Make a factor tree to find the prime factorization of 250.
(64)

**19.** A stop sign has the shape of an eight-sided polygon.
(63) What is the name of an eight-sided polygon?   octagon

**20.** There were 15 boys and 12 girls in the class. What
(29) fraction of the class was made up of girls?  $\frac{4}{9}$

**21.** Instead of dividing $4\frac{1}{2}$ by $1\frac{1}{2}$, Carla doubled both
(42) numbers before dividing mentally. What was Carla's mental division problem and its quotient?  $9 \div 3 = 3$

**22.** What is the reciprocal of $2\frac{1}{2}$?  $\frac{2}{5}$
(30,60)

**23.** There are 1000 grams in a kilogram. How many grams
(15) is 2.25 kilograms?  2250 g

**24.** About how many **millimeters** long is the line?  35 mm
(7)

**25.** The length of $\overline{WX}$ is 53 mm. The length of $\overline{XY}$ is 35 mm.
(68) What is the length of $\overline{WY}$?  88 mm

W          X          Y

**26.** Sketch a cylinder.
(66)

**27.** $\dfrac{8}{25} = \dfrac{?}{100}$   32
(41)

**28.** Arrange these numbers in order from least to greatest:
(49)   −1, 0, 0.1, 1

   0.1, 1, −1, 0

**29.** Draw a circle and shade $\frac{1}{4}$ of it. What percent of the
(33)   circle is shaded?   ; 25%

**30.** How many small cubes are in the big cube?   8
(66)

## LESSON
## 69

# Reducing Fractions Before Multiplying

**Facts Practice:**  30 Fractions to Reduce (Test G in Test Masters)

**Mental Math:** Count up and down by 2's between negative 10 and 10.

| | | |
|---|---|---|
| **a.** $5 \times 280$ | **b.** $476 + 99$ | **c.** $3 \times 54$ |
| **d.** $4.50 + $1.75$ | **e.** $\frac{1}{3}$ of $90.00 | **f.** $\frac{\$250}{10}$ |

**g.** $5 \times 10, \div 2, + 5, \div 2, - 5, \div 10, - 1$
**h.** Hold your hands one yard apart; then two feet apart.

**Problem Solving:** Every even number greater than two is not prime but can be written as a product of primes. Chris thought that even numbers greater than two could also be written as a sum of primes ($4 = 2 + 2$, $6 = 3 + 3$, $8 = 5 + 3$, etc.). Show how the even numbers from 10 to 20 can be written as sums of prime numbers.

The terms of a fraction may be reduced before the fractions are multiplied, even though the terms to be reduced appear in different fractions. Notice that 3 appears as a numerator and as a denominator in these multiplied fractions.

$$\frac{3}{5} \times \frac{2}{3} = \frac{6}{15} \qquad \frac{6}{15} \text{ reduces to } \frac{2}{5}$$

We may reduce the common terms before we multiply. We reduce $\frac{3}{3}$ to $\frac{1}{1}$ by dividing both 3's by 3. Then we multiply the remaining terms.

$$\frac{\overset{1}{\cancel{3}}}{5} \times \frac{2}{\underset{1}{\cancel{3}}} = \frac{2}{5}$$

Reducing before we multiply avoids the need to reduce after we multiply. Reducing before multiplying is also known as **canceling**.

**Example 1**    $\dfrac{5}{6} \times \dfrac{1}{5}$

*Solution*    We will reduce before we multiply. Any numerator may be paired with any denominator to reduce multiplied fractions. Since 5 appears as a numerator and as a denominator, we will reduce $\frac{5}{5}$ to $\frac{1}{1}$ by dividing both 5's by 5. Then we multiply the remaining terms.

$$\dfrac{\overset{1}{\cancel{5}}}{6} \times \dfrac{1}{\underset{1}{\cancel{5}}} = \mathbf{\dfrac{1}{6}}$$

**Example 2**    $1\dfrac{1}{9} \times 1\dfrac{1}{5}$

*Solution*    First we write the numbers in fraction form.

$$\dfrac{10}{9} \times \dfrac{6}{5}$$

We mentally pair 10 with 5 and 6 with 9.

$$\overset{\frown}{10} \underset{\smile}{\times} \overset{\frown}{6} \underset{\smile}{\phantom{}} \; 9 \quad 5$$

We reduce $\frac{10}{5}$ to $\frac{2}{1}$ by dividing 10 and 5 by 5. We reduce $\frac{6}{9}$ to $\frac{2}{3}$ by dividing 6 and 9 by 3.

$$\dfrac{\overset{2}{\cancel{10}}}{\underset{3}{\cancel{9}}} \times \dfrac{\overset{2}{\cancel{6}}}{\underset{1}{\cancel{5}}} = \dfrac{4}{3}$$

We multiply the remaining terms. Then we simplify the product.

$$\dfrac{4}{3} = \mathbf{1\dfrac{1}{3}}$$

**Example 3**    $\dfrac{5}{6} \div \dfrac{5}{2}$

*Solution*    This is a division problem.

$$\dfrac{5}{6} \div \dfrac{5}{2}$$

First we find the number of $\frac{5}{2}$'s in 1. Then we use the reciprocal of $\frac{5}{2}$ to find the number of $\frac{5}{2}$'s in $\frac{5}{6}$.

$$1 \div \frac{5}{2} = \frac{2}{5}$$

$$\frac{5}{6} \times \frac{2}{5}$$

Since this is now a multiplication problem, we may reduce before we multiply.

$$\frac{\overset{1}{\cancel{5}}}{\underset{3}{\cancel{6}}} \times \frac{\overset{1}{\cancel{2}}}{\underset{1}{\cancel{5}}} = \frac{1}{3}$$

**Note:** We only cancel the terms of multiplied fractions. We may cancel the terms of divided fractions only when the problem has been rewritten as a multiplication problem. We do not cancel the terms of added or subtracted fractions.

**Practice** Reduce before multiplying:

a. $\frac{3}{4} \cdot \frac{4}{5}$  $\frac{3}{5}$

b. $\frac{2}{3} \cdot \frac{3}{4}$  $\frac{1}{2}$

c. $\frac{8}{9} \cdot \frac{9}{10}$  $\frac{4}{5}$

Write in fraction form. Then reduce before multiplying.

d. $2\frac{1}{4} \times 4$  9

e. $1\frac{1}{2} \times 2\frac{2}{3}$  4

f. $3\frac{1}{3} \times 2\frac{1}{4}$  $7\frac{1}{2}$

Rewrite each division problem as a multiplication problem. Then reduce before multiplying.

g. $\frac{2}{5} \div \frac{2}{3}$  $\frac{3}{5}$

h. $\frac{8}{9} \div \frac{2}{3}$  $1\frac{1}{3}$

i. $\frac{9}{10} \div 1\frac{1}{5}$  $\frac{3}{4}$

**Problem set 69**

1. Alaska was purchased from Russia in 1867 for seven million, two hundred thousand dollars. Write that amount.
(12)
$7,200,000

2. How many eighth notes equal a half note?  4
(53)

**3.** Instead of dividing $12\frac{1}{2}$ by $2\frac{1}{2}$, Shannon doubled both
(42) numbers and then divided. Write the division problem Shannon formed and its quotient. $25 \div 5 = 5$

In problems 4, 5, and 6, reduce before multiplying:

**4.** $\dfrac{5}{6} \cdot \dfrac{4}{5}$ $\frac{2}{3}$
(69)

**5.** $\dfrac{5}{6} \div \dfrac{5}{2}$ $\frac{1}{3}$
(69)

**6.** $\dfrac{9}{10} \cdot \dfrac{5}{6}$ $\frac{3}{4}$
(69)

**7.** What number is halfway between $\frac{1}{2}$ and 1 on the
(17) number line? $\frac{3}{4}$

**8.** $f - \dfrac{3}{4} = \dfrac{5}{6}$
(42)
$1\frac{7}{12}$

**9.** $3\dfrac{2}{3} + 4\dfrac{5}{6}$ $8\frac{1}{2}$
(58)

**10.** $7\dfrac{1}{8} - 2\dfrac{1}{2}$ $4\frac{5}{8}$
(62)

**11.** $4.37 + 12.8 + 6$ $23.17$
(38)

**12.** $0.46 \div 5$ $0.092$
(44)

**13.** $60 \div 0.8$ $75$
(48)

**14.** What is the average of the three numbers marked by the
(18) arrow on this decimal number line? (First estimate whether the average will be more than 5 or less than 5.)
$5.1$

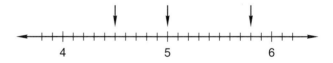

**15.** $1.5 \div 0.06$ is equivalent to which of the following?
(48)
    A. $15 \div 6$      B. $150 \div 6$      C. $150 \div 60$
    B. $150 \div 6$

**16.** There are 1000 milliliters in a liter. How many
(39) milliliters are in 3.8 liters? $3800$ milliliters

19.
$5\overline{)5}\;\dfrac{1}{\phantom{5}}$
$5\overline{)25}$
$3\overline{)75}$
$2\overline{)150}$

**17.** $\dfrac{2}{3} + n = 1$ $\frac{1}{3}$
(42)

**18.** $\dfrac{2}{3}m = 1$ $\frac{3}{2}$
(30)

**19.** Use division by primes to find the prime factorization
(64) of 150.

**20.** Segment *AC* is 47 mm. Segment *AB* is 19 mm. How
(68) long is segment *BC*?   28 mm

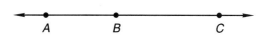

Write problems 21 and 22 in fraction form; then reduce before multiplying.

**21.** $1\frac{2}{3} \times 1\frac{1}{5}$   2
(69)

**22.** $\frac{8}{9} \div 2\frac{2}{3}$   $\frac{1}{3}$
(69)

Use the graph to answer questions 23, 24, and 25:

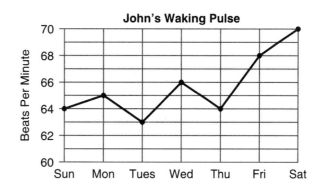

**23.** When John woke on Saturday, his pulse was how many
(15) beats per minute more than it was on Tuesday?
7 beats per minute more

**24.** On Monday, John took his pulse for 3 minutes before
(18) marking the graph. How many times did his heart beat
in those 3 minutes?   195

**25.** Write a question that refers to this graph and answer
(18) the question.   See student work.

**26.** Write the prime factorization of the numerator and
(66) denominator of this fraction. Then reduce the fraction.
$\frac{2 \cdot 2 \cdot 2 \cdot 3 \cdot 3}{2 \cdot 2 \cdot 3 \cdot 5 \cdot 5} = \frac{6}{25}$

$$\frac{72}{300}$$

In rectangle *ABCD*, the length of $\overline{AB}$ is 2.5 cm, and the length of $\overline{BC}$ is 1.5 cm. Use this information and the figure to answer problems 27 through 30.

**27.** What is the perimeter of the rectangle?   8 cm
*(68)*

**28.** What is the area of the rectangle?
*(31)*   3.75 sq. cm

**29.** Name two segments perpendicular to $\overline{DC}$.
*(68)*   $\overline{AD}$ or $\overline{DA}$ and $\overline{BC}$ or $\overline{CB}$

**30.** If segment *BD* were drawn on the figure dividing the rectangle into two equal parts, what would be the area of each part?   1.875 sq. cm
*(68)*

# LESSON 70

# Rectangular Coordinates

Mental Math:
a. 2400
b. 268
c. 344
d. $1.25
e. $4.50
f. $2.50
g. 1
Problem Solving:

**Facts Practice:** 64 Multiplication Facts (Test D in Test Masters)

**Mental Math:** Count by 12's from 12 to 144.

a. $5 \times 480$
b. $367 - 99$
c. $8 \times 43$
d. $10.00 - $8.75$
e. Double $2.25
f. $\frac{\$250}{100}$
g. $8 \times 9, + 3, \div 3, \times 2, - 10, \div 5, + 3, \div 11$
h. Hold your hands one yard apart; then one meter apart.

**Problem Solving:** Copy this factor tree and fill in the missing numbers.

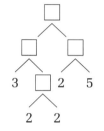

By drawing two number lines perpendicular to each other and by extending the unit marks, we can create a grid or graph called a **coordinate plane.**

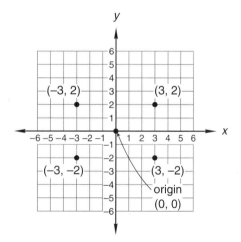

The point at which the number lines intersect is called the **origin.** The horizontal number line is called the **x-axis,** and the vertical number line is called the **y-axis.** We **graph** a point when we make a dot at the location of the point. We can name the location of any point on this coordinate plane with two numbers. The numbers that tell the location of the point are called the **coordinates** of the point.

The coordinates are written as a pair of numbers in parentheses, like (3, −2). The first number is the *x*-coordinate and shows the horizontal (↔) direction and distance from the origin. The second number, the *y*-coordinate, shows the vertical ( ↕ ) direction and distance from the origin. The sign of the coordinate shows direction. Positive coordinates are to the right or up, and negative coordinates are to the left or down.

To graph (3, −2), we begin at the origin and move to the right along the *x*-axis three units to 3 on the number line. From there we move down two units and make a dot. We may label the point we graphed (3, −2). We have graphed and marked the coordinates of three additional points on the coordinate plane. Notice that each pair of coordinates is different and designates a different point.

**Example**   Refer to this coordinate plane to answer questions (a) and (b).

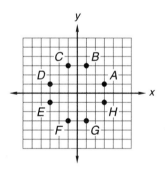

(a) What are the coordinates of point *A*?

(b) Which point has the coordinates (−1, 3)?

*Solution*   (a) We see that point *A* aligns with 3 on the *x*-axis and 1 on the *y*-axis. We write the *x*-coordinate first. So the coordinates of point *A* are **(3, 1).**

(b) We find the point that aligns with −1 on the *x*-axis and 3 on the *y*-axis. This is point **C.** Some people think of starting at the origin and moving to the left one unit and then up three units.

**Practice***  Refer to the coordinate plane in the example to answer questions (a)–(f). Name the points that have the following coordinates:

**a.** $(3, -1)$  $H$      **b.** $(1, 3)$  $B$      **c.** $(-3, 1)$  $D$

Identify the coordinates of the following points:

**d.** $G$  $(1, -3)$      **e.** $E$  $(-3, -1)$      **f.** $F$  $(-1, -3)$

---

**Teacher Note:**  Beginning in Lesson 74, students will be drawing their own graphs. Having graph paper available for Lesson 74 and for subsequent problem sets will be helpful to students. "Activity Master 6" in the Test Masters may also be copied for student use.

---

**Problem set 70**

**1.** What is the least common multiple of 6 and 10?   30
(30)

**2.** The highest point on land is Mt. Everest, which is
(13) 29,028 feet above sea level. The lowest point on land is the Dead Sea, which is 1229 feet below sea level. What is the difference in elevation between these two points?   30,257 ft

**3.** The movie lasted 105 minutes. If it started at 1:15 p.m.,
(32) at what time did it end?   3:00 p.m.

In problems 4 through 7, reduce the fractions, if possible, before multiplying.

**4.** $\dfrac{2}{3} \cdot \dfrac{3}{8}$  $\frac{1}{4}$
(69)

**5.** $1\dfrac{1}{4} \cdot 2\dfrac{2}{3}$  $3\frac{1}{3}$
(69)

**6.** $\dfrac{3}{4} \div \dfrac{3}{8}$  $2$
(69)

**7.** $4\dfrac{1}{2} \div 6$  $\frac{3}{4}$
(69)

**8.** $6 + 3\dfrac{3}{4} + 2\dfrac{1}{2}$
(58)  $12\frac{1}{4}$

**9.** $5 - 3\dfrac{1}{8}$  $1\frac{7}{8}$
(62)

**10.** $5\dfrac{1}{4} - 1\dfrac{7}{8}$  $3\frac{3}{8}$
(62)

**11.** $(437)(86)$
(2)  37,582

**12.** $\dfrac{5472}{18}$  304
(2)

**13.** $15\overline{)\$75.00}$   $\$5.00$
(2)

**14.** $100 - $10.87  $89.13　　**15.** $(1 + 0.6) \div (1 - 0.6)$  4
(1)　　　　　　　　　　　　　　　　　(48)

Refer to this coordinate plane to answer questions 16 and 17:

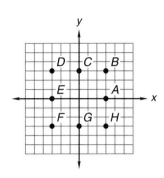

**16.** Name the points that have the following coordinates:
(70)
　(a) $(-3, 3)$  *D*　　　　　　　　(b) $(0, -3)$  *G*

**17.** Identify the coordinates of the following points:
(70)
　(a) *H*  $(3, -3)$　　　　　　　　(b) *E*  $(-3, 0)$

**18.** $1.2f = 120$  100　　　　**19.** $\dfrac{120}{f} = 1.2$  100
(42)　　　　　　　　　　　　　(42)

**20.** Write the prime factorization of the numerator and the
(66) denominator of this fraction. Then reduce the fraction.
　$\dfrac{2 \cdot 2 \cdot 2 \cdot 2 \cdot 2 \cdot 2}{2 \cdot 2 \cdot 2 \cdot 2 \cdot 2 \cdot 7} = \dfrac{2}{7}$　　　　　$\dfrac{64}{224}$

**21.** The perimeter of a square is 6.4 meters. What is its area?
(63) 2.56 sq. m

**22.** Which diagram illustrates a ray?  B.
(68)
　A. ←————→　　B. •————→　　C. •————•

**23.** What fraction of the circle is **not**
(21) shaded?  $\frac{3}{4}$

**24.** A centimeter is about this long ——. About how many
(7) centimeters long is your little finger?  Answers will vary.

**25.** Water freezes at 32° Fahrenheit.
(10) The temperature shown on the thermometer is how many degrees Fahrenheit above the freezing point of water?   4°F

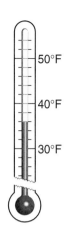

**26.** Ray found that 20% of an hour of TV that he watched
(29,33) was commercial time. Write 20% as a reduced fraction. Then find the number of minutes of commercials there were in the hour.   $\frac{1}{5}$; 12 min

**27.** Name this geometric solid.   cone
(66)

**28.** This square and regular triangle
(63) share a common side. The perimeter of the square is 24 cm. What is the perimeter of the triangle?   18 cm

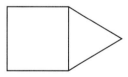

**29.** $\dfrac{7}{20} = \dfrac{?}{100}$   35
(41)

**30.** What is the name of the point on the coordinate plane
(70) that has the coordinates (0, 0)?   origin

# LESSON 71

# Fractions Chart • Multiplying Three Fractions

**Facts Practice:** 72 Mixed Multiplication and Division (Test H in Test Masters)

**Mental Math:** Count up and down by $\frac{1}{8}$'s between $\frac{1}{8}$ and 2.

a. 3 × 125
b. 275 + 50
c. 3 × $0.99   *(3 × $1.00 – 3 × 1¢)*
d. $20.00 – $9.99
e. $\frac{1}{3}$ of $6.60
f. $2.50 × 10
g. 2 × 2, × 2, × 2, × 2, – 2, ÷ 2
h. Hold your hands one foot apart; then six inches apart.

**Problem Solving:** Nelson was thinking of two numbers whose average was 24. If one of the numbers was half of 24, then what was the other number?

**Fractions chart**

We have studied the three steps to take when performing pencil-and-paper arithmetic with fractions and mixed numbers.

**Step 1.** Write the problem in the correct shape.
**Step 2.** Perform the operation.
**Step 3.** Simplify the answer.

The letters S.O.S. may help us remember the steps as "shape," "operate," and "simplify." We will assemble the rules we have learned in a fractions chart. Below the + – signs, we will list the steps we take when adding and subtracting fractions. Below the × ÷ signs, we will list the steps we take when multiplying and dividing fractions.

**Fractions Chart**

| | + − | × ÷ | |
|---|---|---|---|
| **Shape** | Write fractions with common denominators. | Write numbers in fraction form. | |
| **Operate** | Add or subtract the numerators. | ×  cancel. ← $\frac{n \times n}{d \times d}$ | ÷  Find reciprocal of divisor; then |
| **Simplify** | Reduce fractions. Convert improper fractions. | | |

At the "operate" step we separate multiplication and division. When multiplying fractions we may reduce (cancel) before we multiply. Then we multiply the numerators to find the numerator of the product, and we multiply the denominators to find the denominator of the product.

When dividing fractions we first find the reciprocal of the divisor. Then we treat the division problem like a multiplication problem as we multiply by the reciprocal of the divisor.

The "simplify" step is the same for all four operations. We reduce answers when possible and convert answers that are improper fractions to mixed numbers.

**Multiplying three fractions**

To multiply three or more fractions, we follow the same steps we take when multiplying two fractions:

1. We write the numbers in fraction form.
2. We may reduce before we multiply (cancel) by reducing any numerator-denominator pair of terms. Then we multiply the remaining terms.
3. We simplify if possible.

Example $\frac{2}{3} \times 1\frac{3}{5} \times \frac{3}{4}$

Solution First we write $1\frac{3}{5}$ as the improper fraction $\frac{8}{5}$. Then we reduce where possible before multiplying. Multiplying the remaining terms, we find the product.

$$\frac{2}{\cancel{3}} \times \frac{\cancelto{2}{8}}{5} \times \frac{\cancelto{1}{3}}{\cancel{4}} = \frac{4}{5}$$

**Practice** a. Draw the fractions chart from this lesson. See fractions chart.

b. $\frac{2}{3} \cdot \frac{4}{5} \cdot \frac{3}{8}$  $\frac{1}{5}$

c. $2\frac{1}{2} \times 1\frac{1}{10} \times 4$  11

**Problem set
71**

**1.** What is the average of 4.2, 2.61, and 3.6?    3.47
*(18)*

**2.** Four tablespoons equal $\frac{1}{4}$ of a cup. How many
*(53)* tablespoons would equal a full cup?    16

**3.** The temperature on the moon ranges from a high of
*(14)* 134°C to a low of about −170°C. This is a difference of
how many degrees?    304°C

**4.** (a) What fraction of this group is
*(21)*     shaded?    $\frac{3}{10}$

(b) What fraction of this group is
not shaded?    $\frac{7}{10}$

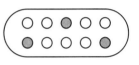

**5.** What fraction of a meter is a centimeter?    $\frac{1}{100}$
*(29)*

**6.** What fraction of a dollar is a nickel?    $\frac{1}{20}$
*(29)*

**7.** $\frac{1}{2} \cdot \frac{5}{6} \cdot \frac{3}{5}$    $\frac{1}{4}$
*(71)*

**8.** $3 \times 1\frac{1}{2} \times 2\frac{2}{3}$    12
*(71)*

**9.** $\frac{3}{4} \div 2$    $\frac{3}{8}$
*(53)*

**10.** $1\frac{1}{2} \div 1\frac{2}{3}$    $\frac{9}{10}$
*(67)*

**11.** $n - \frac{1}{2} = \frac{3}{5}$    $1\frac{1}{10}$
*(42)*

**12.** $1 - w = \frac{7}{12}$    $\frac{5}{12}$
*(42)*

**13.** $w + 2\frac{1}{2} = 3\frac{1}{3}$    $\frac{5}{6}$
*(42)*

**14.** $(1 + 2.3) - 0.45$    2.85
*(38)*

**15.** $(0.12)(0.24)$    0.0288
*(48)*

**16.** $0.6 \div 0.25$    2.4
*(39)*

**17.** Write the standard decimal number for the following:
*(45)*

$$(6 \times 10) + \left(4 \times \tfrac{1}{10}\right) + \left(3 \times \tfrac{1}{100}\right)    60.43$$

**18.** Which is closest to 1?    B. 0.1
*(49)*
A. −1                    B. 0.1                    C. 10

**19.** What is the largest prime number that is less than 100?
*(61)*    97

**20.** $6w = 300$    50
(4)

**21.** $a + 47 = 300$    253
(3)

**22.** A loop of string two feet around is formed to make a
(63)  square.

(a) How many inches long is each side of the square?

(b) What is the area of the square?

(a) 6 in.   (b) 36 sq. in.

Refer to this menu and the following information to answer questions 23, 24, and 25.

**Menu**

| Grilled Chicken Sandwich | $3.49 | Drinks: | Small | $0.89 |
|---|---|---|---|---|
| Taco Salad | $3.29 | | Medium | $1.09 |
| Pasta Salad | $2.89 | | Large | $1.29 |

From this menu the Johnsons ordered two Grilled Chicken Sandwiches, one Taco Salad, a small drink, and two medium drinks.

**23.** What was the total price of the items the Johnsons
(1)  ordered?   $13.34

**24.** If 93¢ tax is added to the bill, and if the Johnsons pay
(12)  for the food with a $20 bill, then how much money should they get back?   $5.73

**25.** Make up an order from the menu. Then calculate the
(10)  bill, not including tax.   See student work.

**26.** If $l$ equals 2.5 and $w$ equals 0.4, then what does $lw$
(45)  equal?   1

**27.** Write the prime factorization of the numerator and
(66)  denominator of this fraction and then reduce the
fraction.   $\frac{2 \cdot 2 \cdot 2 \cdot 3 \cdot 3}{2 \cdot 2 \cdot 2 \cdot 3 \cdot 5}; \frac{3}{5}$

$$\frac{72}{120}$$

Refer to this coordinate plane to answer questions 28 and 29.

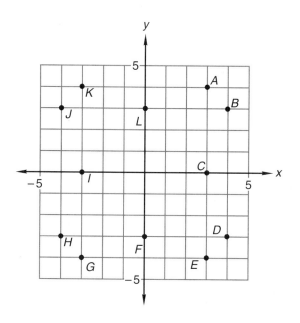

**28.** Identify the coordinates of the following points:
*(70)*
    (a) *K*  (−3, 4)           (b) *F*  (0, −3)

**29.** Name the points that have the following coordinates:
*(70)*
    (a) (3, −4)   *E*         (b) (−3, 0)   *I*

**30.** Draw a pair of parallel lines. Then draw a second pair
*(68)* of parallel lines perpendicular to the first pair of lines
and about the same distance apart. Trace over the
quadrilateral that is formed by the intersecting lines. Is
the quadrilateral a rectangle?        ; yes

# Exponents • Writing Decimal Numbers as Fractions, Part 2

**Mental Math:**
a. 448
b. 325
c. $3.96
d. $4.98
e. $7.00
f. $0.35
g. 21

**Problem Solving:**
1. Shape: $\frac{9}{12} + \frac{8}{12}$
2. Operate: $\frac{17}{12}$
3. Simplify: $1\frac{5}{12}$

**Facts Practice:** Write 24 Mixed Numbers as Improper Fractions (Test J in Test Masters)

**Mental Math:** Count up and down by 25's between 25 and 300.

a. 4 × 112
b. 475 − 150
c. 4 × $0.99
d. $2.99 + $1.99
e. Double $3.50
f. $3.50 ÷ 10
g. 3 × 3, × 3, + 3, ÷ 3, − 3, × 3
h. Hold your hands one yard apart; then one meter apart.

**Problem Solving:** Describe the steps from the fractions chart that would be used to find the answer to the following problem: $\frac{3}{4} + \frac{2}{3}$

**Exponents**   **Exponents** are used to indicate repeated multiplication. The 2 in the following expression is an exponent:

$$5^2$$

Notice that the exponent is elevated and written to the right of the 5. The exponent shows how many times the other number, the **base,** is to be used as a factor. In this case, 5 is to be used as a factor twice.

$$5^2 \text{ means } 5 \cdot 5$$

Since 5 · 5 equals 25, the expression equals 25.

$$5^2 = 25$$

We read numbers with exponents as **powers.** Note that when the exponent is 2 we usually say "squared" and when the exponent is 3 we usually say "cubed."

We read $5^2$ as "five to the second power" or "five squared."

We read $10^3$ as "ten to the third power" or "ten cubed."

We read $3^4$ as "three to the fourth power."

We read $2^5$ as "two to the fifth power."

**Example 1**  Compare: $3^4 \bigcirc 4^3$

**Solution**  We find the value of each expression.

$$3^4 \text{ means } 3 \cdot 3 \cdot 3 \cdot 3, \text{ which equals } 81.$$

$$4^3 \text{ means } 4 \cdot 4 \cdot 4, \text{ which equals } 64.$$

Since 81 is greater than 64, we find that $3^4$ is greater than $4^3$.

$$\mathbf{3^4 > 4^3}$$

**Example 2**  Write the prime factorization of 1000 using exponents to group factors.

**Solution**  Using a factor tree or division by primes, we find the prime factorization of 1000.

$$1000 = 2 \cdot 2 \cdot 2 \cdot 5 \cdot 5 \cdot 5$$

We group the three 2's and the three 5's with exponents.

$$\mathbf{1000 = 2^3 \cdot 5^3}$$

**Example 3**  $100 - 10^2$

**Solution**  We perform operations with exponents before we add, subtract, multiply, or divide. Ten squared is 100. So when we subtract $10^2$ from 100 the difference is zero.

$$100 - 10^2$$

$$\mathbf{100 - 100 = 0}$$

**Writing decimal numbers as fractions, part 2**  We will review changing a decimal number to a fraction or to a mixed number. Recall that the denominator of a decimal number (10 or 100 or 1000 …) is indicated by the number of decimal places in the decimal number. The digits to the right of the decimal point make up the numerator of the fraction.

**Example 4**  Write 0.5 as a common fraction.

**Solution**  We read 0.5 as "five tenths," which also names the fraction $\frac{5}{10}$. We reduce the fraction.

$$\frac{5}{10} = \frac{1}{2}$$

**Example 5**    Write 3.75 as a mixed number.

**Solution**    The whole number part of 3.75 is 3. The fraction part is 0.75, which has two decimal places.

$$3.75 = 3\frac{75}{100}$$

We reduce the fraction.

$$3\frac{75}{100} = 3\frac{3}{4}$$

**Practice**    Find the value of each expression:

**a.** $10^4$    10,000        **b.** $2^3 + 2^4$    24        **c.** $2^2 \cdot 5^2$    100

**d.** Write the prime factorization 72 using exponents.
$72 = 2^3 \cdot 3^2$

Write each decimal number as a fraction or mixed number:

**e.** 12.5    $12\frac{1}{2}$        **f.** 1.25    $1\frac{1}{4}$        **g.** 0.125    $\frac{1}{8}$

**h.** 0.05    $\frac{1}{20}$        **i.** 0.24    $\frac{6}{25}$        **j.** 10.2    $10\frac{1}{5}$

**Problem set 72**

**1.** Mark's temperature was 102°F. Normal body temperature is 98.6°F. How many degrees above normal was Mark's temperature?    3.4°F
(38)

**2.** Jill has read 42 pages of a 180-page book. How many pages are left to read?    138 pages
(11)

**3.** If Jill wants to finish the book in the next three days, then she should read an average of how many pages?    46 pages per day
(18)

**4.** Write 2.5 as a reduced mixed number.    $2\frac{1}{2}$
(72)

**5.** Write 0.35 as a reduced fraction.    $\frac{7}{20}$
(72)

**6.** Write 7% as a fraction. Then write the fraction as a decimal number.    $\frac{7}{100}$; 0.07
(33)

**7.** $\frac{3}{4} \times 2 \times 1\frac{1}{3}$    2
(71)

**8.** $(100 - 10^2) \div 25$    0
(72)

**9.** $3 + 2\frac{1}{3} + 1\frac{3}{4}$    $7\frac{1}{12}$
(59)

**10.** $5\frac{1}{6} - 3\frac{1}{2}$    $1\frac{2}{3}$
(62)

**11.** $\frac{3}{4} \div 1\frac{1}{2}$    $\frac{1}{2}$
(67)

**12.** $7 \div 0.4$    17.5
(72)

**13.** Compare: $5^2$ $\boxed{<}$ $2^5$
(72)

**14.** Compare: $0.3$ $\boxed{>}$ $0.125$
(43)

**15.** $(6.3)(0.48)$    3.0240
(39)

**16.** $0.175 \div 25$    0.007
(44)

**17.** Which digit is in the ten-thousands' place in 123,456.78?
(12)    2

**18.** Arrange in order from least to greatest:    $0, \frac{1}{10}, \frac{1}{4}, \frac{1}{2}, 1$
(57)

$$1, \frac{1}{2}, \frac{1}{10}, \frac{1}{4}, 0$$

**19.** Write the prime factorization of 200 using exponents.
(72)    $200 = 2^3 \cdot 5^2$

**20.** $1.2 + y + 4.25 = 7$    1.55
(42)

**21.** The length of $\overline{AB}$ is 16 mm. The length of $\overline{AC}$ is 50 mm.
(68)    What is the length of $\overline{BC}$?    34 mm

**22.** One half of the area of the square
(38)    is shaded. What is the area of the
shaded region?    18 sq. in.

6 in.

**23.** Is every square a rectangle?    yes
(63)

25. Before we
multiply
fractions, we
write any mixed
numbers as
improper
fractions.

**24.** $\frac{2^2 + 2^3}{2}$    6
(72)

**25.** We read on the fractions chart that the proper "shape"
(71)    for multiplying fractions is "fraction form." What does
that mean?

Refer to this coordinate plane to answer questions 26 and 27:

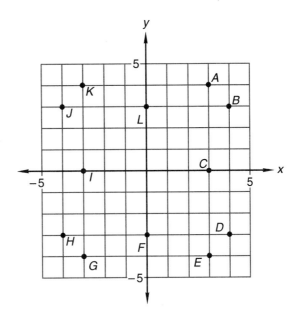

**26.** Identify the coordinates of the following points:
(70)
(a) *H*   (−4, −3)                    (b) *L*   (0, 3)

**27.** Name the points that have the following coordinates:
(70)
(a) (−4, 3)   *J*                    (b) (3, 0)   *C*

**28.** If *s* equals 9, then what does $s^2$ equal?   81
(72)

**29.** Sketch a cylinder.
(66)

**30.** Draw a pair of parallel lines. Then draw a second pair
(68) of parallel lines intersecting but not perpendicular to
the first pair of lines. Trace over the quadrilateral that
is formed by the intersecting lines. Is the quadrilateral
a rectangle?    ; no

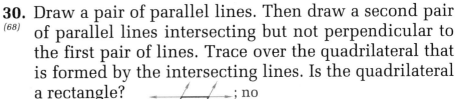

# LESSON 73

# Writing Fractions as Decimal Numbers

**Facts Practice:** 28 Fractions to Simplify (Test I in Test Masters)

**Mental Math:** Count up and down by 5's between negative 25 and 25.

a. 3 × 230          b. 430 + 270          c. 5 × $0.99
d. $5.00 − $1.98    e. $\frac{1}{4}$ of $2.40    f. $1.25 × 10
g. 5 × 5, − 5, × 5, ÷ 2, + 5, ÷ 5
h. Hold your hands one meter apart; then 100 centimeters apart.

**Problem Solving:** In this figure a square and a regular pentagon share a common side. The area of the square is 25 square centimeters. What is the perimeter of the pentagon?

We learned earlier that a fraction bar indicates division. So the fraction $\frac{1}{2}$ also means 1 divided by 2, which we can write as $2\overline{)1}$. By attaching a decimal point and zeros, we can perform the division and write the quotient as a decimal number.

$$\frac{1}{2} \longrightarrow 2\overline{)1.0} \quad \begin{array}{r} 0.5 \\ \hline 1.0 \\ \underline{1\ 0} \\ 0 \end{array}$$

We find that $\frac{1}{2}$ is equivalent to the decimal number 0.5. We divide the numerator by the denominator to find the decimal number that is equivalent to the fraction.

**Example 1**    Convert $\frac{1}{4}$ to a decimal number.

**Solution**    The fraction $\frac{1}{4}$ means 1 divided by 4, which is $4\overline{)1}$. By attaching a decimal point and zeros, we may complete the division.

$$\begin{array}{r} 0.25 \\ 4\overline{)1.00} \\ \underline{8} \\ 20 \\ \underline{20} \\ 0 \end{array}$$

**Example 2**  Use a calculator to convert $\frac{15}{16}$ to a decimal number.

**Solution**  We begin by clearing the calculator. Then we enter the fraction with these key strokes.

After striking the equals sign, the display shows the decimal equivalent of $\frac{15}{16}$.

**0.9375**

The answer is reasonable because both $\frac{15}{16}$ and 0.9375 are less than but close to 1.

**Example 3**  Write $7\frac{2}{5}$ as a decimal number.

**Solution**  The whole number part of $7\frac{2}{5}$ is written to the left of the decimal point. We convert $\frac{2}{5}$ to a decimal by dividing 2 by 5.

$$\frac{2}{5} \longrightarrow 5\overline{)2.0} \quad \overset{0.4}{}$$

Since $\frac{2}{5}$ equals 0.4, the mixed number $7\frac{2}{5}$ equals **7.4.**

**Practice\***  Convert each fraction or mixed number to decimal form:

**a.** $\frac{3}{4}$  0.75  **b.** $4\frac{1}{5}$  4.2  **c.** $\frac{1}{8}$  0.125

**d.** $\frac{7}{20}$  0.35  **e.** $3\frac{3}{10}$  3.3  **f.** $\frac{7}{25}$  0.28

You may use a calculator to convert these fractions to decimals:

**g.** $\frac{11}{16}$  0.6875  **h.** $\frac{31}{32}$  0.96875  **i.** $3\frac{24}{64}$  3.375

**Problem set 73**

**1.** What is the difference when five squared is subtracted *(72)* from four cubed?  39

**2.** On a certain map, 1 inch represents a distance of 10 *(15)* miles. How many miles apart are two towns that are 3 inches apart on the map?  30 mi

**3.** Steve hit the baseball 400 feet. Tom hit the golf ball
*(15)* 300 yards. How many feet farther than the baseball did
the golf ball travel?   500 ft

**4.** Convert $2\frac{3}{4}$ to a decimal number.   2.75
*(73)*

**5.** To what decimal number is $\frac{4}{5}$ equal?   0.8
*(73)*

**6.** Write 0.24 as a reduced fraction.   $\frac{6}{25}$
*(72)*

**7.** If $b$ equals 12 and $h$ equals 8, then what does $bh$ equal?
*(45)* 96

**8.** Compare: $3^2$ $\bigcirc$ 3 + 3
*(72)*

**9.** $\frac{1}{2} + \frac{2}{3} + \frac{1}{6}$   $1\frac{1}{3}$     **10.** $3\frac{1}{4} - 1\frac{7}{8}$   $1\frac{3}{8}$
*(59)*                              *(62)*

**11.** $\frac{5}{8} \cdot \frac{3}{5} \cdot \frac{4}{5}$   $\frac{3}{10}$     **12.** $3\frac{1}{3} \times 3$   10
*(71)*                              *(65)*

**13.** $\frac{3}{4} \div 1\frac{1}{2}$   $\frac{1}{2}$     **14.** $(4 + 3.2) - 0.01$   7.19
*(67)*                              *(38)*

**15.** Sketch a triangular prism.
*(66)*

**16.** Nancy bought a dozen golf balls for $10.44. What was
*(15)* the cost for each golf ball?   $0.87

**17.** Estimate the product of 81 and 38.   3200
*(16)*

**18.** In four days Jill read 42 pages, 46 pages, 35 pages, and
*(18)* 57 pages. What was the average number of pages she
read each day?   45 pages

**19.** What is the least common multiple of 6, 8, and 12?
*(30)* 24

**20.** 24 + $c$ + 96 = 150   30
*(3)*

**21.** Write the prime factorization of the numerator and of
*(66)* the denominator of this fraction. Then reduce the
fraction.   $\frac{2 \cdot 2 \cdot 2 \cdot 5}{2 \cdot 2 \cdot 2 \cdot 2 \cdot 2 \cdot 3}$; $\frac{5}{12}$

$$\frac{40}{96}$$

**22.** What number is $\frac{1}{2}$ of 360?    180
(22)

**23.** Twenty-four of the three dozen bicyclists rode
(29) mountain bikes. What fraction of the bikers rode mountain bikes?    $\frac{2}{3}$

24. All four sides of **24.** Why are some rectangles not squares?
a square are the (63)
same length. Some **25.** Which arrow could be pointing to $\frac{3}{4}$?    B
rectangles are (17)
longer than they are
wide, so not all the
sides are the same
length.

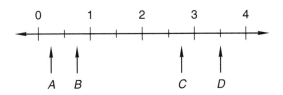

**26.** In quadrilateral *PQRS*, which seg-
(68) ment appears to be
    (a) parallel to $\overline{PQ}$?    $\overline{SR}$ or $\overline{RS}$
    (b) perpendicular to $\overline{PQ}$?    $\overline{PS}$ or $\overline{SP}$

Refer to this coordinate plane to answer questions 27–29:

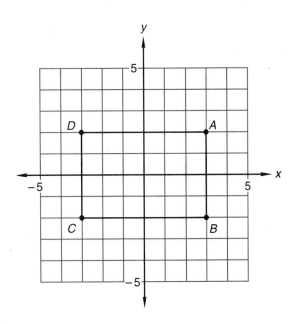

**27.** Identify the coordinates of the following points:
(70)
    (a) *C*    (−3, −2)          (b) Origin    (0, 0)

**28.** Name the points that have the following coordiantes:
(70)
   (a) (−3, 2)   *D*              (b) (3, −2)   *B*

**29.** One pair of parallel segments in rectangle *ABCD* is $\overline{AB}$
(68)
   and $\overline{DC}$. Name a second pair of parallel segments.
   $\overline{DA}$ (or $\overline{AD}$) and $\overline{CB}$ (or $\overline{BC}$)

**30.** Farmer John planted corn on 60% of his 300 acres.
(29,33)
   Write 60% as a reduced fraction. Then find the
   number of acres planted in corn.   $\frac{3}{5}$; 180 acres

# INVESTIGATION
# 2

# Drawing on the Coordinate Plane

Materials needed for investigation:

   • Three sheets of grid paper per student

Christy made the following drawing on a coordinate plane.
Then Christy wrote directions for making the drawing.
These directions are listed on the next page.

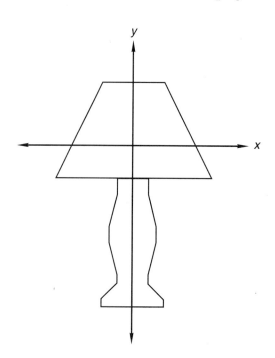

Draw segments to connect the following points in order:

1. $(-1, -2)$    2. $(-1, -3)$    3. $(-1\frac{1}{2}, -5)$    4. $(-1\frac{1}{2}, -6)$

5. $(-1, -8)$    6. $(-1, -8\frac{1}{2})$    7. $(-2, -9\frac{1}{2})$    8. $(-2, -10)$

9. $(2, -10)$    10. $(2, -9\frac{1}{2})$    11. $(1, -8\frac{1}{2})$    12. $(1, -8)$

13. $(1\frac{1}{2}, -6)$    14. $(1\frac{1}{2}, -5)$    15. $(1, -3)$    16. $(1, -2)$

Lift your pencil and restart:

1. $(-2\frac{1}{2}, 4)$        2. $(2\frac{1}{2}, 4)$        3. $(5, -2)$

4. $(-5, -2)$        5. $(-2\frac{1}{2}, 4)$

Refer to the example above to complete the following instructions:

**a.** The coordinates of the vertices are listed in order, as in a dot-to-dot drawing. Follow Christy's directions to make a similar drawing on your own grid paper.

b. See student work. The figure should look like a space shuttle.

**b.** Jenny wrote the following directions for a drawing. Follow her directions to make the drawing on your own grid paper:

1. $(-9, 0)$            2. $(6, -1)$            3. $(8, 0)$

4. $(7, 1)$            5. $(6, \frac{1}{2})$            6. $(6, -1)$

7. $(9, -2\frac{1}{2})$            8. $(10, -2)$            9. $(7, 1)$

10. $(6, 1\frac{1}{2})$            11. $(-10\frac{1}{2}, 3)$            12. $(-11, 2)$

13. $(-10\frac{1}{2}, 0)$            14. $(-10, -1\frac{1}{2})$            15. $(9, -2\frac{1}{2})$

16. $(-3, -3\frac{1}{2})$            17. $(-7, -8)$            18. $(-10, -8)$

19. $(-9, -1\frac{1}{2})$

Lift your pencil and restart:

1. $(-10\frac{1}{2}, 0)$        2. $(-11, -\frac{1}{2})$        3. $(-12, \frac{1}{2})$

4. $(-11\frac{1}{2}, 1)$        5. $(-12, 1\frac{1}{2})$        6. $(-11\frac{1}{2}, 2)$

**7.** $(-12, 2\frac{1}{2})$    **8.** $(-11, 3\frac{1}{2})$    **9.** $(-10\frac{1}{2}, 3)$

**10.** $(-11\frac{1}{2}, 8)$    **11.** $(-9\frac{1}{2}, 8)$    **12.** $(-7, 3)$

**13.** $(-6, 2\frac{1}{2})$    **14.** $(-7, 3)$    **15.** $(-6, 5)$

**16.** $(-4, 5)$    **17.** $(-1, 2)$

**c.** On a coordinate plane make a straight segment drawing. Then write directions for the drawing by listing the coordinates of the vertices of the drawing in "dot-to-dot" order.   See student work.

Selected drawings may be used to provide periodic practice of graphing skills.

## LESSON 74

**Mental Math:**
**a.** 3024
**b.** 375
**c.** $5.97
**d.** $4.49
**e.** $3.20
**f.** $1.25
**g.** 1
**Problem Solving:**

**1.** Shape: $\frac{10}{3} \div \frac{5}{2}$

**2.** Operate: $\frac{\overset{2}{\cancel{10}}}{3} \times \frac{2}{\cancel{5}_{1}} = \frac{4}{3}$

**3.** Simplify: $1\frac{1}{3}$

# Coordinate Geometry

**Facts Practice:**  Linear Measure Facts (Test K in Test Masters)

**Mental Math:**  Count by 12's from 12 to 144.

   **a.** 504 × 6    **b.** 625 − 250    **c.** 3 × $1.99
   **d.** $2.50 + $1.99    **e.** Double $1.60    **f.** $12.50 ÷ 10
   **g.** 6 × 6, − 6, ÷ 6, − 5, × 2, + 1
   **h.** Hold your hands one yard apart; then 18 inches apart.

**Problem Solving:**  Describe the steps from the fractions chart that would be used to find the answer to the following problem:    $3\frac{1}{3} \div 2\frac{1}{2}$

In this lesson we will use graph paper to create a coordinate plane (or use "Activity Master 6" in the Test Masters). Then we will graph points on the coordinate plane that are vertices of a rectangle. We will use the figure that we draw to help us answer questions about the rectangle.

Example   The vertices of a rectangle are located at points (–1, –1), (3, –1), (3, 2), and (–1, 2). Graph the rectangle and find its perimeter and its area.

Solution   Using graph paper we trace over two perpendicular lines on the graph paper to make the x-axis and the y-axis. Then we graph and label the points. The problem states that these points are the vertices of a rectangle. So we draw horizontal and vertical segments to connect the points and draw the rectangle.

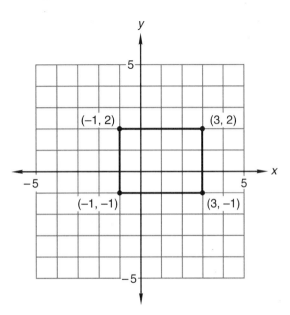

We see that the rectangle is four units long and three units wide. Adding, we find the perimeter is **14 units.** To find the area we may count the unit squares within the rectangle. There are three rows of four squares, so the area of the rectangle is 3 times 4, which is **12 square units.**

Practice   Use graph paper to create a coordinate plane. Then graph the points and use the figure to help you answer the following questions:

*The vertices of a rectangle are located at (–2, –1), (2, –1), (2, 3), and (–2, 3).*

**a.** Graph the rectangle. What do we call this special type of rectangle?   square

**b.** What is the perimeter of the rectangle?   16 units

**c.** What is the area of the rectangle?   16 sq. units

**Problem set 74**
$(30,60)$

**1.** What is the reciprocal of two and three fifths?   $\frac{5}{13}$

**2.** What time is one hour and thirty-five minutes after 2:30 p.m.?   4:05 p.m.
$(32)$

**3.** A 1-pound box of candy cost $4.00. What was the cost per ounce? (1 pound = 16 ounces)   $0.25
$(15)$

**4.** (a) What fraction of the group is shaded?   $\frac{2}{5}$
$(73)$
   (b) Write the fraction in part (a) as a decimal number.   0.4

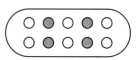

**5.** (a) What fraction of the square is shaded?   $\frac{1}{4}$
$(73)$
   (b) Write the fraction in part (a) as a decimal number.   0.25

**6.** What percent of the circle is shaded?   50%
$(23)$

**7.** Write $3\frac{1}{8}$ as a decimal number.   3.125
$(73)$

**8.** Write 1.8 as a mixed number.   $1\frac{4}{5}$
$(72)$

**9.** Write 12% as a reduced fraction. Then write the fraction as a decimal number.   $\frac{3}{25}$; 0.12
$(33)$

**10.** $\left(\frac{1}{2} + \frac{1}{3}\right) - \frac{1}{6}$   $\frac{2}{3}$
$(56)$

**11.** $5 - m = 3\frac{1}{8}$   $1\frac{7}{8}$
$(42)$

**12.** $3\frac{1}{2} \times 1\frac{1}{3} \times 1\frac{1}{2}$   7
$(71)$

**13.** $m + 1\frac{2}{3} = 3\frac{1}{6}$   $1\frac{1}{2}$
$(42)$

**14.** $4 + $6.37 + 94¢    $11.31
*(1)*

**15.** 1 − 0.95   0.05
*(38)*

**16.** (0.43)(2.6)   1.118
*(39)*

**17.** 0.26 ÷ 5   0.052
*(44)*

**18.** Which digit in 4.87 has the same place value as the 9 in 0.195?   7
*(34)*

**19.** $\dfrac{7}{10} = \dfrac{?}{100}$   70
*(41)*

**20.** $\dfrac{3^3}{0.3}$   90
*(72)*

**21.** Write the prime factorization of the numerator and denominator of $\frac{18}{30}$. Then reduce the fraction.   $\frac{2 \cdot 3 \cdot 3}{2 \cdot 3 \cdot 5}; \frac{3}{5}$
*(66)*

**22.** What is the greatest common factor of 18 and 30?   6
*(20)*

**23.** If the product of two numbers is 1, then the two numbers are which of the following?   B. Reciprocals
*(30)*

A. Equal   B. Reciprocals   C. Opposites   D. Prime

**24.** Why is every rectangle a quadrilateral?   A quadrilateral is a four-sided polygon, and every rectangle has four sides.
*(63)*

**25.** If *b* equals 8 and *h* equals 6, then what does $\frac{bh}{2}$ equal?   24
*(45)*

**26.** Find the prime factorization of 400 using a factor tree. Then write the prime factorization of 400 using exponents.   $400 = 2^4 \cdot 5^2$
*(64,72)*

26.   One possibility:

```
       400
      /   \
    40     10
   /  \   /  \
  8    5 2    5
 / \
4   2
/ \
2   2
```

**27.** Sketch a coordinate plane on graph paper. Then draw a rectangle with vertices located at (3, 1), (3, −1), (−1, 1), and (−1, −1).
*(74)*

27.
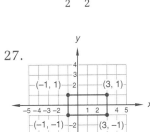

Refer to the rectangle drawn in problem 27 to answer questions 28 and 29.

**28.** What is the perimeter of the rectangle?   12 units
*(8)*

**29.** What is the area of the rectangle?   8 sq. units
*(31)*

**30.** Draw a pair of parallel segments of different lengths. Then form a quadrilateral by drawing two segments that connect the endpoints of the parallel segments. Is the quadrilateral a rectangle?   One example: ⬓ ; no
*(68)*

# LESSON 75

# Comparing Fractions by Converting to Decimal Form

**Mental Math:**
a. 832
b. 535
c. $7.96
d. $5.01
e. $0.90
f. $95.00
g. 5

**Problem Solving:**

$$\begin{array}{r} 1 \\ 7\overline{)7} \\ 5\overline{)35} \\ 3\overline{)105} \\ 2\overline{)210} \\ 2\overline{)420} \end{array}$$

**Facts Practice:** 30 Fractions to Reduce (Test G in Test Masters)

**Mental Math:** Count up and down by 2's between negative 12 and 12.

a. $4 \times 208$  
b. $380 + 155$  
c. $4 \times \$1.99$  
d. $\$10.00 - \$4.99$  
e. $\frac{1}{5}$ of $4.50  
f. $\$0.95 \times 100$  
g. $8 \times 8, - 4, \div 2, + 2, \div 4, \times 3, + 1, \div 5$  
h. Hold your hands one foot apart; then 24 inches apart.

**Problem Solving:** Celina used division by primes to find the prime factorization of a number. Copy her work and fill in the missing numbers.

$$\begin{array}{r} 1 \\ 7\overline{)\square} \\ 5\overline{)\square} \\ 3\overline{)\square} \\ 2\overline{)\square} \\ 2\overline{)\square} \end{array}$$

We have compared fractions by sketching pictures of fractions and by writing fractions with common denominators. Another way to compare fractions is to convert the fractions to decimal form.

**Example 1** To compare these fractions, first convert each fraction to decimal form:

$$\frac{3}{5} \bigcirc \frac{5}{8}$$

**Solution** We convert each fraction to a decimal number by dividing the numerator by the denominator.

$$\frac{3}{5} \longrightarrow 5\overline{)3.0}^{\,0.6} \qquad \frac{5}{8} \longrightarrow 8\overline{)5.000}^{\,0.625}$$

We will write both decimal numbers with the same number of decimal places and compare the decimal numbers.

$$0.600 < 0.625$$

Since 0.6 is less than 0.625, we know that $\frac{3}{5}$ is less than $\frac{5}{8}$.

$$\frac{3}{5} < \frac{5}{8}$$

**Example 2**  Compare: $\frac{3}{4} \bigcirc 0.7$

*Solution*  First we write the fraction as a decimal.

$$\frac{3}{4} \longrightarrow 4)\overline{3.00}^{\,0.75}$$

Then we compare the decimal numbers.

$$0.75 > 0.70$$

Since 0.75 is greater than 0.7, we know that $\frac{3}{4}$ is greater than 0.7.

$$\frac{3}{4} > 0.7$$

**Practice**  Change the fractions to decimal numbers to compare these numbers:

a. $\frac{3}{20} \overset{>}{\bigcirc} \frac{1}{8}$   b. $\frac{3}{8} \overset{<}{\bigcirc} \frac{2}{5}$   c. $\frac{15}{25} \overset{=}{\bigcirc} \frac{3}{5}$

d. $0.7 \overset{<}{\bigcirc} \frac{4}{5}$   e. $\frac{2}{5} \overset{<}{\bigcirc} 0.5$   f. $\frac{3}{8} \overset{>}{\bigcirc} 0.325$

**Problem set 75**

1. What is the product of ten squared and two cubed?
   *(72)*  800

2. What number is halfway between 4.5 and 6.7?   5.6
   *(49)*

3. It is said that each year of a dog's life is equivalent to 7 years of a human's life. In that case, a dog that is 13 years old is the equivalent age of a human that is how many years old?   91 years old
   *(15)*

4. To compare these fractions, first convert each fraction to decimal form:
   *(75)*

$$\frac{2}{5} \overset{>}{\bigcirc} \frac{1}{4}$$

**5.** (a) What fraction of the circle is
(73)　　shaded?　$\frac{3}{4}$

(b) Convert the answer to part (a)
to a decimal number.　0.75

**6.** Convert $2\frac{1}{2}$ to a decimal number.　2.5
(73)

**7.** Write 3.45 as a reduced mixed number.　$3\frac{9}{20}$
(72)

**8.** Write 0.04 as a reduced fraction.　$\frac{1}{25}$
(72)

**9.** Instead of dividing 200 by 18, Sam found half of each
(42)　number and then divided. Show Sam's division
problem and write the quotient as a mixed number.
$100 \div 9 = 11\frac{1}{9}$

**10.** $6\frac{1}{3} + 3\frac{1}{4} + 2\frac{1}{2}$　$12\frac{1}{2}$
(59)

**11.** $\frac{4}{5} = \frac{?}{100}$　80
(41)

**12.** $\left(2\frac{1}{2}\right)\left(3\frac{1}{3}\right)\left(1\frac{1}{5}\right)$　10
(71)

**13.** $5 \div 2\frac{1}{2}$　2
(67)

**14.** $6.7 + 0.48 + n = 8$
(42)　0.82

**15.** $12 - d = 4.75$　7.25
(42)

**16.** $0.35 \times 0.45$　0.1575
(39)

**17.** $4.3 \div 100$　0.043
(51)

**18.** Arrange these numbers in order from least to greatest:
(43)　0.25, 0.3, 0.313　　　　0.3, 0.25, 0.313

**19.** Estimate the sum of 3926 and 5184 to the nearest
(16)　thousand.　9000

**20.** List all the prime numbers between 40 and 50.
(61)　41, 43, 47

**21.** $47.6 - w = 28.4$　19.2
(42)

**22.** What is the perimeter of the tri-
(8)　angle?　36 mm

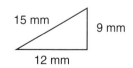

15 mm　9 mm　12 mm

**23.** Draw a quadrilateral that is not a rectangle.　See student
(63)　work.

**24.** About how many **millimeters** long is the line segment?
(7)  45 mm

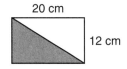

**25.** One half of the area of the rectangle
(31)  is shaded. What is the area of the
shaded region? 120 sq. cm

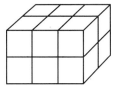
20 cm

12 cm

**26.** How many small cubes were used
(66)  to make this rectangular prism?  12

27.

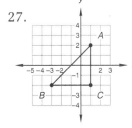

**27.** Sketch a coordinate plane on graph paper. Graph
(74)  point *A* (1, 2), point *B* (−3, −2), and point *C* (1, −2).
Then draw segments to connect each point. What type
of polygon is figure *ABC*?  triangle

**28.** In the figure drawn in problem 27, which segment is
(68)  perpendicular to segment *AC*?  $\overline{BC}$ or $\overline{CB}$

**29.** If *b* equals 12 and *h* equals 9, then what does $\frac{bh}{2}$ equal?
(45)  54

**30.** Draw a pair of parallel lines. Draw a third line
(68)  perpendicular to the parallel lines. Complete a
quadrilateral with a fourth line that intersects but is
not perpendicular to the pair of parallel lines. Trace
over the quadrilateral that is formed. Is the
quadrilateral a rectangle?   no

# LESSON 76

# Finding Unstated Information in Fractional-Part Problems

**Facts Practice:** Linear Measure Facts (Test K in Test Masters)

**Mental Math:** Count up and down by $\frac{1}{8}$'s between $\frac{1}{8}$ and 2.

a. 311 × 5
b. 565 − 250
c. 5 × $1.99
d. $7.50 + $1.99
e. Double 80¢
f. 6.5 ÷ 100
g. 10 × 10, × 10, − 1, ÷ 9, − 11, ÷ 10
h. Hold your hands one meter apart; then one yard apart.

**Problem Solving:** Jill read an average of 45 pages a day for four days. If she read a total of 123 pages during the first three days, then how many pages did she read on the fourth day?

Often fractional-parts statements contain more information than is directly stated. Consider this fractional-part statement.

> *Three fourths of the 28 students in the class are boys.*

This sentence directly states information about the number of boys in the class. It also *indirectly* states information about the number of girls in the class. In this lesson we will practice finding several pieces of information from fractional-part statements.

**Example** Three fourths of the 28 students in the class are boys. Make a sketch that illustrates this statement; then answer the following questions.

(a) Into how many parts is the class divided?

(b) How many students are in each part?

(c) How many parts are boys?

(d) How many boys are in the class?

(e) How many parts are girls?

(f) How many girls are in the class?

*Solution*  We sketch a rectangle to represent the whole class. Since the problem describes $\frac{3}{4}$ of the class, we divide the rectangle into four parts. Dividing the total number of students by four, we find there are seven students in each fourth. We identify three of the four parts as boys. Now we will answer the questions.

28 Students

| |
|---|
| 7 students |
| 7 students |
| 7 students |
| 7 students |

$\frac{3}{4}$ are boys

(a) The denominator of the fraction indicates that the class is divided into **four parts** for the purpose of this statement. It is important to distinguish between the number of *parts* (as indicated by the denominator) and the number of *categories*. There are two categories of students implied by the statement—boys and girls.

(b) In each of the four parts there are **seven students.**

(c) **Three parts are boys.**

(d) Since three parts are boys, and since there are seven students in each part, we find that there are **21 boys** in the class.

(e) Three of the four parts are boys, so only **one part is girls.**

(f) There are seven students in each part, so there are **seven girls.**

**Practice***  Make a sketch to illustrate the following statement, and then answer the questions.

40 Engines

| |
|---|
| 5 Engines |
| 5 Engines |
| 5 Engines |
| 5 Engines |
| 5 Engines |
| 5 Engines |
| 5 Engines |
| 5 Engines |

$\frac{3}{8}$ could climb the hill

*Three eighths of the 40 little engines could climb the hill.*

**a.** Into how many parts was the group divided?  8

**b.** How many engines are in each part?  5

**c.** How many parts could climb the hill?    3

**d.** How many engines could climb the hill?    15

**e.** How many parts could not climb the hill?    5

**f.** How many engines could not climb the hill?    25

---

**Teacher Note:** A tagboard display of a parallelogram is suggested in Lesson 79. You may want to start preparing this early. Please refer to Lesson 79 for instructions.

---

**Problem set 76**

**1.** The weight of an object on the moon is $\frac{1}{6}$ of its weight on earth. A person weighing 114 pounds on earth would weigh how much on the moon?    19 pounds
(29)

**2.** Use the information in problem 1 to calculate what your weight would be on the moon.    Answers vary.
(22)

**3.** Cupid shot 24 arrows and hit 6 targets. What fraction of his shots hit the target?    $\frac{1}{4}$
(29)

4.    30 students

| 6 students |
| 6 students |
| 6 students |
| 6 students |
| 6 students |

$\frac{3}{5}$ are boys

**4.** There are 30 students in the class. Three fifths of them are boys. Make a sketch to illustrate this statement. Then use this information to answer questions (a)–(d).
(76)

(a) Into how many parts was the class divided?    5

(b) How many students are in each part?    6

(c) How many boys are in the class?    18

(d) How many girls are in the class?    12

**5.** (a) Find the fraction of the group that is shaded.    $\frac{3}{8}$
(73)

(b) Convert the fraction in part (a) to a decimal number.    0.375

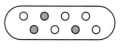

**6.** Write the decimal number 3.6 as a mixed number.    $3\frac{3}{5}$
(72)

**7.** $3^2 - 2^3$   1
(72)

**8.** $\dfrac{2}{5}x = 1$   $\frac{5}{2}$
(30)

**9.** Three fifths of a dollar is how many cents?   60¢
(22)

**10.** Three fifths of a circle is what percent of a circle?   60%
(28)

**11.** A temperature of –3°F is how many degrees below the
(14)   temperature at which water freezes?   35°F

**12.** Compare:  0.35 $\stackrel{=}{\bigcirc}$ $\dfrac{7}{20}$
(75)

**13.** $\dfrac{1}{2} + \dfrac{2}{3}$   $1\frac{1}{6}$   **14.** $3\dfrac{1}{5} - 1\dfrac{3}{5}$   $1\frac{3}{5}$   **15.** $\dfrac{1}{2} + \dfrac{3}{4} + \dfrac{7}{8}$   $2\frac{1}{8}$
(56)               (62)                (59)

**16.** $3 \times 1\dfrac{1}{3}$   4   **17.** $3 \div 1\dfrac{1}{3}$   $2\frac{1}{4}$   **18.** $1\dfrac{1}{3} \div 3$   $\frac{4}{9}$
(65)            (67)            (67)

**19.** What is the perimeter of the
(8)   rectangle?   4.8 cm

**20.** What is the area of the rectangle?
(31)   1.35 sq. cm

1.5 cm

0.9 cm

**21.** Which digit in 6734.2198 is in the ones' place?   4
(12)

**22.** $3.6 + a = 4.15$   0.55
(42)

**23.** Round $357.64 to the nearest dollar.   $358
(50)

**24.** Is every quadrilateral a polygon?   yes
(63)

**25.** What time is one hour and fourteen minutes before noon?
(32)   10:46 a.m.

**26.** What percent of the rectangle
(28)   appears to be shaded?   B. 40%

A. 20%          B. 40%

C. 60%          D. 80%

27.

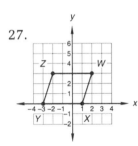

**27.** Sketch a coordinate plane on graph paper. Graph
(74)  point $W$ (2, 3), point $X$ (1, 0), point $Y$ (−3, 0), and
point $Z$ (−2, 3). Then draw $\overline{WX}$, $\overline{XY}$, $\overline{YZ}$, and $\overline{ZW}$.

**28.** (a) Which segment in problem 27 is parallel to $\overline{WX}$?
(68)
(b) Which segment in problem 27 is parallel to $\overline{XY}$?
(a) $\overline{YZ}$ or $\overline{ZY}$   (b) $\overline{ZW}$ or $\overline{WZ}$

**29.** Write the prime factorization of the numerator and the
(66)  denominator of this fraction. Then reduce the fraction.
$\frac{2 \cdot 3 \cdot 5 \cdot 7}{2 \cdot 5 \cdot 5 \cdot 7}, \frac{3}{5}$
$$\frac{210}{350}$$

**30.** The moon has the shape of what geometric solid?
(66)  sphere

# LESSON 77

# Liquid Measure

**Facts Practice:** Write 24 Mixed Numbers as Improper Fractions (Test J in Test Masters)

**Mental Math:** Count up and down by 3's between negative 15 and 15.

**a.** 4 × 325      **b.** 1500 + 275      **c.** 3 × $2.99
**d.** $20.00 − $2.99      **e.** $\frac{1}{3}$ of $2.40      **f.** 1.75 × 100
**g.** 9 × 11, + 1, ÷ 2, − 1, ÷ 7, − 2, × 5
**h.** Hold your hands one foot apart; then 18 inches apart.

**Problem Solving:** Jim was thinking of a prime number between 75 and 100 which did **not** have a 9 as one of its digits. Of what number was he thinking?

To measure quantities of liquid we use units like gallons (gal), quarts (qt), pints (pt), and ounces (oz) in the U.S. Customary System, and we use liters (L) and milliliters (mL) in the metric system. The relationships between the units within each system are shown in the following table.

**Equivalence Table for Units of Liquid Measure**

| U.S. Customary System | Metric System |
|---|---|
| 1 gallon = 4 quarts<br>1 quart = 2 pints<br>1 pint = 2 cups<br>1 pint = 16 ounces<br>1 cup = 8 ounces | 1 liter = 1000 milliliters |

Commonly used container sizes in the U.S. Customary system are illustrated below. Notice that the next smaller container size is half the capacity of the larger container. Also, notice that a quart is a "quarter" of a gallon.

1 gallon    $\frac{1}{2}$ gallon    1 quart    1 pint    1 cup

Food and beverage containers often have both U.S. Customary and metric capacities printed on the containers. Relating the two systems of measure, we find that one liter is a little more than one quart.

**Example 1**  A half-gallon of milk is how many pints of milk?

*Solution*  Two pints equal a quart, and two quarts equal a half-gallon. So a half-gallon of milk is **4 pints.**

**Example 2**  Compare: 12 oz pop can ◯ 1 pint container

*Solution*  A pint equals 16 ounces. **So a pint container is larger than a 12-ounce pop can.**

**Practice**  **a.** What fraction of a gallon is a quart?   $\frac{1}{4}$

**b.** A 2-liter pop bottle has a capacity of how many milliliters?   2000 mL

**c.** A half-gallon of orange juice will fill how many 8-ounce cups?   8 cups

**Problem set 77**

**1.** What is the difference when the product of $\frac{1}{2}$ and $\frac{1}{2}$ is subtracted from the sum of $\frac{1}{2}$ and $\frac{1}{2}$?   $\frac{3}{4}$
$^{(54)}$

**2.** The claws of a Siberian tiger are 10 centimeters long. How many millimeters long is that?   100 mm
$^{(7)}$

**3.** Sue was thinking of a number between 40 and 50 that is a multiple of 3 and 4. Of what number was she thinking?   48
$^{(26)}$

**4.** Make a sketch to illustrate the following statement and use the information to answer questions (a) through (d).
$^{(76)}$

*Four fifths of the 60 lights were on.*

4.
60 lights

12 lights
12 lights
12 lights
12 lights
12 lights
$\frac{4}{5}$ of the lights were on

(a) Into how many parts have the 60 lights been divided?   5

(b) How many lights are in each part?   12

(c) How many lights are "on"?   48

(d) How many lights are "off"?   12

**5.** Which counting number is neither a prime number
(64) nor a composite number?   1

**6.** $\dfrac{4}{5}m = 1$   $\frac{5}{4}$
(30)

**7.** $\dfrac{4}{5} + w = 1$   $\frac{1}{5}$
(42)

**8.** $\dfrac{4}{5} \div x = 1$   $\frac{4}{5}$
(42)

**9.** $y - \dfrac{4}{5} = 1$   $1\frac{4}{5}$
(42)

**10.** (a)  What fraction of the rectangle is shaded?   $\frac{1}{4}$
(73)
     (b)  Write the answer to part (a) as a decimal number.
           0.25

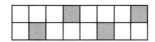

**11.** Convert the decimal number 1.15 to a mixed number.
(72) $1\frac{3}{20}$

**12.** Compare: $\dfrac{3}{5}$ $\bigcirc$ > 0.35
(75)

**13.** $\dfrac{5}{6} - \dfrac{1}{2}$   $\frac{1}{3}$
(56)

**14.** $\dfrac{3}{4} = \dfrac{?}{100}$   75
(41)

**15.** $\dfrac{1}{2} + \dfrac{2}{3} + \dfrac{5}{6}$   2
(59)

**16.** $1\dfrac{1}{2} \times 2\dfrac{2}{3}$   4
(71)

**17.** $1\dfrac{1}{2} \div 2\dfrac{2}{3}$   $\frac{9}{16}$
(67)

**18.** $2\dfrac{2}{3} \div 1\dfrac{1}{2}$   $1\frac{7}{9}$
(67)

**19.** What is the perimeter of the
(38) square?   2 in.

$\frac{1}{4}$ sq. in.  **20.** What is the area of the square?
(38)

**21.** The opposite sides of a rectangle are parallel. True or
(63) false?   true

**22.** What is the average of $3^3$ and $5^2$?   26
(72)

**23.** Round 1.3579 to the hundredths' place.   1.36
(50)

**24.** How many inches is $2\dfrac{1}{2}$ feet?   30 in.
(65)

**25.** Which arrow could be pointing to 0.1?   *C*
(49)

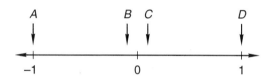

**26.** Draw a polygon that is not a quadrilateral.
(63)   See student work.

**27.** Find the prime factorization of 900 by using a factor
(64,72)   tree. Then write the prime factorization using exponents.
$900 = 2^2 \cdot 3^2 \cdot 5^2$

**28.** Three vertices of a rectangle have the coordinates
(74)   (5, 3), (5, −1), and (−1, −1). What are the coordinates of
the fourth vertex of the rectangle?   (−1, 3)

Refer to this table to answer questions 29 and 30.

| | |
|---|---|
| 3 teaspoons | = 1 tablespoon |
| 16 tablespoons | = 1 cup |
| 2 cups | = 1 pint |
| 2 pints | = 1 quart |
| 4 quarts | = 1 gallon |

**29.** A teaspoon of soup is what fraction of a tablespoon of
(77)   soup?   $\frac{1}{3}$

**30.** How many cups of milk is a gallon of milk?   16 cups
(77)

# LESSON
# 78

# Classifying Quadrilaterals

**Facts Practice:** Linear Measure Facts (Test K in Test Masters)

**Mental Math:** Count up and down by 12's between 12 and 144.

a. $307 \times 6$     b. $1000 - 420$     c. $4 \times \$2.99$
d. $\$5.75 + \$2.99$     e. Double $24     f. $0.125 \times 100$
g. $2 \times 2, \times 2, \times 2, - 1, \times 2, + 2, \div 2, \div 2$
h. Hold your hands one inch apart; then one centimeter apart.

**Problem Solving:** The perimeter of the rectangle is 48 inches. The width is 8 inches. What is the length?

Quadrilaterals are polygons with four sides. Quadrilaterals are classified in the following way:

**Quadrilaterals**

| SHAPE | CHARACTERISTIC | NAME |
|-------|----------------|------|
| | No sides parallel | Trapezium |
| | One pair of parallel sides | Trapezoid |
| | Two pairs of parallel sides | Parallelogram |
| | Parallelogram with equal sides | Rhombus |
| | Parallelogram with right angles | Rectangle |
| | Rectangle with equal sides | Square |

Notice that rhombuses, rectangles, and squares are all parallelograms. Also notice that a square is a special kind of rectangle, which is a special kind of parallelogram, which is a special kind of quadrilateral, which is a special kind of polygon. A square is also a special kind of rhombus.

**Example**   Is the following statement true or false?

"All parallelograms are rectangles."

**Solution**   We are asked to decide if every parallelogram is a rectangle. Since a rectangle is a special kind of parallelogram, some parallelograms are rectangles. However, some parallelograms are not rectangles. So the statement is **false.**

**Practice**   State whether each statement is true or false:

**a.** All quadrilaterals are four-sided polygons.   true

**b.** Some parallelograms are trapezoids.   false

**c.** Every square is a rhombus.   true

**d.** Every rhombus is a square.   false

**e.** Some rectangles are squares.   true

**Problem set 78**

**1.** If you know the perimeter of a rectangle and the length
$^{(8)}$ of the rectangle, how can you figure out the width of the rectangle?   Answers vary. One method is to divide the perimeter by 2 and subtract the length from the quotient.

**2.** A 2-liter beverage bottle contained 2 qt, 3.6 oz of
$^{(77)}$ beverage. Use this information to compare a liter and a quart.

Compare:  1 liter  $\bigodot{>}$  1 quart

**3.** Uncle Bill was 38 when he started his job. He worked
$^{(11)}$ for 33 years. How old was he when he retired?
71 years old

**4.** Is the following statement true or false?   false
$^{(78)}$
"Every rectangle is a square."

**5.** "Every rectangle is a parallelogram." True or false?
$^{(78)}$ true

**6.** Ninety percent of the 30 students were right-handed.
$^{(28)}$ What percent of the students were left-handed?   10%

**7.** If $\frac{3}{4}$ of the 24 runners finished the race, then how many
(76) runners did not finish the race? 6

**8.** $10^3 \div 10^2$ 10
(72)

**9.** 6.42 + 12.7 + 8 27.12
(38)

**10.** $10 - q = 9.87$ 0.13
(42)

**11.** 1.2 × 0.12 0.144
(39)

**12.** 0.288 ÷ 24 0.012
(44)

**13.** 64 ÷ 0.08 800
(48)

**14.** $3\frac{1}{3} + 2\frac{3}{4}$ $6\frac{1}{12}$
(58)

**15.** $w + \frac{1}{4} = \frac{5}{6}$ $\frac{7}{12}$
(42)

**16.** $3\frac{1}{3} \times \frac{1}{5} \times \frac{3}{4}$ $\frac{1}{2}$
(71)

**17.** $2\frac{1}{2} \div 3$ $\frac{5}{6}$
(67)

**18.** The perimeter of a square is 80 cm. What is its area?
(38) 400 sq. cm

**19.** Write the decimal number for the following: 96.03
(45)
$$(9 \times 10) + (6 \times 1) + \left(3 \times \tfrac{1}{100}\right)$$

**20.** If $b$ equals 6 and $h$ equals 8, then what does $\frac{1}{2}bh$ equal?
(45) 24

**21.** Which of these numbers is closest to zero? 0.2
(49)
$$-2, 0.2, 1, \frac{1}{2}$$

**22.** Estimate the product of 6.7 and 7.3 by rounding each
(50) number to the nearest whole number before
multiplying. 49

**23.** The fourth power of 2 (which is $2^4$) equals 16. What
(72) number does the fourth power of 3 equal? 81

**24.** What number is halfway between 0.2 and 0.3? 0.25
(18)

**25.** To what decimal number is the arrow pointing? 10.2
(49)

**26.** Which quadrilateral has one pair of parallel sides but
*(78)* not two pairs of parallel sides?  trapezoid

**27.** The coordinates of the vertices of a quadrilateral are
*(74)* (−5, 5), (1, 5), (3, 1), and (−3, 1). What is the name for
this kind of quadrilateral?  parallelogram

In this figure a square and a regular
hexagon share a common side. The
area of the square is 100 sq. cm. Use
this information to answer problems
28 and 29.

**28.** (a) What is the length of each side of the square? 10 cm
*(63)*
(b) What is the perimeter of the square?  40 cm

**29.** (a) What is the length of each side of the hexagon? 10 cm
*(63)*
(b) What is the perimeter of the hexagon?  60 cm

**30.** Write the prime factorization of the numerator and the
*(66)* denominator of this fraction. Then reduce the fraction.
$\frac{2 \cdot 2 \cdot 2 \cdot 2 \cdot 2}{2 \cdot 2 \cdot 2 \cdot 2 \cdot 3}, \frac{2}{3}$
$$\frac{32}{48}$$

# Area of a Parallelogram

Mental Math:
a. 1260
b. 550
c. $14.95
d. $2.01
e. $1.20
f. 0.375
g. 0
Problem Solving:
   10,000

**Facts Practice:** 28 Fractions to Simplify (Test I in Test Masters)

**Mental Math:** Count up and down by 7's between negative 35
and 35.

**a.** 4 × 315      **b.** 380 + 170      **c.** 5 × $2.99
**d.** $10.00 − $7.99    **e.** $\frac{1}{4}$ of $4.80    **f.** 37.5 ÷ 100
**g.** 5 × 5, × 5, − 25, ÷ 4, ÷ 5, − 5
**h.** Hold your hands a meter apart; then four feet apart.

**Problem Solving:** A seven-digit phone number consists of a
three-digit prefix followed by four digits.
How many different phone numbers are
possible for a particular prefix?

A flexible model of a parallelogram is useful when
discussing the area of a parallelogram. A model can be
constructed of stiff tagboard or cardboard and brads.

Materials needed:

- Two strips of tagboard 1 in. × 10 in.
- Two strips of tagboard 1 in. × 8 in.
- Hole punch
- 4 brads

Assembly:

Lay the two 8 in. strips over the two parallel 10 in.
strips as shown. Punch a hole at the center of the
overlapping ends. Insert and open brads to hold the
strips together.

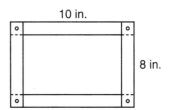

With this model we can demonstrate that the area of the parallelogram changes as the angles between the adjacent sides change. We hold the model with two hands and slide the opposite sides in opposite directions.

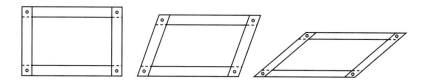

Although the area changes as the angles change, the opposite sides remain parallel, and the perimeter does not change.

The flexible model shows that the two parallelograms may have sides that are equal in length but areas that are different. To find the area of a parallelogram, we multiply two **perpendicular** measurements. We multiply the **base** and the **height** of the parallelogram.

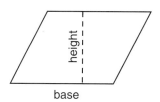

The base of a parallelogram is the length of one of the parallel sides. The height of a parallelogram is the perpendicular distance between the parallel sides. The following activity will illustrate why the area of a parallelogram equals the base times the height.

### Activity: Area of a Parallelogram

Materials needed:

- Graph paper
- Ruler
- Pencil
- Scissors

**Step 1.** Tracing over the lines on the graph paper, draw two parallel segments the same number of units long but shifted slightly as shown.

Then draw segments between the endpoints of the pair of parallel segments to complete the parallelogram.

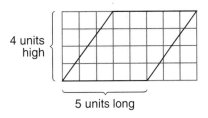

4 units high

5 units long

The parallelogram we drew is 5 units long and 4 units high. Your parallelogram may be different. How many units long and high is your parallelogram? Can you easily count the number of square units in the area of your parallelogram?

**Step 2.** Use your scissors to cut out your parallelogram.

We will cut here.

Then select a line on the graph paper that is perpendicular to one of the parallel sides of the parallelogram and cut the parallelogram into two pieces.

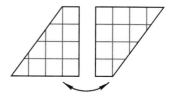

**Step 3.** Rearrange the two pieces of the parallelogram to make a rectangle. What is the length and width of the rectangle? How many square units is the area of the rectangle?

Our rectangle is 5 units long and 4 units wide. The area of the rectangle is 20 square units. So the area of the parallelogram is also 20 square units.

By making a perpendicular cut across the parallelogram and rearranging the pieces, we formed a rectangle with the same area as the parallelogram. The length and width of the rectangle equaled the base and height of the parallelogram. By multiplying the base and height of a parallelogram, we find the area of a parallelogram.

**Example** Find the area of this parallelogram.

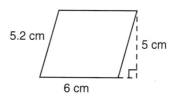

*Solution*   We multiply two perpendicular measurements, the base and the height. The height is often shown as a dashed line segment. The base is 6 cm. The height is 5 cm.

$$6 \text{ cm} \times 5 \text{ cm} = 30 \text{ sq. cm}$$

The area of the parallelogram is **30 sq. cm.**

**Practice**   Find the perimeter and area of these parallelograms:

a.

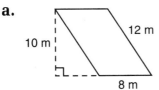

10 m    12 m

8 m

$P = 40$ m; $A = 80$ sq. m

b.

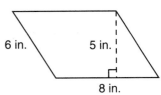

6 in.    5 in.

8 in.

$P = 28$ in.; $A = 40$ sq. in.

**Problem set 79**

1. What is the average of 96, 49, 68, and 75?   72
   *(18)*

2. The average depth of the ocean beyond the edges of
   *(15)* the continents is $2\frac{1}{2}$ miles. How many feet is that?
   (1 mile = 5280 ft)   13,200 ft

3. The 168 girls who signed up for soccer were divided
   *(15)* into 12 teams. How many players were on each team?
   14

4. What is the perimeter of the
   *(78)* parallelogram?   14.4 cm

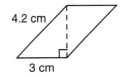

4.2 cm

3 cm

5. This quadrilateral has one pair of
   *(78)* parallel sides. What is the name of
   this kind of quadrilateral?
   trapezoid

6. "All squares are rectangles." True or false?   true
   *(78)*

7. If four fifths of the 30 students in the class were
   *(76)* present, then how many students were absent?   6 students

8. If $\frac{1}{6}$ of the one-hour show was taken up with
   *(29)* commercials, then how many minutes did the
   commercials last?   10 min

**9.** Compare: $0.5 \;\textcircled{<}\; \dfrac{3}{4}$
(75)

**10.** Write 4.4 as a reduced mixed number.   $4\frac{2}{5}$
(72)

**11.** Write $\frac{1}{8}$ as a decimal number.   $0.125$
(73)

**12.** $(6.3)(0.36)$      **13.** $0.36 \div 5$      **14.** $63 \div 0.9$   70
(39)   2.268          (44)   0.072           (48)

**15.** $\dfrac{5}{6} + \dfrac{1}{2}$   $1\frac{1}{3}$     **16.** $\dfrac{5}{8} - \dfrac{1}{4}$   $\frac{3}{8}$     **17.** $2\dfrac{1}{2} \times 1\dfrac{1}{3} \times \dfrac{3}{5}$
(56)                                 (56)                                 (71)                  2

**18.** $\dfrac{17}{20} = \dfrac{?}{100}$   85           **19.** $1\dfrac{1}{2} \div 3$   $\frac{1}{2}$
(41)                                       (67)

**20.** What is the area of the parallelogram?   156 sq. mm
(79)

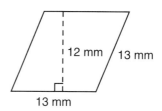

12 mm   13 mm

13 mm

**21.** Round 0.4287 to the hundredths' place.   0.43
(50)

**22.** $4 - a = 2.6$   1.4
(42)

Use the graph of sugar in breakfast cereals to answer questions 23, 24, and 25.

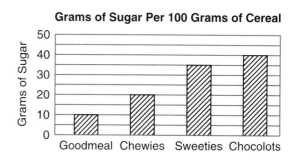

**Grams of Sugar Per 100 Grams of Cereal**

**23.** *Sweeties* contains about how many grams of sugar per
(16)   100 grams of cereal?   35 grams

**24.** Fifty grams of *Chocolots* would contain about how
(16) many grams of sugar?   20 grams

**25.** Write a "larger-smaller-difference" problem that refers
(16) to the bar graph and answer the question.
See student work.

**26.** There was a quart of milk in the bottle. Oscar poured
(77) one cup of milk on his cereal. How many cups of milk
were left in the bottle?   3 cups

**27.** Three vertices of a square are (3, 0), (3, 3), and (0, 3).
(74) What are the coordinates of the fourth vertex of the
square?   (0, 0)

Refer to the square in problem 27 to answer problems 28
and 29.

**28.** What is the perimeter of the square?   12 units
(38)

**29.** What is the area of the square?   9 sq. units
(38)

**30.** Draw a pair of parallel segments that are the same
(78) length. Make a quadrilateral by drawing two more
segments between the endpoints of the parallel
segments. Is the quadrilateral a parallelogram?   yes;

⬜ or ▱

# LESSON 80

# Arithmetic with Units of Measure

---

**Facts Practice:** Linear Measure Facts (Test K in Test Masters)

**Mental Math:** Count up and down by 25's between negative 150 and 150.

**a.** 311 × 7  **b.** 2000 − 1250  **c.** 4 × $9.99
**d.** $2.50 + $9.99  **e.** Double $5.50  **f.** 0.075 × 100
**g.** 8 × 8, + 6, ÷ 2, + 1, ÷ 6, × 3, ÷ 2
**h.** Hold your hands six inches apart; then 6 cm apart.

**Problem Solving:** Copy this problem and fill in the missing digits.

$$\begin{array}{r} 3 \\ \phantom{0}\overline{)\,\_\,\_\,\_} \\ \underline{\phantom{0}\_\,\_} \\ \_\,\_ \\ \underline{\phantom{0}\_\,\_} \\ 2 \end{array}$$

---

Recall that the operations of arithmetic are addition, subtraction, multiplication, and division. In this lesson we will practice adding, subtracting, multiplying, and dividing units of measure.

We may add or subtract measurements that have the same units. If the units are not the same, we first convert one or more measurements so that the units are the same. Then we add or subtract.

**Example 1**  2 ft + 12 in.

**Solution**  The units are not the same. Before we add we either convert 2 feet to 24 inches, or we convert 12 inches to 1 foot.

| CONVERT TO INCHES | CONVERT TO FEET |
|---|---|
| 2 ft + 12 in. | 2 ft + 12 in. |
| 24 in. + 12 in. = **36 in.** | 2 ft + 1 ft = **3 ft** |

Either answer is correct because 3 ft equals 36 in.

Notice that the units of the sum in Example 1 are the same as the units of the addends. The units do not change when we add or subtract measurements. However, the units *do* change when we multiply or divide measurements.

When we find the area of a figure we multiply the lengths. Notice how the units change when we multiply.

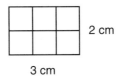

To find the area of this rectangle we multiply 2 cm and 3 cm. The product has a different unit of measure than the factors.

$$2 \textbf{ cm} \times 3 \textbf{ cm} = 6 \textbf{ sq. cm}$$

A centimeter and a square centimeter are two different kinds of units. A centimeter is a line segment used to measure length.

———————
1 cm

A square centimeter is a square used to measure area.

1 sq. cm

The unit of the product is a different unit because we multiplied the units of the factors. When we multiply 2 cm and 3 cm, we multiply the 2 and the 3 and we also multiply the cm and cm.

$$2 \text{ cm} \times 3 \text{ cm} = \underbrace{2 \cdot 3}_{6} \underbrace{\text{cm} \cdot \text{cm}}_{\text{sq. cm}}$$

Instead of writing sq. cm, we may use exponents to write cm · cm as cm². We read cm² as "square centimeters."

$$2 \text{ cm} \times 3 \text{ cm} = \underbrace{2 \cdot 3}_{6} \underbrace{\text{cm} \cdot \text{cm}}_{\text{cm}^2}$$

**Example 2**   6 ft × 4 ft

**Solution**   We multiply the number of units, and we also multiply the units.

$$6 \text{ ft} \times 4 \text{ ft} = \underbrace{6 \cdot 4}_{24} \underbrace{\text{ft} \cdot \text{ft}}_{\text{ft}^2}$$

The product is **24 ft²**, which is also 24 sq. ft.

Units also change when we divide measurements. For example, if we know the area of a rectangle and the length of the rectangle, we can find the width of the rectangle by dividing.

Area = 21 cm²

7 cm

To find the width of this rectangle, we divide 21 cm² by 7 cm.

$$\frac{21 \text{ cm}^2}{7 \text{ cm}} = \frac{\overset{3}{\cancel{21}}}{\underset{1}{\cancel{7}}} \frac{\cancel{\text{cm}} \cdot \text{cm}}{\cancel{\text{cm}}}$$

We divide the numbers and reduce the units. The quotient is 3 cm, which is the width of the rectangle.

**Example 3**   $\dfrac{25 \text{ mi}^2}{5 \text{ mi}}$

*Solution*  To divide the units, we write mi² as  mi · mi  and reduce.

$$\dfrac{\overset{5}{\cancel{25}}}{\underset{1}{\cancel{5}}} \; \dfrac{\cancel{\text{mi}} \cdot \text{mi}}{\cancel{\text{mi}}}$$

The quotient is **5 mi.**

Sometimes when we divide measurements the units will not reduce. When units will not reduce, we leave the units in division form. For example, if a car travels 300 miles in 6 hours, we can find the average speed of the car by dividing.

$$\dfrac{300 \text{ mi}}{6 \text{ hr}} = \dfrac{\overset{50}{\cancel{300}}}{\underset{1}{\cancel{6}}} \; \dfrac{\text{mi}}{\text{hr}}$$

The quotient is $50\frac{\text{mi}}{\text{hr}}$, which is 50 miles per hour (50 mph).

The word "per" means "each" and is used in place of the division sign. Notice that speed is a quotient of distance divided by time.

**Example 4**  $\dfrac{300 \text{ miles}}{10 \text{ gallons}}$

*Solution*  We divide the numbers. The units do not reduce.

$$\dfrac{300 \text{ mi}}{10 \text{ gal}} = \dfrac{\overset{30}{\cancel{300}}}{\underset{1}{\cancel{10}}} \; \dfrac{\text{mi}}{\text{gal}}$$

The quotient is **$30\,\frac{\text{mi}}{\text{gal}}$,** or 30 miles per gallon.

**Practice**   **a.** 2 ft − 12 in. (Write the difference in inches.)   12 in.

**b.** 2 ft × 4 ft   8 ft²

**c.** $\dfrac{12 \text{ cm}^2}{3 \text{ cm}}$   4 cm

**d.** $\dfrac{300 \text{ mi}}{5 \text{ hr}}$   60 $\frac{\text{mi}}{\text{hr}}$

**Problem set**
**80**

**1.** The Jones family had two gallons of milk before
*(77)* breakfast. The family used two quarts of milk during
breakfast. How many quarts of milk did the Jones
family have after breakfast?   6 qt

**2.** One quart of milk is about 945 milliliters of milk. Use
*(77)* this information to help you with this comparison:

Compare:  1 quart ⓒ 1 liter

**3.** Carol cut $2\frac{1}{2}$ inches off her hair three times last year.
*(65)* How much longer would her hair have been if she had
not cut it?   $7\frac{1}{2}$ in.

**4.** The plane flew 1200 miles in 3 hours. Divide the
*(80)* distance by the time to find the average speed of the
plane.   400 $\frac{mi}{hr}$, or 400 mph

**5.** Write the prime factorization of the numerator and
*(66)* denominator of this fraction. Then reduce the fraction.
$\frac{2\cdot3\cdot3\cdot3}{3\cdot3\cdot3\cdot5}, \frac{2}{5}$
$$\frac{54}{135}$$

**6.** The basketball team scored 60% of its 80 points in the
*(29,33)* second half. Write 60% as a reduced fraction. Then
find the number of points the team scored in the
second half.   $\frac{3}{5}$; 48 points

**7.** What is the area of the
*(79)* parallelogram?   600 m²

**8.** What is the perimeter of the
*(78)* parallelogram?   100 m

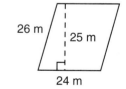

**9.** "Some rectangles are trapezoids." True or false?   false
*(78)*

**10.** If $b$ equals 12 and $h$ equals 16, then what does $\frac{1}{2}bh$
*(45)* equal?   96

**11.** Arrange these numbers in order from least to greatest:
*(75)* $\frac{1}{5}$, 0.4, $\frac{1}{2}$
$$\frac{1}{2}, \frac{1}{5}, 0.4$$

**12.** What decimal number is equal to $\frac{4}{25}$?    0.16
(73)

**13.** $\dfrac{4}{25} = \dfrac{?}{100}$    16        **14.** $(0.4 + 3) \div 2$    1.7
(41)                                        (44)

**15.** $(10 - 0.1) \times 0.1$    0.99
(39)

**16.** $\dfrac{5}{8} + \dfrac{3}{4}$    $1\frac{3}{8}$    **17.** $3 - 1\frac{1}{8}$    $1\frac{7}{8}$    **18.** $4\frac{1}{2} - 1\frac{3}{4}$    $2\frac{3}{4}$
(56)                            (62)                            (62)

**19.** $\dfrac{5}{6} \cdot \dfrac{4}{5} \cdot \dfrac{3}{8}$    $\frac{1}{4}$    **20.** $4\frac{1}{2} \times 1\frac{1}{3}$    6    **21.** $3\frac{1}{3} \div 1\frac{2}{3}$    2
(71)                                  (65)                            (67)

**22.** The perimeter of a square is 2 meters. How many
(38)  centimeters long is each side? (1 meter = 100
      centimeters)    50 cm

**23.** $w - 7.2 = 3.6$    10.8
(42)

**24.** What time is two and one half hours after 10:40 a.m.?
(32)    1:10 p.m.

**25.** Use your ruler to find the length of this line segment
(17)  to the nearest sixteenth of an inch.    $2\frac{5}{8}$ in.

---

**26.** What is the area of a quadrilateral with the vertices
(74)  (0, 0), (4, 0), (6, 3), and (2, 3)?    12 sq. units

**27.** What is the name of this geometric
(66)  solid?    cone

**28.** If the area of a square is one square foot, what is the
(38)  perimeter?    4 ft

**29.** (a) 2 yd + 3 ft (Write the sum in yards.)    3 yd
(80)
      (b) 5 m × 3 m    15 m²

      (c) $\dfrac{36 \text{ ft}^2}{6 \text{ ft}}$    6 ft        (d) $\dfrac{400 \text{ miles}}{20 \text{ gallons}}$    20 $\frac{\text{miles}}{\text{gallon}}$

**30.** Draw a pair of parallel segments that are not the same
(78) length. Form a quadrilateral by drawing two segments
between the endpoints of the parallel segments. What
is the name of this type of quadrilateral?

; trapezoid

## LESSON 81

# Writing Fractions as Percents, Part 1

Mental Math:
a. 400
b. 134
c. $4.98
d. $2.50
e. 25
f. 20
g. 3
Problem Solving:
113

**Facts Practice:** Liquid Measure Facts (Test L in Test Masters)

**Mental Math:** Count by 25's from 25 to 400.

   **a.** $20 \cdot 20$       **b.** $284 - 150$       **c.** $1.99 + $2.99
   **d.** $\frac{1}{3}$ of $7.50      **e.** $2.5 \times 10$       **f.** $\frac{800}{40}$  *(Reduce: $\frac{80\cancel{0}}{4\cancel{0}}$)*
   **g.** $10 \times 10, - 1, \div 3, - 1, \div 4, + 1, \div 3$
   **h.** Hold your thumb and forefinger one inch apart; then one
     centimeter apart.

**Problem Solving:** After three games Beth's average bowling
             score was 110. Her score for her fourth game
             was 115, and the score for her fifth game was
             120. What was her average score for all five
             games?

A percent is actually a fraction with a denominator of 100.
Instead of writing the denominator 100, we write a percent
sign (%). So $\frac{25}{100}$ equals 25%.

**Example 1**   Write $\frac{3}{100}$ as a percent.

*Solution*   A percent is a fraction with a denominator of 100. Instead
of writing the denominator, we write a percent sign. We
write $\frac{3}{100}$ as **3%**.

**Example 2**  Write $\frac{3}{10}$ as a percent.

**Solution**  First we will write an equivalent fraction that has a denominator of 100.

$$\frac{3}{10} = \frac{?}{100}$$

We multiply $\frac{3}{10}$ by $\frac{10}{10}$.

$$\frac{3}{10} \cdot \frac{10}{10} = \frac{30}{100}$$

We write the fraction $\frac{30}{100}$ as **30%**.

**Example 3**  What percent is equal to 1?

**Solution**  A form of 1 is $\frac{100}{100}$, which is **100%**. One hundred percent of a circle is one whole circle. One whole group is 100% of the group.

**Example 4**  Of the 30 students who took the test, 15 earned A's. What percent of the students earned A's?

**Solution**  Fifteen of the 30 students earned A's, so half of the students earned A's.

$$\frac{15}{30} = \frac{1}{2}$$

We know by now that $\frac{1}{2}$ is 50%. To write $\frac{1}{2}$ as a fraction with a denominator of 100, we multiply $\frac{1}{2}$ by $\frac{50}{50}$.

$$\frac{1}{2} \cdot \frac{50}{50} = \frac{50}{100}$$

The fraction $\frac{50}{100}$ equals **50%**.

**Practice**   Write each fraction as a percent:

    **a.** $\dfrac{31}{100}$   31%     **b.** $\dfrac{1}{100}$   1%     **c.** $\dfrac{1}{10}$   10%

    **d.** $\dfrac{3}{50}$   6%     **e.** $\dfrac{7}{25}$   28%     **f.** $\dfrac{2}{5}$   40%

    **g.** Twelve of the 30 students earned a B on the test. What percent of the students earned a B?   40%

**Problem set 81**

**1.** Write the decimal numeral twenty-one and five hundredths.   21.05
<sub>(35)</sub>

**2.** Tennis balls are sold in cans containing 3 balls. What would be the total cost of buying one dozen tennis balls if the price per can was $2.49?   $9.96
<sub>(15)</sub>

**3.** A cubit is about 18 inches. If Ruben was 4 cubits tall, about how many feet tall was he?   6 ft
<sub>(15)</sub>

**4.** (a) Write $\frac{7}{100}$ as a percent.   7%
<sub>(81)</sub>

    (b) Write $\frac{7}{10}$ as a percent.   70%

**5.** Write 90% as a reduced fraction. Then write the fraction as a decimal number.   $\frac{9}{10}$; 0.9
<sub>(33,73)</sub>

**6.** Of the 50 students who took the test, 23 earned A's. What percent of the students earned A's?   46%
<sub>(81)</sub>

**7.** Write $\frac{9}{25}$ as a percent.   36%
<sub>(81)</sub>

**8.** A box of cereal has the shape of what geometric solid?   rectangular prism
<sub>(66)</sub>

**9.** $w - 3\dfrac{5}{6} = 2\dfrac{1}{3}$   $6\frac{1}{6}$       **10.** $3\dfrac{1}{4} - y = 1\dfrac{5}{8}$   $1\frac{5}{8}$
<sub>(42)</sub>                                         <sub>(42)</sub>

**11.** $\dfrac{1}{2} + \dfrac{1}{5} + \dfrac{1}{10}$   $\frac{4}{5}$       **12.** $1\dfrac{4}{5} \times 1\dfrac{2}{3}$   3
<sub>(59)</sub>                                                 <sub>(65)</sub>

**13.** $6 \div 1\frac{1}{2}$    4
(67)

**14.** (a) What fraction of the group is
(21,81)    shaded?   $\frac{3}{5}$

(b) What percent of the group is
shaded?   60%

**15.** Write 0.45 as a reduced common fraction.   $\frac{9}{20}$
(72)

**16.** $0.5 + (0.5 \div 0.5) + (0.5 \times 0.5)$   1.75
(52)

**17.** $6n = 0.12$   0.02          **18.** $6 \div 0.12$   50
(42)                                (48)

**19.** Which digit in 6.3457 has the same place value as the
(12)    8 in 128.90?   6

**20.** Estimate the product of 39 and 41.   1600
(16)

**21.** $5n = 10^2$   20
(72)

**22.** What is the area of the parallel-
(79)    ogram?   500 mm²

**23.** What is the perimeter of the paral-
(78)    lelogram?   94 mm

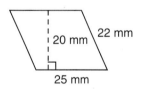

**24.** Write the prime factorization of each number and
(66)    reduce before multiplying:
$\frac{(3 \cdot 7)(2 \cdot 2 \cdot 3)}{2 \cdot 7} = 18$

$$\frac{(21)(12)}{14}$$

**25.** "Some triangles are quadrilaterals." True or False? Why?
(63)    False. Quadrilaterals have four sides, but triangles have three sides.

26.

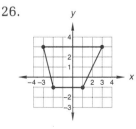

**26.** A quadrilateral has vertices with the coordinates
(74)    $(-2, -1)$,   $(1, -1)$,   $(3, 3)$,   and   $(-3, 3)$.   Graph the
quadrilateral on a coordinate plane. The figure is what
type of quadrilateral?   trapezoid

**27.** (a) 3 quarts + 2 pints (Write the sum in quarts.)   4 qt
<sub>(80)</sub>

(b) $\dfrac{49 \text{ m}^2}{7 \text{ m}}$   7 m

(c) $\dfrac{400 \text{ miles}}{8 \text{ hours}}$   50 mph, or 50 $\frac{\text{mi}}{\text{hr}}$

**28.** If *l* equals 5, *w* equals 4, and *h* equals 3, then what
<sub>(45)</sub> does *lwh* equal?   60

**29.** Three of the dozen eggs were cracked. What percent of
<sub>(81)</sub> the eggs were cracked?   25%

**30.** A pint of milk weighs about a pound. About how
<sub>(77)</sub> many pounds does a gallon of milk weigh?   8 lb

# LESSON 82

# Ratio

---

**Facts Practice:** 28 Fractions to Simplify (Test I in Test Masters)

**Mental Math:** Count by $\frac{1}{4}$'s from $\frac{1}{4}$ to 4.

| | | |
|---|---|---|
| **a.** 30 · 30 | **b.** 1000 − 125 | **c.** 3 × $3.99 |
| **d.** Double $3\frac{1}{2}$ | **e.** 2.5 ÷ 100 | **f.** 20 × 34 |

**g.** 9 × 9, − 1, ÷ 2, + 2, ÷ 6, + 2, ÷ 3

**h.** Hold your hands a meter apart; then a yard apart.

**Problem Solving:** Compare the following and then describe how you performed the comparison:

$$1\tfrac{7}{8} + 2\tfrac{5}{6} + 3\tfrac{4}{5} \bigcirc 2 + 3 + 4$$

---

**Mental Math:**
a. 900
b. 875
c. $11.97
d. 7
e. 0.025
f. 680
g. 3

**Problem Solving:**

(<); Each of the three mixed numbers on the left is less than the respective whole number on the right. So the sum on the left will be less than the sum on the right.

A **ratio** is a way to describe a relationship between numbers. If there are 13 boys and 15 girls in a classroom, then the ratio of boys to girls is 13 to 15. Ratios can be written in several forms. Each of these forms is a way to write the boy-girl ratio.

13 to 15          13:15          $\dfrac{13}{15}$

Each of these forms is read the same, "Thirteen to fifteen."

In this lesson we will focus on the fraction form of a ratio. When writing a ratio in fraction form, we keep the following points in mind:

1. We write the terms of the ratio in the order described in the statement.
2. We reduce ratios in the same manner as we reduce fractions.
3. We leave ratios in fraction form. We do not write ratios as mixed numbers.

**Example 1**  A team lost 3 games and won 7 games. What was the team's won-lost ratio?

*Solution*  The question asks for the ratio in "won-lost" order. The team's won-lost ratio was 7 to 3, which we write as the fraction $\frac{7}{3}$.

$$\frac{\text{Number of games won}}{\text{Number of games lost}} = \frac{7}{3}$$

We leave the ratio in fraction form.

**Example 2**  In a class of 28 students there are 12 boys. What is the ratio of boys to girls in the class?

*Solution*  To write the ratio we need to know the number of girls. If 12 of the 28 students are boys, then 16 of the students are girls. We are asked to write the ratio in "boys to girls" order.

$$\frac{\text{Number of boys}}{\text{Number of girls}} = \frac{12}{16}$$

The ratio 12 to 16 reduces to 3 to 4.

$$\frac{12}{16} = \frac{3}{4}$$

The ratio of boys to girls in the class is $\frac{3}{4}$.

**Practice**  **a.** What is the ratio of dogs to cats in a neighborhood that has 18 cats and 12 dogs?  $\frac{2}{3}$

**b.** What is the girl-boy ratio in a class of 30 students with 14 boys?  $\frac{8}{7}$

**Problem set**  **1.** What is the product when the sum of 0.2 and 0.2 is
**82**  (39) multiplied by the difference of 0.2 and 0.2?  0

**2.** Arabian camels travel about 3 times as fast as Bactrian
(65) camels. If Bactrian camels travel at $1\frac{1}{2}$ miles per hour, at how many miles per hour do Arabian camels travel?  $4\frac{1}{2}$ mph

**3.** Mark was paid at a rate of $4 per hour for cleaning up
(32) a neighbor's yard. If he worked from 1:45 p.m. to 4:45 p.m., how much was he paid?  $12.00

**4.** Write 55% as a reduced fraction.  $\frac{11}{20}$
(33)

**5.** (a) Write $\frac{9}{100}$ as a percent.  9%
(81)
(b) Write $\frac{9}{10}$ as a percent.  90%

**6.** The whole class was present. What percent of the
(81) class was present?  100%

**7.** A century is 100 years. A decade is 10 years.
(29,81)
(a) What fraction of a century is a decade?  $\frac{1}{10}$
(b) What percent of a century is a decade?  10%

**8.** Write 0.48 as a reduced common fraction.  $\frac{12}{25}$
(72)

**9.** Write $\frac{7}{8}$ as a decimal numeral.  0.875
(73)

**10.** $\left(1\frac{1}{3} + 1\frac{1}{6}\right) - 1\frac{2}{3}$  $\frac{5}{6}$      **11.** $1\frac{1}{2} \times 3 \times 1\frac{1}{9}$  5
(47)                                        (71)

**12.** $4\frac{2}{3} \div 1\frac{1}{6}$  4                **13.** $0.1 + (1 - 0.01)$  1.09
(67)                                        (38)

**14.** (0.5)(0.5)(0.5)    0.125
(39)

**15.** 0.4 ÷ (1 ÷ 0.2)    0.08
(48)

**16.** Write the standard numeral for the following:    80,420
(32)
$$(8 \times 10,000) + (4 \times 100) + (2 \times 10)$$

**17.** Compare: $2^4$ ⊜ $4^2$
(72)

**18.** Write the prime factorization of the numerator and
(66) denominator of this fraction. Then reduce the fraction.

$\frac{2 \cdot 2 \cdot 2 \cdot 3}{2 \cdot 2 \cdot 2 \cdot 2 \cdot 2} = \frac{3}{4}$            $\frac{24}{32}$

**19.** What is the greatest common factor of 24 and 32?    8
(20)

**20.** $6n = 360$    60
(4)

**21.** What is the perimeter of the
(8) trapezoid?    56 mm

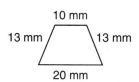

Refer to this parallelogram to answer questions 22 and 23:

**22.** What is the area of the parallel-
(79) ogram?    24 in.²

**23.** One half of the parallelogram is
(79) shaded. What is the area of the
shaded part?    12 in.²

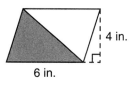

**24.** One fourth of the 120 students took wood shop. How
(76) many students did not take wood shop?    90 students

**25.** How many millimeters is 2.5 centimeters?    25 mm
(7)

**26.** What is the name of this geometric
(66) solid?    pyramid

**27.** (a)  3 quarts + 2 pints (Write the sum in pints.)    8 pt
(80)

(b)  $\dfrac{64 \text{ cm}^2}{8 \text{ cm}}$    8 cm

(c)  $\dfrac{60 \text{ students}}{3 \text{ teachers}}$    20 students per teacher

**28.** Twelve crows and 21 sparrows perched on the wire.
(82) What was the ratio of sparrows to crows perched on the wire?  $\frac{7}{4}$

**29.** Sam answered 20 of the 25 questions correctly. What
(81) percent of the questions did Sam answer correctly?
80%

**30.** Sketch a triangle that has two perpendicular sides.
(68)

---

**LESSON
83**

**Mental Math:**
a. 1600
b. 844
c. $8.98
d. $2.50
e. 750
f. 24
g. 2
**Problem Solving:**
10 cm²; 15 cm²;
25 cm²

# Order of Operations, Part 2

**Facts Practice:**  Linear Measure Facts (Test K in Test Masters)

**Mental Math:**  Count by 12's from 12 to 144.

    **a.** $40 \cdot 40$         **b.** $980 - 136$         **c.** $5.99 + $2.99
    **d.** $\frac{1}{4}$ of $10.00     **e.** $7.5 \times 100$         **f.** $\frac{480}{20}$
    **g.** $8 \times 8, - 4, \div 3, + 4, \div 4, + 2, \div 4$
    **h.** Hold your hands a foot apart; then an inch apart.

**Problem Solving:**  Find  the  area  of  the  two
smaller  shaded  triangles
and  of  the  largest  shaded
triangle.

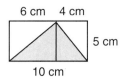

Recall that the four operations of arithmetic are addition, subtraction, multiplication, and division. When more than one type of operation occurs in the same expression, we perform the operations in the order described below.

    1. Perform operations within parentheses.
    2. Multiply and divide in order from left to right.
    3. Add and subtract in order from left to right.

Example 1  $2 \times 8 + 2 \times 6$

*Solution*  Multiplication and addition occur in this expression. We perform the multiplication first.

$$\underbrace{2 \times 8}_{16} + \underbrace{2 \times 6}_{12}$$

Then we perform the addition.

$$16 + 12 = \mathbf{28}$$

**Calculator Test:** Some calculators are designed to recognize the standard order of operations and some are not. If a variety of calculator models are available in the classroom, students may test the design of the calculators from Example 1 with these key strokes.

$$\boxed{2} \boxed{\times} \boxed{8} \boxed{+} \boxed{2} \boxed{\times} \boxed{6} \boxed{=}$$

Calculators with "algebraic logic" should display 28 after the equals-sign key is pressed.

Example 2  $0.5 + 0.5 \div 0.5 - 0.5 \times 0.5$

*Solution*  First we multiply and divide from left to right.

$$0.5 + \underbrace{0.5 \div 0.5}_{1} - \underbrace{0.5 \times 0.5}_{0.25}$$
$$0.5 + \phantom{xx} 1 \phantom{xx} - \phantom{xx} 0.25$$

Then we add and subtract from left to right.

$$0.5 + 1 - 0.25 = \mathbf{1.25}$$

Example 3  $2(8 + 6)$

*Solution*  First we perform the operation within the parentheses.

$$2(8 + 6)$$
$$2(14)$$

Then we multiply.

$$2(14) = \mathbf{28}$$

**Practice***    **a.** $5 + 5 \times 5 - 5 \div 5$    29

       **b.** $2(10) + 2(6)$    32

       **c.** $5 + 4 \times 3 \div 2 - 1$    10

       **d.** $32 + 1.8(20)$    68

       **e.** $3 + 3 \times 3 - 3 \div 3$    11

**Problem set**    **1.** What is the ratio of prime numbers to composite
**83**    (82)   numbers in this list?   $\frac{4}{5}$

$$2, 3, 4, 5, 6, 7, 8, 9, 10$$

**2.** Bianca poured four cups of milk from a full half-
(77)   gallon container. Then how many cups of milk were
left in the container?    4 cups

**3.** $6 + 6 \times 6 - 6 \div 6$    41
(83)

**4.** Write 30% as a reduced fraction. Then write the
(33,73)   fraction as a decimal number.   $\frac{3}{10}$; 0.3

**5.** Write 8% as a reduced fraction.   $\frac{2}{25}$
(33)

**6.** Write $\frac{1}{20}$ as a percent.    5%
(81)

**7.** Write $\frac{1}{20}$ as a decimal number.    0.05
(73)

**8.** "Some parallelograms are rectangles." True or False?
(78)   true

**9.** What is the area of the parallel-
(79)   ogram?    384 cm²

**10.** What is the perimeter of the paral-
(78)   lelogram?    82 cm

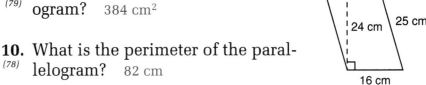

24 cm   25 cm

16 cm

**11.** $\left( 3\frac{1}{8} + 2\frac{1}{4} \right) - 1\frac{1}{2}$   $3\frac{7}{8}$    **12.** $\frac{5}{6} \times 2\frac{2}{3} \times 3$   $6\frac{2}{3}$
(47)                                  (71)

**13.** $8\frac{1}{3} \div 100$   $\frac{1}{12}$
(67)

**14.** $(4 - 3.2) \div 10$   0.08
(51)

**15.** $0.5 \times 0.5 + 0.5 \div 0.5$   **16.** $8 \div 0.04$   200
(83)   1.25              (48)

**17.** Which digit is in the hundredths' place in 12.345678?
(34)   4

**18.** Describe how to round $5\frac{1}{8}$ to the nearest whole
(50) number.   The mixed number $5\frac{1}{8}$ is more than 5 but less than 6. Since $\frac{1}{8}$ is less than $\frac{1}{2}$, $5\frac{1}{8}$ is closer to 5 than 6. Thus, $5\frac{1}{8}$ rounds to 5.

**19.** Write the prime factorization of 700 using exponents.
(72)   $2^2 \cdot 5^2 \cdot 7$

**20.** $8m = 4^2$   2
(72)

**21.** The perimeter of a square is 1 meter. How many
(38) centimeters long is each side?   25 cm

**22.** Sharon scored 9 of the team's 45 points.
(29,81)

(a) What fraction of the team's points did Sharon score?   $\frac{1}{5}$

(b) What percent of the team's points did Sharon score?   20%

**23.** What time is 5 hours and 30 minutes after 9:30 p.m.?
(32)   3:00 a.m.

**24.** $\frac{1}{4} - \frac{1}{2}$ (Careful—the answer is less than zero.)   $-\frac{1}{4}$
(54)

**25.** What is the perimeter of this
(68) triangle?   12 cm

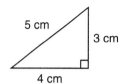

5 cm   3 cm   4 cm

**26.** How many cubes were used to
(66) build this rectangular prism?   40

**27.** 2 ft + 24 in. (Write the sum in inches.)   48 in.
(80)

**28.** (a) $\dfrac{100 \text{ cm}^2}{10 \text{ cm}}$   10 cm
*(80)*

(b) $\dfrac{180 \text{ pages}}{4 \text{ days}}$   45 pages per day

29.

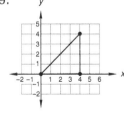

**29.** A triangle has vertices at the coordinates (4, 4), (4, 0),
*(74)* and at the origin. Draw the triangle on graph paper.
Notice that inside the triangle are some full squares
and some half squares.

(a) How many full squares are in the triangle?   6

(b) How many half squares are in the triangle?   4

**30.** What is the ratio of boys to girls in a class of 24
*(82)* students with 16 girls?   $\frac{1}{2}$

## LESSON 84

# Changing Percents to Decimals

**Mental Math:**
a. 2500
b. 375
c. $15.96
d. $2.50
e. 0.75
f. 700
g. 30
**Problem Solving:**
81

**Facts Practice:** Liquid Measure Facts (Test L in Test Masters)

**Mental Math:** Count up and down by 5's between −25 and 25.

a. 50 · 50          b. 1000 − 625          c. 4 × $3.99
d. Double $1.25     e. 7.5 ÷ 10            f. 20 × 35
g. 7 × 7, + 1, ÷ 2, − 1, ÷ 2, × 5, ÷ 2
h. Hold your hands a yard apart; then two feet apart.

**Problem Solving:** Here is part of a multiplication-facts
table, but one number is wrong. What
is the wrong number?

| 48 | 54 |
|----|----|
| 56 | 63 |
| 64 | 81 |

A percent may be quickly changed to a decimal number.
Study the following changes from percent to fraction to
decimal:

$$35\% \longrightarrow \frac{35}{100} \longrightarrow 0.35 \qquad\qquad 5\% \longrightarrow \frac{5}{100} \longrightarrow 0.05$$

Notice that the decimal number has the same digits as
the percent with the decimal point shifted two places to
the left.

**Example 1**  Write 15% in decimal form.

*Solution*  Fifteen percent means $\frac{15}{100}$, which can be written **0.15.**

**Example 2**  Write 115% as a decimal number.

*Solution*  We shift the decimal point two places to the left.

$$115\% = \mathbf{1.15}$$

**Example 3**  What decimal number equals 1%?

*Solution*  One percent equals the fraction $\frac{1}{100}$ and the decimal **0.01.**

**Practice***  Write each of these percents as a decimal number:

    **a.** 65%  0.65     **b.** 9%  0.09     **c.** 150%  1.5

    **d.** 93%  0.93     **e.** 4%  0.04     **f.** 225%  2.25

**Problem set 84**

**1.** Twenty-one of the 25 answers on Scott's test were correct. What percent of the answers were correct?
*(81)* 84%

**2.** By the time the blizzard was over, the temperature had dropped from 17°F to −6°F. This was a drop of how many degrees?
*(14)* 23°F

**3.** The cost to place a telephone call to Tokyo was $1.50 for the first minute plus $1.00 for each additional minute. What was the cost of a 5-minute phone call?
*(12)* $5.50

**4.** Write 25% as a decimal number.  0.25
*(84)*

**5.** Write 125% as a decimal number.  1.25
*(84)*

**6.** What decimal number is equal to 2%?  0.02
*(84)*

**7.** Write 60% as a reduced fraction.  $\frac{3}{5}$
*(33)*

**8.** Write 4% as a reduced fraction.  $\frac{1}{25}$
*(33)*

**9.** Write $\frac{13}{20}$ as a decimal number.  0.65
*(73)*

**10.** Compare: $\frac{3}{8}$ ⓒ 0.38    $<$
(75)

**11.** $2\frac{1}{2} + x = 3\frac{1}{4}$    $\frac{3}{4}$
(42)

**12.** $4\frac{1}{8} - y = 1\frac{1}{2}$    $2\frac{5}{8}$
(42)

**13.** $\frac{3}{4} \times 2\frac{2}{3} \times \frac{1}{2}$    $1$
(71)

**14.** $10 \div 2\frac{1}{2}$    $4$
(67)

**15.** $6.5 - (4 - 0.32)$    $2.82$
(38)

**16.** $(6.25)(1.6)$    $10$
(39)

**17.** $0.06 \div 12$    $0.005$
(44)

**18.** Arrange in order from least to greatest:    $30\%, 0.4, \frac{1}{2}$
(84)

$$\frac{1}{2}, 0.4, 30\%$$

**19.** In a school with 300 students and 15 teachers, what is
(82)  the student-teacher ratio?    $\frac{20}{1}$

**20.** $a - 0.7 = 2.3$    $3$
(42)

**21.** One fourth of the 32 marshmallows burned in the fire.
(76)  How many did not burn?    24

**22.** What is the area of a parallelogram that has vertices
(79)  with the coordinates (0, 0), (4, 0), (5, 3), and (1, 3)?
12 sq. units

**23.** $2 + 2 \times 2 - 2 \div 2$    $5$
(83)

**24.** Jim started the 10-kilometer race at 8:22 a.m. He
(32)  finished the race at 9:09 a.m. How long did it take him
to run the race?    47 min

**25.** Refer to the table below to answer this question: Ten
(15)  kilometers is about how many miles? (Round your
answer to the nearest mile.)    6 mi

| |
| --- |
| 1 meter ≈ 1.093 yards |
| 1 kilometer ≈ 0.621 mile |

**Note:** The symbol ≈ means "approximately equal to."

**26.** Robert packed boxes that were 1
foot long, 1 foot wide, and 1 foot
high into a larger box that was 5 feet
long, 4 feet wide, and 3 feet high.

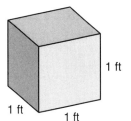

1 ft

1 ft     1 ft

(31)

(a) How many boxes could be
packed on the bottom layer of
the larger box?   20 boxes

(b) Altogether, how many small boxes could be packed
in the larger box?   60 boxes

**27.** (a) 2 ft + 24 in. (Write the sum in feet.)   4 ft
(80)
(b) 3 yd · 3 yd   9 yd²

**28.** Write $\frac{4}{5}$ as a percent.   80%
(81)

**29.** $10^2 - 5^2$   75
(72)

**30.** 3 gallons + 4 quarts (Write the sum in gallons.)   4 gal
(80)

---

**LESSON
85**

# Operations with Fractions
# and Decimals

**Facts Practice:** 30 Fractions to Reduce (Test G in Test Masters)

**Mental Math:** Count up and down by 2's between −10 and 10.

  **a.** 60 · 60      **b.** 850 − 170      **c.** $8.99 + $4.99
  **d.** $\frac{1}{5}$ of $2.50      **e.** 0.08 × 100      **f.** $\frac{360}{120}$
  **g.** 6 × 6, − 6, ÷ 2, − 1, ÷ 2, × 8, − 1, ÷ 5

**Problem Solving:** Copy this problem and fill in the
missing digits. No two digits in the
problem may be alike.

   _ _
×  8
─────
   _ _

When performing operations with fractions and decimals
in the same problem, we will rewrite the problem so that
all numbers are written in the same form, either as
fractions or as decimal numbers.

Example 1    Add 0.5 and $\frac{1}{4}$. Write the answer as a fraction and as a decimal number.

Solution    We show both procedures:

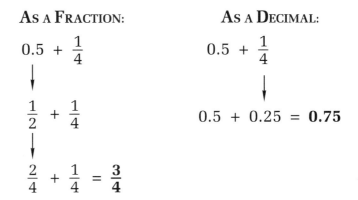

AS A FRACTION:

$$0.5 + \frac{1}{4}$$

$$\downarrow$$

$$\frac{1}{2} + \frac{1}{4}$$

$$\downarrow$$

$$\frac{2}{4} + \frac{1}{4} = \frac{3}{4}$$

AS A DECIMAL:

$$0.5 + \frac{1}{4}$$

$$\downarrow$$

$$0.5 + 0.25 = \mathbf{0.75}$$

The fraction answer $\frac{3}{4}$ is equal to the decimal 0.75, so either answer is correct. In this book the problems will ask you to write an answer in one form or the other.

Example 2    $\frac{1}{2} + 0.3$ (decimal answer)

Solution    Since the problem asks for a decimal answer, we will work the problem in decimal form. First we convert the fraction $\frac{1}{2}$ to a decimal number. Then we add the decimal numbers.

$$\frac{1}{2} + 0.3$$

$$\downarrow$$

$$0.5 + 0.3 = \mathbf{0.8}$$

Example 3    $\frac{1}{3} \times 0.3$ (fraction answer)

Solution    First we convert 0.3 to a fraction. Then we multiply the fractions.

$$\frac{1}{3} \times 0.3$$

$$\downarrow$$

$$\frac{1}{\cancel{3}_{1}} \times \frac{\cancel{3}^{1}}{10} = \frac{\mathbf{1}}{\mathbf{10}}$$

**Practice\***  Write the answers to these problems as decimals:

a. $\frac{3}{5} - 0.4$    0.2    b. $1.2 \times \frac{3}{4}$    0.9    c. $1.5 \div \frac{1}{2}$    3

Write the answers to these problems as fractions:

d. $\frac{2}{3} - 0.5$    $\frac{1}{6}$    e. $\frac{5}{6} \times 0.4$    $\frac{1}{3}$    f. $0.25 \div \frac{1}{2}$    $\frac{1}{2}$

**Problem set 85**

1. What is the quotient when the decimal number ten
   (48) and six tenths is divided by four hundredths?    265

2. The time in Los Angeles is 3 hours earlier than the
   (32) time in New York. If it is 1:15 p.m. in New York, what
   time is it in Los Angeles?    10:15 a.m.

3. Geraldine paid $10 for one dozen photographs costing
   (12) 75¢ each. How much should she get back in change?
   $1.00

4. $32 + 1.8(50)$    122
   (83)

5. How many cubes were used to
   (66) build this rectangular prism?    16

6. $0.25 + \frac{3}{5}$ (decimal)    7. $\frac{3}{5} - 0.4$ (fraction)    $\frac{1}{5}$
   (85)    0.85    (85)

8. $\frac{2}{5} \times 0.12$ (decimal)    9. $0.6 \div \frac{3}{4}$ (fraction)    $\frac{4}{5}$
   (85)    0.048    (85)

10. Write the decimal numeral for 6%.    0.06
    (84)

11. $5\frac{1}{2} + 3\frac{7}{8}$    $9\frac{3}{8}$    12. $3\frac{1}{4} - \frac{5}{8}$    $2\frac{5}{8}$    13. $\left(4\frac{1}{2}\right)\left(\frac{2}{3}\right)$    3
    (58)    (62)    (65)

14. $12\frac{1}{2} \div 100$    $\frac{1}{8}$    15. $5 \div 1\frac{1}{2}$    $3\frac{1}{3}$    16. $\frac{5}{6}$ of $30    $25
    (67)    (67)    (22)

**17.** 4.72 + 12 + $n$ = 50.4    **18.** $10 − $m$ = $9.87   $0.13
(42)  33.68                      (3)

**19.** Write 7% as a fraction.   **20.** 25 ÷ 0.5   50
(33)  $\frac{7}{100}$             (48)

**21.** What number is next in this sequence?
(10)

$$1, 4, 9, 16, 25, 36, \underline{\quad 49 \quad}, ...$$

**22.** 3$n$ = 0.48   0.16
(42)

**23.** The perimeter of the rectangle is
(8)   48 cm. The width is 6 cm. What is
      the length?   18 cm

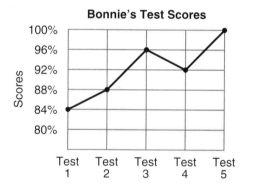

Refer to this line graph to answer questions 24 through 27:

**Bonnie's Test Scores**

**24.** Bonnie's highest score was how many percentage
(18)  points higher than her lowest score?   16

**25.** If Bonnie's five test scores were arranged in order from
(18)  the lowest score to the highest score, then what score
      would be the middle score?   92%

**26.** What was Bonnie's average score on all five tests?   92%
(18)

**27.** Write a question that refers to the line graph and
(18)  answer the question.   See student work.

**28.** What is the area of the parallelogram? 50 cm²
(79)

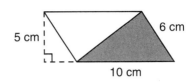

5 cm

6 cm

10 cm

**29.** Fifty percent of the parallelogram is shaded. What is
(79) the area of the shaded region? 25 cm²

**30.** The coordinates of three vertices of a parallelogram
(74) are (−3, 3), (2, 3), and (4, −1). What are the coordinates
of the fourth vertex? (−1, −1), (−5, 7), or (9, −1)

---

**LESSON
86**

**Mental Math:**
a. 4900
b. 625
c. $24.95
d. $1.70
e. 0.625
f. 900
g. 10
**Problem Solving:**
89

# Finding Missing Factors

**Facts Practice:** 64 Multiplication Facts (Test D in Test Masters)

**Mental Math:** Count up and down by $\frac{1}{8}$'s between $\frac{1}{8}$ and 2.

**a.** 70 · 70        **b.** 1000 − 375        **c.** 5 × $4.99
**d.** Double $0.85   **e.** 62.5 ÷ 100        **f.** 20 × 45
**g.** 5 × 5, − 5, × 5, ÷ 2, − 1, ÷ 7, × 3, − 1, ÷ 2
**h.** Hold your hands 50 cm apart; then 25 cm apart.

**Problem Solving:** Samantha averaged 85 points on her first
three tests. She averaged 95 on her next two
tests. What was her average score on her first
five tests?

Since Lesson 4 we have practiced solving missing factor
problems. In this lesson we will solve problems in which
the unknown factor is a mixed number or a decimal
number. Remember, we can find an unknown factor by
dividing the product by the known factor.

Example 1    $5n = 21$

Solution    To find an unknown factor, we divide
the product by the known factor.

$$\begin{array}{r} 4\frac{1}{5} \\ 5\overline{)21} \\ 20 \\ \hline 1 \end{array}$$

$$n = 4\frac{1}{5}$$

**Note:** We will write the answer as a mixed number unless
there are decimal numbers in the problem.

Example 2    $0.6m = 0.048$

Solution    Again we will find the unknown
factor by dividing the product by the
known factor. Since there are decimal
numbers in the problem, we will write
our answer as a decimal number.

$$\begin{array}{r} 0.08 \\ 0.6\overline{)0.0.48} \\ 48 \\ \hline 0 \end{array}$$

$$m = \mathbf{0.08}$$

Example 3    $45 = 4x$

Solution    An equals sign is not directional. It
simply states that the quantities on
either side of the sign are equal. In
this case, the product is 45 and the
known factor is 4. We divide 45 by 4
to find the unknown factor.

$$\begin{array}{r} 11\frac{1}{4} \\ 4\overline{)45} \\ 4 \\ \hline 05 \\ 4 \\ \hline 1 \end{array}$$

$$x = \mathbf{11\frac{1}{4}}$$

**Practice**    **a.** $6w = 21$  $3\frac{1}{2}$    **b.** $50 = 3f$  $16\frac{2}{3}$    **c.** $5n = 36$  $7\frac{1}{5}$

**d.** $0.3t = 0.24$  0.8    **e.** $8m = 3.2$  0.4    **f.** $0.8 = 0.5x$  1.6

**Problem set**    **1.** If the divisor is 12 and the quotient is 24, what is the
**86**    (4)    dividend?  288

**2.** The brachiosaurus, one of the largest dinosaurs,
(22)    weighed only $\frac{1}{4}$ as much as a blue whale weighs. A
blue whale weighs 140 tons when full grown. What
was the weight of the brachiosaurus?  35 tons

**3.** Fourteen of the 32 students in the class are boys. What
(82) is the ratio of boys to girls in the class? $\frac{7}{9}$

**4.** $0.3m = 0.27$   0.9      **5.** $31 = 5n$   $6\frac{1}{5}$
(86)                              (86)

**6.** $3n = 6^2$   12       **7.** $6.5 + \dfrac{3}{5}$ (decimal answer)
(72)                         (85)   7.1

**8.** $3\dfrac{1}{4} + 0.25$ (fraction answer)   $3\frac{1}{2}$
(85)

**9.** Write 175% as a decimal number.   1.75
(84)

**10.** Write 65% as a reduced fraction.   $\frac{13}{20}$
(33)

**11.** $12\dfrac{1}{5} - 3\dfrac{4}{5}$   $8\frac{2}{5}$   **12.** $6\dfrac{2}{3} \times 1\dfrac{1}{5}$   8   **13.** $11\dfrac{1}{9} \div 100$   $\frac{1}{9}$
(62)                   (65)                 (67)

**14.** $4.75 + 12.6 + 10$   27.35    **15.** $0.35 \div 4$   0.0875
(38)                                 (44)

**16.** Write $\frac{8}{25}$ as a percent.   32%
(81)

**17.** Write the decimal numeral twelve and five hundredths.
(35)   12.05

**18.** $35 - (0.35 \times 100)$   0
(83)

**19.** If $a$ equals 15, then what number does $2a - 5$ equal?
(83)   25

**20.** What is the area of the
(79) parallelogram?   450 mm²

**21.** What is the perimeter of
(8) the parallelogram?   90 mm

**22.** "All rectangles are parallelograms." True or False?   true
(78)

**23.** Charles spent $\frac{1}{10}$ of his 100 shillings. How many
(22) shillings did he still have?   90

**24.** The temperature rose from −18°F to 19°F. How many
(14) degrees did the temperature increase?   37°F

**25.** How many **centimeters** long is the line?   4 cm
(7)

mm  10      20      30      40      50

**26.** Nathan poured 500 mL of pop from a full 2-liter
(77) container. How many milliliters of beverage were left
in the container?   1500 mL

**27.** Name this geometric solid.
(66)   triangular prism

**28.** (a) 2 meters + 100 centimeters (Write the answer in
(80)    meters.)   3 m

(b) 2 m · 4 m   8 m²

**29.** 4 + 4 × 4 − 4 ÷ 4   19
(83)

**30.** What is the perimeter of a rectangle with vertices at
(74) (−4, −4), (−4, 4), (4, 4), and (4, −4)?   32 units

# Area of a Triangle

LESSON
87

**Facts Practice:** Liquid Measure Facts (Test L in Test Masters)

**Mental Math:** Count up and down by 25's between −150 and 150.

a. 80 · 80
b. 720 − 150
c. $1.98 + $1.98
d. $\frac{1}{10}$ of $5.00
e. 0.15 × 100
f. $\frac{750}{250}$
g. 4 × 4, − 1, × 2, + 3, ÷ 3, − 1, × 10, − 1, ÷ 9

**Problem Solving:** Silvia was thinking of a number less than 90 that she says when counting by sixes and when counting by fives, but not when counting by fours. Of what number was she thinking?

## Activity: Area of a Triangle

Materials needed:

- Pencil
- Paper
- Ruler
- Scissors

Procedure:

- Fold the paper in half and draw a triangle on the folded paper.

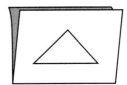

- While the paper is folded, use your scissors to cut out the triangle so that you cut out two congruent triangles.

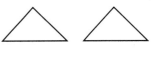

- Arrange the two triangles to form a parallelogram. What fraction of the area of the parallelogram is the area of one of the triangles?

We find that whatever the shape of the triangle, the area of a triangle is half the area of a parallelogram with the same base and height.

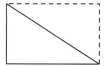 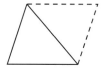 

Recall that the area of a parallelogram can be found by multiplying its base times its height ($A = bh$). So the area of a triangle can be determined by finding half of the product of its base and height.

$$\text{Area of a triangle} = \frac{1}{2}bh$$

Since multiplying by $\frac{1}{2}$ and dividing by 2 are equivalent operations, the formula may also be written

$$A = \frac{bh}{2}$$

We will show the use of both formulas in the examples. When calculating the area of a rectangle, remember that the length of the base and the height are perpendicular measurements.

**Example 1**    Find the area of the triangle.

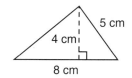

*Solution*    The area of the triangle is half the product of the base and height. The height must be **perpendicular** to the base. The height in this case is 4 cm. Half the product of 8 cm and 4 cm is 16 cm².

$$A = \frac{1}{2}(8 \text{ cm})(4 \text{ cm})$$

$$A = \mathbf{16 \text{ cm}^2}$$

**Example 2**    Find the area of this right triangle.

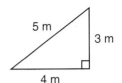

**Solution**    We find the area by multiplying the base and the height, then dividing by 2. With a right triangle two sides are perpendicular, so we use the **perpendicular** sides as the base and height.

$$A = \frac{(4 \text{ m})(3 \text{ m})}{2}$$

$$A = \textbf{6 m}^2$$

**Practice***    Find the area of each triangle:

**a.** 30 ft²

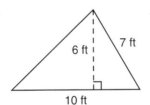

**b.** 24 in.²

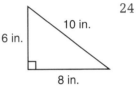

**c.**  420 mm²

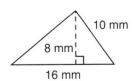

**Problem set 87**

1. Mason scored 12 of the team's 20 points. What percent
   (81) of the team's points did Mason score?    60%

2. If Pinocchio's nose grows $\frac{1}{4}$ inch per lie, then how
   (49) many lies has he told if his nose has grown 4 inches?
   16 lies

3. Mark wants to buy a new baseball glove that costs $50.
   (86) He has $14, and he earns $6 per hour cleaning yards.
   How many hours must he work to have enough money
   to buy the glove?    6 hours

4. Find the area of the triangle.
   (87) 64 mm²

**5.** $10w = 25$ $2\frac{1}{2}$
(86)

**6.** $20 = 9m$ $2\frac{2}{9}$
(86)

**7.** What is the perimeter of this triangle? 24 in.
(8)

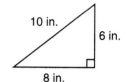
10 in.
6 in.
8 in.

**8.** What is the area of this triangle? 24 in.²
(87)

**9.** Write 5%
(33,84)

    (a) as a decimal number and 0.05

    (b) as a fraction. $\frac{1}{20}$

**10.** $2.5 \times \dfrac{2}{5}$ (decimal answer) 1
(85)

**11.** $\dfrac{2}{3} \div 0.25$ (fraction answer) $2\frac{2}{3}$
(85)

**12.** Compare: $\dfrac{2}{3} + \dfrac{3}{2}$ $\bigcirc\!\!>$ $\dfrac{2}{3} \cdot \dfrac{3}{2}$
(75)

**13.** $\dfrac{1}{3} \times \dfrac{100}{1}$ $33\frac{1}{3}$
(69)

**14.** $6 \div 1\frac{1}{2}$ 4
(67)

**15.** $12 \div 0.25$ 48
(48)

**16.** $0.025 \times 100$ 2.5
(46)

**17.** Multiply $25.00 by 0.07 and round the product to the nearest cent. $1.75
(50)

**18.** The prime factorization of what number is $2^2 \cdot 3^2 \cdot 5^2$? 900
(72)

**19.** Which of these is a composite number? 81
(64)

                  61, 71, 81, 101

**20.** Round the decimal number one and twenty-three hundredths to the nearest tenth. 1.2
(50)

**21.** Albert baked 5 dozen cookies and gave away $\frac{7}{12}$ of them. Then how many cookies were left? 25
(60)

**22.** 6 × 3 − 6 ÷ 3   16        **23.** 76 · 1 = 76 + *w*   0
(83)                              (3)

**24.** How many milliliters is 4 liters?   4000 mL
(77)

**25.** Draw a line segment $2\frac{1}{4}$ inches long. Label the
(68) endpoints *A* and *C*. Then make a dot at the midpoint of
segment *AC* (the point halfway between points *A* and
*C*) and label the dot point *B*. What is the length of $\overline{AB}$
and $\overline{BC}$?  •————————•————————•; $\overline{AB} = \overline{BC} = 1\frac{1}{8}$ in.
                     A          B          C

26.

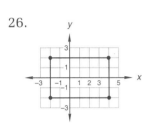

**26.** On a coordinate plane draw a rectangle with vertices
(74) at (−2, −2), (4, −2), (4, 2), and (−2, 2). What is the area
of the rectangle?   24 sq. units

**27.** What is the ratio of the length to the width of the
(82) rectangle in problem 26?   $\frac{3}{2}$

**28.** What percent of the perimeter of a square is the length
(81) of one of its sides?   25%

**29.** Describe how to calculate the area of a triangle. Multiply
(87) the base and height of the triangle, and then divide that answer
by 2.

# LESSON 88

# Comparing Negative Numbers • Square Root

**Mental Math:**
a. 8100
b. 595
c. $47.94
d. $54.00
e. 0.875
f. 720
g. 3
h. 2 m
**Problem Solving:**
  29 cm

**Facts Practice:**  Linear Measure Facts (Test K in Test Masters)

**Mental Math:**  Count up and down by 3's between −15 and 15.

  **a.**  90 · 90          **b.**  1000 − 405          **c.**  6 × $7.99
  **d.**  Double $27.00          **e.**  87.5 ÷ 100          **f.**  20 × 36
  **g.**  3 × 3, + 2, × 5, − 5, × 2, ÷ 10, + 5, ÷ 5
  **h.**  About how many meters high is a classroom door?

**Problem Solving:**  The perimeter of the rectangle is 1 m. What is
  its length?

**Comparing negative numbers**

A number line can help us compare numbers.

Looking at the number line, we see that as we move further and further to the left, the numbers get smaller and smaller. Since −3 is to the left of −2, it is less than −2. This makes sense because a number that is three less than zero is less than a number that is two less than zero.

**Example 1**  Compare: −5 ◯ −2

*Solution*  A number that is 5 less than zero is less than a number that is 2 less than zero.

$$-5 < -2$$

**Example 2**  Arrange in order from least to greatest: 0, 2, −3, −1.

*Solution*  Negative numbers are less than zero, so −3 and −1 are less than 0, and 0 is less than 2. We write the numbers in this order: **−3, −1, 0, 2.**

**Square root**  If we know the area of a square, we can calculate the length of each side. This square has an area of 100 square millimeters.

Area = 100 mm²

We know that the length of each side is 10 mm because

$$10 \text{ mm} \times 10 \text{ mm} = 100 \text{ mm}^2$$

Calculating the length of a side of a square from the area of a square is a picture version of finding the principal **square root** of a number. Finding the square root of a number is the opposite of squaring a number.

Six squared is 36.

The principal square root of 36 is 6.

The square root symbol looks like this:

We read $\sqrt{100}$ as "the square root of 100." This expression means, "What positive number, when multiplied by itself, has a product of 100?" Since 10 times 10 equals 100, the principal square root of 100 is 10.

$$\sqrt{100} = 10$$

A number is a **perfect square** if it has a square root that is a whole number. The first four perfect squares are 1, 4, 9, and 16.

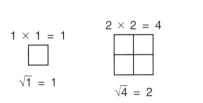

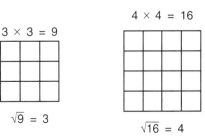

Example 3    $\sqrt{64}$

*Solution*    The square root of 64 can be thought of in two ways:

1. What is the side of a square that has an area of 64?

or    2. What positive number multiplied by itself equals 64?

Either way, we should find that $\sqrt{64}$ equals **8**.

**Practice**    Compare:

**a.** $-3 \enspace \textcircled{>} \enspace -4$    **b.** $3 - 2 \enspace \textcircled{>} \enspace 2 - 3$

Arrange in order from least to greatest:

**c.** $-1, 1, -2, 0$    $-2, -1, 0, 1$

**d.** $\dfrac{1}{2}, -1, 0, 0.1, -\dfrac{1}{2}$    $-1, -\frac{1}{2}, 0, 0.1, \frac{1}{2}$

Find each square root:

**e.** $\sqrt{81}$    9    **f.** $\sqrt{144}$    12    **g.** $\sqrt{400}$    20

**h.** The first four perfect squares are 1, 4, 9, and 16. What are the next four perfect squares?    25, 36, 49, and 64

**i.** $36 - \sqrt{36}$    30

**Problem set 88**

**1.** What is the difference when the product of $\frac{1}{2}$ and $\frac{1}{2}$ is
(24)    subtracted from the sum of $\frac{1}{4}$ and $\frac{1}{4}$?    $\frac{1}{4}$

**2.** A dairy cow can give 4 gallons of milk per day. How
(77)    many cups of milk is that? (1 gallon = 4 quarts, 1 quart = 4 cups)    64 cups

**3.** The recipe called for $\frac{3}{4}$ cup of sugar. If the recipe is
(29)    doubled, how much sugar should be used?    $1\frac{1}{2}$ cups

**4.** Compare: $-5 \enspace \textcircled{>} \enspace -7$
(88)

**5.** Arrange in order from least to greatest: $-4, -2, 0, 6$
(88)
$$-2, 0, -4, 6$$

**6.** $7n = 30$ $4\frac{2}{7}$
(86)

**7.** What is the area of the triangle?
(87) 20 in.²

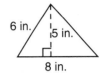

**8.** What is the area of the
(79) parallelogram? 40 in.²

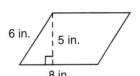

**9.** What is the perimeter of the
(8) parallelogram? 28 in.

**10.** $0.6 \times \dfrac{3}{4}$ (decimal answer) 0.45
(85)

**11.** $3\dfrac{1}{4} - 0.5$ (fraction answer) $2\frac{3}{4}$
(85)

**12.** $0.5 \div \dfrac{2}{3}$ (fraction answer) $\frac{3}{4}$
(85)

**13.** $2 \times 15 + 2 \times 12$ 54 **14.** $\$0.07 \times 10^2$ $7.00
(83) (72)

**15.** $\$6 \div 8$ $0.75 **16.** $1\dfrac{3}{5} \times 10 \times \dfrac{1}{4}$ 4
(2) (65)

**17.** $37\dfrac{1}{2} \div 100$ $\frac{3}{8}$ **18.** $3 \div 7\dfrac{1}{2}$ $\frac{2}{5}$
(67) (67)

**19.** What is the place value of the 7 in 987,654.321?
(12) thousands'

**20.** Write the decimal numeral five hundred ten and five
(35) hundredths. 510.05

**21.** $30 + 60 + m = 180$ 90
(3)

**22.** Half of the students are girls. Half of the girls have
(76) brown hair. Half of the brown-haired girls wear their
hair long. Of the 32 students, how many are girls with
long, brown hair?   4

Refer to this picture graph to answer problems 23–25:

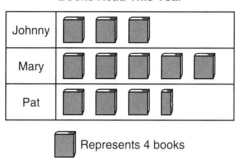

**Books Read This Year**

 Represents 4 books

**23.** How many books has Johnny read?   12 books
(16)

**24.** Mary has read how many more books than Pat? 6 books
(16)

**25.** Write a question that refers to this graph and answer
(16) the question.   See student work.

26.

**26.** This square's area is 25 square
(88) units. This figure illustrates that
25 is a perfect square. Draw a
square on graph paper that
illustrates that 36 is a perfect
square.

**27.** What percent of a gallon is a quart?   25%
(77)

**28.** $25 - \sqrt{25}$   20
(88)

**29.** (a) 100 cm + 100 cm (Write the answer in meters.) 2 m
(80)
　　(b) $\dfrac{(5 \text{ in.})(8 \text{ in.})}{2}$   20 in.²

**30.** How many cubes were used to
(66) build this larger cube?   64

# LESSON
# 89

**Faces, Edges, and Vertices**

Mental Math:
a. 10
b. 746
c. $4.96
d. $8.00
e. 37.5
f. 4
g. 2
h. About 3 ft
**Problem Solving:**
   100,000

**Facts Practice:** Write 24 Mixed Numbers as Improper Fractions (Test J in Test Masters)

**Mental Math:** Count up and down by $\frac{1}{2}$'s between −3 and 3.

  **a.** $\sqrt{100}$          **b.** 781 − 35          **c.** $1.98 + $2.98
  **d.** $\frac{1}{3}$ of $24.00     **e.** 0.375 × 100        **f.** $\frac{1200}{300}$
  **g.** 2 × 2, × 2, × 2, − 1, × 2, + 2, ÷ 4, ÷ 4
  **h.** About how many feet wide is a classroom door?

**Problem Solving:** One state used a license plate that was one letter followed by five digits. How many different license plates could be made that started with the letter *A*?

The illustration below points out a face, an edge, and a vertex of a cube.

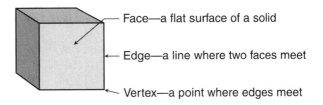

Face—a flat surface of a solid

Edge—a line where two faces meet

Vertex—a point where edges meet

Example   (a)  A cube has how many faces?

(b)  A cube has how many edges?

(c)  A cube has how many vertices?

Solution   (a)  A cube has **6 faces.**

(b)  A cube has **12 edges.**

(c)  *Vertices* is the plural form of *vertex*. A cube has **8 vertices.**

Practice   Here is a pyramid with a square base. One face is a square; the rest are triangles.

  **a.** How many faces are there in all?   5

  **b.** How many edges are there?   8

  **c.** How many vertices are there?   5

Here is a triangular prism.

**d.** How many faces does it have?  5

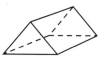

**e.** How many edges?   9

**f.** How many vertices?   6

**Problem set 89**

**1.** What is the average of 4.2, 4.8, and 5.1?   4.7
(18)

**2.** The movie is 120 minutes long. If it begins at
(32) 7:15 p.m., when will it be over?   9:15 p.m.

Fifteen of the 25 students in Room 20 are boys. Use this information to answer problems 3 and 4.

**3.** What percent of the students in Room 20 are boys? 60%
(81)

**4.** What is the ratio of boys to girls in Room 20?   $\frac{3}{2}$
(82)

**5.** This triangular prism has how
(89) many more edges than vertices?
3

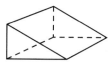

**6.** Name this quadrilateral.   trapezoid
(78)

7. A trapezoid is a polygon with four sides. Two of the sides are parallel. The other two sides are not parallel.

**7.** Describe the appearance of a trapezoid.
(78)

**8.** Arrange in order from least to greatest:   $-4, -2, 0, \frac{1}{2}, 1$
(88)         $1, -2, 0, -4, \frac{1}{2}$

**9.** $25n = 70$   $2\frac{4}{5}$
(86)

**10.** What is the area of the triangle?
(87)   150 mm²

**11.** What is the perimeter of the
(8) triangle?   60 mm

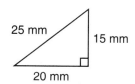

25 mm   15 mm

20 mm

**12.** $6.25 - \dfrac{5}{8}$ (decimal answer)   5.625
(85)

**13.** Write 125% as a decimal number.   1.25
(84)

**14.** Write 28% as a reduced fraction.   $\frac{7}{25}$
(33)

**15.** $\dfrac{n}{0.4} = 0.2$   **16.** $0.625 \div 10$   **17.** $\dfrac{25}{0.8}$   31.25
(42)   0.08   (51)   0.0625   (48)

**18.** $3\dfrac{3}{8} + 3\dfrac{3}{4}$   $7\frac{1}{8}$   **19.** $5\dfrac{1}{8} - 1\dfrac{7}{8}$   $3\frac{1}{4}$   **20.** $6\dfrac{2}{3} \times \dfrac{3}{10} \times 4$
(58)   (47)   (71)   8

**21.** One third of the two dozen knights were on horseback.
(76) How many knights were not on horseback?   16 knights

**22.** Weights totaling 42 ounces were placed on the left-
(18) hand side of the scale while weights totaling 26
ounces were placed on the right-hand side of the
scale. How many ounces of weights should be moved
from the left-hand side to the right-hand side to
balance the scale? (*Hint*: Find the average of the
weights on the two sides of the scale.)   8 oz

**23.** The cube at right is made up of
(38) how many smaller cubes?   27

**24.** Round forty-eight hundredths to the nearest tenth.
(50)   0.5

**25.** $\sqrt{25} - \sqrt{16}$   1
(88)

**26.** The ratio of dogs to cats in the neighborhood is 6 to 5.
*(82)* What is the ratio of cats to dogs?   $\frac{5}{6}$

**27.** $10 + 10 \times 10 - 10 \div 10$   109
*(83)*

**28.** The Thompsons drink a gallon of milk every two days.
*(71)* There are four people in the Thompson family. Each person drinks an average of how many pints of milk each day?   1 pint per day

**29.** (a) 10 cm + 100 mm (Write the answer in mm.) 200 mm
*(80)* (b) 300 books ÷ 30 students   10 books per student

**30.** On a coordinate plane draw a segment from point *A* at
*(74)* (−3, −1) to point *B* at (5, −1). What is the coordinate of the point on $\overline{AB}$ that is halfway from *A* to *B*?   (1, −1)

# INVESTIGATION 3

# Platonic Solids

Recall that polygons are closed two-dimensional figures with straight sides. If every face of a solid figure is a polygon, then the solid figure is called a **polyhedron.** Thus, polyhedrons do not have any curved surfaces. So rectangular prisms and pyramids are polyhedrons, but spheres and cylinders are not polyhedrons.

Remember also that regular polygons have sides of equal length and angles of equal measure. Just as there are regular polygons, so there are regular polyhedrons. A cube is one example of a regular polyhedron. All the edges of a cube are of equal length and all the angles are of equal measure.

There are five regular polyhedrons. These polyhedrons are known as the **Platonic solids,** named after the ancient Greek philosopher Plato. We illustrate the five Platonic solids below.

tetrahedron    cube    octahedron  dodecahedron  icosahedron

In this activity we will construct models of four of the Platonic solids. We will construct an icosahedron in a later investigation.

## Activity: Platonic Solids

Materials needed:

- Copies of "Activity Master 7" and "Activity Master 8" from *Math 76 Test Masters* for each student.
- Ruler
- Scissors
- Glue or tape

Working in pairs or small groups is helpful. Sometimes more than two hands are needed to fold and glue.

Beginning with the tetrahedron pattern, cut around the border of the pattern. The line segments in the pattern are fold lines. Do not cut these. The folds will become the edges of the polyhedron. The triangles marked with "T" are tabs for gluing. These tabs are tucked inside the polyhedron and are hidden from view when the polyhedron is finished.

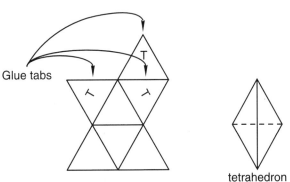

Fold the pattern to make a pyramid with four faces. Glue the tabs or tape across the joining edges to hold the pattern in place.

When you have completed the tetrahedron, select another pattern to cut, fold, and form. All tabs are hidden when the pattern is properly folded, but all other polygons should be fully visible. When you have completed the models, copy this table on a piece of paper and fill in the missing information by studying your models.

| Platonic Solid | Each face is what polygon? | How many faces? | How many vertices? | How many edges? |
|---|---|---|---|---|
| tetrahedron | equilateral triangle | 4 | 4 | 6 |
| cube | squares | 6 | 8 | 12 |
| octahedron | triangle | 8 | 6 | 12 |
| dodecahedron | pentagon | 12 | 20 | 30 |

## Extensions  Alternate patterns:

1. This arrangement of four equilateral triangles was used to make a model of a tetrahedron. Draw another arrangement of four adjoining equilateral triangles that can be folded to make a tetrahedron model. (Omit tabs.)

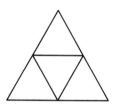

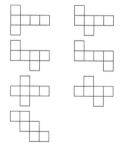

2. This arrangement of six squares was folded to make a model of a cube. How many other different patterns of six adjacent squares can you draw that can be folded to make a model of a cube? (Omit tabs.)

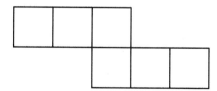

# LESSON
# 90

Mental Math:
a. 35
b. 125
c. $34.95
d. $250.00
e. 0.125
f. 840
g. 7
Problem Solving:

$$\begin{array}{r} 136 \\ \times \quad 7 \\ \hline 952 \end{array}$$

# Geometric Formulas

**Facts Practice:** 72 Mixed Multiplication and Division (Test H in Test Masters)

**Mental Math:** Count by $\frac{1}{3}$'s from $\frac{1}{3}$ to 4.

  **a.** $5^2 + \sqrt{100}$      **b.** $1000 - 875$      **c.** $\$6.99 \times 5$

  **d.** Double $125.00      **e.** $12.5 \div 100$      **f.** $20 \times 42$

  **g.** $3 \times 4, \div 2, \times 3, + 2, \times 2, + 2, \div 2, \div 3$

**Problem Solving:** Copy this problem and fill in the missing digits. No two digits in the problem may be alike.

$$\begin{array}{r} \_\,\_\,\_ \\ \times \quad 7 \\ \hline 9\_\,\_ \end{array}$$

We have found the area of a rectangle by multiplying the length of the rectangle times its width. This procedure can be described with the following formula:

$$A = lw$$

The letter $A$ stands for the area of a rectangle. The letters $l$ and $w$ stand for the length and width of the rectangle. Written side by side, $lw$ means that we multiply the length and width to find the area. The table below lists formulas for the perimeter and area of squares, rectangles, parallelograms, and triangles.

| Figure | Perimeter | Area |
|---|---|---|
| Square | $P = 4s$ | $A = s^2$ |
| Rectangle | $P = 2l + 2w$ | $A = lw$ |
| Parallelogram | $P = 2b + 2s$ | $A = bh$ |
| Triangle | $P = s_1 + s_2 + s_3$ | $A = \frac{1}{2}bh$ |

The letters $P$ and $A$ are abbreviations for "perimeter" and "area." Other abbreviations are illustrated below.

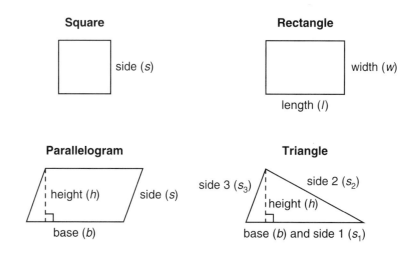

Since squares and rectangles are also parallelograms, the formulas for the perimeter and area of parallelograms may also be used for squares or rectangles.

To use a formula, we substitute a known measure in place of the appropriate letter in the formula. When substituting a number in place of a letter, it is a good practice to write the number in parentheses.

**Example**   Write the formula for the perimeter of a rectangle. Then substitute 8 cm for the length and 5 cm for the width. Solve the equation to find $P$.

*Solution*   The formula for the perimeter of a rectangle is

$$P = 2l + 2w$$

We rewrite the equation, substituting 8 cm for $l$ and 5 cm for $w$. We write these measurements in parentheses.

$$P = 2(8 \text{ cm}) + 2(5 \text{ cm})$$

We multiply 2 times 8 cm and 2 times 5 cm.

$$P = 16 \text{ cm} + 10 \text{ cm}$$

Now we add 16 cm and 10 cm.

$$P = 26 \text{ cm}$$

The perimeter of the rectangle is **26 cm.**

We summarize the steps below to show how your work should look.

$$P = 2l + 2w$$

$$P = 2(8 \text{ cm}) + 2(5 \text{ cm})$$

$$P = 16 \text{ cm} + 10 \text{ cm}$$

$$P = 26 \text{ cm}$$

**Practice**  **a.** Write the formula for the area of a rectangle. Then substitute 8 cm for the length and 5 cm for the width. Solve the equation to find the area of the rectangle. $A = lw$; $A = (8 \text{ cm})(5 \text{ cm})$; $A = 40 \text{ cm}^2$

**b.** Write the formula for the perimeter of a parallelogram. Then substitute 10 cm for the base and 6 cm for the side. Solve the equation to find the perimeter of the parallelogram.   $P = 2b + 2s$; $P = 2(10 \text{ cm}) + 2(6 \text{ cm})$; $P = 32 \text{ cm}$

**Problem set**  **1.** What is the ratio of prime numbers to composite
**90**   *(82)*  numbers in this list?   $\frac{1}{2}$

10, 11, 12, 13, 14, 15, 16, 17, 18, 19, 20, 21

**2.** Sunrise was at 6:15 a.m., and sunset was at 5:45 p.m.
*(32)* How many hours and minutes were there from sunrise to sunset?   11 hr, 30 min

**3.** What number is equal to all of your fingers plus half
*(83)* your toes, minus your knees and elbows?   11

**4.** A rectangular prism has how many more faces than a
*(89)* triangular prism?   1

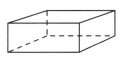 

**5.** What percent of a dollar is a nickel?   5%
*(81)*

**6.** This is a pyramid with a triangular base.

(89)

(a) How many faces does it have?

(b) How many edges does it have?

(c) How many vertices does it have?

(a) 4   (b) 6   (c) 4

**7.** What is the perimeter of the parallelogram?   44 in.

(90)

**8.** What is the area of the parallelogram?   108 in.²

(90)

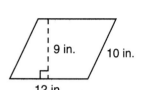

**9.** Write 225% as a decimal numeral.   2.25

(84)

**10.** Write 64% as a reduced fraction.   $\frac{16}{25}$

(33)

**11.** $6\frac{2}{3} + 1\frac{3}{4}$   $8\frac{5}{12}$   **12.** $5 - 1\frac{2}{5}$   $3\frac{3}{5}$   **13.** $4\frac{1}{4} - 3\frac{5}{8}$   $\frac{5}{8}$

(58)                              (62)                              (62)

**14.** $3 \times \frac{3}{4} \times 2\frac{2}{3}$   **15.** $6\frac{2}{3} \div 100$   $\frac{1}{15}$   **16.** $2\frac{1}{2} \div 3\frac{3}{4}$   $\frac{2}{3}$

(71)   6                          (67)                              (67)

**17.** Compare: $\frac{9}{20}$ ⓒ< 50%

(81)

**18.** (a) What fraction of the group is shaded?   $\frac{1}{4}$

(21,81)

(b) What percent of the group is shaded?   25%

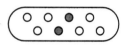

**19.** If $\frac{5}{6}$ of the 300 seeds sprouted, how many seeds did **not** sprout?   50

(76)

**20.** $6y = 10$   $1\frac{2}{3}$        **21.** $6x = 4 \cdot 9$   6

(86)                              (86)

**22.** What is the area of the triangle?

(90)   12 ft²

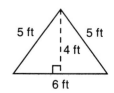

**23.** Round $6.5432 to the nearest cent.  $6.54
(50)

**24.** What time is 2 hours and 15 minutes before 1:45 p.m.?
(32)   11:30 a.m.

**25.** The length of segment *AC* is 56 mm. The length of
(68)   segment *BC* is 26 mm. How long is segment *AB*?  30 mm

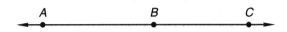

**26.** $9^2 - \sqrt{9}$   78
(88)

**27.** 2 × 15 cm + 2 × 5 cm
(83)   40 cm

28.

*y*

**28.** A square has vertices at the coordinates (2, 0), (0, −2),
(74)   (−2, 0), and (0, 2). Graph the points and draw segments
from point to point in the order given to draw the square.
(The fourth segment is drawn from (0, 2) to (2, 0).)

**29.** The square in problem 28 encloses some whole
(74)   squares and some half squares on the graph paper.

(a) How many whole squares are enclosed by the square?  4

(b) How many half squares are enclosed by the square?  8

**30.** Write the formula for the area of a parallelogram as
(90)   given in this lesson. For the base substitute 15 cm. For
the height substitute 4 cm. Then find the area of the
parallelogram.  $A = bh$; $A = (15 \text{ cm})(4 \text{ cm})$; $A = 60 \text{ cm}^2$

# LESSON 91

# Probability • Chance

**Facts Practice:** Liquid Measure Facts (Test L in Test Masters)

**Mental Math:** Count up and down by 25's between −150 and 150.

   **a.** 30 · 50                        **b.** 486 + 50

   **c.** 50% of 24    *(Think $\frac{1}{2}$ of 24)*       **d.** $20.00 − $14.75

   **e.** 100 × 1.25                    **f.** $\frac{600}{30}$

   **g.** $\sqrt{36}$, + 4, × 3, + 2, ÷ 4, + 1, $\sqrt{}$ †

**Problem Solving:** Jorge's average grade on four tests is 88%. What grade does he need on his fifth test to have a five-test average of 90%?

† Read $\sqrt{}$ as "find the square root."

**Probability**   Imagine you are flipping a coin. How many different outcomes are possible? There are only two: heads and tails. If we ask, "What is the probability of getting heads?" we are asking how likely it is that heads will turn up when a coin is flipped.

Probabilities are stated as ratios. The numerator of the ratio is the number of ways the desired, or favored, event can happen. The denominator of the ratio is the total number of outcomes possible. In this case, the probability of the favored outcome heads is

$$\frac{\text{Number of favorable outcomes}}{\text{Number of possible outcomes}} = \frac{1}{2}$$

**Example 1**   What is the probability of a tossed coin landing tails up?

**Solution**   A coin may land either heads up or tails up. So there are two possible outcomes. The favorable outcome in this question is "tails up," so there is only one favorable outcome. The probability of a tossed coin landing tails up is $\frac{1}{2}$.

$$\frac{\text{Favorable}}{\text{Possible}} = \frac{1}{2}$$

**Example 2**    What is the probability of drawing an ace from a normal deck of 52 cards? (Discussing the composition of a normal deck of 52 cards will help students with the problems in the sets.)

*Solution*    There are 52 possible cards one may draw. There are four favorable cards.

$$\frac{\text{Favorable}}{\text{Possible}} = \frac{4}{52}$$

Recall that we reduce ratios when possible. We reduce $\frac{4}{52}$ to $\frac{1}{13}$. The probability of drawing an ace from a normal deck of 52 cards is $\frac{1}{13}$.

An event that is certain to happen has a probability of 1. If we roll a common number cube, the probability of rolling a number less than 7 is $\frac{6}{6}$ because all 6 possible outcomes are also "favorable" outcomes. The ratio $\frac{6}{6}$ equals 1.

An event that is certain not to happen has a probability of 0. The probability of rolling a 7 with one roll of a single number cube is $\frac{0}{6}$ because no favorable outcomes are possible. The ratio $\frac{0}{6}$ equals 0.

**Chance**    A probability is sometimes expressed as a **chance** written in **percent** form. If the chance of rain is 100%, then it is certain to rain. If the chance of rain is 50%, then it is just as likely to rain as it is not to rain.

**Example 3**    The weather report stated that the chance of rain on Tuesday is 40%. What is the chance that it will not rain?

*Solution*    Either it will rain or it will not rain. The combined probability of the two events is 100%. The probability of rain is 40%, so the probability that it will not rain is **60%**.

## Activity: Coin-Toss

Materials needed:

- A coin for each student or for each pair of students.
- Pencil and paper for recording coin-toss results.
- One calculator would be useful.

Ask students to predict the number of times a coin would land heads up and tails up in 10 flips of the coin. Then have students work in pairs. Each pair of students should record the results of 10 coin flips, noting the number of "heads" and "tails." Collect the results on the board or on an overhead transparency in a form such as this.

| Group | Heads | Tails |
|-------|-------|-------|
| 1 | 6 | 4 |
| 2 | 5 | 5 |
| 3 | 3 | 7 |
| Total | | |

Consider these questions:

**a.** What was the greatest number of "heads" outcomes in any group? What was the greatest number of "tails" outcomes?  Answers will vary.

**b.** Which outcome occurred most frequently?
Answers will vary.

**c.** How do the totals fit with class expectations?
Answers will vary.

**d.** Use a calculator to find the average number of "heads" and "tails" by dividing the totals by the number of groups. Round the quotients to the nearest tenth.
Answers will vary.

**Practice** **a.** What is the probability of rolling a 6 with one roll of a number cube?  $\frac{1}{6}$

**b.** What is the probability of drawing a "spade" from a normal deck of 52 cards? $\frac{1}{4}$

**c.** If the chance of rain tomorrow is 60%, is it more likely to rain or not to rain? to rain

**Problem set 91**

1. It is more likely that it won't rain. If the chance of rain is 40%, then the chance that it won't rain is 60%. So the chance that it won't rain is greater than the chance that it will rain.

**1.** The weather forecast stated that the chance of rain for Wednesday is 40%. Does this forecast mean that it is more likely to rain or not to rain? Why?
(91)

**2.** What is the probability of drawing a "heart" from a normal deck of 52 cards? $\frac{1}{4}$
(91)

**3.** If the sum of three numbers is 144, then what is the average of the three numbers? 48
(18)

**4.** Is it true or false that all quadrilaterals are polygons? true
(63)

**5.** $10^2 - 8^2$ 36
(72)

**6.** $12 - 8 \div 4 + 3 \times 2$ 16
(83)

**7.** Write the formula for the perimeter of a rectangle. Then substitute 12 in. for the length and 6 in. for the width. Solve the equation to find the perimeter of the rectangle. $P = 2l + 2w$; $P = 2(12 \text{ in.}) + 2(6 \text{ in.})$; $P = 36 \text{ in.}$
(90)

**8.** Arrange in order from least to greatest: $-1, 0, 0.1, 1$
(88)
$$1, 0, 0.1, -1$$

**9.** If $\frac{5}{6}$ of the 30 members were present, then how many were absent? 5
(76)

**10.** Reduce before multiplying or dividing: $\dfrac{(24)(36)}{48}$ 18
(69)

**11.** $\dfrac{\sqrt{100}}{\sqrt{25}}$ 2
(88)

**12.** $12\frac{5}{6} + 15\frac{1}{3}$
(58)
$28\frac{1}{6}$

**13.** $100 - 9.9$ 90.1
(38)

$57\frac{1}{7}$ **14.** $\dfrac{4}{7} \times 100$
(29)

**15.** $\dfrac{5}{8} = \dfrac{?}{48}$ 30
(41)

**16.** $0.25 \times \$4.60$ $\$1.15$
(39)

**17.** $7.4 - 3\frac{3}{4}$ (decimal answer)   3.65
(85)

**18.** $16 + 12\frac{3}{10} + 8.4$ (fraction answer)   $36\frac{7}{10}$
(85)

**19.** Write 8% as a decimal.   0.08
(84)

**20.** Write 80% as a reduced fraction.   $\frac{4}{5}$
(33)

**21.** Estimate the product of 6.95 and 12.1 to the nearest whole number.   84
(50)

**22.** $0.5n = 35$   70
(42)

**23.** What is the area of the triangle?   24 cm²
(90)

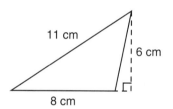

11 cm   6 cm   8 cm

**24.** Here is a rectangular prism.
(89)
(a) How many faces does it have?

(b) How many edges does it have?
(a) 6   (b) 12

Use your ruler to find the length and width of this rectangle to the nearest quarter of an inch. Then refer to the rectangle to answer problems 25 and 26.

$\frac{1}{2}$ in.

$\frac{3}{4}$ in.

**25.** What is the perimeter of the rectangle?
(90)   $2\frac{1}{2}$ in.

**26.** What is the area of the rectangle?   $\frac{3}{8}$ in.²
(90)

**27.** Each term in this sequence is $\frac{1}{16}$ more than the previous term. What are the next four terms in this sequence?
(17)

$\frac{1}{16}, \frac{1}{8}, \frac{3}{16}, \frac{1}{4}, \underline{\quad\frac{5}{16}\quad}, \underline{\quad\frac{3}{8}\quad}, \underline{\quad\frac{7}{16}\quad}, \underline{\quad\frac{1}{2}\quad}, \ldots$

**28.** The coordinates of three vertices of a parallelogram
(74) are (4, 3), (–2, 3), and (0, –2). What are the coordinates
of the fourth vertex?   (6, –2), (–6, –2), or (2, 8)

**29.** (a) (12 cm)(8 cm)   96 cm²   (b) $\dfrac{36 \text{ ft}^2}{4 \text{ ft}}$   9 ft
(80)

**30.** Fernando poured water from one-pint bottles into a
(77) three-gallon bucket. How many pints of water could
the bucket hold?   24 pt

# LESSON 92

# Expanded Notation with Exponents • Order of Operations with Exponents • Powers of Fractions

**Mental Math:**
a. 2400
b. 184
c. 6
d. $8.46
e. 0.012
f. 750
g. 1

**Problem Solving:**
>; 54 is found by
the product 6 × 9.
Each term on the
left is more than the
respective factors
on the right, so the
product on the left
is greater.

---

**Facts Practice:** 28 Fractions to Simplify (Test I in Test Masters)

**Mental Math:** Count up and down by $\frac{1}{8}$'s between $\frac{1}{8}$ and 3.

a. 40 · 60                         b. 234 − 50
c. 25% of 24   *(Think $\frac{1}{4}$ of 24)*   d. $5.99 + $2.47
e. 1.2 ÷ 100                      f. 30 × 25
g. 8 × 9, + 3, ÷ 3, $\sqrt{\phantom{x}}$, × 6, + 3, ÷ 3, − 10

**Problem Solving:** Compare the following and then describe how you performed the comparison:

$$6.142 \times 9.065 \bigcirc 54$$

---

**Expanded notation with exponents**

In Lesson 32 we began writing whole numbers in expanded notation. Here we show 365 in expanded notation.

$$365 = (3 \times 100) + (6 \times 10) + (5 \times 1)$$

When writing numbers in expanded notation we may write the powers of 10 with exponents.

$$365 = (3 \times 10^2) + (6 \times 10^1) + (5 \times 10^0)$$

Notice that $10^0$ equals 1. The table below shows whole number place values with powers of 10.

| Trillions | | | Billions | | | Millions | | | Thousands | | | Ones | | |
|---|---|---|---|---|---|---|---|---|---|---|---|---|---|---|
| hundreds | tens | ones | hundreds | tens | ones | hundreds | tens | ones | hundreds | tens | ones | hundreds | tens | ones |
| $10^{14}$ | $10^{13}$ | $10^{12}$ | $10^{11}$ | $10^{10}$ | $10^9$ | $10^8$ | $10^7$ | $10^6$ | $10^5$ | $10^4$ | $10^3$ | $10^2$ | $10^1$ | $10^0$ |

**Example 1**   The speed of light is about 186,000 miles per second. Write 186,000 in expanded notation using exponents.

*Solution*   We write the non-zero digits (1, 8, and 6) times their place values.

$$\mathbf{186{,}000 = (1 \times 10^5) + (8 \times 10^4) + (6 \times 10^3)}$$

**Order of operations with exponents**   In the order of operations, we simplify expressions with exponents (or square roots) before we multiply or divide.

**Order of Operations**

> **1.** Simplify within parentheses.
>
> **2.** Simplify powers and roots.
>
> **3.** Multiply and divide from left to right.
>
> **4.** Add and subtract from left to right.

Some students remember the order of operations with this memory aid.

**P**lease

**E**xcuse

**M**y **D**ear

**A**unt **S**ally

The first letter of each word is meant to remind us of the order of operations.

**P**arentheses

**E**xponents

**M**ultiplication **D**ivision

**A**ddition **S**ubtraction

**Example 2**    $5 + 3^2 \times 2 - (8 + 8) \div \sqrt{16}$

**Solution**    We follow the order of operations.

| | |
|---|---|
| $5 + 3^2 \times 2 - (8 + 8) \div \sqrt{16}$ | original problem |
| $5 + 3^2 \times 2 - 16 \div \sqrt{16}$ | simplified parentheses |
| $5 + 9 \times 2 - 16 \div 4$ | simplified powers and roots |
| $5 + 18 - 4$ | multiplied and divided |
| **19** | added and subtracted |

**Powers of fractions**    We may use exponents with fractions and with decimals. We use parentheses to include the whole fraction and not just the numerator.

$$\left(\frac{1}{2}\right)^3 \text{ means } \frac{1}{2} \cdot \frac{1}{2} \cdot \frac{1}{2}$$

$$(0.1)^2 \text{ means } 0.1 \times 0.1$$

**Example 3**    Simplify: $\left(\frac{2}{3}\right)^2$

**Solution**    We write $\frac{2}{3}$ as a factor twice and multiply.

$$\frac{2}{3} \cdot \frac{2}{3} = \frac{4}{9}$$

**Practice\***    **a.** Write 2,500,000 in expanded notation using exponents.
$(2 \times 10^6) + (5 \times 10^5)$

**b.** Write this number in standard notation:
5,200,000,000    $(5 \times 10^9) + (2 \times 10^8)$

**c.** $10 + 2^3 \times 3 - (7 + 2) \div \sqrt{9}$   31

**d.** $\left(\dfrac{1}{2}\right)^3$   $\frac{1}{8}$     **e.** $(0.1)^2$   0.01     **f.** $\left(1\dfrac{1}{2}\right)^2$   $2\frac{1}{4}$

**Problem set 92**

**1.** As stated in Example 1, the speed of light is about 186,000 miles per second. The moon is about 250,000 miles from the earth. About how long does it take the light reflected from the moon to reach the earth? (Round your answer to the nearest second.)   1 s
(50)

2. The probability of correctly guessing the answer is $\frac{1}{4}$ because there are four possible answers and only one answer is correct.

**2.** Mitch does not know the correct answer to the multiple choice question. The choices are A, B, C, and D. If Mitch just guesses, what is the probability that Mitch will guess the correct answer? Explain your answer.
(91)

**3.** If the sum of four numbers is 144, then what is the average of the four numbers?   36
(18)

**4.** How many blocks have been put together to form the larger cube?   64
(90)

**5.** Write 225% as a decimal number.   2.25
(84)

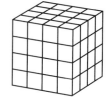

**6.** $3.5 + 3\dfrac{1}{5}$ (decimal answer)   6.7
(85)

**7.** $4.5 - 3\dfrac{3}{4}$ (fraction answer)   $\frac{3}{4}$
(85)

**8.** $(0.3)^3$   0.027     **9.** $\left(2\dfrac{1}{2}\right)^2$   $6\frac{1}{4}$     **10.** $\sqrt{9} \cdot \sqrt{100}$   30
(92)              (92)                        (92)

**11.** Twenty of the two dozen members voted yes. What fraction of the members voted yes?   $\frac{5}{6}$
(76)

**12.** If the rest of the members in Problem 11 voted no, then what was the ratio of "no" votes to "yes" votes?   $\frac{1}{5}$
(82)

**13.** $w + 4\dfrac{3}{4} = 9\dfrac{1}{3}$   $4\frac{7}{12}$     **14.** $\dfrac{3}{8}$ of 100   $37\frac{1}{2}$
(62)                          (69)

**15.** 6.75 + 12 + 4.6   23.35
(38)

**16.** $\frac{6}{5} = \frac{?}{30}$   36
(41)

**17.** $10 + 6^2 \div 3 - \sqrt{9} \times 3$   13
(92)

**18.** A triangular prism has how many faces?   5
(89)

**19.** How many quarts of milk is $2\frac{1}{2}$ gallons of milk?   10 qt
(77)

**20.** Use a factor tree to find the prime factors of 800. Then
(72) write the prime factorization of 800 using exponents.
$2 \times 2 \times 2 \times 2 \times 2 \times 5 \times 5$; $2^5 \times 5^2$

**21.** Round the decimal number one hundred twenty-five
(50) thousandths to the nearest tenth.   0.1

**22.** $0.08n = \$1.20$   $15.00
(86)

**23.** The diagonal segment through this rectangle divides
(87) the rectangle in half. What is the area of one of the
triangles?   234 mm²

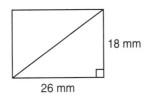
18 mm
26 mm

**24.** Write $\frac{17}{20}$ as a percent.   85%
(81)

**25.** To what decimal number is the arrow pointing?   1.4
(49)

0   1   2

**26.** Write this number in standard notation:   7,250,000,000
(32)
$$(7 \times 10^9) + (2 \times 10^8) + (5 \times 10^7)$$

**27.** (a) What is the probability of rolling a 6 with a single
(91)      roll of a number cube?   $\frac{1}{6}$

    (b) What is the probability of rolling a number less
        than 6 with a single roll of a number cube?   $\frac{5}{6}$

**28.** The coordinates of the four vertices of a quadrilateral
(74) are (−3, −2), (0, 2), (3, 2), and (5, −2). What is the name
for this type of quadrilateral?    trapezoid

**29.** The formula for the area of a triangle is
(90)

$$A = \frac{bh}{2}$$

If the base is 20 cm and the height is 15 cm, then what
is the area?    150 cm²

**30.** What are the next four numbers in this sequence?
(17)

$$\frac{1}{16}, \frac{1}{8}, \frac{3}{16}, \frac{1}{4}, \frac{5}{16}, \frac{3}{8}, \underline{\quad\frac{7}{16}\quad}, \underline{\quad\frac{1}{2}\quad}, \underline{\quad\frac{9}{16}\quad}, \underline{\quad\frac{5}{8}\quad}, \ldots$$

# LESSON 93

# Writing Fractions as Percents, Part 2

Mental Math:
a. 3500
b. 722
c. 40
d. $3.64
e. 2
f. 32
g. 21
Problem Solving:
   24 cm²

**Facts Practice:** Linear Measure Facts (Test K in Test Masters)

**Mental Math:** Count up and down by 12's between 12 and 144.

   **a.** 50 · 70        **b.** 572 + 150        **c.** 50% of 80
   **d.** $10.00 − $6.36    **e.** 100 × 0.02      **f.** $\frac{640}{20}$
   **g.** 4 × 5, + 1, ÷ 3, × 8, − 1, ÷ 5, × 4, − 2, ÷ 2

**Problem Solving:** The perimeter of the triangle is
               24 cm. What is the area of the
               triangle?

10 cm    6 cm

Since Lesson 81 we have practiced changing a fraction to a
percent by writing an equivalent fraction with a
denominator of 100.

$$\frac{3}{5} = \frac{?}{100}$$

Recall that we multiply the fraction by a name for 1 to
rename the fraction.

$$\frac{3}{5} \cdot \frac{20}{20} = \frac{60}{100}$$

Then we write the fraction as a percent.

$$\frac{60}{100} = 60\%$$

In this lesson we will practice another method of changing a fraction to a percent. Since 100% equals 1, we may multiply a fraction by 100% to form an equivalent number. Here we multiply $\frac{3}{5}$ by 100%.

$$\frac{3}{5} \times \frac{100\%}{1} = \frac{300\%}{5}$$

Then we simplify and find that $\frac{3}{5}$ equals 60%.

$$\frac{300\%}{5} = 60\%$$

**To change a number to a percent, multiply the number by 100%.**

**Example 1**   Change $\frac{1}{3}$ to a percent.

*Solution*   We multiply $\frac{1}{3}$ by 100%.

$$\frac{1}{3} \times \frac{100\%}{1} = \frac{100\%}{3}$$

To simplify, we divide 100% by 3 and write the quotient as a mixed number.

$$
\begin{array}{r}
33\frac{1}{3}\% \\
3\overline{)100\%} \\
\underline{9}\phantom{00\%} \\
10\phantom{\%} \\
\underline{9}\phantom{\%} \\
1\phantom{\%}
\end{array}
$$

**Example 2**   Write $\frac{6}{5}$ as a percent.

*Solution*   We multiply $\frac{6}{5}$ by 100%. We will reduce before we multiply.

$$\frac{6}{\cancel{5}_{1}} \times \frac{\cancel{100}\%^{20}}{1} = 120\%$$

In some applications a percent may be greater than 100%.

**Practice***   Change each fraction to a percent by multiplying by 100%:

**a.** $\frac{3}{50}$   6%        **b.** $\frac{1}{2}$   50%        **c.** $\frac{1}{6}$   $16\frac{2}{3}$%

**d.** $\frac{11}{25}$   44%       **e.** $\frac{3}{8}$   $37\frac{1}{2}$%       **f.** $\frac{2}{9}$   $22\frac{2}{9}$%

**g.** $\frac{7}{4}$   175%       **h.** $\frac{4}{7}$   $57\frac{1}{7}$%       **i.** $\frac{1}{30}$   $3\frac{1}{3}$%

**Problem set**  **1.** Copy the boldfaced sentence in this lesson and make
**93**  (55)  up an example problem to show what the sentence
means.   See student work.

**2.** On the Celsius scale water freezes at 0°C and boils at
(18)  100°C. What temperature is halfway between the
freezing and boiling temperatures?   50°C

**3.** If the length of segment $AB$ is $\frac{1}{3}$ the length of segment
(68)  $AC$, and if segment $AC$ is 12 cm long, then how long is
segment $BC$?   8 cm

**4.** What percent of the group is
(81)  shaded?   40%

**5.** Change $\frac{2}{3}$ to a percent by multiplying $\frac{2}{3}$ by 100%.   $66\frac{2}{3}$%
(93)

**6.** $3.3 - 2\frac{1}{5}$ (fraction answer)   $1\frac{1}{10}$
(85)

**7.** $6.4 - 6\frac{1}{4}$ (decimal answer)   0.15
(85)

**8.** $10^4 - 10^3$   9000        **9.** $4 \cdot 12 = 3n$   16
(92)                                (86)

**10.** How much is $\frac{3}{4}$ of 360?      **11.** $0.3 \times 360 = w$   108
(69)  270                            (39)

**12.** $3\frac{1}{2} + 1\frac{3}{4} + 4\frac{5}{8}$   $9\frac{7}{8}$   **13.** $\frac{9}{10} \cdot \frac{5}{6} \cdot \frac{8}{9}$   $\frac{2}{3}$
(59)                                        (71)

**14.** Write 250,000 in expanded notation using exponents.
(92)  $(2 \times 10^5) + (5 \times 10^4)$

**15.** $8.47 + 95¢ + $12        **16.** $37.5 \div 100$   0.375
(1)   $21.42                    (51)

**17.** $\frac{3}{7} = \frac{21}{x}$   49        **18.** $33\frac{1}{3} \div 100$   $\frac{1}{3}$
(41)                            (67)

**19.** If ninety percent of the answers were correct, then
(76) what percent were incorrect?   10%

**20.** Write the decimal number one hundred twenty and
(35) three hundredths.   120.03

**21.** Arrange in order from least to greatest:   $-5.2, -2.5, \frac{2}{5}, \frac{5}{2}$
(88)

$$-2.5, \frac{2}{5}, \frac{5}{2}, -5.2$$

**22.** A pyramid with a square base has how many edges?
(89) 8

**23.** What is the area of this parallelogram?   80 in.²
(79)

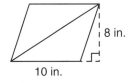

10 in.

8 in.

**24.** During the year in Scott's home town the temperature
(14) ranged from $-37°F$ in winter to $103°F$ in summer. How
many degrees was the range of temperature for the year?
140°F

**25.** How many millimeters long is the segment?   30 mm
(7)

cm   1   2   3   4

**26.** The coordinates of the three vertices of a triangle are
(74) (0, 0), (0, −4), and (−4, 0). Graph the triangle and find
its area.    8 sq. units

**27.** Margie's first nine test scores are shown below.
(9)
$$21, 25, 22, 19, 22, 24, 20, 22, 24$$

(a) Which score did Margie earn the most number of
times?    22

(b) If the scores were listed in order from lowest to
highest, which score would be the middle score in
the list?    22

**28.** $2^3 + \sqrt{25} \times 3 - 4^2 \div \sqrt{4}$    15
(92)

**29.** Sandra filled the aquarium with 24 quarts of water.
(77) How many gallons of water did Sandra pour into the
aquarium?    6 gal

**30.** What is the probability of drawing a red queen from a
(91) normal deck of 52 cards?    $\frac{1}{26}$

**LESSON 94**

# Reducing Units Before Multiplying

**Facts Practice:** 30 Fractions to Reduce (Test G in Test Masters)

**Mental Math:** Count up and down by 20's between −100 and 100.

**a.** 60 · 80  **b.** 437 − 150  **c.** 25% of 80
**d.** $3.99 + $4.28  **e.** 17.5 ÷ 100  **f.** 30 × 55
**g.** $6 \times 8, + 1, \sqrt{\ }, \times 5, + 1, \sqrt{\ }, \times 3, \div 2, \sqrt{\ }$

**Problem Solving:** What are the next four numbers in this sequence?

$$\frac{1}{12}, \frac{1}{6}, \frac{1}{4}, \frac{1}{3}, \underline{\ \ }, \underline{\ \ }, \underline{\ \ }, \underline{\ \ }, \dots$$

Since Lesson 69 we have practiced reducing fractions before multiplying. This is sometimes called *canceling*.

$$\frac{\overset{1}{\cancel{3}}}{\underset{2}{\cancel{4}}} \cdot \frac{\overset{1}{\cancel{2}}}{\underset{1}{\cancel{5}}} \cdot \frac{\overset{1}{\cancel{5}}}{\underset{2}{\cancel{6}}} = \frac{1}{4}$$

We may reduce **units** before multiplying just as we reduce numbers.

$$\frac{4 \text{ miles}}{1 \text{ \cancel{hour}}} \times \frac{2 \text{ \cancel{hours}}}{1} = 8 \text{ miles}$$

**Example 1**  Multiply 55 miles per hour by six hours.

$$\frac{55 \text{ miles}}{1 \text{ hour}} \times \frac{6 \text{ hours}}{1}$$

*Solution*  We write 55 miles per hour as the ratio 55 miles over 1 hour because "per" indicates division. We write six hours as the ratio 6 hours over 1. The unit "hour" appears above and below the division line, so we may cancel "hours."

$$\frac{55 \text{ miles}}{1 \text{ \cancel{hour}}} \times \frac{6 \text{ \cancel{hours}}}{1} = \frac{330 \text{ miles}}{1}$$

Since 330 miles is divided by 1, the answer is **330 miles.** Can you think of a story to fit this problem?

**Example 2**    Multiply 5 feet times 12 inches per foot.

$$\frac{5 \text{ ft}}{1} \cdot \frac{12 \text{ in.}}{1 \text{ ft}}$$

**Solution**    Notice that we write 5 feet as the ratio 5 feet over 1. We cancel units and multiply.

$$\frac{5 \cancel{\text{ ft}}}{1} \times \frac{12 \text{ in.}}{1 \cancel{\text{ ft}}} = \frac{60 \text{ in.}}{1}$$

Since 60 inches is divided by 1, the answer is **60 inches.**

**Practice**    Cancel numbers and units when possible before multiplying:

**a.** $\dfrac{3 \text{ dollars}}{1 \text{ hour}} \times \dfrac{8 \text{ hours}}{1}$    24 dollars

**b.** $\dfrac{6 \text{ baskets}}{10 \text{ shots}} \times \dfrac{100 \text{ shots}}{1}$    60 baskets

**c.** $\dfrac{10 \text{ cents}}{1 \text{ kwh}} \times \dfrac{26.3 \text{ kwh}}{1}$    263 cents

**d.** $\dfrac{29 \text{ students}}{1 \text{ teacher}} \cdot \dfrac{18 \text{ teachers}}{1}$    522 students

**e.** $\dfrac{160 \text{ km}}{2 \text{ hours}} \cdot \dfrac{10 \text{ hours}}{1}$    800 km

**f.** $\dfrac{2.3 \text{ m}}{1} \cdot \dfrac{100 \text{ cm}}{1 \text{ m}}$    230 cm

**Problem set 94**

**1.** If school begins at 8:00 a.m. and ends at 3:10 p.m., then
$^{(32)}$ how many hours and minutes long is the school day?
7 hr, 10 min

**2.** Jeff is 1.67 meters tall. How many centimeters tall is Jeff?
$^{(94)}$ 167 cm

**3.** If $\frac{5}{8}$ of the 40 seeds sprouted, then how many seeds did
$^{(76)}$ not sprout?    15

**4.** Change from expanded notation to standard notation:
(45)
$$(5 \times 100) + (6 \times 10) + \left(7 \times \tfrac{1}{10}\right) + \left(3 \times \tfrac{1}{100}\right)$$
560.73

**5.** Change $\frac{2}{3}$ to its percent equivalent by multiplying $\frac{2}{3}$ by
(93) 100%.   $66\frac{2}{3}\%$

**6.** Write $\frac{3}{2}$ in percent form.   150%
(81)

**7.** What percent is equal to the fraction $\frac{3}{8}$?   $37\frac{1}{2}\%$
(81)

**8.** Ten percent equals what fraction?   $\frac{1}{10}$
(33)

**9.** $\dfrac{25^2}{25}$   25
(92)

**10.** $w = 0.3 \times \$12.00$   $3.60
(39)

**11.** How many cubes formed this
(66) rectangular prism?   36

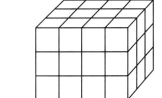

**12.** $\dfrac{3}{4} + \dfrac{3}{5}$   $1\frac{7}{20}$
(56)

**13.** $18\dfrac{1}{8} - 12\dfrac{1}{2}$   $5\frac{5}{8}$
(62)

**14.** $3\dfrac{3}{4} \times 2\dfrac{2}{3} \times 1\dfrac{1}{10}$   11
(71)

**15.** How many fourths are in $2\frac{1}{2}$?   10
(67)

**16.** $12 + 8.75 + 6.8$   27.55       **17.** $(1.5)^2$   2.25
(38)                                   (92)

**18.** $6\dfrac{2}{5} \div 0.8$ (decimal answer)   8
(85)

**19.** Estimate the sum of $6\frac{1}{4}$, 4.95, and 8.21 by rounding each
(50) number to the nearest whole number before adding.
19

**20.** Round three and four hundred fifty-six thousandths to
(50) the nearest hundredth.   3.46

**21.** Arrange in order from least to greatest: $4\%, \frac{1}{4}, 0.4$
(72)

$$\frac{1}{4}, 4\%, 0.4$$

**22.** $y + 3.4 = 5$   1.6
(86)

**23.** $4 \cdot 12 = 8y$   6
(86)

**24.** A cube has edges that are 6 cm long. What is the area
(90) of each face of the cube?   36 cm²

**25.** $\overline{AB}$ is 24 mm long. $\overline{AC}$ is 42 mm long. How long is $\overline{BC}$?
(68) 18 mm

**26.** $6^2 \div \sqrt{9} + 2 \times 2^3 - \sqrt{100}$   18
(92)

**27.** What is the ratio of a pint of water to a quart of water?
(82) $\frac{1}{2}$

**28.** The formula for the area of a parallelogram is $A = bh$.
(90) If the base equals 1.2 m and the height equals 0.9 m,
then what is its area?   1.08 m²

**29.** Multiply 2.5 liters by 1000 milliliters per liter.   2500 mL
(94)

$$\frac{2.5 \text{ liters}}{1} \times \frac{1000 \text{ milliliters}}{1 \text{ liter}}$$

**30.** If the arrow is spun, what is the
(91) probability that the arrow will end
up pointing to an even number?
$\frac{1}{2}$

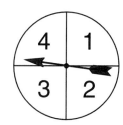

# Writing Decimals as Percents

Mental Math:
a. 6300
b. 614
c. 30
d. $4.11
e. 1.5
f. 25
g. 9
Problem Solving:

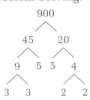

---

**Facts Practice:** 64 Multiplication Facts (Test D in Test Masters)

**Mental Math:** Count by $\frac{1}{16}$'s from $\frac{1}{16}$ to 1.

  **a.** 70 · 90        **b.** 364 + 250        **c.** 50% of 60

  **d.** $5.00 − $0.89      **e.** 100 × 0.015      **f.** $\frac{750}{30}$

  **g.** 6 × 6, − 1, ÷ 5, × 8, − 1, ÷ 11, × 8, × 2, + 1, $\sqrt{\ }$

**Problem Solving:** Copy this factor tree and fill in the missing numbers.

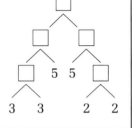

---

In Lesson 93 we saw that a fraction can be named as a percent by multiplying the fraction by 100%. Decimal numbers may be named as percents in the same way.

> **To change a number to a percent, multiply by 100%.**

To change 0.4 to a percent, we multiply 0.4 by 100%.

$$0.4 \times 100\% = 40\%$$

Recall the shortcut for multiplying by 100. When multiplying by 100, we shift the decimal point two places to the right. When we multiply 0.4 by 100 percent, we shift the decimal point two places to the right.

**Example 1** Write 0.12 as a percent.

**Solution** To change a number to a percent, we multiply by 100%. The quick way to multiply by 100% is to shift the decimal point to the right two places and affix a percent sign. Changing a decimal to a percent always shifts the decimal point two places to the right.

$$0.12 \times 100\% = \mathbf{12\%}$$

Example 2   Write 0.125 as a percent.

*Solution*   We multiply 0.125 by 100%.

$$0.125 \times 100\% = \textbf{12.5\%}$$

The result is 12.5%, which may also be written $12\frac{1}{2}\%$.

**Practice***   Change each decimal number to a percent by multiplying by 100%:

| | | |
|---|---|---|
| **a.** 0.5   50% | **b.** 0.06   6% | **c.** 0.375   37.5% |
| **d.** 0.45   45% | **e.** 1.2   120% | **f.** 0.025   2.5% |
| **g.** 0.09   9% | **h.** 1.25   125% | **i.** 0.625   62.5% |

**Problem set 95**

**1.** When the sum of 2.0 and 2.0 is subtracted from the product of 2.0 and 2.0, what is the difference?   0
*(52)*

**2.** An object weighing 4.2 kilograms weighs the same as how many objects each weighing 0.42 kilogram?   10
*(48)*

**3.** If the average of 8 numbers is 12, then what is the sum of the 8 numbers?   96
*(18)*

**4.** What is the name of a quadrilateral that has one pair of sides that are parallel and one pair of sides that are not parallel?   trapezoid
*(78)*

**5.** Write 0.15 as a percent.   15%
*(95)*

**6.** Write 1.5 as a percent.   150%
*(95)*

**7.** Write $\frac{5}{6}$ as a percent.   $83\frac{1}{3}\%$
*(93)*

**8.** Three of these numbers are equivalent. Which one is different?   0.1
*(75,84)*

$$1, 100\%, 0.1, \frac{100}{100}$$

**9.** $11^3$   1331
*(72)*

**10.** How much is $\frac{5}{6}$ of 360?   300
*(69)*

**11.** Factor and reduce: $\dfrac{(45)(54)}{81}$  30
(69)

**12.** $\dfrac{30}{0.08}$  375
(48)

**13.** $16\dfrac{2}{3} \div 100$  $\frac{1}{6}$
(67)

**14.** $2\dfrac{1}{2} + 3\dfrac{1}{3} + 4\dfrac{1}{6}$  10
(59)

**15.** $6 \times 5\dfrac{1}{3} \times \dfrac{3}{8}$  12
(71)

**16.** $\dfrac{2}{5} \times \$12.00$  $\$4.80$
(22)

**17.** $w = 0.12 \times \$6.50$  $\$0.78$
(39)

**18.** $5.3 - 3\dfrac{3}{4}$ (decimal answer)  1.55
(85)

**19.** Copy the boldfaced sentence in this lesson. Then
(95) demonstrate the meaning of the sentence by changing a decimal number of your choice to a percent.
Answers vary.

**20.** Which digit in 6.857 has the same place value as the 3
(12) in 573?  6

**21.** What is the ratio of the number of cents in a dime to
(82) the number of cents in a quarter?  $\frac{2}{5}$

**22.** $4n = 6 \cdot 14$  21
(86)

**23.** $0.3n = 12$  40
(86)

**24.** Draw a segment $1\frac{3}{4}$ inches long. Label the endpoints $R$
(68) and $T$. Then label the midpoint of $\overline{RT}$ point $S$. What is the length of $\overline{RS}$ and $\overline{ST}$?  $\frac{7}{8}$ in.

```
●───────────●───────────●
R           S           T
```

**25.** $\dfrac{6}{9} = \dfrac{36}{?}$  54
(41)

**26.** Multiply 4 hours by 6 dollars per hour:  24 dollars
(94)
$$\dfrac{4 \text{ hr}}{1} \times \dfrac{6 \text{ dollars}}{1 \text{ hr}}$$

**27.** The coordinates of three vertices of a parallelogram
(74) are $(0, 0)$, $(6, 0)$, and $(4, 4)$. What is the area of the parallelogram?  24 units²

**28.** The saying "A pint's a pound the world around" refers
(77) to the fact that a pint of water weighs about one
pound. About how many pounds does a gallon of
water weigh?   about 8 lb

**29.** $3^2 + 2^3 - \sqrt{4} \times 5 + 6^2 \div \sqrt{16}$   16
(92)

**30.** What is the probability of rolling a prime number with
(91) one roll of a number cube?   $\frac{1}{2}$

# LESSON 96

# Writing Mixed Numbers as Percents

**Facts Practice:**  Liquid Measure Facts (Test L in Test Masters)

**Mental Math:** Count up and down by $\frac{1}{2}$'s between –3 and 3.

   **a.** 20 · 50           **b.** 517 – 250         **c.** 25% of 60
   **d.** $7.99 + $7.58        **e.** 0.1 ÷ 100          **f.** 20 × 75
   **g.** 5 × 9, – 1, ÷ 2, – 1, ÷ 3, × 10, + 2, ÷ 9, – 2, ÷ 2

**Problem Solving:** Chad has taken three tests. His lowest score is
70%. His highest score is 100%. What is
Chad's lowest possible and highest possible
three-test average score?

Mixed numbers can be written as percents greater than
100%. The number 1 is equal to 100%, the number 2 is
equal to 200%, and so on.

**We change fractions to percents by multiplying by
100%. We also change mixed numbers to percents by
multiplying by 100%.**

**Example 1**  Write $2\frac{1}{4}$ as a percent.

**Solution**  We will show two methods.

**Method 1:** Split the whole number and fraction. The mixed number $2\frac{1}{4}$ means $2 + \frac{1}{4}$. We change each part to a percent.

$$2 + \frac{1}{4}$$

$$200\% + 25\% = \mathbf{225\%}$$

**Method 2:** Change the mixed number to an improper fraction. The mixed number $2\frac{1}{4}$ equals $\frac{9}{4}$. We change $\frac{9}{4}$ to a percent.

$$\frac{9}{\cancel{4}_{1}} \times \frac{\cancel{100}\%^{25}}{1} = \mathbf{225\%}$$

**Example 2**  Write $2\frac{1}{6}$ as a percent.

**Solution**  In the first example we showed two methods. Method 1 is quick if we can recall the percent equivalent of the fraction. Method 2 can be used if the percent equivalent does not readily come to mind. We will use Method 2 in this example. We write $2\frac{1}{6}$ as the mixed number $\frac{13}{6}$ and multiply by 100%.

$$\frac{13}{6} \times \frac{100\%}{1} = \frac{1300\%}{6}$$

Now we divide 1300% by 6 and write the quotient as a mixed number.

$$\frac{1300\%}{6} = \mathbf{216\frac{2}{3}\%}$$

**Practice**  Change these mixed numbers to percents by first writing each mixed number as an improper fraction.

**a.** $1\frac{1}{4}$  $125\%$  **b.** $2\frac{1}{8}$  $212\frac{1}{2}\%$  **c.** $1\frac{2}{3}$  $166\frac{2}{3}\%$

Change these mixed numbers to percents by first splitting each mixed number into a whole number and a fraction.

**d.** $2\frac{1}{2}$   250%      **e.** $1\frac{1}{8}$   $112\frac{1}{2}\%$      **f.** $2\frac{1}{3}$   $233\frac{1}{3}\%$

**Problem set 96**

**1.** How many quarter-pound hamburgers can be made from 100 pounds of ground beef?   400 hamburgers
*(49)*

**2.** On the Fahrenheit scale, water freezes at 32°F and boils at 212°F. What temperature is halfway between the freezing and boiling temperatures?   122°F
*(18)*

**3.** If the sum of 8 numbers is 48, then the average of the 8 numbers is what number?   6
*(18)*

**4.** Compare: $\frac{5}{8}$ $\underset{<}{\bigcirc}$ 0.675
*(75)*

**5.** Write $2\frac{1}{4}$ as a percent.   225%
*(96)*

**6.** Write $1\frac{2}{5}$ as a percent.   140%
*(96)*

**7.** Write 0.7 as a percent.   70%
*(95)*

**8.** Write $\frac{7}{8}$ as a percent.   $87\frac{1}{2}\%$
*(93)*

**9.** Use division by primes to find the prime factors of 320. Then write the prime factorization of 320 using exponents.   $2^6 \times 5$
*(72)*

**10.** $2^4 - 4^2$   0
*(92)*

**11.** What number is $\frac{1}{8}$ of 360?   45
*(69)*

**12.** $6\frac{3}{4} + 5\frac{7}{8}$   $12\frac{5}{8}$
*(58)*

**13.** $6\frac{1}{3} - 2\frac{1}{2}$   $3\frac{5}{6}$
*(62)*

**14.** $2\frac{1}{2} \div 100$   $\frac{1}{40}$
*(67)*

**15.** 6.93 + 8.429 + 12   27.359
*(38)*

**16.** $(1 - 0.1)(1 \div 0.1)$   9
*(44)*

**17.** $4.2 + \frac{7}{8}$ (decimal answer)   5.075
*(85)*

**18.** $3\frac{1}{3} - 2.5$ (fraction answer)   $\frac{5}{6}$
*(85)*

**19.** If 80% passed, then what percent did not pass?   20%
*(28)*

**20.** Compare: $\dfrac{1}{2} \div \dfrac{1}{3} \; \text{>} \; \dfrac{1}{3} \div \dfrac{1}{2}$
(49)

**21.** What is the next number in this sequence?   0.1 (or $\frac{1}{10}$)
(10)
$$1000, 100, 10, 1, \underline{\hspace{1cm}}, \ldots$$

**22.** $0.4n = \$0.48$   $\$1.20$      **23.** $12w = 8 \cdot 20$   $13\frac{1}{3}$
(42)                          (86)

**24.** The perimeter of the square is 48
(90) inches. What is the area of one of
the triangles?   72 in.²

Refer to this table to answer problems 25, 26, and 27.

**Mark's Personal Running Records**

| Distance | Time (Minutes:Seconds) |
|---|---|
| $\frac{1}{4}$ mile | 0:58 |
| $\frac{1}{2}$ mile | 2:12 |
| 1 mile | 5:00 |

**25.** If Mark set his one-mile record by running at a steady
(32) pace, then what was his half-mile time during the one-
mile race?   2:30

**26.** If Mark ran a 2-mile race, then which of these times
(32) would be a reasonable expectation for the length of
time it would take to run the race?   B. 11:00

   A. 9:30            B. 11:00            C. 15:00

**27.** Write a question that refers to this table and answer the
(N.R.) question.   See student work.

**28.** $\dfrac{7}{4} = \dfrac{w}{44}$   77
(41)

**29.** $10^2 - \sqrt{49} - (10 + 8) \div 3^2$   91
(92)

**30.** What is the probability of rolling a composite number
(91) with one roll of a number cube?   $\frac{1}{3}$

# LESSON 97

Mental Math:
a. 2000
b. 743
c. 24
d. $1.28
e. 1250
f. 9
g. 2
Problem Solving:
  23

**Facts Practice:** Write 24 Mixed Numbers as Improper Fractions (Test J in Test Masters)

**Mental Math:** Count up and down by 7's between 7 and 70.

  **a.** 40 · 50        **b.** 293 + 450        **c.** 50% of 48
  **d.** $20.00 − $18.72    **e.** 12.5 × 100      **f.** $\frac{360}{40}$
  **g.** 8 × 8, − 1, ÷ 9, × 4, + 2, ÷ 2, + 1, $\sqrt{\phantom{x}}$, $\sqrt{\phantom{x}}$

**Problem Solving:** Use "guess and check" to find this square root:

$$\sqrt{529}$$

There are several ways to measure a circle. We may measure the distance around the circle. We may measure the distance across the circle. We may measure the distance from the center of the circle to the circle itself. The pictures below identify these measures.

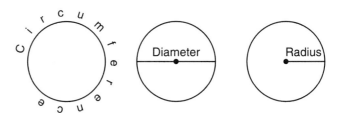

The **circumference** is the distance **around** the circle. This distance is the same as the perimeter of a circle. The **diameter** is the distance **across** a circle through the center. The **radius** is the distance from the center to the circle. The plural of *radius* is **radii.** The length of a diameter is the same as the length of two radii.

**Example 1**   What is the name for the perimeter of a circle?

*Solution*   The distance around a circle is its **circumference.**

**Example 2**   If the radius is 4 cm, what is the length of the diameter?

*Solution*   The diameter of a circle is twice its radius—in this case, **8 cm.**

**Practice**  Give the name for:

**a.** The distance across a circle   diameter

**b.** The distance around a circle   circumference

**c.** The distance from the center to the circle   radius

**d.** If the diameter is 10 in., what is the radius?   5 in.

**Problem set
97**

**1.** When the sum of $\frac{1}{2}$ and $\frac{1}{4}$ is divided by the product of $\frac{1}{2}$
(49)  and $\frac{1}{4}$, what is the quotient?   6

**2.** Jenny is $5\frac{1}{2}$ feet tall. She is how many inches tall? 66 in.
(94)

**3.** If $\frac{4}{5}$ of the 200 runners finished the race, how many
(76)  runners did not finish the race?   40

**4.** If $\overline{BC}$ is 36 cm long and $\overline{AC}$ is 63 cm long, then how
(68)  long is $\overline{AB}$?   27 cm

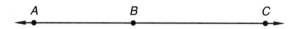

**5.** The circumference of the earth is about 25,000 miles.
(32)  Write that number in expanded notation using
exponents.   $(2 \times 10^4) + (5 \times 10^3)$

**6.** Use your ruler to measure the
(97)  diameter of a quarter to the
nearest sixteenth of an inch.   $\frac{15}{16}$ in.

**7.** Which of these bicycle wheel parts is the best model
(97)  of the circumference of the wheel?   C. Tire

A. Spoke          B. Axle          C. Tire

**8.** As this sequence continues, each number equals the
(10)  sum of the two prior numbers. What is the next
number in this sequence?

1, 1, 2, 3, 5, 8, 13, __21__ , ...

**9.** If there is a 20% chance of rain, then what is the
(91) chance that it will not rain?    80%

**10.** Write $1\frac{1}{3}$ as a percent.    $133\frac{1}{3}\%$
(96)

**11.** $0.08w = \$0.60$    $\$7.50$
(48)

**12.** $\dfrac{1 - 0.001}{0.03}$    33.3        **13.** $\dfrac{3\frac{1}{3}}{100}$    $\frac{1}{30}$
(48)                                        (67)

**14.** How many blocks were used to
(66) build this rectangular prism?    30

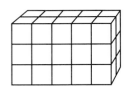

**15.** $6\frac{1}{2} + 4.95$ (decimal)        **16.** $2\frac{1}{6} - 1.5$ (fraction)  $\frac{2}{3}$
(85)                                      (85)
    11.45

**17.** Round $48.3757 to the nearest cent.    $48.38
(50)

**18.** What fraction of a foot is 3 inches?    $\frac{1}{4}$
(94)

**19.** What percent of a meter is 3 centimeters?    3%
(81)

**20.** What is the place value of the 3 in 123,456.789?
(12)    thousands'

**21.** Arrange in order from least to greatest:    $-1, -\frac{1}{2}, 0, \frac{1}{2}, 1$
(88)

$$1, -1, 0, \frac{1}{2}, -\frac{1}{2}$$

**22.** These two triangles together form
(78) what type of quadrilateral?
    trapezoid

**23.** Are the triangles in this quadrilateral
(87) congruent or not congruent?
    not congruent

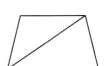

**24.** Write $\frac{1}{2}$
(73,93)
    (a) as a decimal number.    0.5

    (b) as a percent.    50%

**25.** Write 0.3
*(72,95)*
(a) as a fraction. $\frac{3}{10}$

(b) as a percent. 30%

**26.** Write 40%
*(33,84)*
(a) as a reduced fraction. $\frac{2}{5}$

(b) as a simplified decimal number. 0.4

**27.** $\dfrac{4}{10} = \dfrac{20}{w}$ 50
*(41)*

**28.** The diameter of this circle is
*(97)* 20 mm. What is the radius of the circle? 10 mm

20 mm

**29.** $2^3 + \sqrt{81} \div 3^2 + \left(\dfrac{1}{2}\right)^2$ $9\frac{1}{4}$
*(92)*

**30.** Multiply 120 inches by 1 foot per 12 inches. 10 ft
*(94)*
$$\frac{120 \text{ in.}}{1} \times \frac{1 \text{ ft}}{12 \text{ in.}}$$

# LESSON 98

# Fraction-Decimal-Percent Equivalents

**Facts Practice:** Linear Measure Facts (Test K in Test Masters)

**Mental Math:** Count by $\frac{1}{3}$'s from $\frac{1}{3}$ to 4.

a. $60 \cdot 50$　　　　b. $741 - 450$　　　　c. $25\%$ of 48
d. $\$12.99 + \$4.75$　　e. $37.5 \div 100$　　f. $30 \times 15$
g. $7 \times 7, + 1, \div 2, \sqrt{\ }, \times 4, - 2, \div 3, \times 5, + 3, \div 3$

**Problem Solving:** This quadrilateral is a trapezoid, so the 6 cm segment is parallel to the 9 cm segment. In this figure the 4 cm segment is perpendicular to the parallel segments. The figure is divided into two triangles. What is the area of each triangle? *Hint:* Turn the book upside down to view the upper triangle.

Fractions, decimals, and percents are three ways to express parts of a whole. We should be able to change from one form to another. In the following problem sets you will be asked to complete tables that show equivalent fractions, decimals, and percents.

**Example** Complete the table.

| | FRACTION | DECIMAL | PERCENT |
|---|---|---|---|
| 1. | $\frac{1}{2}$ | (a) | (b) |
| 2. | (a) | 0.3 | (b) |
| 3. | (a) | (b) | 40% |

**Solution** For the fraction $\frac{1}{2}$ we write a decimal and a percent. For the decimal 0.3 we write a fraction and a percent. For 40% we write a fraction and a decimal.

1. (a) $\frac{1}{2} = 2\overline{)1.0}^{\,0.5}$　　　　(b) $\frac{1}{2} \times \frac{100\%}{1} = \mathbf{50\%}$

2. (a)  $0.3 = \dfrac{3}{10}$        (b)  $0.3 \times 100\% = \textbf{30\%}$

3. (a)  $40\% = \dfrac{40}{100} = \dfrac{2}{5}$     (b)  $40\% = \textbf{0.4}$

**Practice\***  Complete this table.

| Fraction | Decimal | Percent |
|---|---|---|
| $\dfrac{3}{5}$ | **a.** 0.6 | **b.** 60% |
| **c.** $\frac{4}{5}$ | 0.8 | **d.** 80% |
| **e.** $\frac{1}{5}$ | **f.** 0.2 | 20% |
| $\dfrac{3}{4}$ | **g.** 0.75 | **h.** 75% |
| **i.** $\frac{3}{25}$ | 0.12 | **j.** 12% |
| **k.** $\frac{1}{20}$ | **l.** 0.05 | 5% |

**Problem set 98**

1. A foot-long hot dog can be cut into how many $1\frac{1}{2}$-inch lengths?    8
   <sup>(67)</sup>

2. A can of beans is the shape of what geometric solid? (Name the solid.)   cylinder
   <sup>(66)</sup>

3. If $\frac{3}{8}$ of the group voted yes and $\frac{3}{8}$ voted no, then what fraction of the group did not vote?   $\frac{1}{4}$
   <sup>(76)</sup>

4. Nine months is
   <sup>(29,81)</sup>
   (a) what fraction of a year?   $\frac{3}{4}$
   (b) what percent of a year?   75%

5. This rectangular prism is made up of how many cubes?   48
   <sup>(66)</sup>

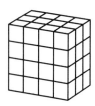

**6.** What percent is equal to 2.5?    250%
(95)

**7.** If $\frac{1}{5}$ of the pie was eaten, then what percent of the pie
(81)    was left?    80%

**8.** Write the percent form of $\frac{1}{7}$.    $14\frac{2}{7}\%$
(93)

**9.** $3^2 - 2^3$    1          **10.** $5 \cdot 4 \cdot 3 \cdot 2 \cdot 1 \cdot 0$    0
(92)                              (5)

**11.** $\dfrac{4.5}{0.18}$    25     **12.** $\sqrt{16} \cdot \sqrt{100}$    40
(48)                              (92)

**13.** $\sqrt{64} + 5^2 - \sqrt{25} \times (2 + 3)$    8
(92)

**14.** $6\dfrac{3}{4} - 6.2$  (decimal answer)    0.55
(85)

**15.** $12\dfrac{1}{2} \times 1\dfrac{3}{5} \times 5$    100     **16.** $(4.2 \times 0.05) \div 7$    0.03
(71)                                              (44)

**17.** Round $7.7777 to the nearest cent.    $7.78
(50)

**18.** Hung earned these scores on his first seven tests:
(9)
$$80\%, 85\%, 100\%, 80\%, 90\%, 80\%, 95\%$$

(a) Which of the scores did Hung earn most often?

(b) If the scores were arranged in order from lowest to
highest, which score would be the middle score?
(a) 80%   (b) 85%

**19.** Write the prime factorization of 900 using exponents.
(72)    $2^2 \cdot 3^2 \cdot 5^2$

**20.** $10n = \$1.20$    $0.12
(4)

**21.** Think of two different prime numbers and write them
(20)    on your paper. Then write the greatest common factor
(GCF) of the two prime numbers.    Selection of prime
numbers will vary. The GCF is 1.

**22.** The perimeter of a square is 2 meters. How many
(94)    centimeters long is each side?    50 cm

**23.** $\dfrac{3}{4} = \dfrac{24}{n}$   32
(41)

Complete the chart to answer problems 24, 25, and 26.

|  | FRACTION | DECIMAL | PERCENT |
|---|---|---|---|
| **24.**<br>(98) | (a) $\frac{3}{5}$ | 0.6 | (b) 60% |
| **25.**<br>(98) | (a) $\frac{3}{20}$ | (b) 0.15 | 15% |
| **26.**<br>(98) | $\frac{3}{10}$ | (a) 0.3 | (b) 30% |

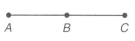

*A        B        C*

**27.** Draw $\overline{AC}$ $1\frac{1}{4}$ inches long. Make a dot at the midpoint of $\overline{AC}$
(68) and label the point *B*. What is the length of $\overline{AB}$ and $\overline{BC}$?
$\frac{5}{8}$ in.

**28.** What is the **chance** of drawing a "diamond" from a
(91) normal deck of 52 cards?   25%

**29.** Compare: 1 gallon $\overset{<}{\bigcirc}$ 4 liters
(77)

**30.** What is the ratio of the radius of a circle to the
(97) diameter of the circle?   $\frac{1}{2}$

# LESSON 99

# Volume of a Rectangular Prism

---

**Facts Practice:** 28 Fractions to Simplify (Test I in Test Masters)

**Mental Math:** Count up and down by 25's between −150 and 150.

   **a.** 50 · 80          **b.** 380 + 550      **c.** 50% of 100
   **d.** $40.00 − $21.89    **e.** 0.8 × 100      **f.** $\frac{750}{25}$
   **g.** 5 + 5, × 10, − 1, ÷ 9, + 1, ÷ 3, × 7, + 2, ÷ 2

**Problem Solving:** One state uses a license plate that is one letter followed by five digits. How many different license plates are possible if all of the letters and digits are used?

---

The **volume** of a shape is the amount of space the shape occupies. To measure volume we use units that take up space, like cubic centimeters or cubic inches.

The volume of a shape is the number of cubic units of space the shape occupies. We will use sugar cubes to help us keep this idea in mind.

We can calculate the volume of a rectangular prism by multiplying the three perpendicular dimensions of the prism: the length, the width, and the height.

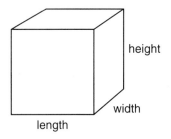

Thus the formula for finding the volume of a rectangular prism is

$$V = lwh$$

**Example 1** How many sugar cubes 1 inch on an edge would be needed to form this rectangular prism?

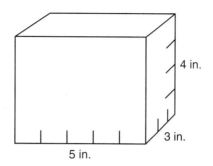

*Solution* The area of the base is 3 inches times 5 inches for 15 square inches. Thus we can set 15 sugar cubes on the bottom layer.

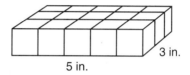

The solid is 4 inches high, so we will have 4 layers for a total of 4 times 15, or **60 sugar cubes** in all.

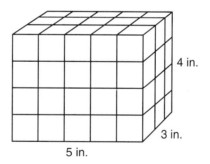

**Example 2** What is the volume of a cube whose edges are 10 centimeters long?

*Solution* The area of the base is 10 cm times 10 cm, or 100 sq. cm. Thus we can set 100 sugar cubes on the bottom layer. There will be 10 layers, so there will be 10 times 100, or 1000, sugar cubes in all. Thus the volume is **1000 cu. cm.**

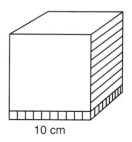

**Example 3**    Dominic used this formula to find the volume of a rectangular prism that was 4 feet long, 3 feet wide, and 2 feet high.

$$V = lwh$$

Use the formula and find the volume of the rectangular prism.

**Solution**    For $l$, $w$, and $h$ we substitute 4 ft, 3 ft, and 2 ft. Then we multiply.

$$V = lwh$$

$$V = (4 \text{ ft})(3 \text{ ft})(2 \text{ ft})$$

$$V = \textbf{24 ft}^3$$

Notice that ft$^3$ means cubic feet.

**Practice**    **a.** How many sugar cubes 1 cm on each edge would be needed to build a cube 4 cm on each edge?
64 cubes

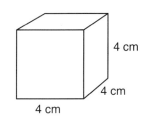

**b.** What is the volume of a rectangular box that is 5 feet long, 3 feet wide, and 2 feet high?    30 ft$^3$

**Problem set 99**    **1.** If 0.6 is the divisor and 1.2 is the quotient, then what
$^{(48)}$ is the dividend?    0.72

**2.** If a number is twelve less than fifty, then it is how
$^{(12)}$ much more than twenty?    18

**3.** If the sum of 4 numbers is 14.8, then what is the
$^{(18)}$ average of the 4 numbers?    3.7

**4.** How many sugar cubes 1 inch on an edge would be
(99) needed to form this rectangular prism?    210 sugar cubes

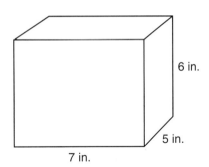

6 in.

5 in.

7 in.

**5.** What is the volume of a cube that has edges
(99) 5 cm long?    125 cm³

**6.** Twelve of the 27 students in the class are boys. What
(82) is the ratio of girls to boys in the class?    $\frac{5}{4}$

**7.** $10^2 + (5^2 - 11) \div \sqrt{49} - 3^3$    75
(92)

**8.** What percent is equivalent to 2.1?    210%
(95)

**9.** The fraction $\frac{2}{3}$ is equal to what percent?    $66\frac{2}{3}\%$
(93)

**10.** If 20% of the students earned A's, then what fraction
(33) of the students did not earn A's?    $\frac{4}{5}$

**11.** $\dfrac{4^2}{2^4}$    1          **12.** $5\dfrac{7}{8} + 4\dfrac{3}{4}$          **13.** $1\dfrac{1}{2} \div 2\dfrac{1}{2}$    $\frac{3}{5}$
(92)                              (58)                                        (67)

$10\frac{5}{8}$

**14.** 8.47 + 9 + 4.6    22.07    **15.** 8.75 × 1.6    14
(38)                                        (39)

**16.** 7.2 ÷ 1.5    4.8          **17.** 198.5 ÷ 100    1.985
(48)                                        (51)

**18.** $3.18 - 3\dfrac{1}{8}$ (decimal answer)    0.055
(85)

**19.** Arrange in order from least to greatest:    100%, 1.2, $\frac{3}{2}$
(81,84)

$$1.2, \frac{3}{2}, 100\%$$

20. Volume is a measure of space. To measure space we use units that take up space-cubes. We do not use squares to measure volume because squares do not take up space.

**20.** We use squares to measure the area of a rectangle. Why do we use cubes instead of squares to measure the volume of a rectangular prism?
*(99)*

**21.** Round $0.16225 to the nearest cent.   $0.16
*(50)*

**22.** 12 · 15 = 9x   20
*(86)*

Rectangle *ABCD* is 8 cm long and 6 cm wide. Segment *AC* is 10 cm long. Use this information to answer problems 23 and 24.

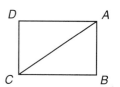

**23.** What is the area of triangle *ABC*?   24 cm²
*(90)*

**24.** What is the perimeter of triangle *ABC*?   24 cm
*(90)*

**25.** Measure the diameter of a nickel to the nearest millimeter.
*(97)*   21 mm

**26.** In a bag are 12 marbles; 8 of the marbles are red and 4 are blue. If a marble is drawn from the bag without looking, what is the probability that the marble will be blue?   $\frac{1}{3}$
*(91)*

Complete the chart to answer problems 27, 28, and 29.

|  | FRACTION | DECIMAL | PERCENT |
|---|---|---|---|
| **27.** *(98)* | $\frac{9}{10}$ | (a) 0.9 | (b) 90% |
| **28.** *(98)* | (a) $1\frac{1}{2}$ | 1.5 | (b) 150% |
| **29.** *(98)* | (a) $\frac{1}{25}$ | (b) 0.04 | 4% |

**30.** A full one-gallon container of milk was used to fill two one-pint containers. Then how many quarts of milk were left in the one-gallon container?   3 qt
*(77)*

# LESSON
# 100

# Circumference Activity

**Mental Math:**
a. 6000
b. 370
c. 25
d. $24.29
e. 0.0375
f. 1000
g. 10

**Problem Solving:**

$$\begin{array}{r} 11 \\ \times\,91 \\ \hline 11 \\ 99 \\ \hline 1001 \end{array} \quad \text{or} \quad \begin{array}{r} 91 \\ \times\,11 \\ \hline 91 \\ 91 \\ \hline 1001 \end{array}$$

**Facts Practice:** 72 Mixed Multiplication and Division (Test H in Test Masters)

**Mental Math:** Count by $\frac{1}{16}$'s from $\frac{1}{16}$ to 1.

a. 20 · 300          b. 920 − 550          c. 25% of 100
d. $18.99 + $5.30          e. 3.75 ÷ 100          f. 40 × 25
g. Find half of 100, − 1, $\sqrt{\phantom{x}}$, × 5, + 1, $\sqrt{\phantom{x}}$, × 3, + 2, ÷ 2

**Problem Solving:** Copy this problem and fill in the missing digits.

$$\begin{array}{r} \_\,1 \\ \times\,\_\,1 \\ \hline \_\,1 \\ \end{array}$$
$$\begin{array}{r} == \\ \hline 1\ 0\ 0\ 1 \end{array}$$

Jennifer used a ruler to measure the diameter of her bicycle tire. She found that the diameter of the tire was two feet. She wondered whether she could figure out the circumference of the tire by knowing just the diameter. She wondered how many diameters equal the circumference.

## Activity:  Circumference

Materials needed:

- String or masking tape
- Scissors
- Tape measure(s)
- Calculator(s)
- Recording Sheet

In this lesson we will perform a two-part activity to find the number of diameters in the circumference of some circular objects. We will measure the circumference and diameter of circles we find. First we will make a list of objects to measure that we could find at school or at home. As a class, suggest objects to add to this list:

Playground circle
Trash can
Plate
Pie pan
Top or bottom of a can
Flying disk
Bicycle tire

This activity is a two-part activity. In the first part you and your partner or group will cut a length of string as long as the diameter of each object you are measuring. (A length of masking tape may be used in place of string.) Then you will begin wrapping the string around the object. Mark the object at the end of the string; then move the string and wrap the object again. You will estimate the number of diameters needed to reach around each object.

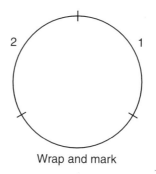

Wrap and mark

In the second part of the activity, you will use a tape measure to measure the circumference and diameter of some circular objects. You will record the measurements on a recording sheet. If you have a metric tape measure, record the measurements to the nearest centimeter. If you have a customary tape measure, record your answer to the nearest quarter inch in decimal form ($\frac{1}{4}$ = 0.25, $\frac{1}{2}$ = 0.5, $\frac{3}{4}$ = 0.75). Using a calculator, you will divide each measured circumference by the diameter to determine the number of diameters in the circumference. Round each quotient to the nearest hundredth.

Make a recording sheet like this to record your work:

**The Number of Diameters in a Circumference**

**Part 1: Estimates (using string or masking tape)**

| Object | Approximate the Number of Diameters in the Circumference. |
|---|---|
| | |
| | |
| | |

**Part 2: Measures (using a tape measure)**

| Object | Circumference | Diameter | Circumference / Diameter |
|---|---|---|---|
| | | | |
| | | | |
| | | | |

**Problem set 100**

**1.** If the cost of calling Hawaii from Denver is $1.48 for the first 3 minutes plus 35¢ for each additional minute, then what would be the total cost of a 10-minute call?   $3.93
(92)

**2.** A shoe box is the shape of what geometric solid?   rectangular prism
(66)

**3.** If the average of six numbers is 12, then what is the sum of the six numbers?   72
(18)

**4.** If $\overline{AB}$ is $\frac{1}{4}$ the length of $\overline{AC}$, and if $\overline{AC}$ is 12 cm long, then how long is $\overline{BC}$?   9 cm
(68)

**5.** What is the name for the perimeter of a circle?   circumference
(97)

**6.** If the radius is 8 cm, what is the length of the diameter?   16 cm
(97)

**7.** A diameter is equal to how many radii?   2
(97)

**8.** What are the next four numbers in this sequence of
(88) perfect squares?

1, 4, 9, 16, 25, 36, 49,  _64_ ,  _81_ ,  _100_ ,  _121_ , ...

**9.** Write $1\frac{1}{2}$ as a percent.   150%
(96)

Complete the chart to answer problems 10, 11, and 12.

| | FRACTION | DECIMAL | PERCENT |
|---|---|---|---|
| **10.** (98) | $\frac{3}{4}$ | (a) 0.75 | (b) 75% |
| **11.** (98) | (a) $1\frac{3}{5}$ | 1.6 | (b) 160% |
| **12.** (98) | (a) $\frac{1}{20}$ | (b) 0.05 | 5% |

**13.** $x + 2\frac{1}{2} = 5$   $2\frac{1}{2}$
(42)

**14.** $\frac{8}{5} = \frac{40}{x}$   25
(41)

**15.** $0.06n = \$0.15$   $2.50
(48)

**16.** $6n = 21 \cdot 4$   14
(86)

**17.** $1\frac{1}{2} \times 4$   6
(65)

**18.** $6 \div 1\frac{1}{2}$   4
(67)

**19.** $0.16 \div 2^3$   0.02
(92)

**20.** $3^2 \div 0.3$   30
(92)

**21.** Sam's garage is 20 feet long, 20 feet wide, and 8 feet
(99) high.

(a) How many 1-foot by 1-foot by 1-foot boxes can he fit on the floor of his garage? (bottom layer)   400

(b) Altogether, how many boxes can Sam fit in his garage if he stacks the boxes 8 feet high?   3200

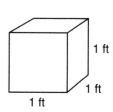

1 ft

1 ft

1 ft

**22.** $9^2 - \sqrt{9} \times 10 - 2^4 \times 2$   19
(92)

**23.** Together, these three triangles
(63) form what polygon?   pentagon

**24.** At 6 a.m. the temperature was −8°F. By noon the
(14) temperature was 15°F. The temperature had risen how
many degrees?   23°F

**25.** To what decimal number is the arrow pointing?   8.8
(49)

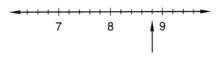

**26.** What is the probability of rolling a perfect square with
(91) one roll of a number cube?   $\frac{1}{3}$

**27.** What is the area of a triangle with vertices at (4, 0),
(87) (0, −3), and (0, 0)?   6 units²

**28.** Multiply 18 feet by 1 yard per 3 feet:   6 yd
(94)
$$\frac{18 \text{ ft}}{1} \times \frac{1 \text{ yd}}{3 \text{ ft}}$$

**29.** If a gallon of milk costs $2.80, then what is the cost per
(77) quart?   $0.70

**30.** Based on the activity in Lesson 100, if a bicycle tire
(100) has a diameter of two feet, then what would be its
approximate circumference?   more than 6 ft, less than 7 ft

# LESSON
# 101

# Proportions •
# Completing Proportions

**Mental Math:**
**a.** 12,000
**b.** 612
**c.** 20
**d.** $52.50
**e.** 6
**f.** 750
**g.** 50
**Problem Solving:**
  6 in.

**Facts Practice:** Percents to Fractions and Decimals (Test M in Test Masters)

**Mental Math:** Count up and down by 12's between 12 and 144.

   **a.** 30 · 400           **b.** 462 + 150      **c.** 50% of 40
   **d.** $100.00 − $47.50    **e.** 0.06 × 100    **f.** 50 × 15
   **g.** 12 + 12, + 1, $\sqrt{\ }$, × 3, + 1, $\sqrt{\ }$, × 2, + 2, × 5

**Problem Solving:** A loop of string was arranged to form a square with sides 9 inches long. If the same loop of string is arranged to form a regular hexagon, how long will each side of the hexagon be?

**Proportions** A **proportion** is a true statement that two ratios are equivalent. Here is an example of a proportion.

$$\frac{3}{4} = \frac{6}{8}$$

We read this proportion, "Three is to four as six is to eight." Two ratios that are not equivalent are not proportional.

**Example 1** Which ratio forms a proportion with $\frac{2}{3}$?

   A. $\frac{2}{4}$     B. $\frac{3}{4}$     C. $\frac{4}{6}$     D. $\frac{3}{2}$

**Solution** Equivalent ratios form a proportion. The ratio equivalent to $\frac{2}{3}$ is $\frac{4}{6}$.

**Example 2** Write this proportion with digits: Four is to six as six is to nine.

**Solution** We write "four is to six" as one ratio and "six is to nine" as the equivalent ratio. We are careful to write the numbers in the order stated.

$$\frac{4}{6} = \frac{6}{9}$$

**Completing proportions**   We may use proportions to solve a variety of problems. Proportion problems often involve finding a missing term in a proportion. The letter $a$ represents a missing term in this proportion.

$$\frac{3}{5} = \frac{6}{a}$$

One way to find a missing term in a proportion is to find a name for 1 by which to multiply one ratio to form the equivalent ratio. The first terms in these ratios are 3 and 6. Since 3 times 2 equals 6, we multiply $\frac{3}{5}$ by $\frac{2}{2}$ to form the equivalent ratio.

$$\frac{3}{5} \cdot \frac{2}{2} = \frac{6}{10}$$

We find that $a$ represents the number 10.

**Example 3**   Find the missing term in this proportion: Two is to six as what number is to 30?

**Solution**   Write the terms of the proportion in the stated order using a letter to represent the unknown number.

$$\frac{2}{6} = \frac{n}{30}$$

We are not given both first terms, but we are given the second terms 6 and 30. Since 6 times 5 is 30, we multiply $\frac{2}{6}$ by $\frac{5}{5}$ to complete the proportion.

$$\frac{2}{6} \times \frac{5}{5} = \frac{10}{30}$$

The missing term of the proportion is **10.**

$$\frac{2}{6} = \frac{10}{30}$$

**Practice***   **a.** Which ratio forms a proportion with $\frac{5}{2}$?   C. $\frac{15}{6}$

A. $\frac{2}{5}$          B. $\frac{4}{10}$          C. $\frac{15}{6}$          D. $\frac{5}{20}$

**b.** Write this proportion with digits: Six is to eight as nine is to twelve.   $\frac{6}{8} = \frac{9}{12}$

**c.** Complete this proportion: Four is to three as twelve is to what number?   9

**d.** Complete this proportion: Six is to nine as what number is to thirty-six?   24

**Problem set 101**

On his first six tests Chris had scores of 90%, 92%, 96%, 92%, 84%, and 92%. Use this information to answer questions 1 and 2.

**1.** (a) Which score occurred most frequently?   92%
   (13)
   (b) The difference between Chris's highest score and his lowest score was how many percentage points?   12%

**2.** What was Chris's average score for the six tests?   91%
   (18)

**3.** In basketball, there are one-point baskets, two-point
   (86) baskets, and three-point baskets. If a team scored 96 points and made 18 one-point baskets and 6 three-point baskets, then how many two-point baskets did the team make?   30

**4.** Which ratio forms a proportion with $\frac{4}{7}$?   C. $\frac{12}{21}$
   (101)

   A. $\frac{7}{4}$          B. $\frac{14}{17}$          C. $\frac{12}{21}$          D. $\frac{2}{3}$

**5.** Complete this proportion: Four is to five as what
   (101) number is to 20?   16

**6.** Arrange in order from least to greatest:   $-1, -0.1, 0, 0.1, 1$
   (88)
   $$-1, 1, 0.1, -0.1, 0$$

**7.** $10^3 - 10^2$   900
   (92)

$\frac{1}{2}$   **8.** What fraction of the diameter of a circle is its radius?
   (97)

Complete the chart to answer problems 9, 10, and 11.

|  | FRACTION | DECIMAL | PERCENT |
|---|---|---|---|
| **9.** (98) | $\frac{4}{25}$ | (a) 0.16 | (b) 16% |
| **10.** (98) | (a) $\frac{1}{100}$ | 0.01 | (b) 1% |
| **11.** (98) | (a) $\frac{9}{10}$ | (b) 0.9 | 90% |

**12.** (59)  $1\frac{2}{3} + 3\frac{1}{2} + 4\frac{1}{6}$   $9\frac{1}{3}$      **13.** (71)  $\frac{5}{6} \times \frac{3}{10} \times 4$   1

**14.** (67)  $6\frac{1}{4} \div 100$   $\frac{1}{16}$      **15.** (38)  $6.437 + 12.8 + 7$   26.237

**16.** (40)  $4.3 \times 0.0067$   0.02881

**17.** (73)  Convert $\frac{1}{7}$ to a decimal number by dividing 1 by 7. Stop dividing after three decimal places and round your answer to two decimal places.   0.14

**18.** (63)  An octagon has how many more sides than a pentagon?   3

**19.** (92)  $4 \times 5^2 - 50 \div \sqrt{4} + (3^2 - 2^3)$   76

**20.** (86)  $2 \cdot m = 3 \cdot 6$   9

**21.** (99)  How many cubes 1 inch on each edge would be needed to build this larger cube?   64

4 in.

**22.** (22)  What number is three tenths of 60?   18

**23.** (18)  The average of four numbers is 5. What is their sum?   20

**24.** (13)  How many years were there from 1215 to 1607?   392

**25.** How many millimeters long is the line?    35 mm
(7)

cm  1  2  3  4

_____

**26.** What is the perimeter of this hexagon? All dimensions are centimeters.    42 cm
(8)

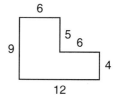

**27.** (a) What is the area of the parallelogram?
(90)

   (b) What is the area of the triangle?

   (c) What is the combined area of the parallelogram and triangle?

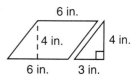

   (a) 24 in.²   (b) 6 in.²   (c) 30 in.²

**28.** How many milliliters is half of a liter?    500 mL
(77)

**29.** The coordinates of the endpoints of a line segment are (3, −1) and (3, 5). The midpoint of the segment is the point halfway between the endpoints. What are the coordinates of the midpoint?    (3, 2)
(74)

**30.** Tania took ten steps to walk across the tetherball circle and 31 steps to walk around the tetherball circle. How many diameters were in the circumference of the tetherball circle?    3.1 $\left(\text{or } 3\frac{1}{10}\right)$
(100)

**LESSON
102**

# Perimeter of Complex Shapes

Mental Math:
a. 3000
b. 293
c. 10
d. $9.64
e. 0.875
f. 25
g. 90
Problem Solving:
  $1.30

**Facts Practice:** Percents to Fractions and Decimals (Test M in Test Masters)

**Mental Math:** Count by 3's from −30 to 30.

   **a.** 50 · 60        **b.** 543 − 250      **c.** 25% of 40

   **d.** $5.65 + $3.99     **e.** 87.5 ÷ 100      **f.** $\frac{500}{20}$

   **g.** 6 × 6, − 1, ÷ 5, × 6, − 2, ÷ 5, × 4, − 2, × 3

**Problem Solving:** Mark has nickels, dimes, and quarters in his pocket. He has half as many dimes as nickels and half as many quarters as dimes. If Mark has four dimes, then how much money does he have in his pocket?

In this lesson we will practice finding the perimeter of complex shapes. The figure below is an example of a complex shape. Notice that the lengths of two of the sides are not given. We will first find the lengths of these sides; then we will find the perimeter of the shape. Assume that angles that look like right angles are right angles unless otherwise stated.

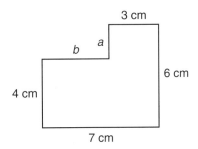

We see that the figure is 7 cm long and 6 cm wide. Notice that the length is also $b$ plus 3 cm. Since $b$ plus 3 cm equals 7 cm, $b$ must equal 4 cm.

$$\text{Length: } b + 3 \text{ cm} = 7 \text{ cm}$$

$$b = 4 \text{ cm}$$

The width is 6 cm, but the width is also 4 cm plus $a$. Since 4 cm + $a$ = 6 cm, $a$ must equal 2 cm.

$$\text{Width: } 4 \text{ cm} + a = 6 \text{ cm}$$

$$a = 2 \text{ cm}$$

We have found that $b$ is 4 cm and $a$ is 2 cm.

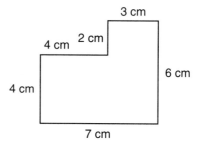

We add the lengths of the sides and find that the perimeter is 26 cm.

$$6 \text{ cm} + 7 \text{ cm} + 4 \text{ cm} + 4 \text{ cm} + 2 \text{ cm} + 3 \text{ cm} = 26 \text{ cm}$$

**Example**  Find the perimeter of this figure.

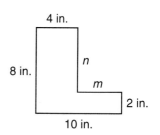

**Solution**  To find the perimeter we add the lengths of the six sides. The lengths of two of the sides are not given in the illustration. We will write two equations using the lengths of the parallel sides to find the lengths of these two sides. The length of the figure is 10 in. The 4 in. side and side $m$, which are parallel to the 10 in. side, together total 10 in. So side $m$ is 6 in.

$$\text{Length: } 4 \text{ in.} + m = 10 \text{ in.}$$

$$m = 6 \text{ in.}$$

The width is 8 in. The parallel sides, side $n$ and the 2 in. side, also total 8 in. So side $n$ is 6 in.

$$n + 2 \text{ in.} = 8 \text{ in.}$$

$$n = 6 \text{ in.}$$

We add the lengths of the six sides and find that the perimeter is **36 in.**

$$10 \text{ in.} + 8 \text{ in.} + 4 \text{ in.} + 6 \text{ in.} + 6 \text{ in.} + 2 \text{ in.} = 36 \text{ in.}$$

**Practice**  Find the perimeters of these complex shapes:

40 cm

**a.**

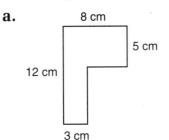

**b.**

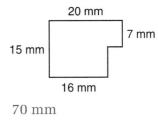

70 mm

**Problem set 102**

**1.** When the sum of $\frac{1}{2}$ and $\frac{1}{3}$ is divided by the product of $\frac{1}{2}$
$^{(49)}$ and $\frac{1}{3}$, what is the quotient?    5

**2.** The average age of three men is 24.
$^{(18)}$
(a) What is the sum of their ages?

(b) If two of the men are 22 years old, how old is the third?
(a) 72 years    (b) 28 years old

**3.** A string one yard long is formed into the shape of a
$^{(38)}$ square.

(a) How many inches long is each side of the square?

(b) How many square inches is the area of the square?
(a) 9 in.    (b) 81 in.$^2$

**4.** Find the missing term in this proportion: Five is to
$^{(101)}$ three as 30 is to what number?    18

**5.** In a class of 30 students there are 14 boys. What is the
$^{(82)}$ boy-girl ratio of the class?    $\frac{7}{8}$

**6.** $100 \div 10^2 + 3 \times \left(2^3 - \sqrt{16}\right)$    13
$^{(92)}$

**7.** If you know the diameter of a circle, how can you find
(97) the radius of the circle?   Divide the diameter of a circle by
2 to find the radius.

**8.** Compare: $\dfrac{5}{8}$ $\bigcirc$ $\dfrac{7}{10}$   <
(75)

Complete the chart to answer problems 9, 10, and 11.

| | Fraction | Decimal | Percent |
|---|---|---|---|
| **9.** (98) | $\dfrac{1}{100}$ | (a) 0.01 | (b) 1% |
| **10.** (98) | (a) $\frac{2}{5}$ | 0.4 | (b) 40% |
| **11.** (98) | (a) $\frac{2}{25}$ | (b) 0.08 | 8% |

**12.** $7\dfrac{1}{2} + 6\dfrac{3}{4} + 1\dfrac{1}{8}$   $15\frac{3}{8}$   **13.** $x + 1\dfrac{3}{4} = 7\dfrac{1}{2}$   $5\frac{3}{4}$
(59)                                                (42)

**14.** $10\dfrac{1}{2} \div 3\dfrac{1}{2}$   3   **15.** $(6 + 2.4) \div 0.04$   210
(67)                              (48)

**16.** Instead of dividing $10\frac{1}{2}$ by $3\frac{1}{2}$, Sam doubled both
(42) numbers before dividing. What was Sam's division
problem and its quotient?   21 ÷ 7 = 3

**17.** Sharon used a tape measure to find the circumference
(100) and the diameter of a plate. The circumference was
about 35 inches, and the diameter was about 11
inches. Find the number of diameters in the
circumference. (Round to the nearest tenth.)   3.2

**18.** Write twenty million, five hundred thousand in
(32) expanded notation using exponents.
$(2 \times 10^7) + (5 \times 10^5)$

**19.** List the prime numbers between 40 and 50.   41, 43, 47
(61)

**20.** $4 \cdot 6 = 3 \cdot n$   8
(86)

**21.** What is the perimeter of the
*(90)* triangle?    60 mm

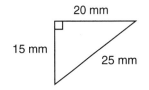

**22.** What is the area of the triangle?
*(87)*    150 mm²

**23.** The Simpsons rented a trailer that was 8 feet long and
*(99)* 5 feet wide. If they load the trailer with 1 foot by 1 foot
by 1 foot wide boxes to a height of 3 feet, how many
boxes can be loaded on the trailer?    120 boxes

**24.** What is the probability of drawing the Queen of
*(91)* Spades from a normal deck of 52 cards?    $\frac{1}{52}$

**25.** What temperature is shown on the
*(10)* thermometer?    −8°F

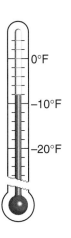

**26.** Find the perimeter of this figure.    140 mm
*(102)*

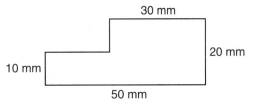

**27.** (a) What is the area of the shaded rectangle?    80 mm²
*(90)*    (b) What is the area of the unshaded rectangle?    140 mm²
(c) What is the combined area of the two rectangles?
220 mm²

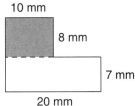

**28.** What are the coordinates of the point halfway between
*(74)* (−3, −2) and (5, −2)?   (1, −2)

**29.** A pint of milk weighs about one pound. About how
*(77)* much does a half gallon of milk weigh?   4 pounds

**30.** $\dfrac{2.5 \text{ m}}{1} \times \dfrac{100 \text{ cm}}{1 \text{ m}}$   250 cm
*(94)*

## LESSON 103

# Cross Products • Using Cross Products to Complete Proportions

**Facts Practice:** Liquid Measure Facts (Test L in Test Masters)

**Mental Math:** Count by $\frac{1}{16}$'s from $\frac{1}{16}$ to 1.

  **a.** 70 · 80                                   **b.** 637 + 250
  **c.** 10% of 40   *(Think $\frac{1}{10}$ of 40)*      **d.** $40.00 − $22.75
  **e.** 0.075 × 100                               **f.** 40 × 22
  **g.** 9 × 9, − 1, ÷ 2, + 2, ÷ 6, × 3, − 1, ÷ 4, × 8

**Problem Solving:** How many six-inch by six-inch square tiles
                     are needed to cover a six-foot by six-foot
                     square porch?

**Cross products**  A test to determine if two fractions are equal is to see if their **cross products** are equal. The cross products of two fractions are found by criss cross multiplication, as we show below.

$$8 \times 3 = \mathbf{24} \qquad 4 \times 6 = \mathbf{24}$$
$$\frac{3}{4} \times\!\!\!\!\diagdown \frac{6}{8}$$

Both cross products are 24. Since the cross products are equal we may conclude that the fractions are equal.

> **Equal fractions have equal cross products.**

**Example 1** Use cross products to determine if $\frac{3}{5}$ and $\frac{4}{7}$ are equal.

**Solution** To find the cross products, we multiply the numerator of each fraction by the denominator of the other fraction. We write the cross product above the numerator that is multiplied.

$$\overset{21}{\underset{5}{3}} \times \overset{20}{\underset{7}{4}}$$

The cross products are not equal, so **the fractions are not equal.** The greater cross product is above the greater fraction. So $\frac{3}{5}$ is greater than $\frac{4}{7}$.

Cross products do not work by magic. When we find the cross products of two fractions, we are simply renaming the fractions with common denominators. The common denominator is the product of the two denominators and is usually not written. Look again at the two fractions we compared.

$$\frac{3}{5} \qquad \frac{4}{7}$$

The denominators are 5 and 7.

If we multiply $\frac{3}{5}$ by $\frac{7}{7}$ and if we multiply $\frac{4}{7}$ by $\frac{5}{5}$, we form two fractions that have common denominators.

$$\frac{3}{5} \times \frac{7}{7} = \frac{21}{35} \qquad \frac{4}{7} \times \frac{5}{5} = \frac{20}{35}$$

The numerators of the renamed fractions are 21 and 20, which are the cross products of the fractions. So when we compare cross products we are actually comparing the numerators of the renamed fractions.

**Example 2** Do these two ratios form a proportion?

$$\frac{8}{12}, \frac{12}{18}$$

*Solution*   Ratios that are equal form a proportion. If the cross products are equal, then the ratios are equal and form a proportion. We multiply 8 by 18, and we multiply 12 by 12.

$$\overset{144}{\underset{12}{8}} \times \overset{144}{\underset{18}{12}}$$

The cross products are 144 and 144, so **the ratios form a proportion.**

$$\frac{8}{12} = \frac{12}{18}$$

**Using cross products to complete proportions**   Since equivalent ratios have equal cross products, we may use cross products to find a missing term in a proportion. By cross multiplying we form an equation. Then we solve the equation to find the missing term of the proportion.

**Example 3**   Complete this proportion: $\dfrac{6}{9} = \dfrac{10}{m}$

*Solution*   The cross products of a proportion are equal. So 6 times $m$ equals 9 times 10, which is 90.

$$\frac{6}{9} = \frac{10}{m}$$

$$6m = 9 \cdot 10$$

We solve this equation.

$$6m = 90$$

$$m = 15$$

The missing term is 15. We complete the proportion.

$$\frac{6}{9} = \frac{10}{15}$$

**Example 4**   Use cross products to find the missing term in this proportion: Fifteen is to twenty-one as what number is to seventy?

*Solution*  We write the ratios in the order stated.

$$\frac{15}{21} = \frac{w}{70}$$

The cross products of a proportion are equal.

$$15 \cdot 70 = 21w$$

To find the missing term we divide $15 \cdot 70$ by 21. Notice how we may reduce.

$$\frac{\overset{5}{\cancel{15}} \cdot \overset{10}{\cancel{70}}}{\underset{\underset{1}{7}}{\cancel{21}}} = w$$

The missing term is **50.**

**Practice**  Use cross products to determine if each pair of ratios forms a proportion:

**a.** $\frac{6}{9}, \frac{7}{11}$  no

**b.** $\frac{6}{8}, \frac{9}{12}$  yes

Use cross products to complete the proportions:

**c.** $\frac{6}{10} = \frac{9}{x}$  15

**d.** $\frac{12}{16} = \frac{y}{20}$  15

**e.** Use cross products to find the missing term in this proportion: 10 is to 15 as 30 is to what number?  45

**Problem set 103**

**1.** A pyramid with a square base has how many more edges than vertices?  3
$^{(89)}$

**2.** Use cross products to find the missing term in this proportion: 15 is to 20 as what number is to 28?  21
$^{(103)}$

**3.** What number is five more than the product of six and seven?  47
$^{(5)}$

**4.** A team won 6 games and lost 10. What was its won-lost ratio?   $\frac{3}{5}$
(82)

**5.** Which ratio forms a proportion with $\frac{2}{3}$?   C. $\frac{4}{6}$
(103)

     A. $\dfrac{2}{4}$        B. $\dfrac{3}{4}$        C. $\dfrac{4}{6}$        D. $\dfrac{3}{2}$

**6.** Solve for the missing term:   $\dfrac{6}{8} = \dfrac{a}{12}$   9
(101)

**7.** What is the perimeter of the hexagon? (All units are centimeters.)   50 cm
(102)

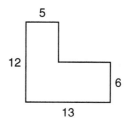

**8.** Compare:   $\dfrac{2}{3}$ $<$ $\dfrac{10}{12}$
(75)

Complete the chart to answer questions 9, 10, and 11.

| | Fraction | Decimal | Percent |
|---|---|---|---|
| **9.** (98) | $\frac{3}{20}$ | (a) 0.15 | (b) 15% |
| **10.** (98) | (a) $1\frac{1}{5}$ | 1.2 | (b) 120% |
| **11.** (98) | (a) $\frac{1}{10}$ | (b) 0.1 | 10% |

**12.** $\left( 3\dfrac{1}{10} + 1\dfrac{1}{5} \right) - 2\dfrac{1}{2}$   $1\frac{4}{5}$      **13.** $6\dfrac{2}{3} \times 2\dfrac{1}{10}$   14
(62)                                                   (65)

**14.** $1\dfrac{2}{3} \div 1\dfrac{1}{2}$   $1\frac{1}{9}$                           **15.** $1 - 0.2 - 0.03$   0.77
(67)                                                       (38)

**16.** $\left(\dfrac{1}{2}\right)^3$    $\dfrac{1}{8}$
(92)

**17.** Divide 0.624 by 0.05 and round the quotient to the
(48) nearest whole number.    12

**18.** The average of three numbers is 20. What is the sum of
(18) the three numbers?    60

**19.** Write the prime factorization of 450 using exponents.
(64)    $2 \cdot 3^2 \cdot 5^2$

**20.** $0.8n = \$12.80$    $\$16.00$
(48)

**21.** $3^4 + 5^2 \times 4 - \sqrt{100} \times 2^3$    101
(92)

**22.** How many blocks 1 inch on each edge would it take to
(99) fill a shoe box that is 12 inches long, 6 inches wide,
and 5 inches high?    360 blocks

**23.** Three fourths of the 60 athletes played. How many
(76) athletes did not play?    15

**24.** Tom lives 15 kilometers south of Jim. Jerry lives 20
(7) kilometers north of Jim. How many kilometers from
Jerry does Tom live?    35 km

**25.** The distance a car travels can be found by multiplying
(94) the **speed** of the car times the amount of **time** the car
. travels at that speed. How far would a car travel in
4 hours at 88 kilometers per hour?    352 km

$$\dfrac{88 \text{ km}}{1 \text{ hr}} \times \dfrac{4 \text{ hr}}{1}$$

**26.** (a) What is the area of the shaded
(31)    rectangle?    60 cm²

(b) What is the area of the
unshaded rectangle?    48 cm²

(c) What is the combined area of
the two rectangles?    108 cm²

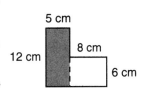

**27.** Simon measured the circumference and diameter of
(50) four circles. Then he divided the circumference by the
diameter for each circle to find the number of
diameters in a circumference. Here are his answers:

3.12, 3.2, 3.15, 3.1

Find the average of Simon's answers. Round the
average to the nearest hundredth.   3.14

28. There are 90
two-digit counting
numbers. Since
Norton was thinking
of only one number,
the probability of
correctly guessing
the number in one
try is $\frac{1}{90}$.

**28.** Norton was thinking of a two-digit counting number,
(91) and he asked Simon to guess the number. Describe
how to find the probability that Simon will guess
Norton's number on the first try.

**29.** The coordinates of three vertices of a triangle are (3, 5),
(74) (−1, 5), and (−1, −3). What is the area of the triangle?
16 sq. units

**30.** $\dfrac{2\ \text{gal}}{1} \times \dfrac{4\ \text{qt}}{1\ \text{gal}} \times \dfrac{2\ \text{pt}}{1\ \text{qt}}$   16 pt
(94)

# LESSON
# 104

# Using Proportions to Solve Ratio Word Problems

**Mental Math:**
a. 8000
b. 417
c. 100
d. $20.19
e. 0.075
f. 22
g. 11
**Problem Solving:**
   6

**Facts Practice:** Percents to Fractions and Decimals (Test M in Test Masters)

**Mental Math:** Count by $\frac{1}{4}$'s from −2 to 2.

   **a.** 200 · 40          **b.** 567 − 150          **c.** 50% of 200
   **d.** $17.20 + $2.99      **e.** 7.5 ÷ 100          **f.** $\frac{440}{20}$
   **g.** 6 × 8, + 1, $\sqrt{\ }$, × 3, − 1, ÷ 2, × 10, − 1, ÷ 9

**Problem Solving:** The numbers in these boxes form number patterns. What one number should be put in both empty boxes to complete the patterns?

| 1 | 2 | 3 |
|---|---|---|
| 2 | 4 |   |
| 3 |   | 9 |

Proportions can be used to solve many types of word problems. In this lesson we will use proportions to solve ratio word problems like the following examples.

**Example 1** The ratio of salamanders to frogs was 5 to 7. If there were 20 salamanders, how many frogs were there?

*Solution* In this problem there are two kinds of numbers, ratio numbers and actual count numbers. The ratio numbers are 5 and 7. The number 20 is an actual count of the number of salamanders. We will arrange these numbers in two columns and two rows to form a ratio box.

|              | RATIO | ACTUAL COUNT |
|--------------|-------|--------------|
| Salamanders  | 5     | 20           |
| Frogs        | 7     | $f$          |

We were not given the actual count of frogs, so we use the letter $f$ to stand for the actual number of frogs. Notice that the ratio and actual count numbers for salamanders and for frogs are in their corresponding rows.

We use the numbers in their positions in the ratio box to write a proportion. By solving the proportion we find the actual number of frogs.

|  | RATIO | ACTUAL COUNT |
|---|---|---|
| Salamanders | 5 | 20 |
| Frogs | 7 | $f$ |

$$\rightarrow \frac{5}{7} = \frac{20}{f}$$

We may solve the proportion two ways. We may multiply $\frac{5}{7}$ by $\frac{4}{4}$, or we may use cross products. Here we show the solution using cross products.

$$\frac{5}{7} = \frac{20}{f}$$

$$5f = 7 \cdot 20$$

$$f = \frac{7 \cdot 20}{5}, \text{ which is } 28$$

We find that there were **28 frogs.**

**Example 2** The ratio of humpback whales to killer whales was 2 to 7. If there were 42 killer whales, how many humpbacks were there?

*Solution* Ratio boxes prove to be very useful, so we begin by drawing a ratio box for this problem.

|  | RATIO | ACTUAL COUNT |
|---|---|---|
| Humpback | 2 | $h$ |
| Killer | 7 | 42 |

$$\rightarrow \frac{2}{7} = \frac{h}{42}$$

We use the ratio box to guide us in writing a proportion. We see that we can solve this proportion by multiplying $\frac{2}{7}$ by $\frac{6}{6}$. We may also solve this proportion using cross products.

$$\frac{2}{7} = \frac{h}{42}$$

$$2 \cdot 42 = 7h$$

$$\frac{2 \cdot 42}{7} = h$$

$$12 = h$$

We find that there were **12 humpback whales.**

**Practice** Draw a ratio box for each problem. Then solve each problem using proportions.

a. There were more dragons than knights in the battle. In fact, the ratio of dragons to knights was 5 to 4. If there were 60 knights, how many dragons were there?
75 dragons

b. At the party the boy-girl ratio was 5 to 3. If there were 30 boys, how many girls were there? 18 girls

**Problem set 104**

1. How far would a car travel in $2\frac{1}{2}$ hours at 50 miles
(94) per hour? 125 mi

$$\frac{50 \text{ mi}}{1 \text{ hr}} \times \frac{2\frac{1}{2} \text{ hr}}{1}$$

2. A map is drawn to this scale: 1 inch = 2 miles. How
(94) many miles apart are two towns that are 3 inches apart on the map? 6 mi

3. The ratio of humpback whales to killer whales was 2
(104) to 7. If there were 28 killer whales, how many humpback whales were there? 8 humpback whales

4. When Robert measured a half-
(99) gallon box of ice cream, he found it had the dimensions shown in the illustration. What was the volume of the box in cubic inches? 122.5 in.[3]

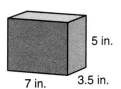
5 in.
7 in.   3.5 in.

**5.** In the class of 30 students there were 12 boys. What
(82) was the boy-girl ratio?  $\frac{2}{3}$

**6.** Which of the following is not a quadrilateral?
(78)
A. Parallelogram    B. Pentagon    C. Rhombus
B. Pentagon

**7.** Marge swung her arm in a circle. If her arm is
(97) 24 inches long, what is the diameter of the circle?
48 in.

**8.** Arrange in order from least to greatest:   $\frac{3}{10}, \frac{1}{3}, \frac{2}{5}$
(75)
$$\frac{1}{3}, \frac{2}{5}, \frac{3}{10}$$

Complete the chart to answer problems 9, 10, and 11.

|   | FRACTION | DECIMAL | PERCENT |
|---|---|---|---|
| **9.** (98) | $\frac{3}{50}$ | (a) 0.06 | (b) 6% |
| **10.** (98) | (a) $\frac{1}{25}$ | 0.04 | (b) 4% |
| **11.** (98) | (a) $1\frac{1}{2}$ | (b) 1.5 | 150% |

**12.** $4\frac{1}{12} + 5\frac{1}{6} + 2\frac{1}{4}$   $11\frac{1}{2}$    **13.** $\frac{4}{5} \times 3\frac{1}{3} \times 3$   8
(59)                                    (71)

**14.** Solve:  $\frac{c}{12} = \frac{3}{4}$   9       **15.** $(1 + 0.5) \div (1 - 0.5)$
(103)                                  (48)   3

**16.** $0.125 \times 80$   10
(39)

**17.** Divide $8.75 by 4 and round the quotient to the
(50) nearest cent.   $2.19

**18.** Write the decimal number one hundred five and
(35) five hundredths.   105.05

**19.** List the factors of 50.   1, 2, 5, 10, 25, 50
(19)

**20.** Write the prime factorization of 50.   $2 \cdot 5 \cdot 5$
(64)

**21.** A quart is a little bit less than a liter, so a gallon is a
(77) little less than how many liters?   4 L

**22.** What number is $\frac{1}{4}$ of 360?   90
(22)

**23.** The perimeter of the triangle is
(90) 18 cm. What is the length of its
longest side?   8 cm

**24.** What is the area of this triangle?
(87) 12 cm²

**25.** The temperature was −5°F at 6:00 a.m. By noon the
(14) temperature had risen 12 degrees. What was the
noontime temperature?   7°F

**26.** The weather report stated that the chance of rain is
(91) 30%. What is the chance that it will not rain?   70%

**27.** Find the perimeter of this figure.
(102) Dimensions are in inches.   48 in.

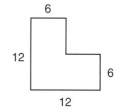

**28.** Rhonda measured the diameter and circumference of a
(100) bowl. The bowl measured 7 inches across and
22 inches around. The circumference was the length
of how many diameters? (Round to two decimal
places.)   3.14

**29.** A room is 15 feet long and 12 feet wide.
(90,94)
(a) The room is how many **yards** long and wide?

(b) What is the area of the room in square yards?
(a) 5 yd by 4 yd   (b) 20 yd²

8, 9, 10, or 11   **30.** Ned has only dimes and nickels in his pocket, and he
(37) has more than one of each. The total value of the coins
is 65¢. How many coins could he have in his pocket?

# LESSON
# 105

# Using a Compass • Pi ($\pi$)

**Facts Practice:** Linear Measure Facts (Test K in Test Masters)

**Mental Math:** Count by 25's from −200 to 200.

    **a.** 40 · 600       **b.** 429 + 350     **c.** 25% of 200
    **d.** $60.00 − $59.45    **e.** 1.2 × 100     **f.** 60 × 12
    **g.** Square 5, − 1, ÷ 4, × 5, + 2, ÷ 4, × 3, + 1, $\sqrt{\phantom{x}}$

**Problem Solving:** Copy this problem and fill in the missing digits:

$$\frac{\square}{4} + \frac{\square}{6} = \frac{11}{12}$$

**Mental Math:**
a. 24,000
b. 779
c. 50
d. $0.55
e. 120
f. 720
g. 5

**Problem Solving:**
$\frac{3}{4} + \frac{1}{6}$ or $\frac{1}{4} + \frac{4}{6}$

**Using a compass**

A compass is a tool for drawing a circle. Here we show two types of compasses.

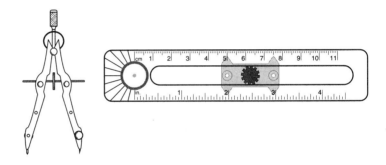

We use a compass by selecting a radius for a circle, then rotating the compass about the center of the circle to draw the circumference.

## Activity: Circles

Materials needed:

- Compass for each student or pair of students
- Plain paper
- Pencils

Draw each circle with the given radius:

**a.** 2 in. radius  See student work.

**b.** 3 cm radius  See student work.

**c.** $1\frac{3}{4}$ in. radius  See student work.

Concentric circles are circles with the same center. A "bull's-eye" target is an example of a concentric circle.

**d.** Draw three concentric circles with radii of 4 cm, 5 cm, and 6 cm.  See student work.

**Pi (π)**  If we know the radius or diameter of a circle, we can calculate the approximate circumference of the circle. Investigating the circumference of some circular objects in Lesson 100, we found that there are a little more than three diameters in a circumference. The actual number of diameters in a circumference is close to $3\frac{1}{7}$, or 3.14. The exact number of diameters in a circumference cannot be expressed as a fraction or as a decimal number, so we use the Greek letter π (pi) to stand for the number of diameters in a circumference.

To find the circumference of a circle, we multiply the diameter of the circle by π. We will use 3.14 as an approximation for π in this book. In the following formula, $C$ stands for the circumference and $D$ stands for the diameter of a circle.

$$C = \pi D$$

**Example**  Sidney drew a circle with a 2-inch radius. What is the circumference of the circle?

**Solution**  The radius of the circle is 2 inches, so the diameter is 4 inches. We multiply 4 inches by π (3.14) to find the circumference.

$$C = \pi D$$
$$C = (3.14)(4 \text{ in.})$$
$$C = 12.56 \text{ in.}$$

The circumference of the circle is about **12.56 inches.**

**Practice**

a. The factors 2 and $r$ in the second equation are equivalent to the $D$ in the first equation because two radii equal one diameter. So two radii times $\pi$ is equivalent to the diameter times $\pi$.

a. The formula for the circumference of a circle presented in this lesson is $C = \pi D$. Another formula for the circumference of a circle using the radius ($r$) instead of the diameter of a circle is $C = 2\pi r$. Explain why these two formulas are equivalent formulas.

Find the circumference of each of these circles. Use 3.14 for $\pi$.

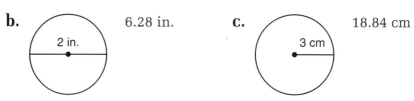

b.    6.28 in.    2 in.

c.    18.84 cm    3 cm

d. The diameter of a penny is about $\frac{3}{4}$ in. (0.75 in.). Find the circumference of a penny. Round your answer to two decimal places.    2.36 in.

e. Roll a penny through one rotation on a piece of paper. Mark the start and the end of the roll. How far did the penny roll in one rotation? Measure the distance to the nearest eighth of an inch.    $2\frac{3}{8}$ in.

**Problem set 105**

1. The average of three numbers is 20. If the greatest is 28, and the least is 15, then what is the third?    17
(18)

2. On a map drawn to the scale of 1 inch = 10 miles, how far apart are two points that are $2\frac{1}{2}$ inches apart on the map?    25 mi
(94)

$$\frac{2\frac{1}{2} \text{ in.}}{1} \times \frac{10 \text{ mi}}{1 \text{ in.}}$$

3. What number is one fourth of 360?    90
(22)

4. What percent of a quarter is a nickel?    20%
(81)

5. If you draw one card from a normal deck of 52 cards, what is the probability that the card will be a face card (jack, queen, king)?    $\frac{3}{13}$
(91)

**6.** One gallon minus one quart equals how many pints?
(77)   6 pints

**7.** The circumference of the front tire on John's bike is
(97)   6 feet. How many turns does the front wheel make as John rides down his 30-foot-long driveway?   5

**8.** The ratio of kangaroos to koalas was 9 to 5. If there
(104)   were 414 kangaroos, how many koalas were there?
230 koalas

Complete the chart to answer questions 9, 10, and 11.

|       | FRACTION | DECIMAL | PERCENT |
|-------|----------|---------|---------|
| **9.**<br>(98) | $\frac{1}{8}$ | (a) 0.125 | (b) 12.5% |
| **10.**<br>(98) | (a) $1\frac{4}{5}$ | 1.8 | (b) 180% |
| **11.**<br>(98) | (a) $\frac{3}{100}$ | (b) 0.03 | 3% |

**12.** $8\frac{1}{3} - 3\frac{1}{2}$   $4\frac{5}{6}$          **13.** $2\frac{1}{2} \times 1\frac{1}{3} \times 1\frac{1}{5}$   4
(62)                                    (71)

**14.** $2\frac{1}{2} \div 100$   $\frac{1}{40}$          **15.** $1 - (0.2 \times 0.3)$   0.94
(67)                                    (83)

**16.** $0.014 \div 0.5$   0.028
(48)

**17.** Find 7% of $14.00 by multiplying 0.07 and $14.00.
(50)   Round the product to the nearest cent.   $0.98

**18.** Write the standard notation for the following:   60,907
(32)
$$(6 \times 10^4) + (9 \times 10^2) + (7 \times 10^0)$$

**19.** The prime factorization of one hundred is $2^2 \cdot 5^2$.
(72)   The prime factorization of one thousand is $2^3 \cdot 5^3$. Write the prime factorization of one million using exponents.   $1{,}000{,}000 = 2^6 \cdot 5^6$

$6\frac{3}{4}$ in.   **20.** A 1-foot ruler broke into two pieces so that one piece
(62)   was $5\frac{1}{4}$ inches long. How long was the other piece?

**21.** $6 + 3^2\left(5 - \sqrt{4}\right)$   33
(92)

**22.** If each small block is one cubic
(99)   centimeter, then what is the volume
of this rectangular prism?
24 cu. cm

**23.** What percent of a meter is 20 centimeters?   20%
(81)

**24.** (a) What is the area of the shaded
(90)       rectangle?   6 cm²

(b) What is the area of the unshaded rectangle?   28 cm²

(c) What is the combined area of
the two rectangles?   34 cm²

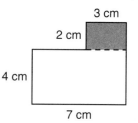

**25.** What is the perimeter of the hexagon in problem 24?
(102)   26 cm

**26.** The diameter of each tire on Jan's bike is two feet.
(105)   What is the circumference of each tire? (Use 3.14 for $\pi$.)
6.28 ft

**27.** What is the area of this triangle?
(87)   14 cm²

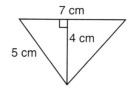

This table shows the number of miles Celina rode her bike
each day during the week. Use this information to answer
questions 28, 29, and 30.

**28.** If the data were rearranged from
(9)   order of days to order of distance
ridden, with 3 miles listed first
and 10 miles listed last, then
which distance would be in the
middle of the list?   6 mi

**Miles of Bike Riding
for the Week**

| Day | Miles |
|-----------|-------|
| Sunday | 7 |
| Monday | 3 |
| Tuesday | 6 |
| Wednesday | 10 |
| Thursday | 5 |
| Friday | 4 |
| Saturday | 7 |

**29.** What was the average number of
(18)   miles Celina rode each day?   6 mi

**30.** Write a "some and some more" question that refers to
(11)   the table and answer the question.   See student work.

# Area of Complex Shapes

LESSON
## 106

Mental Math:
a. 10,000
b. 226
c. 20
d. $22.88
e. 0.06
f. 6
g. 6
Problem Solving:
86

> **Facts Practice:** Percents to Fractions and Decimals (Test M in Test Masters)
>
> **Mental Math:** Count by $\frac{1}{3}$'s from −2 to 2.
>
> **a.** $100 \cdot 100$     **b.** $376 - 150$     **c.** 10% of 200
>
> **d.** $12.89 + $9.99     **e.** $6.0 \div 100$     **f.** $\frac{360}{60}$
>
> **g.** $10 \times 6, + 4, \sqrt{\ }, \times 3, + 1, \sqrt{\ }, \times 7, + 1, \sqrt{\ }$
>
> **Problem Solving:** On his first two tests Jason's average score was 80. On the next three tests his average score was 90. What was Jason's average score on his first five tests?

In this lesson we will practice finding the area of complex shapes. One way to find the area of a complex shape is to divide the shape into two or more parts, find the area of each part, then add the areas. Think how this shape could be divided into two rectangles.

**Example**   Find the area of this figure.

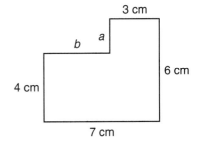

**Solution**   We will show two ways to divide this shape into two rectangles. We use the skills we learned in Lesson 102 to find that side $a$ is 2 cm and side $b$ is 4 cm. We extend side $b$ with a dashed line segment to divide the figure into two rectangles.

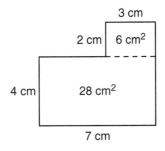

The length and width of the smaller rectangle is 3 cm and 2 cm, so its area is 6 cm². The larger rectangle is 7 cm by 4 cm, so its area is 28 cm². The combined area of the two rectangles is 34 cm².

$$6 \text{ cm}^2 + 28 \text{ cm}^2 = 34 \text{ cm}^2$$

We find that the area of the figure is **34 cm²**.

A second way to divide the figure into two rectangles is to extend side *a*.

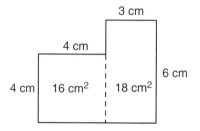

Extending side *a* forms a 4-cm by 4-cm rectangle and a 3-cm by 6-cm rectangle. The combined area of the two rectangles is also 34 cm².

$$16 \text{ cm}^2 + 18 \text{ cm}^2 = 34 \text{ cm}^2$$

Either way we divide the figure we find that its area is 34 cm².

**Practice***  **a.** Find two ways to divide this figure into two rectangles. Then find the area of the figure each way.  50 in.²

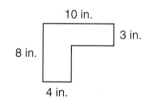

**b.** This trapezoid can be divided into a rectangle and a triangle. Find the area of the trapezoid.  72 cm²

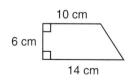

**Problem set 106**  **1.** If the divisor is eight tenths and the dividend is forty-eight hundredths, then what is the quotient?  0.6
(48)

**2.** The plans for the clubhouse were drawn so that 1 inch
(94) equaled 2 feet. On the plans the clubhouse was
4 inches tall. The actual clubhouse will be how tall?
8 ft

**3.** If all the king's horses total 600, and all the king's men
(82) total 800, then what is the ratio of men to horses? $\frac{4}{3}$

**4.** What percent of the perimeter of a regular pentagon is
(63,93) the length of one side? 20%

**5.** What is the area in square feet of a room that is 12 feet
(31) long and 9 feet wide? 108 ft²

**6.** What is the area of the room described in problem 5 in
(94) square yards? 12 yd²

**7.** $10^3 - (10^2 - \sqrt{100}) - 10^3 \div 10^2$ 900
(92)

**8.** What number completes the proportion? $\frac{6}{n} = \frac{8}{12}$
(103) 9

Complete the chart to answer problems 9, 10, and 11.

|  | FRACTION | DECIMAL | PERCENT |
|---|---|---|---|
| **9.** (98) | $1\frac{1}{10}$ | (a) 1.1 | (b) 110% |
| **10.** (98) | (a) $\frac{9}{20}$ | 0.45 | (b) 45% |
| **11.** (98) | (a) $\frac{4}{5}$ | (b) 0.8 | 80% |

**12.** $5\frac{3}{8} + 4\frac{1}{4} + 3\frac{1}{2}$ $13\frac{1}{8}$     **13.** $\frac{8}{3} \cdot \frac{5}{12} \cdot \frac{9}{10}$ 1
(59)                                          (71)

**14.** 64.8 + 8.42 + 24   97.22
(38)

**15.** Find 8% of $6.25 by multiplying 0.08 and $6.25.
(50) Round the product to the nearest cent.   $0.50

**16.** How many ounces is one half of a pint?   8 oz
(77)

**17.** Round the quotient to the nearest hundredth:    0.78
*(50)*
$$0.625 \div 0.8$$

**18.** Write one hundred ten million in expanded notation
*(32)* using exponents.    $(1 \times 10^8) + (1 \times 10^7)$

**19.** What is the greatest common factor of 30 and 45?    15
*(20)*

**20.** A square with sides one inch long
*(31)* is divided into $\frac{1}{2}$-inch by $\frac{1}{4}$-inch
rectangles.

    (a) What is the area of each $\frac{1}{2}$-in. by
$\frac{1}{4}$-in. rectangle?    $\frac{1}{8}$ in.$^2$

    (b) What fraction of the square is
shaded?    $\frac{1}{8}$

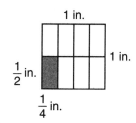

**21.** How many blocks with edges 1 foot long would be
*(99)* needed to fill a cubical box with edges 1 yard long?
27

**22.** $0.3n = \$6.39$    $\$21.30$
*(48)*

**23.** What is the perimeter of this
*(102)* hexagon?    30 cm

**24.** Divide this hexagon into two
*(106)* rectangles. What is the combined
area of the two rectangles? 41 cm$^2$

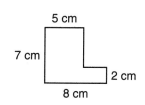

**25.** This trapezoid has been divided
*(106)* into two triangles. What is the
area of the trapezoid?    72 cm$^2$

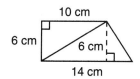

Alberto earned the following scores on his quizzes. Use
this information to answer questions 26 and 27.

$$8, 9, 7, 8, 10, 9, 8, 7, 10$$

**26.** (a) Which score did Alberto earn most often?    8
*(9)*
    (b) If the scores were arranged in order from lowest to
highest, what would be the middle score?    8

**27.** Find Alberto's average quiz score. Round the answer
(50) to the nearest tenth.    8.4

**28.** Instead of dividing 840 by 14, Sam found half of each
(42) number and then divided. What numbers did Sam
divide and what was the quotient?    $420 \div 7 = 60$

**29.** Use your compass to draw a circle that has a **diameter**
(105) of 10 cm.    See student drawing. (a) 5 cm; (b) 31.4 cm

(a) What is the radius of the circle?

(b) Calculate the circumference of the circle.

**30.** $\dfrac{10 \text{ gallons}}{1} \times \dfrac{31.5 \text{ miles}}{1 \text{ gallon}}$    315 mi
(94)

# LESSON 107

# Acute, Obtuse, and Straight Angles • Two-Step Equations

**Facts Practice:** 28 Fractions to Simplify (Test I in Test Masters)

**Mental Math:** Count up and down by 7's between 7 and 70.

**a.** 20 · 500        **b.** 376 + 450        **c.** 50% of $20
**d.** $100.00 − $60.50    **e.** 0.065 × 100    **f.** 25 × 40
**g.** Square 6, − 1, ÷ 5, × 6, − 2, ÷ 5, × 6, + 1, $\sqrt{\phantom{x}}$

**Problem Solving:** If we flip a coin two times there are four possible outcomes: H-H, H-T, T-H, T-T. (H is for "heads," and T is for "tails.") List the possible outcomes if a coin is tossed three times.

**Acute, obtuse, and straight angles**

The words **acute, right, obtuse,** and **straight** are terms we use to name angles of various sizes. Recall that a square corner is a **right angle.** Doors, chalkboards, windows, books, papers, and buildings all contain right angles. An angle smaller than a right angle is an **acute angle.** Some remember this by thinking of "a cute little angle." An angle that makes a straight line is a **straight angle.** An angle that is greater than a right angle but less than a straight angle is an **obtuse angle.** Each type of angle is illustrated below.

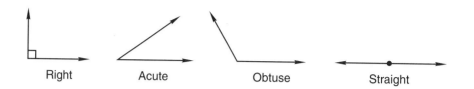

A unit we use for measuring angles is a degree. A full circle or a turn "all the way around" measures 360 degrees. We abbreviate the word **degree** with a small circle above and to the right of the number, as in 360°. A right angle is $\frac{1}{4}$ of a full circle. One fourth of 360° is 90°. A right angle measures 90°. An acute angle measures less than 90°. An obtuse angle measures more than 90° but less than 180°. A straight angle is a half turn and measures 180°.

**Example 1**   If angle $x$ is an acute angle, then what type of angle is angle $y$?

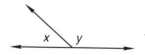

**Solution**   We see that angle $x$ is smaller than a right angle and that angle $y$ is greater than a right angle. Angle $y$ is an **obtuse** angle.

**Example 2**   Together, angle $x$ and angle $y$ form a straight angle. If the measure of angle $x$ is 60°, then what is the measure of angle $y$?

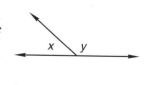

**Solution**   A straight angle measures 180°. Angle $x$ measures 60° of the 180°. So angle $y$ measures the rest of the 180°, which is **120°**.

$$180° - 60° = 120°$$

An angle is formed by the intersection of two lines, rays, or segments. The point of intersection is the vertex of the angle. The lines, rays, or segments form the sides of the angle. A particular angle may be named by a number or letter between the sides of the angle, as in Example 1. An angle may also be named by the letter that identifies its vertex. We may also name an angle with three letters that identify a point on one side of the angle, the vertex of the angle, and a point on the other side of the angle.

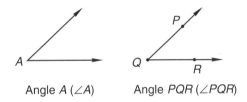

Angle $A$ ($\angle A$)     Angle $PQR$ ($\angle PQR$)

Notice that the symbol $\angle$ may be used to abbreviate the word "angle." We use three letters to name an angle when one letter does not clearly distinguish an angle.

**Example 3**  Name three angles that have their vertex at point $A$.

*Solution*  By tracing the segments from point $D$ to point $A$ to point $C$, we trace over angle $DAC$. Tracing from $C$ to $A$ to $B$, we trace over angle $CAB$. Tracing from $D$ to $A$ to $B$, we trace over the third angle, which is angle $DAB$. The three angles are $\angle DAC$, $\angle CAB$, and $\angle DAB$. When an angle is named with three letters, the letters may be reversed by starting with a point on the other side of the angle. So these three angles could also be named $\angle CAD$, $\angle BAC$, and $\angle BAD$.

**Two-step equations**  Since Lessons 3 and 4 we have solved one-step equations in which we found a missing number in addition, subtraction, multiplication, or division problems. In this lesson we will begin solving two-step equations in which more than one operation is involved.

Example 4    $3n - 1 = 20$

*Solution*    Let us think about what this equation means. When 1 is subtracted from $3n$, the answer is 20. So $3n$ equals 21.

$$3n = 21$$

Since $3n$ means 3 times $n$, and $3n$ equals 21, then $n$ equals 7.

$$n = 7$$

We show our work this way.

$$3n - 1 = 20$$
$$3n = 21$$
$$n = 7$$

**Practice**    **a.** Angle *ABC* is a right angle. If $\angle ABD$ measures 50°, what is the measure of $\angle DBC$?    40°

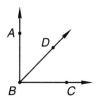

**b.** An angle that measures 108° is what type of angle?

A. Acute      B. Right      C. Obtuse      D. Straight

C. Obtuse

**c.** What type of angle is one half of a straight angle?

right angle

**d.** Figure *ABCD* is a square. The measure of $\angle 1$ equals the measure of $\angle 2$. Angle 1 measures how many degrees?    45°

**e.** Angle *A* is a right angle. The measure of angle *B* appears to be about    C. 30°

A. 60°                    B. 45°                    C. 30°

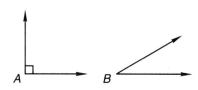

**f.** $3n + 1 = 16$    5                    **g.** $2x - 1 = 9$    5

**Problem set 107**

**1.** Copy this illustrated thermometer
(18) on your paper. The thermometer
shows that the temperature at
which water freezes is 0°C, which
equals 32°F. It also shows that the
temperature at which water boils
is 100°C, which equals 212°F. On
your paper write the temperature
in degrees Celsius and in degrees
Fahrenheit that is halfway between the freezing and boiling
temperature of water.   50°C, 122°F

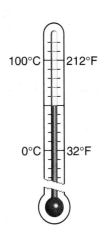

**2.** A set of house plans was drawn to this
(94) scale: 1 in. = 2 ft. On the plans a room measures
5 inches by 6 inches. What is the area of the room in
square feet?   120 ft²

Thanh measured the circumference and diameter of five
circular objects and then divided the circumference by the
diameter to find the number of diameters in the
circumference. He recorded the results in a table. Use this
information to answer questions 3 and 4.

| Object | Circumference | Diameter | Circumference / Diameter |
|--------|---------------|----------|--------------------------|
| Plate | 31 in. | 10 in. | 3.1 |
| Tire | 82 in. | 26 in. | 3.15 |
| Pan | 97 cm | 31 cm | 3.13 |
| Bowl | 22 in. | 7 in. | 3.14 |
| Cup | 25 cm | 8 cm | 3.13 |

**3.** What is the average of the five numbers in the last
(18) column?   3.13

**4.** Explain why the last column is not 3.14 for every object
(105) measured.   All measurement is approximate. Variations in
measurement account for the different quotients.

**5.** The ratio of boys to girls at the party was 2 to 3. If there
(104) were 12 girls at the party, how many boys were there?
8 boys

**6.** Write the prime factorization of the numerator and
*(66)* denominator of $\frac{54}{84}$ and then reduce the fraction.
$\frac{2\cdot3\cdot3\cdot3}{2\cdot2\cdot3\cdot7}, \frac{9}{14}$

**7.** Ol' McDonald's horse was tied to a post in the center
*(97)* of the pasture. What is the shape of the region in
which the horse may roam?   circle

**8.** $3^2 + 4^2 = n^2$   5
*(107)*

Complete the chart to answer problems 9, 10, and 11.

|  | FRACTION | DECIMAL | PERCENT |
|---|---|---|---|
| **9.** *(98)* | $\frac{3}{8}$ | (a) 0.375 | (b) 37.5% |
| **10.** *(98)* | (a) $\frac{3}{50}$ | 0.06 | (b) 6% |
| **11.** *(98)* | (a) $1\frac{2}{5}$ | (b) 1.4 | 140% |

**12.** $5 - \left(6\frac{1}{4} - 2\frac{1}{2}\right)$   $1\frac{1}{4}$     **13.** $3\frac{3}{4} \times 2\frac{2}{5} \times 1\frac{1}{3}$   12
*(62)*                                          *(71)*

**14.** $7 - (4.1 - 0.42)$   3.32     **15.** $(0.6)(\$2.50)$   $1.50
*(38)*                              *(39)*

**16.** $0.0195 \div 30$   0.00065     **17.** $0.6n = \$2.10$   $3.50
*(44)*                               *(48)*

**18.** Divide \$8.78 by 5 and round the quotient to the
*(50)* nearest cent.   \$1.76

**19.** What is the least common multiple of 9 and 12?   36
*(30)*

**20.** This trapezoid is divided into a
*(106)* rectangle and a triangle. Find the
area of the trapezoid.   60 cm²

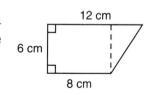

**21.** What type of an angle is an angle that measures 89°?
*(107)*   acute

**22.** The perimeter of the triangle is
*(90)* 16 cm. What is its area?   12 cm²

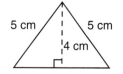

**23.** $3a + 1 = 25$   8
*(107)*

**24.** If each small cube is one cubic
(99) inch, then what is the volume of
this rectangular prism?   48 in.³

**25.** What number is halfway between 82 and 28 on the
(18) number line?   55

**26.** What is the perimeter of this
(102) polygon?   40 cm

**27.** What is the area of this polygon?
(106) 64 cm²

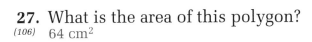

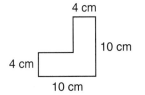

45°    **28.** In this figure right angle *ABC* is
(107) bisected, which means divided in
half, by ray *BD*. The measure of
angle *DBC* is how many degrees?

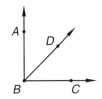

**29.** Robert's bicycle wheel has a diameter of 20 inches.
(105) Find the circumference of the wheel to the nearest inch.
63 in.

**30.** If the probability of winning a prize in the drawing is
(91)   $\frac{1}{1000}$, what is the probability of not winning a prize?
$\frac{999}{1000}$

# LESSON
# 108

# **Transformations**

**Facts Practice:** Percents to Fractions and Decimals (Test M in Test Masters)

**Mental Math:** Count by $\frac{1}{16}$'s from $\frac{1}{16}$ to 1.

**a.** $70 \cdot 70$      **b.** $296 - 150$      **c.** 25% of $20
**d.** $8.23 + $8.99    **e.** $75 \div 100$ (Dec. ans)   **f.** $\frac{800}{40}$
**g.** $8 \times 8, - 4, \div 2, + 5, \div 5, \times 8, - 1, \div 5, \times 2, - 1, \div 3$

**Problem Solving:** The two triangles are congruent. The perimeter of each triangle is 12 cm. What is the area of each triangle?

Two figures are **congruent** if one figure has the same dimensions as the other figure. One way to tell if two figures are congruent is to position one figure "on top of" the other figure. The two triangles below are congruent. Triangle *ABC* can be moved "on top of" triangle *XYZ*, illustrating that it is congruent to triangle *XYZ*.

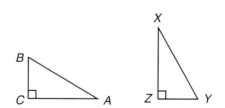

To position triangle *ABC* on triangle *XYZ*, we make three different kinds of moves. First we rotate (turn) triangle *ABC* 90° counterclockwise.

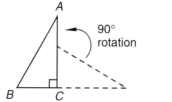

Second, we translate (slide) triangle *ABC* to the right so that side *AC* aligns with side *XY*.

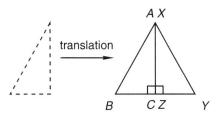

Third, we reflect (flip) triangle *ABC* so that ∠*B* is positioned on top of ∠*Y*.

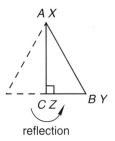

The three different kinds of moves we made are listed in the following table:

**Transformations**

| Rotation | turning a figure about a certain point |
|---|---|
| Translation | sliding a figure in one direction without turning the figure |
| Reflection | reflecting a figure as in a mirror or "flipping" a figure over a certain line |

## Activity: Transformations

Materials needed:

- Scissors
- Pencil
- Paper

Have students work in pairs (or in small groups). Each pair of students (or each group) should cut out a pair of congruent triangles by following these three steps.

**Step 1.** Fold a piece of paper in half.

**Step 2.** Draw a triangle on the folded paper.

**Step 3.** While the paper is folded, cut out the triangle so that two triangles are cut out at the same time.

One person of the pair (or group) places the two triangles on a desk or table so that the triangles are apart and in different orientations. The other person (or another person in the group) moves one of the triangles until it is positioned on top of the other triangle. The moves permitted are rotation, translation, and reflection. The moves should be taken one at a time and described by the student moving the triangle. After the student successfully arranges the triangles, the procedure should be repeated with the roles reversed. Allow each student one or two opportunities to perform and describe the transformation.

**Practice**  Name the transformation(s) necessary to position triangle I on triangle II in each exercise.

**a.**

reflection

**b.**

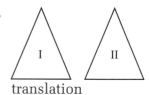

translation

rotation

**c.**

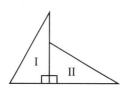

**d.**

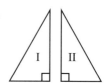

translation and reflection

rotation and reflection

**e.**

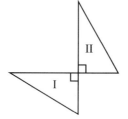

**Problem set 108**

**1.** What is the sum of the first five positive even numbers?
*(10)* 30

**2.** The team's won-lost ratio is 4 to 3. If the team has won
*(104)* 12 games, how many games has the team lost? 9 games

**3.** Thirty-six of the 88 piano keys are black. What is the
*(82)* ratio of black keys to white keys on a piano? $\frac{9}{13}$

**4.** Rollin swung his arm around in a circle. From his
*(105)* shoulder to his fingertips Rollin's arm is 2 feet long.
What is the circumference of the circle traced by his
fingertips when Rollin swings his arm in a circle?
12.56 ft

**5.** Three eighths of the 48 band members played
*(76)* woodwinds. How many woodwind players were in
the band?    18

**6.** What is the least common multiple (LCM) of 6, 8, and 12?
*(30)* 24

7. Rotate tri-
angle I until its
orientation
matches triangle
II. Then translate
triangle I until it
is positioned on
triangle II.

**7.** Triangles I and II are congruent. Describe the transfor-
*(108)* mations necessary to position triangle I on triangle II.

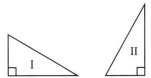

**8.** What number completes the proportion? $\dfrac{7}{20} = \dfrac{n}{100}$
*(103)* 35

Complete the chart to answer problems 9, 10, and 11.

| | Fraction | Decimal | Percent |
|---|---|---|---|
| **9.** *(98)* | $1\frac{2}{5}$ | (a) 1.4 | (b) 140% |
| **10.** *(98)* | (a) $\frac{6}{25}$ | 0.24 | (b) 24% |
| **11.** *(98)* | (a) $\frac{7}{20}$ | (b) 0.35 | 35% |

**12.** $4\frac{3}{4} + \left(2\frac{1}{4} - \frac{7}{8}\right)$   $6\frac{1}{8}$    **13.** $1\frac{1}{5} \div \left(2 \div 1\frac{2}{3}\right)$   1
(62)                                              (67)

**14.** $6.2 + (9 - 2.79)$   12.41    **15.** $9 \div 1.2$   7.5
(38)                                 (48)

**16.** Find 6% of $2.89 by multiplying 0.06 and $2.89.
(50)  Round the product to the nearest cent.   $0.17

**17.** What fraction of a meter is a millimeter?   $\frac{1}{1000}$
(94)

**18.** Arrange these numbers in order from least to greatest:
(43)  0.3, 0.305, 0.31
$$0.3, \ 0.31, \ 0.305$$

**19.** If each edge of a cube is ten centimeters, then its
(99)  volume is how many cubic centimeters?   $1000 \ \text{cm}^3$

**20.** $2^5 - 5^2 + \sqrt{25} \times 2$   17    **21.** $8a = 360$   45
(92)                                 (86)

**22.** Acute angle $a$ is one third of a
(107)  right angle. Its measure is how
many degrees?   30°

**23.** What is the perimeter of this
(102)  polygon?   100 mm

**24.** What is the area of the polygon?
(106)   550 mm²

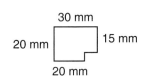

30 mm

20 mm          15 mm

20 mm

16 lb **25.** A pint of water weighs about one pound. About how
(77)  much does a two-gallon bucket of water weigh?

**26.** A trapezoid is a quadrilateral with
(106)  two parallel sides. The parallel
sides of this trapezoid are 10 mm
apart. The trapezoid is divided
into two triangles. What is the
area of the trapezoid?   160 mm²

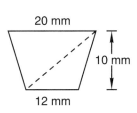

20 mm

10 mm

12 mm

**27.** A cubic container that is 10 cm
<sup>(99)</sup> long, 10 cm wide, and 10 cm deep
can contain one liter of water.
One liter is how many milliliters?
1000 mL

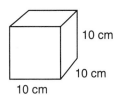

10 cm

10 cm

10 cm

**28.** What is the probability of drawing a red card from a
<sup>(91)</sup> normal deck of 52 cards?   $\frac{1}{2}$

**29.** One and one half kilometers is how many meters?
<sup>(94)</sup>   1500 m

**30.** On a coordinate plane draw a segment from (−3, 4) to
<sup>(107)</sup> (1, −1). Draw another segment from (1, −1) to (5, −1).
Together, the segments form what type of angle?
obtuse angle

# LESSON
# 109

# Corresponding Parts •
# Similar Triangles

**Facts Practice:** 30 Fractions to Reduce (Test G in Test Masters)

**Mental Math:** Count down by 25's from 200 to −200

   **a.** 400 · 30        **b.** 687 + 250      **c.** 10% of $20
   **d.** $10.00 − $6.87    **e.** 0.5 × 100      **f.** 70 × 300
   **g.** Square 7, + 1, ÷ 2, × 3, − 3, ÷ 8, $\sqrt{\phantom{x}}$

**Problem Solving:** One state uses a license plate that is two letters followed by four digits. How many license plates are possible if all of the letters and digits are used?

**Corresponding parts**

The two triangles below are congruent. Each triangle has three angles and three sides. The angles and sides of triangle *ABC* **correspond** to the angles and sides of triangle *XYZ*.

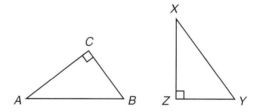

By rotating, translating, and reflecting triangle *ABC*, we could position it on top of triangle *XYZ* and their corresponding parts would be together.

$$\angle A \text{ corresponds to } \angle X$$

$$\angle B \text{ corresponds to } \angle Y$$

$$\angle C \text{ corresponds to } \angle Z$$

$$\overline{AB} \text{ corresponds to } \overline{XY}$$

$$\overline{BC} \text{ corresponds to } \overline{YZ}$$

$$\overline{AC} \text{ corresponds to } \overline{XZ}$$

If two figures are congruent, their corresponding parts are congruent. So the measures of the corresponding parts are equal.

**Example 1** These triangles are congruent. What is the perimeter of each?

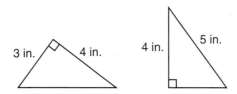

*Solution* We will rotate the triangle on the left so that the corresponding parts are easier to see.

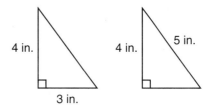

The unmarked side on the left triangle corresponds to the 5-inch side on the right triangle. Since the triangles are congruent, the measures of the corresponding parts are equal. So each triangle has sides that measure 3 inches, 4 inches, and 5 inches. Adding, we find that the perimeter of each triangle is **12 inches.**

$$3 \text{ in.} + 4 \text{ in.} + 5 \text{ in.} = 12 \text{ in.}$$

**Similar triangles** Figures that are the same shape but not necessarily the same size are **similar.** Three of these four triangles are similar.

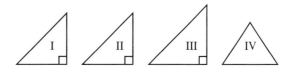

Triangles I and II are similar. They are also congruent. Congruent figures are the same shape (similar) and the same size. Triangle III is similar to triangles I and II. It is also the same shape but not the same size. Triangle III is an enlargement of triangles I and II. Triangle IV is not similar to the other triangles. It cannot be reduced or enlarged to match the other triangles. Its shape is different. Notice that the corresponding angles of similar figures have the same measure.

**Example 2**    The two triangles are similar. What is the measure of angle *A*?

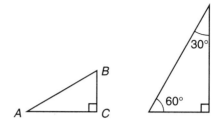

**Solution**    We will rotate and reflect triangle *ABC* so that the corresponding angles are easier to see.

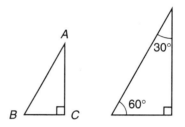

We see that ∠*A* in triangle *ABC* corresponds to the 30° angle of the similar triangle. Since corresponding angles of similar triangles have the same measure, the measure of ∠*A* is **30°**.

**Practice**    **a.** "All squares are similar." True or false?    true

**b.** "All similar triangles are congruent." True or false?    false

**c.** "If two polygons are similar, then their corresponding angles are equal in measure." True or false?    true

**d.** These two triangles are congruent. Which side of triangle *PQR* is the same length as $\overline{AB}$?    $\overline{QR}$

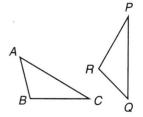

**e.** Which two triangles appear to be similar?   I, II

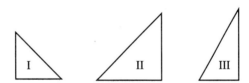

**Problem set 109**

**1.** The first three prime numbers are 2, 3, and 5. Their
(61) product is 30. What is the product of the next three
prime numbers?   1001

**2.** On the map, 2 cm equals 1 km. What is the actual
(94) length of a street that is 10 cm long on the map?
5 km

**3.** Between 8:00 p.m. and 9:00 p.m., the station telecast
(82) 8 minutes of commercials. What was the ratio of
commercial time to program time during that hour?
$\frac{2}{13}$

**4.** (a) Which triangle appears to have a right angle as one
(109)    of its angles?   C.

   (b) In which triangle do all three sides appear to be
   the same length?   A.

**5.** How many degrees would an acute angle measure if it
(107) were two thirds the size of a right angle?   60°

**6.** What is the greatest common factor (GCF) of 10, 15,
(20) and 25?   5

**7.** $10^3 \div 10^2 - 10^1$   0      **8.** $\dfrac{8}{n} = \dfrac{4}{25}$   50
(92)                          (103)

Complete the chart to answer problems 9, 10, and 11.

| | FRACTION | DECIMAL | PERCENT |
|---|---|---|---|
| **9.** (98) | $\frac{5}{8}$ | (a) 0.625 | (b) 62.5% |
| **10.** (98) | (a) $1\frac{1}{4}$ | 1.25 | (b) 125% |
| **11.** (98) | (a) $\frac{7}{10}$ | (b) 0.7 | 70% |

**12.** If the arrow is spun, what is the probability that it will stop on a number less than 4?  $\frac{3}{4}$
(91)

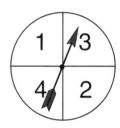

**13.** Convert 200 centimeters to meters by completing this multiplication:    2 meters
(94)

$$\frac{200 \text{ cm}}{1} \cdot \frac{1 \text{ m}}{100 \text{ cm}}$$

**14.** $(6.2 + 9) - 2.79$    12.41    **15.** $0.12m = \$4.20$    $35.00
(38)                                     (48)

**16.** Find 6.5% of $10.80 by multiplying 0.065 and $10.80. Round the product to the nearest cent.    $0.70
(50)

**17.** Write the fraction $\frac{2}{3}$ as a decimal number rounded to the hundredths' place.    0.67
(73)

**18.** The Zamoras rent a storage room that is 10 feet wide, 12 feet long, and 8 feet high. How many cube-shaped boxes one foot on each edge can the Zamoras store in the room?    960 boxes
(99)

19. Similar figures have the same shape. They may or may not be the same size. Congruent figures have the same shape and are the same size. Since congruent figures are the same shape, they are similar.

**19.** Explain why figures that are congruent are also similar.
(109)

**20.** How much money is $\frac{3}{8}$ of $3.60?    $1.35
(22)

**21.** $3w - 1 = 20$ 7
(107)

**22.** Triangle I and triangle II are
(109) congruent. What is the area of
each triangle? 6 in.²

**23.** Name the transformations nec-
(108) essary to position triangle I on
triangle II. rotation and translation

**24.** This trapezoid has been di-
(106) vided into a rectangle and a
triangle. What is the area of
the trapezoid?
51 cm²

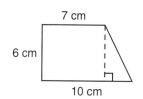

**25.** How many **millimeters** long is this line segment? 34 mm
(7)

**26.** These triangles are similar. What is the measure of
(109) angle $A$? 40°

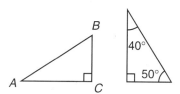

**27.** The ratio of peanuts to cashews in the mix was 9 to 2.
(104) Horace counted 36 cashews in all. How many peanuts
were there? 162 peanuts

**28.** A soup label must be long enough to wrap around a
(105) can. If the diameter of the can is 7 cm, then the label
should be at least how long? (Round up to the nearest
whole number.) 22 cm

**29.** $6\frac{2}{3} \div 100$ $\frac{1}{15}$
(67)

**30.** Compare: $\left(\frac{1}{10}\right)^2$ ⊜ 0.01
(92)

# LESSON
# 110

# Symmetry

**Facts Practice:** Percents to Fractions and Decimals (Test M in Test Masters)

**Mental Math:** Count up and down by $\frac{1}{8}$'s between $\frac{1}{8}$ and 2.

**a.** $90 \cdot 90$  **b.** $726 - 250$  **c.** 50% of $50
**d.** $7.62 + $3.98  **e.** $8 \div 100$ (Dec. Ans.)  **f.** $\frac{350}{50}$
**g.** Square 10, $- 1$, $\div 9$, $\times 3$, $- 1$, $\div 4$, $\times 7$, $+ 4$, $\div 3$

**Problem Solving:** Copy this problem and fill in the missing digits. Use only zeros or ones in the blanks.

### Mental Math:
a. 8100
b. 476
c. $25.00
d. $11.60
e. 0.08
f. 7
g. 20

### Problem Solving:

$$
\begin{array}{r}
91 \\
11\overline{)1001} \\
\underline{99} \\
11 \\
\underline{11} \\
0
\end{array}
$$

A figure is **symmetrical** if it can be divided in half so that the halves are mirror images of each other. We can observe symmetry in nature. A butterfly is symmetrical, most fish are symmetrical, and our bodies are generally symmetrical. Manufactured items may be designed to be symmetrical. A lamp, a chair, and the kitchen sink may be symmetrical. Two-dimensional figures may also be symmetrical. A two-dimensional figure is symmetrical if a line can divide the figure into two mirror images. Line $r$ divides this triangle into two mirror images, so the triangle is symmetrical, and line $r$ is a **line of symmetry.**

**Example 1** This rectangle has how many lines of symmetry?

*Solution*   There are two ways to divide this rectangle into mirror images.

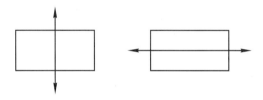

The rectangle has **two lines of symmetry.**

**Example 2**   Which of these triangles does not appear to be symmetrical?

A. 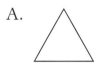   B.    C.

*Solution*   We check each triangle to see if we can find a line of symmetry. In choice A, all three sides of the triangle are the same length. The triangle has three lines of symmetry.

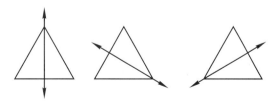

In choice B, two sides of the triangle are the same length. The triangle has one line of symmetry.

In choice C, each side of the triangle is a different length. The triangle has no line of symmetry. The triangle is not symmetrical. The answer is **C.**

**Practice**   **a.** Sketch four squares. Then sketch a different line of symmetry for each square. ▨ ⊟ ⫿ ⊠

**b.** Which of these letters does not have a line of symmetry?
F only

A     B     C     D     E     F

**Problem set**   **1.** When the greatest four-digit number is divided by the
**110**   ⁽²⁾ greatest two-digit number, what is the quotient?   101

**2.** The ratio of the length to the width of a rectangle is 3
⁽¹⁰⁴⁾ to 2. If the width is 60 mm, what is the length?   90 mm

**3.** A box of saltine crackers in the
⁽⁹⁹⁾ shape of a square prism had a
length, width, and height of
4 inches, 4 inches, and 10 inches,
respectively. How many cubic
inches was the volume of the box?
160 in.³

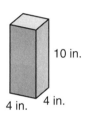

**4.** A full turn is 360°; how many degrees is $\frac{1}{6}$ of a turn?
⁽¹⁰⁷⁾ 60°

Refer to these triangles to answer questions 5, 6, and 7.

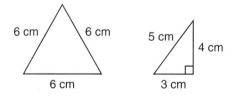

**5.** The three sides of an equilateral triangle are equal in
⁽¹¹⁰⁾ length. The equilateral triangle has how many lines of
symmetry?   3 lines of symmetry

**6.** What is the perimeter of the equilateral triangle?   18 cm
⁽⁹⁰⁾

**7.** A triangle with one right angle is a right triangle. What
(90)    is the perimeter of the right triangle?   12 cm

**8.** What type of angle is greater than an acute angle but
(107)    less than an obtuse angle?   right angle

Complete the chart to answer problems 9, 10, and 11.

|  | FRACTION | DECIMAL | PERCENT |
|---|---|---|---|
| **9.**<br>(98) | $2\frac{3}{4}$ | (a) 2.75 | (b) 275% |
| **10.**<br>(98) | (a) $1\frac{1}{10}$ | 1.1 | (b) 110% |
| **11.**<br>(98) | (a) $\frac{16}{25}$ | (b) 0.64 | 64% |

**12.** $24\frac{1}{6} + 23\frac{1}{3} + 22\frac{1}{2}$   70   **13.** $\left(1\frac{1}{5} \div 2\right) \div 1\frac{2}{3}$   $\frac{9}{25}$
(59)                                                    (67)

**14.** $9 - (6.2 + 2.79)$   0.01       **15.** $0.36m = \$63.00$   $175
(38)                                    (48)

**16.** Find 6.5% of $24.89 by multiplying 0.065 and $24.89.
(50)    Round the product to the nearest cent.   $1.62

**17.** Round the quotient to the nearest thousandth:   0.016
(50)
$$0.065 \div 4$$

**18.** Write the prime factorization of 1000 using exponents.
(72)    $2^3 \cdot 5^3$

**19.** "All squares are similar." True or false?   true
(109)

**20.** $3^3 - 3^2 \div 3 - 3 \times 3$   15
(92)

**21.** What is the perimeter of this
(102)    polygon?   44 m

**22.** What is the area of this polygon?
(106)    106 m²

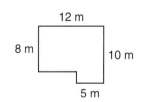

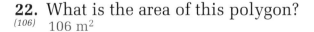

Triangles I and II are congruent. Refer to these triangles to answer questions 23 and 24.

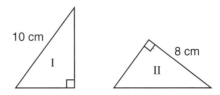

**23.** Name the transformations needed to position triangle I
(108) on triangle II.    rotation, reflection, translation

**24.** The perimeter of each triangle is 24 cm. What is the
(90) length of the shortest side of each triangle?    6 cm

**25.** Sam rolled an old automobile tire down the road. If
(105) the tire had a diameter of two feet, how far down the
road would the tire roll on each complete turn?    6.28 ft

**26.** Use a ruler to draw segment $AB$ $1\frac{3}{4}$ inches long. Then
(68) draw a dot at the midpoint of $\overline{AB}$ and label the point
$M$. How long is $\overline{AM}$?    $B$; $\frac{7}{8}$ in.

**27.** Use a compass to draw a circle on a coordinate plane.
(105) Make the center of the circle the origin, and make the
radius five units. At which two points does the circle
cross the $x$-axis?    (5, 0), (−5, 0)

**28.** What is the circumference of the circle in problem 27?
(105)    31.4 units

**29.** $\dfrac{100}{3}$    $33\frac{1}{3}$
(26)

**30.** $33\frac{1}{3} \div 100$    $\frac{1}{3}$
(67)

# LESSON
# 111

# Applications Using Division

Mental Math:
a. 16
b. 245
c. $24.00
d. $1.41
e. 50
f. 4
g. 25
Problem Solving:
   Saturday

**Facts Practice:** Measurement Facts (Test N in Test Masters)

**Mental Math:** Count up and down by $\frac{1}{2}$'s between $-3$ and $3$.

a. $\frac{2}{3}$ of 24      **b.** $7 \times 35$      **c.** 50% of $48

**d.** $10.00 - $8.59      **e.** $0.5 \times 100$      **f.** $\frac{1600}{400}$

**g.** $8 \times 8, -1, \div 9, \times 4, +2, \div 2, \div 3, \times 5$

**Problem Solving:** Sonya, Sid, and Sharon met at the gym on Monday. Sonya goes to the gym every two days. The next day she will be at the gym is Wednesday. Sid goes to the gym every three days. The next day Sid will be at the gym is Thursday. Sharon goes to the gym every four days. She will next be at the gym on Friday. What day of the week will it be when Sonya, Sid, and Sharon are at the gym on the same day?

When a division problem has a remainder, there are several ways to write the answer. We can write the answer with a remainder. Also, we can write the answer as a mixed number or as a decimal number.

$$
4\overline{)15}^{\,3\text{ r }3} \qquad 4\overline{)15}^{\,3\frac{3}{4}} \qquad 4\overline{)15.00}^{\,3.75}
$$

Sometimes we need to round an answer up, and sometimes we need to round an answer down. The quotient of $15 \div 4$ rounds up to 4 and rounds down to 3. How a division answer should be written depends upon the question to be answered.

**Example 1** One hundred students are to be assigned to 3 classrooms. How many students should be in each class so that the numbers are as balanced as possible?

*Solution* Dividing 100 by 3 gives us $33\frac{1}{3}$ students per class, which is impractical. Assigning 33 students per class takes 99 students. We add the remaining student to one of the classes, giving that class 34 students. We write the answer **33, 33,** and **34.**

**Example 2** Movie tickets cost $4.00. Jim has $15.00. How many tickets can he buy?

*Solution* We divide 15 dollars by 4 dollars per ticket. The quotient is $3\frac{3}{4}$ tickets.

$$\frac{15 \text{ dollars}}{4 \text{ dollars per ticket}} = 3\frac{3}{4} \text{ tickets}$$

Jim cannot buy $\frac{3}{4}$ of a ticket, so we round down to the nearest whole number. Jim can buy **3 tickets.**

**Example 3** Fifteen children need a ride to the fair. Each car can transport 4 children. How many cars are needed to transport 15 children?

*Solution* We divide 15 children by 4 children per car. The quotient is $3\frac{3}{4}$ cars.

$$\frac{15 \text{ children}}{4 \text{ children per car}} = 3\frac{3}{4} \text{ cars}$$

Three cars are not enough. Four cars will be needed. One of the cars will be $\frac{3}{4}$ full. We round $3\frac{3}{4}$ cars up to **4 cars.**

**Example 4** Four workers were paid a total of $15 for cleaning a yard. If the workers divide the money equally, how much money will each worker receive?

*Solution* We divide $15 by 4 workers. This time we write the quotient as a decimal number.

$$\frac{\$15.00}{4 \text{ workers}} = \$3.75 \text{ per worker}$$

Each worker will receive **$3.75.**

**Practice\*** a. Ninety students were assigned to four classrooms as equally as possible. How many students were in each of the four classrooms?   22, 22, 23, 23

b. Movie tickets cost $6.00. Jim has $20.00. How many movie tickets can he buy?   3 tickets

**c.** Twenty-eight children need a ride to the fair. Each van can carry six children. How many vans are needed?
5 vans

**d.** Four workers were paid a total of $25.00 for cleaning a yard. If the workers divide the money equally, how much money will each worker receive?   $6.25

**Problem set 111**

**1.** Eighty students are to be assigned to 3 classrooms. How
(111) many students should be in each class so that the numbers are as balanced as possible? (List the numbers.)
26, 27, 27

**2.** Round ten and eighty-six thousandths to the nearest
(50) hundredth.   10.09

**3.** Shauna bought a sheet of 35¢ stamps at the post office
(48) for $14.00. How many stamps were in the sheet?   40

**4.** Eight sugar cubes were used to
(99) build this 2 by 2 by 2 cube. How many sugar cubes are needed to build a cube that has three sugar cubes along each edge?
27 sugar cubes

**5.** What is the standard number for the following:   5043
(92)
$$(5 \times 10^3) + (4 \times 10^1) + (3 \times 10^0)$$

**6.** You will need a centimeter ruler and an inch ruler to
(7) answer this question. Twelve inches is closest to how many centimeters? Round your answer to the nearest centimeter.   30 cm

**7.** A nickel is what percent of a dollar?   5%
(81)

B. 1 ≠ −1    **8.** The symbol ≠ means **is not equal to.** Which is true?
(84)
A.  1 ≠ 100%      B.  1 ≠ −1        C.  1 ≠ 1.0

Complete the chart to answer problems 9, 10, and 11.

|  | FRACTION | DECIMAL | PERCENT |
|---|---|---|---|
| **9.** (98) | $\frac{11}{20}$ | (a) 0.55 | (b) 55% |
| **10.** (98) | (a) $1\frac{1}{2}$ | 1.5 | (b) 150% |
| **11.** (98) | (a) $\frac{1}{100}$ | (b) 0.01 | 1% |

**12.** (58) $3\frac{2}{3} + 6\frac{5}{6}$   $10\frac{1}{2}$       **13.** (67) $6\frac{1}{4} \div 100$   $\frac{1}{16}$

**14.** (48) $0.3m = \$4.41$   $\$14.70$     **15.** (38) $6 - (0.6 - 0.06)$   5.46

**16.** (18) Andrea received the following scores from the judges:

| 6.7 | 7.6 | 6.6 | 6.7 | 6.5 | 6.7 | 6.8 |
|---|---|---|---|---|---|---|

The highest score and the lowest score are not counted. What is the average of the remaining scores? 6.7

**17.** (N.R.) Refer to problem 16 and write a question about the scores Andrea received from the judges. Then answer your question.   See student work.

**18.** (90) What is the area of this quadrilateral?   40 m²

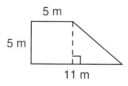

**19.** (89) What is the ratio of vertices to edges on a pyramid with a square base?   $\frac{5}{8}$

**20.** (110) Line $r$ is called a line of symmetry because it divides the equilateral triangle into two mirror images. Which other line is also a line of symmetry?   $t$

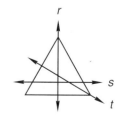

**21.** $3m + 1 = 10$   3
(107)

**22.** Write the prime factorization of 600 using exponents.
(72)   $2^3 \cdot 3 \cdot 5^2$

**23.** The candy bar has 10 sections. If
(94)   one section weighs 12 grams, what
does the whole candy bar weigh?
120 grams

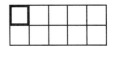

**24.** Find 7% of $0.89 by multiplying 0.07 and $0.89.
(50)   Round the product to the nearest cent.   $0.06

**25.** The probability of winning a prize in the drawing is
(91)   one in a million. What is the probability of not
winning a prize in the drawing?   $\frac{999,999}{1,000,000}$

Triangles *ABC* and *CDA* are congruent. Refer to this figure
to answer questions 26 and 27.

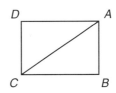

**26.** Which angle in triangle *ABC* corresponds to angle *D* in
(109)   triangle *CDA*?   angle *B*

**27.** Which transformations are needed to position
(108)   triangle *CDA* on triangle *ABC*?   rotation and possibly
translation

**28.** Ted used a compass to draw a circle with a radius of
(105)   five centimeters. What was the circumference of the
circle?   31.4 cm

**29.** $\dfrac{10}{16} = \dfrac{25}{y}$   40
(103)

**30.** Find the value of *d* in $d = rt$ when *r* is $\frac{50 \text{ mi}}{1 \text{ hr}}$ and *t* is 5 hr.
(94)   250 mi

# LESSON 112

# Finding a Given Percent of a Number

**Facts Practice:** Percents to Fractions and Decimals (Test M in Test Masters)

**Mental Math:** Count up and down by 5's between −25 and 25.

a. $\frac{3}{4}$ of 24　　　　b. 6 × 48　　　　c. 25% of $48
d. $4.98 + $2.49　　e. 0.5 ÷ 10　　f. 500 · 30
g. 11 × 4, + 1, ÷ 5, $\sqrt{\ }$, × 4, − 2, × 5, − 1, $\sqrt{\ }$

**Problem Solving:** An auditorium is shaped to have 8 seats in the first row, 10 seats in the second row, 12 seats in the third row, and so on. Altogether, how many seats are in the first 8 rows?

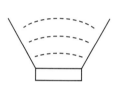

To describe part of a whole group we may use a percent, a fraction, or a decimal number. When we are asked to find a certain percent of a number, we usually change the percent to a fraction or to a decimal number before we perform the calculation.

**Example 1**　What number is 75% of 20?

**Solution**　First we translate the problem into an equation, changing the percent into either a fraction or a decimal. We use a letter for "what number," an equals sign for "is," and a multiplication sign for "of."

PERCENT TO FRACTION:　　　PERCENT TO DECIMAL:

What number is 75% of 20?　　What number is 75% of 20?

$n = \frac{3}{4} \times 20$ 　　　　　 $n = 0.75 \times 20$

We show both the fraction form and the decimal form. Often one form is easier to calculate than the other form.

$$\frac{3}{\overset{1}{\cancel{4}}} \times \overset{5}{\cancel{20}} = 15 \qquad 0.75 \times 20 = 15.00$$

We find that 75% of 20 is **15.**

**Example 2** Jamaal correctly answered 80% of the 25 questions. How many questions did he answer correctly?

*Solution* We want to find 80% of 25. We may change 80% to a fraction $\left(\frac{80}{100} = \frac{4}{5}\right)$ or to a decimal number (80% = 0.80, which is 0.8).

| **Percent to a Fraction:** | **Percent to a Decimal:** |
|---|---|
| 80% of 25 | 80% of 25 |
| $\frac{4}{5} \times 25$ | 0.8 × 25 |

Then we perform the calculations.

$$\frac{4}{\overset{}{\underset{1}{\cancel{5}}}} \times \frac{\overset{5}{\cancel{25}}}{1} = 20 \qquad 0.8 \times 25 = 20.0$$

We find that Jamaal correctly answered **20 questions.**

**Example 3** Find 6% of $12.00.

*Solution* We may change 6% to a fraction $\left(\frac{6}{100} = \frac{3}{50}\right)$ or to a decimal number (6% = 0.06). It seems easier for us to multiply $12.00 by 0.06 than by $\frac{3}{50}$, so we will use the decimal form.

$$6\% \text{ of } \$12.00$$

$$0.06 \times \$12.00 = \$0.72$$

Six percent of $12.00 is **$0.72.**

**Practice\*** **a.** What number is 10% of 350?

35

**b.** Find 25% of 48.

12

**c.** How much money is 8% of $15.00?

$1.20

**d.** Find 7% of $8.98 and round the product to the nearest cent.

$0.63

**e.** Erika correctly answered 80% of the 30 questions. How many questions did she answer correctly?

24

**Problem set 112**

**1.** Two hundred students are traveling by bus on a field
$^{(111)}$ trip. The maximum number of students allowed on
each bus is 84. How many buses are needed for the trip?
3

**2.** Which is the longest distance?    D. 3.41 m
$^{(43)}$
A. 3.14 m    B. 3.4 m    C. 3 m    D. 3.41 m

**3.** What number is 30% of 60?    18
$^{(112)}$

**4.** Complete the proportion: $\dfrac{6}{10} = \dfrac{9}{a}$   15
$^{(103)}$

**5.** Rafael correctly answered 90% of the 30 questions.
$^{(112)}$ How many questions did he answer correctly?    27

**6.** Write twenty million, five hundred ten thousand in
$^{(92)}$ expanded notation using exponents.
$(2 \times 10^7) + (5 \times 10^5) + (1 \times 10^4)$

**7.** Find 8% of \$3.65 and round the product to the
$^{(112)}$ nearest cent.    \$0.29

**8.** $\left(\dfrac{1}{2}\right)^2 + \dfrac{1}{8} \div \dfrac{1}{2}$   $\frac{1}{2}$
$^{(92)}$

Complete the chart to answer problems 9, 10, and 11.

| | FRACTION | DECIMAL | PERCENT |
|---|---|---|---|
| **9.** $^{(98)}$ | $1\frac{4}{5}$ | (a) 1.8 | (b) 180% |
| **10.** $^{(98)}$ | (a) $\frac{3}{5}$ | 0.6 | (b) 60% |
| **11.** $^{(98)}$ | (a) $\frac{1}{50}$ | (b) 0.02 | 2% |

**12.** $5\dfrac{1}{2} - m = 2\dfrac{5}{6}$   $2\frac{2}{3}$     **13.** $\dfrac{2}{3} \times 2\dfrac{1}{4} \times 2$   3
$^{(62)}$                                $^{(71)}$

**14.** 3.45 + 6.7 + 0.429       **15.** $0.05w = 8$   160
$^{(37)}$   10.579                                $^{(48)}$

**16.** All eight books in the stack are the
(15) same size. Three books weigh a
total of six pounds.

(a) How much does each book
weigh?   2 lb

(b) How much do all eight books
weigh?   16 lb

**17.** Find the volume of a rectangular prism using the
(99) formula $V = lwh$ when the length is 8 cm, the width is
5 cm, and the height is 2 cm.   80 cm³

**18.** How many millimeters is 1.2 meters? (1 m = 1000 mm)
(94)   1200 mm

**19.** What is the perimeter of this polygon?   54 mm
(102)

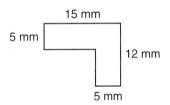

**20.** What is the area of this polygon?   110 mm²
(106)

**21.** If the pattern shown below were cut out and folded on
(66) the dotted lines, would it form a cube, a pyramid, or a
cylinder?   cube

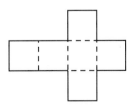

**22.** Which one of these numbers is not a composite number?
(64)
   A. 34          B. 35          C. 36          D. 37
   D. 37

**23.** Debbie wants to decorate a cylindrical wastebasket by
(105) wrapping it with wallpaper. The diameter of the wastebasket is 12 inches. The length of the wallpaper should be at least how many inches? (Round up to the next inch.)   38 in.

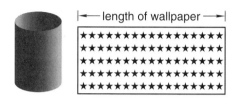

**24.** Which one of these letters has two lines of symmetry?
(110)   H

H     A     V     E

**25.** Which arrow is pointing to $-\frac{1}{2}$?   B
(17)

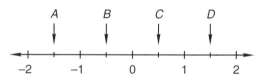

**26.** The ratio of "good guys" to "bad guys" in the movie
(104) was 2 to 3. If there were 18 "bad guys," how many "good guys" were there?   12

**27.** What are the coordinates of the point that is halfway
(74) between $(-2, -3)$ and $(6, -3)$?   $(2, -3)$

**28.** If one card is drawn from a normal deck of 52 cards,
(91) what is the probability that the card will be a red face card (jack, queen, king)?   $\frac{3}{26}$

**29.** Combine the areas of the two
(106) triangles to find the area of the trapezoid.   54 in.²

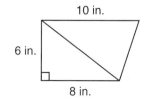

**30.** $3^2 + 2 \times 5^2 - 50 \div \sqrt{25}$   49
(92)

**LESSON
113**

Mental Math:
a. 8
b. 608
c. $3.00
d. $7.02
e. 0.05
f. 3
g. 100
Problem Solving:
   98 in.²

**Facts Practice:** Measurement Facts (Test N in Test Masters)

**Mental Math:** Count up and down by 25's between −100
   and 100.

a. $\frac{2}{5}$ of 20      b. 8 × 76      c. 10% of $30
d. $50.00 − $42.98   e. 5 ÷ 100 (Dec. Ans)   f. $\frac{1200}{400}$
g. 9 × 8, + 3, ÷ 3, $\sqrt{\ }$, × 7, + 1, $\sqrt{\ }$, × 4, + 1, × 4

**Problem Solving:** A corner is clipped off a
   square piece of paper. Find
   the area of the remaining
   shape by adding the areas
   of the two rectangles and
   one triangle.

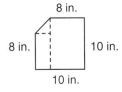

In some ratio problems a total is used as part of the calculation. Consider this problem.

*The ratio of boys to girls in a class was 5 to 4. If there were 27 students in the class, how many girls were there?*

We begin by drawing a ratio box. This time we add a third line for the total number of students. We will use the letters *b* and *g* to represent the actual count of boys and girls.

|       | Ratio | Actual Count |
|-------|-------|--------------|
| Boys  | 5     | *b*          |
| Girls | 4     | *g*          |
| Total | 9     | 27           |

In the ratio column we add the ratio numbers for boys and girls and get the ratio number 9 for the total. We were given 27 as the actual count for the total number of students. We will use two of the three rows from the ratio box to write a proportion. **We use the row we want to complete, and we use the row that is already complete.** Since we were asked to find the actual number of girls we will use the "girls" row. Since we know both "total" numbers we will also use the "total" row. Then we solve the proportion.

|  | RATIO | ACTUAL COUNT |
|---|---|---|
| Boys | 5 | $b$ |
| Girls | 4 | $g$ |
| Total | 9 | 27 |

$$\frac{4}{9} = \frac{g}{27}$$
$$9g = 4 \cdot 27$$
$$g = 12$$

We find that there were 12 girls in the class. If we had wanted to find the number of boys, we would have used the "boys" row and the "total" row to write a proportion.

**Example**    The ratio of football players to band members on the football field was 2 to 5. Altogether there were 175 football players and band members on the football field. How many football players were on the field?

*Solution*    We use the information in the problem to make a table. We include a row for the total. The ratio number for the total is 7.

|  | RATIO | ACTUAL COUNT |
|---|---|---|
| Football Players | 2 | $f$ |
| Band Members | 5 | $b$ |
| Total | 7 | 175 |

Next, we write a proportion using two rows of the table. We are asked to find the number of football players, so we use the "football players" row. We know both totals, so we use the "total" row. Then we solve the proportion.

|  | RATIO | ACTUAL COUNT |
|---|---|---|
| Football Players | 2 | $f$ |
| Band Members | 5 | $b$ |
| Total | 7 | 175 |

$$\frac{2}{7} = \frac{f}{175}$$
$$7f = 2 \cdot 175$$
$$f = 50$$

We find that there were **50 football players** on the field.

**Practice**   Solve these problems. Begin by drawing a ratio box.

**a.** Sparrows and crows perched on the wire had the ratio of 5 to 3. If the total number of sparrows and crows on the wire was 72, how many were crows?   27

**b.** Raisins and nuts were mixed by weight in a ratio of 2 to 3. If 60 ounces of mix were prepared, how many ounces of raisins were used?   24 oz

**Problem set 113**

**1.** The winning pitcher faced 32 batters during the game.
*(111)* If the opposing team had only 9 players, how many of those players did the pitcher face 4 times?   5 players

**2.** The ratio of girls to boys in the class was 4 to 3. If there
*(113)* were 28 students in the class, how many girls were there? Make a ratio box for the problem.   16 girls

**3.** What number is 75% of 24?   18
*(112)*

**4.** Six of the 18 lights were on. What is the ratio of lights
*(82)* on to lights off?   $\frac{1}{2}$

**5.** Write 5300 in expanded notation using exponents.
*(32)* $(5 \times 10^3) + (3 \times 10^2)$

**6.** Write the decimal number twelve and twenty-four
*(35)* thousandths.   12.024

**7.** Find 6% of $5.65 and round the product to the
*(112)* nearest cent.   $0.34

**8.** Arrange in order from least to greatest:   $-2, -\frac{1}{2}, 0, 0.2, \frac{1}{2}$
*(88)*

$$0.2, -2, \frac{1}{2}, 0, -\frac{1}{2}$$

Complete the chart to answer problems 9, 10, and 11.

| | FRACTION | DECIMAL | PERCENT |
|---|---|---|---|
| **9.** (98) | $\frac{3}{25}$ | (a) 0.12 | (b) 12% |
| **10.** (98) | (a) $\frac{7}{20}$ | 0.35 | (b) 35% |
| **11.** (98) | (a) $\frac{1}{25}$ | (b) 0.04 | 4% |

**12.** (62) $\left(3\frac{1}{2} + 2\frac{1}{3}\right) - 1\frac{3}{4}$   $4\frac{1}{12}$   **13.** (67) $1\frac{1}{3} \div 2\frac{2}{3}$   $\frac{1}{2}$

**14.** (92) $(0.1)^2 + 0.1 \div 0.01 - \sqrt{1}$   9.01

**15.** (44) $(1.2 - 0.24) \div 3$   0.32

**16.** (72) Write the prime factorization of 216 using exponents.
$2^3 \cdot 3^3$

**17.** (94) How many millimeters is 12.5 cm? (1 cm = 10 mm)
125 mm

**18.** (106) What is the area of this hexagon?
1700 mm²

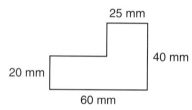

**19.** (102) What is the perimeter of this hexagon?   200 mm

**20.** (99) What is the volume of a cube with edges 10 cm long?
1000 cm³

**21.** (110) A line of symmetry divides a figure into 2 mirror images.
Which line is **not** a line of symmetry in this figure?   r

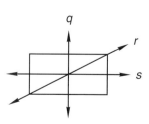

**22.** Make a list of the prime numbers that are even.    2
(61)

**23.** The money was separated into 10
(104) equal parts. The money in 4 of the
parts totaled $12. How much
money was in all 10 parts?
$30.00

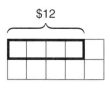

**24.** How much money is 40% of $30.00?    $12.00
(112)

**25.** The center ring at the circus had a diameter of 100
(105) feet. What was the circumference of the center ring?
314 ft

**26.** Line *AC* is a line of symmetry
(108) dividing quadrilateral *ABCD* into
two congruent triangles. Which
transformation(s) would position
one triangle on the other triangle?
reflection

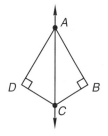

**27.** The ratio of Whigs to Tories was 3 to 4. If the total
(113) number of Whigs and Tories was 84, then how many
Tories were there?    48 Tories

**28.** Jamie's five quiz scores were 10, 7, 8, 9, and 10.
(18)
  (a) Find her average score to one decimal place.    8.8

  (b) If the scores were arranged from highest to lowest,
      what would be her middle score?    9

**29.** What is the probability of rolling an eight with one roll
(91) of a single number cube?    0

**30.** Find a box in the classroom or at home and measure
(99) the length, width, and height of the box. Round each
measure to the nearest inch. Sketch a diagram of the
box on your paper and show the measurements. Then
calculate the approximate volume of the box in cubic
inches.    See student work.

# LESSON 114

# Mean, Median, Mode, and Range

Mental Math:
a. 12
b. 486
c. $300
d. $9.59
e. 1.5
f. 30,000
g. 90
Problem Solving:
   68°F

**Facts Practice:** Percents to Fractions and Decimals (Test M· in Test Masters)

**Mental Math:** Count up and down by 10's between −50 and 50.

   **a.** $\frac{3}{5}$ of 20        **b.** 9 × 54        **c.** 50% of $600

   **d.** $3.60 + $5.99      **e.** 0.015 × 100     **f.** 600 · 50

   **g.** 12 × 2, + 1, × 2, − 1, $\sqrt{\phantom{x}}$ , × 4, − 1, ÷ 3, × 10

**Problem Solving:** Here is a formula that is used to convert degrees Celsius (°C) to degrees Fahrenheit (°F). Use the formula to find the Fahrenheit temperature that is equivalent to 20° Celsius.

$$°F = 1.8°C + 32$$

The words **mean, median, mode,** and **range** are terms used to describe a set of data such as a collection of test scores.

   Mean: the average of the numbers

   Median: the middle number when the data are arranged in order

   Mode: the most frequently occurring number

   Range: the difference between the greatest and least of the numbers

**Example** The following scores were made by the students in the class. Find the mean, median, mode, and range of the scores.

100, 100, 100, 95, 95, 95, 95, 90, 90,
90, 85, 85, 80, 80, 80, 75, 70, 70

**Solution** The mean is the average of the scores. There are 18 scores. We add the scores and divide by 18. Using a calculator is helpful. We find that the sum is 1575, so the **mean is 87.5.**

$$\frac{1575}{18} = 87.5$$

The median is the middle score when the scores are arranged in order. The scores are already ordered. When there are an even number of numbers, there are two middle scores. When there are two middle scores, the median is the average of the two middle scores. Since the two middle scores are 90 and 90, their average is 90, and the **median is 90.**

100, 100, 100, 95, 95, 95, 95, 90, **90,**
**90,** 85, 85, 80, 80, 80, 75, 70, 70

The mode is the score that occurs most frequently. Since 95 appears four times and no other score occurs more than three times, the **mode is 95.**

The range is the difference between the highest and lowest scores. The test scores range from a high of 100 to a low of 70. So the **range is 30** points.

$$100 - 70 = 30$$

**Practice\***   Find the mean, median, mode, and range for each set of data:

**a.** Quiz scores: 10, 9, 7, 8, 10, 6, 9, 7, 9, 10, 9, 8
mean, 8.5; median, 9; mode, 9; range, 4

**b.** Weights of puppies in a litter (in ounces):

6, 8, 7, 8, 5, 8, 6, 8
mean, 7oz; median, 7.5 oz; mode, 8 oz; range, 3 oz

**Problem set 114**

**1.** Eight people will share one dozen sandwiches
$^{(111)}$ equally. How many sandwiches should each person receive? (The sandwiches can be broken into pieces as required.)   $1\frac{1}{2}$ sandwiches

**2.** It is $\frac{3}{4}$ of a mile from Mark's house to school. How far
$^{(65)}$ would Mark walk going to school and back for 5 days?
$7\frac{1}{2}$ mi

**3.** Eighty percent of the 30 students passed the test. How
$^{(112)}$ many students passed the test?   24 students

**4.** Complete the proportion: $\dfrac{12}{25} = \dfrac{y}{100}$   48
$^{(103)}$

**5.** Write the standard number for $(6 \times 10^4) + (2 \times 10^2)$.
(32)  60,200

**6.** Find 8% of $4.65 and round the answer to the
(112) nearest cent.    $0.37

**7.** In three tries, John jumped 4.39 meters, 4.2 meters,
(18) and 4.07 meters. What was the average length of
John's jumps?    4.22 m

**8.** What is the chance a tossed quarter will land heads up?
(91)  50%

Complete the chart to answer problems 9, 10, and 11.

|  | FRACTION | DECIMAL | PERCENT |
|---|---|---|---|
| **9.**<br>(98) | $2\frac{1}{4}$ | (a) 2.25 | (b) 225% |
| **10.**<br>(98) | (a) $\frac{2}{25}$ | 0.08 | (b) 8% |
| **11.**<br>(98) | (a) $\frac{1}{20}$ | (b) 0.05 | 5% |

**12.** $3\frac{1}{2} + 6\frac{2}{3} + 2\frac{5}{6}$   13      **13.** $7\frac{1}{2} \div 1\frac{1}{2}$   5
(59)                                              (67)

**14.** $0.15 \times (3.2 + 12)$      **15.** $(12 - 3.6) \div 0.12$   70
(39)  2.28                        (48)

**16.** Write the prime factorization of 108 using exponents.
(72)  $2^2 \cdot 3^3$

**17.** Ten kilometers is how many meters? (1 km = 1000 m)
(94)  10,000 m

**18.** What is the area of this parallelogram?    72 m²
(79)

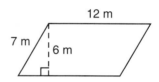

12 m
7 m
6 m

**19.** A pyramid with a triangular base has how many faces?
(89)  4

**20.** A straight angle measures 180
(107) degrees. How many degrees is $\frac{1}{4}$ of
a straight angle?    45°

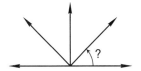

**21.** What is the greatest common factor (GCF) of 40 and 100?
(20)    20

**22.** The boys were divided into 8
(104) equal teams. Fourteen boys made
2 teams. How many boys were
there in all?    56 boys

14

**23.** Draw a triangle that has one obtuse angle.
(107)

**24.** This table shows the value of $2n - 1$ when $n$ is 5, 4,
(107) and 2. For example, $2n - 1$ is 9 when $n$ is 5
because $2(5) - 1$ is 9. What number is missing in the
table?    5

| $n$ | 5 | 4 | 3 | 2 |
|-----|---|---|---|---|
| $2n - 1$ | 9 | 7 | ? | 3 |

**25.** To what decimal number is the arrow pointing?    4.4
(49)

**26.** The radius of this circle is 10 mm.
(97) What is the area of the square?
100 mm²

**27.** Two fifths of the 30 students are boys. How many boys
(76) are there?    12 boys

**28.** The coordinates of three vertices of a rectangle are
(74) (−1, 3), (−1, −3), and (2, −3). What is the perimeter of
the rectangle?    18 units

**29.** If the ratio of boys to girls was 2 to 3, and if there were
(113) 30 students, then how many girls were there?    18 girls

**30.** Find the mean, median, mode, and range of these
(114) ten scores.    mean, 88; median, 90; mode, 90; range, 25

100, 90, 85, 90, 100, 90, 80, 75, 80, 90

## LESSON 115

## Adding and Subtracting Mixed Measures • Multiplying by Powers of Ten

**Mental Math:**
a. 12
b. 152
c. $50.00
d. $90.50
e. 0.012
f. 4
g. 0

**Problem Solving:**

$$\begin{array}{r} 142{,}857 \\ \times \qquad 7 \\ \hline 999{,}999 \end{array}$$

---

**Facts Practice:** Measurement Facts (Test N in Test Masters)

**Mental Math:** Count up and down by $\frac{1}{8}$'s between $\frac{1}{8}$ and 2.

**a.** $\frac{3}{10}$ of 40        **b.** $4 \times 38$        **c.** 25% of $200
**d.** $100.00 − $9.50      **e.** $0.12 \div 10$      **f.** $\frac{2000}{500}$
**g.** $6 \times 8, + 2, \times 2, - 1, \div 3, - 1, \div 4, + 2, \div 10, - 1$

**Problem Solving:** Copy this problem and fill in the missing digits.

$$\begin{array}{r} \_\,\_\,\_{,}\_\,\_\,\_ \\ \times \qquad 7 \\ \hline 9\,9\,9{,}9\,9\,9 \end{array}$$

---

**Adding and subtracting mixed measures**

Measurements that include more than one unit of measurement are mixed measures. If we say that a movie is an hour and 40 minutes long, we have used a mixed measure that includes hours and minutes. When adding and subtracting mixed measures, we may need to convert from one unit to another unit.

**Example 1**

1 hr 40 min
+ 1 hr 50 min

**Solution**   We add 40 minutes and 50 minutes, and their sum equals 90 minutes. Since 60 minutes equals one hour, 90 minutes equals one hour and 30 minutes.

1 hr 40 min
+ 1 hr 50 min
90 min   (which is 1 hr, 30 min)

We change 90 minutes to one hour and 30 minutes. We write 30 minutes in the minutes column and add the one hour to the hour column. Then we add the hours.

$$\overset{1}{1} \text{ hr } 40 \text{ min}$$
$$+ \ 1 \text{ hr } 50 \text{ min}$$
$$\overline{3 \text{ hr } \underset{30}{\cancel{90}} \text{ min}}$$

The sum is **3 hours and 30 minutes.**

Example 2     6 ft 5 in.
       − 4 ft 8 in.

Solution    Before we can subtract inches, we rename 6 feet as 5 feet plus 12 inches. The 12 inches combine with the 5 inches to make 17 inches. Then we subtract.

$$\overset{5}{\cancel{6}} \text{ ft } \overset{17}{\cancel{5}} \text{ in.}$$
$$- \ 4 \text{ ft } 8 \text{ in.}$$
$$\overline{1 \text{ ft } 9 \text{ in.}}$$

The difference is **1 foot and 9 inches.**

**Multiplying by powers of ten**   We can multiply by powers of ten very easily. Multiplying by powers of ten does not change the digits, only the place value of the digits. We can change the place value by moving the decimal point the number of places shown by the exponent. To write $1.2 \times 10^3$ in standard notation, we simply move the decimal point three places to the right and fill the empty places with zero.

$$1.2 \times 10^3 = 1.200 = 1200$$

Example 3   Write $6.2 \times 10^2$ in standard notation.

Solution    To multiply by a power of ten, simply move the decimal point the number of places shown by the exponent. In this case, we move the decimal point two places to the right.

$$6.2 \times 10^2 = \mathbf{620}$$

Sometimes powers of ten are named with words instead of numbers. For example, we might read that there are 5.2 million people living in Hong Kong. The number 5.2 million means 5.2 × 1,000,000. We can write this number by shifting the decimal point six places to the right, which gives us 5,200,000.

**Example 4**    Write $\frac{1}{2}$ billion in standard notation.

**Solution**    The expression $\frac{1}{2}$ billion means $\frac{1}{2}$ of one billion. First we write $\frac{1}{2}$ as the decimal number 0.5. Then we multiply by one billion, which shifts the decimal point nine places.

$$\frac{1}{2} \text{ billion}$$

$$0.5 \times 1,000,000,000 = \mathbf{500,000,000}$$

**Practice\***    **a.**
```
  6 ft 5 in.
+ 4 ft 8 in.
-----------
 11 ft 1 in.
```

**b.**
```
  3 hr 15 min
- 1 hr 40 min
-------------
  1 hr 35 min
```

Write the standard notation for each of the following numbers. Change fractions and mixed numbers to decimal numbers before multiplying.

**c.** $1.2 \times 10^4$    12,000

**d.** 1.5 million    1,500,000

**e.** $2\frac{1}{2}$ billion    2,500,000,000

**f.** $\frac{1}{4}$ million    250,000

**Problem set 115**    **1.** For cleaning the yard four teenagers were paid a total of $35.00. If they divide the money equally, how much money will each teenager receive?    $8.75
*(111)*

**2.** Which of the following is the best estimate of the length of a bicycle?    B. 2 m
*(7)*

A.  1 m        B.  2 m        C.  6 m        D.  36 m

**3.** If the chance of rain is 80%, what is the chance that it
(91) will not rain?    20%

**4.** The team's won-lost ratio was 5 to 3. If the team
(113) played 120 games and did not tie any games, then how
many games did the team win?    75 games

**5.** Write $(6 \times 10^3) + (2 \times 10^1) + (4 \times 10^0)$ as a standard
(92) numeral.    6024

**6.** Write $4.5 \times 10^6$ as a standard numeral.    4,500,000
(115)

**7.** Divide $2.00 by 3 and round the quotient to the
(50) nearest cent.    $0.67

8. A variety of methods are possible. One method is to convert each fraction to a decimal number, order the decimal numbers, and convert the decimal numbers back to fractions.

**8.** Describe a method for arranging these fractions from
(75) least to greatest:

$$\frac{3}{4}, \frac{3}{5}, \frac{4}{5}$$

Complete the chart to answer problems 9, 10, and 11.

| | FRACTION | DECIMAL | PERCENT |
|---|---|---|---|
| **9.** (98) | $\frac{1}{50}$ | (a) 0.02 | (b) 2% |
| **10.** (98) | (a) $1\frac{3}{4}$ | 1.75 | (b) 175% |
| **11.** (98) | (a) $\frac{1}{4}$ | (b) 0.25 | 25% |

**12.** $12\frac{1}{4}$ in. $- 3\frac{5}{8}$ in.  $8\frac{5}{8}$ in.    **13.** $3\frac{1}{3}$ ft $\times 2\frac{1}{4}$ ft  $7\frac{1}{2}$ ft²
(62)                                                              (65)

**14.** $12 + 7.65 + 15.8$   35.45    **15.** 0.6 m $\times$ 0.5 m   0.3 m²
(38)                                    (39)

**16.** $5^2 + 2^5$   57
(92)

**17.** Find the area of the trapezoid by
(106) combining the area of the triangle
and the area of the rectangle.
34 ft²

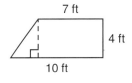

**18.** 2 feet 3 inches − 1 foot 9 inches    6 in.
(115)

**19.** Which line in this figure is not a line of symmetry?    g
(110)

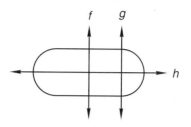

**20.** How many cubes one centimeter
(99)   on each edge would be needed to
fill this box?    30 cubes

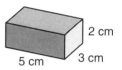

**21.** John worked for three days and earned $150. At that
(104)  rate, how much would John earn in ten days?    $500

**22.** Seventy is the product of which three prime numbers?
(64)   2 · 5 · 7

**23.** Saturn is about 900 million miles from the sun. Write
(12)   that number in standard notation.    900,000,000

**24.** To which number on the scale is the arrow pointing?
(10)   40

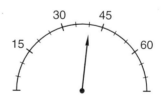

**25.** The ratio of quarters to dimes in the soda machine was
(104)  5 to 8. If there were 120 quarters, how many dimes
were there?    192 dimes

**26.** The coordinates of the three vertices of a triangle are
(87)   (0, 0), (0, 4), and (4, 4). What is the area of the triangle?
8 sq. units

The following list shows the ages of the children attending a party. Use this information to answer questions 27 and 28.

8, 9, 8, 8, 7, 9, 12, 12, 11, 16

**27.** What was the median age of the children attending
(114) the party?   9

**28.** What was the mean age of the children at the party?
(114)   10

**29.** The diameter of a playground ball
(105) is 10 inches. What is the circumference of the ball?   31.4 in.

**30.** Find the value of $A$ in $A = s^2$
(92) when $s$ is 10 m.   100 m²

|←——10 in.——→|

# LESSON
# 116

Mental Math:
a. 28
b. 2880
c. $50.00
d. $5.64
e. 125
f. 36,000
g. 10
Problem Solving:
   17,576,000

# Unit Multipliers

**Facts Practice:** Percents to Fractions and Decimals (Test M in Test Masters)

**Mental Math:** Count by $\frac{1}{4}$'s from −1 to 1.

   **a.** $\frac{7}{10}$ of 40        **b.** 6 × 480        **c.** 10% of $500
   **d.** $4.99 + 65¢      **e.** 0.125 × 1000    **f.** 40 · 900
   **g.** 5 × 7, + 1, ÷ 4, $\sqrt{\;}$, × 7, − 1, × 3, − 10, × 2, $\sqrt{\;}$

**Problem Solving:** How many different license plates can be made if the pattern is three letters followed by three digits, and if all letter and digit combinations are used?

A **unit multiplier** is a fraction equal to one written with two different units of measure. Recall that when the numerator and denominator of a fraction are equal (and are not equal to zero) the fraction equals one. Since one foot equals 12 inches, we can form two unit multipliers using one foot and 12 inches.

$$\frac{1 \text{ ft}}{12 \text{ in.}} \qquad \frac{12 \text{ in.}}{1 \text{ ft}}$$

Each of these fractions equals one because the numerator and denominator of each fraction are equal.

We may use unit multipliers to help us convert from one unit of measure to another. If we want to convert 60 inches to feet, we may multiply 60 inches and the unit multiplier $\frac{1\text{ ft}}{12\text{ in.}}$.

$$\frac{\overset{5}{\cancel{60}}\text{ in.}}{1} \times \frac{1\text{ ft}}{\underset{1}{\cancel{12}}\text{ in.}} = 5\text{ ft}$$

**Example 1** (a) Write two unit multipliers using these equivalent measures: 3 feet equals 1 yard.

(b) Which unit multiplier would you use to convert 30 yards to feet?

**Solution** (a) We write two fractions, reversing the positions of the terms.

$$\frac{\textbf{3 ft}}{\textbf{1 yd}} \qquad \frac{\textbf{1 yd}}{\textbf{3 ft}}$$

(b) The units we change **from** are in the denominator; the units we change **to** are in the numerator. To convert 30 yards to feet, we use the unit multiplier that has 1 yard as the denominator and 3 feet as the numerator.

$$\frac{\textbf{30 yd}}{\textbf{1}} \times \frac{\textbf{3 ft}}{\textbf{1 yd}}$$

Here we show the work. Notice that yards "cancel" and the product is in feet.

$$\frac{30\text{ }\cancel{\text{yd}}}{1} \times \frac{3\text{ ft}}{1\text{ }\cancel{\text{yd}}} = 90\text{ ft}$$

**Example 2** Convert 30 feet to yards using a unit multiplier. (1 yd = 3 ft)

**Solution** We can form two unit multipliers.

$$\frac{1\text{ yd}}{3\text{ ft}} \quad \text{and} \quad \frac{3\text{ ft}}{1\text{ yd}}$$

We are asked to convert from feet to yards, so we use the unit multiplier that has feet in the denominator and yards in the numerator.

$$\frac{\overset{10}{\cancel{30}} \text{ ft}}{1} \times \frac{1 \text{ yd}}{\cancel{3} \text{ ft}} = 10 \text{ yd}$$

Thirty feet converts to **10 yards.**

**Practice**

**a.** Write two unit multipliers for these equivalent measures:
$\frac{1\,\text{gal}}{4\,\text{qt}}, \frac{4\,\text{qt}}{1\,\text{gal}}$
$\qquad$ 1 gal = 4 qt

**b.** Which unit multiplier from problem (a) would you use to convert twelve gallons to quarts?   $\frac{4\,\text{qt}}{1\,\text{gal}}$

**c.** Write two unit multipliers for these equivalent measures:
$\frac{1\,\text{m}}{100\,\text{cm}}, \frac{100\,\text{cm}}{1\,\text{m}}$
$\qquad$ 1 m = 100 cm

**d.** Which unit multiplier in problem (c) would you use to convert 200 cm to meters?   $\frac{1\,\text{m}}{100\,\text{cm}}$

$12\,\text{qt} \times \frac{1\,\text{gal}}{4\,\text{qt}} = 3\,\text{gal}$ **e.** Use a unit multiplier to convert 12 quarts to gallons.

**f.** Use a unit multiplier to convert 200 meters to centimeters.   $200\,\text{m} \times \frac{100\,\text{cm}}{1\,\text{m}} = 20{,}000\,\text{cm}$

**g.** Use a unit multiplier to convert 60 feet to yards. (1 yd = 3 ft)   $60\,\text{ft} \times \frac{1\,\text{yd}}{3\,\text{ft}} = 20\,\text{yd}$

**Problem set 116**

**1.** Tickets to the matinee are $3 each. How many tickets
(111) can Jan buy with $20?   6 tickets

**2.** Maria ran four laps of the track at an even pace. If it
(94) took 6 minutes to run the first three laps, how long did it take to run all four laps?   8 min

**3.** Fifteen of the 25 members played. What fraction of the
(76) members did not play?   $\frac{2}{5}$

**4.** Two fifths of the thirty students in the class are boys.
(76) How many girls are in the class?   18 girls

**5.** Which digit in 94,763,581 is in the ten-thousands' place?
(12)   6

**6.** (a) Write two unit multipliers for these equivalent
(116)       measures:

$\frac{1 \text{ gal}}{4 \text{ qt}}, \frac{4 \text{ qt}}{1 \text{ gal}}$        1 gallon = 4 quarts

(b) Which of the two unit multipliers would you use
to convert 8 gallons to quarts?   $\frac{4 \text{ qt}}{1 \text{ gal}}$

**7.** Estimate the sum of $36.43, $41.92, and $26.70 to the
(50) nearest dollar.   $105.00

**8.** $4 + 4^2 \div \sqrt{4} - \frac{4}{4}$   11
(92)

Complete the chart to answer problems 9, 10, and 11.

|  | FRACTION | DECIMAL | PERCENT |
|---|---|---|---|
| **9.**<br>(98) | $\frac{1}{8}$ | (a) 0.125 | (b) 12.5% |
| **10.**<br>(98) | (a) $\frac{9}{10}$ | 0.9 | (b) 90% |
| **11.**<br>(98) | (a) $\frac{3}{5}$ | (b) 0.6 | 60% |

**12.** $3\frac{1}{4}$ in. + $2\frac{1}{2}$ in. + $4\frac{5}{8}$ in.   $10\frac{3}{8}$ in.
(59)

**13.** $3.25 \div \frac{2}{3}$ (fraction answer)   $4\frac{7}{8}$
(85)

**14.** $m + 1.375 = 5$   3.625    **15.** Solve: $\frac{3}{2} = \frac{18}{m}$   12
(42)                                      (103)

**16.** $\left(\frac{2}{3}\right)^3$   $\frac{8}{27}$
(92)

**17.** If a car travels 6 hours at an average speed of 55 miles
(94) per hour, how far will it travel?    330 mi

$$\frac{6 \text{ hours}}{1} \times \frac{55 \text{ miles}}{1 \text{ hour}}$$

**18.** What is the area of this polygon?    138 m²
(106)

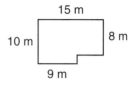

**19.** What is the perimeter of this polygon?    50 m
(102)

**20.** $5w - 1 = 49$    10
(107)

**21.** Which two lines in this figure
(68) appear to be parallel?    r and q

**22.** Which two lines in this figure
(68) appear to be perpendicular?
s and t

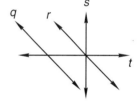

**23.** Think of two different prime numbers and write them
(30) on your paper. Then find the least common multiple
(LCM) of the two prime numbers.    Selected prime numbers
will differ. The LCM will be the product of the prime numbers.

**24.** Write $1.5 \times 10^6$ as a standard number.    1,500,000
(115)

**25.** A classroom that is 30 feet long, 30 feet wide, and 10 feet
(99) high has a volume of how many cubic feet?
9000 ft³

$8 \text{ qt} \cdot \frac{1 \text{ gal}}{4 \text{ qt}} = 2 \text{ gal}$    **26.** Convert 8 quarts to gallons using a unit multiplier.
(116)

**27.** A circle was drawn on a coordinate plane. The coordinates
(97) of the center of the circle were (1, 1). One point on the
circle was (1, −3). What was the diameter of the circle?
8 units

**28.** On the last test the range of scores was 35 points. If the
(114) highest score was 95, what was the lowest score?
60

**29.**    2 hr 15 min          **30.**    4 ft 3 in.
(115) + 3 hr 50 min          (115) − 2 ft 9 in.
───────────              ───────────
6 hr  5 min                  1 ft 6 in.

# LESSON
# 117

# Mass and Weight

**Mental Math:**
a. 25
b. 2135
c. $2.50
d. $11.02
e. 0.096
f. 6
g. 3
**Problem Solving:**
+12; +16

---

**Facts Practice:** 28 Fractions to Simplify (Test I in Test Masters)

**Mental Math:** Count down by 12's from 48 to −48.

   **a.** $\frac{5}{6}$ of 30          **b.** 7 × 305        **c.** 50% of $5.00
   **d.** $20.00 − $8.98     **e.** 9.6 ÷ 100      **f.** $\frac{3000}{500}$
   **g.** 8 × 10, + 1, $\sqrt{\phantom{x}}$ , × 4, $\sqrt{\phantom{x}}$ , × 3, ÷ 2, $\sqrt{\phantom{x}}$

**Problem Solving:** Celina used 4 toothpicks to make a square. Then she used 8 more toothpicks to make a two-by-two square. How many more toothpicks will she need to make a three-by-three square? After making a three-by-three square, predict how many more toothpicks she would need to make a four-by-four square.

←4

+8

---

Physical objects are composed of matter. The amount of matter in an object is its **mass.** In the metric system we measure the mass of objects in milligrams (mg), grams (g), and kilograms (kg).

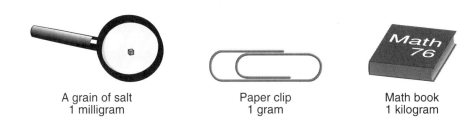

A grain of salt            Paper clip            Math book
1 milligram              1 gram            1 kilogram

1000 mg = 1 g        1000 g = 1 kg

The mass of a particular object is the same on the earth, on the moon, or in orbit. In other words, the mass of an object does not change with changes in the force of gravity. However, the weight of an object does change with changes in the force of gravity.

    When astronauts are in orbit, forces are balanced and the astronauts experience weightlessness. An astronaut who weighs 154 pounds on earth weighs zero pounds in weightless conditions. Although the weight of the astronaut has changed, his or her mass has not changed.

In the U.S. Customary system we measure the weight of objects in ounces (oz), pounds (lb), and tons (t). On earth an object with a mass of one kilogram would weigh about 2.2 pounds.

An envelope and letter
1 ounce

A shoe
1 pound

A small car
1 ton

16 ounces = 1 pound        2000 pounds = 1 ton

**Example 1** Two kilograms is how many grams?

*Solution* One kilogram is 1000 grams. So two kilograms are **2000 grams.**

**Example 2**      9 lb 10 oz
                  − 7 lb 12 oz

*Solution* Before we can subtract ounces, we convert 9 pounds to 8 pounds plus 16 ounces. We combine the 16 ounces and the 10 ounces and get 26 ounces. Then we can subtract.

$$\begin{array}{r} \overset{8}{\cancel{9}} \text{ lb } \overset{26}{\cancel{10}} \text{ oz} \\ - 7 \text{ lb } 12 \text{ oz} \\ \hline 1 \text{ lb } 14 \text{ oz} \end{array}$$

The difference is **1 pound and 14 ounces.**

**Practice**   **a.** Half of a kilogram is how many grams?   500 g

2000 g   **b.** The mass of a liter of water is one kilogram. The mass of two liters of beverage is about how many grams?

**c.**    5 lb 10 oz
    + 1 lb  9 oz
    ―――――――
      7 lb 3 oz

**d.**    9 lb  8 oz
    − 6 lb 10 oz
    ―――――――
      2 lb 14 oz

**e.** A half-ton pickup truck can haul a half-ton load. Half of a ton is how many pounds?    1000 lb

**Problem set
117**

**1.** The outside walls of Mike's house have a surface area
(111) of 1500 square feet. He wants to paint the walls with a paint that covers 400 square feet per gallon. How many 1-gallon cans of paint should he buy?    4 cans

**2.** At the price of 4 pounds for a dollar, how much
(94) money would 10 pounds cost?    $2.50

**3.** How far will a mallard duck fly in 12 hours if it flies at
(94) a rate of 24 miles per hour?    288 mi

$$\frac{12 \text{ hr}}{1} \times \frac{24 \text{ mi}}{1 \text{ hr}}$$

**4.** If the arrow is spun, what is the
(91) probability that it will stop on an even number?    $\frac{1}{3}$

**5.** Write 6010 in expanded notation using exponents.
(72) $(6 \times 10^3) + (1 \times 10^1)$

**6.** In 1990 the population of Georgia was about 6.5
(115) million. Write the population as a standard number.
6,500,000

**7.** Russel sorted through his serving of mixed vegetables
(82) and counted 27 peas, 12 diced carrots, 15 kernels of corn, and 4 lima beans. What was the ratio of peas to kernels of corn in Russel's serving?    $\frac{9}{5}$

**8.** The mixed number $8\frac{5}{9}$ is closest to what whole number?
(17) 9

Complete the chart to answer problems 9, 10, and 11.

| | FRACTION | DECIMAL | PERCENT |
|---|---|---|---|
| **9.** (98) | $\frac{7}{8}$ | (a) 0.875 | (b) 87.5% |
| **10.** (98) | (a) $\frac{12}{25}$ | 0.48 | (b) 48% |
| **11.** (98) | (a) $1\frac{1}{4}$ | (b) 1.25 | 125% |

**12.** (62) $3\frac{1}{3} - 2\frac{1}{2}$   $\frac{5}{6}$

**13.** (67) $16\frac{2}{3} \div 100$   $\frac{1}{6}$

**14.** (112) 16% of $3.75   $0.60

**15.** (92) $\dfrac{\sqrt{100}}{\sqrt{25}}$   2

**16.** (93) Write $\frac{1}{6}$ as a percent by multiplying $\frac{1}{6}$ by 100%.   $16\frac{2}{3}\%$

**17.** (31) A 1-inch by 1-inch square is divided into thirds in one dimension and into fourths in the other dimension. What is the area of the shaded part of the square?   $\frac{1}{12}$ in.²

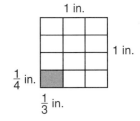

**18.** (110) Which lines are lines of symmetry for the square?   *r, s,* and *t* are all lines of symmetry

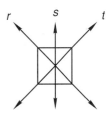

**19.** (112) Find 5% of $2.89 and round the product to the nearest cent.   $0.14

**20.** (92) $\sqrt{100} + 3 \times 2^3 - 10^2 \div \sqrt{16}$   9

**21.** Which angle appears to have a measure of 45°?   *C*
(107)

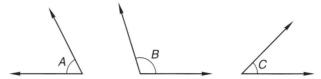

**22.** Each small block in this rectangular
(99)   prism is one cubic inch. What is the
       volume of the rectangular prism?
       54 in.³

**23.** Write the standard number for 2.1 × 10⁶.   2,100,000
(115)

**24.** This map shows that Belmond and Clear Lake are
(94)   about how many miles apart?   about 30 mi

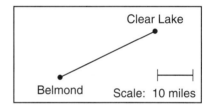

This table shows the scores earned by the 19 students in the
class. Use this information to answer questions 25–27.

**25.** What was the median score?
(114)   23

**26.** What was the mode of the scores?
(114)   22

**27.** Write a question that refers to the
(N.R.)  scores in the table and answer the
        question.   See student work.

**Scores on Test A**

| Number Correct | Number of scores |
|---|---|
| 25 | 3 |
| 24 | 4 |
| 23 | 4 |
| 22 | 5 |
| 21 | 2 |
| 20 | 1 |

**28.** (a) Write two unit multipliers for these equivalent
(117)     measures: 1 lb = 16 oz.   $\frac{1\ lb}{16\ oz}, \frac{16\ oz}{1\ lb}$

      (b) Which unit multiplier would you use to convert
          48 ounces to pounds?   $\frac{1\ lb}{16\ oz}$

**29.**     5 lb 8 oz
(117)    + 3 lb 9 oz
        ─────────────
          9 lb 1 oz

**30.** Half a gram of vitamin C is how many milligrams?
(117)   500 mg

# LESSON
# 118

# **Finding a Percent**

**Mental Math:**
a. 20
b. 2880
c. $2.50
d. $4.73
e. 250
f. 40,000
g. 100
**Problem Solving:**
    98 in.²

**Facts Practice:** Measurement Facts (Test N in Test Masters)

**Mental Math:** Count up by $\frac{1}{16}$'s from $\frac{1}{16}$ and 1.

   **a.** $\frac{2}{3}$ of 30         **b.** 8 × 360        **c.** 25% of $10.00
   **d.** $3.98 + 75¢      **e.** 2.5 × 100       **f.** 200 · 200
   **g.** 7 × 7, + 1, × 2, ÷ 4, √ , × 7, + 1, ÷ 4, × 10, + 10

**Problem Solving:** A corner is clipped off a square piece of paper. Find the area of the remaining shape by subtracting the area of the triangle from the area of the original.

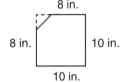

We may choose to name part of a group as a fraction or as a percent.

> One half of this group is shaded.
>
> Fifty percent of this group is shaded.

To name part of a whole or part of a group as a percent, we first name the part as a fraction. Then we convert the fraction to a percent.

**Example 1**  Six of the ten circles are shaded. Six is what percent of ten?

*Solution*  First we find the fraction. Six of ten is $\frac{6}{10}$, which equals $\frac{3}{5}$. Then we convert the fraction to a percent by multiplying by 100%.

$$\frac{6}{\overset{}{\underset{1}{\cancel{10}}}} \times \frac{\overset{10}{\cancel{100\%}}}{1} = \mathbf{60\%}$$

**Example 2**  Six of the nine circles are shaded. Six is what percent of nine?

*Solution*    First we write six of nine as the fraction $\frac{6}{9}$, or $\frac{2}{3}$. Then we convert the fraction to a percent.

$$\frac{2}{3} \times \frac{100\%}{1} = \frac{200\%}{3}$$

We divide 200% by 3 and write the remainder as a fraction.

$$\frac{200\%}{3} = 66\frac{2}{3}\%$$

   In Example 1 we converted the unreduced fraction to a percent. In Example 2 we converted the reduced fraction to a percent. Either the reduced or unreduced form of the fraction may be used. The equivalent percent is the same either way.

**Example 3**    Twelve of the thirty students in the class are boys.

(a) Boys are what percent of the class?

(b) Girls are what percent of the class?

*Solution*    (a) First we find the fraction of the class that is boys. Twelve of 30 is $\frac{12}{30}$, or $\frac{2}{5}$. Now we convert $\frac{2}{5}$ to a percent.

$$\frac{2}{\cancel{5}_{1}} \times \frac{\overset{20}{\cancel{100}}\%}{1} = 40\%$$

We find that boys are **40%** of the class.

(b) To find the percent that is girls, we may convert the fraction that is girls to a percent. However, we already have found that the boys are 40% of the class. So we know that the girls are the rest of the class, which is **60%**.

**Practice***    **a.** Two is what percent of eight?   25%

**b.** Two is what percent of six?   $33\frac{1}{3}\%$

**c.** Two is what percent of five?   40%

**d.** What percent of $10 is $3?   30%

**e.** What percent of $8 is $6?   75%

**f.** Ten of the 25 students are girls. What percent of the students are boys?   60%

**Problem set 118**

**1.** Mrs. Barker wants to cut a 30-inch piece of licorice
(111) into four equal lengths. How long should she cut each length of licorice?   $7\frac{1}{2}$ in.

**2.** If 3 panes of glass cost $18.90, then how much would
(94) 5 panes of glass cost?   $31.50

**3.** $5n + 2 = 42$   8
(107)

**4.** The sail boat traveled 24 miles in three hours. At that
(94) rate, how far could the sail boat travel in five hours?
40 mi

$$\frac{24 \text{ mi}}{3 \text{ hr}} \times \frac{5 \text{ hr}}{1}$$

**5.** $3.5 + 0.35 + n = 5$   1.15
(42)

**6.** Write 500 million in standard form.   500,000,000
(115)

**7.** If the mean of five numbers is 25, what is their sum?
(114) 125

**8.** If these numbers were arranged in order of size, which
(72) number would be between the other two numbers?
7.1

$$7.1, \ 7\frac{1}{2}, \ \frac{20}{3}$$

Complete the chart to answer problems 9, 10, and 11.

|  | FRACTION | DECIMAL | PERCENT |
|---|---|---|---|
| **9.**<br>(98) | $1\frac{1}{5}$ | (a) 1.2 | (b) 120% |
| **10.**<br>(98) | (a) $\frac{1}{20}$ | 0.05 | (b) 5% |
| **11.**<br>(98) | (a) $2\frac{1}{2}$ | (b) 2.5 | 250% |

**12.** $\left(2\dfrac{1}{2}\right)^2$   $6\dfrac{1}{4}$
(92)

**13.** $6\dfrac{2}{3} \div 1\dfrac{2}{3}$   4
(67)

**14.** $(3 + 2.16) \div 0.6$   8.6
(48)

**15.** $\dfrac{2}{p} = \dfrac{10}{15}$   3
(103)

**16.** What is the perimeter of this parallelogram?   12 in.
(90)

**17.** The formula for the area of a parallelogram is $A = bh$. Find the area of a parallelogram with a base of $3\dfrac{1}{2}$ inches and a height of 2 inches.   7 in.²
(90)

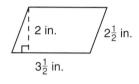

2 in.   $2\dfrac{1}{2}$ in.   $3\dfrac{1}{2}$ in.

Triangle I and triangle II are congruent. Refer to these triangles to answer questions 18, 19, and 20.

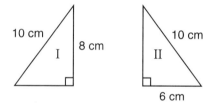

10 cm   8 cm   I   II   10 cm   6 cm

**18.** What is the perimeter of each triangle?   24 cm
(90)

**19.** What is the area of each triangle?   24 cm²
(87)

**20.** What transformations are needed to position triangle I on triangle II?   reflection and translation
(108)

**21.** In 6 years Tom will be 21. How old was he 6 years ago?   9 years old
(12)

**22.** Write the prime factorization of 84 using exponents.   $2^2 \cdot 3 \cdot 7$
(72)

**23.** Write the standard number for $3 \times 10^5$.   300,000
(115)

**24.** During the day the temperature rose from −5°F to 12°F. How many degrees did the temperature rise?   17°F
(14)

**25.** To what fraction is the arrow pointing?   $\frac{5}{6}$
*(17)*

**26.** What percent of the first ten letters of the alphabet
*(112)* are vowels?    30%

**27.** If two fifths of the 30 students in the class are boys,
*(76)* then how many girls are in the class?    18

**28.** What are the coordinates of the point halfway between
*(74)* (0, 0) and (4, 4)?    (2, 2)

**29.** Simon correctly answered 20 of the 25 questions. What
*(118)* percent of the questions did Simon answer correctly?
80%

**30.** Use a unit multiplier to convert 48 ounces to pounds.
*(116)* (1 lb = 16 oz)    48 oz $\cdot \frac{1\,\text{lb}}{16\,\text{oz}}$ = 3 lb

# LESSON
# 119

# Sales Tax • Writing Percents as Fractions, Part 2

**Mental Math:**
**a.** 12
**b.** 4563
**c.** $0.25
**d.** $0.41
**e.** 0.005
**f.** 8
**g.** −1
**Problem Solving:**
  11

**Facts Practice:** 30 Fractions to Reduce (Test G in Test Masters)

**Mental Math:** Count up and down by 5's between −25 and 25.
  **a.** $\frac{3}{4}$ of 16          **b.** 9 × 507          **c.** 10% of $2.50
  **d.** $10.00 − $9.59          **e.** 0.5 ÷ 100          **f.** $\frac{2400}{300}$
  **g.** 10 × 9, − 10, ÷ 2, + 2, ÷ 6, × 10, + 2, ÷ 9, − 9

**Problem Solving:** When Sarah said 7, Tom said 15. When Brad
            said 11, Tom said 23. When Hector said 3,
            Tom said 7. Figure out the rule Tom used to
            change the numbers he was given. What
            number would Tom say if Simon says 5?

**Sales tax**   A **sales tax** is a tax charged on the sale of an item based
upon the selling price. If the sales tax rate is 6%, then for
every dollar of purchase an additional 6¢ is charged as a
tax. The tax is collected by the seller and is sent to the

government. To calculate the sales tax on a purchase, we multiply the purchase price by the tax rate and round the product to the nearest cent.

**Example 1**    If the sales tax rate is 8%, what is the tax on an item with a price of $6.48?

*Solution*    We write 8% as the decimal 0.08 and multiply $6.48.

$$\begin{array}{rl} \$6.48 & \text{price} \\ \times\ 0.08 & \text{tax rate} \\ \hline \$0.5184 & \text{tax} \end{array}$$

We round the product to the nearest cent. We find that the tax is **$0.52.**

**Example 2**    What is the total cost of an $8.96 item plus 6% sales tax?

*Solution*    We find the amount of tax by multiplying $8.96 by 0.06.

$$\begin{array}{l} \$8.96 \\ \times\ 0.06 \\ \hline \$0.5376 \quad \text{which rounds to \$0.54} \end{array}$$

To find the total cost, we add the $0.54 tax to the $8.96 price.

$$\begin{array}{rl} \$8.96 & \text{price} \\ +\ \$0.54 & \text{tax} \\ \hline \$9.50 & \text{total} \end{array}$$

**Writing percents as fractions, part 2**    Recall that a percent is a fraction with a denominator of 100. We write a percent in fraction form by removing the percent sign and writing the denominator 100.

$$50\% = \frac{50}{100}$$

We then reduce the fraction to lowest terms. If the percent includes a fraction, we actually divide by 100 to simplify the fraction.

$$33\frac{1}{3}\% = \frac{33\frac{1}{3}}{100}$$

In this case we divide $33\frac{1}{3}$ by 100. We have performed division problems like this in the problem sets.

$$33\frac{1}{3} \div 100$$

$$\frac{\overset{1}{\cancel{100}}}{3} \times \frac{1}{\underset{1}{\cancel{100}}} = \frac{1}{3}$$

We see that $33\frac{1}{3}\%$ equals $\frac{1}{3}$.

**Example 3** Convert $3\frac{1}{3}\%$ to a fraction.

*Solution* We remove the percent sign and write the denominator 100.

$$3\frac{1}{3}\% = \frac{3\frac{1}{3}}{100}$$

We perform the division.

$$\frac{\overset{1}{\cancel{10}}}{3} \times \frac{1}{\underset{10}{\cancel{100}}} = \frac{1}{30}$$

We find that $3\frac{1}{3}\%$ equals $\frac{1}{30}$.

**Practice** **a.** Find the 8% sales tax on an item that costs $8.75.  $0.70

**b.** What is the total cost of a $12.29 item plus 5% sales tax? $12.90

**c.** Convert $12\frac{1}{2}\%$ to a reduced fraction.  $\frac{1}{8}$

**d.** Write $14\frac{2}{7}\%$ as a reduced fraction.  $\frac{1}{7}$

**Problem set 119** **1.** What is the total cost of a $12.60 item plus 7% sales tax? $13.48
(119)

**2.** Which is the greatest weight?  B. 6.4 lb
(117)
A. 6.24 lb          B. 6.4 lb          C. 6.345 lb

**3.** Seven is what percent of 10?  70%
(118)

**4.** Sound travels about 331 miles per second in air. How
(94)  far will it travel in 60 seconds?    19,860 mi

$$\frac{331 \text{ mi}}{1 \text{ s}} \cdot \frac{60 \text{ s}}{1}$$

**5.** Write the standard number for $(5 \times 10^4) + (6 \times 10^2)$.
(92)  50,600

**6.** If the radius of a circle is seventy-five hundredths of a
(97)  meter, what is the diameter?    1.5 m

**7.** Round the product of $3\frac{2}{3}$ and $2\frac{2}{3}$ to the nearest whole
(65)  number.    10

**8.** Compare:  3.71 ⊘ 3.709
(43)

Complete the chart to answer problems 9 and 10.

|  | FRACTION | DECIMAL | PERCENT |
|---|---|---|---|
| **9.**<br>(98) | $2\frac{2}{5}$ | (a) 2.4 | (b) 240% |
| **10.**<br>(98) | (a) $\frac{17}{20}$ | 0.85 | (b) 85% |

**11.** 30% of 60    18          **12.** $\dfrac{x}{7} = \dfrac{35}{5}$    49
(112)                           (103)

**13.** Write $12\frac{1}{2}\%$ as a reduced fraction.    $\frac{1}{8}$
(119)

**14.** 3.62 + 12 + 16.9          **15.** 0.12 ÷ (12 ÷ 0.4)
(38)   32.52                     (44)   0.004

**16.** Write $\frac{22}{7}$ as a decimal rounded to the hundredths' place.
(50)   3.14

**17.** What whole number multiplied by itself equals 100?
(88)   10

**18.** What is the area of this hexagon?
(106)  68 cm²

**19.** What is the perimeter of this
(102)  hexagon?    36 cm

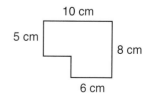

**20.** What is the volume of this cube?
(99)   27 cm³

3 cm

**21.** What is the mode of the number of days in the twelve
(114)   months of the year?   31

**22.** If seven of the containers can hold a
(94)   total of 84 ounces, then how many
   ounces can 10 containers hold?
   120 oz

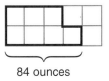

84 ounces

**23.** Write the standard number for $4\frac{1}{2}$ million.   4,500,000
(115)

**24.** Round 58,697,284 to the nearest million.   59,000,000
(16)

**25.** Which arrow is pointing to 0.4?   C
(49)

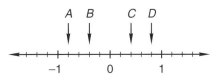

**26.** When Rosita was born, she weighed 7 pounds, 9 ounces.
(117)   Two months later she weighed 9 pounds, 7 ounces. How
   much weight did she gain in two months?   1 lb, 14 oz

**27.** The coordinates of three vertices of a parallelogram
(74)   are (0, 0), (5, 0), and (6, 3).

(1, 3), (11, 3),      (a)  What are the coordinates of the fourth vertex?
or (–1, –3)
         (b)  What is the area of the parallelogram?   15 sq. units

**28.** Convert $16\frac{2}{3}\%$ to a fraction.   $\frac{1}{6}$
(119)

**29.**    2 gal 2 qt 1 pt
(115)  + 2 gal 2 qt 1 pt
   ─────────────
     5 gal 1 qt

**30.** Gilbert started the trip with a full tank of gas. He drove
(94)   323.4 miles then refilled the tank with 14.2 gallons of
   gas. How can Gilbert calculate the average number of
   miles he traveled on each gallon of gas?   Gilbert can divide
   323.4 miles by 14.2 gallons to calculate the miles per gallon.

# INVESTIGATION 4

# Compound Interest

Materials needed for investigation:

- Calculator
- Access to newspapers

When money is loaned or borrowed there is usually an agreement between the lender and the borrower that the borrower will repay the loan amount, called the **principal,** plus an additional amount, called the **interest.** When a person deposits money into a savings account, the person is effectively loaning the money to the bank or savings institution for the institution's use. Therefore, the savings institution agrees to pay interest on the money in the savings account. The following question and explanation describes how interest accumulates in a savings account.

Samantha deposited $2000 in an account that pays 10% per year. If she does not withdraw any money from the account, how much money will be in the account (a) after one year, (b) after two years, and (c) after three years?

We show the arithmetic solution below.

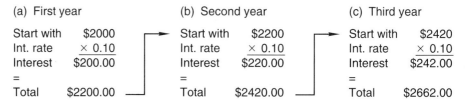

| (a) First year | | (b) Second year | | (c) Third year | |
|---|---|---|---|---|---|
| Start with | $2000 | Start with | $2200 | Start with | $2420 |
| Int. rate | × 0.10 | Int. rate | × 0.10 | Int. rate | × 0.10 |
| Interest | $200.00 | Interest | $220.00 | Interest | $242.00 |
| = | | = | | = | |
| Total | $2200.00 | Total | $2420.00 | Total | $2662.00 |

We found the total amount of money in the account for each year by adding the interest earned that year to the amount of money in the account at the start of that year. Notice that each year the amount of interest earned increases, even though the interest rate stays the same. The interest earned increases because the interest earned in the prior year(s) earned interest along with the principal. Interest earning interest is called **compound interest.** The effect of compound interest becomes more dramatic as the number of years increases.

In our arithmetic solution we multiplied by 10% (0.10) to show the amount of interest earned. Instead of multiplying by 10% and adding, we may multiply by 110% (1.10) to find the total amount in the account after each year.

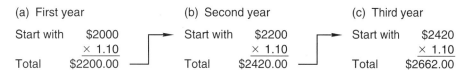

| (a) First year | | (b) Second year | | (c) Third year | |
|---|---|---|---|---|---|
| Start with | $2000 | Start with | $2200 | Start with | $2420 |
| | × 1.10 | | × 1.10 | | × 1.10 |
| Total | $2200.00 | Total | $2420.00 | Total | $2662.00 |

We will use this second method with a calculator. To find the amount of money in Samantha's account after one, two, and three years, we follow this keystroke sequence, using 1.1 for 110%.

Display

| 2 | 0 | 0 | 0 | × | 1 | . | 1 | = | 2200 |
| | | | | × | 1 | . | 1 | = | 2420 |
| | | | | × | 1 | . | 1 | = | 2662 |

**Calculator problems**

1. After three years, $2662 was in Samantha's account. If the account continues to earn 10% interest, how much money would be in the account (a) after 10 years? (b) after 20 years? (Round answers to the nearest cent.)
   (a) $5187.48   (b) $13,455.00

2. Nelson deposited $2000 in an account that pays 9% per year. If he does not withdraw any money from the account, how much will be in the account (a) after three years, (b) after 10 years, and (c) after 20 years? (Multiply by 1.09. Round the answers to the nearest cent.)
   (a) $2590.06   (b) $4734.73   (c) $11,208.82

3. How much more money was in Samantha's account than in Nelson's account (a) after three years, (b) after 10 years, and (c) after 20 years?
   (a) $71.94   (b) $452.75   (c) $2246.18

We may use the memory key to reduce the number of keystrokes. Suppose that Gilbert deposited $2000 in an account that pays 7% interest. To find the amount of money in the account after several years, we will repeatedly multiply by 1.07. We will enter 1.07 into the memory by using the "enter memory" key. Abbreviations on memory keys vary. Determine which memory keys are the "enter memory" →M and "recall memory" MR keys on your calculator. We use this key sequence to enter 107% into the memory.

Now we can use the recall memory key instead of 1.07 to perform the calculations. We find the amount of money in Gilbert's account after one and two years with this sequence of keystrokes.

Display

4. Use the memory keys to find the amount of money in Gilbert's account (a) after three years, (b) after 10 years, and (c) after 20 years. (a) $2450.09   (b) $3934.30 (c) $7739.37

5. A bank offers an annual percentage rate (APR) of 6.29%.

   (a) By what number do we multiply a deposit to find the total amount in an account at this rate after one year?   1.0629

   (b) Maria deposited $1000.00 into an account at this rate. How much money was in the account after three years?   $1200.82

6. Find an advertisement by a bank or other savings institution offering an interest rate to savers. Write a problem based on the advertisement for your classmates to answer. Be sure to provide an answer to your problem.   See student work.

Collected problems may be used to provide distributed practice on this topic during the rest of the year.

# LESSON
# 120

Mental Math:
a. 6
b. 2240
c. $1.25
d. $9.47
e. 37.5
f. 20,000
g. 7
Problem Solving:
$$\begin{array}{r} 19 \\ \times\ 19 \\ \hline 171 \\ 19\ \ \\ \hline 361 \end{array}$$

# Classifying Triangles

**Facts Practice:** Percents to Fractions and Decimals (Test M in Test Masters)

**Mental Math:** Count down by 2's from 10 to −10.

  **a.** $\frac{3}{8}$ of 16          **b.** 4 × 560          **c.** 50% of $2.50
  **d.** $8.98 + 49¢       **e.** 0.375 × 100       **f.** 50 · 400
  **g.** 11 × 6, − 2, $\sqrt{\phantom{x}}$, × 3, + 1, $\sqrt{\phantom{x}}$, × 10, − 1, $\sqrt{\phantom{x}}$

**Problem Solving:** Copy this problem and fill in the missing digits. (*Hint:* The product is a perfect square.)

$$\begin{array}{r} \_\ \_ \\ \times\ \_\ \_ \\ \hline \_\ \_\ \_ \\ \_\ \_\ \_\ \ \\ \hline 3\ \_\ 1 \end{array}$$

All three-sided polygons are triangles, but not all triangles are alike. We distinguish between different types of triangles based on the relative measures of the sides and on the measures of the angles.

We will first consider three different triangles based on the relative measures of their sides.

| Triangles Classified by Their Sides | | |
|---|---|---|
| Name | Example | Description |
| Equilateral | | All three sides are equal in length. |
| Isosceles | | At least two of the three sides are equal in length. |
| Scalene | | All three sides are different lengths. |

All three sides of an **equilateral** triangle are equal in length. All three angles are equal in measure. At least two of the three sides of an **isosceles** triangle are equal in length. At least two of the angles are equal in measure. All three sides of a **scalene** triangle are different lengths. All three angles have different measures.

Next we consider triangles classified by their angles. In an earlier lesson we learned the names of three different kinds of angles: **acute, right,** and **obtuse.** We use these words to describe triangles as well.

| Triangles Classified by Their Angles | | |
|---|---|---|
| Name | Example | Description |
| Acute triangle | | All three angles are acute. |
| Right triangle | | One angle is a right angle. |
| Obtuse triangle | | One angle is an obtuse angle. |

Each angle of an equilateral triangle measures 60°, so an equilateral triangle is also an acute triangle. An isosceles triangle may be an acute triangle, a right triangle, or an obtuse triangle. A scalene triangle may also be an acute, right, or obtuse triangle.

**Practice**   **a.** One side of an equilateral triangle measures 15 cm. What is the perimeter of the triangle?   45 cm

**b.** "An equilateral triangle is also an acute triangle." True or false?   true

**c.** "All acute triangles are equilateral triangles." True or false?   false

**d.** Two sides of a triangle are 3 in. and 4 in. If the perimeter is 10 in., what type of triangle is it?   isosceles (also acute)

**e.** Is every right triangle a scalene triangle? (Yes or No)   no

**Problem set 120**

**1.** The 306 students were assigned to ten rooms so that
*(111)* there were 30 or 31 students in each room. How many
rooms had exactly 30 students?    4

**2.** If 5 feet of ribbon cost $1.20, then 10 feet of ribbon
*(94)* would cost how much?    $2.40

**3.** Six is what percent of 15?    40%
*(118)*

**4.** The multiple choice question has four choices. One of
*(91)* the choices has to be correct, but George had no idea
which one. If George simply guesses, what is the
probability that he will guess the correct answer?    $\frac{1}{4}$

**5.** If $\frac{2}{5}$ of the 30 students in the class are boys, then what
*(76)* is the ratio of boys to girls in the class?    $\frac{2}{3}$

**6.** Write $1.2 \times 10^9$ as a standard number.    1,200,000,000
*(115)*

**7.** The cost ($c$) of produce is related to its price per
*(94)* pound ($p$) and its weight ($w$) by this formula: $c = pw$.
Find the cost when $p$ is $\frac{\$0.65}{1 \text{ pound}}$ and $w$ is 5 pounds.
$3.25

**8.** Arrange these numbers in order from least to greatest:
*(43)*
$$9.9, 9.95, 9.925, 9.09$$
9.09, 9.9, 9.925, 9.95

Complete the chart to answer problems 9 and 10.

| | FRACTION | DECIMAL | PERCENT |
|---|---|---|---|
| **9.** *(98)* | $3\frac{3}{8}$ | (a) 3.375 | (b) 337.5% |
| **10.** *(98)* | (a) $\frac{3}{20}$ | (b) 0.15 | 15% |

**11.** 40% of $3.20    $1.28
*(112)*

**12.** $\frac{x}{3} = \frac{16}{12}$    4
*(103)*

**13.** $1\frac{1}{2} \times 1\frac{2}{3} \times 3\frac{1}{5}$    8
*(71)*

**14.** $6 + 3\dfrac{3}{4} + 4.6$   (decimal answer)   14.35
(85)

**15.** If the sales tax rate is 7%, what is the tax on a $5.85
(119) purchase?   $0.41

**16.** Use division by primes to find the prime factors of
(72) 648. Then write the prime factorization of 648 using
exponents.   $2^3 \cdot 3^4$

**17.** If a 32-ounce box of cereal costs $3.84, what is the cost
(15) per ounce?   $0.12

**18.** Find the area of the trapezoid by
(106) combining the area of the
rectangle and the area of the
triangle.   28 m²

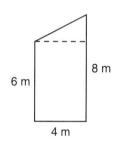

**19.** The radius of a circle is 10 cm. What is the
(105) circumference of the circle?   62.8 cm

**20.** The volume of the pyramid is $\frac{1}{3}$
(99) the volume of the cube. What is
the volume of the pyramid?
9 cm³

**21.** $0.6y = 54$   90
(48)

**22.** Use a number line to find the number that is four more
(14) than −1.   3

**23.** What type of a triangle contains an angle that
(120) measures 90°?   right triangle

**24.** Draw an obtuse triangle.
(120)

**25.** What temperature is shown on the
(10) thermometer?   −2°F

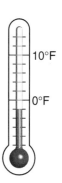

**26.** An equilateral triangle and a
(120) square share a common side. If
the area of the square is 100 mm²,
then what is the perimeter of the
triangle?   30 mm

**27.** Write $11\frac{1}{9}\%$ as a reduced fraction.   $\frac{1}{9}$
(119)

**28.** The heights of the five starters on the basketball team
(114) are listed below. Find the mean, median, and range of
these measures.   mean, 180 cm; median, 181 cm; range, 37 cm

181 cm, 177 cm, 189 cm, 158 cm, 195 cm

**29.** George bought two bunches of bananas. The smaller
(117) bunch weighed 2 lb, 12 oz. The larger bunch weighed
3 lb, 8 oz. What was the total weight of the two
bunches of bananas?   6 lb, 4 oz

**30.** Which type of triangle has no lines of symmetry?
(120)
A. Equilateral     B. Isosceles     C. Scalene
C. Scalene

# LESSON
# 121

# Adding Integers

Facts Practice: Measurement Facts (Test N in Test Masters)

**Mental Math:**

a. $\frac{5}{8}$ of 16                   b. 7 × 406          c. 20% of $5.00
d. 5 is what % of 10?          e. 0.4 × 20          f. $\frac{2000}{400}$
g. 10 × 20, ÷ 4, − 1, $\sqrt{\phantom{x}}$, × 5, + 1, $\sqrt{\phantom{x}}$

**Problem Solving:** How many five-digit zip codes are possible if
                    00000 is not used?

The dots on this number line mark the integers from negative five to positive five (−5 to +5).

Recall that **integers** include all of the counting numbers (1, 2, 3, ...), their negatives (−1, −2, −3, ...), and zero with no fractions between them. In this book we will practice adding, subtracting, multiplying, and dividing integers. This lesson is about adding integers.

If we consider a rise in temperature of five degrees as a positive five (+5) and a fall in temperature of five degrees as a negative five (−5), we may use the scale on a thermometer to keep track of the addition.

Imagine that the temperature is 0°F. If the temperature falls five degrees (−5) and then falls another five degrees (−5), the result is a temperature of −10°F. When we add two negative numbers the sum is negative.

$$-5 + -5 = -10$$

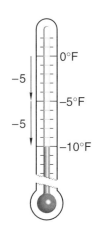

Imagine a different situation. Again the starting temperature is 0°F. First the temperature falls five degrees (−5). Next the temperature rises five degrees (+5). This brings the temperature back to zero. The numbers −5 and +5 are opposites. When we add opposites the sum is zero.

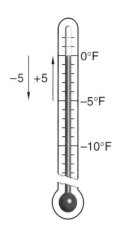

$$-5 + +5 = 0$$

If the temperature rises five degrees (+5) from zero, and then falls ten degrees (−10), the temperature will fall through zero to five degrees below zero (−5). The sum is less than zero because the temperature fell more than it rose.

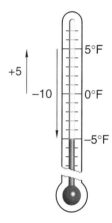

$$+5 + -10 = -5$$

**Example 1**    +8 + −5

*Solution*    We will illustrate this addition with a number line. We begin at zero and move in a positive direction eight units. From +8 we move in a negative direction, or to the left, five units to +3.

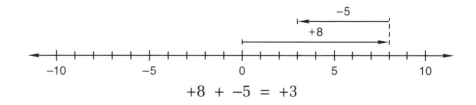

$$+8 + -5 = +3$$

The sum is +3, which we write as **3**.

Example 2   −5 + −3

*Solution*   Again using a number line, we start at zero and move in a negative direction, or to the left, five units to −5. From −5 we continue moving left three units to −8.

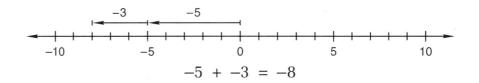

$$-5 + -3 = -8$$

The sum is **−8.**

Example 3   −6 + +6

*Solution*   On a number line we start at zero and return to **zero.**

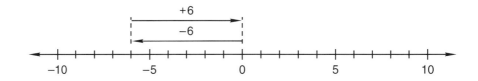

Example 4   (+6) + (−6)

*Solution*   Sometimes positive and negative numbers are written with parentheses. The parentheses help us see that the positive or negative sign is the sign of the number and not an addition or subtraction operation.

$$(+6) + (-6) = 0$$

**Practice***   Find each sum. Illustrate problems (a)–(d) by sketching a number line. Solve (e)–(h) mentally.

**a.** −3 + +4

**b.** +4 + −3

**c.** −3 + +3

**d.** −3 + −4

**e.** (+3) + (−4)   −1

**f.** (+10) + (−5)   +5

**g.** (−10) + (−5)   −15

**h.** (−10) + (+5)   −5

**Problem set 121**

**1.** If Tony reads 30 pages each day, how many days will
(111) it take him to finish a 200-page book?   7 days

**2.** What fraction of the letters in the word **Alabama** are A's?
(29) $\frac{4}{7}$

**3.** A box that is two feet long,
(99) two feet wide, and one foot deep
has a volume of how many cubic
feet?
4 ft³

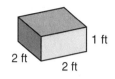

1 ft

2 ft

2 ft

**4.** If Sarah is batting at a rate of 3 hits in every 10 at-bats,
(104) then how many hits is she likely to get in 80 at-bats?
24 hits

**5.** Write the number ninety-six million, fifty thousand,
(12) eight hundred.   96,050,800

**6.** Compare: $(10 + 9) + 8 \;\textcircled{=}\; 10 + (9 + 8)$
(9)

**7.** The mean of 3 numbers is 7. Two of the numbers are 8
(114) and 9. What is the third number?   4

**8.** $(+8) + (-5)$   3
(121)

**9.** Find 30% of $6.40.   $1.92
(112)

Complete the chart to answer problems 10 and 11.

| | Fraction | Decimal | Percent |
|---|---|---|---|
| **10.**<br>(98) | (a) $1\frac{3}{10}$ | 1.3 | (b) 130% |
| **11.**<br>(98) | (a) $\frac{3}{50}$ | (b) 0.06 | 6% |

**12.** $4\frac{1}{4}$ in. $-\ 1\frac{1}{2}$ in.   $2\frac{3}{4}$ in.   **13.** $5 \div 1\frac{2}{3}$   3
(62)                                          (67)

**14.** $5.1 + 4\frac{1}{4}$   (decimal answer)   9.35
(85)

**15.** $4 \div (0.24 \div 6)$   100    **16.** $(-6) + (-3)$   −9
(48)                                  (121)

**17.** What is the area of this parallelogram?    320 mm²
(90)

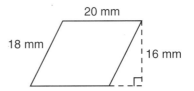

**18.** What is the perimeter of this parallelogram?    76 mm
(90)

**19.** The diameter of a circle is 8 in. What is its circumference?
(105)    25.12 in.

**20.** Complete the proportion: $\dfrac{25}{30} = \dfrac{w}{24}$    20
(103)

**21.** Describe the appearance of an acute triangle and sketch
(120)    an example.    Each angle of an acute triangle is smaller than
a right angle.

**22.** If 12 mongooses weigh 72 pounds, how much would
(104)    100 mongooses weigh?    600 lb

**23.** Pluto's average distance from the sun is about $3\tfrac{1}{2}$
(115)    billion miles. Write that number in standard form.
3,500,000,000

**24.** Illustrate the addition of −4 and +2 on a number line.
(121)

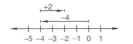

**25.** What is the total cost of a chicken sandwich, a salad,
(119)    and a small juice, including 6% tax?    $5.37

| Menu | |
| --- | --- |
| Chicken Sandwich | $2.99 |
| Salad | $1.29 |
| Juice:  Sm. | $0.79 |
| Lg. | $0.99 |

**26.** Compare: $\dfrac{1}{2}$ ⊙ $\dfrac{1}{2} \cdot \dfrac{1}{2}$
(75)

**27.** The median height of the students in the class was
(114) 60 inches. About what percent of the students were
taller than 60 inches?　50%

**28.** 5 hr, 10 min − 3 hr, 45 min　1 hr, 25 min
(115)

**29.** Convert $1\frac{2}{3}$% to a fraction.　$\frac{1}{60}$
(119)

**30.** Use a unit multiplier to convert 20 bushels to pecks.
(116) (4 pecks = 1 bushel)　80 pecks

---

## LESSON 122

# Finding a Whole When a Fraction is Known

**Facts Practice:** Add Integers (Test O in Test Masters)

**Mental Math:**

　**a.** $\frac{7}{8}$ of 16　　　　**b.** 3 × 760　　**c.** 25% of $80.00
　**d.** 5 is what % of 20?　　**e.** 0.6 × 40　　**f.** 60 · 700
　**g.** 8 × 8, − 1, ÷ 7, $\sqrt{\ }$, × 4, ÷ 2, × 3, ÷ 2

**Problem Solving:** Coins from the vending machine were put
　　　　　　　　　into coin rolls. Forty nickels fill a roll, 50
　　　　　　　　　dimes fill a roll, and 40 quarters fill a roll. The
　　　　　　　　　coins in the machine filled four quarter rolls,
　　　　　　　　　two dime rolls, and three nickel rolls. All nine
　　　　　　　　　rolls equaled how much money?

Consider the following fractional part problem.

*Two fifths of the students in the class are boys. If
there are ten boys in the class, how many students
are in the class?*

A diagram can help us understand
and solve this problem. We have
drawn a rectangle to represent the
whole class. The problem states that
two **fifths** are boys, so we divide the
rectangle into five parts. Two of the
parts are boys, so three of the parts are
girls.

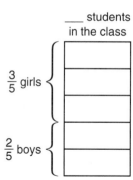

We are also told that there are ten boys in the class. In our diagram ten boys are in two of the parts. Since ten divided by two is five, there are five students in each part. All of the students is all five parts, so there are 25 students in all. We complete the diagram.

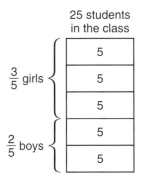

**Example 1**     Three eighths of the people in the town voted. If 120 of the people in the town voted, how many people lived in the town?

*Solution*     We are told that $\frac{3}{8}$ of the town voted, so we divide the whole into eight parts and mark off three of the parts. We are told that these three parts total 120 people. If the three parts are 120, then each part must be 40 ($120 \div 3 = 40$). If each part is 40, then all eight parts must be 8 times 40, which is **320.**

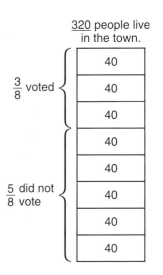

**Example 2**     Six is $\frac{1}{3}$ of what number?

*Solution*     A larger number has been divided into three parts. Six is one of the three parts. Since each part equals six, all three parts equal **18.**

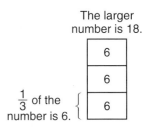

**Example 3**     Six is $\frac{2}{3}$ of what number?

*Solution*   A larger number has been divided into three parts. Two of the three parts total six. So each part equals three (6 ÷ 2 = 3). Since each part equals three, all three parts equal **9.**

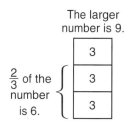

The larger number is 9.

$\frac{2}{3}$ of the number is 6.

**Practice\***   **a.** Eight is $\frac{1}{5}$ of what number?   40

**b.** Eight is $\frac{2}{5}$ of what number?   20

**c.** Eight is $\frac{2}{3}$ of what number?   12

**d.** Nine is $\frac{3}{4}$ of what number?   12

**e.** Sixty is $\frac{3}{8}$ of what number?   160

**f.** Three fifths of the students in the class were girls. If there were 18 girls in the class, how many students were in the class?   30 students

**Problem set 122**   **1.** Three fifths of the people in the town voted. If 120 of *(122)* the people in the town voted, how many people lived in the town?   200

**2.** If 130 children are separated as equally as possible *(111)* into 4 groups, how many will be in each group? (Write the number of children in each of the four groups.)
32, 32, 33, 33

**3.** If the parking lot charges $1.25 per half hour, what is *(94)* the cost of parking a car from 11:15 a.m. to 2:45 p.m.?
$8.75

**4.** (a) What percent of this circle is *(81)* shaded?   25%

(b) What percent of the circle is not shaded?   75%

**5.** Jackson correctly answered 46 of the 50 questions. *(118)* What percent of the questions did Jackson answer correctly?   92%

**6.** The coordinates of the vertices of a triangle are (3, 6),
(87) (5, 0), and (0, 0). What is the area of the triangle?
15 sq. units

**7.** Write one hundred five thousandths as a decimal number.
(35) 0.105

**8.** Round the quotient of $7.00 ÷ 9 to the nearest cent.
(50) $0.78

**9.** Arrange in order from least to greatest:  $\frac{4}{5}$, 81%, 0.815
(95)

$$81\%, \frac{4}{5}, 0.815$$

**10.** What number is 70% of 80?    56
(112)

**11.** Six is $\frac{1}{8}$ of what number?    48
(122)

**12.** Six is $\frac{2}{5}$ of what number?    15
(122)

**13.** $\left(5 - 1\frac{2}{3}\right) - 1\frac{1}{2}$   $1\frac{5}{6}$     **14.** $2\frac{2}{5} ÷ 1\frac{1}{2}$   $1\frac{3}{5}$
(62)                                    (67)

**15.** 0.625 × 2.4    1.5
(39)

**16.** The prime factorization of 24 is 2 × 2 × 2 × 3,
(72) which we can write as $2^3$ × 3. Write the prime
factorization of 36 using exponents.    $2^2$ × $3^2$

**17.** What is the total price of a $12.50 item plus 6% sales tax?
(119) $13.25

**18.** What is the area of this pentagon?
(106) 80 in.$^2$

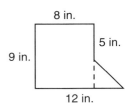

**19.** Write the standard numeral for 6 × $10^5$.    600,000
(115)

**20.** The diameter of a bike wheel is 20 inches. What is the
(105) distance around the wheel?    62.8 in.

**21.** If each small cube is one cubic
(99) inch, what is the volume of this
rectangular solid?  60 in.³

**22.** Draw a triangle in which each angle is smaller than a
(120) right angle. What type of triangle is it?  acute triangle

**23.** The mean, median, and mode of student scores on a test
(114) were 89, 87, and 92, respectively. About half of the
students scored what score or higher?  87

**24.** Illustrate the addition of −2 and +5 on a number line.
(121)

**25.** If the arrow is spun, what is the
(91) probability that it will end up pointing to a number greater than 1?  $\frac{3}{4}$

**26.** By rotation and translation, these
(108) two congruent triangles can be
arranged to form a:  B. Parallelogram

A. Square        B. Parallelogram    C. Hexagon

**27.** −5 + −5 + −5  −15
(121)

**28.** The ratio of cattle to horses on the ranch was 15 to 2.
(113) The combined number of cattle and horses was 1020.
How many horses were on the ranch? Make a ratio box.
120

**29.** $\sqrt{100}$ + 3² × 5 − $\sqrt{81}$ ÷ 3  52
(92)

**30.** Which of these figures has the greatest number of lines
(110) of symmetry?  C.

A. △              B. □              C. ○

# LESSON 123

# Square Roots of Numbers Greater Than 100 • Functions

**Mental Math:**
**a.** 12
**b.** 24
**c.** $3.00
**d.** 50%
**e.** 48
**f.** 5
**g.** 8
**Problem Solving:**
50 cm² − 6 cm²
= 44 cm²

**Facts Practice:** Add Integers (Test O in Test Masters)

**Mental Math:**

**a.** $\frac{1}{2}$ of what number is 6?    **b.** $\frac{3}{10}$ of 80    **c.** 30% of $10.00
**d.** 10 is what % of 20?    **e.** 0.8 × 60    **f.** $\frac{2500}{500}$
**g.** 8 × 7, − 2, ÷ 2, + 9, $\sqrt{\ }$, × 7, − 2, ÷ 5

**Problem Solving:** A small rectangle is cut from a larger rectangular piece of paper. Find the area of the remaining shape by subtracting the area of the smaller rectangle from the area of the larger rectangle.

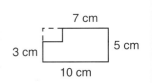

**Square roots of numbers greater than 100**
We have practiced finding square roots of perfect squares from 1 to 100. In this lesson we will find the square roots of perfect squares greater than 100. We will use a "guess and check" method. As we practice, our "guesses" improve and we begin to see clues that help us estimate the answer.

**Example 1**  $\sqrt{400}$

*Solution*  We need to find a number that, when multiplied by itself, has a product of 400.

$$\boxed{\phantom{0}} \times \boxed{\phantom{0}} = 400$$

We know that $\sqrt{400}$ is more than 10 because 10 × 10 equals 100. We also know that $\sqrt{400}$ is much less than 100 because 100 × 100 equals 10,000. Since $\sqrt{4}$ equals 2, the 4 in $\sqrt{400}$ hints that we should try 20.

$$20 \times 20 = 400$$

We find $\sqrt{400}$ equals **20.**

**Example 2**  $\sqrt{625}$

*Solution*　Since $\sqrt{625}$ is greater than $\sqrt{400}$, which we just answered in Example 1, we know that $\sqrt{625}$ is greater than 20. We find that $\sqrt{625}$ is less than 30 because 30 × 30 equals 900. Since the last digit is 5, perhaps $\sqrt{625}$ is 25. We multiply to find out.

$$
\begin{array}{r}
25 \\
\times\ 25 \\
\hline
125 \\
50\phantom{0} \\
\hline
625
\end{array}
$$

We find $\sqrt{625}$ is **25.**

**Functions**　Nathan thought of a rule that would use the length of a side of a square to find the perimeter of the square. He recorded the results in a table in which $S$ stands for the length of a side of a square and $P$ stands for the perimeter of the square.

| $S$ | $P$ |
|---|---|
| 5 | 20 |
| 7 | 28 |
| 10 | 40 |
| 15 | ? |

Nathan created a **function,** which is defined as a pairing of one unknown, in this case the length of a side, with exactly one other unknown, in this case the perimeter. We say the perimeter of a square is a function of the length of each side of the square. The *rule* of the function is to multiply the length of the side by 4 to find the perimeter. The rule can be expressed in a formula.

$$P = 4S$$

We find a missing number in the table by applying the rule to the number we are given. In the table we see that when $S$ is 5, $P$ is 20. When $S$ is 7, $P$ is 28. When $S$ is 10, $P$ is 40. To find $P$ when $S$ is 15, we multiply 15 by 4. So the missing number is 60.

**Example 3** Find the rule for this function. Then use the rule to find the number for $m$ when $l$ is 7.

| $l$ | $m$ |
|---|---|
| 5 | 20 |
| 7 | ? |
| 10 | 25 |
| 15 | 30 |

**Solution** We study the table to discover the rule of the function. We see that when $l$ is 5, $m$ is 20. We might guess that the rule is to multiply $l$ by 4. However, when $l$ is 10, $m$ is 25. Since $10 \times 4$ is not 25, we know that this guess is incorrect. We need to figure out another rule. We notice that 20 is 15 more than 5 and we see that 25 is 15 more than 10. We guess that the rule is to add 15 to $l$. In the last line of the table, $l$ is 15 and $m$ is 30, which fits the rule. So to find $m$ when $l$ is 7, we add 15 to 7.

$$7 + 15 = 22$$

The missing number in the table is **22.**

Instead of using the letter $m$ in the table in this example, we could have written the rule. In this table, $l + 15$ has replaced $m$ which means to add 15 to the number for $l$. We show this type of table in the next example.

| $l$ | $l + 15$ |
|---|---|
| 5 | 20 |
| 7 | ? |
| 10 | 25 |
| 15 | 30 |

**Example 4** Find the missing number in this function table.

| $x$ | 2 | 3 | 4 |
|---|---|---|---|
| $3x - 2$ | 4 | 7 | ? |

**Solution** This table is arranged horizontally. The rule of the function is stated in the table: Multiply the $x$ number by 3 and then subtract 2. To find the missing number in the table, we apply the rule of the function when $x$ is 4.

$$3x - 2$$

$$3(4) - 2 = 10$$

We find that the missing number is **10.**

**Practice** Find each square root:

    **a.** $\sqrt{169}$   13      **b.** $\sqrt{484}$   22      **c.** $\sqrt{961}$   31

Find the missing number in each function:

**d.**   8

| x | y |
|---|---|
| 3 | 1 |
| 5 | 3 |
| 6 | 4 |
| 10 | ? |

**e.**   10

| a | b |
|---|---|
| 3 | 8 |
| 5 | 10 |
| 7 | 12 |
| ? | 15 |

**f.**   25

| x | 3 | 6 | 8 |
|---|---|---|---|
| 3x + 1 | 10 | 19 | ? |

**g.**   4

| x | 3 | ? | 7 |
|---|---|---|---|
| 3x − 1 | 8 | 11 | 20 |

**Problem set 123**

**1.** A 32-ounce box of cereal can fill how many 5-ounce
(111) bowls?   6 bowls

**2.** Which amount of time is shortest?   C. 9.8 s
(43)
     A. 9.99 s      B. 10.0 s      C. 9.8 s      D. 9.85 s

**3.** What percent of this circle is **not**
(81) shaded?   75%

**4.** Three is $\frac{1}{5}$ of what number?   15
(122)

**5.** Write the standard number for $(5 \times 10^6) + (3 \times 10^3)$.
(92)   5,003,000

**6.** How much is the sales tax on an $18,000 car if the
(119) sales tax rate is 7%?   $1260.00

**7.** Estimate the product of 496 and 304.   150,000
(16)

**8.** If you know the circumference of a circle, how can
(105) you calculate the diameter of the circle?

8. You can find
the diameter of a
circle by dividing
the circumference
by $\pi$ (by 3.14).

Complete the chart to answer problems 9 and 10.

| | FRACTION | DECIMAL | PERCENT |
|---|---|---|---|
| **9.** <br> (98) | $\frac{1}{10}$ | (a) 0.1 | (b) 10% |
| **10.** <br> (98) | (a) $1\frac{9}{10}$ | 1.9 | (b) 190% |

**11.** How much money is 70% of $6.30?  $4.41
(112)

**12.** $3\frac{1}{2} + 2\frac{3}{4} + 5\frac{5}{8}$  $11\frac{7}{8}$
(59)

**13.** $\frac{3}{5} \times 1\frac{2}{3} \times 2.5$  (fraction answer)  $2\frac{1}{2}$
(85)

**14.** 0.2 − (1 − 0.875)  **15.** 0.144 ÷ (2 ÷ 0.25)
(38)  0.075         (44)   0.018

**16.** If a 16-ounce can of soup costs 64 cents, what is the
(94)  cost for each ounce of soup?   $0.04

**17.** $\sqrt{900} - \sqrt{9}$  27
(123)

**18.** What is the volume of this
(99)  rectangular prism?  6000 mm³

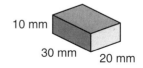

10 mm  30 mm  20 mm

**19.** A circular wading pool that is six feet across is how
(105)  many feet around?   18.84 ft

**20.** A straight angle measures 180°. How
(107)  many degrees is the measure of an
angle that is $\frac{1}{3}$ of a straight angle?
60°

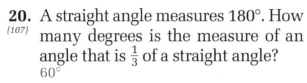

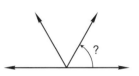

?

**21.** 5 feet, 2 inches − 4 feet, 9 inches   5 inches
(115)

**22.** What number is the largest two-digit prime number?
(61)   97

**23.** Write 200 billion in standard form.   200,000,000,000
(115)

**24.** Illustrate the addition of +4 and −7 on a number line.
(121)

**25.** Find the rule for this function and
(123) use the rule to find the missing
number.  3*a*; 21

| *a* | 3 | 5 | 7 | 10 |
|---|---|---|---|---|
| *b* | 9 | 15 | ? | 30 |

**26.** Drawing one marble from a bag containing only one
(91) red, two white, and three blue marbles, what is the
probability of drawing:

(a) a white marble?  $\frac{1}{3}$

(b) a black marble?  0

**27.** Convert $2\frac{1}{2}\%$ to a fraction.  $\frac{1}{40}$
(119)

**28.** −3 + −3 + −3 + −3  −12
(121)

**29.** The ratio of left-handed to right-handed students in
(113) the room was 1 to 5. If there were 30 students in the
room, how many were left handed? Make a ratio box.
5 students

**30.** The diameter of the circle is one
(105) inch.

(a) What is the perimeter of the
square?  4 in.

(b) What is the circumference of
the circle?  3.14 in.

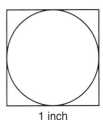

1 inch

# LESSON
# 124

Mental Math:
a. 18
b. 10
c. $8.00
d. 25%
e. 6
f. 90,000
g. 8
Problem Solving:
$n^2 - 1$; 99

---

**Facts Practice:** Percents to Fractions and Decimals (Test M in Test Masters)

**Mental Math:**

  **a.** 6 is $\frac{1}{3}$ of what number?    **b.** $\frac{2}{3}$ of 15    **c.** 40% of $20.00

  **d.** 10 is what % of 40?      **e.** 0.3 × 20    **f.** 300 · 300

  **g.** 10 × 10, − 10, ÷ 2, − 1, ÷ 4, × 3, − 1, ÷ 4

**Problem Solving:** When Tom said 9, Sarah said 80. When Brad said 6, Sarah said 35. When Diana said 7, Sarah said 48. Figure out the rule Sarah used to change the numbers she was given. What number would Sarah say if Sonia said 10?

---

We can estimate the area of a figure using a grid by counting the number of square units enclosed by the figure.

**Example**   This circle is drawn on a grid.

  (a) How many units is the radius of the circle?

  (b) Estimate the area of the circle.

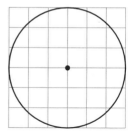

**Solution**   (a) To find the radius of the circle, we may either find the diameter of the circle and divide by two, or we may locate the center of the circle and count units to the circle. We find that the radius is **3 units.**

  (b) To estimate the area of the circle, we count the square units enclosed by the circle. We have shaded the squares that have most of their area within the circle. We have shaded 24 square units. There are eight squares that have about half of their area in the circle. We have marked these squares with a dot. We will count each of these squares as half of a square. Since eight halves is four, we add four square units to 24 square units to make our estimate of the area of the circle **28 square units.**

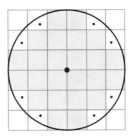

## Activity: Estimating Area

Materials needed:

- One-inch grid paper or graph paper with one-inch divisions emphasized.

On a sheet of grid paper, trace the outline of your shoe or of your hand with your fingers together. Then estimate the area enclosed by the outline.

**Practice** **a.** The radius of this circle is 4 units. Estimate the area of this circle by counting the squares within the circle.
about 50 sq. units

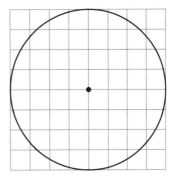

**b.** Draw an irregular shape on grid paper and estimate its area. See student work.

**Problem set**    **1.** If 52 cards are dealt to 7 people as evenly as possible,
**124**    [111] how many people will end up with 8 cards?    3

**2.** About how long is a new pencil?    B. 18 cm
[7]    A.  1.8 cm          B.  18 cm          C.  180 cm

**3.** 2 pounds, 10 ounces + 1 pound, 8 ounces
[117]    4 pounds, 2 ounces

**4.** Recall that the symbol ≠ means "is not equal to."
[73]    Which statement is true?    B. $\frac{3}{4} \neq \frac{9}{16}$

A. $\frac{3}{4} \neq \frac{9}{12}$          B. $\frac{3}{4} \neq \frac{9}{16}$          C. $\frac{3}{4} \neq 0.75$

**5.** How much money is 25% of $48.00?    $12.00
[112]

**6.** As Perry peered out his window he saw 48 trucks, 84
[82]    cars, and 12 motorcycles go by his home. What was
the ratio of trucks to cars that Perry saw?    $\frac{4}{7}$

**7.** What is the mean of 17, 24, 27, and 28?    24
[114]

**8.** Arrange in order from least to greatest:    $\sqrt{36}, 6.1, 6\frac{1}{4}$
[73]

$$6.1, \sqrt{36}, 6\frac{1}{4}$$

**9.** Nine cookies were left in the package. That was $\frac{3}{10}$ of
[53]    the original number of cookies. How many were in the
package originally?    30 cookies

**10.** Buz measured the circumference of the trunk of the
[105]    old oak tree. How can Buz calculate the approximate
diameter of the tree?    Buz can divide the circumference by
π (by 3.14) to calculate the diameter.

**11.** Twelve is $\frac{3}{4}$ of what number?    16
[122]

**12.** $2\frac{2}{3} + \left(5\frac{1}{3} - 2\frac{1}{2}\right)$    $5\frac{1}{2}$      **13.** $6\frac{2}{3} \div 4\frac{1}{6}$    $1\frac{3}{5}$
[62]                                              [67]

**14.** $4\frac{1}{4} + 3.2$    (decimal answer)    7.45
[85]

**15.** $1 - (0.1)^2$   0.99
(92)

**16.** Use a unit multiplier to convert 2.5 pounds to ounces.
(116)   40 oz

**17.** An angle that measures $100°$ is
(107) what type of angle?   obtuse angle

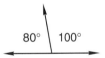

**18.** What is the perimeter of this hexagon?   14 cm
(102)

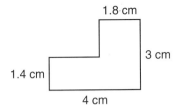

**19.** We show two lines of symmetry
(110) for this square. A square has a total
of how many lines of symmetry? 4

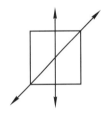

**20.** Each edge of a cube measures 4 feet. What is the
(99) volume of the cube?   64 ft³

**21.** Complete the proportion: $\dfrac{f}{12} = \dfrac{12}{16}$   9
(103)

**22.** Find the rule for this function.
(123) Then use the rule to figure out the
missing number.   5x; 8

| x | y |
|---|----|
| 2 | 10 |
| 3 | 15 |
| 5 | 25 |
| ? | 40 |

**23.** Write the standard number for
(115) $1.25 \times 10^4$.   12,500

**24.** Illustrate the sum of $-4$ and $+7$ on
(121) a number line.

**25.** (a) How many millimeters long is
(7)    this line segment?   26 mm

(b) How many centimeters long is
the line segment? (Write the
answer as a decimal number.)
2.6 cm

**26.** Convert $7\frac{1}{2}\%$ to a fraction.   $\frac{3}{40}$
(119)

**27.** At noon the temperature was −3°F. By sunset the
(14)    temperature dropped another five degrees. Then what
was the temperature?   −8°F

**28.** There were three red, three white, and three blue
(91)    marbles in a bag. Sam drew a white marble out of the
bag and held it. If he draws another marble out of the
bag, what is the probability that the second marble
will also be white?   $\frac{2}{8} = \frac{1}{4}$

**29.** $\sqrt{441}$   21
(123)

**30.** Five dollars is what percent of $25?   20%
(118)

# LESSON
# 125

# Using a Protractor to Measure an Angle

**Facts Practice:** Add Integers (Test O in Test Masters)

**Mental Math:**

  **a.** $\frac{1}{4}$ of what number is 8?    **b.** $\frac{3}{4}$ of 32     **c.** 40% of $30.00

  **d.** 10 is what % of 50?     **e.** $0.5 \times 40$    **f.** $\frac{4000}{80}$

  **g.** $\frac{1}{2}$ of 40, + 1, ÷ 3, × 5, + 1, ÷ 4, × 3, + 1, ÷ 4

**Problem Solving:** Copy the problem and fill in the missing digits.

$$\begin{array}{r} 8\_9 \\ + \ \_8\_ \\ \hline \_\_8 \end{array}$$

In this lesson we will practice using a tool that helps us measure the size of angles. The tool is a **protractor.** To measure an angle, we place the center point of the protractor on the vertex of the angle, and we place one of the zero marks on one ray of the angle. Where the other ray of the angle passes through the scale we can read the size of the angle.

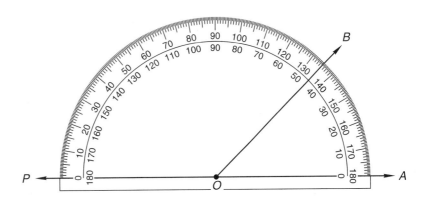

The scale on a protractor has two sets of numbers. One set is for measuring angles starting from the right side, and the other set is for measuring angles starting from the left side. The easiest way to be sure we are reading from the correct scale is to decide if the angle we are measuring is acute or obtuse. Looking at $\angle AOB$ we read the numbers 45° and 135°. Since the angle is less than 90° (acute), it must be 45° and not 135°.

**Practice\***    What is the measure of each of these angles?

      **a.** ∠AOC  15°     **b.** ∠AOE  45°     **c.** ∠AOF  90°

      **d.** ∠AOH  142°     **e.** ∠IOH  38°     **f.** ∠IOE  135°

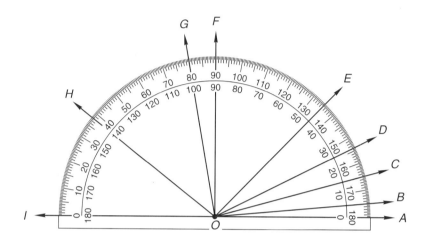

Use your own protractor to find the measure of each of these angles:

      **g.** ∠RMS  60°     **h.** ∠VMT  45°     **i.** ∠VMS  120°

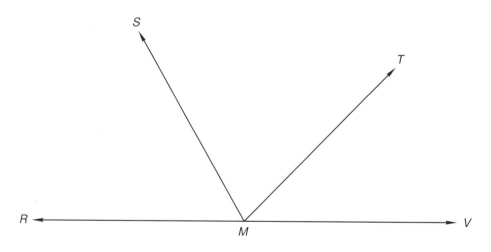

To draw angles with a protractor, follow these steps. Begin by drawing a horizontal ray.

Next, position the protractor so that the center point of the protractor is on the endpoint of the ray and a zero degree mark of the protractor is on the ray.

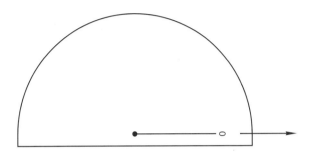

Then, with the protractor in position, make a dot on the paper at the mark on the protractor for the angle you wish to draw. Finally, remove the protractor and draw a ray from the endpoint of the first ray through the dot you made. Use your protractor to draw angles with these measures.

**j.** 30°      **k.** 80° ∟     **l.** 110°

**Problem set
125**

**1.** How many trips would it take to fill a 70-gallon water
(111) tank with a 4-gallon water bucket?    18 trips

**2.** What time is 6 hours and 23 minutes before 8:00 p.m.?
(32)    1:37 p.m.

**3.** The mean, median, and mode of student scores on a
(114) test were 89, 87, and 92, respectively. Which score was made most often on the test?    92

**4.** Fourteen of the 32 students in the class are girls. What
(82) is the boy-girl ratio in the class?    $\frac{9}{7}$

**5.** What number is 75% of 16?    12
(112)

**6.** What is the total price of an $85.00 item including 8%
(119) sales tax?    $91.80

**7.** Use a unit multiplier to convert 10 inches to centimeters.
(116) (1 in. = 2.54 cm)    25.4 cm

**8.** Compare: $\frac{1}{2}$ of 8 $\bigcirc{=}$ $\frac{1}{4}$ of 16
*(22)*

Complete the chart to answer problems 9, 10, and 11.

| | FRACTION | DECIMAL | PERCENT |
|---|---|---|---|
| **9.** *(98)* | $1\frac{2}{5}$ | (a) 1.4 | (b) 140% |
| **10.** *(98)* | (a) $\frac{1}{10}$ | 0.1 | (b) 10% |
| **11.** *(98)* | (a) $1\frac{1}{10}$ | (b) 1.1 | 110% |

**12.** 2.4 + $\frac{3}{5}$   (decimal answer)   3
*(85)*

**13.** 5 × $\frac{3}{4}$ × $2\frac{2}{3}$   10          **14.** 1 − (0.1 − 0.01)   0.91
*(71)*                                      *(38)*

**15.** 0.9 ÷ (3 ÷ 0.5)   0.15    **16.** $40^2$ − $\sqrt{400}$   1580
*(83)*                            *(123)*

**17.** The coordinates of three points that are on the same
*(74)* line are (−2, 3), (0, 1), and (4, $y$). What number should
replace $y$ in the third set of coordinates?   −3

**18.** What is the area of the shaded portion of this
*(79)* parallelogram?   27 cm²

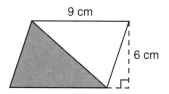

9 cm

6 cm

**19.** What is the circumference of a circle that has a radius
*(105)* of 5 meters?   31.4 m

**20.** For this triangular prism, list the number of its:
*(89)*
   (a) faces   5
   (b) edges   9
   (c) vertices   6

**21.** What is the value of $A$ in $A = \frac{1}{2}bh$ when $b$ is 8 cm and
$^{(45)}$ $h$ is 5 cm?   20 cm²

**22.** Ten is $\frac{2}{3}$ of what number?   15
$^{(122)}$

**23.** In the figure we show one line of
$^{(110)}$ symmetry of an equilateral triangle.
An equilateral triangle has a total
of how many lines of symmetry?   3

**24.** (a) (−12) + (−8)   −20      (b) −12 + +8   −4
$^{(121)}$

**25.** In a bag are four red marbles, five white marbles, and
$^{(91)}$ six blue marbles. If a marble is drawn from the bag,
what is the probability that the marble will be white?
$\frac{1}{3}$

**26.** (a) What is the radius of the circle?
$^{(124)}$ (b) Estimate the area of this circle.
(a) 2 units      (b) about 13 sq. units

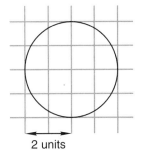

2 units

**27.** 5 lb, 3 oz − 2 lb, 7 oz   2 lb, 12 oz
$^{(117)}$

Refer to this illustration to find the measure of each angle
in problems 28, 29, and 30.

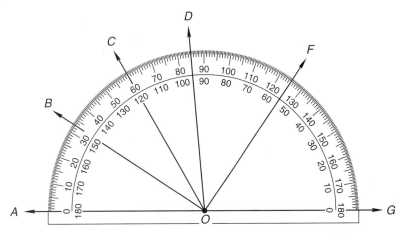

**28.** $\angle AOB$   33°      **29.** $\angle GOF$   55°      **30.** $\angle GOB$   147°
$^{(125)}$                   $^{(125)}$                        $^{(125)}$

# LESSON 126

# Opposites • Algebraic Addition

**Facts Practice:** Add Integers (Test O in Test Masters)

**Mental Math:**

**a.** 10 is $\frac{1}{5}$ of what number?   **b.** $\frac{3}{5}$ of 40   **c.** 60% of $50.00
**d.** 10 is what % of 100?   **e.** 0.7 × 60   **f.** 1000 · 1000
**g.** 6 × 8, + 1, $\sqrt{\ }$, × 5, + 1, $\sqrt{\ }$, × 3, + 2, ÷ 5, $\sqrt{\ }$

**Problem Solving:** The matting of the picture frame surrounded the picture. The outside dimensions of the matting were 11 in. by 13 in. The inside dimensions were 8 in. by 10 in. What was the area of the matting?

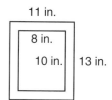

**Opposites**  Opposites are numbers that can be written with the same digits but with opposite signs. The opposite of 3 is −3, and the opposite of −5 is 5 (which can be written +5).

Opposites are the same distance from zero on the number line, but they lie in opposite directions.

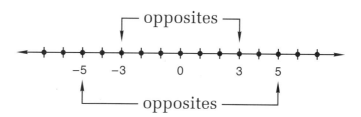

If opposites are added, the sum is zero.

$$-3 + {+3} = 0 \qquad -5 + {+5} = 0$$

**Example 1**  Find the opposite of these numbers:

(a) −7                                    (b) 10

*Solution*  The opposite of a number is written with the same digits but with the sign reversed.

(a) The opposite of −7 is +7, which equals **7.**

(b) The opposite of 10 (which is positive) is **−10.**

**Algebraic addition** Using opposites allows us to change any subtraction problem into an addition problem. Consider this subtraction problem.

$$10 - 6$$

Instead of subtracting 6 from 10, we may add the opposite of 6 to 10. The opposite of 6 is $-6$.

$$10 + -6$$

In both problems the answer is 4. Adding the opposite of a number to subtract is called **algebraic addition.** Instead of subtracting we will use algebraic addition to solve subtraction problems.

**Example 2** $-10 - -6$

*Solution* This problem directs us to subtract a negative six from negative ten. Instead, we may add the opposite of negative six to negative ten.

$$-10 - -6$$
$$\downarrow \quad \downarrow$$
$$-10 + +6 = \mathbf{-4}$$

**Example 3** $(-3) - (+5)$

*Solution* Instead of subtracting a positive five we add a negative five.

$$(-3) - (+5)$$
$$\downarrow \quad \downarrow$$
$$(-3) + (-5) = \mathbf{-8}$$

**Practice*** Find the opposite of each of these numbers:

**a.** $-8$   8          **b.** 4   $-4$          **c.** 0   0

Solve each of these subtraction problems by using algebraic addition:

**d.** $-3 - -4$   1          **e.** $-4 - +2$   $-6$

**f.** $(+3) - (-6)$   9          **g.** $(-2) - (-4)$   2

**Problem set 126**

1. *(111)* If a 36-inch-long sandwich is cut into 8 equal lengths, how long is each length?   $4\frac{1}{2}$ in.

2. *(5)* If photocopies cost 5¢ each for the first hundred copies and 3¢ each for additional copies, what would be the cost of 150 copies?   $6.50

3. *(81)* Thirty people were invited to the party, but only 24 people came. What percent of the people who were invited came to the party?   80%

4. *(112)* How much money is 35% of $80.00?   $28.00

5. *(103)* Complete the proportion: $\dfrac{24}{30} = \dfrac{x}{100}$   80

6. *(116)* Use a unit multiplier to convert 27 tablespoons of ingredients to teaspoons of ingredients. (1 tablespoon = 3 teaspoons)   81 tsp

7. *(50)* Divide $10.00 by 7 and round the quotient to the nearest cent.   $1.43

8. *(72)* Arrange in order from least to greatest:   $0.3, 32\%, \frac{1}{3}$

$$\frac{1}{3}, 32\%, 0.3$$

9. *(122)* Six is $\frac{3}{10}$ of what number?   20

10. *(122)* If $\frac{3}{8}$ of the candy bar weighs 90 grams, then what does the whole candy bar weigh?   240 g

11. *(91)* One thousand people entered the contest but only ten people will win. What is the probability that a person who entered the contest will be a winner?   $\frac{1}{100}$

12. *(62)* $12\frac{1}{2} - 3\frac{5}{8}$   $8\frac{7}{8}$

13. *(67)* $1\frac{2}{3} \div 3\frac{1}{2}$   $\frac{10}{21}$

**14.** $(1 + 0.5)(1 - 0.5)$  0.75   **15.** $5^2 - \sqrt{25}$   20
(39)                                                    (92)

**16.** (a) $(-4) + (-2)$  −6      (b) $(-4) - (-2)$  −2
(126)

**17.** The ratio of roses to camelias in the garden was 3 to 5.
(104)  If there were 45 roses, how many camelias were there?
      75

This pentagon is divided into two rectangles and a triangle. Refer to this figure to answer questions 18 and 19.

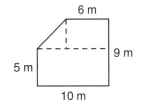

**18.** What is the area of the triangle in
(87)   the figure?   8 m²

**19.** Combine the area of the triangle and the area of the
(106)  two rectangles to find the area of the pentagon.   82 m²

**20.** The area of a square is 25 m². What is the perimeter of
(38)   the square?   20 m

**21.** A pyramid with a rectangular base has how many
(89)   more edges than vertices?   3

**22.** Write $\frac{1}{4}$ million in standard form.   250,000
(115)

**23.** Estimate the area of this circle.
(124)  Less than 4 sq. units (about 3 sq. units)

**24.** What is the total price of a $10.50 item plus 8% sales
(119)  tax?   $11.34

**25.** Figure out the rule for this function.
(123)  Then find the missing number.
      $x + 4$; 18

| $x$ | 2 | 6 | 10 | 14 |
|---|---|---|---|---|
| $y$ | 6 | 10 | 14 | ? |

**26.** $\sqrt{289}$   17          **27.** (a) $-5 - -3$  −2
(123)                          (126)
                                   (b) $-3 - -5$   2

Refer to this illustration to find the measure of the angles in questions 28, 29, and 30.

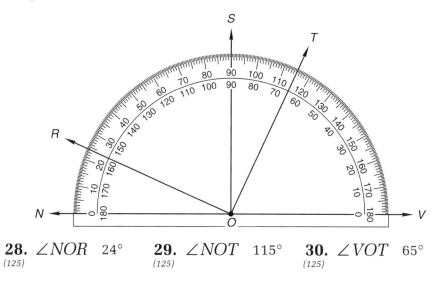

**28.** ∠*NOR*   24°
*(125)*

**29.** ∠*NOT*   115°
*(125)*

**30.** ∠*VOT*   65°
*(125)*

LESSON
**127**

# Finding a Whole When a Percent is Known

---

**Facts Practice:** Measurement Facts (Test N in Test Masters)

**Mental Math:**

**a.** $\frac{2}{3}$ of what number is 6?   **b.** $\frac{7}{10}$ of 60   **c.** 70% of $50.00
**d.** 3 is what % of 6?   **e.** 0.8 × 70   **f.** $\frac{5000}{25}$
**g.** $\frac{1}{2}$ of 50, $\sqrt{\phantom{x}}$, × 6, + 2, ÷ 4, × 3, + 1, × 4, $\sqrt{\phantom{x}}$

**Problem Solving:** At one o'clock the hour and minute hand of a clock form an angle of how many degrees?

---

**Mental Math:**
**a.** 9
**b.** 42
**c.** $35.00
**d.** 50%
**e.** 56
**f.** 200
**g.** 10
**Problem Solving:**
  30°

We have solved problems about fractional parts of a whole. Now we will consider problems about a percent of a whole such as the following problem:

> *Thirty percent of the members of the tribe were warriors. There were 150 warriors in all. What was the population of the tribe?*

The problem tells us that 30% of the members of the tribe were warriors. The entire tribe was the whole group. The warriors were part of the group. We will write an equation using $t$ to stand for the number of members in the whole tribe. We are told that the number of warriors was 150.

30% of the members of the tribe were warriors.

$$30\% \qquad t \qquad\qquad = \qquad 150$$

Now change 30% to a fraction or to a decimal.

30% is changed to $\frac{3}{10}$      30% is changed to 0.3

$$\frac{3}{10}t = 150 \qquad\qquad 0.3t = 150$$

We find $t$ by dividing 150 by three tenths.

$$150 \div \frac{3}{10} \qquad\qquad 0.3\overline{)150.0}^{\,500.}$$

$$\frac{\overset{50}{\cancel{150}}}{1} \times \frac{10}{\underset{1}{\cancel{3}}} = 500$$

We find that there were 500 members in the entire tribe.

**Example 1** Thirty percent of what number is 120?

*Solution* We translate the question into an equation. We translate the word "of" with a multiplication sign and the word "is" with an equals sign. For the words "what number" we write a letter.

Thirty percent of what number is 120?

$$30\% \qquad\qquad n \qquad = 120$$

We may choose to change 30% to a fraction or a decimal number. We choose the decimal form of 30%, which is 0.3.

$$0.3n = 120$$

Now we find $n$ by dividing 120 by 0.3.

$$0.3\overline{)120.0}^{\,400.}$$

The answer is **400.** Thirty percent of 400 is 120.

**Example 2**    Sixteen is 25% of what number?

**Solution**    We translate the question into an equation, using an equals sign for "is," a multiplication sign for "of," and a letter for "what number."

Sixteen is 25% of what number?

$$16 \quad = \quad 25\% \qquad n$$

We see that the way the question was asked, the position of the numbers on the two sides of the equals sign are reversed as compared to Example 1. We may solve the equation in this form or we may rearrange the equation. Either form of the equation may be used.

$$\mathbf{16 = 25\% \mathit{n}}$$

$$\mathbf{25\% \mathit{n} = 16}$$

We will use the translated form of the equation and change 25% to $\frac{1}{4}$.

$$16 = 25\% n$$

$$16 = \frac{1}{4}n$$

We find $n$ by dividing 16 by $\frac{1}{4}$.

$$16 \div \frac{1}{4}$$

$$\frac{16}{1} \times \frac{4}{1} = 64$$

The solution is **64.** Sixteen is 25% of 64.

**Practice\***    **a.** Twenty percent of what number is 120?    600

**b.** Fifty percent of what number is 30?    60

**c.** Twenty-five percent of what number is 12?    48

**d.** Twenty is 10% of what number?    200

**e.** Twelve is 100% of what number? 12

**f.** Fifteen is 15% of what number? 100

**Problem set 127**

**1.** Divide 555 by 12 and write the quotient
(26)
    (a) with a remainder. 46 r 3
    (b) as a mixed number. $46\frac{1}{4}$

**2.** The six gymnasts scored 9.75, 9.8, 9.9, 9.4, 9.9, and
(37) 9.95. The lowest score was not counted. What was the sum of the five highest scores? 49.3

**3.** What time is 3 hours and 55 minutes after 10:10 a.m.?
(32) 2:05 p.m.

**4.** Eight is $\frac{2}{3}$ of what number? 12
(122)

**5.** Write the standard number for the following: 186,000
(92)
$$(1 \times 10^5) + (8 \times 10^4) + (6 \times 10^3)$$

6. One way is to follow the scale all the way from zero. A quick way is to determine whether the angle is acute (less than 90°) or obtuse (greater than 90°) and use the corresponding scale.

**6.** There are two scales on a protractor. When measuring
(125) an angle, how can you tell which scale to use?

**7.** The mean of three numbers is 12. If two of the
(114) numbers are 9 and 10, what is the third number? 17

**8.** Convert $8\frac{1}{3}\%$ to a fraction. $\frac{1}{12}$
(119)

**9.** Nine dollars is what percent of $12? 75%
(118)

**10.** Twenty percent of what number is 12? 60
(127)

**11.** Three tenths of what number is 9? 30
(122)

**12.** $\sqrt{10,000}$    100
(123)

**13.** $(-15) + (+18)$    3
(126)

**14.** $(+8) - (+6)$    2
(126)

**15.** $2\frac{1}{2} - 1\frac{2}{3}$    $\frac{5}{6}$
(62)

**16.** A biathalon is a two-event race that includes biking
(104) and running. If the ratio of the length of the run to the
length of the bike ride in a certain biathalon was 2 to
5, and if the distance run was 10 kilometers, then what
was the total length of the biathalon?   35 km

**17.** The area of the shaded triangle is 2.8 cm². What is the
(79)  area of the parallelogram?   5.6 cm²

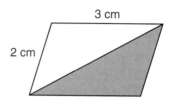

**18.** The figurine was packed in a box that was 10 in. long,
(99)  3 in. wide, and 4 in. deep. What was the volume of
the box?   120 in.³

**19.** A rectangle that is not a square
(110) has a total of how many lines of
symmetry?   2

**20.** If this shape was cut out and
(66)  folded on the dotted lines, would
it form a cube, a pyramid, or a
cone?   pyramid

**21.** $3m - 5 = 25$   10
(107)

**22.** Figure out the rule for this function. Then find the
(123) missing number.   4x; 8

| x | 3 | 4 | 6 | ? |
|---|---|---|---|---|
| y | 12 | 16 | 24 | 32 |

20,000 lb   **23.** How many pounds is 10 tons?
(94)

**24.** Which of these polygons is not a quadrilateral?
(78)

A. Parallelogram  B. Pentagon    C. Trapezoid

B. Pentagon

**25.** Compare: area of the square ⊘ area of the circle
(124)

**26.** The coordinates of three points that are on the same
(74) line are (–3, –2), (0, 0), and (x, 4). What number should replace x in the third set of coordinates?   6

**27.** Use your protractor to draw an angle that is half the
(125) size of a right angle. What is the measure of the angle?
See student work. 45°

**28.** Robert flipped a coin. It landed heads up. He flipped
(91) the coin a second time. It landed heads up. If he flips the coin a third time, what is the probability that it will land heads up?   $\frac{1}{2}$

**29.** The diameter of the circle is 10 cm.
(38) What is the area of the square?
25 cm²

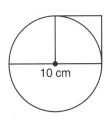

10 cm

**30.** What is the mode and the range of this set of numbers?
(114)

4, 7, 6, 4, 5, 3, 2, 6, 7, 9, 7, 4, 10, 7, 9

mode, 7; range, 8

# INVESTIGATION
# 5

# Sign Wars

One model for the addition of signed numbers is the number line. Students should be able to illustrate the addition of integers on a number line. Another model for the addition of signed numbers is the electrical-charge model, used in the "Sign Wars" game. Learning the "Sign Wars" game is a one-class-period activity. "Screens" should be drawn on the board or should be projected for all to see.

**The Game**  In "Sign Wars" positives battle negatives. After each battle we ask the question, "Who survives?" and write our answer.

**Level 1**  Positive and negative signs are displayed randomly on a screen. During the battle positive and negative pairs are neutralized. (Appropriate sound effects strengthen the experience!)

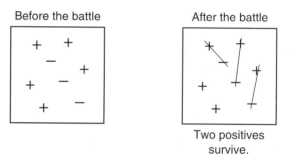

Two positives
survive.

After the battle we count the remaining positives or negatives to determine who survives. See if you can determine the number and type of survivors for the following practice screens.

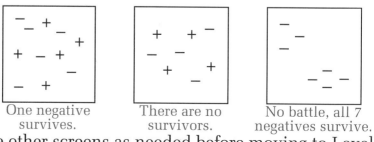

One negative          There are no          No battle, all 7
survives.               survivors.          negatives survive.

Create other screens as needed before moving to Level 2.

**Level 2** Positives and negatives are displayed in counted clusters.

The same rules apply as in Level 1. The suggested strategy is to group forces before the battle. So +3 combines with +1 to make +4, and −5 combines with −2 to make −7.

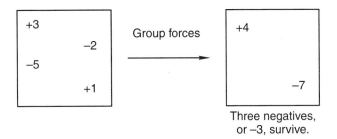

Three negatives, or −3, survive.

Since there are three more negatives than positives, −3 survive. See if you can determine the number and type of survivors for the following practice screens.

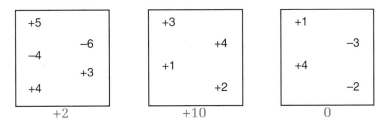

Create additional screens if more practice is needed.

**Level 3** Positive and negative clusters can be displayed with zero, one, or two signs. The same rules apply as in Levels 1 and 2. Clusters appear "in disguise" by taking on an additional sign or by dropping a sign. The first step is to remove the disguise. A cluster with no sign, with − −, or with + + is a positive cluster. A cluster with + − or with − + is a negative cluster. If a cluster has a "shield" (parentheses), look through the shield to see the sign. As examples, −(−3) is really +3, while −(+3) is really −3.

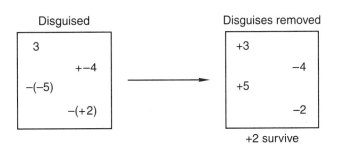

+2 survive

See if you can determine the number and type of survivors for the following practice screens:

| | | |
|---|---|---|
| $--3$ $+(-5)$ $-+6$ $+(+4)$ $-4$ | $+(-3)$ $-2$ $-(+4)$ $-9$ | $-(+6)$ $--3$ $+4$ $-(+2)$ $+-6$ $-7$ |

Extend Level 3 to a line of clusters:

$$-3 + (-4) - (-5) - (+2) + (+6)$$

Use the following steps to find the answer:

**Step 1.** Break code: $-3 - 4 + 5 - 2 + 6$

**Step 2.** Group forces: $-9 + 11$

**Step 3.** Who survives? $+2$

**Practice**

a. $-2 + -3 - -4 + -5$    $-6$

b. $-3 + (+2) - (+5) - (-6)$    $0$

c. $+3 + -4 - +6 + +7 - -1$    $1$

d. $2 + (-3) - (-9) - (+7) + (+1)$    $2$

e. $3 - -5 + -4 - +2 + +8$    $10$

f. $(-10) - (+20) - (-30) + (-40)$    $-40$

## LESSON
## 128

# Estimating Square Roots

Mental Math:
a. 12
b. 12
c. $32.00
d. $33\frac{1}{3}$%
e. 36
f. 1000
g. 6
Problem Solving:
   31.4 ft

**Facts Practice:**  Add and Subtract Integers (Test P in Test Masters)

**Mental Math:**

    **a.** 8 is $\frac{2}{3}$ of what number?   **b.** $\frac{2}{5}$ of 30    **c.** 80% of $40.00

    **d.** 3 is what % of 9?      **e.** 0.9 × 40   **f.** 10 · 10 · 10

    **g.** 3 × 3, × 3, + 3, ÷ 3, − 3, × 3, − 3, ÷ 3

**Problem Solving:** There were two circles of horses on the carousel. The diameter of the inner circle of horses was 30 feet, while the diameter of the outer circle of horses was 40 feet. In each turn of the carousel, a horse in the outer circle travels how much farther than a horse in the inner circle?

We have practiced finding the square roots of numbers that are perfect squares. All of the following numbers are perfect squares:

$$1, 4, 9, 16, 25, 36, 49, 64, 81, 100$$

In this lesson we will practice estimating the square root of numbers that are not perfect squares.

**Example 1**  Between which two consecutive whole numbers is $\sqrt{20}$?

*Solution*  Notice that we are not asked to find the square root of 20. To find the whole numbers on either side of $\sqrt{20}$, we may first think of the perfect squares that are on either side of 20. Looking at the list at the beginning of this lesson we see that 20 is between the perfect squares 16 and 25. Since $\sqrt{16}$ is 4, and $\sqrt{25}$ is 5, we see that $\sqrt{20}$ **is between 4 and 5.**

Since 4 × 4 is 16, and 5 × 5 is 25, there must be some number between 4 and 5 that is the square root of 20. We could try 4.5.

$$4.5 \times 4.5 = 20.25$$

We see that 4.5 is too large. We could try 4.4.

$$4.4 \times 4.4 = 19.36$$

We see that 4.4 is too small. So $\sqrt{20}$ is more than 4.4 but less than 4.5, and it is closer to 4.5. We could continue this process and never find the exact decimal number or fraction that equals $\sqrt{20}$. The square root of 20 belongs to a class of numbers called **irrational numbers.**

Irrational numbers cannot be exactly expressed as a ratio—that is, as a fraction or decimal. We may use fractions or decimals to express the approximate value of an irrational number.

$$\sqrt{20} \approx 4.5$$

The wavy equals sign means "approximately equal to." The square root of 20 is approximately equal to 4.5.

**Example 2**   Use a calculator to approximate the value of $\sqrt{20}$ to two decimal places.

*Solution*   We clear the calculator and then enter $\boxed{\sqrt{\phantom{x}}}$ $\boxed{2}$ $\boxed{0}$ . The display reads 4.472135955. The actual value of the $\sqrt{20}$ contains an infinite number of decimal places. The display approximates $\sqrt{20}$ to nine decimal places. We are asked to show two decimal places, so we round the displayed number to **4.47.**

**Practice***   Each of these square roots is between which two consecutive whole numbers? Find the answer without the aid of a calculator.

**a.** $\sqrt{2}$   1 and 2   **b.** $\sqrt{15}$   3 and 4   **c.** $\sqrt{40}$   6 and 7

**d.** $\sqrt{60}$   7 and 8   **e.** $\sqrt{70}$   8 and 9   **f.** $\sqrt{80}$   8 and 9

Using a calculator, approximate each of these square roots to two decimal places.

**g.** $\sqrt{3}$   1.73          **h.** $\sqrt{10}$   3.16          **i.** $\sqrt{50}$   7.07

**Problem set 128**

**1.** Deborah ordered a meal priced at $6.95 and a beverage priced at $1.25. The sales tax rate was 6%. What was the total price including food, drink, and tax?   $8.69
(119)

**2.** The weather forecast stated that the chance for rain is 80%. What is the chance that it will not rain?   20%
(91)

**3.** Eight is 20% of what number?   40
(127)

**4.** $\dfrac{3}{5} \neq$   D. 6%
(95)

A. 0.6          B. $\dfrac{15}{25}$          C. 60%          D. 6%

**5.** Forty-five of the 60 trees in the orchard were apple trees. What fraction of the trees were apple trees?   $\frac{3}{4}$
(29)

**6.** Two thirds of an hour is how many minutes?   40 min
(29)

**7.** Find the mean, median, mode, and range for this set of numbers:   mean, 8; median, 7.5; mode, 7; range, 5
(114)

$$11, 10, 9, 9, 8, 7, 7, 7, 6, 6$$

**8.** Compare: 10% of 30 $\;=\;$ 30% of 10
(112)

Complete the chart to answer problems 9, 10, and 11.

|  | FRACTION | DECIMAL | PERCENT |
|---|---|---|---|
| **9.** (98) | $\dfrac{12}{25}$ | (a) 0.48 | (b) 48% |
| **10.** (98) | (a) $1\frac{4}{5}$ | 1.8 | (b) 180% |
| **11.** (98) | (a) $\frac{9}{25}$ | (b) 0.36 | 36% |

**12.** $3\frac{2}{3} + 1\frac{5}{6}$   $5\frac{1}{2}$
(58)

**13.** $2\frac{1}{2} \div 1\frac{2}{3}$   $1\frac{1}{2}$
(67)

**14.** $0.3 \div (3 \div 0.03)$   0.003
(48)

**15.** $(-7) + (+16)$   9
(126)

**16.** Between which two consecutive whole numbers is $\sqrt{30}$?
(128)   5 and 6

**17.** If 2.5 pounds of beef cost $4.50, what is the price per
(94)   pound?   $1.80

**18.** What is the area of the shaded part of this rectangle?
(87)   20 cm²

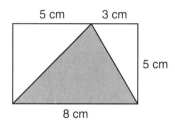

**19.** What is the name for the shape of a basketball?   sphere
(66)

**20.** 5 hr, 10 min, 15 s − 1 hr, 25 min, 30 s
(115)   3 hr, 44 min, 45 s

**21.** Which of these shapes is *not* symmetrical (has no lines
(110)   of symmetry)?   C.

A.      B.      C.

**22.** Write the prime factorization of 96 using exponents.
(72)   $2^5 \times 3$

**23.** Write the standard number for $1.25 \times 10^6$.   1,250,000
(115)

**24.** $(-6) - (+8) + (+4) - (-10)$   0
(126)

**25.** The graph shows the percentage of the Smiths' income
(40) that is spent on various items. The circle represents
100% of their income. What percent of their income
goes into savings?   8%

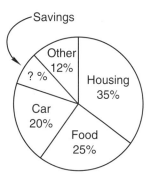

**26.** On a coordinate plane draw a ray from (0, 0) through
(125) (10, 10). Draw a second ray from (0, 0) through (10, 0).
Use your protractor to find the measure of the angle
formed by the rays.   See student work.; 45°

**27.** The measure of angle $a$ is $\frac{1}{6}$ of 360°.
(107)
(a)  What is the measure of angle $a$?

(b)  What type of angle is angle $a$?

(a) 60°   (b) acute

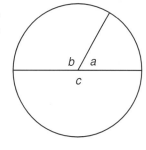

**28.** $20^2 - \sqrt{100} \times 5 + \sqrt{225}$   365
(92)

**29.** What percent of 16 is $\sqrt{16}$?   25%
(118)

**30.** Sarah is reading a book with 350 pages. She calculated
(113) that the ratio of the pages she has read to the pages she
has not read is 2 to 3. How many pages has Sarah read?
140 pages

# LESSON 129

# Using Proportions to Solve Percent Problems

**Facts Practice:** Add and Subtract Integers (Test P in Test Masters)

**Mental Math:**

**a.** $\frac{2}{3}$ of what number is 10?  **b.** $\frac{5}{6}$ of 30  **c.** 80% of $50.00
**d.** 3 is what % of 12?  **e.** 0.2 × 200  **f.** $\frac{4500}{50}$
**g.** 7 × 7, + 1, × 2, − 1, ÷ 9, + 1, ÷ 3, × 4, − 1, ÷ 3

**Problem Solving:** Niki constructed a kite with sticks, paper, string, and glue. The cross sticks were two feet long and three feet long. As the wind lifted the kite, it blew against the paper that had an area of how many square feet?

We know that a percent may be expressed as a fraction with a denominator of 100.

$$30\% \text{ equals } \frac{30}{100}$$

A percent may also be regarded as a ratio in which 100 represents the total number in the group, as we show in this example.

**Example 1** Thirty percent of the students earned an A on the test. If twelve students earned an A, how many students were there in all?

**Solution** We will construct a ratio box. The ratio numbers we are given are 30 and 100, *which represents the total.* The actual count we are given is 12. Our categories are "A's" and "not A's."

|  | RATIO | ACTUAL COUNT |
|---|---|---|
| A's | 30 | 12 |
| Not A's |  |  |
| Total | 100 |  |

Since the ratio total is 100, the ratio number for "not A's" is 70. We use $n$ to stand for "not A's" and $t$ for "total" in the actual count column. We use two rows from the table to write a proportion. Since we know both numbers in the "A's" row, we use the numbers in the "A's" row for the proportion. Since we want to find the total number of students, we also use the numbers from the "total" row.

| | Ratio | Actual Count |
|---|---|---|
| A's | 30 | 12 |
| Not A's | 70 | $n$ |
| Total | 100 | $t$ |

$$\frac{30}{100} = \frac{12}{t}$$

Now we solve the proportion using cross products.

$$\frac{30}{100} = \frac{12}{t}$$

$$30t = 12 \cdot 100$$

$$t = \frac{\overset{4}{\cancel{12}} \cdot \overset{10}{\cancel{100}}}{\underset{\underset{1}{\cancel{3}}}{\cancel{30}}}$$

$$t = 40$$

The total number of students was **40.**

In the above problem we did not need to use the 70% who were "not A's." In the next problem we need to use the percent obtained from subtracting a given percent from 100%.

Example 2   Only 40% of the team members played in the game. If 24 team members did not play, then how many did play?

*Solution*  We construct a ratio box. The categories are "played," "did not play," and "total."

|  | RATIO | ACTUAL COUNT |
|---|---|---|
| Played | 40 | $p$ |
| Did not Play | 60 | 24 |
| Total | 100 | $t$ |

$$\frac{40}{60} = \frac{p}{24}$$

$$60p = 40 \cdot 24$$

$$p = \frac{\overset{4}{\cancel{40}} \cdot \overset{4}{\cancel{24}}}{\underset{\underset{1}{\cancel{6}}}{\cancel{60}}}$$

$$p = 16$$

We find that **16** team members played.

**Practice**  Solve these percent problems using proportions. Make a ratio box for each problem.

**a.** Forty percent of the students earned an A on the test. If 24 students did not earn an A, how many students were there in all?  40

**b.** Seventy percent of the team members played in the game. If 21 team members played, how many team members did not play?  9

$\frac{70}{100} = \frac{21}{t}$  **c.** Referring to problem (b), what proportion would we use to find the number of members on the team?

**Problem set 129**  **1.** Fifty-eight players were divided as evenly as possible into 8 teams. How many teams had exactly 7 players?
*(111)*  6

**2.** To the nearest cent, what is $\frac{1}{3}$ of $10?  $3.33
*(50)*

50%  **3.** What percent of the letters in the word **Alaska** are A's?
*(81)*

**4.** From a normal deck of 52 cards, two aces were
(91) removed leaving only 50 cards. If Sammy randomly
draws a card from this deck of 50 cards, what is the
probability

(a) of drawing an ace?   $\frac{1}{25}$

(b) of drawing a king?   $\frac{2}{25}$

**5.** Use digits to write the number fifteen million, nine
(12) hundred eighty-five thousand.   15,985,000

**6.** Use a unit multiplier to change 4000 ounces to
(116) pounds. (1 pound = 16 ounces)   250 lb

**7.** Arrange in order from greatest to least:   $\sqrt{26}, 5, 4.99$
(128)
$$5, \sqrt{26}, 4.99$$

**8.** What is the sales tax on an $8.79 item if the tax rate is 6%?
(119) $0.53

**9.** Fifteen is 30% of what number?   50
(127)

**10.** Fifteen is $\frac{5}{6}$ of what number?   18
(122)

**11.** (a) (8) + (−13)   −5        (b) (−8) + (+13)   5
(126)

**12.** How many small cubes are in this large cube?   64
(99)

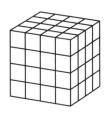

**13.** $4\frac{1}{2} \div 0.09$   (decimal answer)   50
(85)

**14.** $\frac{7}{8} + \left(4 - 1\frac{1}{4}\right)$   $3\frac{5}{8}$        **15.** $2\frac{1}{2} \div \left(1\frac{1}{2} \times 1\frac{2}{3}\right)$   1
(62)                                     (67)

**16.** Between which two consecutive whole numbers on
*(128)* the number line is $\sqrt{12}$?   3 and 4

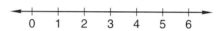

**17.** When the 48 passengers took their seats, the bus was $\frac{2}{3}$
*(122)* full. How many passengers can sit in the bus when it
is full?   72

The following scores were made on a test: 72, 80, 84, 88,
100, 88, and 76. Using these scores, answer problems 18,
19, 20, and 21.

**18.** Which score was earned most often (mode)?   88
*(114)*

**19.** If the scores were listed in order, what would be the
*(114)* middle score (median)?   84

**20.** What is the average of all the scores (mean)?   84
*(114)*

**21.** What is the difference between the highest score and
*(114)* the lowest score (range)?   28

**22.** Use the rule of the function to
*(123)* find the missing number.   20

| $a$ | 6 | 10 | 12 | 15 |
|---|---|---|---|---|
| $b$ | 16 | ? | 22 | 25 |

**23.** In the figure, $\angle ABC$ is a right
*(107)* angle, and $\angle CBD$ is a right angle.
What type of angle is $\angle ABD$?
straight angle

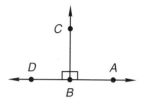

**24.** $-8 - (-6) - (+4) + (-5) + (+7)$   $-4$
*(126)*

**25.** At the local track the ratio of joggers to walkers was 2
*(113)* to 1. If 24 people were on the track, how many were
jogging?   16

**26.** Compare:  area of the circle $\textcircled{<}$ 400 cm²
(124)

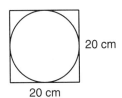

20 cm

20 cm

**27.** Sixty percent of the students in the auditorium were
(129) girls. If there were 120 boys in the auditorium, how
many girls were there? (Make a ratio box for the
problem.)    180

**28.** The coordinates of the vertices of an isosceles triangle
(87) are (0, 5), (3, 0), and (−3, 0). What is the area of the
triangle?    15 sq. units

**29.** 3 gal, 2 qt, 1pt + 1 gal, 1 qt, 1 pt    5 gal
(115)

**30.** Which transformations would posi-
(108) tion triangle I on triangle II?
rotation and reflection

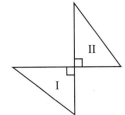

# LESSON
# 130

# Area of a Circle

**Facts Practice:** Add and Subtract Integers (Test P in Test Masters)

**Mental Math:**

   **a.** $\frac{3}{4}$ of what number is 6?  **b.** $\frac{9}{10}$ of 50   **c.** 90% of $40.00
   **d.** 3 is what % of 15?        **e.** 0.4 × 300   **f.** 20 · 20 · 20
   **g.** 8 × 7, − 6, ÷ 5, − 4, ÷ 3, − 2, × 1

**Problem Solving:** Copy the problem and fill in the missing digits. Can you find more than one solution?

$$\begin{array}{r} \_\ \_\ r\ 7 \\ \_\overline{)\_\ 7\ \_} \\ \underline{=\ =\ =} \\ =\ = \\ \underline{=\ =} \\ = \end{array}$$

We have estimated the areas of circles drawn on a grid by counting squares within a circle. In this lesson we will learn another method to calculate the area of a circle.

To find the area of a circle, we must first find the area of a square that could be drawn on the radius of the circle. This circle has a radius of 10 mm, so the area of the square is 100 mm². 

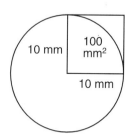

The area of the circle is exactly equal to the area of $\pi$ of these squares. To find the area of this circle, we multiply the area of the square by $\pi$. We will continue to use 3.14 for the approximation of $\pi$.

$$3.14 \times 100 \text{ mm}^2 \text{ or } 314 \text{ mm}^2$$

The area of the circle is approximately 314 mm².

**Example**   The radius of a circle is 3 cm. What is the area of the circle? (Use $\pi = 3.14$.)

*Solution*   We will find the area of a square whose sides equal the radius. Then we multiply that area by 3.14.

Area of square: 3 cm × 3 cm = 9 cm²

Area of circle: $(3.14)(9 \text{ cm}^2) = 28.26 \text{ cm}^2$

The area of the circle is approximately **28.26 cm²**.

**Practice***   Find the approximate areas of the circles that have the following measures.

    **a.** Radius, 2 ft   12.56 ft²      **b.** Diameter, 2 ft   3.14 ft²

    **c.** Radius, 8 in.   200.96 in.²    **d.** Diameter, 8 in.   50.24 in.²

**Problem set 130**

    **1.** The quotient of a division problem is 5 and the
    (2) remainder is 7. The divisor must have been larger than which number?   larger than 7

    **2.** The four judges awarded scores of 9.9, 9.8, 9.6, and
    (114) 10.0 to the contestant. The highest and lowest scores were not counted. What was the mean of the two middle scores?   9.85

    **3.** What number is 32% of 50?   16
    (112)

    **4.** Using 3 feet = 1 yard, write two ratios equal to 1.
    (116) Which one would you use to find the number of yards in 342 feet?   $\frac{3\,\text{feet}}{1\,\text{yard}}, \frac{1\,\text{yard}}{3\,\text{feet}}$; *use* $\frac{1\,\text{yard}}{3\,\text{feet}}$

    **5.** What decimal number is three tenths more than
    (38) twenty-five thousandths?   0.325

    **6.** John was thinking of a counting number from 1 to 10.
    (91) He gave James three tries to guess the number. If James does not correctly guess the number on his first try, what is the probability that he will guess the correct number on his second try?   $\frac{1}{9}$

**7.** Round the product of $3\frac{1}{3}$ and $2\frac{1}{3}$ to the nearest whole
(65) number.   8

**8.** Compare: $\dfrac{1}{2}$ of 17 $\bigcirc\!=$ 50% of 17
(112)

**9.** After reading page 132, Susan figured she had read $\frac{3}{4}$
(122) of her book. How many pages are in her book?
176 pages

**10.** Twenty is 40% of what number?   50
(127)

**11.** Thirty is 30% of what number?   100
(127)

**12.** $4\frac{1}{2} + 3\frac{1}{4} + 2\frac{1}{6}$   $9\frac{11}{12}$      **13.** $3\frac{1}{3} \times 2\frac{1}{3}$   $7\frac{7}{9}$
(59)                                            (65)

**14.** $1.2 + (4 - 1.86)$   3.34     **15.** $3.3 \times 2.3$   7.59
(38)                                (39)

**16.** (a) $(-12) + (-8)$   −20      (b) $(-3) - (+12)$   −15
(126)

**17.** $-3 + (-2) - (-4) + (-6) - (+5)$   −12
(126)

**18.** The radius of a circle is 4 cm.
(130)   (a) What is the area of the square?
(b) What is the area of the circle?
(a) 16 cm²   (b) 50.24 cm²

**19.** "Two polygons that are congruent are also similar."
(109) True or false?   true

**20.** $40 + 50 + a = 180$   90
(3)

**21.** Find the value of $y$ in $y = mw + 2$ when $m = 3$ and
(45) $w = 4$.   14

**22.** Which of the following letters has two lines of
(110) symmetry?   H

M     A     T     H

**23.** The park had a season attendance of 3.5 million
(115) people. Write the standard number for that amount.
3,500,000

**24.** The ratio of brooms to mops in the custodian's closet
(113) was 2 to 3. If the total number of brooms and mops in
the closet was 30, how many mops were there?
18

**25.** Which arrow could be pointing to $\sqrt{3}$?   *D*
(128)

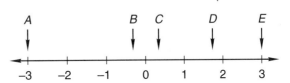

**26.** A cord of wood was stacked 4 feet wide, 4 feet high,
(99) and 8 feet long. How many cubic feet of wood were in
the cord?   128 ft³

**27.** The Smiths spend 35% of their income on housing. If
(127) their housing expenses are $840 per month, then what
is the Smiths' monthly income?   $2400

The diameter of a CD is about 12 cm. Use this information
to answer problems 28 and 29.

**28.** What is the circumference of a
(105) CD?   37.68 cm

**29.** What is the area of a CD?
(130)   113.04 cm²

**30.** The measure of $\angle b$ is $\frac{1}{3}$ of 360°.
(107)
(a) What is the measure of $\angle b$?

(b) What type of angle is $\angle b$?
(a) 120°   (b) obtuse

# LESSON
# 131

# Probability of a Series of Events

---

**Facts Practice:** Add and Subtract Integers (Test P in Test Masters)

**Mental Math:**

**a.** $\frac{4}{5}$ of 35

**b.** 70% of $30.00

**c.** 12 is $\frac{3}{4}$ of what number?

**d.** 3 is what % of 30?

**e.** 0.6 × 300

**f.** $\frac{4800}{60}$

**g.** 9 × 9, − 1, ÷ 4, − 2, ÷ 3, × 5, ÷ 2, + 1, $\sqrt{\phantom{x}}$

**Problem Solving:** How many three-digit area codes are possible if zero cannot be used for the first digit and if zero and one cannot be used for the second digit?

---

We have practiced finding the probability that a single event will occur. For example, we found that the probability that a coin will land heads up on a single toss is one chance in two, which is $\frac{1}{2}$. In this lesson we will practice finding the probability **that a series of events will occur.**

**Example 1** What is the probability that a coin will land heads up twice in two tosses?

**Solution** Recall that probability is the ratio of the number of favorable outcomes to the number of possible outcomes.

$$\text{Probability} = \frac{\text{Number of favorable outcomes}}{\text{Number of possible outcomes}}$$

We list the possible outcomes below.

First toss heads, second toss heads (HH).
First toss heads, second toss tails (HT).
First toss tails, second toss heads (TH).
First toss tails, second toss tails (TT).

We see that there are four possible outcomes. In this case, the favorable outcome is heads on the first toss followed by heads on the second toss. Since only one of the four possible outcomes is heads twice, the probability is $\frac{1}{4}$.

We may also multiply the probability of each of the single events to find the probability of a series of events. The probability of the coin landing heads up is $\frac{1}{2}$ on the first toss and $\frac{1}{2}$ on the second toss. So the probability of the coin landing heads up twice in a row is $\frac{1}{2} \cdot \frac{1}{2}$, which is $\frac{1}{4}$.

**Example 2**   There were two red marbles, three white marbles, and four blue marbles in a bag. One marble will be drawn from the bag and held. Then a second marble will be drawn from the bag. What is the probability that both marbles drawn from the bag will be white?

*Solution*   We will calculate the probability of each event separately. Then we will multiply the probabilities to find the probability of the series of events.

There are nine marbles in the bag, and three of them are white. So the probability of drawing a white marble on the first draw is $\frac{3}{9}$, which equals $\frac{1}{3}$.

After one marble is drawn there are eight marbles left in the bag. Since the probability we are calculating is that both marbles drawn will be white, we assume that the first draw removed a white marble from the bag, leaving two white marbles for the second draw. So the probability of drawing a white marble from the bag on the second draw is $\frac{2}{8}$ which equals $\frac{1}{4}$. Thus the probability of drawing a white marble on both draws is $\frac{1}{3} \cdot \frac{1}{4}$, which is $\frac{1}{12}$.

**Note:** We are calculating the probability of a series of *future* events. The probability that a coin will land heads up twice in a row is $\frac{1}{4}$ if both tosses lie in the future. Once one toss is completed, the probability of the coin landing heads up on the next toss is $\frac{1}{2}$ because only one toss lies in the future.

**Practice**   **a.** What is the probability that a coin will land heads up three times in three tosses?   $\frac{1}{8}$

**b.** A bag contains two red marbles, three white marbles, and four blue marbles. If one marble will be removed from the bag and then another marble will be removed from the bag, what is the probability that both marbles will be blue?   $\frac{1}{6}$

**Problem set**    **1.** The price of the television was $399.00. The sales tax
**131**    (119)  was 7%. What was the total cost of the television
including sales tax?   $426.93

**2.** If the taxi charges $1.25 for the first mile and 95¢ for
(12)  each additional mile, what would be the cost of a
7-mile ride?   $6.95

**3.** Use a unit multiplier to change 5000 decimeters to
(116)  centimeters. (10 centimeters = 1 decimeter)
$$\frac{5000\ \text{decimeters}}{1} \cdot \frac{10\ \text{centimeters}}{1\ \text{decimeter}} = 50{,}000\ \text{cm}$$

**4.** Twenty-four is 60% of what number?   40
(127)

**5.** Twenty-four is $\frac{2}{3}$ of what number?   36
(122)

**6.** During the basketball game Sandra made 8 shots and
(129)  missed 12 shots. What percent of her shots did Sandra
make? (Make a ratio box for this problem. Remember
that the total number of shots is 100%.)   40%

**7.** Albert noticed that the cookies could be separated into
(15)  2 equal groups, 3 equal groups, or 4 equal groups. If
there were less than 20 cookies, how many cookies
were there?   12 cookies

**8.** Which of these numbers is closest to 1000?   C. 999.1
(31)  A. 999        B. 1001        C. 999.1        D. 1001.1

Complete the chart to answer problems 9, 10, and 11.

|  | FRACTION | DECIMAL | PERCENT |
|---|---|---|---|
| **9.** (98) | $\frac{3}{100}$ | (a) 0.03 | (b) 3% |
| **10.** (98) | (a) $2\frac{7}{10}$ | 2.7 | (b) 270% |
| **11.** (98) | (a) $1\frac{9}{20}$ | (b) 1.45 | 145% |

$10\frac{1}{2}$ in.   **12.** 2 ft, 6 in. − 1 ft, $7\frac{1}{2}$ in.   **13.** $5\frac{1}{3}$ yd ÷ 2   $2\frac{2}{3}$ yd
(115)                                          (67)

**14.** $5\dfrac{1}{4} + 2.3$   (decimal answer)   7.55
(85)

**15.** $0.25 \div (2 \div 0.04)$   0.005
(48)

**16.** Arrange in order from least to greatest:   $1^3, \sqrt{3}, 2$
(128)
$$2, \sqrt{3}, 1^3$$

**17.** Combine the area of the two
(106) rectangles and the triangle to find the area of the pentagon.   43 ft²

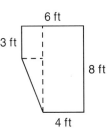

**18.** What is the area of this circle?
(130)   314 m²

**19.** What is the circumference of this
(105) circle?   62.8 m

**20.** A soup can is what geometric shape?   cylinder
(66)

**21.** What is the probability that a coin will land tails up
(131) three times on three tosses?   $\frac{1}{8}$

**22.** (a) $(-15) + (+24)$   9       (b) $(-8) - (+3)$   −11
(126)

**23.** Find the missing number in this function:   26
(123)

| $x$ | 1 | 2 | 3 | 4 |
|---|---|---|---|---|
| $3x^2 - 1$ | 2 | 11 | ? | 47 |

**24.** What is the smallest prime number?   2
(61)

**25.** Which of the following shapes could not fold into a cube?

(66)

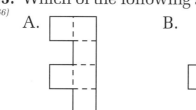  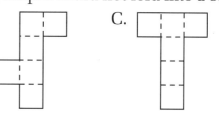

A.    B.    C.    A.

**26.** A bag contains two red, three white, and four blue
(131) marbles. If one marble is removed and then another,
what is the probability that both marbles removed will
be red?    $\frac{1}{36}$

**27.** $-2 - -4 + -6 + +8 - +10 - -12$    6
(126)

**28.** What percent of the months of the year begin with the
(81) letter *J*?    25%

**29.** A classroom cabinet is 3 ft wide,
(99) 2 ft deep, and 6 ft high. What is
the volume of the cabinet?    36 ft³

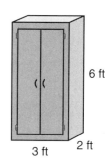

6 ft

3 ft    2 ft

**30.** On a coordinate plane draw a ray from (0, 0) through
(125) (−10, 10). Draw a second ray from (0, 0) through (12, 0).
Use a protractor to find the measure of the angle formed
by the two rays.    See student work. 135°

# LESSON
# 132

# Volume of a Cylinder

**Facts Practice:** Percents to Fractions and Decimals (Test M in Test Masters)

**Mental Math:**

| | |
|---|---|
| **a.** $\frac{2}{3}$ of 27 | **b.** 80% of $60.00 |
| **c.** $\frac{3}{4}$ of what number is 9? | **d.** 5 is what % of 5? |
| **e.** 0.8 × 400 | **f.** 10 · 20 · 30 |

**g.** $\frac{1}{4}$ of 24, × 5, + 5, ÷ 7, × 8, + 2, ÷ 7, + 1, ÷ 7

**Problem Solving:** The first three prime numbers are 2, 3, and 5. These numbers can be arranged to form a three-digit number that is also a prime number. What is that three-digit prime number?

Mental Math:
a. 18
b. $48.00
c. 12
d. 100%
e. 320
f. 6000
g. 1
Problem Solving:
    523

Imagine pressing a quarter down into a block of soft clay.

As the quarter moves into the clay, it creates a hole in the clay the shape of a cylinder. The area of the quarter sweeps out a cylinder as it moves through the clay. We can calculate the volume of the cylinder by multiplying the area of the circular face of the quarter times the distance it moved through the clay.

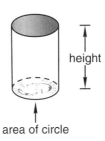

height

area of circle

**Example**  The diameter of this cylinder is 20 cm. Its height is 10 cm. What is its volume?

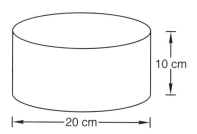

**Solution**  To calculate the volume of a cylinder, we find the area of a circular end of the cylinder and multiply that area by the height of the cylinder—by the distance between the circular ends.

Since the diameter of the cylinder is 20 cm, the radius is 10 cm. A square with a side the length of the radius has an area of 100 cm². So the area of the circle is 3.14 times 100 cm², which is 314 cm².

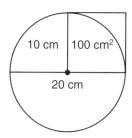

Now we multiply the area of the circular end of the cylinder by the 10 cm height of the cylinder.

$$314 \text{ cm}^2 \times 10 \text{ cm} = 3140 \text{ cm}^3$$

We find that the volume of the cylinder is approximately **3140 cubic centimeters.**

**Practice**

a. 600 cm³

**a.** A large can of soup has a diameter of about 8 cm and a height of about 12 cm. The volume of the can is about how many cubic centimeters? (Round your answer to the nearest hundred cubic centimeters.)

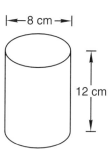

**Problem set 132**

1. Write the prime factorization of 750 using exponents.
(72)   $2 \cdot 3 \cdot 5^3$

2. About how long is your little finger?   C. 50 mm
(7)
A. 0.5 mm    B. 5 mm    C. 50 mm    D. 500 mm

3. If 3 parts weigh 24 grams, how much do 8 parts weigh?   64 g
(104)

4. Complete the proportion: $\dfrac{3}{24} = \dfrac{8}{w}$   64
(103)

5. Write the standard number for $(7 \times 10^3) + (4 \times 10^0)$.
(92)   7004

6. Use digits to write two hundred five million, fifty-six thousand.   205,056,000
(12)

7. The mean of four numbers is 25. Three of the numbers are 17, 23, and 25.
(114)

(a) What is the fourth number?   35

(b) What is the range of the four numbers?   18

8. Sketch a number line to show this addition:
(121)
$$(-4) + (-4) + (-4)$$

9. Three scruples equal one dram. Make two unit multipliers using these units, and select one to change 24 drams to scruples.
(116)
$$\frac{3\ \text{scrupels}}{1\ \text{dram}}, \frac{1\ \text{dram}}{3\ \text{scrupels}}; \quad \frac{24\ \text{drams}}{1} \cdot \frac{3\ \text{scruples}}{1\ \text{dram}} = 72 \text{ scruples}$$

10. Twenty-four guests came to the party. This was $\frac{4}{5}$ of those who were invited. How many guests were invited?   30
(122)

11. $1\dfrac{1}{3} + 3\dfrac{3}{4} + 1\dfrac{1}{6}$   $6\frac{1}{4}$
(59)

12. $\dfrac{5}{6} \times 3 \times 2\dfrac{2}{3}$   $6\frac{2}{3}$
(71)

13. $5.62 + 0.8 + 4$   10.42
(38)

14. $0.08 \div (1 \div 0.4)$   0.032
(48)

15. $(-2) + (-2) + (-2)$   $-6$
(126)

16. $\sqrt{2500} + \sqrt{25}$   55
(123)

**17.** At \$1.12 per pound, what is the price per ounce?
*(116)* (1 pound = 16 ounces)   \$0.07

**18.** The children held hands and stood in a circle. The
*(105)* diameter of the circle was 10 m. What was the circumference of the circle?   31.4 m

**19.** If the area of a square is 36 cm², what is the perimeter
*(38)* of the square?   24 cm

**20.** If each small cube is 1 cm³, what is
*(99)* the volume of the rectangular solid?
24 cm³

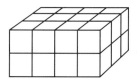

**21.** Write two formulas for the circumference of a circle.
*(105)* $C = \pi D$, $C = 2\pi r$

**22.** What is the probability of guessing the right answer to
*(91)* a multiple choice question if the choices are $a$, $b$, $c$,
and $d$?   $\frac{1}{4}$

**23.** On a 20-question multiple choice test with four
*(113)* choices for each question, how many questions are
likely to be answered correctly simply by guessing
each answer?   5

**24.** (a) $(-8) - (+7)$   $-15$     (b) $(-8) - (-7)$   $-1$
*(126)*

**25.** $+3 + -5 - -7 - +9 + +11 + -7$   0
*(126)*

**26.** On a coordinate plane draw a ray from (0, 0) through
*(125)* (−8, 0). Draw a second ray from the origin through
(−8, −8). Use your protractor to find the measure of the
angle formed by the two rays.   See student work.; 45°

**27.** Jan tossed a coin and it landed heads up. What is the
*(131)* probability that her next two tosses of the coin will
also land heads up?   $\frac{1}{4}$

**28.** The inside diameter of the mug is
(132) 8 cm. The depth of the mug is 7 cm.
What is the capacity of the mug in
cubic centimeters? (Regard the
capacity of the mug as a cylinder
with the given dimensions.)
351.68 cm³

**29.** A cubic centimeter of liquid is a milliliter of liquid.
(77) The mug in problem 28 will hold how many
milliliters of hot chocolate? (Round to the nearest ten
milliliters.)   350 mL

**30.** Ricardo correctly answered 90% of the questions on
(129) the test. If he incorrectly answered four questions,
how many questions did he answer correctly? (Make a
ratio box for this problem.)   36

# INVESTIGATION 6

# Icosahedron • Buckyball

**Icosahedron**   Recall from the investigation following Lesson 89 that
there are five regular polyhedrons and that they are called
the Platonic solids.

tetrahedron   cube   octahedron   dodecahedron   icosahedron

In this investigation we will construct a model of an
icosahedron and see how it is modified to form a
Buckyball.

## Activity: Icosahedron

Materials needed: icosahedron

- One icosahedron pattern and two Buckyball patterns for each student. ("Activity Master 9" and "Activity Master 10" in *Math 76 Test Masters*)
- Scissors
- Glue or tape

Working in pairs or in small groups is helpful. Cut out the icosahedron pattern. We suggest pre-folding the pattern before making the cuts to separate the tabs. Remember that the triangles marked with a "T" are tabs and are hidden from view when the model of the icosahedron is finished.

When you have completed the model, hold it lightly between your thumb and forefinger. You should be able to turn the icosahedron while it is in this position. Since an icosahedron is a regular polyhedron, you should be able to reposition the polyhedron so that your fingers are touching two different vertices without changing the appearance of the figure.

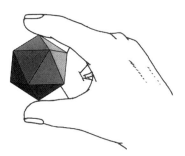

In this position, your thumb and finger each touch a vertex. As you turn the icosahedron there are more vertices you can count. How many vertices are there in all? How many faces are there in all? What is the shape of each face? An icosahedron has 12 vertices and 20 faces. Each face is an equilateral triangle.

**Buckyball** Examples of the Platonic solids occur in some of the tiniest structures known. Molecules exist that have the structure of each of the Platonic solids. In addition, a molecule called *Buckyball* was recently discovered that is a variation of an icosahedron. We found that an icosahedron has 20 triangular faces and 12 vertices. Notice that if a vertex were cut off a solid icosahedron, a pentagon would appear in its place.

Also notice that the five triangles that met at the vertex are no longer triangles. If each of the 12 vertices were cut off, each triangle would become a hexagon instead. The result would be a polyhedron with 12 regular pentagons and 20 regular hexagons. You may recognize that the resulting shape resembles a soccer ball.

You can demonstrate the pattern to yourself by drawing a pentagon around each vertex of your model of an icosahedron. Remarkably, a form of the element carbon has been formed in this shape and has been named *Buckyball*[†]. The three scientists who discovered and studied this molecule won the 1996 Nobel Prize in Chemistry[††]. To build a model of a Buckyball requires two Buckyball patterns from the *Math 76 Test Masters.* After cutting out the patterns, fold them together as you would fold your fingers together. You can learn more about the Buckyball on the Internet by using a search engine to look for "Buckyball."

---

[†]Also called *Buckminsterfullerine*, or C60, in honor of Buckminster Fuller, architect of the geodesic dome of this shape.
[††]The scientists are Robert F. Curl, Jr., Sir Harold W. Kroto, and Richard E. Smalley.

# LESSON
# 133

# Experimental and
# Theoretical Probability

**Facts Practice:** Add and Subtract Integers (Test P in Test Masters)

**Mental Math:**

**a.** $\frac{7}{10}$ of 40

**b.** 90% of $80.00

**c.** $\frac{2}{5}$ of what number is 10?

**d.** 5 is what % of 15?

**e.** 0.1 × 200

**f.** $\frac{2000}{40}$

**g.** 50% of 20, × 10, ÷ 2, − 1, $\sqrt{\phantom{x}}$, × 3, − 1, ÷ 2, − 1, $\sqrt{\phantom{x}}$

**Problem Solving:** A window has the shape of a rectangle with a half circle above the rectangle. Find the area of the window with the given dimensions.

3 ft

4 ft

## Activity: Probability

Materials needed:

- One or more pairs of dice

Tally the results of 36 rolls of a pair of dice in a form such as the following.

**Results of Dice Roll**

| Number | Count |
|--------|-------|
| 2 | I |
| 3 | II |
| 4 | IIII |
| 5 | III |
| 6 | ЖН I |
| 7 | ЖН II |
| 8 | IIII |
| 9 | ЖН |
| 10 | II |
| 11 | I |
| 12 | I |

Using your own results, complete the following exercises:

**a.** Which number or numbers occurred most frequently?
    See student work.

**b.** Which number or numbers occurred least frequently?

  **c.** Describe any pattern you notice in your results.
  See student work.

  **d.** Sketch a bar graph of your results in this form.
  See student work.

**Results of Dice Roll**

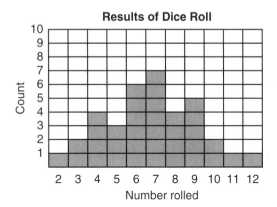

Recording the results of coin tosses or dice rolls creates data that can be used to determine the likelihood of an event. Probabilities that are determined by data collection are **experimental probabilities.** The data from the dice-roll activity should show that the probability of rolling a 6, 7, or 8 with a pair of dice is greater than the probability of rolling a 2 or 12.

**Theoretical probability** is the calculation of a probability by analyzing a particular event and not by performing it repeatedly. Using this chart we can calculate the theoretical probability of rolling a selected number with a pair of dice.

|       | ⚀ | ⚁ | ⚂ | ⚃ | ⚄ | ⚅ |
|-------|---|---|---|----|----|----|
| ⚀ | 2 | 3 | 4 | 5 | 6 | 7 |
| ⚁ | 3 | 4 | 5 | 6 | 7 | 8 |
| ⚂ | 4 | 5 | 6 | 7 | 8 | 9 |
| ⚃ | 5 | 6 | 7 | 8 | 9 | 10 |
| ⚄ | 6 | 7 | 8 | 9 | 10 | 11 |
| ⚅ | 7 | 8 | 9 | 10 | 11 | 12 |

The chart shows 36 equally likely results from rolling a pair of dice. Only one of the results is a 2, and only one of the results is a 12. So the probability of rolling a 2 is $\frac{1}{36}$, and the probability of rolling a 12 is $\frac{1}{36}$.

The chart shows that three of the results are 4. The result is 4 if the first die is ⚀ and the second die is ⚂, if the first die is ⚂ and the second die is ⚀, or if both dice are ⚁. So the probability of rolling a 4 is $\frac{3}{36}$, which reduces to $\frac{1}{12}$.

**Example**  What is the probability of rolling a six with one roll of a pair of dice?

*Solution*  The table shows that there are five ways to roll a six. So the probability of rolling a six is $\frac{5}{36}$.

**Practice**  **a.** This bar graph displays the theoretical probability of rolling the numbers 2 through 12 with one pair of fair dice. Discuss the similarities and differences between this theoretical bar graph and your experimental bar graph. How would you explain any differences?  See student work.

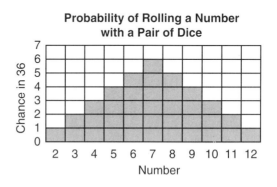

**b.** Which number is just as likely to be rolled as six?  8

**c.** What is the probability of rolling a five with one roll of a pair of dice?  $\frac{1}{9}$

**Problem set**
**133**

**1.** Divide 315 by 25 and write the quotient
*(26)*
(a) with a remainder.  12 r 15

(b) as a decimal number.  12.6

**2.** What time is 3 hours and 45 minutes before noon?
*(32)* 8:15 a.m.

**3.** If 3 pounds of grapes cost $1.59, what is the cost of
*(15)* 1 pound of grapes?  $0.53

**4.** Use digits to write the number one and one half
*(115)* million.  1,500,000

**5.** Use a calculator to approximate $\sqrt{17}$ to the hundredths'
*(128)* place.  4.12

**6.** Use digits to write the number one hundred five and
*(35)* five hundredths.  105.05

**7.** The noontime temperatures for the week were 68°F,
*(114)* 70°F, 76°F, 75°F, 76°F, 74°F, and 72°F. Find the mean,
median, and range of the noontime temperatures for
the week.  mean, 73°F; median, 74°F; range, 8°F

**8.** Compare:  6% of 50 $\textcircled{<}$ 10% of 40
*(112)*

**9.** Fifty percent of what number is 30?  60
*(127)*

**10.** Thirty percent of the boats in the harbor were capsized
*(129)* by the high winds. If 12 boats were capsized, how
many boats were in the harbor?  40 boats

**11.** What is the probability of rolling a nine on one roll of
*(133)* a pair of dice?  $\frac{1}{9}$

**12.** $5 - \left(4\frac{1}{3} - 1\frac{1}{2}\right)$  $2\frac{1}{6}$      **13.** $3\frac{1}{3} \div 2\frac{1}{2}$  $1\frac{1}{3}$
*(62)*                                      *(67)*

3.276  **14.** $3.6 - (0.36 - 0.036)$      **15.** $5.2 \times 3.6 \times 0.27$  5.0544
*(37)*                                  *(39)*

**16.** (−4) + (−4) + (−4)  −12   **17.** (−15) − (+3)   −18
<sub>(126)</sub>                              <sub>(126)</sub>

**18.** This isosceles triangle has how
<sub>(110)</sub> many lines of symmetry?   1

**19.** Between which two consecutive whole numbers is $\sqrt{45}$ ?
<sub>(128)</sub>  6 and 7

**20.** Find the value of $y$ if $y = rs + t$ and if $r = 3$, $s = 4$,
<sub>(45)</sub>  and $t = 1$.   13

**21.** What is the greatest common factor (GCF) of 15 and 24?
<sub>(20)</sub>   3

**22.** Change 400 ounces to pints. (2 pints = 32 ounces)
<sub>(116)</sub>   25 pints

**23.** In a bag there are 4 green marbles and 12 red marbles.
<sub>(91)</sub>
   (a) If one marble is drawn from the bag, what is the
       probability that the marble will be green?   $\frac{1}{4}$

   (b) If a green marble is drawn from the bag, what is
       the probability that the next marble drawn from
       the bag will be green?   $\frac{1}{5}$

**24.** What is the volume of this cube?
<sub>(99)</sub>   216 m³

**25.** The volume of the pyramid is $\frac{1}{3}$ of
<sub>(29)</sub>  the volume of the cube. What is
   the volume of the pyramid?   72 m³

6 m

**26.** −3 + −2 − −6 − +4 + +5   +2
<sub>(126)</sub>

**27.** Nathan tossed a coin 20 times and tallied the results.
<sub>(133)</sub> How do these experimental results differ from the
   theoretical probability?   Tails occurred slightly more often than
   heads. Theoretically, both would have occurred ten times in 20 tosses.

**Results of 20 Coin Tosses**

| Heads | ЖHT IIII |
|-------|----------|
| Tails | ЖHT ЖHT I |

**28.** Use a calculator to find $\sqrt{45}$. Round the square root to
(128) the nearest hundredth.    6.71

**29.** If the edges of a cube are 1 cm, then the edges are also
(99) 10 mm. One cubic centimeter is how many cubic
millimeters?    1000 mm³

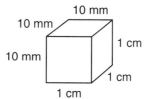

**30.** A birthday candle in the shape of a
(132) cylinder has a diameter of 6 mm
and a height of 60 mm. What is the
volume of a birthday candle? Round
your answer to the nearest hundred
cubic millimeters.    1700 mm³

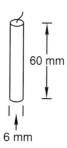

# LESSON 134

# Multiplying and Dividing Integers

Mental Math:
a. 18
b. $100.00
c. 20
d. 25%
e. 120
f. 24
g. 4
Problem Solving:
2

**Facts Practice:** Measurement Facts (Test N in Test Masters)

**Mental Math:**

**a.** $\frac{3}{8}$ of 48   **b.** 10% of $1000.00

**c.** 6 is $\frac{3}{10}$ of what number?   **d.** 5 is what % of 20?

**e.** 0.3 × 400   **f.** 12 is 50% of what number?

**g.** 2 × 2, + 2, × 2, − 2, × 2, − 2, ÷ 2, − 2, × 2, + 2, $\sqrt{\phantom{x}}$

**Problem Solving:** If $x$ is a whole number, if $x^2 = y$ and $y^2 = z$, and if $z^2$ equals a three-digit number, then what number is $x$?

We know that when we multiply two positive numbers the product is positive.

$$(+3)(+4) = +12$$

**Positive × positive = positive**

Notice that when we write (+3)(+4) there is no + or − sign between the sets of parentheses.

When we multiply a positive number and a negative number, the product is negative. We show an example on this number line by multiplying 3 and −4.

$$3 \text{ times } {-4} \quad \text{means} \quad (-4) + (-4) + (-4)$$

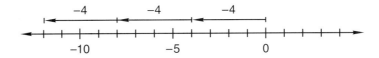

We write the multiplication this way.

$$(+3)(-4) = -12$$

*Positive* three times *negative* four equals *negative* 12.

**Positive × negative = negative**

When we multiply two negative numbers the product is positive. Consider this sequence of equations.

1. Three times 4 is 12 ($3 \times 4 = 12$).
2. Three times the opposite of 4 is the opposite of 12 ($3 \times -4 = -12$).
3. The opposite of 3 times the opposite of 4 is the opposite of the opposite of 12 ($-3 \times -4 = +12$).

### Negative × negative = positive

Recall that we may rearrange the numbers of a multiplication fact to make two division facts.

| Multiplication Facts | Division Facts | |
|---|---|---|
| $(+3)(+4) = +12$ | $\dfrac{+12}{+3} = +4$ | $\dfrac{+12}{+4} = +3$ |
| $(+3)(-4) = -12$ | $\dfrac{-12}{+3} = -4$ | $\dfrac{-12}{-4} = +3$ |
| $(-3)(-4) = +12$ | $\dfrac{+12}{-3} = -4$ | $\dfrac{+12}{-4} = -3$ |

Studying these nine facts, we can summarize the results in two rules.

1. **If the two numbers in a multiplication or division problem have the same sign, the answer is positive.**
2. **If the two numbers in a multiplication or division problem have different signs, the answer is negative.**

**Examples and *Solutions***

1. $(+8)(+4) = +32$
2. $(+8) \div (+4) = +2$
3. $(+8)(-4) = -32$
4. $(+8) \div (-4) = -2$
5. $(-8)(+4) = -32$
6. $(-8) \div (+4) = -2$
7. $(-8)(-4) = +32$
8. $(-8) \div (-4) = +2$

**Practice\***    **a.** $(-5)(+4)$   $-20$         **b.** $(-5)(-4)$   $+20$

**c.** $(+5)(+4)$   $+20$         **d.** $(+5)(-4)$   $-20$

**e.** $\dfrac{+12}{-2}$   $-6$   **f.** $\dfrac{+12}{+2}$   $+6$   **g.** $\dfrac{-12}{+2}$   $-6$   **h.** $\dfrac{-12}{-2}$   $+6$

**Problem set**
**134**

**1.** Divide 315 by 20 and write the quotient
$^{(26)}$   (a) with a remainder.   15 r 15

(b) as a decimal number.   15.75

**2.** Jenny ran 4 laps in 5 minutes. How many seconds did it
$^{(15)}$ take to run each lap if she ran at a steady pace?   75 s

**3.** Fifteen is 25% of what number?   60
$^{(127)}$

**4.** Complete the proportion: $\dfrac{35}{w} = \dfrac{70}{100}$   50
$^{(103)}$

**5.** Write the prime factorization of 225 using exponents.
$^{(72)}$   $3^2 \cdot 5^2$

**6.** $(-3) + (-5) + (+4) - (-6) - (+2)$   0
$^{(126)}$

**7.** What is the sales tax on a $20 purchase if the tax rate
$^{(119)}$ is 7.5%?   $1.50

**8.** Six out of every 100 fans cheered for the visiting team.
$^{(104)}$ If 60 people cheered for the visiting team, how many
fans were there?   1000

Complete the chart to answer problems 9, 10, and 11.

|  | FRACTION | DECIMAL | PERCENT |
|---|---|---|---|
| **9.**<br>$^{(98)}$ | $\frac{3}{6}$ | (a) 0.5 | (b) 50% |
| **10.**<br>$^{(98)}$ | (a) $2\frac{3}{5}$ | 2.6 | (b) 260% |
| **11.**<br>$^{(98)}$ | (a) $\frac{4}{25}$ | (b) 0.16 | 16% |

**12.** $6.4 + 3\dfrac{1}{2}$ (fraction answer)   $9\frac{9}{10}$
(85)

**13.** $\dfrac{9}{10} \cdot \dfrac{5}{12} \cdot \dfrac{8}{15}$   $\frac{1}{5}$       **14.** $\sqrt{225}$   15
(71)                                      (123)

**15.** $5.35 + 6 + 2\dfrac{1}{8}$ (decimal answer)   13.475
(85)

**16.** On the number line, $\sqrt{31}$ is between which two
(128) consecutive whole numbers?   5 and 6

At right is a list of scores earned in a
diving competition. Use this list to
answer problems 17, 18, 19, and 20.

| 6.0 |
|-----|
| 6.5 |
| 7.0 |
| 7.5 |
| 6.5 |
| 6.5 |
| 7.0 |

**17.** What score was made most often
(114) (mode)?   6.5

**18.** If the scores were arranged in
(114) order of size, which would be the
middle score (median)?   6.5

**19.** What is the average of all the scores? (Round the mean
(114) to the nearest tenth.)   6.7

**20.** What is the difference between the highest and the
(114) lowest score (range)?   1.5

**21.** A cylinder has a diameter of 20 cm
(132) and a height of 20 cm. What is the
volume of the cylinder?   6280 cm³

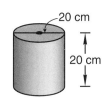
20 cm
20 cm

**22.** What is the probability of rolling a seven on one roll of
(133) a pair of dice?   $\frac{1}{6}$

**23.** It was estimated that three quarters of a billion people
(115) watched the closing ceremonies of the Olympics.
Write that number.   750,000,000

**24.** (a) (−6)(+3)   −18          (b) (−6) ÷ (+3)   −2
(134)

**25.** Use a unit multiplier to change 4.2 liters to milliliters.
(116) (1 liter = 1000 milliliters)   4200 mL

**26.** Compare: (−3)(+4) $\lessdot$ (−3) + (+4)
(134)

**27.** Angle *AOD* is a straight angle. Angle *BOD* is a right
(107) angle. The measure of ∠*COD* is half the measure of
∠*BOD*. What is the measure of ∠*BOC*?   45°

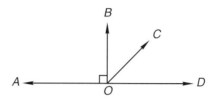

**28.** If the arrow on this spinner is spun
(133) 100 times, then the theoretical
probability is that it would stop on
4 how many times?   25

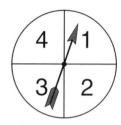

**29.** Convert $6\frac{2}{3}\%$ to a fraction.   $\frac{1}{15}$
(119)

**30.** What are the coordinates of the point halfway between
(74) (1, 3) and (3, 1)?   (2, 2)

# LESSON
## 135

# Constructing Bisectors

Mental Math:
a. 4
b. $16.00
c. 10
d. 50%
e. 300
f. 16
g. 1
Problem Solving:

| -9 | -6 | -3 | 3 | 3 | 6 | 9 |
|----|----|----|---|---|---|---|
| -6 | -4 | -2 | 2 | 2 | 4 | 6 |
| -3 | -2 | -1 | 1 | 1 | 2 | 3 |
| -3 | -2 | -1 | 0 | 1 | 2 | 3 |
| 3 | 2 | 1 | -1 | -1 | -2 | -3 |
| 6 | 4 | 2 | -2 | -2 | -4 | -6 |
| 9 | 6 | 3 | -3 | -3 | -6 | -9 |

**Facts Practice:** Multiply and Divide Integers (Test Q in Test Masters)

**Mental Math:**

**a.** $\frac{2}{9}$ of 18

**b.** 20% of $80.00

**c.** $\frac{3}{5}$ of what number is 6?

**d.** 20 is what % of 40?

**e.** 0.5 × 600

**f.** 25% of what number is 4?

**g.** 7 × 4, + 2, × 2, + 4, $\sqrt{\ }$, ÷ 2, − 2, ÷ 2

**Problem Solving:** Celina made a multiplication table that included negative numbers. The center row and center column contain the factors for the table. Copy this table on your paper and fill in the missing products.

| -9 |  | 3 |  | 9 |
|----|----|----|----|----|
|  |  | 2 |  |  |
|  |  | 1 |  |  |
| -3 | -2 | -1 | 0 | 1 | 2 | 3 |
|  |  | -1 |  |  |
|  |  | -2 |  |  |
| 9 |  | -3 |  | -9 |

The word "bisect" means to cut into two equal parts. We bisect a line segment when we draw a line or segment through the midpoint of the segment. Here segment $AB$ is bisected by line $r$ into two line segments, $\overline{AM}$ and $\overline{MB}$, whose lengths are equal.

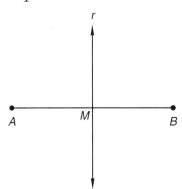

We bisect an angle by drawing a ray that divides the original angle into two smaller angles of equal measure. Below $\angle RST$ is bisected by ray $SB$.

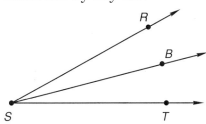

In this activity we will use a compass, a ruler, and a pencil to bisect segments and angles.

### Activity: Bisectors

Materials needed:

- Besides pencil and unlined paper, each student or pair of students needs a compass and a ruler or an unmarked straight edge.

If students are working in pairs, one student will draw a line segment and the other student will construct a perpendicular bisector. Then the activity is repeated with the roles reversed. The same procedure may be used for the angle bisector activity.

**Perpendicular Bisector**  Draw a line segment on an unlined sheet of paper. Set a compass so that the distance between the point of the compass and the pencil point is more than half the length of the segment. Then place the point of the compass on an endpoint of the segment and "swing an arc" on both sides of the segment, as illustrated.

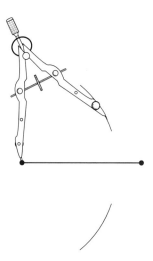

Without resetting the radius of the compass, lift the point of the compass and place the point on the other endpoint of the segment. Swing an arc on both sides of the segment so that the arcs intersect as shown. (It may be necessary to return to the first endpoint to extend the first set of arcs until the arcs intersect on both sides of the segment.)

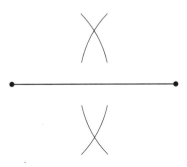

A line drawn through the two points where the arcs intersect will bisect the segment and will also be perpendicular to it. The line is a perpendicular bisector of the segment.

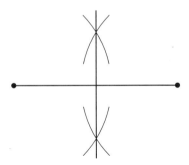

**Angle Bisector** Use a pencil and straight edge to draw an angle on a sheet of unlined paper. Placing the point of the compass on the vertex of the angle, sweep an arc across both sides of the angle. The arc intersects the sides of the angle at two points, which we have labeled $A$ and $B$. Point $A$ and point $B$ are both the same distance from the vertex.

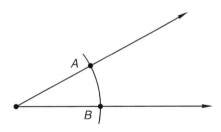

Now we set the compass so that the distance between the point of the compass and the pencil point is more than half the distance from point *A* to point *B*. Placing the point of the compass at point *A* we sweep an arc as shown.

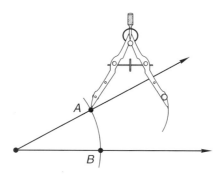

Without resetting the radius of the compass, move the point of the compass to point *B* and sweep an arc to intercept the first arc.

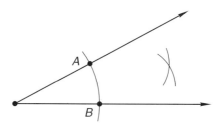

A ray drawn from the vertex of the angle through the intersection of the arcs bisects the angle. The ray is the angle bisector of the angle.

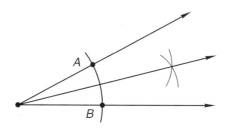

**Practice**

See student work.

**a.** Use your protractor to make a 60° angle. Then use a compass and a straight edge to bisect the angle.

**b.** Use your ruler to draw a segment 10 cm long. Then use a compass and straight edge to construct a perpendicular bisector of the segment. See student work.

**Problem set 135**

**1.** Divide 315 by 24 and write the quotient
(26)
(a) as a mixed number.   $13\frac{1}{8}$

(b) as a decimal number.   13.125

**2.** Find the volume of a can with a diameter of 2 in. and a height of 5 in.   15.7 in.³
(132)

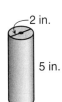
-2 in.
5 in.

**3.** Six of the 14 players were left-handed. What was the ratio of left-handed players to right-handed players? $\frac{3}{4}$
(82)

**4.** 24% ≠   D. 24
(84)

A. $\dfrac{12}{50}$        B. 0.24        C. $\dfrac{6}{25}$        D. 24

**5.** Write the standard number for the following:   60,050,000
(92)
$$(6 \times 10^7) + (5 \times 10^4)$$

**6.** Estimate the sum of 6.9, $3\frac{1}{3}$, 7.01, and $3\frac{5}{6}$ to the nearest whole number.   21
(50)

**7.** Reduce units before multiplying:   384 oz
(94)
$$\frac{3 \text{ gal}}{1} \times \frac{4 \text{ qt}}{1 \text{ gal}} \times \frac{2 \text{ pt}}{1 \text{ qt}} \times \frac{16 \text{ oz}}{1 \text{ pt}}$$

**8.** Arrange in order from greatest to least:   $1\frac{1}{2}$, 1.39, 125%
(84)
$$1\frac{1}{2}, 125\%, 1.39$$

**9.** Ten percent of the books were damaged. If 20 books were damaged, how many were not damaged? Make a ratio box for the problem.   180 books
(129)

**10.** Eight is 20% of what number?   40
(127)

**11.** Eight is $\frac{2}{5}$ of what number?   20
(122)

**12.** If the spinner is spun twice, what
(131) is the probability that the spinner
will stop on 3 both times?   $\frac{1}{16}$

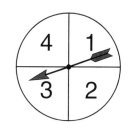

**13.** $5\frac{1}{2} - \left(4\frac{1}{4} - 3\frac{1}{3}\right)$   $4\frac{7}{12}$   **14.** $3 \div \left(1\frac{2}{3} \div 3\right)$   $5\frac{2}{5}$
(62)                                         (67)

**15.** $0.1 - 0.0986$   0.0014     **16.** $3.5 \times 1.2 \times 100$   420
(37)                                    (39)

**17.** What is the cost per doughnut if two dozen doughnuts
(15) cost $4.32?   $0.18

**18.** What is the area of this circle?
(130)   1256 m²

**19.** What is the circumference of this
(105) circle?   125.6 m

20 m

Use 3.14 for $\pi$

**20.** Each face of a cube is a square.
(38) What is the area of each square
face of this cube?   25 cm²

5 cm

**21.** What is the value of $y$ if $y = t^2 + c$ and if $t = 6$ and
(92)   $c = 7$?   43

**22.** Which positive one-digit numbers are **not** divisors of
(19)   420?   8 and 9

**23.** (a) $(-12) + (-3)$   −15     (b) $(-12) - (-3)$   −9
(126)

**24.** (a) $(-12) \times (-3)$   36     (b) $(-12) \div (-3)$   4
(134)

**25.** Use your ruler to draw a line segment that is $2\frac{1}{4}$ inches
$^{(135)}$ long. Then use a compass and straight edge to construct a perpendicular bisector of the segment.
See student work.

**26.** Use your protractor to make an 80° angle. Then use a
$^{(135)}$ compass and straight edge to construct an angle bisector of the angle. See student work.

**27. (a)** $\dfrac{-12}{+6}$ $-2$        **(b)** $\dfrac{-12}{-6}$ $2$
$^{(134)}$

**28.** The area of this square is 20 cm$^2$.
$^{(128)}$ Use your calculator to find the length of each side to the nearest tenth of a centimeter. 4.5 cm

20 cm$^2$

**29.** $-10 + -20 - -40 + +10 - +30$   $-10$
$^{(126)}$

**30.** What is the area of a triangle whose vertices have the
$^{(87)}$ coordinates $(2, 0)$, $(0, -2)$, and $(-2, 0)$? 4 sq. units

# LESSON 136

# Surface Area of a Prism

**Facts Practice:** Multiply and Divide Integers (Test Q in Test Masters)

**Mental Math:**

a. $\frac{4}{5}$ of 30

b. 30% of $200.00

c. 12 is $\frac{3}{10}$ of what number?

d. 6 is what % of 24?

e. 0.7 × 400

f. 5 is 10% of what number?

g. 7 × 9, − 3, ÷ 2, + 10, ÷ 2, − 5, ÷ 5, − 3

**Problem Solving:** A social security number is three digits plus two digits plus four digits. If any digit may be used in any position, how many different social security numbers are possible?

We have measured the volumes of rectangular prisms and special rectangular prisms called *cubes*. Besides measuring the volume of a solid, we can also measure the total area of all of its surfaces. This is called the **surface area** of a solid. A cube puzzle can help us understand this idea.

9   squares each face
× 6   faces
54   squares total

How many square stickers are needed to cover this cube? We could just begin counting and hope that we count them all, or we can be systematic in our approach to the problem. How many squares are needed to cover one face? How many faces are there in all? What is the total number of squares needed to cover all the faces?

**Example 1**  How many squares, 1 inch on a side, would be needed to cover this prism?

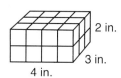

2 in.

3 in.

4 in.

*Solution*  The rectangular prism has 6 surfaces. We find the area of each surface, then add to find the total surface area. The front and back faces are 2-inch by 4-inch rectangles. The area of each is 8 in.². The top and bottom faces are 3-inch by 4-inch rectangles with areas of 12 in.². The left and right rectangles each have an area of 6 in.². We add the areas of the six rectangles to find the total surface area.

$$8 \text{ in.}^2 + 8 \text{ in.}^2 + 12 \text{ in.}^2 + 12 \text{ in.}^2 + 6 \text{ in.}^2 + 6 \text{ in.}^2 = \textbf{52 in.}^2$$

**Example 2** Find the surface area of a cube with edges 5 cm long.

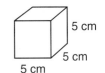

5 cm
5 cm
5 cm

*Solution* Each face of the cube is a square with sides that are 5 cm long. So the area of each square face is 25 cm². A cube has six faces. Thus the total surface area of the cube is six times 25 cm².

$$6 \times 25 \text{ cm}^2 = \textbf{150 cm}^2$$

**Practice** Find the surface area of each rectangular prism:

**a.**

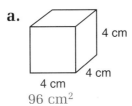

4 cm
4 cm
4 cm
96 cm²

**b.**

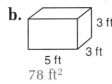

3 ft
3 ft
5 ft
78 ft²

**c.**

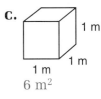

1 m
1 m
1 m
6 m²

**Problem set 136**

**1.** Divide 938 by 40 and write the quotient
(26)
(a) as a mixed number.   $23\frac{9}{20}$
(b) as a decimal number.   $23.45$

**2.** One fifth of the 300 troops were injured. How many
(76) were not injured?   240 troops

**3.** Complete the proportion: $\frac{12}{20} = \frac{18}{g}$   30
(103)

**4.** Write the standard number for twenty million, one
(12) hundred thousand, fifty.   20,100,050

**5.** Twenty is 25% of what number?   80
(127)

**6.** If the mean of 10 numbers is 6.4, what is their sum?  64
*(114)*

**7.** What is 1% of one million?   10,000
*(112)*

**8.** Use a unit multiplier to change 16,000 acres to square miles. (1 square mile = 640 acres)   25 sq. mi
*(116)*

**9.** Write $\frac{1}{6}$ as a percent by multiplying $\frac{1}{6}$ and 100%.  $16\frac{2}{3}\%$
*(93)*

**10.** $(1.2)^2 - 1.2$   0.24
*(92)*

**11.** A bag contains one red marble, two white marbles, and four blue marbles.
*(91)*

   (a) If one marble is drawn from the bag, what is the probability that the marble will be red?   $\frac{1}{7}$

   (b) If a red marble is drawn from the bag and is not replaced, then what is the probability that the next marble drawn will be white?   $\frac{1}{3}$

**12.** Each face of this cube has an area of 36 cm². What is the total surface area of the cube?   216 cm²
*(136)*

6 cm
6 cm
6 cm

**13.** $\left(3\frac{3}{4} + 2\frac{1}{2}\right) \times 1\frac{1}{3}$   $8\frac{1}{3}$
*(65)*

**14.** $\left(3\frac{1}{2} - 1\frac{2}{3}\right) \div 1\frac{1}{3}$   $1\frac{3}{8}$
*(67)*

**15.** (a) $(+12)(-6)$   $-72$
*(134)*

   (b) $\dfrac{+12}{-6}$   $-2$

**16.** The ratio of orangutans to chimpanzees was 2 to 5. If there were 40 chimpanzees, how many orangutans were there?   16 orangutans
*(104)*

**17.** What is the circumference of this circle?   125.6 mm
*(105)*

40 mm

**18.** What is the area of this circle?
*(130)*   1256 mm²

**19.** What is the area of this parallelogram? 17.92 in.²
(79)

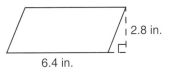

2.8 in.

6.4 in.

**20.** An octagon has how many more sides than a
(63) quadrilateral? 4

**21.** How many square stickers, one inch
(136) on a side, would be needed to cover
this prism? 90 stickers

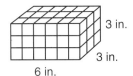

3 in.

3 in.

6 in.

**22.** Twenty-three thousand is not divisible by which of
(19) these numbers? B. 3

A. 2          B. 3          C. 5          D. 10

**23.** What is the probability of an event that is **certain** to
(91) happen? 1

**24.** 75 + 50 + $a$ = 180    55
(3)

**25.** To what fraction on the number line is the arrow
(17) pointing? $\frac{1}{3}$

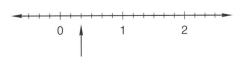

0          1          2

**26.** Draw a line segment 5 cm long. Then use a compass
(135) and straight edge to construct a perpendicular bisector
of the segment. See student work.

310 cm³   **27.** A cylindrical jelly jar has an
(132) inside diameter of 6 cm and a
height of 11 cm. How many cubic
centimeters of jelly can fit in the
jar? Round your answer to the
nearest ten cubic centimeters.

11 cm

6 cm

**28.** $(+5) + (-4) - (+3) - (-2) + (+1)$    1
(126)

**29.** What is the probability of rolling 11 with one toss of a
(133)    pair of dice?    $\frac{1}{18}$

**30.** If an obtuse angle is bisected, then each smaller angle
(107)    formed is what kind of angle?    acute

---

**LESSON
137**

Mental Math:
a. 27
b. $160.00
c. 16
d. $33\frac{1}{3}\%$
e. 630
f. 50
g. 2
Problem Solving:
    $-40°F$

# Sum of the Angle Measures of a Triangle

**Facts Practice:** Multiply and Divide Integers (Test Q in Test
Masters)

**Mental Math:**

  **a.** $\frac{3}{4}$ of 36         **b.** 80% of $200.00
  **c.** 12 is $\frac{3}{4}$ of what number?   **d.** 7 is what % of 21?
  **e.** 0.9 × 700           **f.** 20% of what number is 10?
  **g.** $\frac{1}{3}$ of 30, × 4, + 2, ÷ 6, × 7, + 1, × 2, $\sqrt{\phantom{x}}$, − 1, $\sqrt{\phantom{x}}$, + 1, $\sqrt{\phantom{x}}$

**Problem Solving:** Here is a formula used to convert degrees
Celsius (°C) to degrees Fahrenheit (°F). Use
the formula to find the Fahrenheit
temperature that is equivalent to −40°C.
°F = 1.8°C + 32°

## Activity: Angles of a Triangle

Materials needed:

- Pencil
- Paper
- Ruler
- Compass
- Scissors

Draw two different triangles on a sheet of paper using a
pencil and ruler. The triangles may be acute, right, or
obtuse. Make each side of the triangles more than one inch
long.

Use your compass to draw arcs at each angle of both triangles as shown. (Keep the compass setting the same for all the arcs.) Use scissors to cut out one triangle. Then cut off the "corners" of the triangle by following the arcs and fit the corners together to make a half circle.

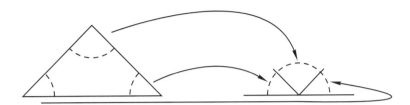

Repeat the cutting and fitting with the second triangle. The corners again fit together to form a half circle.

If we cut circular corners off any triangle we can fit the corners together to make half a circle, as we show here. This tells us something about the sum of the angles of a triangle. A full circle measures 360°, so a half circle measures 180°. Together, the three angles of a triangle are equivalent to a half circle, so the sum of their measures is 180°.

> **The sum of the angle measures of any triangle is 180°.**

**Example**  The measures of two of the angles of the triangle are given. What is the measure of the third angle?

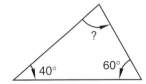

**Solution**  The sum of the three angles must total 180°. The two angles given total 100°. Subtracting 100° from 180°, we find that the third angle measures **80°**.

**Practice**  Find the measure of the angle not given:

a. 90°

b. 58°

c. 41°

**a.**

**b.**

**c.**

**d.** If the three angles of a triangle are all the same measure, then each angle measures how many degrees?
60°

**Problem set**
**137**

**1.** The league is forming soccer teams so that there are 14
(111) or 15 players on each team. If 300 players sign up for soccer, what is the greatest number of teams that can be formed?    21 teams

**2.** If the sales tax rate is 6 cents for every one dollar of
(119) sales, how much is the tax on a television set that sells for $350?    $21.00

**3.** What is the area of this circle?
(130) 113.04 m²

**4.** What is the circumference of this
(105) circle?    37.68 m

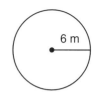

6 m

**5.** Write a quarter of a million as a standard number.
(115) 250,000

**6.** If the sum of 12 numbers is 288, what is the mean of
(114) the numbers?    24

**7.** Use a unit multiplier to change 1.25 meters to
(116) millimeters. (1 meter = 1000 millimeters)    1250 mm

**8.** $(1.1)^3 - 1.1$    0.231
(92)

Complete the chart to answer problems 9, 10, and 11.

|        | FRACTION | DECIMAL | PERCENT |
|--------|----------|---------|---------|
| **9.** (98) | $\frac{19}{20}$ | (a) 0.95 | (b) 95% |
| **10.** (98) | (a) $1\frac{9}{10}$ | 1.9 | (b) 190% |
| **11.** (98) | (a) $\frac{16}{25}$ | (b) 0.64 | 64% |

**12.** $\dfrac{4.32}{0.003}$    1440
(48)

**13.** $1\frac{2}{3} \div \left(3 \div \frac{3}{5}\right)$    $\frac{1}{3}$
(67)

**14.** 16% of $3.75 $0.60
(112)

**15.** 60° + 70° + $n$ = 180° 50°
(137)

**16.** Write $1\frac{2}{3}$% as a reduced fraction. $\frac{1}{60}$
(119)

**17.** What is the probability that the spinner will stop on a number less than 4? 1
(91)

**18.** What is the probability that the spinner will stop on a 1 twice in a row? $\frac{1}{9}$
(131)

**19.** What is the probability of an event that **cannot** happen? 0
(91)

**20.** What is the measure of angle $A$? 40°
(137)

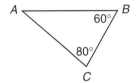

**21.** How many square tiles 1 foot on a side would be needed to cover this cube? 96 tiles
(136)

4 ft

**22.** What is the volume of this cube? 64 ft³
(99)

The table shows the number of students in a class of 25 students who received certain scores on a class quiz. Use this table to answer problems 23, 24, and 25.

**Class Quiz Scores**

| Score | Number of Students |
|-------|--------------------|
| 10 | 2 |
| 9 | 3 |
| 8 | 7 |
| 7 | 5 |
| 6 | 5 |
| 5 | 3 |

**23.** Which score was made most often (mode)? 8
(114)

**24.** What was the median score? 7
(114)

**25.** What percent of the class scored 8 or more? 48%
(114)

**26.** Use a protractor to make a 100° angle. Then use a
$_{(135)}$ compass and straight edge to bisect the angle.
See student work.

**27.** (a) $\dfrac{-27}{-3}$   +9          (b) $\dfrac{-27}{+3}$   −9
$_{(134)}$

**28.** (−3) − (−3) − (+3) + (−3) + (+3)   −3
$_{(126)}$

**29.** The coordinates of the vertices of a triangle are (3, 0),
$_{(87)}$ (0, 3), and (−3, 0). What is the area of the triangle?
9 sq. units

**30.** The area of this square is 10 in.²
$_{(128)}$ Use your calculator to find the
length of each side to the nearest
tenth of an inch.   3.2 in.

10 in.²

---

# LESSON
# 138

# Roman Numerals

**Facts Practice:** Multiply and Divide Integers (Test Q in Test
Masters)

**Mental Math:**

   **a.** $\frac{5}{8}$ of 40          **b.** 90% of $300.00

   **c.** $\frac{2}{3}$ of what number is 20?     **d.** 8 is what % of 40?

   **e.** 0.3 × 500          **f.** 8 is 25% of what number?

   **g.** 6 × 8, + 1, $\sqrt{\ }$, × 3, − 1, × 2, ÷ 5, + 1, $\sqrt{\ }$, × 5, + 1, $\sqrt{\ }$, $\sqrt{\ }$, × 5

**Problem Solving:** A label is wrapped around a
soup can that has a diameter of
8 cm and a height of 12 cm.
What is the area of the label?

The numerals we normally use to write numbers are
called *Arabic numerals*. There are other ways to write
numbers. One ancient form of numerals that we still use
today is *Roman numerals*. We see Roman numerals used
to number chapters in books, to mark hours on clocks, to

date buildings, and to number Olympiads and Super Bowl games. The table below lists values of some Roman numerals.

| NUMERAL | I | V | X | L | C | D | M |
|---------|---|---|---|---|---|---|---|
| VALUE | 1 | 5 | 10 | 50 | 100 | 500 | 1000 |

The Roman numeral system does not use place value. The numeral II does not stand for eleven, it stands for two. The value of the numerals are added together unless a numeral of lesser value is written in front of a numeral of greater value, in which case the smaller is subtracted from the larger.

**Examples and *Solutions***

1. III = **3**
2. IX = **9**
3. XXX = **30**
4. DC = **600**
5. IV = **4**
6. XIII = **13**
7. XL = **40**
8. MM = **2000**
9. VI = **6**
10. XIV = **14**
11. LXX = **70**
12. MCM = **1900**
13. VIII = **8**
14. XVI = **16**
15. XC = **90**
16. MCMXC = **1990**

**Practice*** Write the Arabic numeral for each of the Roman numerals:

**a.** XXIII   23
**b.** XLII   42
**c.** CXC   190

**d.** LXXIX   79
**e.** CCC   300
**f.** DCC   700

**g.** XCIV   94
**h.** DCCLXVI   766
**i.** MCMXXI   1921

Write the Roman numeral for each of these numbers:

**j.** 7   VII
**k.** 19   XIX
**l.** 24   XXIV

**m.** 80   LXXX
**n.** 140   CXL
**o.** 400   CD

**p.** 750   DCCL
**q.** 900   CM
**r.** 2001   MMI

**Problem set**
**138**

**1.** Divide 400 by 32 and write the quotient as a mixed
(26) number.    $12\frac{1}{2}$

**2.** Divide 100 by 8 and write the quotient as a decimal
(44) number.    12.5

**3.** The team scored 27 points in the first half. If the team
(122) scored $\frac{3}{4}$ of their points in the first half, how many
points did the team score in the whole game?    36 points

**4.** Twenty is what percent of 25?    80%
(118)

**5.** Compare: $(0.1)^2$ ⊘ $(0.1)^3$
(92)

Complete the chart to answer problems 6 through 11.
(138)

| ROMAN NUMERAL | ARABIC NUMERAL |
|---|---|
| CCXXXIV | **6.**    234 |
| CLXVI | **7.**    166 |
| MDCXL | **8.**    1640 |
| **9.**    CXXIV | 124 |
| **10.**    DLV | 555 |
| **11.**    MCCXXXIV | 1234 |

**12.** $1\frac{7}{8} + 3\frac{1}{2}$    $5\frac{3}{8}$          **13.** $1\frac{2}{3} \times 3$    5
(58)                                        (65)

**14.** $12 \div (0.12 \div 12)$          **15.** $(-6) - (+15)$    $-21$
(48)    1200                        (126)

**16.** $(-6)(+15)$    $-90$
(134)

**17.** Write the prime factorization of 64 using exponents.
(72)    $2^6$

**18.** A corner was clipped from a 10 mm by 20 mm
(106) rectangular piece of paper. What was the area of the
triangular corner that was clipped?    5 mm²

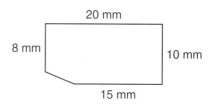

20 mm

8 mm

10 mm

15 mm

**19.** What is the circumference of this
(105) circle?    12.56 ft

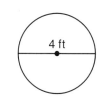
4 ft

**20.** What is the area of this circle?
(130)    12.56 ft²

**21.** What is the volume of this prism?
(99)    24 m³

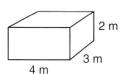
2 m
3 m
4 m

**22.** What is the surface area of this
(136) prism?    52 m²

**23.** In triangle *ABC*, the measure of
(137) ∠*A* is 80°, and the measure of ∠*B*
is 50°. What is the measure of
∠*C*?    50°

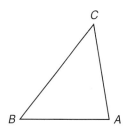
C
B    A

**24.** What number is 5 more than half the product of 12
(12) and 16?    101

**25.** To what number on the scale is
(10) the arrow pointing?    225

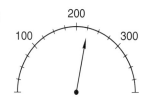
200
100    300

**26.** −15 + −20 − −10 + −5 + +30    0
(126)

**27.** (a) $\dfrac{-20}{-5}$    +4             (b) $\dfrac{+20}{-5}$    −4
(134)

In this figure, a cone is in a cylinder. Refer to this figure to
answer problems 28 and 29.

**28.** What is the volume of the cylinder?
(132)    169.56 in.³

**29.** The volume of the cone is $\frac{1}{3}$ of the
(29) volume of the cylinder. What is
the volume of the cone?    56.52 in.³

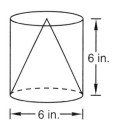
6 in.
6 in.

**30.** What is the probability of rolling a 7 twice in two rolls
(133) of a pair of dice?    $\frac{1}{36}$

# Appendix

## *Supplemental Practice Problems for Selected Lessons*

This appendix contains additional practice problems for concepts presented in selected lessons. It is very important that no problems in the regular problem sets be omitted to make room for these problems. This book is designed to produce long-term retention of concepts, and long-term practice of all the concepts is necessary. The practice problems in the problem sets provide enough initial exposure to concepts for most students. If a student continues to have difficulty with certain concepts, some of these problems can be assigned as remedial exercises.

# Supplemental Practice Problems
# for Selected Lessons

**Supplemental Practice for Lesson 2**
**Set A**

1. 576 × 8    4608
2. $3.08 × 7    $21.56
3. 784 × 6    4704
4. 4306 × 9    38,754
5. 42¢ × 30    $12.60
6. 56 × 40    2240
7. 60 × 78    4680
8. 70¢ × 64    $44.80
9. 90 × 70    6300
10. 300 × 60    18,000
11. 400 × 50    20,000
12. 80 × 500    40,000
13. 37 × 43    1591
14. 62¢ × 74    $45.88
15. 86 × 27    2322
16. 94 × 63    5922
17. $4.08 × 24    $97.92
18. 507 × 37    18,759
19. 62 × 409    25,358
20. 84 × $3.06    $257.04
21. 520 × 36    18,720
22. 940 × 42    39,480
23. $7.90 × 86    $679.40
24. 243 × 67    16,281

**Set B** Write uneven division with a remainder.

1. 357 ÷ 5    71 r 2
2. $2.44 ÷ 4    $0.61
3. 892 ÷ 7    127 r 3
4. 143 ÷ 4    35 r 3
5. $4.12 ÷ 4    $1.03
6. 423 ÷ 6    70 r 3
7. $7.28 ÷ 7    $1.04
8. 812 ÷ 9    90 r 2
9. 1206 ÷ 6    201
10. $8.24 ÷ 4    $2.06
11. 906 ÷ 9    100 r 6
12. 3492 ÷ 7    498 r 6
13. $1.44 ÷ 12    $0.12
14. 472 ÷ 10    47 r 2
15. 893 ÷ 15    59 r 8
16. 762 ÷ 25    30 r 12
17. 432 ÷ 20    21 r 12
18. 986 ÷ 50    19 r 36
19. 1427 ÷ 25    57 r 2
20. 3819 ÷ 19    201
21. 4126 ÷ 32    128 r 30
22. 968 ÷ 24    40 r 8
23. 377 ÷ 18    20 r 17
24. 566 ÷ 42    13 r 20

**Supplemental Practice for Lesson 3**

Find the missing number in each problem.

$$
\textbf{1.}\quad
\begin{array}{r}
12 \\
+\;A \quad {\scriptstyle 15}\\
\hline
27
\end{array}
\qquad
\textbf{2.}\quad
\begin{array}{r}
B \quad {\scriptstyle 25}\\
+\;15 \\
\hline
40
\end{array}
\qquad
\textbf{3.}\quad
\begin{array}{r}
8 \\
+\;C \quad {\scriptstyle 25}\\
\hline
33
\end{array}
\qquad
\textbf{4.}\quad
\begin{array}{r}
D \quad {\scriptstyle 29}\\
+\;21 \\
\hline
50
\end{array}
$$

$$
\textbf{5.}\quad
\begin{array}{r}
16 \\
+\;E \quad {\scriptstyle 29}\\
\hline
45
\end{array}
\qquad
\textbf{6.}\quad
\begin{array}{r}
F \quad {\scriptstyle 46}\\
+\;26 \\
\hline
72
\end{array}
\qquad
\textbf{7.}\quad
\begin{array}{r}
36 \\
+\;G \quad {\scriptstyle 28}\\
\hline
64
\end{array}
\qquad
\textbf{8.}\quad
\begin{array}{r}
H \quad {\scriptstyle 26}\\
+\;55 \\
\hline
81
\end{array}
$$

$$
\textbf{9.}\quad
\begin{array}{r}
25 \\
-\;J \quad {\scriptstyle 13}\\
\hline
12
\end{array}
\qquad
\textbf{10.}\quad
\begin{array}{r}
K \quad {\scriptstyle 60}\\
-\;36 \\
\hline
24
\end{array}
\qquad
\textbf{11.}\quad
\begin{array}{r}
40 \\
-\;L \quad {\scriptstyle 23}\\
\hline
17
\end{array}
\qquad
\textbf{12.}\quad
\begin{array}{r}
M \quad {\scriptstyle 49}\\
-\;17 \\
\hline
32
\end{array}
$$

$$
\textbf{13.}\quad
\begin{array}{r}
38 \\
-\;N \quad {\scriptstyle 22}\\
\hline
16
\end{array}
\qquad
\textbf{14.}\quad
\begin{array}{r}
P \quad {\scriptstyle 62}\\
-\;43 \\
\hline
19
\end{array}
\qquad
\textbf{15.}\quad
\begin{array}{r}
63 \\
-\;Q \quad {\scriptstyle 15}\\
\hline
48
\end{array}
\qquad
\textbf{16.}\quad
\begin{array}{r}
R \quad {\scriptstyle 63}\\
-\;24 \\
\hline
39
\end{array}
$$

**17.** $S + 26 = 62$ {36}          **18.** $T - 26 = 43$ {69}

**19.** $35 + U = 57$ {22}          **20.** $42 - V = 15$ {27}

**21.** $W + 54 = 80$ {26}          **22.** $X - 38 = 14$ {52}

**23.** $27 + Y = 72$ {45}          **24.** $60 - Z = 32$ {28}

**Supplemental Practice for Lesson 4**

Find the missing number in each problem.

$$
\textbf{1.}\quad
\begin{array}{r}
A \quad {\scriptstyle 6}\\
\times\;5 \\
\hline
30
\end{array}
\qquad
\textbf{2.}\quad
\begin{array}{r}
7 \\
\times\;B \quad {\scriptstyle 9}\\
\hline
63
\end{array}
\qquad
\textbf{3.}\quad
\begin{array}{r}
C \quad {\scriptstyle 15}\\
\times\;8 \\
\hline
120
\end{array}
\qquad
\textbf{4.}\quad
\begin{array}{r}
9 \\
\times\;D \quad {\scriptstyle 20}\\
\hline
180
\end{array}
$$

$$
\textbf{5.}\quad
\begin{array}{r}
E \quad {\scriptstyle 25}\\
\times\;6 \\
\hline
150
\end{array}
\qquad
\textbf{6.}\quad
\begin{array}{r}
4 \\
\times\;F \quad {\scriptstyle 14}\\
\hline
56
\end{array}
\qquad
\textbf{7.}\quad
\begin{array}{r}
G \quad {\scriptstyle 26}\\
\times\;9 \\
\hline
234
\end{array}
\qquad
\textbf{8.}\quad
\begin{array}{r}
8 \\
\times\;H \quad {\scriptstyle 22}\\
\hline
176
\end{array}
$$

**9.** $J\overline{)96}$ $\;^{8}$ {12}  **10.** $8\overline{)K}$ $\;^{7}$ {56}  **11.** $L\overline{)105}$ $\;^{7}$ {15}  **12.** $12\overline{)M}$ $\;^{15}$ {180}

**13.** $\dfrac{N}{5} = 14$ {70}   **14.** $\dfrac{90}{P} = 6$ {15}   **15.** $\dfrac{Q}{25} = 20$ {500}   **16.** $\dfrac{84}{R} = 7$ {12}

**17.** $6S = 90$ {15}                    **18.** $T \div 15 = 9$ {135}

**19.** $7U = 126$ {18}                  **20.** $152 \div V = 8$ {19}

**21.** $128 = 8W$ {16}                  **22.** $X \div 16 = 8$ {128}

**23.** $153 = 9Y$ {17}                  **24.** $144 \div Z = 9$ {16}

**Supplemental Practice for Lesson 12**

Use digits to write the following:

1. Five thousand    5000
2. Two hundred eight    208
3. One thousand, two hundred    1200
4. Six thousand, fifty    6050
5. Nine hundred forty-three    943
6. Eight thousand, one hundred ten    8110
7. Ten thousand    10,000
8. Twenty-one thousand    21,000
9. Forty thousand, nine hundred    40,900
10. One thousand, ten    1010
11. Fifteen thousand, twenty-one    15,021
12. Nineteen thousand, eight hundred    19,800
13. One hundred thousand    100,000
14. Two hundred ten thousand    210,000
15. Four hundred five thousand    405,000
16. Three hundred twenty-five thousand    325,000
17. One million    1,000,000
18. One million, two hundred thousand    1,200,000
19. Ten million, one hundred fifty thousand    10,150,000
20. Five hundred million    500,000,000
21. Two million, fifty thousand    2,050,000
22. Twenty-five million, seven hundred fifty thousand    25,750,000
23. Five billion    5,000,000,000
24. One billion, two hundred fifty million    1,250,000,000
25. Twenty-one billion, five hundred ten million    21,510,000,000
26. Two hundred billion    200,000,000,000
27. One trillion    1,000,000,000,000
28. Ten trillion    10,000,000,000,000
29. Two trillion, five hundred billion    2,500,000,000,000
30. Two hundred trillion    200,000,000,000,000

**Supplemental Practice for Lesson 16**

Round each of these numbers to the nearest ten:

**1.** 678   *680*   **2.** 83   *80*   **3.** 575   *580*   **4.** 909   *910*

**5.** 99   *100*   **6.** 1492   *1490*   **7.** 104   *100*   **8.** 1321   *1320*

Round each of these numbers to the nearest hundred:

**9.** 678   *700*   **10.** 437   *400*   **11.** 846   *800*   **12.** 1587   *1600*

**13.** 1023   *1000*   **14.** 987   *1000*   **15.** 3679   *3700*   **16.** 4981   *5000*

Round each of these numbers to the nearest thousand:

**17.** 1986   *2000*   **18.** 2317   *2000*   **19.** 1484   *1000*

**20.** 3675   *4000*   **21.** 5280   *5000*   **22.** 1760   *2000*

**23.** 36,102   *36,000*   **24.** 57,843   *58,000*   **25.** 375,874   *376,000*

**Supplemental Practice for Lesson 18**

Find the average of each set of numbers:

**1.** 15, 18, 21   *18*   **2.** 16, 18, 20, 22   *19*

**3.** 5, 6, 7, 8, 9   *7*   **4.** 2, 4, 6, 8, 10, 12   *7*

**5.** 100, 200, 300, 400   *250*   **6.** 20, 30, 40, 50, 60   *40*

**7.** 23, 35, 32   *30*   **8.** 136, 140, 141   *139*

**9.** 94, 94, 98, 98   *96*   **10.** 68, 72, 68, 76, 76   *72*

**11.** 6847, 6951   *6899*   **12.** 86, 86, 86, 86, 86   *86*

**13.** 562, 437, 381   *460*   **14.** 6, 6, 3, 9, 3, 6, 9   *6*

What number is halfway between each pair of numbers?

**15.** 47 and 91   *69*   **16.** 56 and 88   *72*

**17.** 75 and 57   *66*   **18.** 1 and 101   *51*

**19.** 92 and 136   *114*   **20.** 253 and 325   *289*

**21.** 548 and 752   *650*   **22.** 1776 and 1986   *1881*

**Supplemental Practice for Lesson 20**

List the factors of each number:

**1.** 30    **2.** 40    **3.** 50    **4.** 60    **5.** 35
1, 5, 7, 35

**6.** 36    **7.** 37  1, 37  **8.** 38    **9.** 39    **10.** 49
1, 7, 49

1. 1, 2, 3, 5, 6, 10, 15, 30
2. 1, 2, 4, 5, 8, 10, 20, 40
3. 1, 2, 5, 10, 25, 50
4. 1, 2, 3, 4, 5, 6, 10, 12, 15, 20, 30, 60
6. 1, 2, 3, 4, 6, 9, 12, 18, 36
8. 1, 2, 19, 38
9. 1, 3, 13, 39

Find the Greatest Common Factor (GCF) of each set of numbers:

**11.** 14, 28  14    **12.** 12, 20  4    **13.** 15, 16  1

**14.** 15, 25  5    **15.** 25, 50  25    **16.** 40, 70  10

**17.** 24, 42  6    **18.** 12, 21  3    **19.** 22, 55  11

**20.** 12, 30  6    **21.** 4, 3, 2  1    **22.** 2, 4, 6  2

**23.** 4, 8, 12  4    **24.** 6, 12, 20  2    **25.** 24, 30, 12, 15
3

**Supplemental Practice for Lesson 22**

**1.** $\frac{1}{2}$ of 42  21    **2.** $\frac{1}{3}$ of $42  $14.00

**3.** $\frac{2}{3}$ of 42  28    **4.** $\frac{1}{4}$ of $60  $15.00

**5.** $\frac{3}{4}$ of 60  45    **6.** $\frac{2}{3}$ of $60  $40.00

**7.** $\frac{1}{5}$ × 60  12    **8.** $\frac{2}{5}$ × $60  $24.00

**9.** $\frac{3}{5}$ × 20  12    **10.** $\frac{3}{8}$ × $24  $9.00

**11.** $\frac{5}{6}$ × 24  20    **12.** $\frac{3}{10}$ × $100  $30.00

**13.** What number is $\frac{2}{3}$ of 48?  32

**14.** How much money is $\frac{1}{5}$ of $90?  $18.00

**15.** What number is $\frac{5}{8}$ of 40?  25

**16.** How much money is $\frac{1}{10}$ of $200?  $20

**17.** What number is $\frac{9}{10}$ of 60?  54

**18.** How much money is $\frac{3}{4}$ of $28?  $21

**19.** One third of 27 is what number?  9

**20.** Two thirds of 36 is what number?  24

**21.** Three fourths of 24 is what number?   18

**22.** Four fifths of 35 is what number?   28

**23.** Two ninths of 36 is what number?   8

**24.** Seven tenths of 30 is what number?   21

**25.** Five twelfths of 24 is what number?   10

**Supplemental Practice for Lesson 26**

Write each of these improper fractions as a mixed number:

**1.** $\frac{3}{3}$   1    **2.** $\frac{5}{4}$   $1\frac{1}{4}$    **3.** $\frac{7}{3}$   $2\frac{1}{3}$    **4.** $\frac{17}{10}$   $1\frac{7}{10}$    **5.** $\frac{24}{6}$   4

**6.** $\frac{24}{5}$   $4\frac{4}{5}$    **7.** $\frac{24}{4}$   6    **8.** $\frac{32}{15}$   $2\frac{2}{15}$    **9.** $\frac{32}{16}$   2    **10.** $\frac{27}{5}$   $5\frac{2}{5}$

**11.** $\frac{36}{7}$   $5\frac{1}{7}$    **12.** $\frac{25}{6}$   $4\frac{1}{6}$    **13.** $\frac{35}{5}$   7    **14.** $\frac{12}{5}$   $2\frac{2}{5}$    **15.** $\frac{31}{10}$   $3\frac{1}{10}$

**16.** $1\frac{5}{2}$   $3\frac{1}{2}$    **17.** $3\frac{6}{3}$   5    **18.** $7\frac{9}{4}$   $9\frac{1}{4}$    **19.** $6\frac{8}{2}$   10    **20.** $4\frac{5}{3}$   $5\frac{2}{3}$

**21.** $11\frac{6}{5}$   $12\frac{1}{5}$    **22.** $4\frac{11}{10}$   $5\frac{1}{10}$    **23.** $2\frac{13}{12}$   $3\frac{1}{12}$    **24.** $1\frac{10}{3}$   $4\frac{1}{3}$    **25.** $23\frac{7}{2}$   $26\frac{1}{2}$

**Supplemental Practice for Lesson 29 Set A**

Reduce each fraction to lowest terms:

**1.** $\frac{2}{6}$   $\frac{1}{3}$    **2.** $\frac{3}{6}$   $\frac{1}{2}$    **3.** $\frac{4}{6}$   $\frac{2}{3}$    **4.** $\frac{2}{8}$   $\frac{1}{4}$    **5.** $\frac{4}{8}$   $\frac{1}{2}$

**6.** $\frac{6}{8}$   $\frac{3}{4}$    **7.** $\frac{3}{9}$   $\frac{1}{3}$    **8.** $\frac{2}{10}$   $\frac{1}{5}$    **9.** $\frac{4}{10}$   $\frac{2}{5}$    **10.** $\frac{5}{10}$   $\frac{1}{2}$

**11.** $\frac{8}{10}$   $\frac{4}{5}$    **12.** $\frac{2}{12}$   $\frac{1}{6}$    **13.** $\frac{3}{12}$   $\frac{1}{4}$    **14.** $\frac{4}{12}$   $\frac{1}{3}$    **15.** $\frac{6}{12}$   $\frac{1}{2}$

**16.** $\frac{8}{12}$   $\frac{2}{3}$    **17.** $\frac{9}{12}$   $\frac{3}{4}$    **18.** $3\frac{10}{12}$   $3\frac{5}{6}$    **19.** $4\frac{6}{15}$   $4\frac{2}{5}$    **20.** $1\frac{18}{24}$   $1\frac{3}{4}$

**21.** $2\frac{15}{18}$   $2\frac{5}{6}$    **22.** $6\frac{16}{24}$   $6\frac{2}{3}$    **23.** $8\frac{12}{24}$   $8\frac{1}{2}$    **24.** $9\frac{8}{24}$   $9\frac{1}{3}$    **25.** $10\frac{10}{24}$   $10\frac{5}{12}$

**Set B**   Add or subtract then simplify the answer if possible.

**1.** $\frac{5}{8} + \frac{2}{8}$   $\frac{7}{8}$    **2.** $\frac{5}{8} - \frac{2}{8}$   $\frac{3}{8}$    **3.** $\frac{3}{6} + \frac{2}{6}$   $\frac{5}{6}$

**4.** $\dfrac{3}{6} - \dfrac{2}{6}$ $\frac{1}{6}$ 　　**5.** $\dfrac{1}{3} + \dfrac{1}{3}$ $\frac{2}{3}$ 　　**6.** $\dfrac{1}{3} - \dfrac{1}{3}$ $0$

**7.** $\dfrac{4}{9} + \dfrac{1}{9}$ $\frac{5}{9}$ 　　**8.** $\dfrac{4}{9} - \dfrac{2}{9}$ $\frac{2}{9}$ 　　**9.** $\dfrac{1}{4} + \dfrac{1}{4} + \dfrac{1}{4}$ $\frac{3}{4}$

**10.** $\dfrac{1}{7} + \dfrac{2}{7} + \dfrac{3}{7}$ $\frac{6}{7}$ 　**11.** $\dfrac{3}{4} + \dfrac{2}{4}$ $1\frac{1}{4}$ 　　**12.** $\dfrac{3}{4} - \dfrac{1}{4}$ $\frac{1}{2}$

**13.** $\dfrac{2}{3} + \dfrac{2}{3}$ $1\frac{1}{3}$ 　　**14.** $\dfrac{3}{8} - \dfrac{1}{8}$ $\frac{1}{4}$ 　　**15.** $\dfrac{4}{5} + \dfrac{4}{5}$ $1\frac{3}{5}$

**16.** $\dfrac{6}{5} - \dfrac{1}{5}$ $1$ 　　**17.** $\dfrac{5}{8} + \dfrac{3}{8}$ $1$ 　　**18.** $\dfrac{5}{8} - \dfrac{1}{8}$ $\frac{1}{2}$

**19.** $\dfrac{3}{10} + \dfrac{2}{10}$ $\frac{1}{2}$ 　**20.** $\dfrac{9}{10} - \dfrac{1}{10}$ $\frac{4}{5}$ 　**21.** $\dfrac{5}{12} + \dfrac{5}{12}$ $\frac{5}{6}$

**22.** $\dfrac{5}{12} - \dfrac{1}{12}$ $\frac{1}{3}$ 　**23.** $\dfrac{3}{10} + \dfrac{7}{10}$ $1$ 　**24.** $\dfrac{7}{10} - \dfrac{3}{10}$ $\frac{2}{5}$

**Supplemental Practice for Lesson 30**

Find the Least Common Multiple (LCM) of each set of numbers.

**1.** 3, 4 　12 　　**2.** 3, 5 　15 　　**3.** 3, 6 　6 　　**4.** 4, 6 　12

**5.** 6, 8 　24 　　**6.** 4, 8 　8 　　**7.** 3, 8 　24 　　**8.** 2, 8 　8

**9.** 3, 9 　9 　　**10.** 6, 9 　18 　　**11.** 6, 10 　30 　**12.** 4, 10 　20

**13.** 8, 12 　24 　**14.** 9, 12 　36 　**15.** 10, 12 　60 　**16.** 2, 5, 10 　10

**17.** 2, 3, 4 　12 　**18.** 2, 3, 6 　6 　**19.** 2, 4, 8 　8 　**20.** 2, 4, 6 　12

**Supplemental Practice for Lesson 32**

Write each of these numbers in standard form:

**1.** $(6 \times 100) + (7 \times 10)$ 　670

**2.** $(5 \times 1000) + (4 \times 100)$ 　5400

**3.** $(7 \times 100) + (3 \times 1)$ 　703

**4.** $(8 \times 10) + (1 \times 1)$ 　81

**5.** $(9 \times 1000) + (5 \times 10)$ 　9050

**6.** $(7 \times 100) + (3 \times 10)$ 　730

7. $(5 \times 100) + (6 \times 10)$

8. $(5 \times 1000) + (6 \times 100)$

9. $(7 \times 100) + (6 \times 1)$

10. $(5 \times 1000) + (2 \times 100) + (8 \times 10)$

Write each of these numbers in expanded notation:

**7.** 560 　　　**8.** 5600 　　　**9.** 706 　　　**10.** 5280

Find the time elapsed from:

**11.** 3:00 a.m. to 8:30 a.m.
5 hr, 30 min

**12.** 7:15 a.m. to 10:00 a.m.
2 hr, 45 min

**13.** 8:45 a.m. to 11:20 a.m.
2 hr, 35 min

**14.** 9:30 a.m. to 1:15 p.m.
3 hr, 45 min

**15.** 10:25 a.m. to 2:00 p.m.
3 hr, 35 min

**16.** 9:40 a.m. to 2:30 p.m.
4 hr, 50 min

17. 3 hr, 50 min

**17.** 5:15 p.m. to 9:05 p.m.

**18.** 2:50 p.m. to 6:15 p.m.

18. 3 hr, 25 min

**19.** 10:35 a.m. to 6:20 p.m.
7 hr, 45 min

**20.** 10:53 a.m. to 2:27 p.m.
3 hr, 34 min

**Supplemental Practice for Lesson 33**

Write each percent as a fraction. Reduce when possible.

**1.** 50% $\frac{1}{2}$  **2.** 25% $\frac{1}{4}$  **3.** 75% $\frac{3}{4}$  **4.** 10% $\frac{1}{10}$

**5.** 20% $\frac{1}{5}$  **6.** 90% $\frac{9}{10}$  **7.** 30% $\frac{3}{10}$  **8.** 60% $\frac{3}{5}$

**9.** 80% $\frac{4}{5}$  **10.** 1% $\frac{1}{100}$  **11.** 5% $\frac{1}{20}$  **12.** 99% $\frac{99}{100}$

**13.** 2% $\frac{1}{50}$  **14.** 35% $\frac{7}{20}$  **15.** 45% $\frac{9}{20}$  **16.** 4% $\frac{1}{25}$

**17.** 14% $\frac{7}{50}$  **18.** 24% $\frac{6}{25}$  **19.** 40% $\frac{2}{5}$  **20.** 70% $\frac{7}{10}$

**Supplemental Practice for Lesson 35**

Write each of these numbers as a decimal number:

**1.** Five tenths    0.5

**2.** Three hundredths    0.03

**3.** Eleven hundredths    0.11

**4.** One thousandth    0.001

**5.** Twenty-five thousandths    0.025

**6.** One and two tenths    1.2

**7.** Ten and four tenths    10.4

**8.** Two and one hundredth    2.01

**9.** Five and twelve hundredths    5.12

**10.** One hundred twenty thousandths    0.12

**11.** Two hundred five thousandths    0.205

**12.** Six and fifteen hundredths    6.15

**13.** Ten and one hundred thousandths    10.1

**14.** Twelve and six hundredths    12.06

**15.** Ten and twenty-two thousandths    10.022

Write each fraction or mixed number as a decimal number:

**16.** $\dfrac{5}{100}$  0.05  **17.** $\dfrac{12}{1000}$  0.012  **18.** $1\dfrac{3}{10}$  1.3  **19.** $10\dfrac{1}{10}$  10.1  **20.** $15\dfrac{23}{100}$  15.23

**21.** $\dfrac{124}{1000}$  0.124  **22.** $1\dfrac{1}{1000}$  1.001  **23.** $1\dfrac{45}{100}$  1.45  **24.** $8\dfrac{3}{100}$  8.03  **25.** $9\dfrac{52}{1000}$  9.052

**Supplemental Practice for Lesson 36**

**1.** $1 - \dfrac{2}{3}$  $\frac{1}{3}$  **2.** $2 - 1\dfrac{1}{3}$  $\frac{2}{3}$  **3.** $6 - 3\dfrac{3}{4}$  $2\frac{1}{4}$

**4.** $1 - \dfrac{2}{5}$  $\frac{3}{5}$  **5.** $3 - 1\dfrac{4}{5}$  $1\frac{1}{5}$  **6.** $7 - 3\dfrac{1}{2}$  $3\frac{1}{2}$

**7.** $1 - \dfrac{3}{8}$  $\frac{5}{8}$  **8.** $4 - 1\dfrac{1}{4}$  $2\frac{3}{4}$  **9.** $8 - 3\dfrac{1}{3}$  $4\frac{2}{3}$

**10.** $1 - \dfrac{7}{10}$  $\frac{3}{10}$  **11.** $3 - 1\dfrac{1}{2}$  $1\frac{1}{2}$  **12.** $10 - 4\dfrac{5}{8}$  $5\frac{3}{8}$

**13.** $1 - \dfrac{3}{4}$  $\frac{1}{4}$  **14.** $5 - 3\dfrac{3}{8}$  $1\frac{5}{8}$  **15.** $12 - 4\dfrac{3}{10}$  $7\frac{7}{10}$

**Supplemental Practice for Lesson 40 Set A**

**1.** $0.62 + 0.4$  1.02  **2.** $0.62 - 0.4$  0.22

**3.** $1.5 + 0.15$  1.65  **4.** $1.2 - 0.15$  1.05

**5.** $0.5 + 0.41$  0.91  **6.** $0.5 - 0.41$  0.09

**7.** $0.23 + 0.6 + 1.4$  2.23  **8.** $5.3 - 4.29$  1.01

**9.** $3.6 + 2 + 0.75$  6.35  **10.** $1 - 0.3$  0.7

**11.** $4.75 + 3 + 12.5$  20.25  **12.** $15.4 - 15.40$  0

**13.** $0.3 + 0.4 + 0.5$  1.2  **14.** $5 - 1.25$  3.75

**15.** $0.36 + 0.4 + 0.575$  1.335  **16.** $0.3 - 0.036$  0.264

**17.** $1 + 0.2 + 3.456$  4.656  **18.** $10 - 0.7$  9.3

**19.** $0.6 + 0.7 + 0.8$  2.1  **20.** $1 - 0.21$  0.79

**Set B**

**1.** $0.3 \times 4$  1.2  **2.** $0.4 \times 0.6$  0.24  **3.** $0.3 \times 0.2$  0.06

**4.** $0.4 \times 0.3$  0.12  **5.** $7 \times 0.21$  1.47  **6.** $0.6 \times 1.24$  0.744

**7.** $0.36 \times 0.4$  0.144  **8.** $0.012 \times 10$  0.12  **9.** $1.2 \times 8$  9.6

10. 0.434
11. 0.144  **10.** $6.2 \times 0.07$  **11.** $1.2 \times 0.12$  **12.** $1.25 \times 10$  12.5

**13.** $3.6 \times 1.2$ _4.32_  **14.** $4.5 \times 9$ _40.5_  **15.** $0.015 \times 0.03$
   _0.00045_
**16.** $6.75 \times 0.1$   **17.** $0.01 \times 3.75$   **18.** $1.5 \times 1.5$ _2.25_
   _0.675_       _0.0375_
**19.** $0.25 \times 0.25$   **20.** $6.3 \times 0.24$   **21.** $4.2 \times 100$ _420_
   _0.0625_       _1.512_

**Supplemental Practice for Lesson 44**

**1.** $4.8 \div 6$ _0.8_    **2.** $0.48 \div 4$ _0.12_  **3.** $0.48 \div 8$ _0.06_

**4.** $0.125 \div 5$    **5.** $1.44 \div 6$ _0.24_  **6.** $0.018 \div 3$
   _0.025_          _0.006_
**7.** $0.24 \div 12$ _0.02_  **8.** $5.6 \div 8$ _0.7_  **9.** $17.1 \div 9$ _1.9_

**10.** $3.65 \div 5$ _0.73_  **11.** $42.80 \div 10$   **12.** $3.10 \div 10$ _0.31_
         _4.28_
**13.** $0.190 \div 5$   **14.** $0.234 \div 9$   **15.** $5.00 \div 4$ _1.25_
   _0.038_       _0.026_
**16.** $0.7 \div 5$ _0.14_  **17.** $0.4 \div 4$ _0.1_  **18.** $0.5 \div 4$ _0.125_

**19.** $3.6 \div 10$ _0.36_  **20.** $0.24 \div 10$   **21.** $0.12 \div 8$ _0.015_
         _0.024_
**22.** $0.9 \div 4$ _0.225_  **23.** $1.1 \div 8$   **24.** $0.51 \div 10$
         _0.1375_        _0.051_

**Supplemental Practice for Lesson 45**

Write each of these numbers in expanded notation.

**1.** $3.5$   $(3 \times 1) + \left(5 \times \frac{1}{10}\right)$    **2.** $0.26$   $\left(2 \times \frac{1}{10}\right) + \left(6 \times \frac{1}{100}\right)$
**3.** $4.08$   $(4 \times 1) + \left(8 \times \frac{1}{100}\right)$    **4.** $3.14$
**5.** $0.015$  $\left(1 \times \frac{1}{100}\right) + \left(5 \times \frac{1}{1000}\right)$   **6.** $0.09$   $\left(9 \times \frac{1}{100}\right)$
**7.** $12.5$           **8.** $0.405$   $\left(4 \times \frac{1}{10}\right) + \left(5 \times \frac{1}{1000}\right)$

4. $(3 \times 1) +$
   $\left(1 \times \frac{1}{10}\right) +$
   $\left(4 \times \frac{1}{100}\right)$

7. $(1 \times 10) +$
   $(2 \times 1) +$
   $\left(5 \times \frac{1}{10}\right)$

Write each number in decimal form.

**9.** $(6 \times 1) + \left(5 \times \dfrac{1}{10}\right)$   _6.5_

**10.** $\left(7 \times \dfrac{1}{10}\right) + \left(5 \times \dfrac{1}{100}\right)$   _0.75_

**11.** $(5 \times 10) + \left(5 \times \dfrac{1}{10}\right)$   _50.5_

**12.** $\left(8 \times \dfrac{1}{100}\right)$   _0.08_

**13.** $(7 \times 1) + \left(5 \times \dfrac{1}{100}\right)$   _7.05_

**14.** $\left(3 \times \dfrac{1}{100}\right) + \left(9 \times \dfrac{1}{1000}\right)$   _0.039_

**15.** $(8 \times 10) + (3 \times 1) + \left(2 \times \dfrac{1}{10}\right)$   83.2

**16.** $(7 \times 10) + \left(8 \times \dfrac{1}{10}\right) + \left(1 \times \dfrac{1}{100}\right)$   70.81

**Supplemental Practice for Lesson 47**

**1.** $1 - \dfrac{1}{5}$   $\frac{4}{5}$    **2.** $1 - \dfrac{3}{8}$   $\frac{5}{8}$    **3.** $2 - \dfrac{1}{2}$   $1\frac{1}{2}$

**4.** $2 - \dfrac{1}{3}$   $1\frac{2}{3}$    **5.** $2 - 1\dfrac{1}{4}$   $\frac{3}{4}$    **6.** $3 - 1\dfrac{3}{8}$   $1\frac{5}{8}$

**7.** $3 - 2\dfrac{5}{8}$   $\frac{3}{8}$    **8.** $8 - 3\dfrac{3}{4}$   $4\frac{1}{4}$    **9.** $8 - 5\dfrac{1}{8}$   $2\frac{7}{8}$

**10.** $10 - 4\dfrac{2}{5}$   $5\frac{3}{5}$    **11.** $4\dfrac{1}{3} - 1\dfrac{2}{3}$   $2\frac{2}{3}$    **12.** $4\dfrac{1}{5} - 1\dfrac{3}{5}$   $2\frac{3}{5}$

**13.** $6\dfrac{1}{10} - 3\dfrac{4}{10}$   $2\frac{7}{10}$   **14.** $5\dfrac{3}{8} - 3\dfrac{6}{8}$   $1\frac{5}{8}$    **15.** $2\dfrac{1}{4} - 1\dfrac{2}{4}$   $\frac{3}{4}$

**16.** $5\dfrac{2}{5} - 3\dfrac{4}{5}$   $1\frac{3}{5}$    **17.** $7\dfrac{3}{8} - 4\dfrac{4}{8}$   $2\frac{7}{8}$    **18.** $9\dfrac{1}{10} - 3\dfrac{5}{10}$   $5\frac{3}{5}$

**19.** $4\dfrac{2}{4} - 1\dfrac{3}{4}$   $2\frac{3}{4}$    **20.** $8\dfrac{3}{5} - 1\dfrac{4}{5}$   $6\frac{4}{5}$    **21.** $4\dfrac{1}{4} - 1\dfrac{3}{4}$   $2\frac{1}{2}$

**22.** $4\dfrac{3}{8} - 1\dfrac{5}{8}$   $2\frac{3}{4}$    **23.** $3\dfrac{1}{6} - 1\dfrac{5}{6}$   $1\frac{1}{3}$    **24.** $6\dfrac{1}{10} - 4\dfrac{3}{10}$   $1\frac{4}{5}$

**Supplemental Practice for Lesson 48**

**1.** $5.2 \div 0.4$   13    **2.** $0.144 \div 0.8$   0.18    **3.** $3.21 \div 0.3$   10.7

**4.** $1.00 \div 0.4$   2.5    **5.** $0.525 \div 0.05$   10.5    **6.** $8.1 \div 0.09$   90

**7.** $1.2 \div 0.003$   400    **8.** $0.54 \div 0.006$   90    **9.** $1.2 \div 0.12$   10

**10.** $0.12 \div 1.2$   0.1    **11.** $0.5 \div 0.04$   12.5    **12.** $3.6 \div 0.5$   7.2

**13.** $0.12 \div 10$   0.012    **14.** $6.4 \div 100$   0.064    **15.** $3.5 \div 0.08$   43.75

**16.** $8 \div 0.5$   16    **17.** $4 \div 0.4$   10    **18.** $12 \div 0.06$   200

**19.** $18 \div 0.20$   90    **20.** $16 \div 0.008$   2000    **21.** $5 \div 0.25$   20

74   **22.** $4.44 \div 0.06$    **23.** $16 \div 0.25$   64    **24.** $0.3 \div 0.4$   0.75

**Supplemental Practice for Lesson 50**

Round each number to the nearest tenth.

**1.** 0.48   0.5    **2.** 0.133  0.1    **3.** 0.375  0.4    **4.** 4.28   4.3

**5.** 62.84  62.8    **6.** 0.0984  0.1    **7.** 6.25   6.3    **8.** 1.97   2

Round each number to the nearest hundredth (or cent).

**9.** 0.8181    **10.** 0.6666    **11.** 1.333    **12.** 4.321
   0.82           0.67           1.33           4.32

**13.** $0.2345    **14.** $7.675    **15.** $0.166    **16.** $3.422
   $0.23          $7.68          $0.17          $3.42

Round each number to the nearest whole number.

**17.** 12.34  12    **18.** 4.567   5    **19.** 91.66  92    **20.** 142.8  143

**Supplemental Practice for Lesson 51**

Solve mentally.

**1.** 4.2 × 10   42                **2.** 0.35 × 10   3.5

**3.** 0.178 × 10   1.78         **4.** 3.65 × 10   36.5

**5.** 4.21 × 100   421          **6.** 0.375 × 100   37.5

**7.** 6.5 × 100   650           **8.** 4.323 × 100   432.3

**9.** 7.275 × 1000   7275      **10.** 6.4 × 1000   6400

**11.** 0.86 × 1000   860       **12.** 0.01625 × 1000   16.25

**13.** 4.2 ÷ 10   0.42           **14.** 0.42 ÷ 10   0.042

**15.** 42.1 ÷ 10   4.21          **16.** 6 ÷ 10   0.6

**17.** 87.5 ÷ 100   0.875      **18.** 6.5 ÷ 100   0.065

**19.** 0.4 ÷ 100   0.004       **20.** 372.8 ÷ 100   3.728

**21.** 123.4 ÷ 1000   0.1234    **22.** 42.5 ÷ 1000   0.0425

**23.** 7.6 ÷ 1000   0.0076     **24.** 4 ÷ 1000   0.004

**Supplemental Practice for Lesson 56**

**1.** $\frac{1}{2} + \frac{1}{8}$   $\frac{5}{8}$        **2.** $\frac{1}{2} - \frac{1}{8}$   $\frac{3}{8}$        **3.** $\frac{3}{4} + \frac{1}{8}$   $\frac{7}{8}$

**4.** $\frac{3}{4} - \frac{1}{8}$   $\frac{5}{8}$        **5.** $\frac{2}{3} + \frac{1}{6}$   $\frac{5}{6}$        **6.** $\frac{2}{3} - \frac{1}{6}$   $\frac{1}{2}$

**7.** $\frac{1}{3} + \frac{1}{4}$   $\frac{7}{12}$       **8.** $\frac{1}{3} - \frac{1}{4}$   $\frac{1}{12}$       **9.** $\frac{3}{4} + \frac{2}{3}$   $1\frac{5}{12}$

**10.** $\frac{3}{4} - \frac{2}{3}$   $\frac{1}{12}$      **11.** $\frac{1}{2} + \frac{1}{10}$   $\frac{3}{5}$      **12.** $\frac{1}{2} - \frac{1}{10}$   $\frac{2}{5}$

**13.** $\dfrac{3}{4} + \dfrac{3}{8}$   $1\frac{1}{8}$    **14.** $\dfrac{3}{4} - \dfrac{3}{8}$   $\frac{3}{8}$    **15.** $\dfrac{2}{3} + \dfrac{1}{2}$   $1\frac{1}{6}$

**16.** $\dfrac{2}{3} - \dfrac{1}{2}$   $\frac{1}{6}$    **17.** $\dfrac{7}{10} + \dfrac{1}{2}$   $1\frac{1}{5}$    **18.** $\dfrac{7}{10} - \dfrac{1}{2}$   $\frac{1}{5}$

**19.** $\dfrac{1}{4} + \dfrac{1}{5}$   $\frac{9}{20}$    **20.** $\dfrac{1}{4} - \dfrac{1}{5}$   $\frac{1}{20}$    **21.** $\dfrac{3}{5} + \dfrac{1}{2}$   $1\frac{1}{10}$

**Supplemental Practice for Lesson 62**

**1.** $3\dfrac{1}{8} + 2\dfrac{1}{4}$   $5\frac{3}{8}$    **2.** $3\dfrac{1}{4} - 2\dfrac{1}{8}$   $1\frac{1}{8}$    **3.** $1\dfrac{1}{6} + 1\dfrac{1}{3}$   $2\frac{1}{2}$

**4.** $2\dfrac{1}{3} - 1\dfrac{1}{6}$   $1\frac{1}{6}$    **5.** $3\dfrac{3}{4} + 4\dfrac{1}{8}$   $7\frac{7}{8}$    **6.** $4\dfrac{3}{4} - 3\dfrac{1}{8}$   $1\frac{5}{8}$

**7.** $5\dfrac{3}{5} + 1\dfrac{3}{10}$   $6\frac{9}{10}$   **8.** $5\dfrac{3}{5} - 1\dfrac{3}{10}$   $4\frac{3}{10}$   **9.** $4\dfrac{1}{2} + 2\dfrac{1}{12}$   $6\frac{7}{12}$

**10.** $4\dfrac{1}{2} - 2\dfrac{1}{12}$   $2\frac{5}{12}$   **11.** $6\dfrac{1}{2} + 2\dfrac{1}{3}$   $8\frac{5}{6}$   **12.** $4\dfrac{1}{2} - 2\dfrac{1}{3}$   $2\frac{1}{6}$

**13.** $5\dfrac{1}{2} + 1\dfrac{2}{3}$   $7\frac{1}{6}$    **14.** $5\dfrac{1}{2} - 1\dfrac{2}{3}$   $3\frac{5}{6}$    **15.** $1\dfrac{1}{2} + \dfrac{3}{4}$   $2\frac{1}{4}$

**16.** $1\dfrac{1}{2} - \dfrac{3}{4}$   $\frac{3}{4}$    **17.** $6\dfrac{3}{5} + 1\dfrac{1}{2}$   $8\frac{1}{10}$   **18.** $6\dfrac{3}{5} - 1\dfrac{1}{2}$   $5\frac{1}{10}$

**19.** $2\dfrac{7}{10} + 1\dfrac{1}{5}$   $3\frac{9}{10}$   **20.** $2\dfrac{7}{10} - 1\dfrac{1}{5}$   $1\frac{1}{2}$   **21.** $8\dfrac{2}{3} + 1\dfrac{3}{4}$   $10\frac{5}{12}$

**22.** $8\dfrac{2}{3} - 1\dfrac{3}{4}$   $6\frac{11}{12}$   **23.** $3\dfrac{1}{2} + 1\dfrac{1}{3}$   $4\frac{5}{6}$   **24.** $5\dfrac{1}{4} + 3\dfrac{1}{2}$   $8\frac{3}{4}$

**Supplemental Practice for Lesson 64**

21. $2 \times 3 \times 7$
22. $2 \times 2 \times 2 \times 2 \times 3$
23. $2 \times 2 \times 3 \times 5$
24. $2 \times 2 \times 5 \times 5$

Write the prime factorization of each number:

**1.** 6   $2 \times 3$    **2.** 7   $1 \times 7$    **3.** 8   $2 \times 2 \times 2$   **4.** 9   $3 \times 3$

**5.** 10   $2 \times 5$    **6.** 11   $1 \times 11$    **7.** 12   $2 \times 2 \times 3$   **8.** 13   $1 \times 13$

**9.** 14   $2 \times 7$    **10.** 15   $3 \times 5$    **11.** 16   $2 \times 2 \times 2 \times 2$   **12.** 18   $2 \times 3 \times 3$

**13.** 20   $2 \times 2 \times 5$   **14.** 21   $3 \times 7$    **15.** 24   $2 \times 2 \times 2 \times 3$   **16.** 30   $2 \times 3 \times 5$

**17.** 36   $2 \times 2 \times 3 \times 3$   **18.** 39   $3 \times 13$   **19.** 40   $2 \times 2 \times 2 \times 5$   **20.** 41   $1 \times 41$

**21.** 42    **22.** 48    **23.** 60    **24.** 100

**Supplemental Practice for Lesson 65**

1. $3 \times 1\frac{1}{4}$   $3\frac{3}{4}$    2. $1\frac{1}{2} \times 3$   $4\frac{1}{2}$    3. $1\frac{1}{2} \times 1\frac{1}{4}$   $1\frac{7}{8}$

4. $1\frac{2}{3} \times 2\frac{1}{2}$   $4\frac{1}{6}$    5. $3\frac{1}{2} \times 5$   $17\frac{1}{2}$    6. $1\frac{3}{4} \times 1\frac{1}{2}$   $2\frac{5}{8}$

7. $3\frac{1}{3} \times 1\frac{2}{3}$   $5\frac{5}{9}$    8. $7\frac{1}{2} \times 2$   $15$    9. $\frac{4}{5} \times 1\frac{1}{5}$   $\frac{24}{25}$

10. $\frac{5}{6} \times 1\frac{1}{5}$   $1$    11. $1\frac{1}{2} \times 1\frac{1}{3}$   $2$    12. $1\frac{1}{2} \times 1\frac{2}{3}$   $2\frac{1}{2}$

13. $1\frac{1}{4} \times 2\frac{2}{5}$   $3$    14. $3\frac{2}{3} \times 3$   $11$    15. $4 \times 3\frac{1}{2}$   $14$

16. $\frac{5}{6} \times 3\frac{3}{5}$   $3$    17. $3\frac{1}{3} \times 2\frac{1}{10}$   $7$   18. $5\frac{1}{3} \times 1\frac{1}{8}$   $6$

19. $2\frac{1}{2} \times 1\frac{1}{3}$   $3\frac{1}{3}$   20. $\frac{7}{8} \times 2\frac{2}{3}$   $2\frac{1}{3}$   21. $1\frac{2}{5} \times 2\frac{1}{2}$   $3\frac{1}{2}$

**Supplemental Practice for Lesson 67**

1. $1\frac{1}{2} \div 3$   $\frac{1}{2}$    2. $3 \div 1\frac{1}{2}$   $2$    3. $1\frac{2}{3} \div 2$   $\frac{5}{6}$

4. $2 \div 1\frac{2}{3}$   $1\frac{1}{5}$    5. $\frac{3}{4} \div 1\frac{1}{2}$   $\frac{1}{2}$    6. $1\frac{1}{2} \div \frac{3}{4}$   $2$

7. $1\frac{2}{3} \div 1\frac{1}{2}$   $1\frac{1}{9}$    8. $1\frac{1}{2} \div 1\frac{2}{3}$   $\frac{9}{10}$    9. $\frac{3}{8} \div 2$   $\frac{3}{16}$

10. $2 \div \frac{3}{8}$   $5\frac{1}{3}$    11. $1\frac{3}{5} \div 2\frac{1}{3}$   $\frac{24}{35}$   12. $2\frac{1}{3} \div 1\frac{3}{5}$   $1\frac{11}{24}$

13. $4\frac{1}{2} \div 2\frac{1}{4}$   $2$    14. $2\frac{1}{4} \div 4\frac{1}{2}$   $\frac{1}{2}$    15. $5 \div 1\frac{1}{4}$   $4$

16. $1\frac{1}{4} \div 5$   $\frac{1}{4}$    17. $2\frac{2}{3} \div 2$   $1\frac{1}{3}$    18. $2 \div 2\frac{2}{3}$   $\frac{3}{4}$

19. $2\frac{1}{2} \div 1\frac{3}{4}$   $1\frac{3}{7}$   20. $1\frac{3}{4} \div 2\frac{1}{2}$   $\frac{7}{10}$   21. $\frac{3}{4} \div 2\frac{1}{4}$   $\frac{1}{3}$

**Supplemental Practice for Lesson 70**

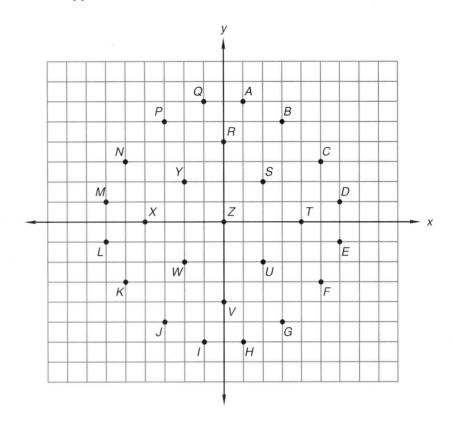

1. What is the name of the vertical axis?   *y*-axis

2. What is the name of the horizontal axis?   *x*-axis

3. What is the name given to the point at which the *x* and *y* axes cross?   origin

4. What name do we use to describe the numbers that give the location of a point?   coordinates

Which points have these coordinates?

5. $(3, 5)$   *B*    6. $(0, 4)$   *R*    7. $(-2, -2)$   *W*   8. $(-4, 0)$   *X*

9. $(2, -2)$   *U*   10. $(5, -3)$   *F*   11. $(-1, 6)$   *Q*   12. $(-3, -5)$   *J*

What are the coordinates of these points?

13. *L*  $(-6, -1)$    14. *A*  $(1, 6)$   15. *C*  $(5, 3)$   16. *D*  $(6, 1)$   17. *G*  $(3, -5)$

18. *I*  $(-1, -6)$    19. *K*  $(-5, -3)$   20. *V*  $(0, -4)$   21. *M*  $(-6, 1)$   22. *P*  $(-3, 5)$

$(-2, 2)$   23. *Y*    24. *S*  $(2, 2)$   25. *Z*  $(0, 0)$

**Supplemental Practice for Lesson 73**

Write each fraction as a decimal number:

**1.** $\frac{1}{2}$   0.5   **2.** $\frac{1}{4}$   0.25   **3.** $\frac{1}{8}$   0.125   **4.** $\frac{1}{10}$   0.1   **5.** $\frac{3}{4}$   0.75

**6.** $1\frac{3}{8}$   1.375   **7.** $2\frac{3}{10}$   2.3   **8.** $4\frac{3}{5}$   4.6   **9.** $7\frac{5}{8}$   7.625   **10.** $3\frac{7}{10}$   3.7

Write each decimal number as a reduced fraction or mixed number.

**11.** 0.1   $\frac{1}{10}$   **12.** 1.2   $1\frac{1}{5}$   **13.** 0.4   $\frac{2}{5}$   **14.** 2.5   $2\frac{1}{2}$

**15.** 0.8   $\frac{4}{5}$   **16.** 3.9   $3\frac{9}{10}$   **17.** 0.12   $\frac{3}{25}$   **18.** 4.15   $4\frac{3}{20}$

**19.** 0.25   $\frac{1}{4}$   **20.** 3.75   $3\frac{3}{4}$   **21.** 0.025   $\frac{1}{40}$   **22.** 0.005   $\frac{1}{200}$

**Supplemental Practice for Lesson 76**

Two fifths of the 25 ballplayers played.

**1.** Into how many parts was the team divided?   5

**2.** How many were in each part?   5

**3.** How many parts played?   2

**4.** How many players played?   10

**5.** How many parts did not play?   3

**6.** How many players did not play?   15

Five sixths of the 300 members had paid their dues.

**7.** Into how many parts was the group divided?   6

**8.** How many members are in each part?   50

**9.** How many parts paid their dues?   5

**10.** How many members paid their dues?   250

**11.** How many parts did not pay their dues?   1

**12.** How many members did not pay their dues?   50

Three tenths of the $6000 in prize money went to pay taxes.

**13.** Into how many parts was the prize money divided?   10

**14.** How much money was in each part?   $600

**15.** How many parts went to pay taxes?   3

**16.** How much money went to pay taxes? $1800

**17.** How many parts did not go to pay taxes? 7

**18.** How much money did not go to pay taxes? $4200

Out of 800 students, $\frac{27}{100}$ rode their bikes to school.

**19.** Into how many parts were the students divided? 100

**20.** How many students were in each part? 8

**21.** How many parts rode bikes? 27

**22.** How many students rode their bikes? 216

**23.** How many parts did not ride bikes? 73

**24.** How many students did not ride their bikes? 584

**Supplemental Practice for Lesson 83**

**1.** $3 + 3 \div 3 + 3 \times 3$  13

**2.** $3 \times 3 - 3 - 3 \div 3$  5

**3.** $3 + 3 \times 3 \div 3 - 3$  3

**4.** $3 - 3 \div 3 + 3 \times 3$  11

**5.** $4 + 4 \times 4 + 4 \div 4$  21

**6.** $4 \div 4 + 4 \times 4 - 4$  13

**7.** $5 - 4 \div 2 + 3 \times 6$  21

**8.** $6 - 3 \times 2 + 5 - 4$  1

**9.** $5 \times 5 - 5 \div 5 - 5$  19

**10.** $6 + 5 \times 4 - 3 - 2 \div 1$  21

**11.** $4(5) - 4 + 5(4)$  36

**12.** $3(2 + 1) - 2 + 3 \times 2$  13

**13.** $4(5 - 4) + 5 - 4$  5

**14.** $32 + 1.8 \times 10$  50

**15.** $2(5 + 4) - 2(4 + 3)$  4

**16.** $6 \times 4 \div 2 - 6 \div 2 \times 4$  0

**17.** $(5 + 3)(5 - 3)$  16

**18.** $32 + 1.8(50)$  122

**19.** $10 + 10 \times 10 - 10 \div 10$  109

**20.** $2(5) + 2(4) - 2(5 + 4)$  0

**Supplemental Practice for Lesson 84**

| | PERCENT | FRACTION | | DECIMAL | |
|---|---|---|---|---|---|
| 1. | 10% | (a) | $\frac{1}{10}$ | (b) | 0.1 |
| 2. | 20% | (a) | $\frac{1}{5}$ | (b) | 0.2 |
| 3. | 30% | (a) | $\frac{3}{10}$ | (b) | 0.3 |
| 4. | 40% | (a) | $\frac{2}{5}$ | (b) | 0.4 |
| 5. | 50% | (a) | $\frac{1}{2}$ | (b) | 0.5 |
| 6. | 15% | (a) | $\frac{3}{20}$ | (b) | 0.15 |
| 7. | 25% | (a) | $\frac{1}{4}$ | (b) | 0.25 |
| 8. | 45% | (a) | $\frac{9}{20}$ | (b) | 0.45 |
| 9. | 75% | (a) | $\frac{3}{4}$ | (b) | 0.75 |
| 10. | 1% | (a) | $\frac{1}{100}$ | (b) | 0.01 |
| 11. | 2% | (a) | $\frac{1}{50}$ | (b) | 0.02 |
| 12. | 4% | (a) | $\frac{1}{25}$ | (b) | 0.04 |
| 13. | 5% | (a) | $\frac{1}{20}$ | (b) | 0.05 |
| 14. | 6% | (a) | $\frac{3}{50}$ | (b) | 0.06 |
| 15. | 12% | (a) | $\frac{3}{25}$ | (b) | 0.12 |
| 16. | 24% | (a) | $\frac{6}{25}$ | (b) | 0.24 |
| 17. | 90% | (a) | $\frac{9}{10}$ | (b) | 0.9 |
| 18. | 95% | (a) | $\frac{19}{20}$ | (b) | 0.95 |
| 19. | 36% | (a) | $\frac{9}{25}$ | (b) | 0.36 |
| 20. | 150% | (a) | $1\frac{1}{2}$ | (b) | 1.5 |
| 21. | 250% | (a) | $2\frac{1}{2}$ | (b) | 2.5 |
| 22. | 110% | (a) | $1\frac{1}{10}$ | (b) | 1.1 |
| 23. | 125% | (a) | $1\frac{1}{4}$ | (b) | 1.25 |
| 24. | 120% | (a) | $1\frac{1}{5}$ | (b) | 1.2 |
| 25. | 105% | (a) | $1\frac{1}{20}$ | (b) | 1.05 |

**Supplemental Practice for Lesson 85**

Write each answer as a fraction:

**1.** $0.5 + \dfrac{1}{3}$   $\frac{5}{6}$    **2.** $0.8 - \dfrac{2}{5}$   $\frac{2}{5}$    **3.** $\dfrac{3}{4} - 0.1$   $\frac{13}{20}$

**4.** $\dfrac{1}{3} \times 0.6$   $\frac{1}{5}$    **5.** $0.2 \times \dfrac{1}{2}$   $\frac{1}{10}$    **6.** $0.75 \div \dfrac{3}{4}$   $1$

**7.** $\dfrac{3}{4} \div 0.25$   $3$    **8.** $\dfrac{7}{10} + 0.3$   $1$    **9.** $\dfrac{1}{10} + 0.3$   $\frac{2}{5}$

**10.** $0.4 - \dfrac{3}{10}$   $\frac{1}{10}$    **11.** $\dfrac{2}{3} \times 0.75$   $\frac{1}{2}$    **12.** $\dfrac{1}{5} \div 0.6$   $\frac{1}{3}$

Write each answer as a decimal:

**13.** $3.6 + \dfrac{1}{2}$   $4.1$    **14.** $\dfrac{1}{4} - 0.2$   $0.05$    **15.** $1.2 \times \dfrac{1}{5}$   $0.24$

**16.** $\dfrac{3}{5} \div 0.3$   $2$    **17.** $4.4 + \dfrac{3}{5}$   $5$    **18.** $\dfrac{3}{4} - 0.15$   $0.6$

**19.** $1.2 \times \dfrac{3}{4}$   $0.9$    **20.** $\dfrac{3}{10} \div 0.3$   $1$    **21.** $1 + \dfrac{1}{2}$   $1.5$

**22.** $\dfrac{3}{8} - 0.3$   $0.075$    **23.** $0.8 \times \dfrac{1}{8}$   $0.1$    **24.** $\dfrac{1}{2} \div 0.2$   $2.5$

**Supplemental Practice for Lesson 87**

Find the area of each triangle or shaded triangle.

**1.**   24 cm²    **2.**   16 cm²

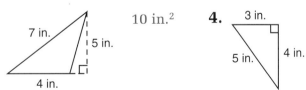
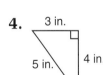

**3.**   10 in.²    **4.**   6 in.²

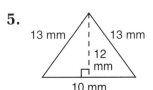
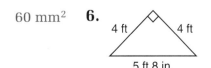

**5.**   60 mm²    **6.**   8 ft²

**7.** 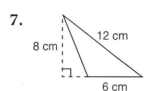 24 cm² **8.** 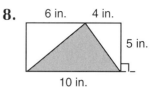 25 in.²

**9.** 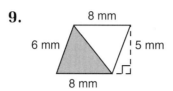 20 mm² **10.** 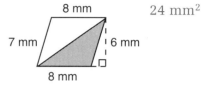 24 mm²

**11.** 39 m² **12.** 45 cm²

Write each number in expanded notation using exponents.

**1.** 450,000     **2.** 25,000,000     **3.** 16,000,000,000
$(4 \times 10^5) + (5 \times 10^4)$   $(2 \times 10^7) + (5 \times 10^6)$   $(1 \times 10^{10}) + (6 \times 10^9)$

Write each number in standard notation.

**4.** $5 \times 10^6$   5,000,000

**5.** $(3 \times 10^4) + (6 \times 10^3)$   36,000

**6.** $(1 \times 10^9) + (5 \times 10^8)$   1,500,000,000

Find each power.

**7.** $\left(\dfrac{1}{3}\right)^3$   $\frac{1}{27}$   **8.** $\left(2\dfrac{1}{2}\right)^2$   $6\frac{1}{4}$   **9.** $(0.1)^3$   **10.** $\left(1\dfrac{1}{2}\right)^3$   $3\frac{3}{8}$
                                                                              0.001

Simplify each expression using the proper order of operations.

**11.** $20 + 3^2 \times 2 - (8 + 2) \div \sqrt{25}$   36

**12.** $(2 + 3)^2 - 5(4) + \sqrt{100} \div \sqrt{25}$   7

**13.** $2 \times 3^2 - 2^3 + \sqrt{64} - 2(3)$   12

**14.** $\sqrt{9} + 5^2 - \sqrt{36} \div 3 - 2 \times 1^4$   24

**15.** $4^2 \div \sqrt{16} \times (2 + 1)^2 \div \sqrt{36} - 3 \times 2$   0

**Supplemental Practice for Lesson 93**

Write each fraction as a percent.

1. $\dfrac{1}{10}$  10%  2. $\dfrac{9}{10}$  90%  3. $\dfrac{1}{5}$  20%  4. $\dfrac{3}{4}$  75%  5. $\dfrac{3}{20}$  15%

6. $\dfrac{3}{25}$  12%  7. $\dfrac{3}{50}$  6%  8. $\dfrac{3}{100}$  3%  9. $\dfrac{11}{100}$  11%  10. $\dfrac{11}{50}$  22%

11. $\dfrac{11}{25}$  44%  12. $\dfrac{11}{20}$  55%  13. $\dfrac{1}{3}$  14. $\dfrac{2}{3}$  15. $\dfrac{1}{8}$

16. $\dfrac{3}{8}$  17. $\dfrac{1}{9}$  18. $\dfrac{5}{4}$  125%  19. $\dfrac{1}{6}$  20. $\dfrac{5}{8}$

21. $\dfrac{1}{7}$  $14\frac{2}{7}\%$  22. $\dfrac{5}{2}$  250%  23. $\dfrac{5}{6}$  $83\frac{1}{3}\%$  24. $\dfrac{7}{9}$  $77\frac{7}{9}\%$  25. $\dfrac{5}{12}$  $41\frac{2}{3}\%$

13. $33\frac{1}{3}\%$
14. $66\frac{2}{3}\%$
15. $12\frac{1}{2}\%$
16. $37\frac{1}{2}\%$
17. $11\frac{1}{9}\%$
19. $16\frac{2}{3}\%$
20. $62\frac{1}{2}\%$

**Supplemental Practice for Lesson 95**

Write each decimal as a percent.

1. 0.6  60%  2. 3.4  340%  3. 0.01  1%  4. 1.2  120%  5. 0.5  50%

6. 1.0  100%  7. 0.37  37%  8. 4.5  450%  9. 2.0  200%  10. 0.1  10%

11. 1.05  105%  12. 0.6  60%  13. 3.0  300%

Write each percent as a decimal.

14. 25%  0.25  15. 20%  0.2  16. 120%  1.2  17. 125%  1.25

18. 3%  0.03  19. 70%  0.7  20. 1%  0.01  21. 200%  2

22. 6%  0.06  23. 24%  0.24  24. 375%  3.75  25. 9%  0.09

| | FRACTION | | DECIMAL | | PERCENT | |
|---|---|---|---|---|---|---|
| **1.** | | $\frac{1}{100}$ | (a) | 0.01 | (b) | 1% |
| **2.** | (a) | $\frac{4}{5}$ | | 0.8 | (b) | 80% |
| **3.** | (a) | $\frac{1}{4}$ | (b) | 0.25 | | 25% |
| **4.** | | $\frac{3}{4}$ | (a) | 0.75 | (b) | 75% |
| **5.** | (a) | $\frac{7}{10}$ | | 0.7 | (b) | 70% |
| **6.** | (a) | $\frac{9}{10}$ | (b) | 0.9 | | 90% |
| **7.** | | $\frac{1}{20}$ | (a) | 0.05 | (b) | 5% |
| **8.** | (a) | $\frac{1}{2}$ | | 0.5 | (b) | 50% |
| **9.** | (a) | $\frac{1}{25}$ | (b) | 0.04 | | 4% |
| **10.** | | $\frac{1}{50}$ | (a) | 0.02 | (b) | 2% |
| **11.** | (a) | $\frac{9}{20}$ | | 0.45 | (b) | 45% |
| **12.** | (a) | $\frac{23}{100}$ | (b) | 0.23 | | 23% |
| **13.** | | $1\frac{1}{2}$ | (a) | 1.5 | (b) | 150% |
| **14.** | (a) | $\frac{3}{20}$ | | 0.15 | (b) | 15% |
| **15.** | (a) | $\frac{1}{10}$ | (b) | 0.1 | | 10% |
| **16.** | | $\frac{1}{8}$ | (a) | 0.125 | (b) | 12.5% |
| **17.** | (a) | $\frac{1}{5}$ | | 0.2 | (b) | 20% |
| **18.** | (a) | $\frac{7}{20}$ | (b) | 0.35 | | 35% |

**Supplemental Practice for Lesson 101**

**1.** $\dfrac{3}{4} = \dfrac{a}{20}$   15

**2.** $\dfrac{4}{6} = \dfrac{12}{b}$   18

**3.** $\dfrac{c}{6} = \dfrac{8}{12}$   4

**4.** $\dfrac{4}{d} = \dfrac{24}{60}$   10

**5.** $\dfrac{8}{10} = \dfrac{12}{e}$   15

**6.** $\dfrac{9}{10} = \dfrac{f}{1000}$   900

**7.** $\dfrac{g}{4} = \dfrac{27}{36}$   3

**8.** $\dfrac{15}{h} = \dfrac{30}{42}$   21

**9.** $\dfrac{12}{15} = \dfrac{i}{25}$   20

**10.** $\dfrac{7}{8} = \dfrac{700}{j}$   800

**11.** $\dfrac{k}{60} = \dfrac{4}{5}$   48

**12.** $\dfrac{12}{l} = \dfrac{60}{100}$   20

**13.** $\dfrac{3}{25} = \dfrac{m}{100}$   12

**14.** $\dfrac{3}{8} = \dfrac{9}{n}$   24

**15.** $\dfrac{p}{20} = \dfrac{35}{100}$   7

**16.** $\dfrac{12}{q} = \dfrac{10}{20}$   24

**17.** $\dfrac{27}{50} = \dfrac{r}{100}$   54

**18.** $\dfrac{6}{18} = \dfrac{7}{s}$   21

**19.** $\dfrac{t}{4} = \dfrac{75}{100}$   3

**20.** $\dfrac{27}{u} = \dfrac{15}{20}$   36

**Supplemental Practice for Lesson 106**

Find the perimeter and area of each polygon. Assume that angles that look like right angles are right angles.

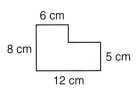

1. Perimeter   40 cm
2. Area   78 cm²

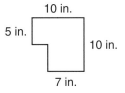

3. Perimeter   40 in.
4. Area   85 in.²

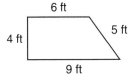

5. Perimeter   24 ft
6. Area   30 ft²

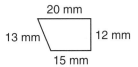

7. Perimeter   60 mm
8. Area   210 mm²

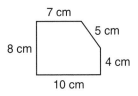

9. Perimeter   34 cm
10. Area   74 cm²

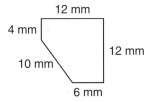

11. Perimeter   44 mm
12. Area   120 mm²

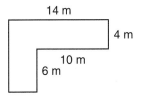

13. Perimeter   48 m
14. Area   80 m²

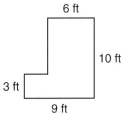

15. Perimeter   38 ft
16. Area   69 ft²

**Supplemental Practice for Lesson 111**

Write each quotient in three forms.

| | PROBLEM | WITH REMAINDER | FRACTION | DECIMAL |
|---|---|---|---|---|
| **1.** | $100 \div 8$ | 12 r 4 | $12\frac{1}{2}$ | 12.5 |
| **2.** | $50 \div 4$ | 12 r 2 | $12\frac{1}{2}$ | 12.5 |
| **3.** | $56 \div 10$ | 5 r 6 | $5\frac{3}{5}$ | 5.6 |
| **4.** | $65 \div 10$ | 6 r 5 | $6\frac{1}{2}$ | 6.5 |
| **5.** | $63 \div 12$ | 5 r 3 | $5\frac{1}{4}$ | 5.25 |
| **6.** | $72 \div 5$ | 14 r 2 | $14\frac{2}{5}$ | 14.4 |
| **7.** | $49 \div 4$ | 12 r 1 | $12\frac{1}{4}$ | 12.25 |
| **8.** | $38 \div 8$ | 4 r 6 | $4\frac{3}{4}$ | 4.75 |
| **9.** | $47 \div 4$ | 11 r 3 | $11\frac{3}{4}$ | 11.75 |
| **10.** | $146 \div 8$ | 18 r 2 | $18\frac{1}{4}$ | 18.25 |
| **11.** | $390 \div 20$ | 19 r 10 | $19\frac{1}{2}$ | 19.5 |
| **12.** | $625 \div 10$ | 62 r 5 | $62\frac{1}{2}$ | 62.5 |
| **13.** | $432 \div 5$ | 86 r 2 | $86\frac{2}{5}$ | 86.4 |
| **14.** | $650 \div 8$ | 81 r 2 | $81\frac{1}{4}$ | 81.25 |
| **15.** | $325 \div 20$ | 16 r 5 | $16\frac{1}{4}$ | 16.25 |
| **16.** | $562 \div 8$ | 70 r 2 | $70\frac{1}{4}$ | 70.25 |
| **17.** | $530 \div 40$ | 13 r 10 | $13\frac{1}{4}$ | 13.25 |
| **18.** | $375 \div 50$ | 7 r 25 | $7\frac{1}{2}$ | 7.5 |
| **19.** | $240 \div 100$ | 2 r 40 | $2\frac{2}{5}$ | 2.4 |
| **20.** | $534 \div 10$ | 53 r 4 | $53\frac{2}{5}$ | 53.4 |

**Supplemental Practice for Lesson 112**

**1.** What is 25% of 100?    25    **2.** What is 25% of 200?    50

**3.** What is 25% of 400?    100    **4.** What is 25% of 40?    10

**5.** What is 25% of 20?    5    **6.** What is 20% of 100?    20

**7.** What is 20% of 50?    10    **8.** What is 20% of 5?    1

**9.** What is 50% of 200?    100    **10.** What is 50% of 100?    50

**11.** What is 50% of 50?    25    **12.** What is 50% of 12?    6

**13.** What is 60% of 100? 60  **14.** What is 60% of 200? 120

**15.** What is 60% of 50?  30  **16.** What is 60% of 25?  15

**17.** What is 75% of 100? 75  **18.** What is 75% of 400? 300

**19.** What is 75% of 40?  30  **20.** What is 75% of 4?  3

**Supplemental Practice for Lesson 114**

1. a. mean, 7.7;
   b. median, 8;
   c. mode, 8;
   d. range, 6
3. a. mean, 8.6 yr;
   b. median, 9 yr;
   c. mode, 10 yr;
   d. range, 4 yr

Find the (a) mean, (b) median, (c) mode, and (d) range for each set of data. (Round decimal answers to one decimal place.)

**1.** Quiz scores:  10, 8, 7, 8, 6, 9, 8, 4, 9, 8

**2.** Best times in 50 m race: 8.7 s, 9.3 s, 7.9 s, 9.8 s, 8.7 s, 9.6 s    a. mean, 9 s; b. median, 9 s; c. mode, 8.7 s; d. range, 1.9 s

**3.** Ages of children in club: 6 yr, 8 yr, 9 yr, 10 yr, 10 yr

**4.** Number of students in each classroom: 24, 23, 21, 24, 28, 25, 30, 27, 32    a. mean, 26; b. median, 25; c. mode, 24; d. range, 11

**Supplemental Practice for Lesson 115**

**1.**      2 hr 45 min
       + 3 hr 25 min
       —————————
        6 hr  10 min

**2.**      10 min 15 s
        −  5 min 50 s
       —————————
         4 min  25 s

**3.**      1 yd 2 ft 8 in.
       + 2 yd 1 ft 9 in.
       —————————
        4 yd 1 ft  5 in.

**4.**      6 ft 3 in.
        − 5 ft 7 in.
       —————————
            8 in.

**5.**      6 lb 10 oz
       + 3 lb  8 oz
       —————————
        10 lb   2 oz

**6.**      8 lb 3 oz
        − 6 lb 9 oz
       —————————
         1 lb 10 oz

**7.**      2 gal 3 qt
       + 3 gal 2 qt
       —————————
        6 gal  1 qt

**8.**      5 gal 2 qt
        − 1 gal 3 qt
       —————————
         3 gal  3 qt

Write each of these numbers in standard notation:

**9.** $\frac{1}{2}$ million   500,000

**10.** $2.5 \times 10^7$   25,000,000

**11.** $7 \times 10^5$   700,000

**12.** $1\frac{1}{2}$ billion   1,500,000,000

**13.** $1.25 \times 10^9$  1,250,000,000

**14.** 15 million   15,000,000

**15.** $3.5 \times 10^6$   3,500,000

**16.** $\frac{1}{2}$ billion   500,000,000

**Supplemental Practice for Lesson 118**

1. Six is what percent of 12?   50%

2. Six is what percent of 10?   60%

3. Six is what percent of 8?   75%

4. Six is what percent of 6?   100%

5. Twelve is what percent of 120?   10%

6. Twelve is what percent of 60?   20%

7. Twelve is what percent of 48?   25%

8. Twelve is what percent of 24?   50%

9. Twelve is what percent of 12?   100%

10. Twelve is what percent of 16?   75%

11. Twelve is what percent of 15?   80%

12. Twelve is what percent of 100?   12%

13. What percent of 100 is 8?   8%

14. What percent of 10 is 8?   80%

15. What percent of 16 is 8?   50%

16. What percent of 8 is 8?   100%

17. What percent of 80 is 8?   10%

18. What percent of 100 is 20?   20%

19. What percent of 80 is 20?   25%

20. What percent of 40 is 20?   50%

21. What percent of 25 is 20?   80%

22. What percent of 20 is 20?   100%

23. What percent of 15 is 3?   20%

24. What percent of 100 is 30?   30%

25. What percent of 40 is 30?   75%

**Supplemental Practice for Lesson 121**

1. $-3 + (-4)$   $-7$    2. $(-5) + (-8)$   $-13$    3. $+3 + (-5)$   $-2$

4. $3 + (-8)$   $-5$    5. $-3 + 4$   $1$    6. $(-4) + (+3)$   $-1$

7. $-7 + 6$   $-1$    8. $(-6) + (+6)$   $0$    9. $5 + (-11)$   $-6$

**10.** (+5) + (+7)  12   **11.** (−12) + (−12)  −24  **12.** −12 + 12  0

**13.** (−12) + (+15)  3   **14.** (+8) + (−1)  7   **15.** (−8) + (+1)  −7

**16.** −5 + 8  3   **17.** +15 + (−18)  −3   **18.** −25 + (−30)  −55

**19.** (+15) + (−20)  −5   **20.** +8 + (−16)  −8   **21.** −9 + 15  6

**22.** (−6) + (+20)  14   **23.** (−20) + (−12)  −32   **24.** (+6) + (−4)  2

**25.** +8 + (−18)  −10

**Supplemental Practice for Lesson 122**

**1.** Fifty is $\dfrac{1}{2}$ of what?  100  **2.** Forty is $\dfrac{1}{4}$ of what?  160

**3.** Thirty is $\dfrac{1}{5}$ of what?  150  **4.** Twenty is $\dfrac{1}{10}$ of what?  200

**5.** Ten is $\dfrac{2}{5}$ of what?  25  **6.** Twenty is $\dfrac{2}{3}$ of what?  30

**7.** Thirty is $\dfrac{3}{4}$ of what?  40  **8.** Forty is $\dfrac{2}{5}$ of what?  100

**9.** Fifty is $\dfrac{5}{8}$ of what?  80  **10.** Twelve is $\dfrac{1}{4}$ of what?  48

**11.** Twelve is $\dfrac{3}{4}$ of what?  16  **12.** Twelve is $\dfrac{1}{3}$ of what?  36

**13.** Twelve is $\dfrac{3}{5}$ of what?  20  **14.** Sixty is $\dfrac{1}{10}$ of what?  600

**15.** Sixty is $\dfrac{1}{5}$ of what?  300  **16.** Sixty is $\dfrac{3}{10}$ of what?  200

**17.** Sixty is $\dfrac{2}{5}$ of what?  150  **18.** Sixty is $\dfrac{1}{2}$ of what?  120

**19.** Sixty is $\dfrac{3}{5}$ of what?  100  **20.** Thirty-five is $\dfrac{7}{10}$ of what?  50

**21.** Forty is $\dfrac{4}{5}$ of what?  50  **22.** Forty-five is $\dfrac{9}{10}$ of what?  50

**23.** Thirty is $\dfrac{3}{4}$ of what?  40  **24.** Twenty is $\dfrac{1}{4}$ of what?  80

**Supplemental Practice for Lesson 125**

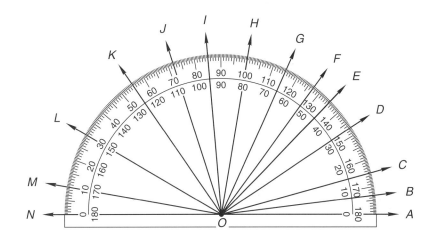

Using the protractor, find the measure of each of the following angles.

**1.** ∠AOB 7°  **2.** ∠AOE 45°  **3.** ∠AOH 80°  **4.** ∠AOK 125°

**5.** ∠AON 180°  **6.** ∠AOD 33°  **7.** ∠AOG 65°  **8.** ∠AOJ 108°

**9.** ∠AOM 170°  **10.** ∠AOC 15°  **11.** ∠AOF 53°  **12.** ∠AOI 95°

**13.** ∠AOL 150°  **14.** ∠NOL 30°  **15.** ∠NOI 85°  **16.** ∠NOF 127°

**17.** ∠NOC 165°  **18.** ∠NOK 55°  **19.** ∠NOH 100°  **20.** ∠NOE 135°

**21.** ∠NOM 10°  **22.** ∠NOJ 72°  **23.** ∠NOG 115°  **24.** ∠NOD 147°

**Supplemental Practice for Lesson 126**

**1.** 3 − (−5)  8    **2.** −3 − 5  −8    **3.** −3 − (−5)  2

**4.** (−5) − (−3)  −2  **5.** (−5) − (+3)  −8  **6.** 5 − (−6)  11

**7.** 7 − (−12)  19  **8.** −7 − (−12)  5  **9.** (−7) − (+12) −19

**10.** −12 − 7  −19  **11.** −12 − (−7) −5  **12.** 12 − (−7)  19

**13.** (−12) − (+7) −19  **14.** −6 − (−6)  0  **15.** (+6) − (−6) 12

**16.** (−10) − (+5) −15  **17.** −10 − (−5) −5  **18.** −5 − 10  −15

**19.** −5 − (−10) 5  **20.** 10 − (−5) 15  **21.** −12 − (−8)  −4

**22.** (−12) − (+8) −20  **23.** −8 − 12 −20  **24.** −8 − (−12)  4

**25.** 8 − (−12)  20

**Supplemental Practice for Lesson 127**

1. Ten is 10% of what number?   100
2. Ten is 20% of what number?   50
3. Ten is 40% of what number?   25
4. Ten is 25% of what number?   40
5. Ten is 5% of what number?   200
6. Ten is 2% of what number?   500
7. One hundred is 100% of what number?   100
8. Twenty is 20% of what number?   100
9. Twenty is 10% of what number?   200
10. Twenty is 1% of what number?   2000
11. Six is 10% of what number?   60
12. Six is 25% of what number?   24
13. Six is 1% of what number?   600
14. Five is 100% of what number?   5
15. Fifty is 50% of what number?   100
16. Fifty is 100% of what number?   50
17. Fifty is 10% of what number?   500
18. Six is 75% of what number?   8
19. Ten is 100% of what number?   10
20. Fifty is 25% of what number?   200
21. Forty is 100% of what number?   40
22. Forty is 40% of what number?   100
23. Forty is 50% of what number?   80
24. Forty is 25% of what number?   160
25. Twenty is 25% of what number?   80

**Supplemental Practice for Lesson 128**

1. $\sqrt{36}$   6      2. $\sqrt{4}$   2      3. $\sqrt{81}$   9      4. $\sqrt{49}$   7

5. $\sqrt{121}$   11   6. $\sqrt{16}$   4      7. $\sqrt{64}$   8      8. $\sqrt{100}$   10

9. $\sqrt{25}$   5     10. $\sqrt{9}$   3      11. $\sqrt{144}$   12   12. $\sqrt{1}$   1

Each square root is between which two consecutive whole numbers?

**13.** $\sqrt{10}$     **14.** $\sqrt{30}$     **15.** $\sqrt{40}$     **16.** $\sqrt{50}$     **17.** $\sqrt{60}$
3, 4          5, 6          6, 7          7, 8          7, 8

**18.** $\sqrt{70}$     **19.** $\sqrt{80}$     **20.** $\sqrt{90}$     **21.** $\sqrt{5}$     **22.** $\sqrt{2}$
8, 9          8, 9          9, 10         2, 3          1, 2

**Supplemental Practice for Lesson 130**

Complete the chart for each circle. (Use $\pi = 3.14$.)

| RADIUS | DIAMETER | CIRCUMFERENCE | AREA |
|---|---|---|---|
| 1 in. | **1.** 2 in. | **2.** 6.28 in. | **3.** 3.14 in.$^2$ |
| **4.** 2 ft | 4 ft | **5.** 12.56 ft | **6.** 12.56 ft$^2$ |
| 3 cm | **7.** 6 cm | **8.** 18.84 cm | **9.** 28.26 cm$^2$ |
| **10.** 4 m | 8 m | **11.** 25.12 m | **12.** 50.24 m$^2$ |
| 5 mm | **13.** 10 mm | **14.** 31.4 mm | **15.** 78.5 mm$^2$ |
| **16.** 6 yd | 12 yd | **17.** 37.68 yd | **18.** 113.04 yd$^2$ |
| 10 km | **19.** 20 km | **20.** 62.8 km | **21.** 314 km$^2$ |
| **22.** 50 mi | 100 mi | **23.** 314 mi | **24.** 7850 mi$^2$ |

**25.** What special word is used to describe the perimeter of a circle?    circumference

**Supplemental Practice for Lesson 134**

**1.** $(-3)(+4)$   $-12$

**2.** $(-8)(-12)$   96

**3.** $(+12)(-15)$   $-180$

**4.** $(-18)(-20)$   360

**5.** $(+21)(-7)$   $-147$

**6.** $(-8)(+17)$   $-136$

**7.** $(-25)(-15)$   375

**8.** $(+18)(+5)$   90

**9.** $(-7)(+43)$   $-301$

**10.** $(-12)(-24)$   288

**11.** $(+6)(-18)$   $-108$

**12.** $(-9)(-25)$   225

**13.** $(-24) \div (+2)$   $-12$

**14.** $(-24) \div (-3)$   8

**15.** $-72 \div 8$   $-9$

**16.** $400 \div (-5)$   $-80$

**17.** $(-234) \div (-6)$   39

**18.** $(-144) \div (+12)$   $-12$

**19.** $-125 \div 25$   $-5$

**20.** $(-375) \div (-15)$   25

**Supplemental Practice for Lesson 138**

Write the Arabic numeral.

**1.** XIX  19     **2.** XVII  17     **3.** CCCXCI  391

**4.** CDXXIV  424     **5.** MCC  1200     **6.** LIV  54

**7.** CCLVI  256     **8.** MMCLX  2160     **9.** XCII  92

**10.** CDXXV  425     **11.** XXIV  24     **12.** CCXLIV  244

**13.** MCMLXIX  1969     **14.** MLXVI  1066     **15.** MCMLXXXIV  1984

Write the Roman numeral.

**16.** 63  LXIII     **17.** 89  LXXXIX     **18.** 101  CI     **19.** 651  DCLI     **20.** 44  XLIV

**21.** 99  XCIX     **22.** 156  CLVI     **23.** 490  CDXC     **24.** 2310  MMCCCX     **25.** 1907  MCMVII

# Glossary

**acute angle**   An angle that has a measure greater than 0° and less than 90°.

**acute triangle**   A triangle in which each of the three angles measures less than 90°.

**addend**   A number that is added in an addition problem.

**addition sequence**   An ordered list of numbers in which the same number is added to the previous term to get the following term.

**algebraic addition**   The addition of the opposite of a number; used to replace subtraction.

**a.m.**   Before noon (*ante meridiem*).

**angle**   An opening between two intersecting lines, rays, or segments.

**Arabic numerals**   The digits (0, 1, 2, 3, 4, 5, 6, 7, 8, and 9) used in combination with place value to express numbers. For example, 475 is an Arabic numeral.

**area**   The number of square units of a given size that cover the surface of a figure.

**average**   The amount found by dividing the sum of a set of numbers by the number of numbers in the set, also known as arithmetic average or mean.

**base**   In a triangle or parallelogram, the side from which the height of the triangle or parallelogram is measured.

**Celsius scale**   One of the scales used on a thermometer to measure temperature. On this scale, water boils at 100°C and freezes at 0°C. Normal body temperature is 37°C.

**century**   One hundred years.

**chance**   The likelihood that something will happen, expressed as a percentage.

**circle**   A round graph in which every point on the graph is the same distance from a center point.

**circumference**   The distance around a circle, also known as the perimeter of a circle.

**common number**   A number shared by two or more sets, as in common factor, common multiple, and common denominator.

**compare**   To determine whether one number or expression is greater than, less than, or equal to another number or expression.

**compass**   A tool that aids in the drawing of circles, as well as in other geometric applications.

**composite**   A number that has more than two factors.

**cone**   A three-dimensional solid with a circular base and a single vertex.

**congruent**   A set of figures that have the same shape and size. Also, angles or line segments that have the same measure.

**coordinate plane**   A graph of two perpendicular number lines that have scale marks extended to form a grid on which to plot points.

**coordinates**   A paired set of numbers like (3, −2) that indicates the location of a point on a coordinate plane. The first number shows the horizontal direction and distance from the origin (on the *x*-axis); the second number shows the vertical direction and distance from the origin (on the *y*-axis).

**counting numbers** The numbers in this sequence: 1, 2, 3, 4, 5, ....

**cross products** The result of taking a pair of fractions and multiplying the numerator of the first fraction by the denominator of the second fraction and vice versa.

**cube** A three-dimensional solid with six square faces. Adjacent faces are perpendicular, and opposite faces are parallel.

**cylinder** A three-dimensional solid with two circular bases, that are opposite and parallel to each other.

**decade** Ten years.

**decimal places** All of the place values to the right of the decimal point.

**decimal point** A period used to separate the ones' place from the tenths' place.

**degree (°)** The unit used to measure angles. Also, the symbol used to denote unit divisions on a temperature scale.

**denominator** The bottom number of a fraction, designating the number of equal parts in a whole.

**diameter** The distance across a circle through the center of the circle.

**difference** The result of subtraction.

**digit** Any one of the following ten numerical symbols: 0, 1, 2, 3, 4, 5, 6, 7, 8, 9.

**dividend** The number that is divided in a division problem.

**divisible** The ability to be divided without a remainder; for example, 6 is divisible by 1, 2, 3, and 6.

**divisor** The number by which another number is divided.

**edge**   A line at which two faces of a solid come together.

**endpoints**   The points at which a line segment ends.

**equals sign (=)**   A symbol that indicates that two numbers or expressions are equivalent.

**equilateral triangle**   A triangle in which all three sides and all three angles are equal in measure.

**equivalent**   Expressions that have the same value; for example, $\frac{2}{4}$ is equivalent to $\frac{1}{2}$, or $\frac{2}{4} = \frac{1}{2}$.

**estimate**   To roughly determine a size or value; to calculate approximately using rounded numbers.

**even numbers**   Those numbers that can be divided by 2 without a remainder. The digit in the ones' place of an even number is 0, 2, 4, 6, or 8.

**experimental probability**   The probability of an event occurring as determined by data collection.

**exponent**   A number that indicates repeated multiplication of the base. For example, in $5^2$, 2 is the exponent and 5 is the base, and this means $5 \times 5$, or 25.

**face**   A flat surface of a solid.

**fact families**   Sets of three numbers which can be formed into two addition facts and two subtraction facts, or two multiplication facts and two division facts.

**factor**   A number being multiplied. Also, a whole number which divides another whole number without a remainder.

**Fahrenheit scale**   One of the scales used on a thermometer to measure temperature. On this scale, water boils at 212°F and freezes at 32°F. Normal body temperature is 98.6°F.

**fraction**   A common fraction is part of a whole, expressed as a numerator over a denominator.

**geometry**  The study of shapes.

**graph**  A diagram such as a bar graph, a circle graph (pie chart), or a line graph that displays quantitative information.

**greater than/less than sign (<>)**  A symbol placed between two numbers or expressions to indicate which is greater or which is less.

**greatest common factor (GCF)**  The largest whole number that is a factor of all members of a given set of whole numbers.

**height**  In a triangle or parallelogram, the perpendicular distance from the base to the opposite vertex of a triangle or from the base to the parallel side of a parallelogram.

**hexagon**  Any six-sided polygon.

**histogram**  A special type of bar graph that displays data in equivalent intervals with no space between the bars.

**horizontal**  Parallel with the horizon; perpendicular to vertical.

**hundredths' place**  The place value two places to the right of the decimal point. Each hundredth equals $\frac{1}{100}$.

**improper fraction**  A fraction in which the numerator is equal to or greater than the denominator; a fraction that is equal to or greater than one.

**integers**  The set of numbers that includes all the counting numbers, their opposites, and zero.

**intersecting lines**  Lines that cross; lines which share a common point.

**irrational number**  A number that cannot be expressed as a fraction. Examples are $\pi$ and $\sqrt{2}$.

**isosceles triangle**  A triangle in which at least two of the three sides and angles are equal in measure.

**length**    A longer side of a rectangle.

**least common multiple (LCM)**    The smallest number that is a multiple of a given set of whole numbers.

**line**    A continuous string of points extending in two opposite directions without end.

**line of symmetry**    A line that divides a figure into two mirror images.

**mass**    The amount of matter in an object.

**mean**    The average of a set of numbers.

**median**    In a set of numbers arranged in order from least to greatest, the middle number, or the average of the two middle numbers.

**metric system**    An international system of measure based on multiples of ten using units such as meters, liters, and grams.

**mixed number**    An expression made up of a whole number and a fraction, such as $2\frac{3}{4}$.

**mode**    The most frequently occurring number or numbers in a set of numbers.

**multiple**    A number found by multiplying a given number by a whole number greater than zero; for example, the multiples of 5 are 5, 10, 15, 20, ....

**multiplication sequence**    An ordered list of numbers in which the same number is multiplied by the previous term to get the following term.

**negative**    A number less than zero; the opposite of positive.

**noon**    Midday; 12:00 p.m.

**number line**    A line with evenly spaced marks on which a number is associated with each mark.

**numeral**   A written symbol for a number.

**numerator**   The top number of a fraction, designating the number of parts being used.

**oblique**   Slanted, sloped, or inclined lines; neither horizontal nor vertical; neither parallel nor perpendicular.

**obtuse angle**   An angle that has a measure greater than 90° but less than 180°.

**obtuse triangle**   A triangle in which one angle measures greater than 90°.

**octagon**   Any eight-sided polygon.

**odd numbers**   Those numbers that have a remainder of 1 when divided by 2. The digit in the ones' place of an odd number is 1, 3, 5, 7, or 9.

**operations of arithmetic**   Mathematical processes performed according to specific rules. These processes are addition, subtraction, multiplication, and division.

**opposites**   Those numbers that can be written with the same digits but with opposite signs. For example, the opposite of 5 is −5. The sum of a number and its opposite is zero.

**origin**   The point (0, 0) on a coordinate plane at which the $x$-axis and $y$-axis intersect.

**parallel**   Lines, rays, or segments that remain the same distance apart and do not intersect.

**parallelogram**   A quadrilateral that has two pairs of parallel sides.

**pentagon**   Any five-sided polygon.

**percent**   A fraction with the denominator 100 expressed with a percent sign, %. For example, $99\% = \frac{99}{100}$.

**perfect square**   A number that has as its square root a whole number. Examples of perfect squares are 1, 4, and 9.

**perimeter**   The distance around a shape.

**perpendicular**   Lines, rays, or segments that intersect to form right angles.

**pi ($\pi$)**   The Greek letter that stands for the number of diameters in a circumference (approximately equal to 3.14).

**place value**   The value of a digit determined by its position within the numeral.

**plane**   A flat surface in mathematics that has no boundaries.

**p.m.**   After noon (*post meridiem*).

**polygon**   Any straight-sided closed plane figure.

**polyhedron**   A solid figure on which every face is a polygon.

**positive**   A number greater than zero; the opposite of negative.

**prime**   A counting number that has exactly two factors, the number 1 and itself.

**prime factorization**   The breakdown of a counting number by writing it as a product of its prime factors.

**prism**   A three-dimensional solid that has two congruent, parallel polygons as its bases.

**probability**   The likelihood that something will happen expressed as a ratio.

**product**   The result of multiplying.

**proper fraction**   A fraction in which the numerator is less than the denominator.

**proportion**   A true statement that demonstrates two ratios are equivalent.

**protractor**   A tool that is used to measure and draw angles.

**pyramid**   A three-dimensional solid with a polygon as its base and triangular sides that meet at a vertex.

**quadrilateral**   Any four-sided polygon.

**quantitative**   Expressed as or relating to a quantity or number.

**quotient**   The result of division.

**radius**   The distance from the center of a circle to a point on the circle. The plural of *radius* is *radii*.

**range**   The difference between the greatest and the least in a set of numbers.

**ratio**   An expression of the relationship between two numbers using a colon, a fraction, or words, such as 3:2, $\frac{3}{2}$, or 3 to 2.

**ray**   The portion of a line that begins at one point and continues without end.

**reciprocal**   The fraction resulting from inverting a given fraction (reversing the numerator and denominator). The product of a fraction and its reciprocal is one.

**rectangle**   A four-sided polygon that has four right angles.

**rectangular prism**   A prism with rectangles as bases.

**rectangular solid**   A three-dimensional solid where all six faces are rectangles. Opposite faces are parallel and adjacent faces are perpendicular.

**reduce**   To divide a fraction by another fraction equal to 1 in order to form an equivalent fraction in which both the numerator and denominator have lesser values. For example, $\frac{2}{4}$ reduces to $\frac{1}{2}$.

**reflection**   A transformation performed by reflecting a figure as in a mirror or flipping a figure over a certain line.

**regular polygon**   A polygon in which all sides and angles are equal in measure.

**remainder**   In subtraction, the difference; in division, any number that is left over after dividing integers.

**rhombus**   A parallelogram that has sides of equal length.

**right angle**   A square angle, often marked with a square, that has a measure of 90°.

**right triangle**   A triangle in which one angle measures 90°.

**Roman numerals**   An ancient form of numbering that does not use place value; for example, II is a Roman numeral equivalent to the Arabic numeral 2.

**rotation**   A transformation performed by turning a figure about a certain point.

**rounding**   Finding another number that is near the number given; for example, 587 rounds to 600.

**sales tax**   The tax charged on the sale of an item based upon the selling price.

**scale**   A system of marks at regular intervals used for measurement. Also, an instrument that displays such marks.

**scalene triangle**   A triangle in which all three sides and all three angles are not equal in measure.

**segment**   A part of a line that has two endpoints.

**sequence**   An ordered list of numbers that follows a certain rule.

**side**   A line segment of a polygon; the number of sides indicates the type of polygon.

**similar**   A set of figures or angles that are the same shape but not necessarily the same size.

**solid**   A geometric shape that occupies space.

**sphere**   A smooth geometric solid that is shaped like a ball.

**square**   A rectangle in which all sides are the same length.

**square root**   A number that, when multiplied by itself, equals the given number. The square root of 49 is 7 because $7 \cdot 7 = 49$. The principal of the positive square root of a number is indicated by this symbol, $\sqrt{\phantom{x}}$ .

**straight angle**   An angle that forms a straight line and has a measure of 180°.

**sum**   The result of addition.

**surface area**   The total area of all of the surfaces of a geometric solid.

**survey**   A method of collecting data about a particular population.

**tenths' place**   The place value one place to the right of the decimal point. Each tenth equals $\frac{1}{10}$.

**theoretical probability**   The probability of an event occurring as determined by analysis rather than by experimentation.

**thousandths' place**   The place value three places to the right of the decimal point. Each thousandth equals $\frac{1}{1000}$.

**transformation**   Any of the three forms of movement (rotation, reflection, and translation) made to reposition a figure.

**translation**   A transformation performed by sliding a figure in one direction without turning the figure.

**trapezium**   A quadrilateral in which no sides are parallel.

**trapezoid**   A quadrilateral in which one pair of sides are parallel.

**triangle**   A polygon that has three sides and three angles, the sum of which measure 180°.

**unit multiplier**   A fraction equal to one, written with two different but equivalent units of measure; for example, $\frac{1\,\text{ft}}{12\,\text{in.}}$ is a unit multiplier.

**U.S. Customary System**   A U.S. system of measure using units such as feet, gallons, and pounds.

**vertex**   The point at which two sides of a polygon or three or more edges of a polyhedron intersect. The plural of *vertex* is *vertices*. Note that a *cone* also has a vertex. This vertex is not made from the intersection of edges, but rather the intersection of the lines that would make up the non-base surface of the cone.

**vertical**   Upright; perpendicular to horizontal.

**volume**   The amount of space a given shape occupies.

**whole numbers**   All the counting numbers and zero, as in the sequence: 0, 1, 2, 3, 4, ....

**width**   A shorter side of a rectangle.

**x-axis**   The horizontal number line of the coordinate plane.

**y-axis**   The vertical number line of the coordinate plane.

# Index

## Symbols

$\approx$ (approximately equals sign), 408
$\angle$ (angle), 515
¢ (cent sign), 7
: (colon)
    for ratios, 398
    for time, 159
. (decimal point), 2, 168–169
° (degree symbol)
    for angles, 514
    for temperature, 44
— (division or fraction bar), 8, 26
$\overline{)}$ (division box), 8
÷ (division sign), 8
$ (dollar sign), 2
= (equals sign), 2, 40
< > (greater than/less than sign), 40
– (minus sign), 2
× (multiplication sign), 6
· (multiplication sign), 222
≠ (not equals sign), 539
( ) (parentheses), 23
% (percent), 164
$\pi$ (pi), 505
+ (plus sign), 1
$\sqrt{\phantom{x}}$ (square root), 423

## A

Abbreviation(s)
    cubic (cu.) units, 472
    for patterns
        equal groups (EG), 68
        larger-smaller-difference (L-S-D), 59
        later-earlier-difference (L-E-D), 59
        some and some more (SSM), 49
        some went away (SWA), 49

Abbreviation(s) (*Cont.*)
    square (sq.) units, 154, 389–390
    for units of length, 30
    for units of liquid measure, 373
    for units of mass, 566
    for units of weight, 567
Acute
    angles, 513–514
    triangles, 584
Addend(s)
    definition of, 1
    missing, 13–14
Addition
    of decimals, 183–184
        with whole numbers, 187–188
    of fractions
        with common denominators, 115–117
            in mixed numbers, 129–130
        steps for, 274–275
        with unlike denominators, 255
            in mixed numbers, 281–282
    of integers, 588–590
    with missing addends, 13–14
    of mixed measures, 556–557
    with money, 1–2
    as multiplication, 6
    order of operations for, 22–23
    with whole numbers, 1
Algebraic addition, 615
Angle(s)
    bisectors, 667–668